Colonial Governors
from the Fifteenth Century to the Present

Colonial Governors
from the Fifteenth Century to the Present

A Comprehensive List by
David P. Henige

The University of Wisconsin Press
Madison, Milwaukee, and London
1970

Published by
The University of Wisconsin Press
Box 1370, Madison, Wisconsin 53701

The University of Wisconsin Press, Ltd.
27–29 Whitfield Street, London, W.1

Printed in the United States of America by
Cushing-Malloy, Inc., Ann Arbor, Michigan

Standard Book Number 299-05440-3
Library of Congress Catalog Card Number 73-81320

To my mother

in gratitude for everything

Acknowledgments

It is obviously almost beyond comment that a work of this nature cannot be the production of a single individual. I have been most fortunate in the amount of help I have received throughout the course of my research. This will be evident from the citations, and to the individuals there mentioned I would like to express my gratitude. Some among them were particularly and repeatedly helpful. This was notably so in respect to the personnel of the various French archives in Paris. My particular gratitude goes, therefore, to Mlle. Marie-Antoinette Menier, Conservateur, Archives nationales, Section Outre-mer, to Contre-admiral C.-R. Fliche, Chef du Service historique de la marine, to F. Mealin, Sous-Directeur du Service des Personnels de l'Ancienne Administration d'Outre-Mer, to F. Dousset, Adjoint du Directeur-Général des Archives de France, and to Pierre Brasseur, Directeur des Territoires d'Outre-Mer. Their assistance was in every sense indispensable to the completion of the French section of this book and their patience never seemed to wilt under my incessant demands.

In like fashion A. E. M. Ribberink and Mrs. Dr. M. A. P. Meilink-Roelofsz, successively Keepers of the First Section of the Algemeen Rijksarchief, The Hague, graciously, fully, and promptly answered my several inquiries and provided me with data which were not available elsewhere.

The following individuals provided assistance of various kinds which has not always been acknowledged in the citations because it applied in many cases to information on several colonies: J.-Fr. Maurel, Conservateur, Archives du Sénégal, Dakar; Y. Arbellot-Repaire, Administrateur civil, Saint-Pierre et Miquelon; P. C. Soeters, Head, Department of Genealogy, Koninklijke Bibliotheek, The Hague; J. Lambert, Conservateur, Bibliothèque royale de Belgique, Brussels; André Scherer, Archiviste de la Réunion, Saint-Denis; L. van Meerbeeck, Archiviste général *p.i.*, Archives générales du Royaume, Brussels; M. van Grieken-Taverniers, L'Archiviste-Adjoint, Direction générale A, Archives africaines, Brussels; C. Bataille, Directeur du Service des Archives, Fort-de-France, Martinique; John Sutherland Thomson, Administrator of the British Virgin Islands; D. E. Howland, New Zealand Department of Island Territories (now Department of Maori and Island Affairs), Wellington; M. I. Moir, India Office Records, London; A. G. Davey, Army Records Center, Hayes, Middlesex, England; J. Wright, Assistant Librarian, The Royal Military Academy, Sandhurst, Camberley, England; Dr. Enders, Deutsches Zentralarchivs, Potsdam; H. L. White, National Librarian, National Library of Australia, Canberra; Y. Sakai, Director, Division for Interlibrary Services, National Diet Library, Tokyo; and Jorge Ignacio Rubio Mañé, Director, Archivo general de la Nación, Mexico City.

Acknowledgments

Señor Guillermo Porras Muñoz of Mexico City provided me with much data and advice in addition to the list of the governors of Nueva Vizcaya.

In the course of the past several years I have found it necessary to exploit printed sources which were not always readily available. In this I have had the good fortune to secure the support and interest of John M. Morgan, Reference Librarian at the University of Toledo Library. Mr. Morgan's willingness to aid researchers well beyond the norms of simple duty can be readily attested to by others as well as myself. But his friendship and criticisms have been valued even more than his professional assistance. I am also grateful to Mrs. Jacqueline Kelly and the staff of the Interlibrary Loan Department of the University of Wisconsin Memorial Library for their assistance, and to Bruce G. Inksetter of the Department of Hebrew and Semitic Studies of the University of Wisconsin for his generous and unselfish assistance at diverse points along the way. Professor Philip D. Curtin of the University of Wisconsin Department of History took an instrumental interest in my work and thereby provided no little encouragement. John Paul Irwin, friend and colleague, provided assistance with some of the German sources, but most importantly offered constructive critical commentary on matter included in the various colony descriptions. It is not too much to say that they are better for his informed interest.

It is customary to include a disclaimer at this point to the effect that all errors are solely the author's responsibility. Even were it not customary I would feel compelled to do so, for the assistance rendered by the myriad of individual named above and throughout this work—as well as those who have remained unnamed—has benefitted this work materially. It would have been much the poorer—indeed impossible of completion—without them.

This work has claimed much of my time—time which has necessarily been taken from my wife, Suzanne, and children, Cynthia, Christopher, and Brian. Their tolerance and their encouragement have in no small measure made the task an easier one. Appropriately my greatest debt is expressed, however inadequately, by the dedication.

D. P. H.

Madison, Wisconsin
September, 1969

Preface

A major theme of the modern era has been the expansion of Europe, a small segment of civilization, into nearly every part of the globe, and the consequent imposition of its political control and the transplantation of its cultural values throughout the world. This process of spreading political control endured over four centuries, and then within the space of scarcely more than half a century began rapidly to reverse itself. It may conveniently be divided into two parts, with the year 1800 as a useful, if somewhat rough, dividing point. During the first period, initiated by the voyages sponsored by Henry the Navigator, prince of Portugal, the "Iberian" expansion was most spectacular and certainly dominant. The rapid disintegration of the Spanish Empire in the early years of the 19th century and the loss by Portugal of Brazil, her most prized overseas possession, ushered in a new phase of colonial activity. Nineteenth-century colonial expansion was dominated by Great Britain and latterly France, but was participated in as well by the Netherlands, Germany, Portugal, and others. Several of these nations had acquired overseas possessions from as early as the 15th century, and the 19th century represented for them a culmination of a long process rather than a significant change in activity.

Four centuries of overseas expansion by a dozen countries resulted in a large variety of colonies.[1] Some were merely small enclaves, acquired because of their strategic locations in terms of commercial or military activities, and reflecting the early inability of most European countries to engage in large-scale colonial ventures. Others, acquired, except in the case of Spain, much later, covered much larger land areas, but were occupied by only the handful of Europeans needed as administrators. British India and most of the African colonies are standard examples of this form of colonialism. Many areas, though, were settled by relatively large numbers of Europeans. If these areas already possessed a large and dynamic indigenous population, a "plural society" would often develop, as in Mexico. In areas of little or no previous habitation, such as Canada, Australia, or Réunion, more faithful replicas of European societies could emerge.

Responding to the exigencies of time and place, the extension of European control assumed many guises. Consequently, in official, administrative, or diplomatic parlance various areas might come to be termed "protectorates" or

---

1. The term colony is used generically in this introduction. It includes all forms of European control, i.e., possessions which were not officially termed colonies as well as those that were.

"mandates" or "territories," but a common feature was that they represented areas administratively controlled and subject to exploitation by some European nation.[2]

The purpose of this work, which is intended as a work of reference and makes no pretense whatever to any broader aim, is to present lists of the governors[3] of the European colonies from 1415, when the Portuguese occupied Ceuta, to the present time.[4] It seems appropriate to present this at a time when decolonization has reached a point where colonialism can be regarded as a historical occurrence rather than a contemporary phenomenon. Its prime justification is simply that no one has seen fit to produce a similar compilation in the past.[5] As a result, what can be considered an integrated and self-defining body of information has lain scattered in a legion of sources. The lists of governors of British colonies in the annual *Colonial Office Lists* are unduly simplistic in many cases, unnecessarily complex in others, often distorted, and admittedly incomplete, and their value is thereby vitiated. In any event few libraries possess complete files of the *List*. The annual *India Office List* and its predecessors represents a more systematic attempt to include this information, but omissions, particularly that of Aden, can be cited. In the British imperial system only the Australian colonies are well served—by the *Australian Encyclopaedia*—and the lists presented here for these colonies are essentially a distillation of information contained in these volumes.

Nothing is available for the French colonies as a unit, or for any substantial segment of them, and the same must be said for the Spanish colonies after 1700 and for the Portuguese colonies as well. Except for Germany, this lack extends to the lesser imperial systems as well. In sum, then, it might fairly be observed that there is a distressing lack of printed material available and this work is specifically designed to remedy this deficiency.

---

2. "European" includes American and Australian when used in this context, as they were essentially European societies transplanted.

3. Again, "governor" is used generically although it was but one, albeit the most common, of many titles bestowed on colonial administrators.

4. For the brief colonial efforts of Brandenburg and Kurland in the 17th and 18th centuries, see the Appendix.

5. This is not to imply that no efforts have been made on more limited bases. For example, Ernst Schäfer in his appendices to his two-volume *El consejo real y supremo de las Indias* (Seville: Imp. m. Carmona, 1935–47) included much information on the governors and lesser officials of Spanish America before 1700. However, his perspective is admittedly that of the Council of the Indies rather than of the colonies themselves. Consequently he includes only the governors appointed by royal *titulos*, thereby omitting many acting-governors who served for extended periods. Furthermore, by using the dates of appointments rather than of assumption of office, in most cases he presented a distorted picture of actual service in office. A. M. H. J. Stokvis in his compendious *Manuel d'histoire, de généalogie et de chronologie de tous les états du globe depuis les temps les reculés jusqu'à nos jours*, 3 vols. (Leiden: E. J. Brill, 1888–93), tried to include data on colonies existing prior to that time but his information is skeletal and often inaccurate and is of little value today.

Each imperial system had, of course, its own administrative procedures, and even within a given imperial system wide variation could and did exist. While wishing to avoid procrustean rigidity, I believed that certain uniformities should be observed throughout this work. In terms of deciding what should be included I have descended to what might be called "the second echelon of administration." This situation most commonly arises in areas governed by viceroys or governors-general. Mexico and Peru in the Spanish system, India in the British system, and French West Africa and French Equatorial Africa can be cited as examples of administrative units whose components have been included. These major components, although often arbitrarily and carelessly delineated, merit inclusion insofar as they became the foci around which newly independent states were formed—as in the case of Peru or French West Africa or French Equatorial Africa, or they have survived in virtually unaltered form as administrative units within their successor states—as in the case of Mexico or British India. Under these circumstances I have not thought it logical to include the Canadian provinces or the Australian states after confederation, when they became only very indirectly connected administratively with the metropolis. In any case their inclusion would not fill a historiographical gap since information on the lieutenant governors of all of them can conveniently be found in the respective national encyclopedias.

A rational grouping of colonies within their imperial systems has proven elusive. Most of the colonies during their existence underwent administrative changes. Thus, certain British West Indian islands were initially subject to Barbados, later formed parts of the Leeward or Windward Islands governments, then were joined together as the West Indies Federation, and finally became each a completely separate administrative unit. Since this kind of administrative legerdemain occurred in the other imperial systems as well, to choose one grouping to the exclusion of others would have been unduly arbitrary and synchronic. Consequently I have adopted an alphabetical arrangement within each imperial system. This may not be an ideal solution and can present its own difficulties but these have been minimized by appropriate remarks in the introductions and by extensive cross-referencing both in the colony descriptions and in the general index.

The form of the colony name used is for the most part that used in the *Columbia Lippincott Gazetteer*. Sometimes, for consistency, names like Nueva España have been retained, although their English counterparts are in wide usage. Sufficient cross-references have been included in the general index to obviate any problems arising from the sometimes arbitrary decisions made in this matter.

The problem of whether to list acting-governors has been a particularly thorny one. Almost every colony had many periods during which an acting-governor administered the colony during the absence or incapacity of the substantive governor. Normally these periods were of brief duration—a matter of a few weeks or months—but they occasionally became quite extended. The diversity of practice between, and indeed within, the various imperial systems renders it impossible to adopt a uniform policy in dealing with this problem. The fact that many acting-governors were subsequently appointed substantively further muddies the waters. Generally, however, I have included only those acting-governors who served consecutively for a reasonably long period—for instance a year. Only those who served between administrations of different governors are shown. Those who served within the administration of a governor who was serving a single appointment are not included. However, I have felt advisable to modify this practice for the earlier centuries of colonization. During this period colonial administration was often casual, or in the hands of private chartered companies, and well-articulated practices had not yet fully matured. As a result, the distinction between acting-governor and substantive governor was blurred, if, indeed, there was an implicit distinction made. This system has resulted in some inconsistencies, but I have felt that any alternative would be less satisfactory. Certainly the inclusion of all acting-governors would often prove confusing and it would have inflated the dimensions of this work beyond reasonable limits.

Another problem concerns the accuracy of the sources in regard to the actual administrative titles in use. Where information as to the precise titles—administrator, captain-general, resident, etc.—was available, these distinctions have been made. However, where the sources do not make such distinctions, the term governor has been used, in its generic sense. Titles have been anglicized except when the English was thought to distort the meaning.

Only a governor's personal name and, where applicable, his title in peerage (when different from his given name), are shown. No military or naval rank or titles of knighthood or any other indication of knighthood (K.C.I.E., G.C.B., etc.) have been shown. This differs from the system adopted in the *Colonial Office Lists*, the *India Office Lists*, and the French *Annuaires*, each of which meticulously includes information of this kind, but I cannot discern any useful purpose in including these data, which are almost always quite irrelevant for purposes of identification.

In the earlier centuries of colonization one often finds the names of a given individual spelled several ways. This was true in every imperial system. I have attempted to include such variations only when they seem necessary for basic identification. For the French colonies I have generally used the forms given in the *Dictionnaire de biographie française* and the *Dictionary of Canadian Biography*. On the point of general orthography it should be noted that I have followed, for all Portuguese names, the orthography adopted by the Lisbon Academia das Ciências in 1940 and accepted by the Brazilian Academia das Letras in 1943.[6]

Particular pains have been taken to include the full name of each incumbent and it is here that I feel that this work makes its most original contribution. Only the sources for the Spanish and Portuguese colonies habitually include this information. The sources available for the other imperial systems include it only occasionally—the French sources almost never. I believe this information to be useful to the point of necessity to ensure completeness and accuracy and to avoid confusion in cases of common surnames. Although the individual colony descriptions include sources for specific colonies, it may be useful to note here the sources which include information of this kind for several colonies.

---

6. Under this agreement the Brazilian and Portuguese orthographies are practically identical. However in cases of disagreement, as in the name António, I have adopted the orthography used in Portugal.

For the British colonies the most obvious as well as the most useful sources have been the "Records of Services" sections of the *Colonial Office Lists* and *India Office Lists* and their respective predecessors. Frederick Boase's *Modern English Biography* includes sketches of several thousand Britishers who died between 1850 and 1900 and therefore it has information on many colonial governors. *Who's Who* and to a lesser extent *The Dictionary of National Biography* have been helpful, but both, and particularly the latter, include data only on those governors who reached high rank. The "Gazette Appointments" sections of the *Annual Registers* to 1872 have provided information on several of the more adamantine cases. For the Canadian colonies *The Encyclopedia Canadiana* and François Joseph Audet's *Canadian Historical Dates and Events, 1492–1915* have been used. For the Indian colonies, in addition to the *India Office Lists* I have consulted C. E. Buckland's *Dictionary of Indian Biography* and V. C. P. Hodson's *List of Officers of the Bengal Army, 1758–1834.* For the Australian colonies one need only refer to *The Australian Encyclopaedia*, truly a paradigm of a national encyclopedia. Finally, Eric A. Walker's *A History of Southern Africa* is useful for the several British colonies in that area.

Much less is available for the French colonies. The value of the *Dictionnaire de biographie française* is marred by the fact that it has not yet progressed through the letter "D." The *État général de la marine et des colonies*, published from 1763 to 1852, and its successors, the *Annuaire de la marine et des colonies* to 1886, the *Annuaire coloniale* of the Ministère des Colonies to 1896, the *Annuaire* of the same ministry to 1942, and the *Annuaire* of the Ministère de la France d'Outre-Mer from 1946 to 1954 are collectively an indispensable source for securing full names of French colonial administrators. Initially these were merely registers but latterly their value has been enhanced by the inclusion of brief "administrative biographies." Information for the Indochinese colonies may be found in J.-F.-A. Brébion's *Dictionnaire de bio-bibliographique générale, ancienne et moderne de l'Indo-Chine française.*

For the colonies in the other imperial systems various sources have been used. But in all cases much is owed to the kindness of the persons of the various archives included in the acknowledgments.

The description included for each colony is not intended to serve as a short administrative or political history of the colony but rather is designed to give a short sketch of the colony's position in its particular imperial system and to include miscellaneous relevancies such as changes in name or in administrative status or whatever else is thought necessary. Furthermore the descriptions are intended to include whatever cross-referencing is considered necessary. References to colonies within the same imperial system are simply indicated by "(q.v.)." If the colony belongs to a different imperial system, the number of the colony is given in parentheses.

In the lists, the divisions imposed on the basic data—the chronological list of governors—are designed to show changes in administrative title, changes in the name or composition of the colony, or the various administrative divisions of the colony, and changes in the governing imperial power. Where there were no known official appointments of governor to a colony during a period of rule by another imperial power, this period is indicated parenthetically in the list rather than by a separate heading. Periods of temporary supression of a colony, or of council rule—that is, when no governor served—are also shown in paren theses in the lists.

When a man served more than one term in a colony, this is shown by figures in parentheses following his name.

The device of underlining a date has been used in situations where exact be ginning and ending dates of a man's term are not known. A single underlined date represents the only known date that the individual was in office. Two underlined dates indicate the earliest and latest dates that an individual is known to have held the office. He may have held office for several years before and after these dates, and conceivably, in some cases, he may not have served con secutively between the two dates. If one of the two dates is underlined this means that the date of the beginning (or ending) of the man's term is not certain but the other date is certain. The references shown for each list include only the most important sources used in constructing the list. It would have been impossible to be more comprehensive since in some cases there were as many sources as individuals in the list.

It is fully realized that the quality of the lists included in this work varies. Many can be offered only as points of departure. This is especially true in the case of the Spanish colonies where obvious discrepancies will be seen as occurring. Often the data in Spanish archival sources are not adequate to the task of allaying these difficulties, particularly where an appointment was not royally conferred. It is hoped that the level of error and confusion for the other imperial systems is significantly less but the scope and complexity of the subject matter renders some error inevitable. Thus this work cannot be offered as a definitive contribution, but it is hoped that it will serve as a stimulus to further research in the area. In this regard it is strongly urged that corrections and additions as well as any other emendations be brought to the notice of the author.

Contents

Contents

Contents

Colonies
and Governors

Belgium

Belgium, of course, had not participated in the early colonial activities of the 17th and 18th centuries. After 1830 the Belgian government showed little interest in colonial matters, and it is unlikely that this policy would have been altered had it not been for the personality of the Belgian monarch Leopold II (1865–1909). Before his accession he had travelled in North Africa and had developed into an ardent imperialist, one who could write that "all the non-appropriated lands on the surface of the globe can become the field of our operation and of our success."[1] The Belgian government was indifferent to such lofty ambitions, and in 1876 Leopold formed the International African Association. This was ostensibly designed to foster international cooperation in exploring and civilizing Africa but in fact the Association was international in name only; it was dominated by Leopold and became the vehicle for his ambitions. His attention turned to the area of the Congo basin, whose hinterland lay unclaimed by any European country (any other claims were immaterial). The International African Association was replaced by the International Association of the Congo and Leopold's agents began to explore and lay claim to the area. The Belgian king's apparently quixotic hopes of securing possession of this vast area were abetted and in fact made possible by the mutual jealousies of the major European powers. France and Great Britain each dreaded the possibility of the other's staking a claim to the area, and they came to regard Leopold as an innocuous and therefore acceptable alternative. Consequently the Congress of Berlin in 1885 recognized Leopold's claims to the area and the Congo Free State was established.

The Congo Free State was unique in modern colonial expansion. It was the private domain—seventy-five times as large as Belgium—of Leopold, who was in effect his own chartered company. He regarded the Congo Free State as a business enterprise, himself as a royal entrepreneur—a kind of latter-day *roi épicier*. And on this basis the Free State was administered. Rubber, ivory, and, later, copper were extracted with no consideration for human costs, and exploitation of the Congolese people was unprecedentedly harsh and cruel. Fiscal profit was the only rationale for the Congo Free State. Eventually this situation created a level of international concern that made reform necessary. In 1908 Leopold reluctantly transferred sovereignty of the Congo Free State to the government of Belgium, and it was renamed the Belgian Congo. Belgian administra-

---

1. Quoted in William L. Langer, *European Alliances and Alignments, 1871–1890* (New York: Alfred A. Knopf, 1931), p. 290.

tion after 1908 was efficient but benevolent and paternal. Belgium governed
through a system of indirect rule, but indirect rule of the French variety where
traditional sanctions were ignored and the indigenous rulers were merely agents
of the government upon which they depended for their tenure. In 1919 the area
of Ruanda-Urundi, formerly part of German East Africa, was added to the Belgian
colonial empire and attached to the Belgian Congo, but with special administrative provisions since it was governed first as a mandate, then a trusteeship.

The paternalism of Belgian rule in the Congo included no provisions for an
orderly evolution to self-rule, and no measures were taken to prepare the Congolese people for independence. Indeed, when nationalism erupted in 1959 it
surprised, then mortified, the Belgian government which, with its limited experience, overreacted and granted almost immediate and complete independence
to the Congo, wholly neglecting or impossibly telescoping the intermediate
steps necessary for an orderly transition. In 1960 the Belgian Congo became
independent as the Republic of the Congo. Two years later Ruanda-Urundi likewise became independent, forming the two kingdoms of Rwanda and Burundi.

1 BELGIAN CONGO

As a source for slaves the area around the mouth of the Congo River had been frequented for
centuries by traders of many European nations. In 1876 Leopold II, king of Belgium, long in-
terested in African matters, formed the International African Association. The Association was
ostensibly a multi-national, non-political organization, interested only in the exploration of
Africa, but from the beginning it was dominated by Leopold, whose aims were of a greater scope.
By 1885 expeditions authorized by him had laid claim to much of the Congo River basin, and the
Congress of Berlin recognized his sovereignty over this area in that year. As a result, the Congo
Free State was organized and governed, not by Belgium, but by Leopold himself on a personal
basis. Under his tenure the colony was exploited by concessionnaires interested in ivory and
rubber production. In 1908 Belgium assumed sovereignty and the colony was renamed the Belgian Congo. Nationalist pressure resulted in an abrupt granting of independence in 1960, long
before the colony was ready to assume this burden. The present name is Republic of the Congo.

Congo Free State
Governors

1887-1890	Camille Janssen
1890-1891	Herman Ledeganck
1891	Henri-Ernest Gondry
1891-1892	Camille-Aimé Coquilhat
1892-1896	Théophile-Théodore-Joseph-Antoine Wahis (1)
1896-1900	François-Ernest-Joseph-Marie Dhanis
1900-1908	Théophile-Théodore-Joseph-Antoine Wahis (2)

Belgian Congo
Governors

1908-1912	Théophile-Théodore-Joseph-Antoine Wahis
1912-1916	Félix-Alexandre Fuchs
1916-1921	Eugène-Joseph-Marie Henry
1921-1923	Maurice-Eugène-Auguste Lippens
1923-1927	Martin-Joseph-Marie-Réne Rutten
1927-1934	Auguste-Constant Tilkens
1934-1946	Pierre-Marie-Joseph Ryckmans
1946-1952	Eugène-Jacques-Pierre-Louis Jungers
1952-1958	Léon-Antonin-Marie Pétillon
1958-1960	Henri Arthur Adolf Antoon Marie Christophe Cornelis

Information from L. van Meerbeeck, Archiviste général *p.i.*, Archives générales du Royaume,
Brussels; *Biographie coloniale belge*, under individual names.

2 RUANDA-URUNDI

The kingdoms of Rwanda and Burundi were among the last areas added to German East Africa (71)
and were administered separately from the rest of that colony. During World War I the two kingdoms were occupied by troops from the Belgian Congo (q.v.), and they were granted as a mandate
to Belgium after the war. Ruanda-Urundi was governed as a part of the Belgian Congo and the
governor of Ruanda-Urundi was also vice governor-general of the Belgian Congo. In 1962, after
the Belgian Congo had been granted its independence, Ruanda-Urundi became separately independent as two countries, Rwanda and Burundi.

Belgium

Governors
1916–1919 Justin-Prudent-François-Marie Malfeyt
1920–1930 Alfred-Frédéric-Gérard Marzorati
1930–1932 Charles-Henri-Joseph Voisin
1932–1946 Eugène-Jacques-Pierre-Louis Jungers
1946–1952 Léon-Antonin-Marie Pétillon
1952–1955 Alfred Maria Josephus Ghislencus Claeys-Boúúaert
1955–1962 Jean-Paul Harroy

Ruanda
High Representative
1962   Guillaume-Auguste-Émile Logiest

Urundi
High Representative
1962   Édouard Hennequiau

Information from L. van Meerbeeck, Archiviste général *p.i.*, Archives générales du Royaume, Brussels; *Biographie coloniale belge* , under individual names.

Bibliography: Belgium

Academie royale des Sciences d'Outre-Mer. *Biographie coloniale belge*. 6 vols. Brussels: Librairie Falk fils, 1948—62.

Denmark

Denmark, through its union with Norway, had administered Iceland since 1380 and in this sense may be considered to have been among the earliest of colonial powers. Between 1605 and 1607 three expeditions had been dispatched to Greenland in the hope of locating earlier settlements there or of establishing new ones, but neither hope was realized. In 1616 Denmark turned its attention to the tropical world with the formation of the Danish East India Company which established a post at Tranquebar and later at other points in India. In the 1650's posts were established along the Guinea coast and on the Gold coast of West Africa. Danish seamen began to visit the West Indies in 1654, and in 1671 the Danish West Indies Company was formed to establish settlements, rather than simply posts, there. In due time three islands came under Danish control and inevitably they were organized on the plantation system, then universal in the West Indies, with sugar as the staple commodity.

In the middle of the 18th century the Danish crown assumed control of the country's overseas possessions, and the chartered companies lost their administrative functions. Denmark, in 1792 (effective in 1803), was the first European nation to prohibit the slave trade from its African possessions.

Increasingly heavier commitments to colonial ventures by the larger European powers in the 19th century rendered Denmark, with its limited resources and capabilities, obsolete as a colonial power. The British occupation of India, and greater British and French interest in West Africa, resulted in a precipitate decline—indeed, almost a disappearance—of the trade of Denmark's colonies. They became "fantastical monsters, annually demanding their tribute of money and human lives without adequate return."[1] Under these circumstances the Danish government authorized the sale of its African and Asian possessions in 1840. The buyer in each case proved to be Great Britain, which regarded the Danish possessions in India as an administrative nuisance and feared that the French might ultimately seek to purchase Denmark's Gold Coast posts. The Danish West Indies, the most important, lingered under Danish ownership until 1917, although nearly purchased by the United States (no one wanted them) in the 1860's. The strategic considerations of World War I finally prompted the United States to purchase the three islands and Denmark's colonial "empire" came to an end.

The example of Denmark is particularly revealing of the trend of the expan-

---

1. [Georg Nørregård] "The English Purchase of the Danish Possessions in the East Indies and Africa," *Revue française d'histoire des colonies* 9(1933):ix.

sion of Europe. Before the 18th century the objectives of the various European countries, Spain and to some extent Portugal being excepted, were limited both by resources and interest. In this competition any nation with a modicum of maritime strength could engage, and most did. After about 1800, while the field of colonial activity widened, the number of participants was limited to those with sufficient national resources to devote to colonialism as well as to colonization. Denmark was not among this select group.

3 DANISH GOLD COAST

In 1657 the Danes expelled Sweden from the latter's posts on the Gold Coast and established themselves in the Swedish fort of Osu near Accra. The post was renamed Christiansborg and it became the headquarters for Danish commercial activities along the Guinea coast. During the period of their establishment on this coast, the Danes built or purchased further posts at Keta (Fort Prinzenstein), Teshi (Fort Augustaborg), Ningo (Fort Friedensborg), and Ada (Fort Konigstein), which were all situated to the east of Accra along the coast. The prosperity of these trading centers depended in large measure on the traffic in slaves, but Denmark abolished this trade in 1792 (in force, 1803). Without the slave trade the posts had little function, and by the accession of Christian VIII in 1839 Denmark had become desirous of ridding herself of both her Indian and African posts. Great Britain, interested in forestalling further French expansion in this area, purchased all the Danish forts in 1850 and integrated them into her colony of the Gold Coast (136).

Governors

1659-1662	Jost Cramer
1662-1669	Henning Albrecht
1669-1674	Bartolomaus von Gronestein
1674-1680	Conrad Crul[1]
1680-1681	Peter With
1681-1687	Hans Lykke
1687-1691	Nikolaj Fensman
1691-1692	Jørgen Meyer
1692-1694	Harding Petersen
1694-1697	Thomas Jacobsen
1697-1698	Erik Olsen Lygaard (1)
1698-1703	Johan Trane
1703-1704	Hartvig Meyer
1704-1705	Peder Sverdrup
1705-1711	Erik Olsen Lygaard (2)
1711-1717	Frantz Boye
1717-1720	Knud Rost
1720-1722	Peder Østrup
1722-1723	David Herrn
1723	Niels Jensen Østrup
1723-1724	Christian Andreas Syndemann
1724-1727	Henrik Suhm
1727	Frederik Pahl
1727-1728	Andreas Willumsen
1728-1735	Anders Pedersen Waerøe
1735-1736	Søren Schiellerup
1736-1740	Enevold Nielson Boris
1740-1743	Peter Nikolaj Jørgensen
1743-1744	Christian Glob Dorph
1744-1745	Jørgen Billsen
1745-1746	August Frederik Hackenburg
1746-1751	Joost Platfus[s]
1751	Magnus Christopher Lützow
1751-1752	Magnus Hacksen
1752-1757	Carl Engman

1757-1762	Christian Jessen
1762-1766	Carl Gottleb Resch
1766-1768	Christian Tychsen
1768-1769	Frantz Joachim Kuhberg
1769-1770	Gerhard Friedrich Wresberg
1770	Joachim Christian Otto
1770-1772	Johan Daniel Frölich
1772-1777	Niels Urban Aarestrup
1777-1779	Johan Conrad von Hemsen
1779-1789	Jens Adolf Kiøge
1789	Johan Friedrich Kipnasse
1789-1792	Andreas Riegelsen Bjørn
1792-1793	Bendt Olrik
1793-1795	Christian Friedrich von Hager
1795-1807	Johan Peter David Wrisberg
1807-1816	Christian Schiønning
1816-1817	Johan Emanuel Rechter
1817-1819	Jens Nikolaj Cornelius Reiersen
1819-1820	Christian Svanekiaer
1820-1821	Peter Svane Steffens
1821-1822	Mathias Thønning
1822-1825	Johan Christopher Richelieu
1825-1826	Niels Brock (1)
1826-1828	Jens Peter Findt
1830-1831	Ludvig Vincent Hein
1831	Helmuth von Ahrensdorff
1831-1832	Niels Brock (2)
1832-1833	Henrik Gerhard Lind
1833-1834	Edvard von Gandil
1834-1839	Frederik Siegfried Mørch
1839	Hans Angel Gjede
1839-1841	Lucas Dall
1841-1842	Bernhard Johan Christian Wilkens
1842-1847	Edvard James Arhold Carstensen
1847-1850	Rasmus Emil Schmidt

Larsen, *Guvernører, residenter*, pp. 24–25; Nørregård, passim.

9

4 DANISH WEST INDIES

In 1672 the island of Saint Thomas in the West Indies was settled under the aegis of the Danish West Indies Company. The company took possession of the neighboring island of Saint Johns in 1684 but only settled it in 1716. In 1733 Saint Croix, French since 1650 but never settled, was purchased. These three islands comprised the Danish West Indies. From 1734 to 1756 Saint Thomas and Saint Johns were administered as a unit, and Saint Croix was administered separately except that from 1736 to 1744 a governor-general administered all three islands. In 1755 control of the islands was transferred from the Danish West Indies Company to the crown, and in 1756 the office of governor-general was reinstituted. From 1756 to 1871 the seat of the governor-general was on Saint Croix and the other two islands retained a separate but subordinate administration. From 1801 to 1802 and again from 1807 to 1815 the Danish West Indies, like almost all overseas European colonies, were occupied by the British, but they were returned in 1815. In 1862 the post of governor of Saint Thomas-Saint Johns was abandoned, and nine years later the governor-general removed to Saint Thomas. By 1850 Denmark had disposed of its other colonies and was willing to dispose of the Danish West Indies as well. A treaty of sale was concluded with the United States in 1867 but never ratified by the U.S. Senate. Denmark therefore retained the islands for another fifty years until 1917 when altered circumstances found the United States a more willing purchaser—at a price vastly greater than that agreed upon in 1867 (v. Virgin Islands, 411).

Saint Croix
Governors
1734-1736	Frederik Moth
1736-1744	Gregers Hög Nissen
1744-1747	Poul Jensen Lindemark
1747-1751	Jens Hansen
1751-1756	Peter Clausen (1)

Danish West Indies
Governors-General
1756-1766	Christian Leberecht von Prøck
1766-1771	Peter Clausen (2)
1771-1773	Ulrich Wilhelm von Roepstorff
1773-1785	Peter Clausen (3)
1785-1787	Henrik Ludvig Ernst von Schimmelmann
1787-1794	Ernst Frederik von Walterstorff (1)
1794-1796	Wilhelm Anton Lindemann (1)
1796-1799	Thomas de Malleville
1799-1801	Wilhelm Anton Lindemann (2)
1801-1802	(under Great Britain)
1802-1803	Ernst Frederik von Walterstorff (2)
1803-1807	Balthazar Frederik Mühlenfels
1807	Hans Christopher Lillienskjøld
1807-1815	(under Great Britain)
1815-1816	Peter Lotharius von Oxholm
1816-1820	Adrian Benjamin Bentzon
1820-1822	Carl Adolph Rothe
1822-1827	Johan Frederik Bardenfleth
1827-1848	Peter Carl Frederik von Scholten
1848-1851	Peder Hansen
1851-1855	Hans Ditmar Frederik Feddersen
1855-1861	Johan Frederik Schlegel
1861-1872	Vilhelm Ludvig Birch
1872-1881	Janus August Garde
1881-1893	Christian Henrik Arendrup
1893-1903	Carl Emil Hedemann
1904-1905	Frederik Theodor Martin Mortensen Nordlien
1905-1908	Christian Magdalus Thestrup Cold
1908-1912	Peter Carl Limpricht
1912-1916	Lars Christian Helweg-Larsen
1916-1917	Henrik Konow

Saint Thomas-Saint Johns
Governors
1672-1680	Jørgen Iversen Dyppel
1680-1682	Nicolaj Esmit
1682-1684	Adolph Esmit
1684-1686	Gabriel Milan
1686	Mikkel Mikkelsen
1686-1689	Christopher Heins
1689-1702	Johan Lorentz[en]
1702-1706	Claus Hansen
1706-1708	Joachim Melchior von Holten
1708-1710	Diderich Mogensen
1710-1716	Mikkel Knudsen Crone
1716-1724	Erik Bredal
1724	Otto Jacob Thambsen
1724-1727	Frederik Moth (1)
1727-1733	Henrik Suhm
1733-1736	Philip Gardelin
1736-1740	Frederik Moth[1] (2)
1740-1744	Jacob Schönemann
1744-1747	Christian Schweder
1747-1758	Christian Suhm
1758-1760	Harrien Felchenhauer
1760-1764	Johan Georg von John
1764-1765	Peter Gynthelberg
1765-1766	Ulrich Wilhelm Roepstorff
1766-1773	Jens Nielsen Kragh
1773-1796	Thomas de Malleville
1796-1800	Balthazar Frederik von Mühlenfels
1800-1801	Casimir Wilhelm von Scholten (1)

1801–1802	(under Great Britain)	1823–1826	Peter Carl Frederik von Scholten (2)
1802–1803	Willum von Rømeling		
1803–1807	Casimir Wilhelm von Scholten (2)	1826–1829	Johannes Söbötker (1)
1807–1815	(under Great Britain)	1829–1834	Frederik Ludvig Christian Pentz Rosenørn
1815–1818	Christian Ludvig von Scholten		
1818–1820	Peter Carl Frederik von Scholten (1)	1834–1836	Frederick von Oxholm (1)
		1836–1848	Johannes Söbötker (2)
1820–1822	Carl Gotlieb Fleischer	1848–1852	Frederick von Oxholm (2)
1822–1823	Carl Vilhelm Jessen	1853–1862	Hans Henrik Berg

1. Governor-General of Danish West Indies.

Most lists of the governors and governors-general of the Danish West Indies are distorted because they fail to distinguish between the posts of governor of Saint Croix and governor of Saint Thomas-Saint Johns in the period from 1733 to 1756 when they were separate and usually equal. The above lists are based on Larsen, *Dansk Vestindien*, pp. 371–85, with modifications provided by Det kongelige Bibliothek, Copenhagen. See also Westergaard, pp. 285–89, for the period 1733 to 1756.

5 TRANQUEBAR

The Danish East India Company, formed in 1611, purchased Tranquebar, on the Coromandel coast of southeastern India near the French post at Pondichéry (v. French India, 21), from the raja of Tanjore in 1620, and Tranquebar remained the headquarters for Danish commercial activities in the area. Later, Denmark acquired posts at Dannemarksnagore (1698) and Frederiksnagore (1755) in Bengal. The Nicobar Islands were occupied in 1756. Tranquebar was occupied by the British, although they did not administer it separately, from 1808 to 1815. The three mainland posts were sold to Great Britain in 1845. The Nicobar Islands were gradually abandoned after 1848 and were ceded to Great Britain in 1869 (v. Andaman and Nicobar Islands, 81).

Governors

1620–1621	Ove Gedde	1733–1741	Poul Krisk Panck
1621–1636	Roland Crappé	1741–1744	Ivar Bonsack
1636–1643	Bernt Pessart	1744–1754	Hans Ernst Bonsack
1643–1648	Willum Leyel	1754–1759	Hans Georg Krog
1648–1655	Poul Hansen Korsør	1759–1760	Christian Frederik Høyer
1655–1669	Eskild Andersen Kongsbakke	1760–1761	Herman Jacob Forck
1669–1673	Henrik Eggers	1761–1775	Peter Herman Abbestee (1)
1673–1682	Sigvart Adeler	1775–1779	David Brown
1682–1686	Axel Juel	1779–1788	Peter Herman Abbestee (2)
1686–1687	Wolff Heinrich von Calnein	1788–1806	Peter Anker
1687–1689	Christian Porck (1)	1806–1808	Johan Peter Hermanson (1)
1689–1690	Mourids Hartmann	1808–1815	(under Great Britain)
1690–1694	Christian Porck (2)	1815–1816	Gerhard Sievers Bille
1694–1701	Claus Vogdt (Voigt)	1816–1822	Johan Peter Hermanson (2)
1701	Andreas Andrae	1822–1823	Jens Kofoed
1701–1702	Mikkel Knudsen Crone	1823–1825	Ulrich Anton Schönheyder
1702–1704	Jørgen Hermansen Bjørn	1825–1829	Hans Diderich Brinck-Seidelin
1704–1716	Johan Sigismund Hassius	1829–1832	Lauritz Christensen
1716–1720	Christen Brun-Lundegaard	1832–1838	Conrad Emil Mourier
1720–1726	Christian Ulrich von Nissen	1838–1841	Johannes von Rehling
1726–1730	Rasmus Hansen Attrup	1841	Christian Tiemroth
1730–1733	Diderich Mühlenport	1841–1845	Peder Hansen

Denmark

Larsen, *De dansk-ostindiske koloniers historie*, 1:170–71; idem, *Guvernører, residenter*, p. 18. The latter work also includes material on the subordinate administrators at Dannemarksnagore, Frederiksnagore, and the Nicobar Islands, on pp. 19, 21, and 28, respectively.

Bibliography: Denmark

Larsen, Kay. *De dansk-ostindiske koloniers historie*. 2 vols. Copenhagen: Centralforlaget, 1907–8.
——. *Dansk vestindien (1666–1917)*. Copenhagen: C. A. Reitzel, 1928.
——. *Guvernører, residenter, kommandanter og chefer samt enkelte andre fremtra edende personer i de tidligere danske tropekolonier*. Copenhagen: Arthur Jensen forlag, 1940.
Nørregård, Georg. *Danish Settlements in West Africa, 1658–1850*. Translated by Sigurd Mammen. Boston: Boston University Press, 1966.
Westergaard, Waldemar. *The Danish West Indies under Company Rule (1671–1754)*. New York: Macmillan Co., 1917.

France

The Crusades provided the first budding of French overseas expansion. French rulers played a prominent role in the Crusades from 1097 to 1270, and France's later intense interest in North Africa and the Levant can be traced to this period. During the 14th and 15th centuries France was active in the western Mediterranean and along the coast of North Africa. Indeed, there exists a persistent but unsubstantiated tradition that Dieppois traders frequented the Guinea coast between 1364 and 1413 and established posts there at Elmina and elsewhere, but the tradition is of suspiciously late origin. In any case, it is historically certain that the Norman Jean de Bethencourt explored and colonized several of the Canary Islands in the years after 1402, although he later acknowledged Castilian rather than French sovereignty over his rights to them.

France, of course, was not included in Pope Alexander VI's arbitrary division of the New World by the Treaty of Tordesillas in 1494, but this exclusion scarcely stifled French interests in the newly discovered areas. Frenchmen were in Brazil at least as early as 1504 and twenty years or so later established a settlement there, only to be driven out by the Portuguese, "rightful" proprietors under the terms of the Papal Bull. Later in the century they returned to establish a settlement on Guanabara Bay, known as France Antarctique, partly as a Huguenot refuge. Again, early in the 17th century a French settlement, grandiloquently termed France Équinoxiale, was established at the mouth of the Amazon. In each instance the settlement was destroyed by the Portuguese. Efforts to found a Huguenot haven also led to an abortive colonizing effort in Florida. In this case it was the Spanish who suppressed it. The French navigator Jacques Cartier discovered the Saint Lawrence River in northern North America in 1534, but even before this time French fishermen had exploited the rich preserves of the Grand Banks area off the coast of Newfoundland. In the East the French had reached Sumatra in 1529, and in Africa they were the first to dispute the Portuguese monopoly of trade along the Guinea coast.

Nevertheless, none of these widespread, if disjointed, activities resulted in any permanent French settlement. It was the 17th century which was to be the great era of French overseas expansion and the vehicles for this expansion were the private chartered companies. For France was the most extreme example of this phenomenon so typical of early European expansion. No less than seventy-five such companies were created between 1599 and 1789 for the purposes of trade and colonization.[1] These companies were under royal control, though pri-

---

1. J. Chailley-Bert, *Les compagnies de colonisation sous l'ancien régime* (Paris: Armand Colin, 1898), pp. 21–25.

vately financed. The state thereby retained its sovereignty with minimal capi
tal investment. By 1674 most of the French colonies had reverted to the complete control of the crown, although they continued to be chartered for purpose
of trade.

French colonial activity under the *ancien régime* was primarily confined to
northern North America, the West Indies and the Guiana coast of South Americ
and India and points along the sea route to India. In each area French efforts
were rewarded with a certain success. The rich fur trade of Canada was profi
ably exploited; Saint-Domingue was the largest sugar producer in the world in
the 18th century; and in India the French were able, in the mid-18th century, t
make a serious bid to become the dominant European power in the subcontinen
But the lack of sea power, and heavy French commitments to the politics of
Europe, militated against lasting success in each of these promising areas.
Furthermore, it was only in the West Indies that French settlement reached the
proportions of English and Spanish settlement in the New World, and even her
it was based on slave societies. As a result of every major European war of t
18th century France lost some of its colonies to Great Britain and by 1815 it
was left with only French Guiana, a few of the less important Indian islands,
Senegal in West Africa, Réunion in the Indian Ocean, five vestigial enclaves i
India, and a small group of islands off the Newfoundland coast. The largest
and richest of its possessions had been irretrievably lost.

The second phase of the French imperial effort was confined to regions not
exploited earlier, that is, Africa, Southeast Asia, and the Pacific. It began in
1830 with the invasion of Algeria on highly questionable pretexts. After 1843
some islands in the Pacific Ocean were annexed as a balance to Great Britain
increasing interest in the area. Further trading posts were established along
the west coast of Africa, and under the governorship of Faidherbe (1854—65) th
old French colony of Senegal began to expand inland—the first European effor
in West Africa to penetrate beyond the coast. French imperial ventures in the
19th century were often spearheaded by missionary activities and this was pa
ticularly true in Indochina where missionary efforts dated from the 18th centu
After 1858 these religious activities were transformed into political and military conquest. By 1897 the whole area of French Indochina had been added as
a major colony to the French empire.

But the greatest French activity was confined to Africa. During the classical years of the "scramble," France added most of West Africa and West Equa
torial Africa to the empire. Its 17th-century interest in Madagascar provided
claim which, however tenuous, allowed France to claim priority and annex tha
island in 1897. French activity in Africa, and to a lesser degree in Indochina
was stimulated by the desire to forestall possible British control of these are
and by a militaristic, chauvinist reaction to the great humiliation of the Franc
Prussian War of 1870—71, which furthermore provided the justification for ove
seas empire-building.

The French Empire in 1900 was large and, at least in Africa, largely contigu
ous, but it had been frantically acquired and very incompletely integrated into
a unified whole. Of all the French colonies of the post-1815 period only Alge
had received a large influx of French emigrants. The French empire, then, rep
sented the classical typology of colonialism—large numbers of aliens ruled l

14

insignificant numbers of Europeans whose primary interests were administrative and exploitative. The French propounded a series of ethical—not as mystical as those of the Portuguese—bases to justify as well as regulate the relationship of the subject peoples to the French colonial government, or to France itself in theory. Initially the policy of *assimilation*, moderately successful earlier in Senegal, was adopted. Briefly and simply stated this theory maintained that all of the subject peoples were capable, and would eventually be desirous, of being gallicized culturally, socially, and linguistically—in fine, that each of the colonies could and would become replicas of the motherland through the medium of the *mission civilatrice* and would in time be glad to leave behind their previous, inferior cultural milieu. The basic unsoundness of this policy soon manifested itself, and assimilation was gradually, if unofficially, replaced by *association*, which professed to recognize the intrinsic worth of all cultures and allowed colonial peoples to retain, therefore, most aspects of their particular cultures. Neither the policy of assimilation nor that of association envisioned substantial autonomy for the French colonies, and like metropolitan France itself they were tightly controlled from Paris. Until 1884 all the French colonies, logically enough, were administered by the Ministry of the Navy. After 1884 there was a separate colonial department but only in 1897 was the Ministry of Colonies created.

Despite the pretense of equality among French colonies, only a minuscule percentage of their inhabitants had become French citizens by the beginning of World War II. There was no French colonial equivalent to the British dominion, although a few French colonies were allowed to send a representative to the Chamber of Deputies. This situation was radically altered by the course of World War II. During the war France lost control of all its colonies and mandates and, like the Netherlands, resumption of control after the war had perforce to be on a different basis. In 1946 the empire was renamed the French Union. Martinique, Guadeloupe, and Réunion—all old French colonies with French populations—became overseas departments of France. Most of the other colonies became overseas territories and their inhabitants became French citizens. The Ministry of Colonies was replaced by a Ministry of Overseas Territories (Ministère d'Outre-Mer). Except for the citizenship aspect, however, little had changed in the relation of the territories to France. Another category in the French Union were the associated states. These included the former protectorates of Tunisia, Morocco, and Indochina. They were putatively autonomous except in matters of foreign affairs and were thus analogous to the early forms of British dominions. The French Union never reached the stage of functioning fully since events moved too rapidly for its cumbrous structure. The associated states became independent between 1954 and 1956. Incipient nationalism in the overseas territories also necessitated a reevaluation of their roles. In 1958 the Community replaced the Union and all but a few colonies became substantially independent and then became completely independent within a few years. In 1961 the Community was dissolved. Algeria, nominally an integral part of France, secured its independence, after a bitter struggle, in 1963. Since that time only a few small and scattered overseas territories remain as vestiges of the former French Empire.

6 ACADIA

Acadia, in what is now Nova Scotia, was the first French colony in the New World. The first settlement occurred in 1604, followed by subsequent ones, undertaken by private concession-naires. The colony was subjected to several English raids from New England and Acadia was occupied by the English in 1654, but returned in 1670. In 1710, during the War of the Spanish Succession, Acadia was again occupied by the English, this time permanently as confirmed by the Treaty of Utrecht in 1713. In return, France received the lesser prize of Île Royale (q.v.).

The following list of governors is somewhat arbitrary in that the office was constantly dis-puted among various claimants, especially before 1654, because of the issuance of conflicting patents by the French king. Furthermore there was a high degree of absenteeism among these earlier governors, who were substituted for, on varying bases, by lieutenants or deputies.

Governors
1604-1606	Pierre du Gua de Monts
1606-1611	Jean de Biencourt de Poutrincourt
1611-1623	Charles de Biencourt de Saint-Just
1623-1632	Charles de Saint-Étienne de la Tour (1)
1632-1635	Isaac de Razilly
1635-1650	Charles de Menou d'Aulnay Charnisay
1635-1643	Charles de Saint-Étienne de la Tour (2)
1650-1654	Charles de Saint-Étienne de la Tour (3)

under Great Britain

Governors
1654-1657	John Leverett

1657-1670	Thomas Temple

under France

Governors
1668-1670	Alexandre Le Borgne de Bellisle
1670-1673	Héctor d'Andigné de Grandfontain
1673-1677	Jacques de Chambly
1677-1678	Pierre de Joybert de Soulanges
1678-1684	Michel Le Neuf de la Vallière
1684-1687	François-Marie Perrot
1687-1690	Louis-Alexandre des Friches de Menneval
1690-1700	Joseph Robinau de Villebon
1700-1701	Sébastien de Villieu
1701-1705	Jacques-François de Brouillan
1705-1706	Simon-Pierre Denys de Bonaventu
1706-1710	Daniel d'Auger de Subercase

Després, pp. 219–88; *Dictionary of Canadian Biography*, I, under individual names.

7 ALGERIA

European interest in North Africa began as a logical sequel to the end of the *Reconquista* in Spain in 1492. In the middle of the 16th century the area of Algeria came under nominal Ottoman suzerainty, but from 1509 to 1792 the Spaniards held Orán (368) and occasionally other coastal towns as well. In 1705 the ruler of Algiers repudiated Ottoman control. The piratical tendencie of all the North African rulers attracted European and even American interest around the turn of the 19th century. French interest dated to 1797 and seemed to revolve almost exclusively, at least in form, around debt problems.

Disputes over a debt owed by France to the dey of Algiers led to a French invasion of Algeria in 1830. Dispensing with the form of a protectorate the French deposed the dey and began from the first to rule the area directly. The coastal areas were easily conquered, but it was not until 1847 that the near interior was controlled. Until 1879 Algeria was a military province, but after that date it had a civil government and a quasi-colonial relationship with the metropolis. After 1900 France began to extend her control over the vast desert interior, bringing the boundaries of the colony limitrophe to her other West African possessions. By the end of World War II Algiers had a very large French immigrant population—a population which vigorously resisted any concessions to Algerian nationalism. As a result a revolt broke out in 1954 which, though not militarily successful, nonetheless forced France to concede complete independence to Algeria under a native government in 1962.

Governors

1830	Louis-Auguste-Victor de Bourmont, Comte de Ghaisnes
1830-1831	Bertrand Clauzel (1)
1831-1832	Pierre Bethezène
1832-1833	Anne-Jean-Marie-René Savary, Duc de Rovigo
1833-1834	Théophile Voirol
1834-1835	Jean-Baptiste Drouet d'Erlon
1835-1837	Bertrand Clauzel (2)
1837	Charles-Marie Denys de Damrémont
1837-1841	Sylvain-Charles Valée
1841-1845	Thomas-Robert Bugeaud de la Piconnerie, Duc d'Isly
1845-1847	Louis-Christophe-Léon Juchault de Lamorisière
1847	Marie-Alphonse Bedeau
1847-1848	Henri-Eugène-Philippe-Louis d'Orléans, Duc d'Aumale
1848	Louis-Eugène Cavaignac
1848	Nicolas-Anne-Théodule Changarnier
1848	Gerald-Stanislas Marey-Monge, Comte de Peluse
1848-1850	Viala Charon
1850-1851	Alphonse-Henri d'Hautpoul
1851	Aimable-Jean-Jacques Pelissier (1)
1851-1858	Jean-Louis-Cesar-Alexandre Randon

Ministers

1858-1859	Napoléon-Charles-Paul Bonaparte
1859-1860	Justin-Napoléon-Samuel-Prosper de Chasseloup-Laubat

Governors-General

1860-1864	Aimable-Jean-Jacques Pelissier, Duc de Malakoff (2)
1864	Édouard-Charles de Martimprey
1864-1870	Marie-Edme-Patrice-Maurice de MacMahon, Duc de Magenta
1870	François-Louis-Alfred Durrieu
1870	Jean-Walsin Esterhazy

1870-1871	Alexandre-Charles-Auguste du Bouzet
1871	Arsène-Mathurin-Louis-Marie Lambert
1871-1873	Louis-Henri de Gueydon
1873-1879	Antoine-Eugène-Alfred Chanzy
1879-1881	Jules-Philippe-Louis-Albert Grévy
1881-1891	Louis Tirman
1891-1897	Jules-Martin Cambon
1897-1898	Louis Lépine
1898-1900	Édouard Julien-Laferrière
1900-1901	Célestin-Auguste-Charles Jonnart (1)
1901-1903	Amédée-Joseph-Paul Revoil
1903	Maurice Varnier
1903-1911	Célestin-Augustin-Charles Jonnart (2)
1911-1918	Charles Lutaud
1918-1919	Célestin-Augustin-Charles Jonnart (3)
1919-1921	Jean-Baptiste-Eugène Abel
1921-1925	Jules-Joseph-Théodore Steeg
1925	Henri Dubief
1925-1927	Maurice Viollette
1927-1930	Pierre-Louis Bordes
1930-1935	Jules-Gaston-Henri Carde
1935-1940	Georges Le Beau
1940-1941	Jean-Charles Abrial
1941-1943	Yves-Charles Châtel
1943	Bernard-Marcel Peyrouton
1943-1944	Georges-Albert-Julien Catroux (1)
1944-1948	Yves Chataigneau
1948-1951	Marcel-Édmond Naegelen
1951-1955	Roger-Étienne-Joseph Leonard
1955-1956	Jacques-Émile Soustelle

Ministers-Resident

1956	Georges-Albert-Julien Catroux (2)
1956-1958	Robert Lacoste

Delegates-General

1958	Raoul Salan
1958-1960	Paul-Albert-Louis Delouvrier
1960-1962	Jean Morin
1962	Christian Fouchet

Information from the Press and Information Service, Embassy of France, Washington, D.C. Also, J.P.

8 ANNAM

French interest in Annam, already exemplified in Cochin China and Cambodia (qq.v.) continued and intensified in the 1870's. In 1875 the Annamite ruler accepted, under duress, a resident at his court in Hué. In 1883 the powers of this resident were expanded so that he became de facto ruler of the kingdom. The protectorate of Annam became a component of the Union of Indochina in 1887. Under the Japanese occupation during World War II the post of resident was suppressed. After French withdrawal in 1954 the area of Annam was divided between North and South Vietnam.

Annam-Tonkin		Residents-Superior	
Residents-General		1886-1888	Charles Dillon
1884-1885	Victor-Gabriel Lemaire	1888-1889	Séraphin Hector (1)
1885-1886	Philippe-Marie-André Roussel de	1889	Léon-Jean-Laurent Chavassieux
	Courcy	1889-1891	Séraphin Hector (2)
1886	Paul Bert	1891-1897	Ernest-Albert Brière
1886-1887	Paulin-François-Alexandre Vial	1897-1898	Jean-Calixte-Alexis Auvergne (1)
1887	Pierre-Louis-Georges Bihouard	1898-1900	Léon-Jules-Pol Boulloche
1887-1888	Étienne-Antoine-Guillaume	1900-1904	Jean-Calixte-Alexis Auvergne (2)
	Richaud	1904-1906	Jean-Ernest Moulié
1888-1889	Pierre-Paul Rheinart	1906-1908	Fernand-Ernest Levecque
		1908-1910	Élie-Jean-Henri Groleau
Annam		1910-1912	Henri-Victor Sestier
Chargés d'Affaires		1912-1913	Georges-Marie-Joseph Mahé
1875-1876	Pierre-Paul Rheinart (1)	1913-1920	Jean-François-Eugène Charles
1876-1897	Paul-Louis-Félix Philastre	1920-1927	Pierre-Marie-Antoine Pasquier
1879-1880	Pierre-Paul Rheinart (2)	1927-1928	Jules Fries
1880-1881	Louis-Eugène Palasme de	1928-1931	Aristide-Eugène Le Fol
	Champeaux	1931-1934	Yves-Charles Châtel
1881-1883	Pierre-Paul Rheinart (3)	1934-1940	Maurice-Fernand Graffeuil
1883-1884	François-Jules Harmand	1940-1942	Émile-Louis-François Grandjean

Information from Duong Sanh, Conservateur, National Library, Saigon, South Vietnam, and from the Archives nationales, section outre-mer, Paris. Also, Brébion, pp. 10—11 and under individual names.

9 CAMBODIA

Taking advantage of a succession dispute and professing a desire to protect Christian missionaries, France proclaimed a protectorate over the kingdom of Cambodia in 1863. In 1887 Cambodia became a constituent member of the Indochinese Union. During World War II the Japanese suppressed the French administration in Cambodia. In 1945 French control was reimposed on a different basis than before the war and in 1949 Cambodia became an associated state of the French Union. It became fully independent in 1954.

Residents		1870	Armand Pottier (2)
1863-1866	Ernest-Marc-Louis de Gonzague	1870-1871	Jules-Marcel Brossard de Corbigny
	Doudart de Lagrée	1871-1879	Jean Moura
1866-1868	Armand Pottier (1)	1879-1881	Étienne-François Aymonier
1868-1870	Jean Moura	1881-1885	Augustin-Julien Fourès

Residents-General
1885-1886 Pierre de Badens
1886-1887 Georges-Jules Piquet
1887-1889 Louis-Eugène Palasme de
          Champeaux

Residents-Superior
1889-1897 Albert-Louis Huyn de
          Vernéville
1897-1900 Alexandre-Antoine-Étienne-
          Gustave Ducos
1900-1901 Louis-Paul Luce (1)
1901-1902 Léon-Jules-Pol Boulloche

1902-1904 Henri-Félix de Lamothe
1904-1905 Jules-Louis Morel
1905-1911 Louis-Paul Luce (2)
1911-1914 Antoine-Georges-Amédée-Ernest
          Outrey
1914 Xavier Tessarech
1914-1926 François-Marius Baudoin
1926-1928 Aristide-Eugène Le Fol
1928-1932 Fernand-Marie-Joseph-Antoine
          Lavit
1932-1937 Achille-Louis-Auguste Silvestre
1937-1942 Léon-Emmanuel Thibeaudeau
1942-1945 Jean de Lens

Information from Duong Sanh, Conservateur, National Library, Saigon, and from Archives nationales, section outre-mer, Paris. Also, Brébion, pp. 58—59 and under individual names.

10 CAMEROUN

During World War I France occupied the eastern and major part of the German colony of Kamerun (75), the remainder accruing to Great Britain (v. Nigeria, 180). From 1922 Cameroun was administered under a mandate from the League of Nations. In 1946 France accepted a trusteeship for the territory from the United Nations, although reluctantly, for it wished to rule Cameroun directly as a colony. Cameroun continued as a trust territory until 1960 when it became independent.

Governors
1916 Joseph-Gaudérique Aymerich
1916-1920 Lucien-Louis Fourneau
1920-1921 Jules-Gaston-Henri Carde

High Commissioners
1921-1923 Jules-Gaston-Henri Carde
1923-1932 Théodore-Paul Marchand
1932-1935 Auguste-François Bonnecarrère
1935-1936 Jules-Vincent Repiquet
1936-1939 Pierre-François Boisson
1939-1940 Richard-Édmond-Maurice-Édouard
          Brunot

1940 Philippe-François-Marie Leclerc
          de Hauteclocque
1940-1943 Pierre-Charles-Albert Cournarie
1943-1944 Hubert-Eugène-Paul Carras
1944-1946 Henri-Pierre Nicolas
1946-1947 Robert-Louis Delavignette
1947-1949 René Hoffherr
1949-1954 Jean-Louis-Maurice-André
          Soucadaux
1954-1956 Roland-Joanes-Louis Pré
1956-1957 Pierre-Auguste-Joseph Messmer
1958 Jean-Paul Ramadier
1958-1960 Xavier-Antoine Torré

Gardinier, passim; Gifford and Louis, p. 773.

11 CHAD

The area of Chad became subject to French penetration soon after 1890, but no administrative structure was established until after the defeat of the Sudanese adventurer Rabeh in 1900. From 1906 to 1920 Chad and Ubangi-Shari (q.v.) were administered as a unit. After 1920 Chad became a separate colony within French Equatorial Africa (q.v.). The colony was ruled by lieutenant governors until 1946 when the rank was raised to governor. In the referendum of 1958 Chad voted to become an autonomous state within the French Community and in 1960 it became independent as Chad.

Ubangi-Shari and Chad
Lieutenant Governors
1906-1911	Émile Merwart
1911	Jean-Baptiste-Ernest Noirot
1911-1913	Frédéric Estèbe
1913-1916	Pierre-Pascal-Marie-Georges Adam
1916-1918	Victor-Emmanuel Merlet
1918-1920	Ernest-François-Maurice Delafosse

Chad
Military Commandants
1900-1920	Georges-Mathieu Destenave
1902-1904	Victor-Emmanuel-Étienne Largeau (1)
1904-1906	Henri-Joseph-Eugène Gouraud
1906-1908	Victor-Emmanuel-Étienne Largeau (2)
1908-1909	Constant Millot
1909-1910	Alexandre-Marie-Henry Moll
1910-1911	Joseph-Édmond Maillard
1911-1912	Victor-Emmanuel-Étienne Largeau (3)
1912	James-Édouard Hirtzman
1912-1913	Gabriel-Julien-Joseph Briand (1)
1913-1915	Victor-Emmanuel-Étienne Largeau (4)
1915-1916	Gabriel-Julien-Joseph Briand (2)
1916-1918	Clément-Léon Martelly
1918-1920	Albert Ducarre

Lieutenant Governors
1920-1925	Fernand-Marie-Joseph-Antoine Lavit
1925	Antoine Touzet
1925-1928	Dieudonné-François-Joseph-Marie Reste
1928-1929	Adolphe Deitte
1929-1932	Jules-Marcel de Coppet
1933-1934	Richard-Édmond-Maurice-Édouard Brunot
1934-1938	Charles-Jean-Jacques-Émile Dagain
1939-1941	Adolphe-Félix-Sylvestre Eboué
1941-1942	Pierre-Olivier Lapie
1943-1944	André-Jean-Gaston Latrille
1944-1946	Jacques-Camille-Marie Rogué

Governors
1946-1949	Jacques-Camille-Marie Rogué
1949	Paul-Hippolyte-Julien-Marie Le Layec
1950-1951	Henri-Jean-Marie de Mauduit
1951	Charles-Émile Hanin
1951-1956	Ignace-Jean-Aristide Colombani
1956-1958	Jean-René Troadec

High Commissioner
1959-1960	Daniel-Marius Doustin

Information from Le Chef du Service des Archives, Administration provisoire des Services du Ministère de la France d'Outre-Mer, Paris, and from Archives nationales, section outre-mer, Paris.

12 COCHIN CHINA

Cochin China was the southernmost part of the kingdom of Annam (q.v.). French interest in the area culminated with the occupation of the area around the Mekong River delta beginning in 1858. In 1862 this conquest was recognized by Annam which ceded the provinces to France. The colony soon expanded both north and south of the nuclear provinces. Until 1879 the governors of Cochin China were all admirals of the French navy; civil government was instituted in that year. On the establishment of the Indochinese Union (v. Indochina) in 1887, the colony came to be governed by lieutenant governors, but in 1911 this rank was changed to governor. Cochin China was the only component of Indochina officially ruled directly. All the others were nominally protectorates. Cochin China was occupied by the Japanese in 1942. In 1946 it was created an autonomous republic—a fiction designed to stifle nationalist desires. On the division of the eastern part of French Indochina in 1954 into North and South Vietnam, Cochin China became a part of the latter.

Governors

1858-1859	Charles Rigault de Genouilly
1859	Jean-Bernard Jauréguiberry
1859-1860	Théogène-François Page
1860-1861	Joseph-Hyacinthe-Louis-Jules d'Ariès
1861	Léopold-Victor-Joseph Charner
1861-1863	Louis-Adolphe Bonard
1863-1868	Pierre-Paul-Marie de la Grandière
1868-1869	Marie-Gustave-Hector Ohier
1870-1871	Alphonse-Jean-Claude-René-Théodore de Cornulier-Lucinière
1871-1874	Marie-Jules Dupré
1874-1875	Jules-François-Émile Krantz
1875-1877	Victor-Auguste Duperré
1877-1879	Louis-Charles-Georges-Jules Lafont
1879-1883	Charles-Marie Le Myre de Vilers
1883-1885	Charles-Antoine-François Thomson
1885-1886	Charles-Auguste-Frédéric Bégin
1886-1887	Ange-Michel Filippini

Lieutenant Governors

1887	Jean-Antoine-Ernest Constans
1887-1888	Georges-Jules Piquet

1888	Auguste-Eugène Navelle
1888-1889	(abolished)
1889	Augustin-Julien Fourès (1)
1889-1892	Henri-Eloi Danel
1892-1895	Augustin-Julien Fourès (2)
1895-1897	Alexandre-Antoine-Étienne-Gustave Ducos
1897-1898	Ange-Eugène Nicolai
1898-1901	Édouard Picanon
1901-1902	Henri-Félix de Lamothe
1902-1906	François-Pierre Rodier
1906-1907	Olivier-Charles-Arthur de Lalande de Calan
1907-1909	Louis-Alphonse Bonhoure
1909-1911	Jules-Maurice Gourbeil

Governors

1911-1916	Jules-Maurice Gourbeil
1916-1921	Maurice-Joseph Le Gallen
1921-1926	Maurice Cognacq
1926-1929	Paul-Marie-Alexis-Joseph Blanchard de la Brosse
1929-1934	Jean-Félix Krautheimer
1934-1939	Pierre-André-Michel Pagès
1939-1940	René Veber
1940-1942	André-Georges Rivoal

Information from Duong Sanh, Conservateur, National Library, Saigon, and from Archives nationales, section outre-mer, Paris. Also, Brébion, pp. 84–85.

13 COMORO ISLANDS

The Comoro Islands, the islands previously comprising the colony of Mayotte (q.v.), were separated from Madagascar (q.v.) in 1947 and erected into a separate colony. In the referendum of 1958 the inhabitants voted to remain within the French Republic. However, internal autonomy was granted in 1961 and the governors became high commissioners. Since then, the status of the islands has not changed.

Governors

1947-1949	Eugène-Alain-Charles-Louis Alaniou
1949-1950	Marie-Emmanuel-Adolphe-Roger Remy
1950-1957	Pierre-Léonard-Alphonse Coudert

France

1957-1960   Georges Arnaud
1961   Louis-Joseph-Édouard Saget

High Commissioners
1961-1963   Louis-Joseph-Édouard Saget
1963-1966   Henri-Joseph-Marie Bernard
1966——   Antoine-Padouan Columbani

Information from Archives nationales, section outre-mer, Paris.

14 DAHOMEY

From 1671 the port of Ouidah (Whydah) on the Gulf of Guinea was the site of several European factories, established to engage in the slave trade. After the conquest of Ouidah by the African kingdom of Dahomey (or Abomey) in 1727 these factories continued to exist, but under the strict control of the Dahomean ruler's representative. The Dutch and Danes departed from the Guinea coast in the middle of the 19th century (v. Danish Gold Coast, 3, and the Netherlands colony, Gold Coast, 268); Britain was engaged elsewhere; but French interest in the Dahomey area increased. A protectorate was established over the small coastal state of Porto Novo in 1863 but withdrawn in 1867 only to be reasserted in 1883. From 1878 to 1894 French influence along the coast was broadened. In 1894 the interior kingdom of Dahomey was conquered and a temporary protectorate was established there. In 1900 the kingdom was abolished and the territory annexed. In 1899 Dahomey became a part of French West Africa (q.v.). Until 1886 the French settlements were under Gabon (q.v.). From 1886 to 1894 under Rivières du Sud (v. French Guinea). In 1894 Dahomey became a separate colony. In 1937 the lieutenant governors of Dahomey became governors. In 1958 Dahomey became an autonomous member of the French Community and in 1960 it became independent as the Republic of Dahomey.

Cotonou

Consuls
1878-1881   Albert-Richard Ardin d'Elteil
1881-1883   Victor Bareste

Porto Novo

Residents
1883   Bonaventure Colonna de Lecca
1883-1884   D. Germa
1884-1886   Charles Disnematin-Dorat
1886-1887   Emmanuel Roget
1887   Gentien-Antonin-Marie Péréton
1887-1888   Victor-Marie-Louis Ballot (1)
1888-1889   Paul-Alphonse-Frédéric-Marie
              de Beeckmann
1889   Louis-Frédéric-Émile Tautain
1889-1891   Victor-Marie-Louis Ballot (2)

Dahomey

Lieutenant Governors
1891-1900   Victor-Marie-Louis Ballot
1900-1906   Victor-Théophile Liotard
1906-1908   Charles-Emmanuel-Joseph Marchal
1809-1909   Jean-Jules-Émile Peuvergne

1901-1911   Henri-Jules-Jean-Baptiste Malan
1911-1912   Émile Merwart
1912-1917   Charles-Henri-Adrien Noufflard
1917-1928   Gaston-Léopold-Joseph Fourn
1929-1931   Dieudonné-Jean-François Reste
1931-1932   Théophile-Antoine-Pascal Tellier
1932   Louis-Placide Blacher
1932-1934   Jules-Marcel de Coppet
1934-1935   Marcel-Alexandre-Jean
              Marchessou
1935-1937   Maurice-Léon Bourgine

Governors
1937-1938   Louis-Alexandre-Étienne Bonvin
1938-1940   Armand-Léon Annet
1940-1943   Léon-Hippolyte Truitard
1943-1945   Charles-André-Maurice Assier
              de Pompignan
1945-1946   Marc-Antoine-Christian Laurent
              de Villedeuil
1946-1948   Robert Legendre
1948   Jean-Georges Chambon
1948-1949   Jacques-Alphonse Boissier
1949-1951   Claude Valluy

1951-1955 Charles-Henri Bonfils   *High Commissioner*
1955-1958 Casimir-Marc Biros   1959-1960 René Tirant

Information from Jacques Lombard, Institut français [now fondamental] d'Afrique noire, centre du Dahomey, Porto Novo, Dahomey. For the directors of the French post at Ouidah in the 18th century, see Akinjogbin, p. 216; Dunglas, pp. 183—84; and Schefer, 1:215—24. For the English directors at Ouidah in the 18th century, see Akinjogbin, pp. 218—19. For the directors of the Portuguese post in the 18th and 19th centuries, see Pierre Verger, *Le Fort St. Jean-Baptiste d'Ajuda* (Porto Novo: Institut des recherches appliquées du Dahomey, 1966), passim. The Portuguese retained sovereignty over their fort until 1961 when it was ceded to the new Republic of Dahomey.

15 DIÉGO-SUAREZ

After the French intervention in Madagascar (q.v.) in 1886, by which the Merina kingdom became a protectorate, the colony of Diégo-Suarez was established in the far north of the island, designed as a beachhead for future French interests. With the establishment of the colony of Madagascar and of French control over the whole island in 1896, Diégo-Suarez no longer served any function and the colony was abolished, becoming a district of Madagascar.

Governors
1886-1887 Henri-Paul-Marie Caillet
1887-1896 Ernest-Emmanuel Froger

Ministère des Colonies, *Annuaire coloniale*, 1887—97.

16 FORT-DAUPHIN

Fort-Dauphin, on the southeastern tip of Madagascar, was founded in 1642 by the French, who hoped to use it as a base from which to compete with the Dutch and English in the Indian Ocean. Fort-Dauphin never achieved that purpose and was used only for trade with its own interior, and later as a way-station to India. From 1667 to 1671 Fort-Dauphin served briefly as the headquarters of the Compagnie des Indes orientales, but it was replaced by India in this respect and by Bourbon (v. Réunion) as the way-station to India. Its utility ended, and subjected to the attacks of hostile Malagasy, Fort-Dauphin was abandoned in 1674. Its brief existence was inglorious, but Fort-Dauphin repaid the French in the 19th century, serving to authenticate French claims to the entire island of Madagascar (q.v.).

Governors			
1642-1648	Jacques Pronis (1)	1655-1656	Gueston
1648-1655	Étienne de Flacourt	1656-1657	de Champmargou (1)
1655	Jacques Pronis (2)	1657-1660	du Rivau
1655	des Perriers	1661-1665	de Champmargou (2)
		1665	Pierre de Beausse

France

1665-1666	Montaubon	1670-1671	Jacob Blanquet de la Haye
1667-1670	François de Lopis, Marquis de Montdevergue	1671-1672	de Champmargou (3)
		1672-1674	Jean de la Bretesche

Barassin; Froidevaux.

17 FRENCH ANTILLES

The various French possessions in the West Indies were, except for brief periods, privately owned and administered before 1667. In that year a governor-general was appointed, although crown control over the islands was deferred until 1674. The governor-general resided on Martinique. The government of the French Antilles included Martinique (q.v.), Guadeloupe (q.v.), part of Saint-Christophe (q.v.) (to 1702 when it was conquered by the English, v. Saint Kitts, 208), Saint-Croix (to 1733 when it was sold to Denmark, v. Danish West Indies, 4), Désirade, Marie-Galante, Grenada (q.v.), and various minor islands. These islands were captured by the English between 1759 (v. Guadeloupe, 141) and 1762 (v. Martinique, 158), and on their return the government-general was not reestablished. In 1768 it was reinstituted on a limited scale, but it was finally abolished in 1775. During the period from 1667 to 1762 the component islands had their own administrations.

Governors-General

1628-1638	Pierre Belain d'Esnambuc	1702-1703	Nicolas de Gabaret (1)
1638-1645	Philippe Lonvilliers de Poincy	1703-1709	Charles-François de Machault de Bellemont
1645-1647	Noël Patrocles de Thoisy		
1647-1663	(none)	1709-1710	Nicolas de Gabaret (2)
1663-1665	Alexandre de Prouville de Tracy	1710-1713	Raimond-Balthasar Phélypeaux, Sieur du Verger
1665-1667	(none)		
1667-1677	Jean-Charles de Baas-Castelmore	1713-1715	Hemon Coinard de La Malmaison
1667-1690	Charles de La Roche-Courbon, Comte de Blénac (1)		
		1715-1717	Abraham de Belébat de Duquesne-Guitton
1690-1692	François d'Alesso, Marquis d' Eragny	1717	Antoine Arcy de la Varenne
		1717-1728	François de Pas de Feuquières
1692-1696	Charles de La Roche-Courbon, Comte de Blénac (2)	1728-1744	Jacques-Charles Bochart, Sieur de Champigny
1696-1700	Thomas-Claude Renart de Fuchsamberg, Marquis d' Amblimont	1744-1750	Charles de Tubières de Pastel de Levoy de Grimoire, Marquis de Caylus
1700-1701	Charles de Peychpeyrou-Comminge de Guitaut (1)	1750-1757	Maximin de Bompar
		1757-1761	François de Beauharnais de Beaumont
1701	Charles d'Esnotz de Forbonest		
1701-1702	Charles de Peychpeyrou-Comminge de Guitaut (2)	1761-1762	Louis-Charles Le Vassor de La Touche

Information from Le Sous-Préfet, Directeur du Cabinet, Fort-de-France, Martinique. Also, Chauleau, pp. 36—72.

18 FRENCH EQUATORIAL AFRICA

French interest in what was to become the area covered by French Equatorial Africa dates from 1838 when trade began along the coast of Gabon (q.v.). By 1847 exploration into the hinterland had begun but with no significant results before the expeditions of Savorgnan de Brazza, which began in 1877. In 1882 the French Congo was created. In 1886 de Brazza was appointed commissioner-general, having authority over both Gabon and French Congo while personally governing the former. French authority continued to expand, necessitating the creation of Ubangi-Shari-Chad (later separated into Ubangi-Shari and Chad) in 1906. In 1910 the name French Congo was changed to French Equatorial Africa and the title of commissioner-general was changed to governor-general. In 1958 the federation was dissolved as each of its four component colonies chose autonomy.

French Congo
Commissioners-General
1886-1898	Pierre-Paul-François-Camille Savorgnan de Brazza
1898-1901	Henri-Félix de la Mothe
1901-1904	Louis-Albert Grodet
1904-1908	Émile Gentil
1908-1910	Martial-Henri Merlin

French Equatorial Africa
Governors-General
1910-1917	Martial-Henri Merlin
1918-1919	Gabriel-Louis Angoulvant
1920-1924	Jean-Victor Augagneur
1924-1934	Raphaël-Valentin-Marius Antonetti
1934-1935	Georges-Édouard-Alexandre Renard

1935-1939	Dieudonné-François-Joseph-Marie Reste
1939-1940	Pierre-François Boisson
1940	Louis Husson
1940	René de Larminat
1940-1944	Félix-Adolphe-Sylvestre Eboué
1944-1947	Ange-Marie-Charles-André Bayardelle
1947	Charles-Jean Luizet

High Commissioners
1947-1951	Bernard Cornut-Gentille
1951-1958	Paul-Louis-Gabriel Chauvet
1958	Pierre-Auguste-Joseph Messmer
1958	Yvon Bourges

High Commissioner-General
1959-1960	Yvon Bourges

L'Encyclopédie coloniale et maritime: Afrique equatoriale française, pp. vii-x.

19 FRENCH GUIANA

A French attempt to settle in Guiana in 1604 was unsuccessful but in 1644 a settlement was effected by the Compagnie du Cap Nord. The settlement was captured by the Dutch in 1653 and held by them until 1664 when it was resettled by the French Compagnie de la France équinoxiale. In 1674 French Guiana came under royal control. In 1809 the colony was occupied by the Portuguese from Brazil, but it was returned to the French in 1817. After 1852 French Guiana served as the main penal colony for France. In 1930 the interior of the colony, known as Inini, was administratively detached, although the governor of French Guiana was ex officio governor of Inini. In 1946 French Guiana became an overseas department of France and the governor was replaced by a prefect.

Governors
1664-1665	Joseph-Antoine Lefebvre de la Barre (1)
1665	Antoine de Noël de la Trompe d'Or
1665-1668	Cyprien Lefebvre de Lézy (1)
1668-1670	Joseph-Antoine Lefebvre de la Barre (2)
1670-1679	Cyprien Lefebvre de Lézy (2)

France

1679-1684	Pierre-Eléonore de la Ville, Marquis de Férolles (1)	1827-1829	Louis-Henri Desaulses de Freycinet
1684-1687	Pierre de Sainte-Marthe de Lalande	1829-1836	Jean-Guillaume Jubelin
1687-1688	Pierre-Eléonore de la Ville, Marquis de Férolles (2)	1836-1837	François-Dominique Laurens de Choisy
1688-1691	François Lefebvre de la Barre	1837-1839	Paul de Nourquer du Camper
1691-1700	Pierre-Eléonore de la Ville, Marquis de Férolles (3)	1839-1841	Jean-Baptiste-Marie-Augustin Gourbeyre
1700-1701	Rémi Guillouet d'Orvilliers (1)	1841-1843	Pons-Guillaume-Basile Charmasson du Puy-Laval
1701-1705	Pierre-Eléonore de la Ville, Marquis de Férolles (4)	1843-1845	Marie-Jean-François Layrle
1705-1706	Antoine de Querci de Rionville	1845-1846	Jean-Baptiste-Armand-Bertrand Cadéot
1706-1713	Rémi Guillouet d'Orvilliers (2)	1846-1850	André-Aimé Pariset
1713-1716	Pierre de Morthon de Laumière de Grandville	1850-1851	Louis-Eugène Maissin
1716-1720	Claude Guillouet d'Orvilliers (1)	1851	Jean-François-Marie-Félix-Stanislas Vidal de Lingendes
1720-1722	François de la Motte-Aigron	1851-1852	Octave-Pierre-Antoine-Henri de Chabannes-Curton
1722-1729	Claude Guillouet d'Orvilliers (2)	1852-1853	Joseph-Napoléon Sarda-Garriga
1729-1730	Michel Narshalek de Charanville	1853-1854	Martin Fourichon
1730	Gilbert Guillouet d'Orvilliers (1)	1854-1855	Louis-Adolphe Bonard
1730-1736	Henri Dussault de Lamirande	1855-1856	Antoine-Alphonse Masset
1736	Henri de Poilvillain de Grênay	1856-1859	Auguste-Laurent-François Baudin
1736-1738	Gilbert Guillouet d'Orvilliers (2)	1859-1864	Louis-Marie-François Tardy de Montravel
1738-1743	Antoine Le Moyne de Châteauguay	1864-1865	Antoine Favre
1743-1751	Gilbert Guillouet d'Orvilliers (3)	1865-1870	Privat-Antoine-Agathon Hennique
1751-1752	Jean-Baptiste-Hyacinthe de Saint-Michel Dunezat (1)	1870-1877	Jean-Louis Loubère
1752-1753	Gilbert Guillouet d'Orvilliers (4)	1877-1880	Marie-Alfred-Armand Huart
1753-1757	Jean-Baptiste-Hyacinthe de Saint-Michel Dunezat (2)	1880-1883	Charles-Alexandre Lacouture
		1883-1884	Henri-Isidore Chessé
1757-1763	Gilbert Guillouet d'Orvilliers (5)	1884-1885	Jean-Baptiste-Antoine Lougnon
1763-1764	Jean-Pierre-Antoine de Béhague (1)	1885-1887	Léonce-Pierre-Henri Le Cardinal
1764	Louis-Thomas Jacau de Fiedmond (1)	1888-1891	Anne-Léodor-Philotée-Metellus Gerville-Réache
1764-1765	Étienne-François de Turgot	1891-1893	Louis-Albert Grodet (1)
1765-1766	Jean-Pierre-Antoine de Béhague (2)	1893	Paul-Émile-Joseph-Casimir Fawtier
1766-1781	Louis-Thomas Jacau de Fiedmond (2)	1893-1895	Camille Charvein
1781-1785	Ferdinand-Alexandre de Bessner	1895-1896	Henri-Félix de Lamothe
1785	Louis de Lavallière	1896-1898	Henri-Eloi Danel
1785-1787	Thomas de FitzMaurice	1898-1899	Henri-Charles-Victor-Amédée Roberdeau
1787-1788	Pierre-François de Mareuilh de Villeboi	1899	Louis Mouttet
1788-1789	Charles-Guillaume Vial d'Alais	1899-1903	Émile Merwart
1789-1791	Jacques-Martin de Bourgon	1903-1905	Louis-Albert Grodet (2)
1791-1792	Henri Bénoit	1905	Charles-Emmanuel-Joseph Marchal
1792-1793	Frédéric Guillot (or Guyot)		
1793-1794	Nicolas-Georges Jeannet-Oudin (1)	1905-1906	Victor-François-Ferdinand Rey
1794-1796	François-Maurice Cointet	1906	Louis-Alphonse Bonhoure
1796-1798	Nicolas-Georges Jeannet-Oudin (2)	1906-1907	Édouard Picanon
1798-1799	Étienne-Laurent-Pierre Burnel	1907-1909	François-Pierre Rodier
1799-1800	Étienne Franconie	1909-1910	William-Maurice Fawtier
1800-1809	Jean-Baptiste-Victor Hugues	1910	Fernand-Ernest Thérond
1809-1817	(under Portugal)	1910-1911	Paul Samary
1817-1819	Jean-François Carra Saint-Cyr	1911	Denis-Joseph Goujon
1819-1823	Pierre-Clément de Laussat	1911-1914	Pierre-Jean-Henri Didelot (1)
1823-1825	Pierre-Bernard de Milius	1914-1916	Fernand-Ernest Levecque
1825-1826	Charles-Emmanuel de Muyssard	1916	Pierre-Jean-Henri Didelot (2)
1826-1827	Joseph Burgues de Missiessy		

1916-1917	Georges Lévy
1917	Jules-Gérard-Auguste Lauret
1917-1918	Antoine-Joseph-Xavier Barre
1918-1923	Henri-Alphonse-Joseph Lejeune
1923	Julien-Edgard Cantau
1923-1926	Marc-Émile-Charles-Jean Chanel
1926-1927	Gabriel-Henri-Joseph Thaly
1927	François-Adrien Juvanon
1927-1928	Émile Buhot-Launay
1928-1929	Camille-Théodore-Raoul Maillet
1929-1931	Bernard-Jacques-Victorin Siadous
1931-1933	Louis-Joseph Bouge
1933-1935	Julien-Geroges Lamy
1935-1936	Charles-Max Masson de Saint-Félix
1936	Pierre Tap
1936-1938	René Veber (1)
1938-1942	Robert-Paul Chot-Plassot
1942-1943	René Veber (2)
1943-1944	Jean-Alexandre-Léon Rapenne
1944-1946	Jules-Eucher Surlemont
1946	Jean Pezet

Information from A. Dubois-Chabert, Le Préfet de la Guyane Française, Cayenne, French Guiana.

20 FRENCH GUINEA

The Compagnie du Sénégal and its successors began trading, along with the English and Portuguese, on the coasts of what was later to be French Guinea in the 18th century. After 1850 the French began to conclude treaties of cession with the local rulers and to construct forts. In 1882 the colony of Rivières du Sud was created. After 1886 this included the French establishments along the Gulf of Guinea as well (v. Dahomey and Ivory Coast). Until 1891 Rivières du Sud was subordinated to Senegal, but in 1893 the name of the colony was changed to French Guinea and it was given separate status. Between 1881 and 1897 the interior, known as Futa Jallon, was occupied and added to the colony. French Guinea was made a component of French West Africa (q.v.) in 1895. In the referendum of 1958 it was the only colony to vote for complete and immediate independence, becoming the Republic of Guinea (Guinée).

Rivières du Sud
Lieutenant Governors

1882-1890	Jean-Marie Bayol
1890-1893	Noël-Eugène-Victor Ballay

French Guinea
Lieutenant Governors

1893-1900	Noël-Eugène-Victor Ballay
1900-1904	Paul-Jean-François Cousturier
1904-1906	Antoine-Marie-Auguste Frezouls
1906-1908	Joost van Vollenhoven
1908-1910	Victor-Théophile Liotard
1910-1913	Camille-Lucien-Xavier Guy
1913-1916	Jean-Jules-Émile Peuvergne
1916-1929	Jean-Louis-Georges Poiret
1930-1931	Louis-Jean Antonin
1931-1932	Robert-Paul-Marie de Guise
1932-1936	Joseph-Zébédée-Olivier Vadier

Governors

1936-1940	Louis-Placide Blacher
1940-1942	Félix Giacobbi
1942-1944	Horace-Valentin Crocicchia
1944-1946	Jacques-Georges Fourneau
1946-1948	Édouard-Louis-Barthélemy-Marie-Joseph Terrac
1948-1950	Roland-Joanes-Louis Pré
1950-1953	Paul-Henri Siriex
1953-1955	Jean-Paul Parisot
1955-1956	Charles-Henri Bonfils
1956-1957	Jean-Paul Ramadier
1958	Jean Mauberna

Information from Ministère de l'Information et du Tourisme, Conakry, Republic of Guinea.

21 FRENCH INDIA

French efforts to secure a foothold in India had failed in 1603 and 1642 but were successful in 1672. In 1674 the site of Pondichéry was acquired although the capital was not moved there until 1683. Other sites were acquired during the next seventy-five years, and in 1750, under the administration of Dupleix, France was the strongest European power in India. However, the French government chose to avoid a policy of intervention in India, and as a result the British soon achieved predominance, several times occupying the French possessions. In 1816 they were permanently returned to the French. After 1816 French India, known as the Établissements français dans l'Inde, consisted of Pondichéry, Karikal, and Yanaon (Yanam) on the Coromandel coast, Mahé on the Malabar coast, and Chandernagore in Bengal, a total of less than 200 square miles. Nonetheless, the French retained possession of these enclaves until after the British departure from India in 1947. Between 1950 and 1954 the French possessions were transferred to India.

Governors

1668-1671	François Caron
1671-1681	François Baron
1681-1693	François Martin (1)
1693-1699	(under the Netherlands)
1699-1706	François Martin (2)
1706-1708	Pierre Dulivier (1)
1708-1713	Guillaume-André Hébert (1)
1713-1715	Pierre Dulivier (2)
1715-1718	Guillaume-André Hébert (2)
1718-1721	Pierre-André Prévost de la Prévostière
1721-1723	Pierre-Christophe Le Noir (1)
1723-1726	Joseph Beauvollier de Courchant
1726-1735	Pierre-Christophe Le Noir (2)
1735-1741	Pierre-Benoît Dumas
1741-1754	Joseph-François Dupleix
1754-1755	Charles-Robert Godeheu de Zaimont
1755-1758	Georges Duval de Leyrit
1758-1761	Thomas-Arthur de Lally Tollendal
1761-1765	(under Great Britain)
1765-1766	Jean Law de Lauriston (1)
1766-1767	Antoine Boyelleau
1767-1777	Jean Law de Lauriston (2)
1777-1778	Guillaume-Léonard de Bellecombe
1778-1783	(under Great Britain)
1783-1785	Charles-Joseph Pâtissier, Marquis de Bussy-Castelnau
1785	François de Souillac
1785-1787	David Charpentier de Cossigny
1787-1789	Thomas de Conway
1789-1793	Camille-Charles Leclerc de Fresne
1793	Dominique-Prosper de Chermont
1793-1803	(under Great Britain)
1803	Charles-Matthieu-Isidore Décaen
1803-1816	(under Great Britain)
1816-1825	André-Julien du Puy
1825-1828	Philippe Panon, Vicomte des Bassayns de Richemont
1829-1835	Auguste-Jacques-Nicolas Peureux de Mélay
1835-1840	Hubert-Jean-Victor, Marquis de Saint-Simon
1840-1844	Paul de Norquer du Camper
1844-1849	Louis Pujol
1849-1851	Hyacinthe-Marie de Lalande de Calan
1851	Philippe-Achille Bédier
1852-1857	Raimond-Jean-Baptiste de Verninac de Saint-Maur
1857-1863	Alexandre-Jean-Baptiste-Joseph-Jacques Durand d'Ubraye
1863-1871	Napoléon-Joseph-Louis Bontemps
1871-1875	Pierre-Aristide Faron
1875-1878	Adolphe-Joseph-Antoine Trillard
1878-1881	Léonce Laugier
1881-1884	Julien-Théodore Drouhet
1884-1886	Étienne-Antoine-Guillaume Richaud
1886-1888	Louis-Evenor-Édouard Manès
1888-1889	Georges-Jules Piquet
1889-1891	Louis-Hippolyte-Marie Nouët
1891-1896	Léon-Émile Clément-Thomas
1896-1898	Louis-Jean Girod
1898-1902	François-Pierre Rodier
1902-1904	Victor-Louis-Marie Lanrezac
1904-1905	Jean-Baptiste-Philémon Lemaire
1905-1906	Joseph-Pascal François
1906-1908	Gabriel-Louis Angoulvant
1908-1909	Adrien-Jules-Jean Bonhoure
1909-1910	Ernest-Fernand Levecque
1910-1912	Pierre-Louis-Alfred Duprat
1912-1918	Alfred-Albert Martineau
1918-1926	Louis-Martial-Innocent Gerbinis
1926-1928	Pierre-Jean-Henri Didelot
1928-1931	Robert-Paul-Marie de Guise
1931-1934	François-Adrien Juvanon
1934-1936	Léon Solomiac
1936-1938	Horace-Valentin Crocicchia
1938-1945	Louis-Alexandre-Étienne Bonvin
1945-1947	Nicolas-Ernest-Marie-Maurice Jeandin
1947-1948	Charles-François-Marie Baron

Commissioners
1948-1949 Charles-François-Marie Baron

1949-1950 Charles Chambon
1950-1954 André Ménard

Information from Archives nationales, section outre-mer, Paris.

22 FRENCH POLYNESIA

French Polynesia consists of Tahiti and the Society Islands, together with numerous islets and atolls, the most important of which are the Marquesas, Gambier Island, and the Tuamotu archipelago, located in the eastern Pacific. In 1841 the ruler of Tahiti sought and received French protection. When she repented of her decision the French governors promptly annexed Tahiti. In 1847 the French government rescinded the annexation but retained the protectorate. Finally, in 1880 Pomare V ceded Tahiti to France. Neighboring islands were acquired from 1842 onwards. From 1853 to 1860 New Caledonia (q.v.) was administered from Tahiti. From 1843 to 1849 and 1854 to 1860, and after 1881, the colony was administered by governors. During the intervening periods the rank was reduced to commandant. Until 1957 French Polynesia was called Établissements français de l'Océanie. In 1958 French Polynesia voted to remain within the French Community as an overseas territory.

Governors
1843-1847 Armand-Joseph Bruat
1847-1849 Charles-François Lavaud

Commandants
1849-1850 Charles François Lavaud
1850-1852 Louis-Adolphe Bonard
1852-1854 Théogène-François Page

Governors
1854-1858 Joseph-Fidele-Eugène du Bouzet
1858   Jean-Marie-Joseph-Théodose
           Saysset de Mars
1858-1860 Louis-Eugène Gualtier de la
           Richerie

Commandants
1860-1864 Louis-Eugene Gualtier de la
           Richerie
1864-1869 Émile-François-Guillaume-
           Clément de la Roncière
1869-1871 Michel-Louis-Isidore de Jouslard
1871-1873 Hippolyte-Auguste Girard
1873-1876 Octave-Bernard Gilbert-Pierre
1876-1877 Antoine-Léonce Michaux
1877   Joseph-Henri Brunet-Millet
1877-1878 Auguste-Marie-Édouard d'Oncieu
           de la Bâthie
1878-1880 Jacques-Ferdinand Planche
1880-1881 Henri-Isidore Chessé

Governors
1881-1883 Frédéric-Jean Dordolot des Essarts

1883-1885 Marie-Nicolas-François-Auguste
           Morau
1885-1893 Étienne-Théodore Lacascade
1893-1896 Pierre-Louis-Clovis Papinaud
1896-1901 Gustave-Pierre-Théodore Gallet
1901   Victor-François-Ferdinand Rey
1901-1904 Édouard-Georges-Théophile
           Petit
1904   Victor-Louis-Marie Lanrezac
1904-1905 Henri-François-Charles Cor
1905-1907 Philippe-Émile Jullien
1907-1908 Élie-Adrien-Édouard Charlier
1908-1910 Joseph-Pascal François
1910-1912 Adrien-Jules-Jean Bonhoure
1912   Charles Hostein
1912-1913 Baptiste-Léon Géraud
1913-1915 William-Maurice Fawtier
1915-1919 Gustave-Jacques-Henri Julien
1919-1921 Jocelyn Robert
1921-1922 Auguste-André-Marius Guédès
1922-1927 Louis-Félix-Marie-Édouard Rivet
1927-1928 Jean-Baptiste-Dominique Solari
1928-1930 Joseph-Louis Bouge
1930-1932 Léonce-Alphonse-Noël-Henri Jore
1932-1933 Alfred-Léon Bouchet
1933-1935 Michel-Lucien Montagné
1935-1937 Henri-Camille Sautot
1937-1940 Frédéric-Marie-Jean-Baptiste
           Chastenet de Géry
1940-1941 Émile de Curton
1941-1945 Georges-Louis-Joseph Orselli
1945-1947 Jean-Camille Haumant
1947-1949 Pierre-Louis Maestracchi

France

1949-1950	Armand Anziani	1958-1961	Pierre-René-Jean Sicaud
1950-1954	Jean-Albert-René Petitbon	1961-1965	Aimé-Marius-Louis Grimald
1954-1958	Jean-François Toby	1965-1969	Jean-Charles Sicurani
1958	Camille-Victor Bailly	1969——	Pierre-Louis Angeli

Information from M. J. Huber, Le Secrétaire-Général, Gouvernement de la Polynésie Française, Papeete, French Polynesia.

23 FRENCH SOMALILAND

Obock, at the southern end of the Red Sea, was acquired by France in 1862, but it was not occupied until 1884. Subsequently, protectorates were extended over neighboring sultanates, particularly Tadjoura, and the colony was extended. In 1892 the capital was transferred to the more advantageously located Djibouti, and in 1896 the colony was renamed Côte français des Somalis (previously it had been called Obock). The British occupied the colony during part of World War II although the administration remained French. In 1958 the inhabitants voted to become an overseas territory of the French Union rather than to become autonomous. In 1967 the territory was renamed Territoire des Afars et Issas.

Commandant

1884-1887	Antoine-Marie-Joseph-Léonce Lagarde

Governors

1887-1899	Antoine-Marie-Joseph-Léonce Lagarde
1899-1900	Alfred-Albert Martineau
1900-1904	Adrien-Jules-Jean Bonhoure (1)
1904-1913	Pierre-Hubert-Auguste Pascal
1913-1915	Adrien-Jules-Jean Bonhoure (2)
1915-1916	Paul Simoni
1916-1918	Victor-Marie Fillon
1918-1924	Jules-Gérard-Auguste Lauret
1924-1934	Pierre-Amable Chapon-Baissac
1934-1935	Jules-Marcel de Coppet
1935-1936	Achille-Louis-Auguste Silvestre
1936-1937	Armand-Léon Annet
1937-1938	Marie-François-Julien Pierre-Alype
1938-1940	Hubert-Jules Deschamps

1940	Gaëtan-Louis-Élie Germain
1940-1942	Pierre-Marie-Élie-Louis Nouailhetas
1942	Christian-Raimond Dupont
1942-1943	Ange-Marie-Charles-André Bayardelle
1943-1944	Michel-Raphaël-Antoine Saller
1944-1946	Jean-Victor-Louis-Joseph Chalvet
1946-1950	Paul-Henri Siriex
1950-1954	Numa-Henri-François Sadoul
1954	Roland-Joanes-Louis Pré
1954-1957	Jean-Albert-René Petitbon
1957-1958	Maurice Meker
1958-1962	Jacques-Marie-Julien Compain
1962-1966	René Tirant
1966-1967	Louis-Joseph-Édouard Saget

High Commissioners

1967-1969	Louis-Joseph-Édouard Saget
1969——	Dominique Ponchardier

Information from Ministère des Affaires intérieurs, Service de l'Information, Djibouti, Somaliland.

24 FRENCH SOUTHERN AND ANTARCTIC LANDS

The colony Terres australes et antarctiques françaises, or T.A.A.F., was created in 1955 and consists of Saint Paul and Amsterdam islands, the Kerguélen and Crozet archipelagoes, and Adélie Land (Terre Adélie) on Antarctica. These islands were claimed by France after their discovery by French navigators in 1772 and 1774, but no settlement was made until 1950 when Saint Paul, Amsterdam, and Kerguelen were occupied, primarily for use as bases for scientific experiments.

Administrators-Superior
1954-1959   Xavier Richert
1959——   Pierre-Charles Rolland

Statesman's Year Book, 1955 to date.

25 FRENCH SUDAN

French interest in what was to become French Sudan began under the expansionist governor of Senegal, Louis-Léon-César Faidherbe, in the 1850's. In 1879 the desire to build a railroad connecting the Senegal and Niger rivers quickened this interest and in 1880 a commandant-supérieur was appointed and French control began expanding eastward along the Niger. Until 1892 and from 1899 to 1904 the colony was subordinate to Senegal. It was a part of French West Africa (q.v.) from 1895 to 1958. During its existence the colony was known under several different names:

    1880-1890   Upper River
    1890-1899   French Sudan
    1899-1902   Upper Senegal-Middle Niger
    1902-1904   Senegambia-Niger
    1904-1920   Upper Senegal-Niger
    1920-1958   French Sudan

From 1932 to 1947 part of the suppressed colony of Upper Volta (q.v.) was attached to French Sudan. In 1958 French Sudan voted to become an autonomous member of the French Community, and two years later it became independent as Mali.

Commandants-Supérieurs
1880-1883   Gustave Borgnis-Desbordes
1883-1884   Charles-Émile Boilève
1884-1885   Antoine-Vincent-Auguste Combes
1885-1886   Henri-Nicolas Frey
1886-1888   Joseph-Simon Galliéni
1888-1891   Louis Archinard (1)
1891-1892   Pierre-Marie-Gustave Humbert

Lieutenant Governors
1892-1893   Louis Archinard (2)
1893-1895   Louis-Albert Grodet
1895-1898   Louis-Edgard de Trentinian (1)
1898   Marie-Michel-Alexandre-René Audéoud
1898-1899   Louis-Edgard de Trentinian (2)

Delegate
1899-1904   Amédée-Guillaume Merlaud-Ponty

Lieutenant Governors
1904-1908   Amédée-Guillaume Merlaud-Ponty
1908-1915   Marie-François-Joseph Clozel
1915-1918   Raphaël-Valentin-Marius Antonetti
1918-1919   Auguste-Charles-Désire-Emmanuel Brunet
1919-1924   Marcel-Achille-Henry-Raymond Olivier
1924-1931   Jean-Henri Terrasson de Fougères
1931-1935   Louis-Jacques-Eugène Fousset
1935-1936   Matthieu-Maurice Alfassa
1936-1937   Ferdinand-Jacques-Louis Rougier

France

Governors
1937-1938 Ferdinand-Jacques-Louis Rougier
1938-1940 Jean-Hyacinthe Desanti
1940-1942 Jean-Alexandre-Léon Rapenne
1942-1946 Auguste-Maurice-Léon Calvel
1946-1952 Édmond-Jean Louveau
1952   Camille-Victor Bailly

1952-1953 Salvador-Jean Etcheber
1953   Albert-Jean Mouragues
1953-1956 Lucien-Eugène Geay
1956-1958 Henri-Marie-Joseph Gipoulon

High Commissioner
1959-1960 Jean-Charles Sicurani

Information from Le Commissaire de l'Information, Koulouba, Mali.

26 FRENCH WEST AFRICA

In 1895 French Guinea, French Sudan, Ivory Coast, and Senegal (qq.v.) were administratively united in a federation known as French West Africa. Dahomey joined in 1899, and Mauritania, Niger, and Upper Volta joined as they became separate colonies (qq.v.). Since the capital of the federation was in Dakar, the governor-general served as lieutenant governor of Senegal until 1902 when Senegal was reconstructed as a colony. In 1937 the heads of the eight constituent colonies in French West Africa were raised to the rank of governors. In 1958 the federation was dissolved.

Governors-General
1895-1900 Jean-Baptiste-Émile-Louis-
               Barthélemy Chaudié
1900-1902 Noël-Eugène-Victor Ballay
1902-1908 Ernest-Nestor Roume
1908-1916 Amédée-Guillaume Merlaud-Ponty
1916-1917 Marie-François-Joseph Clozel
1917-1918 Joost van Vollenhoven
1918-1919 Gabriel-Louis Angoulvant
1919-1923 Martial-Henri Merlin
1923-1930 Jules-Gaston-Henri Carde
1930-1936 Jules Brévié
1936-1940 Jules-Marcel de Coppet

1940   Léon-Henri-Charles Cayla

High Commissioners
1940-1943 Pierre-François Boisson
1943-1946 Pierre-Charles-Albert
               Cournarie
1946-1948 René-Victor-Marie Barthes
1948-1951 Paul-Léon-Albin Bechard
1951-1956 Bernard Cornut-Gentille
1956-1958 Gaston Cusin

High Commissioner-General
1958-1959 Pierre-Auguste-Joseph Messmer

L'Encyclopédie coloniale et maritime: Afrique occidentale française, pp. vii-ix.

27 GABON

French settlements on the Gabon coast were organized under a commandant-particulier, subject to Senegal, in 1843. After 1859 the commandant-supérieur of Gabon and the Gulf of Guinea settlements had the title Commandant of the Naval Division of the West Coast of Africa, while a commandant-particulier remained in Gabon. In 1881 this individual became commandant-supérieur of Gabon and the Gulf of Guinea settlements, but the latter were removed from his jurisdiction in 1886. In 1891 Gabon became subordinated to French Congo (v. French Equatorial Africa), with a lieutenant governor. After 1910 it was a component colony of French Equatorial Africa. In 1946 governors replaced the lieutenant governors. In 1958 Gabon became an autonomous member of the French Community and it achieved independence in 1960, retaining the name Gabon.

Gabon and dependencies
Commandants-Supérieurs
1845-1848	Jean-Baptiste Montagniès de la Roque
1848	Auguste-Laurent-François Baudin (1)
1848-1850	Louis-Édouard Bouët-Willaumez
1850-1851	Charles Penaud
1851-1854	Auguste-Laurent-François Baudin (2)
1854-1856	Jérôme-Félix Monléon
1856-1859	Auguste-Leopold Prôtet
1859-1861	Auguste Bosse
1861-1863	Octave-François-Charles Didelot
1863-1866	André-Émile-Léon Laffon de Ladébat
1866-1868	Alphonse-Jean-René Fleuriot de Langle
1868-1869	Alexandre-François Dauriac
1869-1870	Victor-Auguste Duperré
1870-1872	Siméon Bourgois
1872-1874	Antoine-Louis-Marie Le Couriault de Quillio
1874-1875	Charles-Henri-Jules Panon du Hazier
1875-1877	Amédée-Louis Ribourt
1877-1879	François-Hippolyte Allemand
1879-1881	Bernard-Ernest Mottez
1881-1884	Louis-Antoine Rischill Grivel
1885-1886	Jules-Marie-Armand Cavelier de Cuverville

Gabon
Commandants-Particuliers
1843-1844	Antoine Devoisins
1844	Joseph-Marie Millet
1844-1846	André Brisset (1)
1846	Clément Grosjean
1846-1847	Carrilès
1847	André Brisset (2)
1847-1848	Victor-Joseph Roger
1848	Alphonse-Alexandre Sourdeaux
1848	Eugène-Jean-Antoine Desperles
1848-1849	Étienne-Charles Deschanel
1849-1850	Jean-Auguste Martin
1850-1853	Alexis-Édouard Vignon (1)
1853-1857	Peters-Théophile Guillet
1857-1859	Alexis-Édouard Vignon (2)
1859-1860	Pierre-Alexandre Mailhetard
1860-1861	César-Charles-Joseph Pradier
1861	Paul-Claude-Nicolas Brüe
<u>1863</u>	Charles-Ferdinand-Eugène Baur
1866-1867	Joseph-Henri Brunet-Millet
1867-1868	Hyacinthe-Laurent-Théophile Aube

1868-1869	Frédéric-Aimable Bourgarel
1869-1871	Hippolyte-Adrien Bourgoin
1871-1873	Gustave-Aristide-Léopold Garraud
1873-1875	Charles-Henri-Jules Panon du Hazier
1875-1876	Félix-Ambroise Clément
1876-1878	Jules Boitard
1878-1879	Paul-Michel-Frédéric Caudière
1879-1880	Augustin-Ernest Dumont
1880-1881	Jules-Émile Hanet-Cléry

Gabon and Gulf of Guinea Settlements
Commandants-Particuliers
1881-1882	Jules-Émile Hanet-Cléry
1882-1884	Émile Masson
1884-1885	Jean-Joseph-Alfred Cornut-Gentille
1885-1886	Georges-Élie Pradier

Gabon
Lieutenant Governors
1886-1889	Noël-Eugène-Victor Ballay
1889-1891	Fortuné-Charles de Chavannes
1891-1904	(under French Congo)
1904-1905	Louis-Auguste-Bertrand Ormières
1905-1906	Alfred-Louis Fourneau
1906-1907	Fernand-Ernest Thérond
1907-1909	Alfred-Albert Martineau
1909-1910	Léon-Félix Richaud
1910	Joseph-Pascal François
1910-1911	Adolphe-Louis Cureau
1911-1913	Georges-Virgile Poulet
1913-1918	Marie-Casimir-Joseph Guyon
1918-1919	Maurice-Pierre Lapalud
1919-1922	Jean-Henri Marchand
1922-1923	Édmond-Émilien Cadier
1923	Jocelyn Robert
1923-1924	Louis-Nicholas-Marie Cercus
1924-1931	Marie-Joseph-Jules-Pierre Bernard
1931-1934	Marcel-Alexander-Jean Marchessou
1934-1935	Louis-Alexis-Étienne Bonvin (1)
1935-1936	Charles-André-Maurice Assier de Pompignan (1)
1936-1937	Louis-Alexis-Étienne Bonvin (2)
1937-1938	Georges-Hubert Parisot
1938-1940	Georges-Pierre Masson
1941-1942	Victor Valentin-Smith
1942-1943	Charles-André-Maurice Assier de Pompignan (2)
1943-1944	Paul Vuillaume
1944-1946	Numa-François-Henri Sadoul (1)

France

Governors

1946-1947	Roland-Joanes-Louis Pré
1947-1949	Numa-François-Henri Sadoul (2)
1949-1951	Pierre-François Pelieu
1951-1952	Charles-Émile Hanin

1952-1958	Yves-Jean Digo
1958	Louis-Marius-Pascal Sanmarco

High Commissioner

1959-1960	Jean Risterucci

Information from Le Chef du Service des Archives, Administration provisoire des Services du Ministère de la France d'Outre-Mer, Paris, and from Archives du Sénégal, Dakar, Senegal, from their dossier 6 G 14. Also, Atger, pp. 14—15; Deschamps; Ministère de La Marine et des Colonies, *Annuaire*, 1854—86; Schefer, 2:447-540.

28 GORÉE AND DEPENDENCIES

The islet of Gorée off Cape Verde in Senegal (q.v.) was occupied by the French in 1677 and has been held by them for most of the time since then. From 1763 to 1778 Gorée was the only part o Senegal retained by the French (for its commandants, see Senegal). Until 1854, however, Gorée was always subordinate to the governor of Senegal when Senegal was held by the French. In 1854 it was detached from Senegal and, together with the French posts in Gabon (q.v.) and along the Guinea coast (v. French Guinea), erected into a separate colony. The commandant-supérieur had overall responsibility for the colony and had simultaneously the title Commandant of Naval Division of the West Coast of Africa. The commandant-particulier resided in Gorée and administered that island only, thus being analogous to the commandant-particulier in Gabon during this same period. This arrangement was short lived, for in 1859 Gorée was reattached to Senega and the remaining posts were erected into a separate colony which had its headquarters in Gabo

Commandants-Supérieurs[1]

1854-1856	Jérôme-Félix Monléon
1856-1859	Auguste-Léopold Prôtet

Commandants-Particuliers

1854-1856	Timoléon-Jean-François Ropert
1856-1859	Jean-Isidore-Raoul-Paul d'Alteyrac
1859	Georges-Étienne-Catherine de Cools

1. For earlier governors of Gorée, see under Senegal.

Gaffiot, p. 242; Schefer, 2:407—45.

29 GREAT LEBANON

At the partition of the Ottoman Empire after World War I Syria (q.v.) fell to France. In 1920 the predominantly Christian *sanjaks* (administrative districts) were separated and formed into a government called Great Lebanon. Although other states were formed within Syria, Great Lebanon always retained a special status. In 1926 a republic was proclaimed and the French governor was replaced by a president elected by a representative council, although Lebanon (as it was now called) continued to fall under the jurisdiction of the high commissioner of Syria until 1944 when it became fully independent.

Governors
1920-1923   Georges Trabaud
1923-1924   Privat-Antoine Audouard
1924-1925   Charles-Alexis Vandenburg
1925-1926   Léon-Henri-Charles Cayla

Salibi, p. 174.

30 GRENADA

Grenada, the most southerly of the windward islands of the Lesser Antilles, was discovered by Columbus in 1498. In 1609 a settlement was established by the English, but they abandoned it before the end of the year. Finally it was settled from Martinique (q.v.) in 1649. The island was owned by various private individuals until 1664 when it was purchased by the Compagnie des Indes occidentales. Ten years later it, like the other French possessions in the West Indies, came under royal control. Grenada remained a French colony, subject to the authority of the governor-general of the French Antilles (q.v.), until 1762 when the island was captured by the British. Grenada was geographically well apart from the other French islands in the Lesser Antilles, and by the Treaty of Paris of 1763 Great Britain retained possession of the island, although it was briefly reoccupied by the French from 1779 to 1784.

Governors
1649-1654   Jean Le Comte
1654-1658   Louis Cacqueray de Valminière
1658   Dubuc
1658-1664   Jean Faudoas de Cérillac
1666   Vincent
1671-1674   de Canchy
1675-1679   Pierre de Sainte-Marthe de Lalande
1679-1680   Jacques de Chambly
1680-1689   Nicolas de Gabaret
1690-1693   Louis Ancelin de Gémosat
1697   Jean-Léon Fournier de Carles de
            Pradine
1700   de Bellair

1701-1708   Joseph de Bouloc
1711-1716   Guillaume-Emmanuel-Théodore de
            Maupeou, Comte de l'Estrange
1717-1721   Jean-Michel l'Épinay de la
            Longueville
1721-1722   Jean Balthazard du Houx
1723-1727   Robert Giraud du Poyet
1727-1734   Charles Brunier, Marquis de
            Larnage
1734-1748   Jean-Louis Fournier de Carles de
            Pradine
1748-1757   Longvilliers de Poincy
1757-1762   Pierre-Claude Bonvoust d'Aulnay
            de Prulay

Information from Le Directeur-Général des Archives de France, Paris. Also, Debien, p. 449.

31 GUADELOUPE

Guadeloupe is located in the Lesser Antilles and is the largest of the French possessions in the Caribbean. It was first occupied by the French in 1635 under the auspices of the Compagnie de îles de l'Amérique. From 1649 to 1664 it was privately owned; from 1664 to 1674 it was administered by the Compagnie des Indes occidentales. After 1674 it was directly administered by the crown. It was occupied by the British from 1759 to 1763, from 1810 to 1814, and from 1815 t 1816. From 1674 to 1759 and from 1768 to 1775 Guadeloupe was subordinated to the governor-general of the French Antilles (q.v.) at Martinique (q.v.) but it always retained a governor of its own. Attached to Guadeloupe for administrative purposes were Marie Galante, Désirade, Les Saintes, Saint Barthélemy (from 1878 on), and part of Saint Martin (or Maarten). Saint Martin ha been wholly occupied by the French in 1638, but after 1703 the southern section was occupied by the Dutch (v. Saint Eustatius, 280). In 1946 Guadeloupe became an overseas department of France.

Governors
1635	Jean Duplessis, Sieur d' Ossonville
1635-1640	Charles Liénard de l'Olive
1640-1643	Jean Aubert
1643-1664	Charles Houël, Sieur de Petit-Pré
1664-1669	Claude-François du Lion
1669-1677	(under Martinique)
1677-1695	Pierre Hencelin
1695-1704	Charles Auger
1704-1717	Hemon Coinard de la Malmaison
1717-1719	Michel-Savinien Lagarigue de Savigny
1719-1728	Alexandre Vaultier, Comte de Moyencourt
1728-1734	Robert Giraud du Poyet
1734-1737	Charles Brunier, Marquis de Larnage
1737-1753	Gabriel d'Erchigny de Clieu
1753-1757	Jean-Antoine-Joseph de Mirabeau
1757-1759	Charles-François-Emmanuel Nadau du Treil

under Great Britain

Governors
1759-1760	Byam Crump
1760-1763	Campbell Dalrymple

under France

Governors
1763-1764	François-Charles de Bourlamaque
1764-1765	Édouard de Copley
1765-1768	Pierre-Gédéon de Nolivos
1768-1769	Anne-Joseph-Hippolyte de Maurès de Malartic
1769-1771	François-Claude-Amour de Bouillé du Chariol
1771-1773	Louis-François de Dion
1773-1775	Édouard-Hilaire-Louis de Tilly
1775-1782	Bache-Elzéar-Alexandre d'Arbaud de Jouques

1782-1783	Claude-Charles Damas de Marillac
1783-1784	Beaumé de la Saulais
1784-1792	Charles-François de Clugny de Thénissey
1792-1793	René-Marie d'Arrot
1793	Jean-Baptiste-Raimond Lacrosse (1)
1793-1794	Georges-Henri-Victor Collot
1794-1798	Jean-Baptiste-Victor Hugues
1798-1801	Edme-Étienne Borne-Desfourneau
1801-1802	Magloire Pélage
1802	Antoine Richepanse
1802-1803	Jean-Baptiste-Raimond Lacrosse (2)
1803-1810	Manuel-Louis-Jean-Augustin Ernouf

under Great Britain

Governors
1810-1813	Alexander Forrester Inglis Cochrane
1813-1814	John Skinner

under France

Governors
1814-1815	Charles-Alexandre-Léon Durand, Comte de Linois
1815-1816	(under Great Britain)
1816-1823	Antoine-Philippe de Lardenoy
1823-1826	Louis-Léon Jacob
1826-1830	Jean-Julien Angot des Rotours
1830-1831	Louis-François Vatable
1831-1837	René Arnous Dessaulsay
1837-1841	Jean-Guillaume Jubelin
1841-1845	Jean-Baptiste-Marie-Augustin Gourbeyre
1845-1848	Marie-Jean-François Layrle
1848-1851	Jacques-Amédée-Philippe Fiéron
1851-1854	Tranquille Aubry-Bailleul
1854-1857	Philibert-Augustin Bonfils

1857-1859	Philippe-Victor Touchard	1911-1913	Jean-Jules-Émile Peuvergne
1859-1860	Napoléon-Joseph-Louis Bontemps	1913-1917	Émile Merwart
1860-1864	Charles-Victor Frébault	1917-1920	Jules-Maurice Gourbeil
1864-1870	Louis-Hippolyte de Lormel	1920-1924	Pierre-Louis-Alfred Duprat
1870-1880	Gabriel Couturier	1924	Jocelyn Robert
1880-1886	Léonce Laugier	1924-1926	Maurice Beurnier
1886-1891	Antoine-Frédéric-Henri Le Boucher	1926-1929	Louis-Martial-Innocent Gerbinis
1891-1894	Louis-Hippolyte-Marie Nouët	1929-1931	Théophile-Antoine-Pascal Tellier
1894-1895	Noël Pardon	1931-1934	Alphonse-Paul-Albert Choteau
1895-1901	Dauphin Moracchini	1934-1936	Louis-Joseph Bouge
1901-1903	Martial-Henri Merlin	1936-1939	Adolphe-Félix-Sylvestre Eboué
1903-1905	Paul-Marie-Armand de La Loyère	1939-1940	Marie-François-Julien Pierre-Alype
1905-1907	Léon-Jules-Pol Boulloche	1940-1944	Constant-Louis-Sylvain Sorin
1907-1909	Victor-Marie-Louis Ballot	1944-1946	Maurice-Pierre-Eugène Bertaut
1909-1911	Henri-François-Charles Cor	1946-1947	Ernest de Nattes

Information from Le Secrétaire-Général, Préfecture de la Guadeloupe, Basse-Terre, Guadeloupe. For a detailed account of the complex earlier period, see Crouse, *French Pioneers*, and idem, *The French Struggle*.

32 ÎLE DE FRANCE

Mauritius (q.v.), occupied by the Dutch (v. 272) from 1638 to 1658 and 1664 to 1710, was finally abandoned by them as useless. It was claimed by France in 1715 and settled from Réunion (q.v.) in 1722. Until 1767 it was administered by the Compagnie des Indes which valued it for its strategic location on the route to the French possessions in India. Cultivation from cloves and nutmeg began during the French occupation. After 1767 the island was directly ruled by the French government. The governor at Île de France was governor-general of the French possessions in the Indian Ocean after 1727. During the Napoleonic Wars Île de France was a headquarters for privateers who preyed on British shipping in the Indian Ocean. As a result Great Britain occupied the island in 1810 and renamed it with the former Dutch name Mauritius. Great Britain retained possession of the island at the Treaty of Paris in 1814 (v. 161).

Governors

1722-1726	Denis de Nyon	1772-1776	Charles-Henri-Louis d'Arsac de Ternay
1726-1727	Denis de Brousse	1776-1779	Antoine de Guiran de la Brillane
1727-1729	Pierre-Benoît Dumas		
1729-1735	Nicolas de Maupin	1779-1787	François de Souillac
1735-1746	Bertrand-François Mahé de Labourdonnais	1787-1789	Joseph-Antoine-Raimond de Bruni d'Entrecasteaux
1746-1753	Pierre-Félix-Barthélemy David	1789-1790	Thomas de Conway
1753-1756	Jean-Baptiste-Charles Bouvet de Lozier	1790-1792	David Charpentier de Cossigny
		1792-1800	Anne-Joseph-Hippolyte de Maurès de Malartic
1756-1759	René Magon de la Villebague		
1759-1767	Antoine Desforges Boucher	1800-1803	François-Louis de Magallon de la Morlière
1767-1768	Jean-Daniel Dumas		
1768-1772	François-Julien du Dresnay Desroches	1803-1810	Charles-Matthieu-Isidore Décaen

Toussaint, pp. 119–20. See also d'Épinay, passim.

33 ÎLE ROYALE

Île Royale, or Cape Breton, was occupied by the French after the British conquest of Acadia (q.v.) in 1710. Île Royale commanded the entrance to the Saint Lawrence River and the French fortified its capital, Louisburg, in order to exploit this. However, Île Royale was occupied by the British from 1745 to 1749 and again in 1758 when the whole of New France (q.v.) was taken from the French. The British government long discouraged settlement on Île Royale, and it was only settled during and after the American Revolution by Loyalists from the American colonies. In 1784 it was constituted a separate British colony (v. Cape Breton, 114).

Governors
1714-1717 Philippe de Pastour de
           Costebelle
1717-1739 Joseph Brouillan de Saint-Ovide
1739-1740 Isaac-Louis Forant
1740-1744 Jean Baptiste Prévost du Quesnel
1744-1745 Louis du Pont du Chambon

under Great Britain

Governors
1745-1746 Peter Warren

1746-1747 Charles Knowles
1747-1749 Peregrine Thomas Hopson

under France

Governors
1749-1751 Charles des Herbiers de la
           Ralière
1751-1753 Jean-Louis de Raymond
1753-1754 Charles-Joseph d'Ailleboust
1754-1758 Augustin de Drucourt

Audet, pp. 50—51. This list contains some distortions.

34 ÎLE SAINT-JEAN

Île Saint-Jean lay directly north of the French colony of Acadia (q.v.), across the Strait of Northumberland. Until 1720, when it was settled by refugees from Acadia, there was no permanent settlement on the island. It remained a French possession, with an interval of English occupation from 1744 to 1748, until 1758 when, like France's other North American colonies, it was permanently occupied by the British, who later called it Prince Edward Island (198).

Governors
1720-1722 David de Gotteville de Bellisle
1722-1723 Jean-Maurice-Josué du Bois-
           Berthélot de Beaucours
1726-1732 Jacques d'Espiet de Pensens (1)
1732-1733 François Eurry de la Pérelle

1733-1737 Jacques d'Espiet de Pensens (2)
1737-1744 Louis du Pont du Chambon
1744-1748 (under Great Britain)
1749-1754 Claude-Elisabeth Denys de
           Bonaventure
1754-1758 Gabriel Rosseau de Villejoin

Harvey, p. 239 and passim.

35 INDOCHINA

Indochina was a federation formed in 1887 from the colony of Cochin China and the protectorates of Annam, Cambodia, and Tonkin (qq.v.). To these, Laos (q.v.) was added in 1897, as a protectorate, and Kouang-Tchéou-Wan (q.v.) in 1900. Indochina became the richest of France's colonies. From 1941—42 to 1945 it was occupied by the Japanese, although the Vichy-appointed governor-general was retained. In 1945 and 1946 Indochina was temporarily occupied by British and Chinese troops pending the ability of the French government to reassert its control. Kouang-Tchéou-Wan was returned to China, and in 1949 and 1950 Cambodia, Laos, and Vietnam (comprising Cochin China, Annam, and Tonkin) were recognized as independent within the French Union, although the French presence, in the persons of the high commissioners and later the commissioners-general, was retained. In 1954 the French, after a severe military defeat, were forced to withdraw completely.

Governors-General

1887-1888	Jean-Antoine-Ernest Constans
1888-1889	Étienne-Antoine-Guillaume Richaud
1889-1891	Georges-Jules Piquet
1891-1894	Jean-Marie-Antoine de Lanessan
1894-1895	Léon-Armand Rousseau
1895-1897	Augustin-Julien Fourès
1897-1902	Joseph-Athanase-Paul Doumer
1902-1907	Jean-Baptiste-Paul Beau
1907-1908	Louis-Alphonse Bonhoure
1908-1910	Antony-Wladislas Klobukowsky
1910-1911	Albert-Jean-Georges-Marie-Louis Picquié
1911	Louis-Paul Luce
1911-1914	Albert-Maurice Sarraut
1914-1915	Joost van Vollenhoven
1915-1916	Ernest-Nestor Roume
1916-1917	Jean-Eugène Charles
1917-1919	Albert-Maurice Sarraut
1919-1920	Maurice-Antoine-François Monguillot

1920-1922	Maurice Long
1922-1925	Martial-Henri Merlin
1925-1928	Alexandre Varenne
1928-1934	Pierre-Marie-Antoine Pasquier
1934-1936	Eugène-Jean-Louis-René Robin
1936-1939	Jules Brévié
1939-1940	Georges-Albert-Julien Catroux
1940-1945	Jean Decoux

High Commissioners

1945-1947	Georges Thierry d'Argenlieu
1947-1948	Émile-Édouard Bollaert
1948-1950	Léon-Marie Pignon
1950-1952	Jean de Lattre de Tassigny
1952-1953	Jean Letourneau

Commissioners-General

1953	Jean Letourneau
1953-1954	Maurice Dejean
1954	Paul Ely

Blanchard, "Indo-Chine"; Brébion, pp. 200—201; Hall, pp. 895—96 (although Hall implies that the governors of Cochin China from 1879 to 1887 were governing all of Indochina, which is incorrect).

36 IVORY COAST

An attempt by the French to establish a trading post at Assinie in the last years of the 17th century was soon abandoned. However, in 1843 "protectorates" were established at Grand-Bassam and Assinie, and posts were established there and later at Dabou nearby. The commandant at Grand-Bassam often carried the title Commandant-Particulier of the French Establishments on the Gold Coast. These establishments, like those in Gabon (q.v.) were under the general authority of the commandant of the Naval Division of the West Coast of Africa. The French government abandoned its claims to the posts in 1871 and French influence was left to be carried on by agents of the trading firm of A. Verdier et Cie. In 1881 the commandant-supérieur at Gabon was granted responsibility for French interests in the Ivory Coast area but nothing further was done.

France

From 1886 to 1893 the area fell under the jurisdiction of the lieutenant-governor of Rivières du Sud (v. French Guinea). Finally a resident was appointed at Assinie in 1889. In order effectively to occupy the interior under the terms of the Berlin Conference the French began to penetrate inland. The extent of this expansion became great enough to warrant the creation of a separate colony, called Côte d'Ivoire, in 1893. In 1895 the Ivory Coast became a part of French West Africa, and it remained so until 1958. Until 1937 the colony was governed by lieutenant governors, thereafter by governors. From 1932 to 1947 the largest part of the suppressed colony of Upper Volta (q.v.) was attached to the Ivory Coast. In 1958 the colony voted to become an autonomous member of the French Community, and two years later it became fully independent, retaining the name Ivory Coast.

Grand-Bassam

Commandants

1843	Charles-Marie Philippe de Kerhallet
1843-1844	Thomas-Jules-Séraphin Besson
1844-1845	Joseph Pellegrin
1845-1847	Conjard
1847-1848	Camille-Adolphe Pigeon
1849-1850	Jean-Jules-Charles Boulay
1851-1853	Charles-Gabriel-Felicité Martin des Pallières
1853-1854	François Chirat
1854-1855	Pierre-Alexander Mailhetard (1)
1856	Noël Bruyas
1857	Charles-Paul Brossard de Corbigny
1858-1859	Pierre-Alexandre Mailhetard (2)
1860-1862	Charles-René-Gabriel Liébault
1862-1863	Joseph Alem
1863-	Jean-Antoine-Léonard-Eudore Noyer
-	Jacques-Bertrand-Oscar Desnouy
1864	Jean-Auguste Martin
1866	Léon Noël
1867	Alfred Pouzols
1869	Jean-Louis Vernet

Assinie

Residents

1889-1890	Marcel Treich-Laplène
1890	Jean-Joseph-Étienne-Octave Péan
1890-1892	Jean-Henry-Auguste Desailles
1892	Julien-François Voisin
1892-1893	Bricard

Ivory Coast

Lieutenant Governors

1893-1895	Louis-Gustave Binger
1895-1896	Pierre-Hubert-Auguste Pascal
1896	Eugène Bertin
1896-1898	Louis Mouttet
1898-1899	Adrien-Jules-Jean Bonhoure
1899	Pierre-Paul-Marie Capest
1899-1902	Henri-Charles-Victor-Amédée Roberdeau
1902-1908	Marie-François-Joseph Clozel
1908-1916	Louis-Gabriel Angoulvant
1916-1918	Maurice-Pierre Lapalud (1)
1918-1924	Raphaël-Valentin-Marius Antonetti
1924-1925	Richard-Édmond-Maurice-Édouard Brunot
1925-1930	Maurice-Pierre Lapalud (2)
1930	Jules Brévié
1931-1935	Dieudonné-François-Joseph-Marie Reste
1935-1936	Adolphe Deitte
1936-1937	Gaston-Charles-Julien Mondon

Governors

1937-1939	Gaston-Charles-Julien Mondon
1939-1941	Horace-Valentin Crocicchia
1941-1942	Hubert-Jules Deschamps
1942-1943	Georges-Pierre Rey
1943-1947	André-Jean-Gaston Latrille
1947-1948	Oswald-Marcellin-Maurice-Marius Durand
1948	Georges-Louis-Joseph Orselli
1948-1951	Laurent-Élisée Pechoux
1951-1952	Pierre-François Pelieu
1952-1954	Camille-Victor Bailly
1954-1956	Pierre-Joseph-Auguste Messmer
1956-1957	Pierre-Auguste-Michel-Marie Lami
1957-1958	Ernest de Nattes

High Commissioners

1959	Ernest de Nattes
1959-1960	Yves-René-Henri Guéna

Information from Le Chef de l'Information, Abidjan, Ivory Coast, and from Camille-Victor Bailly, Le Gouverneur, Le Chef de l'Administration provisoire des Services de la France d'Outre-Mer, Paris. Also, Atger, pp. 132–33 and passim; Ministère de la Marine et des Colonies, *État général*, 1843–52; idem., *Annuaire*, 1853–70; Schnapper, pp. 39–50, 185–200, and passim; Rambosson, p. 171.

37 KOUANG-TCHÉOU-WAN

Kouang-Tchéou-Wan is located in the northeast part of the Liuchow peninsula in Kwangtung province, China. It was occupied by France in 1898 for use as a naval station and coaling depot like Great Britain's Weihaiwei (241) and Germany's Kiaochow (76). In 1900 it was leased from China, and in the same year it was attached administratively to Indochina (q.v.). In 1943 Kouang-Tchéou-Wan was occupied by the Japanese, and after World War II it reverted to China.

Administrators

1898-1900	Charles-Louis-Théobald Courrejolles
1900-1902	Gustave Alby (1)
1902-1903	Théophile-Henri Bergès
1903-1906	Gustave Alby (2)
1906-1908	Jean-Edme-Fernand Gautret
1908-1910	Henri-Victor Sestier
1910-1911	Paul-Edgard Dufrénil
1911-1912	Jean-Ernest Moulié
1912	Pierre-Stephane Salabelle
1912-1915	Henri-Jean-Auguste Caillard
1915-1919	Marius-Albert Garnier
1919-1922	Jean-Félix Krautheimer (1)
1922	Paul-Marie-Alexis-Joseph Blanchard de la Brosse (1)
1922-1923	Jean-Félix Krautheimer (2)
1923-1925	Paul-Michel-Achille Quesnel
1925-1927	Paul-Marie-Alexis-Joseph Blanchard de la Brosse (2)
1927-1929	Louis-Félix-Marie-Édouard Rivet
1929-1932	Achille-Louis-Auguste Silvestre
1932-1933	Pierre-Charles-Édmond Jabouille
1933-1934	Paul Delamarre
1934-1936	Maurice-Émile-Henri de Tastes
1936-1937	Camille-Fernand Chapoulart
1937-1942	Jacques-Henri-Paul Le Prevôt
1942	Louis-Frédéric-Claire-Guillaume Marty
1942-1943	Pierre-Marie-Jean Domec

Information from Duong Sanh, Conservateur, National Library, Saigon, South Vietnam, and from Archives nationales, section outre-mer, Paris. Also, Brébion, p. 215.

38 LAOS

A French consulate was established in the kingdom of Luang Prabang in Laos in 1886. After a decade of tripartite negotiations between France, Siam, and Great Britain an agreement was reached in which the area of Laos was left to the French, while the independence of Siam was guaranteed against foreign encroachment. As a result of this agreement France proclaimed a protectorate over Luang Prabang as well as additional territory, and attached it to Indochina (q.v.) under the control of a resident-general. French control was restored in 1945–46 after an interlude of Japanese control during World War II. In 1949 France recognized Laos as independent within the French Union. Laos is an excellent example of a modern state whose territorial boundaries, although highly artificial, have remained intact from the period of colonial rule.

Residents-Superior

1897-1899	Louis-Paul Luce
1899-1905	Marcel-Auguste-Armand Tournier
1905-1907	Georges-Marie-Joseph Mahé (1)
1907-1909	Élie-Jean-Henri Groleau
1909-1910	Georges-Marie-Joseph Mahé (2)
1910-1911	Antoine-Georges-Amédée-Ernest Outrey
1911-1912	Georges-Marie-Joseph Mahé (3)
1912-1913	Louis-Antoine Aubry de la Noë
1913-1916	Claude-Léon-Lucien Garnier
1917-1931	Jules-Georges-Théodore Bosc
1931	Yves-Charles Châtel
1931-1934	Aristide-Eugène Le Fol
1934-1938	Eugène-Henri-Roger Eutrope
1938-1941	André Touzet
1941-1945	Louis-Marie-Antoine Brasey

Information from Duong Sanh, Conservateur, National Library, Saigon, South Vietnam, and from Archives nationales, section outre-mer, Paris. Also Brébion, pp. 223—24.

39 LOUISIANA

In 1682 Robert Cavelier de La Salle had claimed all the lands drained by the Mississippi River to be French, and two years later he tried unsuccessfully to plant a colony at the mouth of the river. In 1699 Biloxi was settled from New France (q.v.) and in 1718 the capital of the colony was removed to New Orleans. From 1699 to 1713 Louisiana was under crown rule, from 1713 to 1716 it was a proprietary colony of Antoine Crozat, from 1716 to 1733 it was administered by the Compagnie de l'Ouest, and after 1733 it was again under the direct rule of the French crown. Several posts were erected along the Mississippi River as far north as the Illinois, but little control or settlement occurred beyond the southern reaches of the river. In 1762, to forestall a British takeover, Louisiana was ceded to Spain by the Treaty of Fontainebleu, but the colony only came under Spanish authority in 1765 (v. 352).

Governors

1699–1701	Sieur de Sauvolle de la Villantray
1701–1704	Jean-Baptiste Le Moyne de Bienville (1)
1704–1706	Pierre Le Moyne d'Iberville
1706–1712	Jean-Baptiste Le Moyne de Bienville (2)
1712–1716	Antoine de La Mothe-Cadillac
1716–1717	Jean-Michel l'Épinay de La Longueville
1717–1726	Jean-Baptiste Le Moyne de Bienville (3)
1726–1732	Étienne Boucher de Périer de Salvert
1732–1743	Jean-Baptiste Le Moyne de Bienville (4)
1743–1752	Pierre-François de Rigaud, Marquis de Vaudreuil-Cavagnal
1752–1763	Louis Billouard de Kerlérec de Kervasegan
1763–1765	Jean-Jacques-Blaise d'Abbadie
1765–1766	Charles-Philippe Aubry

Davis, pp. 37—94; Lauvrière, passim.

40 MADAGASCAR

The coastline of Madagascar was discovered by the Portuguese around 1500, but no settlements existed there until the 17th century. French interest in the island of Madagascar dated from the early 17th century, and from 1643 to 1674 there was a French colony at Fort-Dauphin (q.v.) intended as a way-station on voyages to the East Indies and India. In 1750 France obtained Sainte Marie de Madagascar (q.v.) by cession, and in 1841 the island of Nosy Bé (q.v.). Nonetheless the French government wished to secure the entire island, and in 1885 French forces invaded the Merina kingdom, which controlled most of the island's interior, and proclaimed a protectorate. At the same time the Merina ruler ceded Diégo-Suarez (q.v.). In 1896 a second invasion resulted in the abolition of the Merina kingdom and the erection of Madagascar into a colony. At the same time the government of Madagascar incorporated the three colonies mentioned above. In 1947 a widespread rebellion was suppressed. In 1958 Madagascar voted to become autonomous within the French Community, and in 1960 it became independent as the Malagasy Republic.

Residents-General

1886-1889	Charles-Marie Le Myre de Vilers
1889-1892	Louis-Maurice Bompard
1892-1894	Arthur-André-Henri Larrouy
1895-1896	Jacques-Charles-René-Achille Duchesne
1896	Hippolyte-Joseph Laroche

Governors-General

1896-1905	Joseph-Simon Galliéni
1905-1910	Jean-Victor Augagneur
1910-1914	Albert-Jean-Georges-Marie-Louis Picquié
1914-1917	Hubert-Auguste Garbit (1)
1917-1918	Martial-Henri Merlin
1918-1919	Abraham Schrameck
1919-1920	Marie-Casimir-Joseph Guyon

1920-1924	Hubert-Auguste Garbit (2)
1924-1930	Marcel-Achille-Henry-Raymond Olivier
1930-1939	Léon-Henri-Charles Cayla (1)
1939-1940	Jules-Marcel de Coppet (1)
1940-1941	Léon-Henri-Charles Cayla (2)
1941-1942	Armand-Léon Annet
1942-1943	Paul-Louis de Gentilhomme
1943-1944	Pierre-Marie de Saint-Mart
1944-1946	Paul de Saint-Mart

High Commissioners

1946-1948	Jules-Marcel de Coppet (2)
1948-1950	Pierre de Chevigné
1950-1954	Isaac-Robert Bargues
1954-1960	Jean-Louis-Maurice-André Soucadaux

Information from Michel Perrin, Service des Archives, Secrétariat-Général du Gouvernement, Tananarive, Malagasy Republic.

41 MARTINIQUE

France took possession of the Lesser Antilles island of Martinique in 1625 but only began to settle it ten years later under the Compagnie des îles de l'Amérique which governed it until 1650 when it was purchased by Jacques Dyel du Parquet. In 1664 the Compagnie des Indes occidentales purchased the island from the heir of Dyel du Parquet, but only retained it until 1674 when it came under the direct authority of the French crown. From 1667 to 1762 Martinique was the headquarters of the governor-general of the French Antilles (q.v.). From 1768 to 1775 the government-general was briefly revived. Martinique was occupied and governed by the British from 1762 to 1763, from 1794 to 1802, and from 1809 to 1814. In 1946 Martinique, like Guadeloupe (q.v.), became an overseas department of France, and the governor was replaced by a prefect.

Governors

1635-1646	Jacques Dyel du Parquet (1)
1646-1647	Jérôme du Sarrat, Sieur de la Pierrière
1647-1658	Jacques Dyel du Parquet (2)
1658-1659	Marie Bonnard du Parquet
1659-1662	Adrien Dyel de Vaudroques
1662-1663	Médéric Roolle, Sieur de Goursolas
1663-1665	Adrien-Jacques Dyel de Clermont
1665-1669	Robert le Fichot des Friches de Clodoré
1669-1670	François Roolle de Loubière
1670-1679	Antoine-André de Sainte-Marthe de Lalande
1680-1687	Jacques de Chambly
1689	Claude de Roux de Saint-Laurent
1689-1711	Nicolas de Gabaret

1717-1721	de Hurault
1721-1728	Jean-Charles de Bochart, Sieur de Champigny
1728-1742	de Brach
1742-1749	Martin de Pointesable
1752-1757	Rouillé de Rocourt

under Great Britain

Governor

1762-1763	William Rufane

under France

Governors

1763-1765	François-Louis de Salignac

France

1771-1772	Louis-Florent de Valière	1848-1851	Armand-Joseph Bruat
1772-1776	Vital-Auguste de Grégoire, Comte d'Énnery	1851-1853	Auguste-Napoléon Vaillant
		1853-1856	Louis-Henri de Gueydon
1771-1772	Louis-Florent de Valière	1856-1859	Armand-Louis-Joseph-Denis Fitte de Soucy
1772-1776	Vital-Auguste de Grégoire, Comte de Nozières	1859-1864	Antoine-Marie-Ferdinand de Maussion de Candé
1776-1777	Robert d'Argout		
1777-1783	François-Claude-Amour de Bouillé du Chariol	1864-1867	François-Théodore de Lapelin
		1867-1870	Louis-Auguste Bertier
1783-1789	Claude-Charles Damas de Marillac (1)	1870-1871	Charles-Louis-Constant Menche de Loisne
1789-1790	Joseph-Hyacinthe-Charles du Houx, Comte de Vioménil	1871-1875	Georges-Charles Cloué
		1875-1877	Thomas-Louis-Kirkland Le Normant de Kergrist
1790-1791	Claude-Charles Damas de Marillac (2)	1877-1879	Marie-Bruno-Ferdinand Grasset
1791-1793	Jean-Pierre-Antoine de Béhague	1879-1881	Hyacinthe-Laurent-Théophile Aube
		1881-1887	Vincent-Gaëtan Allègre

under Great Britain

		1887-1889	Louis-Albert Grodet
		1889-1891	Germain Casse
Governors		1891-1895	Dauphin Moracchini
1794	Robert Prescott	1895-1898	Noël Pardon
1794-1795	John Vaughan	1898-1901	Marie-Louis-Gustave Gabrié
1795-1796	Robert Shore Milnes	1901-1902	Louis Mouttet
1796-1802	William Keppel	1902-1904	Jean-Baptiste-Philémon Lemaire
		1904-1907	Louis-Alphonse Bonhoure
		1907-1908	Charles-Jules-Louis Lepreux

under France

		1908-1913	Fernand Foureau
Governor		1913-1914	Joseph-Henri-Alfred Vacher
1802-1809	Louis-Thomas Villaret de Joyeuse	1914-1915	Georges-Virgile Poulet
		1915-1920	Camille-Lucien-Xavier Guy

under Great Britain

		1920-1921	Jules-Maurice Gourbeil
		1921-1923	Fernand-Ernest Levecque
Governors		1923-1926	Henri-Marius Richard
1809	George Beckwith	1926-1928	Robert-Paul-Marie de Guise
1809-1812	John Broderick	1928-1933	Louis-Martial-Innocent Gerbinis
1812-1814	Charles Wale	1933-1934	Adolphe-Félix-Sylvestre Eboué
		1934	René Veber

under France

		1934-1935	Mathieu-Maurice Alfassa
Governors		1935-1936	Louis-Jacques-Eugène Fousset
1814-1818	Pierre-Marie-René de Vaugiraud	1936	Marie-Marc-Georges Pelicier
1818-1826	François-Xavier de Donzelot	1936-1938	Jean-Baptiste Alberti
1826-1829	François-Marie-Michel de Bouillé	1938	Léopold-Arthur-André Allys
1829-1830	Louis-Henri Desaulses de Freycinet	1938-1939	Maurice-Xavier-Joseph Dechartre
1830-1834	Jean-Henri-Joseph Dupôtet	1939-1940	Georges-Aimé Spitz
1834-1836	Emmanuel Halgan	1940-1941	Louis-Henri-François-Denis Bressoles
1836-1838	Ange-René-Armand de Mackau		
1838-1840	Alphonse-Louis-Théodore de Mogès	1941-1943	Yves-Maurice Nicol
1840-1844	Étienne-Henri Mengin Duval d'Ailly	1943-1944	Louis-Georges-André Ponton
1844-1848	Pierre-Louis-Aimé Mathieu	1944-1945	Antoine-Marie Angelini
1848	François-Auguste Perrinon	1945-1946	Georges-Hubert Parisot
		1946	Georges Louis-Joseph Orselli

Information from Le Sous-Préfet, Directeur du Cabinet, and from Le Directeur du Service des Archives de la Martinique, both in Fort-de-France, Martinique. For the 17th-century governors, see Chauleau, pp. 20-36; Crouse, *French Pioneers*, passim; and idem, *French Struggle*, passim.

42 MAURITANIA

Vague French rights to Mauritania had been recognized by Great Britain as early as 1857. Until 1900, however, the French government made no efforts to exercise these rights beyond occupying a few coastal posts and the north bank of the Senegal River to protect riverain trade. Beginning in 1900 full-scale occupation was begun, but it was only after 1914 that the territory was reasonably pacified. From 1902 to 1920 Mauritania was only a military district ruled by a commandant, but in 1920 it became a colony and a member of French West Africa (q.v.). The colony was so desolate that until 1958 it was administered from Saint Louis in Senegal. In 1958 Mauritania, like all but one of France's West African colonies, voted to become autonomous within the French Community. Two years later it became independent as the Islamic Republic of Mauritania.

Commandants
1902-1905 Xavier Coppolani
1905-1907 Bernard-Laurent Montané-
           Capdebosq
1907-1910 Henri-Joseph-Eugène Gouraud
1910-1912 Henri-Hippolyte Patey
1912-1914 Charles-Paul-Isidore Mouret
1914-1916 Louis-Jules-Albert Obissier
1916-1920 Nicolas-Jules-Henri Gaden

Governors
1920-1927 Nicolas-Jules-Henri Gaden
1928-1929 Alphonse-Paul-Albert Choteau
1929-1931 René-Hector-Émile Chazal
1931-1934 Gabriel-Omer Descemet
1934-1935 Jean-Victor Chazelas
1935-1936 Jules-Marcel de Coppet

1936-1942 Jean-Louis Beyriès
1942-1944 Jean-Victor-Louis-Joseph
           Chalvet
1944-1946 Christian-Robert-Roger Laigret
1947-1948 Lucien-Eugène Geay
1948-1949 Henri-Jean-Marie de Mauduit
1949-1950 Édouard-Louis-Barthélemy-
           Marie-Joseph Terrac
1950-1951 Jacques-Camille-Marie Rogué
1951-1954 Pierre-Auguste-Joseph Messmer
1954-1955 Albert-Jean Mouragues (1)
1955-1956 Jean-Paul Parisot
1956-1958 Albert-Jean Mouragues (2)

High Commissioner
1959-1960 Pierre-Amédée-Joseph-Émile-
           Jean Anthonioz

Information from Félix Brigaud, Directeur du Centre, Institut français d'Afrique noire, St. Louis, Senegal, and from J. C. Pansard, Cabinet du Premier Ministre, Nouakchott, Mauritania.

43 MAYOTTE

Mayotte, one of the Comoro Islands, was ceded to France by its ruler Andriantsuli in 1841, and it was occupied two years later. Beginning in 1886 the remaining islands of the Comoros—Great Comoro, Anjuan (Anjouan), and Mohilla (Mohéli)—were proclaimed protectorates. In 1912 their protectorate status was abolished and they became direct dependencies of Mayotte. In 1914 all four islands were annexed to Madagascar and the colony ceased to exist. In 1947, however, the Comoro Islands (q.v.) were detached by Madagascar and once again given an autonomous status.

Governors
1843-1844 Paul-Charles-Alexandre-Léonard
           Rang
1844-1846 Auguste-Noël Lebrun
1846-1849 Pierre Passot
1849-1851 Stanislas-Fortuné Livet

1851-1853 Philibert-Augustin Bonfils
1853-1855 André Brisset
1855-1857 André-César Vérand
1857-1860 Charles-Auguste-Joseph Morel
1860-1864 Charles-Louis-Benjamin Gabrié
1864-1871 Joseph-Vincent-Christophe Colomb

France

1871-1878	Patrice-Louis-Jules Ventre de la Touloubre	1896-1897	Gentien-Antonin-Victor Pereton
1878-1879	Charles-Henri Vassal	1897-1899	Louis-Alexandre Mizon
1880-1885	François-Aimé-Marie-Édmond Ferriez	1899-1901	Pierre-Louis-Clovis Papinaud (2)
		1901-1903	Pierre-Hubert-Auguste Pascal
		1903-1905	Albert-Alfred Martineau
1885-1887	Anne-Léodor-Philotée-Metellus Gerville-Réache	1905-1906	Jean-Auguste-Gaston Joliet
		1906-1908	Fernand Foureau
1887-1888	Paul-Louis-Maxime Céloron de Blainville	1908-1911	Charles-André-Édouard Vergnes
		1911	Frédéric Estèbe
1888-1893	Pierre-Louis-Clovis Papinaud (1)	1911-1913	Gabriel-Samuel Garnier-Mouton
1893-1896	Étienne-Théodore Lacascade	1913-1914	Honoré Cartron

Information from Archives nationales, section outre-mer, Paris.

44 MIDDLE CONGO

A separate administration for Middle Congo was established under French Congo (v. French Equatorial Africa) in 1897. Subsequently, in hopes that it would be developed, nearly the whole of the colony was given over to concessionary companies, but actual development was minimal. In 1911 a large chunk of the colony was ceded to Germany and attached to Kamerun (75) in return for German non-interference with French interests in Morocco (q.v.). After the Allied conquest of the German colonies, this territory was restored to Middle Congo. Three times during its existence Middle Congo was suppressed as a separate colony and directly administered by the governor-general of French Equatorial Africa. In 1958 the colony became autonomous within the French Community, and it became independent in 1960 as the Congo Republic.

Lieutenant-Governors

1894-1899	Albert Dolisie	1932-1941	(under French Eq. Africa)
1899-1902	Jean-Baptiste-Philémon Lemaire	1941-1945	Gabriel-Émile Fortune
1902-1903	Emile Gentil	1945-1946	Ange-Marie-Charles-André Bayardelle
1903-1906	(under French Eq. Africa)	1946	Christian-Robert-Roger Laigret
1906-1911	Adolphe-Louis Cureau	1946-1947	Numa-Henri-François Sadoul
1911-1912	Charles-André-Édouard Vergnes	1947-1950	Jacques-Georges Fourneau
1912-1916	Lucien-Louis Fourneau	1950-1952	Paul-Hippolyte-Julien-Marie Le Layec
1916-1917	Jules-Gaston-Henri Carde	1952-1953	Jean-Jacques Chambon
1917-1919	René-Victor Fournier	1953-1956	Ernest-Eugène Rouys
1919-1924	Matthieu-Maurice Alfassa	1956-1958	Jean-Michel Soupault
1924-1925	Jean-Henri Marchand	1958	Paul-Charles Dériaud
1925-1929	(under French Eq. Africa)		
1929-1930	Adolphe Deitte		
1930-1932	Charles-Max Masson de Saint-Félix		

High Commissioner

1959-1960 Gui-Noël Georgy

Information from Le Chef du Service des Archives, Administration provisoire des Services du Ministère de la France d'Outre-Mer, Paris, and from Le Directeur des Services de l'Information, Ministère de l'Information, Brazzaville, Congo Republic.

45 MINORCA

For the French governors of Minorca from 1756 to 1763, see the British colony, Minorca, 162.

46 MONTREAL

The town of Montreal was founded from Quebec in 1642, and it remained a separate jurisdiction under New France (q.v.) from that date until its capture by the English in 1760. It developed into the center of New France's lucrative fur trading expeditions.

Governors

1642-1665	Paul de Chomedey de Maisonneuve
1665-1668	Zacharie Depuy
1669-1670	Paul de Lamotte de Saint-Paul
1670-1684	François-Marie Perrot
1684-1698	Louis-Héctor de Callières
1698-1703	Pierre de Rigaud, Marquis de Vaudreuil
1704-1724	Claude de Ramezay
1724-1729	Charles Le Moyne de Longueuil I
1730-1733	Jean Bouillet de la Chassaigne
1733-1748	Jean-Maurice-Josué du Bois-Berthélot de Beaucours
1749-1755	Charles Le Moyne de Longueuil II
1757-1760	François-Pierre de Rigaud de Vaudreuil

Audet, pp. 78—79 (but for the period from 1733 to 1749 this list is incorrect).

47 MOROCCO

For early European interests in Morocco, see the British colony, Tangier (228), and the Portuguese colony, Ceuta (290). France wanted to secure control over Morocco in order to round off its North African possessions (see Tunis and Algeria), but was unable to do so before 1912 because of German opposition. In 1911, however, Germany withdrew its opposition in return for the cession of a large slice of Middle Congo (q.v.) which Germany attached to its colony of Kamerun (75). Morocco was then substantially divided into a Spanish zone (v. 357) and a French zone, with the city of Tangiers becoming an internationally controlled area. This division remained intact until 1956 when increasing Moroccan nationalist pressure forced France to grant the country complete independence. Spain followed suit almost immediately.

Residents-General

1912-1925	Louis-Hubert-Gonzalve Lyautey
1925-1928	Jules-Joseph-Théodore Steeg
1928-1933	Lucien Saint
1933-1936	Henri Ponsot
1936	Bernard-Marcel Peyrouton
1936-1943	Augustin-Paul-Charles Nogues
1943-1946	Gabriel Puaux
1946-1947	Eirik Labonne
1947-1951	Alphonse-Pierre Juin
1951-1954	Augustin-Léon Guillaume
1954-1955	François Lacoste
1955	Gilbert-Yves-Édmond Grandval
1955	Pierre-Georges-Jacques-Marie Boyer de la Tour du Moulin
1955-1956	André-Louis Dubois

Spuler, 1:271, and 2:353—54.

48 NEW CALEDONIA

The island of New Caledonia, discovered by James Cook in 1774, was occupied by the French in 1853. Until 1884 the governor of New Caledonia was also the commander of the French naval forces in the Pacific. From 1864 to 1894 the island served as a penal colony, but it was superseded in this respect by French Guiana (q.v.). New Caledonia voted to remain within the French Community as an overseas territory in 1958. The governor of New Caledonia currently serves also as high commissioner for French possessions in the Pacific, that is, French Polynesia and the Wallis and Futuna Islands (qq.v.).

Governors

1853	Auguste Febvrier des Pointes
1854	Louis-Marie-François Tardy de Montravel
1855-1858	Joseph-Fidèle-Eugène de Bouzet
1858-1860	Jean-Marie-Joseph-Théodose Saysset de Mars
1860-1862	Jean-Pierre-Thomas Durand
1862-1869	Charles Guillain
1869-1870	Jacques-Eugène-Barnabe Ruillier
1870-1874	Eugène Gualtier de la Richerie
1874-1875	Louis-Eugène Alleyron
1875-1879	Léopold-Eberhard-Ludwig de Pritzbuer
1879-1880	Jean-Baptiste-Léon Olry
1880-1882	Amédée-Anatole-Prosper Courbet
1882-1884	Léopold-Augustin-Charles Pallu de la Barrière
1884-1886	Antoine-Frédéric-Henri Le Boucher
1886-1888	Louis-Hippolyte-Marie Nouët
1888-1889	Léon-Émile Clément-Thomas
1889-1891	Noël Pardon
1891-1892	Émile-Gustave Laffon
1892-1894	Albert-Jean-Georges-Marie-Louis Picquié
1894-1902	Paul-Théodore-Ernest-Marie Feillet
1902-1905	Édouard Picanon
1906-1908	Victor-Théophile Liotard
1909-1910	Louis-Alphonse Bonhoure
1910-1914	Auguste-Charles Désiré-Emmanuel Brunet
1915-1919	Jules-Vincent Repiquet (1)
1919-1920	Joseph-Marie-Eugène Joulia
1921-1923	Jules-Vincent Repiquet (2)
1923-1925	Henri-Joseph-Marie d'Arboussier
1925-1932	Marie-Joseph-Casimir Guyon
1932-1933	Léonce-Alphonse-Nöel-Henri Jore (1)
1933-1936	Bernard-Jacques-Victorin Siadous
1936-1938	Alexandre-Jean-Marcel Marchessou
1938-1939	Léonce-Alphonse-Nöel-Henri Jore (2)
1939	René-Victor-Marie Barthès
1939-1940	Marie-Marc-Georges Pelicier
1940-1942	Henri-Camille Sautot
1942-1943	Marie-Henri-Ferdinand-Auguste Montchamp
1943-1944	Christian-Robert-Roger Laigret
1944-1947	Jacques-Victor-François Tallec
1947-1948	Georges-Hubert Parisot
1948-1951	Pierre-Charles-Albert Cournarie
1951-1954	Raoul-Eugène Angammarre
1954-1956	René Hoffherr
1956-1959	Aimé-Marius-Louis Grimald
1959-1963	Laurent-Elisée Péchoux
1963-1965	Casimir-Marc Biros
1965—	Jean Risterucci

Information from Le Haut-Commissaire de la République dans l'Océan Pacifique et aux Nouvelles Hébrides, Nouméa, New Caledonia. Also, O'Reilly, "Chronologie de la Nouvelle-Calédonie, 1774—1903."

49 NEW FRANCE

The area of what was to become New France was first visited by Jacques Cartier in 1535—36 but early attempts at settlement were unsuccessful. In 1603 colonizing efforts began in Acadia (q.v.) and in 1608 Quebec, which became the capital of New France, was founded. Later, Trois-Rivière and Montreal (q.v.), further up the Saint Lawrence River, were established. In 1629 the colony was occupied by the English, but it was returned in 1632. Other colonies were established in time around the littorals of New France over which the governor-general in Quebec exercised a nominal control (see, besides Acadia and Montreal, Plaisance, Île Royale, and Louisiana). The encroachments of the English, already begun in 1629, intensified with the occupation of Acadia (78) in 1710, and during the Seven Years' War all the remaining French settlements in Canada were occupied. By the Treaty of Paris in 1763 France ceded them to Great Britain (v. Newfoundland, 169, Nova Scotia, 187, and Prince Edward Island, 198).

Governors

1612-1629	Samuel de Champlain (1)
1629-1632	Lewis Kirke
1632-1633	Emery de Caën
1633-1635	Samuel de Champlain (2)
1635-1636	Marc-Antoine Bras-de-fer de Châteaufort
1636-1648	Charles Huault de Montmagny
1648-1651	Louis d'Ailleboust de Coulonges et d'Argentenay (1)
1651-1656	Jean de Lauzon
1656-1657	Charles de Lauson de Charny
1657-1658	Louis d'Ailleboust de Coulonges et d'Argentenay (2)
1658-1661	Pierre Voyer d'Argenson
1661-1663	Pierre Dubois d'Avaugour
1663-1665	Augustin de Saffray de Mézy
1665-1672	Daniel de Rémy de Courcelle
1672-1682	Louis de Buade, Comte de Frontenac et Palluau (1)
1682-1685	Joseph-Antoine Lefebvre de la Barre
1685-1689	Jacques-René de Brisay, Marquis de Denonville
1689-1698	Louis de Buade, Comte de Frontenac et Palluau (2)
1698-1703	Louis-Héctor de Callières
1703-1725	Philippe de Rigaud, Marquis de Vaudreuil
1725-1726	Charles Le Moyne, Baron de Longueuil I
1726-1747	Charles de la Boische, Marquis de Beauharnois
1747-1749	Roland-Michel Barrin, Comte de la Galissonière
1749-1752	Jacques-Pierre de Taffenel, Marquis de la Jonquière de la Pomarède
1752-1755	Michel-Ange Duquesne de Menneville
1755-1760	Pierre de Rigaud, Marquis de Vaudreuil-Cavagnal

Lemieux, pp. 1—81.

50 NEW HEBRIDES CONDOMINIUM

For the description of this colony, see the British colony New Hebrides Condominium, 172.

Resident Commissioners

1901-1904	Gaudence-Charles Faraut
1904-1908	Charles Bord
1908-1909	Charles-Henri-Adrien Noufflard
1909-1911	Jules Martin
1911-1913	Jules-Vincent Repiquet
1913-1916	Jacques-Louis Miramende (1)
1916-1918	Édmond Lippmann
1918-1919	Lucien-Hugues-Arthur Nielly
1919-1920	Alfred Solari
1920-1921	Jacques-Louis Miramende (2)
1921-1923	Henri-Joseph-Marie d'Arboussier (1)
1923-1925	Auguste-Adolphe-Joseph-Marie-Raoul de La Vaissière
1925-1929	Henri-Joseph-Marie d'Arboussier (2)
1929-1930	Gabriel-Henri-Joseph Thaly
1930-1931	Maurice-Georges Tronet
1931-1933	Antoine-Louis Carlotti
1933-1935	Henri-Camille Sautot (1)
1935-1937	Fernand-Gaston-Georges-Émile-Robert Casimir
1937-1940	Henri-Camille Sautot (2)
1940-1947	Robert-Charles-Henri Kuter
1947-1949	André Ménard

France

1949-1958	Pierre-Amédée-Joseph-Émile-Jean Anthonioz	1960-1965	Maurice-Charles-Jules Delauney
1958-1960	Benjamin-Marcel Favreau	1965 —	Jacques Mouradian

Information from C. Coldeboeuf, Le Directeur du Cabinet de Résidence de France, Port Vila, New Hebrides.

51 NIGER

French penetration east of the Niger river increased the size of the colony of Upper Senegal-Niger (v. French Sudan) beyond the point of efficiency and forced the creation of a new colony, Niger, in 1911. Niger remained under military rule until 1922 when civil government was introduced and it was raised to a colony. In 1937 the lieutenant governors were replaced by governors. In 1958 Niger became autonomous within the French Community, and it attained independence in 1960 as the Republic of Niger.

Commissioners

1912-1913	Charles-Camille Thierry de Maugras
1914-1916	Paul-Celestin-Marie-Joseph Venel
1916-1918	Charles-Henri Mourin
1918-1919	Marie-Joseph-Félix Méchet
1919-1920	Claude-Paul-Émile Lefebvre
1920-1921	Maurice-Gustave-Fernand Renauld
1921-1922	Lucien-Émile Ruef

Lieutenant Governors

1922-1929	Jules Brévié
1930	Alphonse-Paul-Albert Choteau
1931	Louis-Placide Blacher
1932-1933	Théophile-Antoine-Pascal Tellier

1933-1934	Maurice-Léon Bourgine
1934-1935	Léon-Charles-Adolphe Pêtre
1936-1937	Joseph-Urbain Court

Governors

1937-1938	Joseph-Urbain Court
1939-1940	Jean-Alexandre-Léon Rapenne
1941-1942	Maurice-Émile Falvy
1942-1954	Jean-François Toby
1955-1956	Jean-Paul Ramadier
1956-1958	Paul-Camille Bordier
1958	Louis-Félix Rollet
1958	Don-Jean Colombani

High Commissioner

1959-1960	Don-Jean Colombani

Information from A. Gayot, Service de l'Information, Niamey, Republic of Niger. Also, Séré de Rivières, pp. 266—68.

52 NOSY BÉ

Nosy Bé, a small island off the northwest coast of Madagascar, was ceded to France by its Sakalava ruler in 1840. It was used as a naval station almost exclusively, although some settlement was attempted. Until 1843 it was under Réunion (q.v.), then under Mayotte (q.v.) to 1878 when it was made a separate colony. In 1896, like Diégo-Suarez (q.v.), it was of no further use as a distinct colony and was subsumed into Madagascar (q.v.).

Governors

1841-1842	François Gouhot
1842	Pierre Passot
1842-1845	Charles-Auguste-Joseph Morel
1845-1848	Henri-Martin Lamy
1848-1851	Jean-Ernest Marchaisse
1851	Alexandre-Louis Berg
1851-1852	Jean-Théophile Lapeyre-Bellair
1852-1853	Thomas-Joseph Dupuis (1)
1853-1854	André Brisset
1854-1855	Louis-Antoine-Ernest Arnoux
1855-1856	Joseph-Méciste Septans
1856-1858	Thomas-Joseph Dupuis (2)
1858-1860	Paul-Gustave Sachet
1860-1861	Justin-Jean-Baptiste-Clément Duperier
1861-1865	Vincent Derussat
1865-1866	Pierre Lucas
1866-1868	Joseph-Jean-Ferdinand Hayes
1868-1869	Louis-Jean Chériner
1869-1870	Aimé-Ernest-Justin Champy
1870-1871	Patrice-Louis-Jules Ventre de la Touloubre
1871-1872	Jean-Baptiste-Joseph-Charles Barnier
1872-1873	Marie-Alexandre Leclos
1873-1874	Honoré-Henri Léchelle
1874-1875	Claude-Michel-Jacques-Louis-François Fontaine
1875-1876	Joseph-Marie Carle
1876	Arthur-Paul Feutray
1877-1878	François-Aimé-Marie-Édmond Ferriez
1878-1883	Alphonse Seignac-Lesseps
1883-1886	Alexandre-Charles LeMaître
1886-1888	Léon-Émile Clément-Thomas
1888-1889	Furcy-Augustin Armanet
1890-1895	Joseph François

Decary, *L'île Nosy Bé*, pp. 186–87.

53 PLAISANCE

Plaisance, situated on an inlet in southern Newfoundland, was established by the French ca. 1640 to serve as a base for their fishing activities in the Grand Banks. In 1662 it was colonized on a small scale and provided with a rudimentary administration. Plaisance was surrendered to Great Britain by the terms of the Treaty of Utrecht in 1713 (v. Newfoundland, 169). Its inhabitants emigrated to Île Royale (q.v.).

Governors

1662-1663	Thalour du Perron
1663-1664	Nicolas Gargot de la Rochette
1664-1667	Bellot Lafontaine
1667-1670	Sieur de la Palme
1670-1684	Sieur de Poippe
1685-1690	Antoine de Parat
1690-1697	Jacques-François de Brouillan
1697-1702	Joseph de Monic
1702-1706	Daniel d'Auger de Subercase
1706-1713	Philippe de Pastour de Costebelle

La Morandière, 1:403–507.

54 RÉUNION

Réunion, one of the Mascarenes, was claimed by France as early as 1639, but the first settlement was not made until 1664—by emigrants from Fort-Dauphin (q.v.) in Madagascar (q.v.). Later this nucleus was supplemented by pirates from Madagascar whose lairs had been destroyed. Réunion was governed by the Compagnie des Indes until 1764 when the crown assumed

France

control. After 1727 it was subject to the authority of the governor-general at Île de France (q.v.). From 1810 to 1815 it was occupied by the British, and afterward, with the retention of Île de France and the Seychelles (q.v.) by the English, it became the only French colony in the Indian Ocean east of Madagascar. Réunion underwent an uncommonly large number of name changes:

1649-1793	Bourbon
1793-1806	Réunion
1806-1810	Bonaparte
1810-1848	Bourbon
1848—	Réunion

In 1947 Réunion became an overseas department of France governed by a prefect.

Commandants

1665-1671	Étienne Regnault
1671-1674	Jacques de Lahure
1674-1678	Henri Esse d'Orgeret
1678-1680	Germain de Fleuricourt
1680-1686	Hyacinthe-Bernardin de Quimper
1686-1689	Jean-Baptiste Drouillard
1689-1690	Henri Habet de Vauboulon
1690-1696	Michel Firélin
1696-1698	Joseph Bastide
1698-1701	Jacques de la Cour de la Saulais
1701-1709	Jean-Baptiste de Villers
1709-1710	François-Michel Desbordes de Charanville
1710-1715	Pierre-Antoine Parat de Chaillenest
1715-1718	Henri Justamont
1718-1723	Joseph Beauvollier de Courchant
1723-1725	Antoine Boucher-Desforges
1725-1727	Hélie Dioré
1727-1735	Pierre-Benoît Dumas
1735-1739	Lémery-Dupont
1739-1744	Pierre-André d'Héguerty
1744-1745	Didier de Saint-Martin (1)
1745	Jean-Baptiste Azéma
1745-1746	Gaspard de Ballade (1)
1746-1748	Didier de Saint-Martin (2)
1748-1749	Gaspard de Ballade (2)

Governors

1750-1753	Jean-Baptiste-Charles Bouvet de Lozier (1)
1753-1756	Joseph Brénier
1756-1763	Jean-Baptiste-Charles Bouvet de Lozier (2)

Commandants

1763-1767	François-Jacques Bertin d'Avesnes
1767	Martin-Adrien Bellier

Governors

1767-1773	Guillaume-Léonard de Bellecombe
1773-1776	Jean-Guillaume Steinauer
1776-1779	François de Souillac
1779-1781	Joseph Murinay de Saint-Maurice
1781-1785	André-Joseph-François Chalvet de Souville
1785-1787	Hélie Dioré
1787-1790	David Charpentier de Cossigny
1790-1792	Dominique-Prosper de Chermont
1792-1794	Jean-Baptiste Vigoureux du Plessis
1795-1803	Philippe-Antoine Jacob de Cordemoy
1803-1806	François-Louis Magallon de Lamorlière
1806-1809	Nicolas-Arnault de Regnac des Brulys
1809-1810	Jean-Chrysostome Bruneteau de Sainte-Suzanne

under Great Britain

Governors

1810-1811	Robert Townsend Farquhar
1811	Henry Warde
1811-1815	Henry Sheehy Keating

under France

Governors

1815-1817	Athanase-Hyacinthe Bouvet de Lozier
1817-1818	Hilaire-Urbain Lafitte de Courteil
1818-1821	Pierre-Bernard de Milius
1821-1826	Louis-Henri Desaulses de Freycinet
1826-1830	Achille-Gui-Marie-Michel de Penfentenio de Cheffontaines
1830-1832	Étienne-Henri Mengin Duval d'Ailly
1832-1838	Jacques-Philippe Cuvillier
1838-1841	Anne-Chrétien-Louis de Hell
1841-1846	Charles-Louis-Joseph Bazoche
1846-1848	Emmanuel-François-Joseph Graëb
1848-1850	Joseph-Napoléon Sarda-Garriga
1850-1852	Louis-Isaac-Pierre-Hilaire Doret
1852-1858	Louis-Henri Hubert-Delisle
1858-1864	Rodolphe-Augustin Darricau
1864-1869	Marc-Jules Dupré
1869-1875	Louis-Hippolyte de Lormel

1875–1879	Pierre-Aristide Faron	1910–1913	François-Pierre Rodier
1879–1886	Pierre-Étienne Cuinier	1913–1920	Pierre-Louis-Alfred Duprat
1886–1888	Étienne-Antoine-Guillaume Richaud	1920–1923	Frédéric Estèbe
1888–1893	Louis-Evenor-Édouard Manès	1923–1925	Maurice-Pierre Lapalud
1893–1896	Henri-Eloi Danel	1925–1934	Jules-Vincent Repiquet
1896–1901	Laurent-Marie-Émile Beauchamp	1934–1936	Alphonse-Paul-Albert Choteau
1901–1906	Paul Samary	1936–1938	Léon-Hippolyte Truitard
1906–1908	Adrien-Jules-Jean Bonhoure	1938–1940	Joseph-Urbain Court
1908–1910	Camille-Lucien-Xavier Guy	1940–1942	Pierre-Émile Aubert
1910	Philippe-Émile Jullien	1942–1947	André-Jean-Charles Capagorry

Information from André Scherer, Directeur des Services d'Archives de La Réunion, Saint-Denis, Réunion.

55 SAINT-CHRISTOPHE

Saint-Christophe was the first French settlement in the West Indies. From the beginning the island of Saint Christopher was shared with the English. Until 1674 the French portion of the island was privately owned and administered. The Compagnie de Saint-Christophe held the colony from 1628 to 1635, the Compagnie des îles de l'Amérique from 1635 to 1651, the Knights of Malta from 1651 to 1665, and the Compagnie des Indes occidentales from 1665–1674. In 1666 the French drove the British from the island, but five years later the island was again divided between the two nations. In 1702 the French were finally expelled from the island, and British sole possession was confirmed by the Treaty of Utrecht in 1713 (v. Saint Kitts-Nevis-Anguilla, 208).

Governors

1628–1636	Pierre Belain d'Esnambuc	1646–1660	Philippe Lonvilliers de Poincy (2)
1636–1638	Pierre du Halde	1660–1666	Charles de Sales
1638–1639	René de Béculat, Sieur de La Grange Fromenteau	1666–1689	Claude de Roux de Saint-Laurent
		1689–1690	Charles Peychpeyrou-Comminge de Guitaut
1639–1644	Philippe Lonvilliers de Poincy (1)	1690–1698	(under Great Britain)
1644–1646	Robert Lonvilliers de Poincy	1698–1702	Jean-Baptiste de Gennes

Crouse, *French Pioneers*, passim; idem, *French Struggle*, passim; Servant, pp. 436–41.

56 SAINT-DOMINGUE

Tortuga, an island off the northwest coast of the Spanish colony of Santo Domingo (387) (also known as Hispaniola) was occupied by French freebooters in 1641 and shortly thereafter subjected to a more formal form of government. By the Treaty of Ryswick in 1697 France obtained the western part of Hispaniola, renaming it Saint-Domingue. During the 18th century Saint-Domingue became France's most valuable colony and the largest sugar producer in the world. By 1791 it contained a large French settler population but a much larger Negro population. The ideas of the French Revolution brought a decade of chaotic strife to Saint-Domingue. By 1802 the French had lost control, although Toussaint L'Ouverture was nominally the French governor-general. A brief effort to reconquer the island in 1802–3 was disastrous and the French withdrew completely in 1803. Subsequently the former French portion of the island became known as Haiti.

Governors

1641–1652	Le Vasseur
1652–1654	Timoléon Hotman de Fontenay[1]
1656–1665	Jérémie Deschamps, Chevalier du Raussac et du Moussac
1665–1676	Bertrand d'Ogeron de la Bouère
1676–1683	Jacques Nepveu, Sieur de Pouançay
1684–1691	Pierre-Paul Tarin de Cussy
1691–1700	Jean-Baptiste Ducasse
1700–1703	Joseph d'Honon de Galiffet
1703–1705	Charles Auger
1705–1707	Jean-Pierre de Casamajor de Charritte
1707–1710	François-Joseph de Choiseul-Beaupré
1710–1711	Laurent de Valernod
1711–1712	Nicolas de Gabaret
1712–1713	Paul-François de La Grange, Comte d'Arquian
1713–1714	Louis de Courbon, Comte de Blénac

Governors-General

1714–1716	Louis de Courbon, Comte de Blénac
1716–1719	Charles Joubert de La Bastide, Marquis de Châteaumorand
1719–1723	Leon, Marquis de Sorel
1723–1731	Gaspard-Charles de Goussé, Chevalier de La Roche-Allard
1731–1732	Antoine-Gabriel de Vienne de Busserrolles
1732	Étienne Cochard de Chastenoye (1)
1732–1737	Pierre de Fayet de Peychaud
1737–1746	Charles Brunier, Marquis de Larnage
1746–1748	Étienne Cochard de Chastenoye (2)
1748–1751	Hubert de Brienne, Comte de Conflans

1751–1753	Emmanuel-Auguste de Cahideux, Comte du Bois de La Mothe
1753–1757	Joseph-Hyacinthe de Rigaud, Marquis de Vaudreuil
1757–1762	Philippe-François Bart
1762–1763	Gabriel de Bory
1763	Armand de Belzunce
1763–1764	Pierre-André de Gohin de Montreuil
1764–1766	Charles-Henri-Théodat d'Estaing du Saillans
1766–1769	Louis-Armand Constantin, Chevalier de Rohan-Montbazon
1769–1771	Pierre-Gédéon de Nolivos
1772–1775	Louis-Florent de Valière
1775–1776	Victor-Thérèse Charpentier, Comte d'Ennery
1776–1777	Jean-Baptiste de Tastes de Lilancour
1777–1780	Robert d'Argout
1780–1781	Jean-François Reynaud de Villeverd
1781–1782	Jean-Baptiste de Tastes de Lilancour
1782–1785	Guillaume-Léonard de Bellecombe
1785–1786	Gui-Pierre de Coustard
1786–1787	César-Henri de La Luzerne
1787–1788	Alexandre de Vincent de Mazade
1788–1789	Marie-Charles du Chilleau, Marquis d'Airvault
1789–1790	Louis-Antoine Thomassin, Comte de Peynier
1790–1792	Philibert-François Rouxel de Blanchelande
1792–1793[2]	François-Thomas Galbaud
1793–1796	Étienne Maynaud de Laveaux
1796–1797	Léger-Félicité Sonthonax
1797–1802	Pierre-Dominique Toussaint l'Ouverture
1802	Charles-Victor-Emmanuel Leclerc
1802–1803	Donatien-Marie-Joseph de Vimeur, Comte de Rochambeau

1. The index to Moreau de Saint-Méry refers to this governor as Louis d'Aché de Fontenay, but this is an error. The form used in this list is that used by Crouse, *French Pioneers*. See further, Raul Alejandro Molina, "Don Timoleón d'Osmat, Señor de Fontenay," *Historia* (Buenos Aires), no. 14 (1958), pp. 19–34.

2. From 1793 to 1798 British forces occupied the southern part of Saint-Domingue. The effort to retain this foothold was abandoned because of the adverse climate and the hostility of the blacks. The military governors during this period were:

1793–1794	John Whitelocke	1796–1797	John Graves Simcoe
1794–1796	Adam Williamson	1797–1798	Thomas Maitland

Moreau de Saint-Méry, 1:17–20, and 3:1443–1559.

57 SAINTE-LUCIE

Between 1638 and 1763 the island of Sainte-Lucie was settled intermittently by the French and English who seemed to delight in turning one another out. From 1723 to 1743 and 1748 to 1756 the island was officially declared neutral. France occupied it in 1756, lost it in 1762, and regained it in 1763. For most of the period from 1763 to 1803 it was in French hands. After 1803 it became permanently British. For supplementary data as well as for the British governors before 1803, see Saint Lucia, 209, in the Great Britain section.

Governors			
1763-1764	Pierre-Lucien de La Chapelle de Jumilhac	1781-1784	(under Great Britain)
		1784-1789	Jean-Zénon-André de Véron de Laborie
1764-1771	Claude-Anne de Micoud	1789-1793	Jean-Joseph de Gimat
1771-1773	Claude-Anne-Gui de Micoud (1)	1793-1794	Nicolas-Xavier de Ricard
1773-1775	Frédéric Laure de Kearney	1794-1795	(under Great Britain)
1775-1776	Alexandre Potier de Courcy	1795-1796	Goyrand
1776-1778	Marc-Étienne de Joubert	1796-1802	(under Great Britain)
1778-1781	Claude-Anne-Gui de Micoud (2)	1802-1803	Jean-François-Xavier Nogues

Information from the Administrator of Saint Lucia, Castries, Saint Lucia. Also, Dermigny and Debien; Micoud.

58 SAINTE MARIE DE MADAGASCAR

Sainte Marie, a small island off the northeastern coast of Madagascar, was ceded to the French by its Malagasy ruler in 1750, but it remained unoccupied until 1819. Until 1843 it was under Bourbon (v. Réunion). From 1843 to 1853 it was subject to Mayotte, and from 1853 to 1877 it was a separate colony. In 1878 it was returned to Réunion's jurisdiction where it remained until 1896 when, like France's other small colonies on Madagascar, Nosy Bé and Diégo-Suarez (qq.v.), it was annexed to Madagascar (q.v.).

Commandants			
1819-1821	Jean-Louis-Joseph Carayon (1)	1849-1850	Pierre-Balthasar Mermier (1)
1821-1823	Jean-Baptiste-Sylvain Roux	1850-1851	André Brisset
1823-1827	Bertrand-Hercule Blévec (1)	1851-1853	Pierre-Balthasar Mermier (2)
1827-1829	Jean-Louis-Joseph Carayon (2)	1853	Félix-Sylvain Grébert
1829	Bertrand-Hercule Blévec (2)	1853-1855	Jean-Pierre-Thomas Durand
1829-1830	Jean-Louis-Joseph Carayon (3)	1855-1858	Anne-Jean-Baptiste Raffenel
1830-1841	(none)	1858-1868	Jean-Paul de la Grange
1841-1849	Raimond Vergès	1868-1874	Louis-Justin-Ignace Blandinières
		1874-1878	Charles-Henri Vassal

Decary, "Bertrand Hercule Blévec"; Ministère de la Marine et des Colonies, *Annuaire*, 1865–78; Rambosson, p. 300.

59 SAINT EUSTATIUS

For the French governors of Saint Eustatius from 1781 to 1784, see the Dutch colony, Saint Eustatius, 280.

60 SAINT PIERRE AND MIQUELON

Saint Pierre and Miquelon, a group of eight small islands off the southern coast of Newfoundland, are the relics of France's once vast possessions in North America. They are used as a base for France's fishing fleet in the Grand Banks, a role previously filled by Plaisance (q.v.). The islands were occupied by England during the American Revolution and the Napoleonic Wars but were not separately administered.

Commandants

1763-1773	François-Gabriel Dangeac
1773-1778	Charles-Gabriel Sébastien, Baron de l'Espérance
1778-1783	(under Great Britain)
1783-1793	Antoine-Nicolas Dandasne-Danseville
1793-1816	(under Great Britain)
1816-1819	Jean-Philippe Bourilhon
1819-1825	Philippe-Athanase-Hélène Fayolle
1825-1828	Augustin-Valentin Borius
1828-1839	Joseph-Louis-Michel Bruë
1839-1842	Louis-Alexandre Mamyneau
1842-1845	Joseph-Alphonse Desrousseaux
1845-1850	Joseph-Marie-Fidèle Delécluse
1850-1859	Jacques-François Gervais
1859-1864	Émile-François-Guillaume-Clément de la Roncière
1864-1873	Pierre-Vincent Cren
1873-1878	Charles-Henri-Alfred Joubert
1878-1880	Antoine-Étienne Guien
1880-1887	Gaston-Louis, Comte de Saint-Phalle

Governors[1]

1887-1891	Henri-Félix de La Mothe
1891-1895	Paul-Théodore-Ernest-Marie Feillet
1895-1897	Laurent-Marie-Émile Beauchamp
1897-1900	Paul-Émile Daclin-Sibour
1900-1901	Paul Samary
1901-1905	Philippe-Émile Jullien
1905-1906	Paul-Jean-François Cousturier
1906-1909	Raphaël-Valentin-Marius Antonetti
1909-1912	Pierre-Jean-Henri Didelot
1912-1915	Charles-Rémy-Victor-Omard Marchand
1915-1922	Ernest-Philippe-François Lachat
1922-1928	Jean-Henri-Émile Bensch
1928-1929	François-Adrien Juvanon
1929-1932	Henri-Camille Sautot
1932-1933	Georges-Marie-Roger Chanot
1933-1937	Georges-Jules-Eugène Barrillot
1937-1942	Gilbert de Bournat
1942-1943	Alain-François Savary
1943-1946	Pierre-Marie-Jacques-François Garrouste
1946-1947	Maurice-René-Charles-Victor Marchand
1947-1949	Jean-René Moisset
1949-1950	Guy Clech
1950-1952	Eugène-Alain-Charles Louis Alaniou
1952-1955	Irenée-François-Antoine Davier
1955-1958	Pierre-René-Jean Sicaud
1958-1961	René-Louis Pont
1961-1962	Pierre-Jean-Charles Maillard
1962-1965	Jacques-Emmanuel Herry
1965-1967	Georges-Marie-Joseph Poulet
1967—	Jean-Jacques Buggia

1. From 1906 to 1923, and 1933 to 1946, called administrators.

Information from P. Fonteney, Le Chef du Cabinet de Saint-Pierre et Miquelon, and from Y. Arbellot-Répaire, Administrateur Civil, Saint-Pierre et Miquelon. Also, Ribault.

61 SENEGAL

The mouth of the Senegal River had been visited by Europeans regularly since the first Portuguese arrived in 1445. In 1659 the French built Saint Louis at the mouth of the river, and thereafter, except for brief periods, they controlled the area around the town. In 1677 they occupied Gorée (q.v.). From 1626 to 1758 French activities along the Senegal coast were controlled by the following chartered companies:

1626-1658	Compagnie Normand
1658-1664	Compagnie du Cap Vert et du Sénégal
1664-1673	Compagnie des Indes occidentales
1673-1682	Compagnie d'Afrique
1682-1718	Compagnies (3) du Sénégal
1718-1758	Compagnie des Indes orientales

In 1758 the English seized the French forts. They returned Gorée in 1763 and erected the remainder into the colony of Senegambia (213). The French retook the British possessions in 1778 but lost them all again in 1809, recovering them finally in 1817. Until the middle of the 19th century French interest in Senegal was limited to the coastal and riverain trade, but French authority began to expand rapidly after the arrival of Faidherbe in 1854. In 1895 Senegal became the seat of French West Africa (q.v.) and lost its own individual administration until 1902. In 1958 Senegal became an autonomous member of the French Community, and it became fully independent in 1960.

Directors[1]

1674-1682	Jacques Fuméchon
1682-1685	Denis Basset
1685-1689	Louis Moreau de Chambonneau (1)
1689-1693	Michel Jajolet de la Courbe (1)
1693-1695	Louis Moreau de Chambonneau (2)
1695-1697	Jean Bourguignon
1697-1702	André Bruë (1)
1702-1706	Lamaître
1706-1710	Michel Jajolet de la Courbe (2)
1710-1711	Guillaume-Joseph de Mustellier
1712-1713	de Richebourg
1714-1720	André Bruë (2)
1720-1723	Nicolas Després de Saint-Robert (1)
1723-1725	Julien Dubellay
1725-1726	Nicolas Després de Saint-Robert (2)
1726	Arnaud Plumet
1726-1733	Jean Levens de la Roquette
1733-1738	Sébastien-Auguste Devaulx
1738-1746	Pierre-Félix-Barthélemy David
1747-1758	Jean-Baptiste Estoupan de la Bruë

under Great Britain

Governors

1758-1763	Richard Alchorne Worge

under France

Gorée[2]

Commandants

1763-1764	Pierre-François-Guillaume Poncet de la Rivière

1764-1767	Jean-Georges Le Baillif de Mesnager
1767-1768	Claude Le Lardeux de la Gastière
1768-1772	Pierre-Louis de Rastel de Rocheblave
1772	Antoine-Jean-Baptiste-Georges-Louis Desmarets de Montchaton
1772-1774	Charles-Hippolyte Boniface
1774-1777	Joseph-Alexandre Le Brasseur
1777-1778	Alexandre-David Armény de Paradis
1778	Charles-Joseph-Bonaventure Boucher

Senegal

Commandants

1778-1779	Armand-Louis de Gontaut Biron, Duc de Lauzun
1779-1781	Jacques-Joseph Eyriès
1781-1783	Anne-Guilin Dumontêt
1783-1786	Louis Le Gardeur de Repentigny
1786-1788	Stanislas-Jean de Boufflers
1788-1801	François-Michel-Émile Blanchot de Verly (1)
1801-1802	Louis-Henri-Pierre Lasserre
1802-1807	François-Michel-Émile Blanchot de Verly (2)
1807-1809	Pierre-François Levasseur

under Great Britain

Governors

1809-1811	Charles William Maxwell
1811-1814	Charles MacCarthy
1814-1816	Thomas Brereton

under France

Commandants

1817–1820	Julien-Désiré Schmaltz
1820–1822	Louis-Jean-Baptiste Lecoupé de Montereau
1822–1828	Jacques-François Roger

Governors

1828–1829	Jean-Guillaume Jubelin
1829–1831	Pierre-Édouard Brou
1831–1833	Thomas-Xavier Renault de Saint-Germain
1833–1834	Eustache-Louis-Jean Quernel
1834–1836	Louis Pujol
1836	Louis-Augustin-Médéric Malavois
1836–1837	Louis-Laurent-Auguste Guillet
1837–1839	Julien-Armand Soret
1839–1841	Pons-Guillaume-Basile Charmasson de Puy-Laval
1841–1842	Jean-Baptiste Montagniès de la Roque
1842–1843	Édouard-Paul Pageot des Noutières
1843–1844	Louis-Édouard Bouët-Willaumez
1844–1845	Pierre-Maurice Thomas
1845–1846	François-Marie-Charles Ollivier
1846–1847	Ernest Bourdon de Grammont
1847–1848	Auguste-Laurent-François Baudin (1)
1848	Léandre-Adolphe-Joseph Bertin-Duchâteau
1848–1850	Auguste-Laurent-François Baudin (2)
1850–1854	Auguste-Léon Protêt
1854–1861	Louis-Léon-César Faidherbe (1)
1861–1863	Jean-Bernard Jauréguiberry
1863–1865	Louis-Léon-César Faidherbe (2)
1865–1869	Jean-Marie-Émile Pinet-Laprade
1869–1876	François-Xavier-Michel-Victorien Valière
1876–1881	Louis-Alexandre-Esprit-Gaston Brière de l'Isle
1881	Louis-Ferdinand de Lanneau
1881–1882	Henri-Philibert Canard
1882	Aristide-Louis-Antoine-Maximien-Marie Vallon
1882–1884	René-Camille-Gaston Servatius
1884–1886	Alphonse Seignac-Lesseps
1886–1888	Jules-Eugène Genouille
1888–1890	Léon-Émile Clément-Thomas
1890–1895	Henri-Félix de la Mothe

Lieutenant Governors

1902–1908	Camille-Lucien-Xavier Guy
1908–1909	Jules-Maurice Gourbeil
1909–1911	Jean-Jules-Émile Peuvergne
1911–1914	Henri-François-Charles Cor
1914–1916	Raphaël-Valentin-Marius Antonetti
1916–1921	Fernand-Ernest Lévecque
1921–1924	Pierre-Jean-Henri Didelot
1924–1926	Camille-Théodore-Raoul Maillet
1926–1929	Léonce-Alphonse-Noël-Henri Jore
1929–1936	Maurice Beurnier
1936–1937	Louis-Charles Lefebvre

Governors

1937–1938	Louis-Charles Lefebvre
1938–1941	Georges-Hubert Parisot
1941–1943	Georges-Pierre Rey
1943–1944	Hubert-Jules Deschamps
1944–1945	Charles-Jean-Jacques-Émile Dagain
1945–1946	Pierre-Louis Maestracci
1946–1947	Oswald-Marcellin-Maurice-Marius Durand
1947–1950	Laurent-Marcel Wiltord
1950–1952	Camille-Victor Bailly
1952–1953	Lucien-Eugène Geay
1953–1954	Daniel-Henri-Marie Goujon
1954–1955	Maxime-Marie-Antoine Jourdain
1955–1957	Don-Jean Colombani
1957–1958	Pierre-Auguste-Michel-Marie Lami

High Commissioner

1959–1960	Pierre-Auguste-Michel-Marie Lami

1. Most of the lists of the early governors begin with Thomas Lambert in 1626 and continue unbroken from that time. However, there was no permanent French occupation at this early period, and even after 1659 the sources are confusing and contradictory (see Cultru, pp. xxix–xxxi, and Ritchie, pp. 289, 302, 309n). For this reason the governors are given only from 1674, from which time they can be ascertained with a reasonable degree of certainty.

2. The British held Senegal until 1778.

Information from Abdoulaye Ly, Le Directeur-Adjoint de l'Institut français d'Afrique noire, Dakar, Senegal. Also, Delcourt, pp. 106–13; Jore, pp. 32–251; Schefer, passim.

62 SEYCHELLES ISLANDS

For the French commandants of the Seychelles Islands from 1788 to 1810, see the British colony, Seychelles Islands, 214.

63 SYRIA

Syria fell to France as a League of Nations mandate after World War I. France divided the country into five states—Aleppo, Damascus, Jabal Druze, the Alawis, and Great Lebanon (q.v.), and referred to them collectively as the Levant States. Although the last became a separate government, and later a country, the remaining four remained loosely united in spite of French efforts at decentralization. The mandate remained in effect until 1946, although heavy nationalist pressure led to the granting of nominal independence in 1941 after the occupation of the country by Free French troops supported by the British.

High Commissioners
1919-1923   Henri-Joseph-Eugène Gouraud
1923-1925   Maxime Weygand (1)
1925   Maurice-Paul-Emmanuel Sarrail
1925-1926   Henri de Jouvenel
1926-1933   Henri Ponsot
1933-1938   Damien de Martel
1938-1939   Gabriel Puaux
1939-1940   Maxime Weygand (2)

1940   Eugène Mittelhauser
1940   Jean Chiappe
1940-1941   Henri-Fernand Dentz

Delegates-general
1941-1943   Georges-Albert-Julien Catroux
1943   Jean Helleu
1943-1944   Yves Chataigneau
1944-1946   Paul-Émile-Marie-Étienne Beynet

Longrigg, p. 236 and passim.

64 TOBAGO

For the French governors of Tobago from 1781 to 1793, see the British colony, Tobago, 230.

65 TOGO

The German colony of Togo (77) was occupied by British and French forces in 1914. In 1922 France and Great Britain were awarded mandates for their two parts of Togo. The British administered their portion as part of the Gold Coast (136), while France administered hers separately. In 1946 Togo became a United Nations trusteeship. In 1956 Togo was granted a measure of internal autonomy, followed four years later by full independence.

France

Governors
1916-1917 Gaston-Léopold-Joseph Fourn
1917-1921 Alfred-Louis Woelfel

High Commissioners
1921-1922 Alfred-Louis Woelfel
1922-1931 Auguste-François Bonnecarrère
1931-1933 Robert-Paul-Marie de Guise
1933-1934 Léon-Charles-Adolphe Pêtre
1934-1935 Maurice-Léon Bourgine
1935-1936 Léon Geismar
1936-1941 Michel-Lucien Montagné

1941   Léonce-Joseph Delpech
1941-1942 Jean-François-Marie de Saint-
              Alary
1942-1943 Pierre-Jean Saliceti
1943-1944 Albert Mercadier
1944-1948 Jean Noutary
1948-1951 Jean-Henri-Arsène Cédile
1951-1952 Yves-Jean Digo
1952-1954 Laurent-Elisée Péchoux
1955-1957 Jean-Louis-Philippe Bérard
1957-1960 Georges-Léon Spénale

Cornevin, p. 239 and passim.

66 TONKIN

Tonkin was the northern viceroyalty of the kingdom of Annam. In 1873–74 the French, already heavily involved in Indochina (v. Cochin China, Annam, Cambodia), made an abortive effort to occupy Tonkin. In 1886 a resident was appointed, but he was subject to the resident-general of Annam. Finally in 1888 Tonkin was raised to a parity with Annam as a member of the Indochinese Union. Japanese forces occupied Tonkin during World War II. After the war French influence was quickly undermined by the Viet Minh until in 1954 France withdrew from Tonkin and all of Indochina. Tonkin became a part of North Vietnam.

Annam-Tonkin
Residents-General
1884-1885 Victor-Marie Lemaire
1885-1886 Philippe-Marie-André Roussel de
              Courcy
1886   Paul Bert
1886-1887 Paulin-François-Alexandre Vial
1887   Pierre-Louis-Georges Bihouard
1887-1888 Étienne-Antoine Guillaume Richaud
1888-1889 Pierre-Paul Rheinart

Tonkin
Residents-Superior
1886   Paulin-François-Alexandre Vial
1886-1887 Jean-Thomas-Raoul Bonnal
1887-1888 (abolished)
1888-1889 Eusèbe-Irenée Parreau
1889-1891 Ernest-Albert Brière
1891-1893 Léon-Jean-Laurent Chavassieux

1893-1895 François-Pierre Rodier
1895-1897 (abolished)
1897-1904 Augustin-Julien Fourès
1905-1907 Élie-Jean-Henri Groleau
1907   Louis-Alphonse Bonhoure
1907-1909 Louis-Jules Morel
1909-1912 Paul Simoni
1912-1915 Léon-Louis-Jean-Georges
              Destenay
1915-1916 Maurice-Joseph Le Gallen
1917-1921 Jean-Baptiste-Édouard Bourcier
              Saint-Gaffray
1921-1925 Maurice-Antoine-François
              Monguillot
1925-1930 Eugène-Jean-Louis-René Robin
1930-1937 Auguste-Eugène-Ludovic Tholance
1937-1940 Yves-Charles Châtel
1940-1941 Émile-Louis-François Grandjean
1941-1942 Pierre-Abel Delsalle

Information from Duong Sanh, Conservateur, National Library, Saigon, South Vietnam, and from Archives nationales, section outre-mer, Paris. Also, Brébion, pp. 409–10.

67 TUNIS

In 1881 French forces occupied Tunis, alleging defalcation of debts by the bey, perhaps profiting by the example of Great Britain in Egypt. A protectorate was proclaimed and, as in most protectorates, the resident-general became the effective executive head of the country. A measure of autonomy was granted in 1951 but nationalist pressure forced France to grant complete independence in 1956.

Residents-General

1882	Théodore-Justin-Dominique Roustan
1882-1886	Pierre-Paul Cambon
1886-1892	Justin Massicault
1892-1894	Maurice Rouvier
1894-1901	René-Philippe Millet
1901-1906	Eugène-Jean-Marie Pichon
1906-1918	Gabriel-Ferdinand Alapetite
1918-1921	Pierre-Étienne Flandin
1921-1929	Lucien Saint
1929-1933	François Manceron
1933-1936	Bernard-Marcel Peyrouton (1)
1936-1938	Armand Guillon
1938-1940	Eirik Labonne
1940	Bernard-Marcel Peyrouton (2)
1940-1943	Jean-Pierre Estéva
1943-1946	Charles-Emmanuel Mast
1946-1950	Jean Mons
1950-1952	Louis-Marcelin-Marie Perillier
1952-1953	Jean de Hauteclocque
1953-1954	Pierre Voizard
1954-1955	Pierre-Georges-Jacques-Marie Boyer de la Tour du Moulin
1955-1956	Roger Seydoux Fornier de Clausonne

Spuler, 1:406, and 2:591—92.

68 UBANGI-SHARI

The French expansion inland from French Congo (v. French Equatorial Africa) led to the creation of the province of Ubangi-Shari in 1894. Ubangi-Shari was one of the four colonies comprising French Equatorial Africa. From 1906 to 1920 the lieutenant governors of Ubangi-Shari also administered Chad (q.v.). In 1958 Ubangi-Shari became an autonomous member of the French Community, and two years later it became independent, renaming itself the Central African Republic.

Lieutenant Governors

1894-1899	Victor-Théophile Liotard
1899-1906	Adolphe-Louis Cureau

Ubangi-Shari and Chad
Lieutenant Governors

1906-1911	Émile Merwart
1911	Jean-Baptiste-Ernest Noirot
1911-1913	Frédéric Estèbe
1913-1916	Pierre-Pascal-Marie-Georges Adam
1916-1918	Victor-Emmanuel Merlet
1918-1919	Ernest-François-Maurice Delafosse
1919-1920	Auguste Lamblin (1)

Ubangi-Shari
Lieutenant Governors

1920-1922	Henri-Auguste-Alphonse Dirat
1922-1926	Auguste Lamblin (2)
1926-1928	Georges-David Prouteaux
1928-1929	Auguste Lamblin (3)
1930-1935	Adolphe Deitte
1935-1936	Richard-Édmond-Marie-Édouard Brunot
1936	Émile Buhot-Launay
1936-1939	Charles-Max Masson de Saint-Félix
1939-1942	Pierre de Saint-Mart
1942-1946	Henri-Camille Sautot

France

Governors
1946-1948   Jean-Victor-Louis-Joseph Chalvet
1949-1950   Pierre-Jean-Marie Delteil
1950-1951   Ignace-Jean-Aristide Colombani
1951-1954   Aimé-Marius-Louis Grimald

1954-1958   Louis-Marius-Pascal Sanmarco
1958   Paul-Camille Bordier

High Commissioner
1959-1960   Paul-Camille Bordier

Information from Le Chef du Service des Archives, Administration provisoire des Services du Ministère de la France d'Outre-Mer, Paris.

69 UPPER VOLTA

The provinces of Upper Senegal-Niger (v. French Sudan) composed of the Mossi people were detached in 1919 and formed into the colony of Upper Volta. This colony was dismembered in 1932 and its territory divided among Dahomey (q.v.), French Sudan, and Ivory Coast (q.v.). In 1947 it was re-created. In 1958 Upper Volta became an autonomous member of the French Community and in 1960 it became independent as Upper Volta, or the Voltaic Republic.

Governors
1919-1928   Frédéric-Charles-Édouard-
                 Alexandre Hesling
1928-1931   Alberic-Auguste Fournier
1931-1932   Gabriel-Omer Descemet
1932   Henri-Louis-Joseph Chessé
1932-1947   (abolished)
1947-1948   Gaston Mourgues

1948-1952   Albert-Jean Mouragues
1952-1953   Roland-Joanes-Louis Pré
1953-1956   Salvador-Jean Etcheber
1956-1958   Yvon Bourges

High Commissioner
1959-1960   Paul-Jean-Marie Masson

Information from the Ministère de la France d'Outre-Mer, Service des Archives, Paris.

70 WALLIS AND FUTUNA ISLANDS

The Wallis Islands were governed as a protectorate under French Polynesia beginning in 1842. In 1887 a protectorate was proclaimed over the Futuna Islands and the two groups were administered from New Caledonia (q.v.). In 1917 they were made a colony, and in 1961 their status changed to that of an overseas territory under the high commissioner at New Caledonia. The residents were usually French military doctors.

Residents
1887-1892   Maurice-Antoine Chauvot
1892-1896   Henri-Valentin Dodun de Kéroman
1896-1897   Henri-Dominique Lefebvre de
                 Sainte-Marie
1897-1898   Émile Proche
1898-1902   Étienne-Joseph Ponge
1902-1905   Édouard Chaffaud

1905-1909   Maxime Viala
1909-1914   Victor-Jean Brochard
1914-1916   Édouard-Victor Magnien
1916-1921   Georges Mallet
1921-1924   Gaston-Marius Bécu
1924-1928   Georges-Charles-Paul Barbier
1928-1931   Jean Marchat
1921-1933   Georges-Jean-Louis Rénaud

1933-1938	Joseph-Jean David	1955-1956	Bernard-François-Joseph Heintz
1938-1940	Eugène-Auguste Lamy	1956-1958	Maurice-Antoine Rougetet
1940-1942	Léon-Émile-Marie-Prosper-	1958-1961	Pierre Fauché
	Jacques Vrignaud	1961	Jacques-Emmanuel Herry
1942-1944	Jean-Baptiste Mattei		
1944-1946	Robert-Maxime Charbonnier		*Administrators-Superior*
1946-1947	Pierre-Robert-Jean-Marie	1961-1962	Jean Perié
	Farges	1962-1964	Jean-Marie Bertrand
1947-1949	Marcel-Alexandre-Étienne Chomet	1964-1967	André-Pierre-François Duc-
1949-1951	Michel Cresson		Dufayard
1951-1953	Jean-Flavien Folie-Desjardins	1967-1968	Fernand Lamodière
1953-1955	Charles André	1968——	Jacques-Frédéric Bach

"Liste des résidents français aux Iles Wallis et Futuna."

Bibliography: France

Akinjogbin, Isaac Adeagbo. *Dahomey and Its Neighbours, 1708–1818.* Cambridge: Cambridge University Press, 1967.

Atger, Paul. *La France en Côte d'Ivoire de 1843 à 1893: Cinquante ans d'hésitations politiques et commerciales.* Publications de la section d'histoire, no. 2. Dakar: University of Dakar, 1962.

Audet, François J[oseph]. *Canadian Historical Dates and Events, 1492–1915.* Ottawa: Public Archives of Canada, 1917.

Azéma, Georges. *Histoire de l'île Bourbon depuis 1643 jusqu'au 20 décembre 1848.* Paris: Henri Plon, 1859.

Barassin, Jean. "Un registre de Fort-Dauphin (1665–1670)." *Recueil de documentation et travaux inédits pour servir à l'histoire de la Réunion (ancien île Bourbon),* n.s. 1 (n.d.): 69–87.

Blanchard, Marcel. "Administrateurs d'Afrique Noire." *Revue française d'histoire des colonies* 40 (1953): 377–430.

——. "Administrateurs d'Indo-Chine (1880–1890)." *Revue française d'histoire des colonies* 39 (1952): 1–34.

Brébion, Jean-François-Antoine. *Dictionnaire de bio-bibliographie générale, ancienne et moderne de l'Indo-Chine Française.* Paris: Société d'éditions géographique, maritime et coloniale, 1935.

Chauleau, Liliane. *La société à la Martinique au XVIIe siècle (1645-1713).* Caen: Impr. Ozanne et cie., 1955.

Cornevin, Robert. *Histoire du Togo.* Paris: Berger-Levrault, 1960.

Couillard-Després, Azarie. "Les gouverneurs de l'Acadie sous le régime française, 1660–1710." *Mémoires et comptes-rendus de la Société royale du Canada,* 3d ser. 33 (1939): 219–88.

Crouse, Nellis Maynard. *French Pioneers in the West Indies, 1624–1664.* New York: Columbia University Press, 1940.

——. *The French Struggle for the West Indies, 1665–1713.* New York: Columbia University Press, 1943.

Cultru, Prosper, ed. *Premier voyage du Sieur de La Courbe fait à la coste d'Afrique en 1685.* Paris: Edouard Champion, 1913.

Davis, Edwin A. *Louisiana: A Narrative History.* Baton Rouge: Claitor's Book Store, 1961.

Debien, Gabriel. "Une branche des Sainte-Marthe aux îles au XVIIe siècle." *Bulletin de la Société des antiquaries de l'ouest,* 4th ser. 7 (1963/64): 435–65.

Decary, Raymond. "Bertrand Hercule Blévec, successeur de Sylvain Roux à Sainte-Marie de Madagascar (1823–1830)." *Revue française d'histoire des colonies* 38 (1951): 385–426.

————. *L'île Nosy Bé de Madagascar: Histoire d'une colonisation.* Paris: Éditions maritimes et d'outre-mer, 1960.

Delcourt, André. *La France et les établissements français au Sénégal entre 1713 et 1763.* Mémoires de L'Institut français d'Afrique noire, no. 17. Dakar: IFAN, 1952.

Dermigny, L., and Debien, G. "La révolution aux Antilles." *Revue d'histoire de l'Amérique française* 8(1954/56):55—73, 250—71.

Deschamps, Hubert. "Quinze ans du Gabon (les débuts de l'établissements français, 1839—1853)." *Revue française d'histoire d'outre-mer* 50(1963):283—345, and 52(1965):92—126.

Dictionary of Canadian Biography. 1 vol. to date. Toronto: University of Toronto Press, 1966—

Dictionnaire de biographie française. Parts 1—67, Paris: Letouzey et Ané, 1933—.

Dunglas, Édouard. "Contribution à l'histoire du Moyen-Dahomey (Royaumes d'Abomey, de Kétou et de Ouidah)." *Études dahoméennes* 19(1957):1—185, 20(1957):1—152, and 21(1958):1—118

Encyclopédie coloniale et maritime. Edited by Eugène-Léonard Guernier and G. Froment-Guieysse. 8 vols. Paris: Encyclopédie coloniale et maritime, 1944—51.

Épinay, Adrien d'. *Renseignements pour servir à l'histoire de l'Île de France jusqu'à l'année 1810, inclusivement.* Port Louis: Imprimerie Dupuy, 1890.

Fauteux, Aegidius. *Les chevaliers de Saint-Louis en Canada.* Montreal: Les Éditions des Dix, 1940.

France, Ministère de la Guerre. *Annuaire official des officiers de l'armée active,* 1819—1939; *Annuaire de l'état militaire,* 1819—47; *Annuaire militaire,* 1848—70; *Annuaire de l'armée française,* 1873—1905; *Annuaire official de l'armée française,* 1906—21; *Annuaire official de l'armée active,* 1922—39.

————. *Annuaire official des troupes coloniales,* 1894—1923.

————, Ministère de la Marine et des Colonies. *Annuaire,* 1853—86.

————, Ministère de la Marine et des Colonies. *État général de la marine et des colonies,* 1763—1852; *Annuaire,* 1853—86.

————, Ministère des Colonies. *Annuaire coloniale,* 1887—97; *Annuaire,* 1898—1942.

Froidevaux, Henri. "Les premiers successeurs de Flacourt à Madagascar (février 1655—janvier 1656)." *Revue de l'histoire des colonies françaises* 7(1919):5—34.

Gaffiot, R. *Gorée, capitale déchue.* Paris: L. Fournier, 1933.

Gardinier, David E. *Cameroon. United Nations Challenge to French Policy.* London: Institute of Race Relations, 1963.

Gifford, Prosser, and Louis, William R. *Britain and Germany in Africa: Imperial Rivalry and Colonial Rule.* New Haven: Yale University Press, 1967.

Goepp, Édouard, and Mannoury d'Ectot, Henri de. *La France: Biographique illustrée: Marins* 2 vols. Paris: Furne, Jouvet et cie., 1877.

Hall, D. G. E. *A History of South-East Asia.* 2nd ed. London: Macmillan & Co., 1964.

Harvey, Daniel Cobb. *The French Régime in Prince Edward Island.* New Haven: Yale University Press, 1926.

J. P. "Liste chronologique des gouverneurs de l'Algérie." *Revue africaine* 31(1887):427—35.

Jore, Léonce. "Les établissements français sur la côte occidentale d'Afrique de 1758 à 1809." *Revue française d'histoire d'outre-mer* 51(1964):7—477.

Lacour-Gayet, Jean-Marie-Georges-Ferdinand. *La marine militaire de la France sous le règne de Louis XV.* Paris: H. Champion, 1910.

————. *La marine militaire de la France sous le règne de Louis XVI.* Paris: H. Champion, 1905.

La Morandière, Charles de. *Histoire de la pêche française de la morue de l'Amérique septentrionale des origines à 1789.* 2 vols. Paris: G.-P. Maisonneuve et Larose, 1962—63.

Lauvrière, Émile. *Histoire de la Louisiane française (1673—1939).* Paris: G.-P. Maisonneuve, 1940.

Lémery, Henry. *La révolution française à la Martinique.* Paris: Larose, 1936.

Lemieux, Louis Joseph. *The Governors-General of Canada, 1608—1931.* London: Lake and Bell, 1931.

"Liste des résidents français aux Iles Wallis et Futuna." *Bulletin de la Société des océanistes* 19(1963):227—28.

Longrigg, Stephen Hemsley. *Syria and Lebanon under French Mandate.* London: Oxford University Press, 1958.

Mazas, Alexandre. *Histoire de l'ordre royal et militaire de Saint-Louis depuis son institution en 1693 jusqu'en 1830.* 3 vols. Paris: Firmin Didot frères, 1860—61.

Micoud, Claude-Anne-Gui. "Mémoire sur l'affaire de Sainte-Lucie." *Annales des Antilles*, no. 13 (1966), pp. 29−33.

Ministère de la Guerre. See under France.

Ministère de la Marine et des Colonies. See under France.

Ministère des Colonies. See under France.

Moreau de Saint-Méry, Médéric-Louis-Elie. *Description topographique, physique, civile, politique et historique de la partie française de l'île Saint-Domingue*. 3 vols. Paris: Société de l'histoire des colonies françaises, 1958.

O'Reilly, Patrick. *Calédoniens—Repertoire bio-bibliographique de la Nouvelle-Calédonie*. Paris: Musée de l'Homme, 1953.

——. "Chronologie de la Nouvelle-Calédonie (1774−1903)." *Bulletin de la Société des océanistes* 9 (1953):25−54.

——. "Chronologie de Wallis et Futuna." *Bulletin de la Société des océanistes* 19 (1963):12−45.

——. "Essai de chronologie des Nouvelles-Hebrides." *Bulletin de la Société des océanistes* 12 (1956):5−61.

Rambosson, J. *Les colonies françaises: Géographie, histoire, productions, administration et commerce*. Paris: Charles Delagrave et cie., 1868.

Ribault, Jean-Yves. "La population des îles Saint-Pierre et Miquelon de 1763 à 1793." *Revue française d'histoire d'outre-mer* 53 (1966):5−66.

Ritchie, Carson I. A. "Deux textes sur le Sénégal (1673−1677)." *Bulletin de l'Institut fondamental d'Afrique noire* 30, no. 1 (1968):289−353.

Robinet, Jean-Baptiste-Eugène. *Dictionnaire historique et biographique de la révolution et de l'empire, 1789−1815*. 2 vols. Paris: Librairie historique de la révolution et de l'empire, 1899.

Salibi, Kamal S. *The Modern History of Lebanon*. London: Weidenfeld and Nicholson, 1965.

Schefer, Christian. *Instructions générales données de 1763 à 1870 aux gouverneurs et ordonnateurs des établissements français en Afrique occidentale*. 2 vols. Paris: Société de l'histoire des colonies françaises, 1927.

Schnapper, Bernard. *La politique et le commerce français dans le Golfe de Guinée de 1838 à 1871*. Paris: Mouton & cie., 1961.

Séré de Rivières, Édmond. *Histoire du Niger*. Paris: Éditions Berger-Levrault, 1965.

Servant, Georges. "Les compagnies de Saint-Christophe et des îles de l'Amérique (1625−1653)." *Revue de l'histoire des colonies françaises* 1 (1913):385−482.

Six, Georges. *Dictionnaire biographique des généraux et amiraux français de la révolution et de l'empire (1792−1814)*. 2 vols. Paris: G. Saffroy, 1934.

Spuler, Berthold. *Regenten und Regierungen der Welt*. 2 vols. Würzburg: A. G. Ploetz, 1962−63.

Statesman's Year Book: Statistical and Historical Annual of the States of the World. London: Macmillan & Co., 1864−.

Taboulet, Georges. *La geste français en Indochine*. 2 vols. Paris: Adrien-Maisonneuve, 1956.

Toussaint, Auguste. *L'administration française de l'île Maurice et ses archives (1721−1810)*. Port Louis: Imprimerie Commerciale, 1965.

Viata, M. "Les îles Wallis et Horn." *Bulletin de la Société neuchâteloise de géographie* 28 (1919):209−83.

Germany

The German Empire became the third largest of all imperial systems and then completely disappeared, all within scarcely more than a generation. More than any other empire it typifies the extent to which the various imperial systems were linked to the political realities of Europe and were, in fact, the product of them. In 1884 Germany could still be represented as "collect[ing] colonists without colonies," whereas Great Britain "made colonies with colonists" and France "set up colonies without colonists."[1] But this was the last year such a statement could be made. The German Chancellor Otto von Bismarck was scarcely an ardent colonialist, for he regarded colonies as a needless drain on German resources, resources that would be better spent maintaining German paramountcy on the Continent. Nonetheless, he came to realize that the acquisition of colonies could be useful for diplomatic leverage, particularly in his efforts to alienate France from Great Britain. Consequently Germany staked out claims to miscellaneous areas in Africa that were subsequently expanded into full-scale colonies, and one school of thought has it that Germany's entry into the colonial field precipitated the "scramble for Africa." Germany now had overseas colonial possessions but Bismarck, in his belief that they should not become economic liabilities, granted the administration of all of them but Kamerun and Togo (and later Kiaochow) to a series of chartered companies. However, the day of the chartered company as a widespread initiator of colonial enterprise was over and the experiment failed. By 1899 the German government was forced to assume direct control of and responsibility for all of the German colonies. The Kolonialamt (Colonial Office) was created in 1907 to administer this responsibility. But the existence of the Kolonialamt was brief. At the outbreak of World War I in 1914 all of the German colonies except German East Africa (which was not conquered until 1918) were occupied by the troops of one or another of the Allied Powers.

Historically, wartime occupation of an enemy's colonies was more often temporary than permanent. But at the end of the war in 1918 none of Germany's colonies was returned. Instead of being absorbed directly into one of the vic-

---

1. *The Times*, August 27, 1884, quoted in William R. Louis, "Great Britain and German Expansion in Africa, 1884—1919," in Prosser Gifford and W. R. Louis (eds.), *Britain and Germany in Africa. Imperial Rivalry and Colonial Rule* (New Haven, 1967), p. 3.

torious imperial systems, however—diplomacy had progressed to a stage of greater sophistication than that—they were deposited in the lap of the Leag of Nations which in turn granted them as mandates to the various occupying powers. After 1918 Germany made sporadic demands for the return of its for colonies, but with no success.

71 German East Africa

German merchants had traded extensively in eastern Africa since the 1850's. In 1884 Carl Peters, together with some associates, formed the Gesellschaft für deutsche Kolonisation, which was transformed in 1885 into the Deutsche-Ostafrikanische Gesellschaft. Through a series of questionable "treaties," Peters had acquired extensive lands for his company, and official German protection was extended to them. In 1886 eastern Africa was unofficially divided into northern and southern spheres of influence between Germany and Great Britain. In 1890, under the terms of the Heligoland Treaty, Germany abandoned, in favor of Great Britain, its claims to Zanzibar (248), the Sultanate of Witu (in Kenya, 151), and Nyasaland (188), in return for Heligoland (142), which had been governed by the British since 1807. Like the other German chartered companies the German East African Company was unable to exploit the potential of German East Africa, and it relinquished its territorial rights to the German government in 1891 while retaining many of its economic privileges. The outbreak of World War I saw a German offensive from East Africa into neighboring British territories, the only such action from any German colony during the war. While unable to maintain this initiative, the German forces did sustain resistance throughout the war and only surrendered to British colonial forces after the armistice of November, 1918. Subsequently, German East Africa was divided by the League of Nations. By far the greater part of the territory was awarded to Great Britain as a mandate and renamed Tanganyika (227). However, the interlacustrine states of Rwanda and Burundi, bordering on the Belgian Congo, were awarded to Belgium and administered by that country through the government of the Belgian Congo (v. Ruanda-Urundi, 2).

The administrators of German East Africa were designated reichskommissars under the company's rule, governors from 1891 on.

Reichskommissars	1893-1895 Friedrich von Schele
1885-1889 Karl Peters	1895-1896 Hermann von Wissmann (2)
1889-1891 Hermann von Wissmann (1)	1896-1901 Eduard von Liebert
	1901-1906 Adolf von Götzen
Governors	1906-1912 Albrecht von Rechenberg
1891-1893 Julius von Soden	1912-1918 Heinrich Schnee

Kienitz, pp. 75—99.

72 GERMAN NEW GUINEA

The New Guinea Company was formed in 1884 and within a year German sovereignty had been proclaimed over northeastern New Guinea, the islands to the north, which were known as the Bismarck Archipelago, and the Marshall Islands. The phosphate-rich atoll of Nauru was annexed in 1888, and in 1899 Germany purchased the Mariana Islands (except Guam), the Caroline Islands, and the Palau Islands from Spain (v. Guam, 341). Initially the New Guinea Company administered the mainland territory, christened Kaiser Wilhelmsland, and the Jaluit Company (Jaluit Gesellschaft), the islands. The former relinquished its sovereignty to the German government in 1899, the latter in 1906. Immediately after the outbreak of World War I, British, Australian, New Zealand, and Japanese forces occupied all German territories in the Pacific Ocean. In the Allies' disposition of the German colonial territories in 1920 Japan received the Mariana, Caroline, Marshall, and Palau groups (v. Pacific Islands Mandate, 251), and Australia received a mandate to the Bismarck Archipelago, Nauru, and Kaiser Wilhelmsland (v. British New Guinea, 106, and Nauru, 166).

Germany

Landeshauptmanns
1886–1888   Georg van Schleinitz
1888—1889   Reinhold Krätke

Reichskommissar
1889–1892   Fritz Rose

Landeshauptmanns
1892–1895   Georg Schmiele
1895–1896   Rüdiger
1896–1897   Kurt von Hagen
1897–1898   Hugo Skopnik

Governors
1899–1902   Rudolf von Bennigsen
1902–1914   Albert Hahl

Kienitz, pp. 103—15.

73 GERMAN SAMOA

The intense commercial interest of Great Britain, the United States, and Germany in the Samoa
Islands in the 19th century led to an agreement, in 1879, by which the islands were to be unde
the joint supervision of the three countries represented by their respective consuls in Apia, th
capital of the islands. This unwieldy arrangement failed to survive the strains put on it by the
rivalries of the various Samoan factions contesting for the "kingship" of the island, itself a ne
institution imposed by the Western Powers. As a result of tortuous negotiations, concluded in
the Tripartite Treaty of 1899, Germany and the United States divided the Samoan group betweer
them (v. American Samoa, 405) with Great Britain receiving as compensation half the Solomon
Islands (108), as well as a free hand in the Tonga Islands (231) and certain other colonial ces
sions from Germany. The western part of the Samoan group, known as the Territory of Western
Samoa, was administered by Germany until 1914 when it was seized by New Zealand, which in
1920 received mandatory rights to former German Samoa (v. Western Samoa, 244).

Governors
1900–1911   Wilhelm Heinrich Solf
1911–1914   Erich Schultz-Ewerth

Kienitz, p. 103.

74 GERMAN SOUTHWEST AFRICA

In 1882 a German merchant had solicited the protection of the German government for his facto
at Angra Pequena on the coast of southwest Africa. After a period of diplomatic sparring with
Great Britain, Bismarck, in April 1884, proclaimed the area to be under German protection. It v

ermany's first official colonial venture. The political boundaries of German Southwest Africa
ere demarcated in the Heligoland Treaty of 1890 which established the Caprivi Strip extending
o the Zambezi River. In the previous year the German government had taken over direct control
f the area from the Southwest Africa Colonial Company because of the latter's financial and
dministrative difficulties. Extensive military campaigns against the Herero and Hottentot rulers
ere necessary before effective control could be established. In 1915, as a result of the out-
reak of World War I, troops from the Union of South Africa invaded and conquered German
outhwest Africa and the territory was later awarded as a mandate to the Union by the League of
ations (v. Union of South Africa, 237, in Great Britain).

andeshauptmanns
885-1890 Heinrich Göring
890-1894 Kurt von François
894-1899 Theodor Gotthilt Leutwein

Governors
899-1905 Theodor Gotthilt Leutwein
905-1907 Friedrich von Lindequist
907-1910 Bruno von Schuckmann
910-1915 Theodor Seitz

Kienitz, pp. 31—46.

75 KAMERUN

A foothold was secured by German mercantile interests on the Cameroon coast near Duala in
1884, in order to forestall British efforts to extend their own control along the coast eastward
from the Niger. Subsequent exploration into and "pacification" of the interior expanded this
foothold considerably. In 1912, 107,000 square miles of the French colony of Middle Congo (44)
was added to Kamerun as one by-product of the Agadir crisis, and the colony thereby extended
its boundaries to the Congo River. Kamerun was conquered by the British and French in 1916 and
during the remainder of the war was occupied by troops of both nations jointly. After the war it
was divided. Britain secured a slice along its western boundary which it administered through
Nigeria (180). France received the vastly larger share which it governed independently as
Cameroun (10). The League of Nations formalized this arrangement in 1922 by granting mandates.

Reichskommissar
1884-1885 Max Buchner

Governors
1885-1891 Julius von Soden
1891-1895 Eugen von Zimmerer
1895-1907 Jesko von Puttkamer
1907-1910 Theodor Seitz
1910-1912 Otto Gleim
1912-1916 Karl Ebermaier

Kienitz, pp. 61—73.

76 KIAOCHOW

In pursuit of an ice-free port in the Far East, Germany decided on the Kiaochow peninsula in China's Shantung province. In 1898 China was induced to lease the peninsula to Germany for period of ninety-nine years. Because of the nature of Germany's interest in the area Kiaochow was not governed through the regular German colonial administrative structure but rather by th Naval Ministry (Reichsmarineamt). The governor always held the high naval rank of Kapitän z See. In October 1914 Japan occupied the German territory on the Kiaochow and administered i directly, that is, not as a League of Nations mandate. In 1922 Japan returned it to China.

Governors
1898-1899	Kurt Rosendahl	1901-1911	Oskar von Truppel
1899-1901	Paul Jäschke	1911-1914	Alfred Meyer-Waldeck

Kienitz, pp. 117—20.

77 TOGO

German factories were established along the Togo coast in 1880. In 1884, in Togo as elsewhe German commercial agents began to sign "treaties of protection" with the chiefs in the area. However, company rule was never tried in Togo and the German government assumed direct re- sponsibility from the beginning. Eventually a long thin strip of territory was demarcated and i remained under German rule until 1914 when, surrounded as it was by British and French territ it was easily occupied. As small as the colony was, it was divided between France and Great Britain, each of which was granted a League of Nations mandate in 1922. Again, Britain, as wi the former Kamerun, chose to administer the territory through one of its existing colonies, in th case the Gold Coast (136). France administered its area separately, using the name Togo (65)

Kommissars
1885-1887	Ernst Falkenthal	1902-1903	Waldemar Horn
1888-1890	Eugen von Zimmerer	1903-1910	Julius Zech
1890-1895	Jesko von Pettkamer	1911-1912	Edmund Brückner
1895-1898	August Köhler	1912-1914	Adolf Friedrich, Herzog zu Mecklenburg

Governors
1898-1902   August Köhler

Kienitz, pp. 51—58.

Bibliography: Germany

Kienitz, Ernst. *Zeittafel zur deutschen Kolonialgeschichte*. Munich: Paul Wustrow, 1941.

Great Britain

The British Empire came to be considered the paradigm of successful European domination of the world—surpassing all other colonial empires in its wealth, population, and geographical distribution. Furthermore, the British seem to have possessed an unusual flexibility in governing which allowed them to profit from the mistakes of their imperial past. Hence when the empire, characterized by overt political control, dissolved in the 20th century, its end was less accompanied by prolonged violent spasms than that of any of the other major empires. Nor did it in fact entirely disappear since it was replaced by the Commonwealth, to which most of the former members of the British Empire adhered, doubtless induced by the practical advantages it offered, but not seldom prompted by a sense of sentiment—an apprehension of a common heritage. Surprisingly these sentiments were not endemic to those areas largely settled from and reflective of Great Britain, but also found expression in the many former possessions in which the British themselves were but a tiny majority amidst "alien" peoples. It is not possible nor pertinent to seek to explain here the manifold factors which accounted for the undenied success of the British imperial experience but it may be useful to outline, if only in an episodic fashion, the broad course of that experience.

There was little in the first two centuries of Great Britain's colonial activity to foreshadow its later preeminence. Like its European competitors, England's interest in acquiring overseas possessions was, at this time, with a single, albeit important, exception, economic, and its performance, if adequate, was scarcely extraordinary. In the last years of the 16th century England, as a feature of its conflict with Spain, began to ply the seas in earnest in search of profitable commercial opportunities. In 1600 the East India Company was formed to partake of the rich trade of the East. Together with the Dutch United East India Company (V.O.C.), the English destroyed the spice monopoly of Portugal, then unhappily united with Spain and recipient of the favors of its enemies. Nonetheless, at the time the English were much less successful than their Dutch rivals, who had effectively ousted them from the East Indies trade by the middle of the 17th century. Thenceforth English interest turned to India where several trading factories had been established. The trade was profitable but the French, the Danes, the Dutch, and the Portuguese had posts in India also and the prospects of extensive influence seemed remote, indeed undesireable, until the collapse of the Mughal Empire after about 1700.

During the 17th century several of the West Indian islands were occupied by English settlers, and Jamaica was seized from the Spaniards. The most impor-

tant, if not initial, motivation for this settlement was the success of the suga
plantation system in the West Indies which resulted from the introduction of
sugar technology by the Dutch from Brazil towards the middle of the century.
The European market for sugar grew rapidly and seemed to be infinitely capab.
of absorbing the production of the New World. As a result these islands flour
ished. Barbados became England's most valuable colony during the last half
the 17th century and remained so during much of the 18th.[1]

In order to provide the necessary manpower for the sugar plantations—for
the raising, harvesting, and processing of the cane was labor-intensive and tl
death rate was high—several posts were established along the west coast of
Africa designed to serve as entrepots for the trade in slaves. Through these
African posts the British also bought slaves for the Spanish colonies, and the
asiento, the license granted by the Spanish government for this purpose, was
highly valued in British commercial and political circles.

The third major area of English interest at this time was the eastern seaboa
of North America from Georgia north to the Saint Lawrence River. The colonie:
established here, except for the southernmost of them whose cotton and tobac
plantation societies identified them more closely with the West Indian coloni(
were unique insofar as they were purely settlement colonies. That is, they w(
faithful replicas of metropolitan British society. In contrast the Spanish and
Portuguese colonies in the New World were, in effect, plural societies, for bo'
the culture of the indigenous peoples and the peoples themselves were subsumed into the new societies. The indigenous Indian population of North Amei
ica, sparse in numbers and with little of cultural value to offer the English
colonists other than foodstuffs, was largely excluded from the settlements.
The importance of these colonies was less contemporary than retrospective. I
truth the English government "had the highest opinion of those colonies which
most closely resembled Brazil [that is, the sugar colonies], and the lowest of
those which were most like herself."[2] They did offer useful markets for Britis!
domestic manufactures, but the cotton and tobacco produced in the southern
colonies was also available from the West Indies. Furthermore, many of these
colonies, settled by religious and civil dissidents from Great Britain, all too
often proved impatient of imperial restrictions, and the cost of their defense
must have at times seemed unnecessarily prohibitive to the British governmen1
The value of these colonies, then, lay more in their "Britishness" and in their
strategic location flanking both the French and Spanish possessions in North
America, than in their intrinsic economic worth.

Great Britain made every effort to create an integrated mercantilist system
within which each colony or group of colonies could contribute. The Indian
posts provided pepper and tea and cotton and silk, the African posts provided

---

1. The value of Barbadian sugar exported to England in 1680, for example,
was "almost certainly" greater than the value of all commodities exported fron
all of England's North American colonies in the same year. Richard S. Dunn,
"The Barbados Census of 1680: Profile of the Richest Colony in English America," *William and Mary Quarterly*, 3d ser. 26 (1969):4.

2. David K. Fieldhouse, *The Colonial Empire* (London: Weidenfeld and
Nicolson, 1966), p. 58.

the slave labor necessary for the functioning of the sugar plantations in the West Indies, which in turn provided sugar; and the North American colonies provided cotton and tobacco and a market for British finished goods. Tight restrictions were enacted to ensure that all trade would be transacted within the confines of this system. In this sense it closely parallelled the economic practices of the other colonial systems during this period.

Great Britain had used the numerous major European wars, as well as lesser international tensions of the 17th and 18th centuries, to seize colonial possessions of her enemy of the moment. Jamaica and New York were seized from Spain and the Netherlands respectively in 1656 and 1664. During the War of the Spanish Succession (1702—13) Gibraltar and Minorca were taken from Spain, and Acadia (or Nova Scotia) and part of Newfoundland from France. Great Britain's overseas acquisitions during the Seven Years' War (1756—63) were to have important ramifications for the future development of the British Empire. France's possessions in North America, nibbled at by Britain during the previous century, were, with the exception of a small group of offshore islands, occupied by British forces, and were ceded by France under terms of the Treaty of Paris in 1763. The removal of the French presence from North America had serious implications for the older British colonies to the south, as will be noted.

In India, France and to a lesser degree Great Britain found themselves drawn into the political vacuum created by the Mughal collapse. At first the French, judiciously exploiting the rivalries of the Indian rulers, seemed more likely to become the dominant European influence. However, the British, better supported by their home government and emulating many of the French practices, ultimately triumphed and established their own preponderant influence while eliminating the French as potential rivals. Nonetheless the British did not yet feel sufficiently strong to act independently and therefore initially legitimized their presence by extorting a position within the traditional indigenous framework from the moribund but still conveniently prestigious Mughal Empire.

Thus in 1763 the British possessions stood at the pinnacle of two centuries of accumulation—unchallenged in most of North America and in India and become economically potent in the Spanish and Portuguese empires in America. Within the next half century Great Britain was to lose, by the unprecedented means of an internal rebellion, part of her empire, while gaining a greater one in other regions of the world.

The North American colonists had long been restive under the mercantilist restrictions placed upon them. They deplored the monopsynistic practices of the metropolitan government, and resented what they regarded as unwarranted and unjust efforts to impose tighter royal control throughout the colonies. Heretofore these recalcitrant tendencies had been tempered by the presence of the French in Canada and the colonists' consequent need of imperial protection. Thus, the British success in seizing Canada militated against the continuance of its control to the south, for once the danger from France was removed the colonists were obviously less reliant on imperial defense. But the effort in Canada had been expensive and, not unreasonably, the British government expected those who benefited most from it to contribute proportionately towards the extinguishment of the debt. A new series of taxes was levied, each one in its turn resented. Equally resented was the British effort to curb the westward expansion of the colonies in order to facilitate the defense of—and concomitantly the control of—these colonies. Further exacerbating this situation wa the congruence of a ruler and of a set of ministries determined to maintain th prerogatives of the metropolis and at the same time lacking in experiences of similar nature to guide them. The result was a progressive abandonment of mutually acceptable compromises. Rebellion ensued and the British governme perhaps not completely certain of the rectitude of its own position and in any event more interested in preserving its other possessions from its rivals on t Continent, recognized, after several years of desultory warfare, the independence of the American colonies, doubtless relieved to have salvaged Canada a its West Indian possessions from the rubble.

Great Britain, in 1783, nevertheless found itself in the happy position of being able to replace twelve lost sheep with a single but splendid elephant. The East India Company had found itself becoming involved, often unwillingly in disputes throughout the subcontinent. In 1767 the secretary of the compan Robert James, observed that the company's military operations "grew insensib from one trouble to another—we could form no judgment of their progress."[3] This progressive involvement and expansion on the local level was to recur time and again in the next 125 years and many government officials were to echo James's lament. Certainly his observation was borne out by subsequent developments in India where, by 1818, British influence had been replaced by overt political control over nearly all of the subcontinent. Until 1858 this control was exercised by the East India Company—the greatest of all the colonia chartered companies—although its activities were increasingly scrutinized b the British government.

The wars of the French Revolution between 1793 and 1815 saw Great Britai acquire its largest number of overseas colonies at the expense of wartime enemies. Cape Colony and Ceylon were taken from the Netherlands, and Mauritius from France, all to protect the increasingly vital route to India. Strateg and economic considerations demanded that the West Indies be made complete safe for British interests, so part of Guiana was seized from the Dutch, Trinid from Spain, and Tobago from France. Naval strategists saw Heligoland and Malta as useful bases for ensuring British naval supremacy in the North and Mediterranean Seas and they, too, became British possessions as a result of these wars.

It has been fashionable to distinguish between a "first" British Empire, end ing in 1783, and a "second" British Empire, arising after that date. Doubtless it is true that "the British Empire did not merely evolve: it underwent reconstruction" during this period,[4] and that the identity of many of the British colonies changed, but certain analogies exist in the patterns of expansion and settlement during these two periods. Considerations of strategy, particularly naval strategy, still dominated in the selection of acquisitions during the late period. Australia, New Zealand, Cape Colony, and Canada replaced the American colonies as areas of white settlement. And of course many colonies

---

3. Quoted in Price J. Marshall, *Problems of Empire: Britain and India, 1757–1813* (London: George Allen & Unwin, 1968), p. 17.

4. Fieldhouse, *Colonial Empires*, p. 55.

existed throughout both periods. Again, in each of the periods an economic theory was devised to allow each colony to become a contributing member to the empire as a whole. The American Revolution had given the lie to those theorists who advocated mercantilism. As a result, the policy of free trade, mooted as early as 1776 by Adam Smith, emerged triumphant, and by 1830 the trade of all of the British colonies had been opened to all nations who would extend reciprocal advantages. It was expected that their naval supremacy and "Anglo-Saxon enterprise" would enable the British to dominate the trade throughout the world whereas heretofore they could only be certain of a reasonable monopoly within their own imperial system. The truly new element in the "second" British Empire was India—a possession so rich, so populous, so enormous, and so prestigious that it continued to the end of its colonial status to be treated as a category of its own.

In 1807 Great Britain, emulating the example of Denmark, abolished the slave trade between Africa and its West Indian possessions. Satisfied of the righteousness of their new position, the British sought to impose this abolition on the other nations engaging in the trade. These efforts were initially unsuccessful and the numbers of slaves transported to the New World scarcely diminished, if at all. Gradually, however, through cajolery or force, the West African trade was abolished. But it was only after about 1865 that shipments to Cuba and Brazil ceased entirely. The motivations of the British government in this matter were both numerous and ambiguous. A surge of humanitarian sentiment proved influential in the implementation of the policy of abolition but this would never have sufficed of itself. More potent was the death of mercantilism and the consequent decline of the sugar industry—the major market for the several millions of slaves that had been shipped from Africa. Slavery itself was only abolished in the British West Indian islands in 1833.

The increasing complexity of the empire required both stronger efforts at metropolitan coordination and a new flexibility in the approach to government at local, colonial levels. Quite obviously India could not be governed in the same fashion as Canada, nor could Jamaica be compared to Australia, or Gibraltar to the Gold Coast.

The most important problems were those presented by the increasingly numerous areas of white settlement. By 1850 these included New Zealand, Cape Colony, and the Australian and Canadian colonies, as well as several less important areas. Some of these colonies, as well as those in the West Indies, had been granted representative institutions before 1800. However, a strong sentiment for responsible, that is, cabinet, government was developing. This sentiment manifested itself, for example, in a rebellion in Canada in 1837. Not serious of itself, this revolt impelled the British government to reconsider its policies toward the settlement colonies. The Earl of Durham was despatched to investigate the causes for the uprising and his report urged that certain colonies be granted responsible government in matters not of broadly imperial concern. Between 1848 and 1893 all of the white settlement colonies were granted responsible government. It was assumed in London that certain criteria would be met before a colony could be considered qualified to receive the privileges of responsible government. Most importantly, if a colony included a large non-white majority likely to be dominated or exploited by the white settlers it would not be given responsible government without offering safeguards considered adequate by the home government. For this reason Cape Colony and Natal only achieved responsible government at a late date (1872 and 1893 respectively), preferring representative government and imperial defense without imperial control of native policy to responsible government com bined with the onus of paying for their own native wars should they arise despite the safeguards. And the West Indies colonies, with miniscule white populations, attained responsible government only after 1950.

The many British possessions which had little or no white settlement were directly ruled from London through a governor and collectively styled crown colonies. These possessed no representative institutions and were ruled by the governor autocratically. India, as we have seen, was governed by the Ea India Company until 1858, and thereafter directly by the British government through the agency of the India Office. Effective control was always exercise however, from Calcutta (later from Delhi) by the viceroy himself, who exercis the prerogative indicated by his title, adopted at the time of the transfer of power. Finally, still other areas, which it was not thought convenient to rule directly, were termed protectorates. Here, power nominally rested with the local ruler. In fact, however, real power lay with the British "resident" or "a visor."

"We seem, as it were," commented Sir John Seeley in 1883, "to have conquered and peopled half the world in a fit of absence of mind."[5] Uttered, sig nificantly, before the more systematic dissection of Africa after 1885, the statement, stripped of its hyperbole, contained elements of truth. In the century before Seeley's comment there was probably never a period during which any British government frankly pursued an imperialistic policy. There were e and flows of interest in colonization and "imperialism," of course, but the ex pansion of British interests, whether formally or informally, continued unabate no less during periods of "anti-imperialist" ministries than during those of g ernments characterized as "imperialist."[6] Yet little of this expansion occurre at the instance or prompting of the British government itself. Seizure of an enemy's colonies ceased after 1815 when the balancing of power and the avo ance of tensions were the rule in Europe. New Zealand, and parts of Australi and the Cape Colony, were settled under the aegis of private chartered companies, resurrected from their long slumber. The activities of these companie were tolerated and oftentimes encouraged by the government, but the initiativ remained private.

How, then, can we account for the almost disguised but nevertheless stea growth of the British Empire during the 19th century? Obviously no single an swer will suffice, but there were several factors which were more than simply idiosyncratic. Much of the expansion was initiated at the local level, and th

5. John R. Seeley, *The Expansion of England* (London: Macmillan & Co., 1889), p. 8.

6. See, for instance, John Gallagher and Ronald Robinson, "The Imperialis of Free Trade," *Economic History Review*. 2d ser. 6 (1953):3–4, and W. Dav McIntyre, *The Imperial Frontier in the Tropics* (London: Macmillan & Co., 1967).

metropolitan government was often presented with a fait accompli which it found less convenient to reject than to accept, albeit often grudgingly. The steady expansion of Cape Colony and India, always in search of "stable" frontiers, are particular cases in point, but examples abound.

Humanitarian motives, often construed in the very broadest possible sense, often impelled the British government to annex areas which could not hope to fulfil the ubiqitous requirement of paying their own way. The concept of the "white man's burden," so evident in British thought about India, found further utility in parts of Africa and in the island groups of the Pacific. Often, of course, it was used as a convenient and acceptable justification to mask less lofty motives.

Commercial considerations, as always, played an important part in the imperial argumentation of the 19th century. Hong Kong was annexed because it offered attractive commercial as well as strategic advantages. The West African posts, although bereft of their utility for the slave trade, were retained in the hopes that they would now serve as equally useful bases for exploiting the products and presumed markets in the interior. Nonetheless, it would be unreasonable to assign to these considerations the magnitude that is the wont of the school of "economic imperialists."

Another and perhaps the most important consideration for the expansion of the British Empire during the 19th century was a desire, almost an obsession, to maintain the balance of power that was the cardinal policy of European diplomacy during this period. This seems to have been especially true for Africa. The continent was opened for expansion at a time when the number of actual and potential imperial powers was greater than ever and even the most sanguine observers could not descry any great value in much of the area suddenly become available. For Great Britain control of the Nile valley and hence of Egypt was axiomatic. Consequently England's participation in the "scramble" was less designed to gain sheer territorial bulk, as in the case of France, than to secure those areas the British governments regarded as vital to their own strategic interests. The westward expansion of India was nearly always justified in terms of securing a "natural boundary" (a conveniently ambiguous concept), and of keeping Russia, expanding eastwards, at a safe distance from Britain's most prized colonial possession. The result was two ill-advised and disastrous wars with Afghanistan as well as a much larger India than might otherwise have been the case. Likewise Burma was annexed at least partly to forestall feared French penetration from Indochina. This type of "defensive imperialism" often intruded unreasonably; it was used as justification, for example, for the extension of British control to, and for the colonization of, Western Australia, for which an unwelcome and probably nonexistent French interest was raised as a bête noire.

It is significant that many British possessions were retained long after they had lost their original utility. The habit of expansion seems to have become reflexive on occasion. The critics of imperial expansion, derisively labelled "little Englanders," habitually pointed to Gibraltar as an example of a possession which was retained long after it had lost both its strategic value and its defensibility, and whose continued possesion merely provided a point of excerbation with an otherwise friendly nation.[7] The controversy over the cession, in 1860, of the Bay Islands, of no real value to Great Britain, underscored the "prestige" that seemed to many to be so pleasant a concomitant of empire.

By the end of the 19th century the British Empire had nearly approached the limit of its expansion. All that remained was the filling out of some African colonies and the areas mandated to Britain after World War I. But already the essential nature of the empire had begun to be transformed. The advent of responsible government in all of the most important colonies (except, of course, India) and the confederation of the Canadian colonies in 1867 heralded a substantial reorientation of the concept of empire. The American Revolution had clearly demonstrated the dangers of metropolitan obduracy. The Durham *Report* and its implementation equally showed that this lesson had not been lost on the British governments of the 19th century. But surprisingly, this reformulation of imperial relationships occurred first with regard to the white settlement colonies; only much later was it applied to the vast areas of the British Empire which were inhabited by non-whites.

The beginnings of the Commonwealth (the name itself was officially applied only in 1926) may be traced to the confederation of the Canadian provinces (except Newfoundland) in 1867. Canada became the first of a series of dominions—Australia in 1901, New Zealand in 1907, the Union of South Africa in 191 Newfoundland in 1918, the Irish Free State in 1922.[8] The British government was represented in these dominions by governors-general whose duties were now much more restricted than those of governors of crown colonies. They were therefore supplemented by high commissioners who were responsible for diplomatic functions—were, in effect, ambassadors. In theory, the dominions were still bound by parliamentary statutes, and the conduct of foreign affairs was to be exercised on their behalf by the British government. In practice these limitations were seldom exercised. The British Parliament consulted the dominions as a matter of practice before acting on legislation affecting them. Routine foreign matters were habitually conducted by the dominion governments and the assistance of the dominions to the British war effort of 1914–18 result in further prerogatives, such as the negotiation of treaties without necessary reference to the position of the British government, being formally extended. A the Imperial Conference of 1926 it was decided that the dominions were "autonomous communities ..., equal in status ... and freely associated" as members of the Commonwealth.[9] The Statute of Westminster, enacted five years later, formally exempted the dominions from British parliamentary supremacy of any kind, although any dominion could choose to accept an act of Parliament.

---

7. See, for example, Goldwin Smith, *The Empire* (London: John Henry and James Parker, 1863), pp. 207–9, 216.

8. The term "dominion" was not actually new to British imperial history. T short-lived Dominion of New England had included the colonies of Connecticu Massachusetts, New Jersey, New Plymouth, New York, and Rhode Island withir it during all or part of the period from 1686 to 1689.

9. Arthur Berriedale Keith, *Speeches and Documents on the British Dominions, 1918–1931: From Self-Government to Sovereignty* (London: Oxford University Press, 1932), p. 161.

This evolution from empire to Commonwealth affected only the dominions before 1947. Indeed, it was only in 1919 that representative government was attempted in India and then only on a very limited basis. The official majorities in the Council of State and Legislative Assembly were abolished and the franchise was extended to a small percentage of the Indian people. In the provinces the principle of "dyarchy" was established. The provincial ministries were to have Indian as well as British ministers, and jurisdiction in certain unimportant areas was "transferred" to the Indian members. In 1935 the dyarchical principle was extended to the Indian government but nothing more was done before the outbreak of World War II. Only in 1947 did India become an independent dominion after an indefensibly long hiatus.

Two years later India expressed its intention to become a republic, that is, to replace the British monarch as head of state by a locally chosen president. Heretofore the concept of a republic within the Commonwealth had seemed incongruous. For this reason the Irish Free State, a republic in all but name after 1937, only became one formally after its withdrawal from the Commonwealth. Faced with the prospect of losing India, Commonwealth theoreticians concluded that in fact there was nothing really incongruous about a republic within the Commonwealth, and India became a republic the following year, while remaining a Commonwealth member.

The rest of the British Empire in 1947 consisted of a mélange of crown colonies of one sort or another, "protectorates" (another ambiguous term), and mandates. The Gold Coast was the first of these to become independent—as Ghana in 1957, and in the succeeding dozen years most of the other independencies capable of a viable independence have become independent. Most have chosen to become republics, either at or soon after the attainment of independence, and nearly all have chosen to remain in the Commonwealth. The Commonwealth has ceased to be a kind of Anglo-Saxon federation—indeed, certain of the more "Anglo-Saxon" of the former British colonies have found themselves, or have considered themselves to be no longer welcome in the Commonwealth and have chosen to withdraw from it—and now represents an expression of a community of interests based on a common institutional heritage.

In closing it may be useful to present graphically the Commonwealth of Nations as it is presently (August, 1969) composed.

Independent countries recognizing the British monarch as sovereign:

United Kingdom (1800)	Trinidad and Tobago (1962)
Canada (1867)	Malta (1962)
Australia (1901)	The Gambia (1965)
New Zealand (1910)	Guyana (1966)
Ceylon (1948)	Barbados (1966)
Sierra Leone (1961)[10]	Mauritius (1968)
Jamaica (1962)	

Independent republics within the Commonwealth:

India (1950)	Ghana (1960)
Pakistan (1956)	Cyprus (1960)

---

10. Sierra Leone is expected to become a republic during 1969.

Tanzania (1962)   Zambia (1964)
Nigeria (1963)   Singapore (1965)
Uganda (1963)   Malawi (1966)
Kenya (1964)   Botswana (1966)

Independent monarchies within the Commonwealth:
Malaysia (1957 as Malaya;   Lesotho (1966)
      1963 as Malaysia)   Swaziland (1968)

States in association with Great Britain (i.e., the Associated States of the West Indies):[11]
Antigua (1967)   Saint Kitts-Nevis (1967)
Dominica (1967)   Saint Lucia (1967)
Grenada (1967)

"Protectorates," i.e., states for whose foreign relations Great Britain is responsible under treaty provisions:
Persian Gulf sheikhdoms   Brunei (1888)
      and sultanates (1853)   Tonga (1900)

Dependent territories of varying types:
Bahama Islands
Bermuda
British Honduras
British Indian Ocean Territory
British Virgin Islands
Cayman Islands
Falkland Islands and dependencies
Fiji
Gibraltar
Hong Kong
Montserrat
Pitcairn Island
Saint Vincent[11]
Saint Helena and dependencies
Seychelles Islands
Turks and Caicos Islands
Western Pacific High Commission
    British Solomon Islands Protectorate
    Gilbert and Ellice Islands
    New Hebrides Condominium (with France)
Australian External Territories
    Norfolk Island
    Papua-New Guinea
    miscellaneous island groups
New Zealand Territories
    Niue
    Cook Islands[12]

---

11. Saint Vincent is scheduled to join the Associated States of the West Indies in October, 1969.
12. The Cook Islands are nominally independent but maintain themselves in "association" with New Zealand.

78 ACADIA

For the English governors of Acadia from 1654 to 1670, see the French colony, Acadia, 6.

79 ADEN

The British established themselves at the strategic port of Aden, near the southwestern corner of the Arabian peninsula, in 1839 when they seized the town from the sultan of Lahej. The settlement was subject to the presidency of Bombay under the Government of India until 1947. It included, as dependencies, the islands of Karaman and Perim in the Red Sea, and Socotra and Kuria Muria in the Indian Ocean. In addition to the colony itself the Aden government exercised jurisdiction, very vague until the 1930's, over the "states" of the Eastern and Western Protectorates. In 1959 these states began to unite into the South Arabian Federation. In 1963 Aden itself joined the federation and ceased to exist as a separate colony.

Political Agents
1840-1854   Stafford Bettesworth Haines
1854-1856   James Outram
1856-1859   William Marcus Coghlan

Political Residents
1859-1863   William Marcus Coghlan
1863-1869   William Lockyer Merewether
1869-1871   Edward Lechmere Russell
1871-1872   Charles William Tremenheere
1872-1877   John William Schneider
1877-1882   Francis Adam Ellis Loch
1882-1885   James Blair
1885-1890   Adam George Forbes Hogg
1890-1895   John Jopp
1895-1899   Charles Alexander Cuningham
1899-1901   O'Moore Creagh
1901-1904   Pelham James Maitland
1904-1906   Henry Macan Mason

1906-1910   Ernest De Brath
1910-1915   James Alexander Bell
1915-1916   Charles Henry Uvedale Price
1916-1920   James Marshall Stewart
1920-1925   Thomas Edwin Scott
1925-1928   John Henry Keith Stewart
1928-1931   George Stewart Symes
1931-1932   Bernard Rawdon Reilly

Chief Commissioner and Resident
1932-1937   Bernard Rawdon Reilly

Governors
1937-1940   Bernard Rawdon Reilly
1940-1944   John Hathorn Hall
1944-1951   Reginald Stuart Champion
1951-1956   Tom Hickinbotham
1956-1960   William Henry Tucker Luce
1960-1963   Charles Hepburn Johnston

Information from M. I. Moir, India Office Records, London.

80 AJMER-MERWARA

Ajmer and Merwara were ceded to the British by the Sindhia ruler of Gwalior in 1818, and between 1832 and 1871 were part of the North-West Frontier Provinces (q.v.). Until 1871 the area was governed by superintendents. In 1871 the agent to the viceroy for Rajputana became, ex officio, chief commissioner of Ajmer-Merwara. In 1947 Ajmer-Merwara acceded to the Indian Union (v. India).

Great Britain

Chief Commissioners
1871-1873 Richard Harte Keatinge
1873-1878 Lewis Pelly
1878-1887 Edward Ridley Colborne Bradford
1887-1890 Charles Kenneth Mackenzie Walter
1890-1895 George Herbert Trevor
1895-1898 Robert Joseph Crosthwaite
1898-1905 Arthur Henry Temple Martindale

1905-1918 Elliott Graham Colvin
1918-1919 John Manners Smith
1919-1925 Robert Erskine Holland
1925-1927 Stewart Blakeley Agnew Patterson
1927-1932 Leonard William Reynolds
1932-1937 George Drummond Ogilvie
1937-1944 Arthur Cunningham Lothian
1944-1947 Hiranand Rupchand Shivdasani

India Office List and Burma Office List, 1940, p. 126.

81 ANDAMAN AND NICOBAR ISLANDS

The Andaman Islands, located in the Bay of Bengal, had been used as a penal colony by the British in India from 1789 to 1796 when the colony was abandoned. Soon after 1850 the penal colony was reestablished, and a superintendent was appointed in 1858. From 1872 the administering officer was known as chief commissioner, although this title was not formally recognized until 1919. In 1869 the adjacent Nicobar Islands were obtained from Denmark, which had occupied them since the middle of the 18th century (v. Tranquebar, 51). From 1942 to 1945 the Andaman and Nicobar Islands were occupied by the Japanese, and in 1947 the islands acceded to the Indian Union (v. India).

Superintendents
1858-1859 James Pattison Walker
1859-1862 James Colpoys Haughton
1862-1864 Robert Christopher Tytler
1864-1868 Barnet Ford
1868-1871 Henry Stuart Man
1871-1872 Donald Martin Stewart

Chief Commissioners
1872-1875 Donald Martin Stewart
1875-1879 Charles Arthur Barwell
1879-1892 Thomas Cadell
1892-1894 Norman Macleod Thomas Horsford

1894-1904 Richard Carnac Temple
1904-1906 William Rudolph Henry Merk
1906-1913 Herbert Arrott Browning
1913-1920 Montague William Douglas
1920-1923 Henry Cecil Beadon
1923-1931 Michael Lloyd Ferrar
1931-1935 John William Smyth
1935-1938 William Alexander Cosgrave
1938-1942 Charles Francis Waterfall (1)
1942-1945 (under Japan)
1945-1946 Charles Francis Waterfall (2)
1946-1947 Noel Kennedy Paterson

India Office List and Burma Office List, 1940, pp. 126—27; Portman, passim.

82 ANGLO-EGYPTIAN SUDAN

The vast area of the Nilotic Sudan was occupied by Egyptian forces in a series of campaigns which ended in 1821, and it was administered by Egypt until 1881 when the Mahdist rebellion erupted and drove the Egyptians and their British supporters from the entire area. In 1898 British and Egyptian forces reoccupied the Sudan and established an administration over the area. This administration was nominally condominial, but in practice Egyptian claims to the

84

area were disregarded and all high-level officials were British. In 1951 the Egyptian government attempted to reassert its historic claims to the Anglo-Egyptian Sudan but without success. In 1956 the Anglo-Egyptian Sudan became independent as the Republic of Sudan.

Governors-General			
1899	Horatio Herbert Kitchener, Viscount Kitchener	1926-1934	John Loader Maffey
		1934-1940	George Stewart Symes
1899-1916	Francis Reginald Wingate	1940-1947	Hubert Jervoise Huddleston
1916-1924	Lee Oliver Fitzmaurice Stack	1947-1954	Robert George Howe
1924-1926	Geoffrey Francis Archer	1954-1955	Alexander Knox Helm

Statesman's Year Book, 1899-1956.

83 ANTIGUA

Antigua was discovered by Columbus in 1493. It was settled by the British from Saint Kitts (q.v.) in 1632, and except for a brief period of French occupation in 1666-67 has remained a British possession ever since. In 1671 Antigua became the seat of the newly created Leeward Islands government (q.v.) but was locally administered by a deputy governor. This office lapsed after 1747. After 1871 Antigua was administered by the colonial secretary of the Leeward Islands. In 1936 the office of Administrator of Antigua was created. From 1958 to 1962 Antigua was a member of the West Indies Federation (q.v.). It ceased to be a member of the Leeward Islands at that government's dissolution in 1960. Since 1967 Antigua has been a member of the Associated States of the West Indies.

Governors
1635-1639	Edward Warner
1639-1640	Rowland Thompson
1640-1652	Henry Ashton
1652-1660	Christopher Keynell
1661-1664	John Bunckley
1664-1666	Robert Carden
1666	Daniel Fish
1666-1667	(under France)
1667-1670	Henry Willoughby
1670-1671	Samuel Winthrop

Deputy or Lieutenant Governors
1671-1675	Philip Warner
1675-1678	Rowland Williams (1)
1678-1680	James Vaughan
1680-1682	Valentine Russell
1682-1683	Paul Lee
1683-1688	Edward Powell
1689-1692	Rowland Williams (2)

1692-1698	(none)
1698-1715	John Yeamans
1715-1741	Edward Byam
1742-1747	George Lucas

Administrators
1936	Hubert Eugene Bader
1936-1941	James Dundas Harford
1941-1944	Herbert Boon
1944-1946	F. S. Harcourt
1946-1947	Leslie Stuart Greening
1947-1954	Richard St. John Omerad Wayne
1954-1958	Alec Lovelace
1958-1964	Ian Graham Turbott
1964-1966	David James Gardiner Rose
1966-1967	Wilfred Ebenezer Jacobs

Governors
1967—	Wilfred Ebenezer Jacobs

Harper, pp. 1-3, 18-24; Higham, passim; Williamson, passim.

84 ASHANTI

With the conquest of the Ashanti kingdom in 1896 a resident was appointed by the governor of the Gold Coast (q.v.) to administer the territory of the conquered kingdom. In 1902 the resident was replaced by a chief commissioner, a position similar to that later established in the Gold Coast Colony and Gold Coast, Northern Territories (qq.v.). With the granting of internal autonomy to the Gold Coast in 1951 the administrators of Ashanti were designated regional officers. In 1957, upon the independence of the Gold Coast of which Ashanti became a part, the office was abolished.

Resident
1896-1902   Donald William Stewart

Chief Commissioners
1902-1904   Donald William Stewart
1905-1920   Francis Charles Fuller
1920-1923   Charles Henry Harper
1923-1931   John Maxwell
1931-1933   Harry Scott Newlands
1933-1936   Francis Walter Fitton Jackson

1936-1941   Hubert Craddock Stevenson
1941-1946   Edward Gerald Hawkesworth
1946-1951   Charles Owen Butler
1951-1952   William Hugh Beaton

Regional Officers
1952-1954   William Hugh Beaton
1954-1955   Arthur John Loveridge
1955-1957   Arthur Colin Russell

Statesman's Year Book, 1896—1957.

85 ASSAM

The region of Assam, that is, the area representing the former Ahom kingdom of Assam, was under Bengal (q.v.), until 1874 when a commissioner was appointed. From 1905 to 1912 Assam was part of the short-lived government of East Bengal and Assam, but after 1912 it again became a separate government. In 1921 it was elevated to a governor's province. In 1947 Assam became a part of the Union of India (v. India). Three years later the state of Assam was created within the Union of India, based largely on the former province.

Commissioners
1874-1878   Richard Harte Keatinge
1878-1881   Steuart Colvin Bayley
1881-1885   Charles Bletterman Elliott
1885-1887   William Erskine Ward (1)
1887-1889   Dennis Fitzpatrick
1889-1891   James Wallace Quinton
1891-1896   William Erskine Ward (2)
1896-1902   Henry John Stedman Cotton
1902-1905   Joseph Bampfylde Fuller

East Bengal and Assam
Lieutenant Governors
1905-1906   Joseph Bampfylde Fuller
1906-1911   Lancelot Hare
1911-1912   Charles Stuart Bayley

Assam
Chief Commissioners
1912-1918   Archdale Earle
1918-1921   Nicholas Dodd Beatson Bell

Governors
1921   Nicholas Dodd Beatson Bell
1921-1922   William Sinclair Marris
1922-1927   John Henry Kerr
1927-1932   Egbert Laurie Lucas Hammond
1932-1937   Michael Keane
1937-1942   Robert Niel Reid
1942-1947   Andrew Gourlay Clow

India Office List and Burma Office List, 1940, pp. 120—21.

86 ASSINIBOIA

The area of Assiniboia in western Canada was granted to the Scot Lord Selkirk by the Hudson's Bay Company (q.v.) to be settled by Irish and Scotch tenants. Most of the settlement was along the Red River, and Assiniboia was commonly referred to as the Red River Settlement. Opposition from the North West Company, a rival of the Hudson's Bay Company, resulted in the settlements' twice being scattered, but each time resettlement occurred. Until 1836 Assiniboia was governed by Lord Selkirk and his heirs and thereafter, until 1870, directly by the Hudson's Bay Company. In 1870 Assiniboia was absorbed into the newly created province of Manitoba.

Governors

1811-1818	Miles Macdonell	1833-1839	Alexander Christie (1)
1818-1822	Alexander McDonell	1839-1844	Duncan Finlayson
1822-1823	Andrew Bulger	1844-1848	Alexander Christie (2)
1823-1825	Robert Parker Pelly	1848-1855	William Bletterman Caldwell
1825-1833	Donald Mackenzie	1855-1858	Francis Godschall Johnson
		1858-1870	William Mactavish

Audet, pp. 67–68; *Encyclopedia Canadiana*, passim.

87 AUSTRALIA

Until 1901 the Australian continent and its neighboring islands were occupied by the separate British colonies of New South Wales, Northern Australia, Queensland, South Australia, Tasmania, Victoria, and Western Australia (qq.v.). As each colony filled out its allotted territory, thereby becoming limitrophe with its neighbors, and after the imperial forces left in 1870, and fortified by the example of Canada (q.v.), thoughts of federation became persistent. A political effort, the movement culminated in the establishment of the Commonwealth of Australia in 1901. Australia is a federal state, with each of the former colonies now individual states within it. It has remained a member of the British Commonwealth and the British monarch is represented by an appointed governor-general.

Governors-General

1901-1903	John Adrian Louis Hope, Earl of Hopetoun	1931-1936	Isaac Alfred Isaacs
1903-1904	Hallam Tennyson, Baron Tennyson	1936-1944	Alexander Gore Arkwright Hore-Ruthven, Baron Gowrie
1904-1908	Henry Stafford Northcote, Baron Northcote	1945-1947	Henry William Frederick Albert, Duke of Gloucester
1908-1911	William Humble Ward, Earl of Dudley	1947-1953	William John McKell
1911-1914	Thomas Denman, Baron Denman	1953-1959	William Joseph Slim
1914-1920	Ronald Craufurd Munro-Ferguson, Viscount Novar	1959-1961	William Shepherd Morrison, Viscount Dunrossil
1920-1925	Henry William Forster, Baron Forster	1961-1965	William Philip Sidney, Viscount de l'Isle
1925-1930	John Lawrence Baird, Baron Stonehaven	1965-1969	Richard Gardiner Casey, Baron Casey
		1969——	Paul Meernaa Caedwalla Hasluck

Australian Encyclopaedia, under individual names.

88 BAHAMA ISLANDS

The Bahamas are a group of about 700 small islands lying off the southwestern coast of the United States and north of Cuba. Watlings Island in the Bahamas was the site of Columbus's first landfall in 1492. The islands were sporadically occupied by Spaniards until 1629 when they were occupied by the English. Some settlement was made after 1649 by the English Company of Eleutherian Adventurers, but civil government was actually inaugurated only after the grant of the islands to six of the lords proprietors of South Carolina (q.v.) in 1670. The islands became a haven for piracy during this period, and this occasioned the assumption of direct crown control in 1717. During the American Revolution the islands were occupied by both the Americans and the Spaniards. From 1799 to 1848 the Turks and Caicos Islands (q.v.) were subject to the governor of the Bahamas. The Bahamas remain a crown colony of Great Britain.

Governors

1671–1676	John Wentworth
1676–1677	Charles Chillingsworth
1677–1682	Robert Clarke
1682–1684	Richard Lilburne
1684–1687	(abandoned)
1687–1690	Thomas Bridges
1690–1693	Cadwallader Jones
1693–1697	Nicholas Trott
1697–1699	Nicholas Webb
1700–1701	Elias Haskett
1701–1704	Ellis Lightwood
1704	Edward Birch
1704–1717	(unadministered)
1717–1721	Woodes Rogers (1)
1721–1728	George Phenney
1729–1732	Woodes Rogers (2)
1732–1733	Richard Thompson[1]
1733–1738	Richard Fitzwilliam
1738–1758	John Tinker
1758–1760	John Gambier[1] (1)
1760–1768	William Shirley
1768–1774	Thomas Shirley
1774–1776	Montfort Browne (1)
1776–1778	John Gambier[2] (2)
1778–1789	Montfort Browne (2)
1779–1782	John Maxwell (1)
1782–1783	(under Spain)
1784	John Maxwell (2)
1784–1786	James Edward Powell[2]
1786–1787	John Brown[1]
1787–1796	John Murray, Earl of Dunmore
1796–1797	Robert Hunt[1]
1797–1801	William Dowdeswell
1801–1804	John Halkett
1804–1820	Charles Cameron
1820–1829	Lewis Grant
1829–1833	James Carmichael Smyth
1833–1835	Blayney Townley Balfour
1835–1837	William Macbean George Colebrooke
1837–1844	Francis Cockburn
1844–1849	George Benvenuto Mathew
1849–1854	John Gregory
1854–1857	Alexander Bannerman
1857–1864	Charles John Bayley
1864–1869	Rawson William Rawson
1869–1871	John Walker
1871–1873	George Cumine Strahan
1873–1874	John Pope Hennessey
1874–1880	William Robinson
1880–1882	Jeremiah Thomas Fitzgerald Callaghan
1882–1884	Charles Cameron Lees
1884–1887	Henry Arthur Blake
1887–1895	Ambrose Shea
1895–1898	William Frederick Haynes Smith
1898–1904	Gilbert Thomas Carter
1904–1912	William Grey-Wilson
1912–1914	George Basil Haddon-Smith
1914–1920	William Lamond Allardyce
1920–1926	Harry Edward Spiller Cordeaux
1926–1932	Charles William James Orr
1932–1936	Bede Edmund Clifford
1936–1940	Charles Cecil Farquharson Dundas
1940–1945	Edward Alfred Christian, Duke of Windsor
1945–1950	William Lindsay Murphy
1950–1951	George Ritchie Sandford
1951–1953	Robert Arthur Neville
1953–1956	Thomas David Knox, Earl of Ranfurly
1956–1960	Oswald Raynor Arthur
1960–1964	Robert Stapledon de Stapledon
1964–1968	Ralph Francis Alnwick Grey
1968–—	Francis Edward Hovell Thurlow Cumming-Bruce

1. President
2. Lieutenant Governor

Burns, pp. 358–62, 397–400, 425–26, 499–500, 513–14, 549–50, 601, 647, 761; Public Record Office, *Journal of Board of Trade*, 1719–22 to 1776–82, passim.

89 BAHRAIN

Bahrain, an island and sheikhdom in the Persian Gulf, was brought under British protection as a result of a series of treaties during the 19th century. In 1900 a political agent was appointed to the court of Bahrain to preserve British interests. Until 1947 this agent was appointed by the Government of India. Like the former political agent at Kuwait (q.v.), he is subject to the authority of the chief political resident of the Persian Gulf (q.v.).

Political Agents

1900-1904	John Calcott Gaskin	1932-1937	Percy Gordon Loch (2)
1904-1909	Francis Beville Prideaux	1937	Tom Hickinbotham (1)
1909-1910	Charles Fraser Mackenzie	1937-1940	Hugh Weightman
1910-1911	Stuart George Knox	1940-1941	Reginald George Evelyn William
1911-1912	David Lockhart Robertson Lorimer		Alban
1912-1914	Arthur Prescott Trevor	1941-1943	Edward Birkbeck Wakefield (1)
1914-1916	Terence Humphrey Keyes	1943-1945	Tom Hickinbotham (2)
1916-1917	Trenchard Craven William Fowle	1945-1947	Edward Birkbeck Wakefield (2)
1917-1918	Percy Gordon Loch (1)	1947-1951	Cornelius James Pelly
1918	George Alexander Gavin Mungavin	1951-1952	William Scott Laver
1918-1919	Arthur Gordon Phillips	1952-1955	John William Wall
1919-1921	Harold Richard Patrick Dickson	1955-1959	Charles Alexander Gault
1921-1926	Clive Kirkpatrick Daly	1959-1962	Edward Parr Wiltshire
1926-1929	Cyril Charles Johnson Barrett	1962-1965	John Peter Tripp
1929-1932	Charles Geoffrey Prior	1965-1969	Anthony Derrick Parsons
		1969—	Alexander John Stirling

Information from M. I. Moir, *India Office Records*, London. Also, *Statesman's Year Book*, 1947 to date.

90 BALUCHISTAN

The British began to assume control over the rough desert region in extreme western India known as Baluchistan in the 1870's. British protectorates were established over the states of Kalat and Las Bela and a chief commissioner was appointed in 1877. The area had little commercial worth and was valued for its strategic location at the borders of both Persia and Afghanistan. In 1947 Baluchistan became part of Pakistan, but Pakistani administration was inaugurated only in 1949.

Chief Commissioners

1877-1892	Robert Groves Sandeman	1922-1927	Frederick William Johnston
1892-1896	James Browne	1927-1931	Henry Beauchamp St. John
1896-1900	Hugh Shakespear Barnes	1931-1938	Alexander Norman Ley Cater
1900-1904	Charles Edward Yate	1938-1939	Arthur Edward Broadbent Parsons
1905-1907	Alexander Lauzun Pendock Tucker	1939-1943	Herbert Aubrey Metcalfe
1907-1909	Arthur Henry McMahon	1943-1946	William Rupert Hay
1909-1911	Charles Archer	1946	Charles Geoffrey Prior
1911-1917	John Ramsay	1946-1947	Henry Mortimer Poulton
1917-1919	Henry Robert Conway Dobbs	1947-1948	Ambrose Dundas Flux Dundas
1919-1922	Armine Brereton Dew	1948-1949	Cecil Arthur Grant Savidge

India Office List and Burma Office List, 1940, p. 124.

91 BANTAM

After 1603 Bantam, in West Java, was the most important English post in the East Indies. In 1613 a chief factor was appointed by the East India Company. In 1617 Bantam was raised to a presidency and had control over the English posts on the Coromandel coast and in the East Indies. From 1630 to 1634 it was reduced to an agency under Surat (q.v.). In 1634 it again became a presidency. In 1652 the presidency was moved to Madras (q.v.) and Bantam again became an agency, but until 1652 Bantam and Surat were the only presidencies among the East India Company's posts in and around the Eastern seas. Bantam remained an agency until 1682 when the growing Dutch power in Java (v. Netherlands East Indies, 275) forced the English to abandon the post, which was shortly afterwards transferred to Bencoolen (q.v.) on the west coast of Sumatra.

Chief Factors
1613-1615	John Jourdain (1)
1615	Thomas Elkington
1615-1616	John Jourdain (2)
1616-1617	George Berkley

Presidents
1617-1618	George Ball
1618-1619	John Jourdain (3)
1620-1623	Richard Fursland
1623-1625	Thomas Brockeden
1625-1628	Henry Hawley
1628-1629	Richard Bix
1629-1630	George Muschamp (1)

Agents
1630-1631	George Willoughby (1)

1631-1632	William Hoare
1632-1633	Thomas Woodson
1633-1634	John Ling

Presidents
1634-1636	George Willoughby (2)
1636-1637	Robert Coulson
1637-1638	William Johnson
1638-1639	Gerald Pinson
1639-1640	George Muschamp (2)
1640-1643	Aaron Baker (1)
1643-1645	Ralph Cartwright
1645-1649	Aaron Baker (2)
1649-1650	Thomas Peniston
1650-1652	Aaron Baker (3)

Chaudhuri, p. 224; Foster, vols. 1 to 9, passim.

92 BARBADOS

Barbados, in the Lesser Antilles, was discovered by Spaniards in 1519. In 1627 the British began to settle there under the patronage of James Ley, Earl of Marlborough. In 1628 the original colonists were expelled by another English group sponsored by James Hay, Earl of Carlisle. Until 1652 it was privately governed. In 1662 the British crown assumed direct control. During the 17th and 18th centuries Barbados was a large producer of sugar and England's richest West Indies colony. From 1833 to 1885 the governor of Barbados was also governor-in-chief of the Windward Islands, which included Grenada, Saint Lucia, Saint Vincent, and Tobago (qq.v.). In 1885 the Windward Islands government was reconstructed without Barbados which again became a separate crown colony. In 1966 Barbados became an independent member of the British Commonwealth.

Governors
1628-1629	Charles Wolferston
1629	John Powell
1629	Robert Wheatley

1629-1630	William Tufton
1630-1639	Henry Hawley
1639-1641	Henry Huncks
1641-1650	Philip Bell[1]

1650-1651	Francis Willoughby (1)
1651-1652	George Ayscue
1652-1660	Daniel Searle[1]
1660	Thomas Modyford
1660-1663	Humphrey Walrond[2]
1663-1667	Francis Willoughby (2)
1667-1668	William Willoughby (1)
1668-1669	Christopher Codrington (1)
1669-1670	William Willoughby (2)
1670-1672	Christopher Codrington (2)
1672-1673	William Willoughby (3)
1673-1674	Peter Colleton[2]
1674-1680	Jonathan Atkins
1680-1685	Richard Dutton
1685-1690	Edwin Stede[1]
1690-1694	James Kendall
1694-1696	Francis Russell
1696-1698	Francis Bond[2]
1698-1701	Ralph Grey
1701-1703	John Farmer[2]
1703-1706	Beville Granville
1706-1707	William Sharpe[2]
1707-1710	Metford Crowe
1710-1711	George Lillington[2]
1711-1720	Robert Lowther
1720	John Frere[1]
1720-1722	Samuel Cox[1]
1722-1731	Henry Worsley
1731-1733	Samuel Barwick[1]
1733-1735	Emanuel Scrope, Viscount Howe
1735-1739	James Dotin[2] (1)
1739-1740	Robert Byng
1740-1742	James Dotin[2] (2)
1742-1747	Thomas Robinson
1747-1753	Henry Grenville
1753-1756	Ralph Weekes[2]
1756-1766	Charles Pinfold
1766-1768	Samuel Rous[2]
1768-1772	William Spry
1773-1780	Edward Hay
1780-1783	James Cunninghame
1784-1793	David Parry
1794-1800	George Poyntz Rickets
1801-1806	Francis Humberstone Mackenzie, Baron Seaforth
1806-1810	John Spooner[2]
1810-1814	George Beckwith
1815-1816	James Leith
1817-1820	Stapleton Cotton, Baron Combermere
1821-1827	Henry Warde
1827-1829	John Brathwaite Skeete[2]
1829-1832	James Lyon
1833-1836	Lionel Smith
1836-1841	Evan Murray John McGregor
1841-1846	Charles Edward Grey
1846-1848	William Reid
1848-1856	William Macbean George Colebrooke
1856-1862	Francis Hincks
1862-1868	James Walker
1868-1875	Rawson William Rawson
1875-1876	John Pope Hennessey
1876-1880	George Cumine Strahan
1880-1885	William Robinson
1885-1889	Charles Cameron Lees
1889-1891	Walter Joseph Sendall
1891-1900	James Shaw Hay
1900-1904	Frederic Mitchell Hodgson
1904-1911	Gilbert Thomas Carter
1911-1918	Leslie Probyn
1918-1925	Charles Richard Mackey O'Brien
1925-1933	William Charles Fleming Robertson
1933	Harry Scott Newlands
1933-1938	Mark Aitchison Young
1938-1941	Eubule John Waddington
1941-1947	Henry Grattan Bushe
1947-1949	Hilary Rudolph Blood
1949-1953	Alfred William Lungley Savage
1953-1959	Robert Duncan Arundell
1959-1966	John Montague Stow

Governors-General

1966	John Montague Stow
1966——	Arleigh Winston Scott

1. Lieutenant Governor.
2. President.

Burn, pp. 351—56, 394—96, 432—34, 499, 508, 548—49, 605, 645, 761—62; Schomburgk, pp. 684—86.

93 BASUTOLAND

The Sutu ruler Moshoeshoe requested the protection of Great Britain against the Boers, and in 1868 the area occupied by the Sutu was proclaimed a protectorate. In 1871 it was attached to the Cape Colony (q.v.) but with special legislative provisions which ensured its autonomy. The inability of the Cape authorities to control the area effectively and the disenchantment of the Sutu with the Cape government led to the Disannexation Act of 1883 by which Great Britain assumed direct responsibility. A resident commissioner replaced the government agent in 1884. Subsequently the resident commissioner was subject to the high commissioner for South Africa (q.v.) but not to the Union of South Africa (q.v.). Despite efforts of the Union to annex Basutoland the protectorate remained separate until 1966 when it gained its independence under the name Lesotho. Lesotho remains within the Commonwealth as an independent monarchy.

Government Agents		1916–1917	Robert Thorne Coryndon
1868	Walter Currie	1917–1926	Edward Charles Frederick
1868–1870	James Henry Bowker		Garraway
1870–1881	Charles Duncan Griffith	1926–1935	John Christian Ramsay Sturrock
1881–1883	Joseph Millerd Orpen	1935–1942	Edmund Charles Smith Richards
1883–1884	Matthew Smith Blyth	1942–1946	Charles Noble Arden-Clarke
		1947–1951	Aubrey Denzil Forsyth Thompson
Resident Commissioners		1951–1955	Edwin Porter Arrowsmith
1884–1893	Marshall James Clarke	1955–1961	Alan Geoffrey Tunstal Chaplin
1893–1901	Godfrey Yeatman Lagden	1961–1966	Alexander Falconer Giles
1901–1915	Herbert Cecil Sloley		

Information from Director of Information, Department of Information, Maseru, Basutoland, and from A. E. H. Sammons, Colonial Office, London. Also, Lagden, 2:676.

94 BAY ISLANDS

The colony of the Bay Islands consisted of Ruatan and several other islands in the Bay of Honduras. Minor British settlement had occurred on Ruatan in the 17th and 18th centuries but in each case it was of brief duration. After 1838 considerable immigration from the Cayman Islands took place, and from 1841 Great Britain definitely claimed the islands—a claim contested by Honduras. In 1852 the islands were erected into a distinct crown colony. The governor-in-chief of the Bay Islands was the governor of Jamaica and the lieutenant governor was the superintendent of British Honduras. Resident British authority was vested in presiding magistrates. Britain claims of sovereignty over the islands were never fully authenticated, nor logically advanced, and in 1860 Great Britain ceded the islands to Honduras, which took possession in the following year.

Presiding Magistrates
1852–1855   Charles Henry Johnes Cuyler
1855–1860   Alexander Wilson Moir

Waddell, pp. 59–77.

95 BECHUANALAND

The barren area occupied by the various Tswana tribes offered a buffer area for Britain's South African possessions, and a protectorate was proclaimed over the area in 1885 although it was only in 1891 that Bechuanaland was delimited. In that same year the administrator was replaced by a resident commissioner later subject directly to the high commissioner for South Africa (q.v.) rather than to the authorities of the Union of South Africa (q.v.), although in 1895 the southern part of Bechuanaland was annexed to the Cape Colony (q.v.). Bechuanaland remained a protectorate until 1966 when it became independent as Botswana. Botswana continues to be a member of the Commonwealth.

Commissioners			
1885-1895	Sidney Godolphin Alexander Shippard	1928-1930	Rowland Mortimer Daniel
		1930-1937	Charles Fernand Rey
1895-1897	Francis James Newton	1937-1942	Charles Noble Arden-Clarke
1897-1901	Hamilton John Goold-Adams	1942-1946	Aubrey Denzil Forsyth Thompson
1901-1906	Ralph Champneys Williams	1946-1950	Anthony Sillery
1907-1916	Francis William Panzera	1950-1953	Edward Betham Beetham
1916-1917	Edward Charles Frederick Garraway	1953-1955	William Forbes MacKenzie
1917-1923	James Comyn Macgregor	1955-1959	Martin Osterfield Wray
1923-1927	Jules Ellenberger	1959-1965	Robert Peter Fawcus
		1965-1966	Hugh Selby Norman-Walker

Information from A. E. H. Sammons, Colonial Office, London.

96 BENCOOLEN

Early English interest in the East Indies had been centered at Bantam (q.v.) since 1609, but the growing preponderance of Dutch power on Java caused the British to move the focus of their attention to the west coast of Sumatra where they established York Fort in the Bencoolen area in 1685. After 1714 the British center was at Fort Marlborough, with a group of posts farther north along the coasts at Tapanuli, Natal, and Air Bangis. Until 1760 the Bencoolen posts were subordinate to Madras (q.v.). In 1760 Bencoolen was raised to the status of a presidency but the inability of the British on Sumatra profitably to exploit the pepper trade resulted in the suppression of the presidency in 1785 when Bencoolen became subordinate to Bengal. Great Britain retained control of Bencoolen until 1825 when it was ceded to the Netherlands (v. Netherlands East Indies, 275) as a result of the agreement of 1824 by which Great Britain renounced interest in the East Indian archipelago in return for a free hand in Malaya (q.v.).

Deputy Governors			
1685	Ralph Ord	1708	John Delapie
1685-1690	Benjamin Bloome	1708-1710	Robert Skingle
1690-1691	James Sowdon	1710	Jeremiah Harrison[1]
1691-1695	Charles Fleetwood	1710-1711	Anthony Ettricke
1695-1696	Charles Barwell	1711-1712	John Daniell
1696-1699	Matthew Mildmay	1712	John Hunter
1699-1700	Robert Broughton	1712-1716	Joseph Collett
1700-1705	Richard Watts	1716-1717	Theophilus Shyllinge
1705-1708	Matthew Ridley	1717-1718	Richard Farmer
1708	James Cross	1718-1719	Thomas Cooke[1]
1708	Abraham Hoyle	-1723	Thomas Dunster
		1723-1728	Joseph Walsh

Great Britain

1728-1730	Nicholas Morse
1730-1731	Stephen Newcome
1731-1736	Francis Everest
1736-1746	Robert Lennox
1746-1752	Joseph Hurlock
1752-1754	Robert Hindley
1754-1755	John Walsh[1]
1754-1757	John Pybus
1757-1758	Randolph Marriott
1758-1760	Roger Carter

Governors/Presidents
1760-1767	Roger Carter
1767-1776	Richard Wyatt
1776	Robert Hay
1776-1780	William Broff

Governors
| 1780-1781 | Hew Steuart |
| 1781-1785 | Edward Coles |

Deputy Governors
1785-1786	John Crisp (1)
1786-1787	Thomas Palmer
1787-1789	George Salmon[1]
1789-1793	John Crisp (2)
1793-1799	Robert Broff
1799	John Crisp (3)
1799-1800	Philip Braham
1800-1805	Walter Ewer

Residents
1805-1807	Thomas Parr
1808-1810	Richard Parry
1810-1812	William Parker
1812-1818	George John Siddons

Lieutenant Governor
| 1818-1824 | Thomas Stamford Raffles |

Resident
| 1824-1825 | John Prince |

1. Supervisor.

Bastin, pp. xli-xlii; Wink, pp. 125-26.

97 BENGAL

Bengal was the first large area of India to come under direct British control (v. Fort William). In 1774 the governor of Bengal became governor-general of all the British possessions in India. Until 1834 the governor-general continued to administer directly the growing possessions of Great Britain in India (q.v.) except for Bombay and Madras (qq.v.). In 1834 Agra, later the North-West Provinces (v. United Provinces), was carved from Bengal. In 1854 a separate lieutenant governor was appointed for Bengal, freeing the governor-general from this local responsibility. Initially the province of Bengal covered all of northeastern India but in the course of time Assam, Bihar, and Orissa (qq.v.) were removed from Bengal and created separate provinces. In 1912 the lieutenant governor became governor. In 1947 the province of Bengal was divided between India and Pakistan.

Lieutenant Governors
1854-1859	Frederick James Halliday
1859-1862	John Peter Grant
1862-1867	Cecil Beadon
1867-1871	William Grey
1871-1874	George Campbell
1874-1877	Richard Temple
1877-1879	Ashley Eden
1879-1882	Steuart Colvin Bayley (1)
1882-1885	Augustus Rivers Thompson
1885-1890	Steuart Colvin Bayley (2)
1890-1895	Charles Alfred Elliott
1895-1898	Alexander Mackenzie

1898-1903	John Woodburn
1903-1908	Arthur Henderson Leith Fraser
1908-1912	Edward Norman Baker

Governors
1912-1917	Thomas David Gibson-Carmichael, Baron Carmichael
1917-1922	Laurence John Lumley Dundas, Earl of Ronaldshay
1922-1927	Victor Alexander George Robert Bulwer-Lytton, Earl of Lytton
1927-1930	Francis Stanley Jackson
1930-1932	Hugh Lansdown Stephenson

1932-1937	John Anderson	1939-1944	John Arthur Herbert
1937-1939	Michael Herbert Rudolf Knatchbull-	1944-1946	Richard Gardiner Casey
	Hugessen, Baron Brabourne	1946-1947	Frederick John Burrows

Buckland, passim; *India Office List and Burma Office List*, 1947, p. 27.

98 BERMUDA

The Bermuda Islands were discovered in about 1515 by the Spaniard Juan Bermúdez, but first settled in 1609 by a colony sent by the Virginia Company. During the 17th century the islands were known as the Somers Islands after the first governor. In 1615 the Virginia Company sold its rights to the Somers Islands Company which exercised control over the islands until 1684 when royal control was established. Since that time Bermuda has remained a crown colony.

Governors

1609-1610	George Somers	1701-1713	Benjamin Bennett (1)
1610-1611	Matthew Somers	1713-1715	Henry Pulleine
1611-1612	Richard Walters	1715-1722	Benjamin Bennett (2)
1612-1616	Richard Moore	1722-1728	John Bruce Hope
1616-1619	Daniel Tucker	1728-1737	John Pitt
1619-1622	Nathaniel Butler	1737-1744	Alured Popple
1622	John Harrison (1)	1745-1747	Francis Jones
1622-1623	John Bernard	1747-1764	William Popple
1623	John Harrison (2)	1764-1780	George James Bruere
1623-1627	Henry Woodhouse	1780-1781	George Bruere
1627-1629	Philip Bell	1781-1788	William Browne
1629-1637	Roger Wood	1788-1794	Henry Hamilton
1637-1641	Thomas Chaddock	1794-1796	James Craufurd
1641-1642	William Sayle	1796	William Campbell
1642-1643	Josias Forster (1)	1796-1798	Henry Tucker
1643-1645	William Sayle[1] (1)	1798-1805	George Beckwith
1644-1645	Samuel Paynter (1)	1805-1806	Francis Gore
1644-1645	William Wilkinson (1)	1806-1811	John Hodgson
1645-1646	Josias Forster (2)	1811-1819	James Cockburn
1646-1647	William Sayle[1] (2)	1819-1826	William Lumley
1646-1647	Samuel Paynter (2)	1826-1832	Hilgrove Turner
1646-1647	William Wilkinson (2)	1832-1839	Stephen Remnant Chapman
1647-1649	Thomas Turnor	1839-1846	William Reid
1649-1650	John Trimingham	1846-1854	Charles Elliot
1650	James Jennings	1854-1861	Freeman Murray
1650-1659	Josias Forster (3)	1861-1867	Harry St. George Ord
1659-1662	William Sayle (3)	1867-1870	Francis Edward Chapman
1662-1668	Florentia Seymour (1)	1870-1871	Thomas Gore Browne
1668-1669	Samuel Whatley	1871-1877	John Henry Lefroy
1669-1681	John Heydon	1877-1882	Robert Michael Laffan
1681-1682	Florentia Seymour (2)	1882-1888	Thomas Lionel John Gallwey
1682-1683	Henry Durham	1888-1892	Edward Newdigate Newdegate
1683-1687	Richard Cony	1892-1896	Thomas Casey Lyons
1687-1691	Robert Robinson	1896-1902	George Digby Barker
1691-1693	Isaac Richier	1902-1904	Henry LeGuay Geary
1693-1698	John Goddard	1904-1907	Robert Macgregor Stewart
1698-1701	Samuel Day	1907-1908	Joscelyn Heneage Wodehouse
		1908-1912	Frederick Walter Kitchener

Great Britain

1912–1917	George Mackworth Bullock	1943–1946	David George Brownlow Cecil, Marquess of Exeter
1917–1922	James Willcocks	1946–1949	Ralph Leatham
1922–1927	Joseph John Asser	1949–1955	Alexander Hood
1927–1931	Louis Jean Bols	1955–1959	John Dale Wooddall
1931–1936	Thomas Astley-Cubitt	1959–1964	Julian Alvery Gascoine
1936–1939	Reginald John Thoroton Hildyard	1964——	John Roland Robinson, Baron Martonmere
1939–1941	Denis John Charles Kirwan Bernard		
1941–1943	Francis Knollys		

1. During these periods rule was collegial.

Andrews, pp. 416–23; Burns, pp. 180–84, 356–58, 400–401, 466–68, 500, 514–15, 549, 601, 762–63; Wilkinson, passim.

99 BIHAR

The East India Company acquired the rights to Bihar, directly west of Bengal, in 1765. Until 1912 Bihar remained part of Bengal, but on the dissolution of the East Bengal-Assam province (v. Assam) Bihar and Orissa were detached from Bengal and erected into a separate province under a lieutenant governor. In 1919 Bihar-Orissa became a governor's province. In 1936 Orissa was detached from Bihar, which remained a province until it became part of India in 1947.

Bihar and Orissa

Lieutenant Governors

1912–1915	Charles Stuart Bayley
1915–1919	Edward Albert Gait

Governors

1919–1920	Edward Albert Gait
1920–1922	Satyendra Prasanna Sinha, Baron Sinha
1922–1927	Henry Wheeler

1927–1932	Hugh Lansdown Stephenson
1932–1936	James David Sifton

Bihar

Governors

1936–1937	James David Sifton
1937–1939	Maurice Garnier Hallett
1939–1943	Thomas Alexander Stewart
1943–1946	Thomas George Rutherford
1946–1947	Hugh Dow

India Office List and Burma Office List, 1940, pp. 122–23.

100 BOMBAY

The island of Bombay on the western coast of India was ceded to Great Britain by Portugal in 1661 as part of the dowry of Catarina of Bragança, wife of Charles II. In 1668 the crown granted Bombay to the East India Company and it replaced Surat (q.v.) as the chief British factory in western India, although until 1687 the governor of Bombay continued to reside at Surat while governing Bombay through deputy governors. After 1708 Bombay was the center of British authority in India until replaced more than half a century later by Bengal. Bombay continued as a governor's province of India until 1947. From 1839 to 1937 Aden (q.v.) was subject to Bombay and from 1843 to 1936 Sind (q.v.) was also subordinate to the governor of Bombay. In 1947 Bombay became a state of the Indian Union.

Governors

1664-1666	Humphrey Cooke
1666-1667	Gervase Lucas
1667-1668	Henry Gary
1668	George Oxinden
1668-1669	Henry Young
1669-1670	James Adams
1670	Matthew Gray
1670-1672	Philip Gifford (1)
1672-1674	John Shaxton
1675-1676	Philip Gifford (2)
1676-1677	John Petit
1677-1679	Henry Oxinden
1679-1681	John Child (1)
1681-1682	Mansell Smith
1682-1684	Charles Ward
1684-1685	Charles Zinzan
1685-1687	John Wyborne
1687-1690	John Child (2)
1690-1694	Bartholomew Harris
1694-1704	John Gayer
1704-1708	Nicholas Waite
1708-1715	William Aislabie
1715-1716	Stephen Strutt
1716-1720	Charles Boone
1720-1728	William Phipps
1728-1734	Robert Cowan
1734-1739	John Horne
1739-1742	Stephen Law
1742-1750	William Wake
1750-1760	Richard Bourchier
1760-1767	Charles Crommelin
1767-1771	Thomas Hodges
1771-1784	William Hornby
1784-1788	Rawson Hart Boddam
1788	Andrew Ramsay
1788-1790	William Medows
1790-1795	Robert Abercromby
1795-1811	Jonathan Duncan
1811-1812	George Brown
1812-1819	Evan Nepean
1819-1827	Montstuart Elphinstone

1827-1830	John Malcolm
1830-1831	Thomas Beckwith
1831	John Romer
1831-1835	John Fitzgibbon, Earl of Clare
1835-1838	Robert Grant
1838-1839	James Farish
1839-1842	James Rivett-Carnac
1842-1846	George Arthur
1846-1847	Lestock Robert Reid
1847-1848	George Russell Clerk (1)
1848-1853	Lucius Bentinck Cary, Viscount Falkland
1853-1860	John Elphinstone, Baron Elphinstone
1860-1862	George Russell Clerk (2)
1862-1867	Henry Bartle Edward Frere
1867-1872	William Robert Seymour Vesey Fitzgerald
1872-1877	Philip Edmond Wodehouse
1877-1880	Richard Temple
1880-1885	James Fergusson
1885-1890	Donald James Mackay, Baron Reay
1890-1895	George Robert Canning Harris, Baron Harris
1895-1899	William Mansfield, Baron Sandhurst
1899-1903	Henry Stafford Northcote
1903-1907	Charles Wallace Cochrane-Baillie, Baron Lamington
1907-1913	George Sydenham Clarke, Baron Sydenham
1913-1918	Freeman Freeman-Thomas, Marquess of Willingdon
1918-1923	George Ambrose Lloyd, Baron Lloyd
1923-1928	Leslie Orme Wilson
1928-1933	Frederick Hugh Sykes
1933-1937	Michael Herbert Rudolf Knatchbull-Hugessen, Baron Brabourne
1937-1943	Laurence Roger Lumley, Earl of Scarbrough
1943-1947	David John Colville

Fawcett, vols. 1 and 3, passim; *India Office List and Burma Office List*, 1947, pp. 22—23.

101 BRITISH COLUMBIA

Vancouver Island off Canada's western coast was granted to the Hudson's Bay Company (q.v.) in 1849. The mainland, known before 1858 as New Caledonia, was settled from Vancouver Island and made a separate colony in 1858 but with the same governor as Vancouver Island. From 1864 to 1866 the two colonies were divided, but in 1866 they were united under a single governor and called British Columbia. In 1871 British Columbia became a province of the new Confederation of Canada (v. Canada).

Great Britain

Vancouver Island

Governors
1849-1851 Richard Blanshard
1851-1864 James Douglas
1864-1866 Arthur Edward Kennedy

British Columbia

Governors
1858-1864 James Douglas
1864-1866 Frederick Seymour

the united colony

Governors
1866-1869 Frederick Seymour
1869-1871 Anthony Musgrave

Audet, p. 71; *Encyclopedia Canadiana*, 2:66.

102 BRITISH GUIANA

In 1803 Great Britain permanently occupied the Dutch Guianese settlements of Berbice (260), Demerara (266), and Essequibo (267). In 1831 these colonies were united to form British Guiana. Much of British Guiana's history has been consumed with boundary disputes with Venezuela and Brazil, arbitrated in 1899 and 1904 respectively. In 1966, after a hectic period of transition, British Guiana became, as Guyana, an independent member of the British Commonwealth.

Demerara-Essequibo

Lieutenant Governors
1803-1804 Robert Nicholson (1)
1804-1805 Antony Beaujon
1805-1807 James Montgomery
1807-1808 Robert Nicholson (2)
1808-1809 Charles Bayne Hodgson Ross
1809   Samuel Dalrymple
1809-1812 Henry William Bentinck
1812-1813 Hugh Lyle Carmichael
1813-1824 John Murray
1824-1831 Benjamin D'Urban

Berbice

Lieutenant Governors
1803-1804 Robert Nicholson (1)
1804-1806 Abraham Jacob van Imbijze van
           Batenburg
1806-1807 Robert Nicholson (2)
1807-1809 James Montgomery
1809-1810 William Woodly
1810   Samuel Dalrymple
1810-1812 Robert Gordon (1)
1812-1813 John Murray
1813   Robert Gordon (2)
1814-1820 Henry William Bentinck
1821-1831 Henry Beard

British Guiana

Governors
1831-1833 Benjamin D'Urban

1833-1838 James Carmichael Smyth
1838-1848 Henry Light
1848-1854 Henry Barkly
1854-1862 Philip Edmond Wodehouse
1862-1869 Francis Hincks
1869-1874 John Scott
1874-1877 James Robert Longden
1877-1882 Cornelius Hendricksen Kortright
1882-1887 Henry Turner Irving
1887-1893 Jenico William Joseph Preston,
           Viscount Gormanston
1893-1896 Charles Cameron Lees
1896-1898 Augustus William Lawson
           Hemming
1898-1901 Walter Joseph Sendall
1901-1904 James Alexander Swettenham
1904-1912 Frederick Mitchell Hodgson
1912-1917 Walter Egerton
1918-1923 Wilfrid Collet
1923-1925 Graeme Thomson
1925-1928 Cecil Hunter Rodwell
1928-1930 Frederick Gordon Guggisberg
1930-1935 Edward Brandis Denham
1935-1937 Geoffrey Alexander Northcote
1937-1941 Wilfrid Edward Jackson
1941-1947 Gordon James Lethem
1947-1953 Charles Campbell Woolley
1953-1955 Alfred William Lungley Savage
1955-1959 Patrick Muir Renison
1959-1964 Ralph Francis Alnwick Grey
1964-1966 Richard Edmonds Luyt

Guyana
Governors General
1966   Richard Edmonds Luyt
1966-1969   David James Gardiner Rose

Information from H. R. Persaud, Archivist of British Guiana, Georgetown, British Guiana.

103 BRITISH HONDURAS

It appears that some English settlement occurred on the Central American coast as early as 1638. About 1660 the ruler of the Moskito Indians placed himself under British protection and settlement increased. From 1740 to 1782 the British settlements were governed by the superintendent of the Moskito Coast (q.v.). In 1786 most of the Moskito Coast was abandoned as a result of treaty arrangements with Spain. The area around Belize was governed before 1786 and from 1791 to 1797 by annual magistrates who varied in number. The superintendent, first appointed in 1786, was replaced by a lieutenant governor in 1862 and finally by a governor in 1884. From 1862 to 1884 British Honduras was under Jamaica (q.v.), but it became a separate crown colony in 1884 and remains so today.

Superintendents
1786-1790	Edward Marcus Despard
1790-1791	Peter Hunter
1791-1797	(annual magistrates)
1797-1800	Thomas Barrow (1)
1800-1803	Richard Bassett
1803-1805	Thomas Barrow (2)
1805-1806	Gabriel Gordon
1806-1809	Andrew Mark Kerr Hamilton
1809-1814	John Nugent Smyth
1814-1822	George Arthur
1822-1823	Aleyne Hampden Pye
1823-1829	Edward Codd
1829-1830	Alexander McDonald (1)
1830-1837	Francis Cockburn
1837-1843	Alexander McDonald (2)
1843-1851	Charles St. John Fancourt
1851-1854	Philip Edmond Wodehouse
1854-1857	William Stevenson
1857-1862	Frederick Seymour

Lieutenant Governors
1862-1864	Frederick Seymour
1864-1867	John Gardiner Austin
1867-1870	James Robert Longden
1870-1874	William Wellington Cairns
1874-1877	Robert Miller Mundy
1877-1882	Frederick Palgrave Barlee
1882-1884	Robert William Harley
1884	Roger Tuckfield Goldsworthy

Governors
1884-1891	Roger Tuckfield Goldsworthy
1891-1897	Cornelius Alfred Moloney
1897-1904	David Wilson
1904-1906	Ernest Bickham Sweet-Escott
1906-1913	Eric John Eagles Swayne
1913-1918	Wilfrid Collet
1918-1919	William Hart Bennett
1919-1925	Eyre Hutson
1925-1932	John Alder Burdon
1932-1934	Harold Baxter Kittermaster
1934-1940	Alan Cuthbert Maxwell Burns
1940-1947	John Adams Hunter
1947-1948	Edward Gerald Hawkesworth
1948-1952	Robert Herbert Garvey
1952-1955	Patrick Muir Renison
1955-1961	Colin Hardwick Thornley
1961-1966	Peter Hyla Gawne Stallard
1922——	John Warburton Paul

Burdon, 1:47; 2:43, 3:48a.

104 BRITISH INDIAN OCEAN TERRITORY

The British Indian Ocean Territory was created in 1965. Its commissioner is the governor of the Seychelles Islands (q.v.). The territory consists of the Chagos Archipelago, Aldabra, Farquhar, and Des Roches Islands.

Commissioners

1965–1966 Julian Edward Asquith, Earl of
            Oxford and Asquith

1966—   Hugh Selby Norman-Walker

Statesman's Year Book, 1965 to date.

105 BRITISH KAFFRARIA

As British authority extended eastward from the Cape Colony (q.v.), the area just west of the River Kei was erected into a separate crown colony in 1847 and called British Kaffraria. The colony was an anomaly, too small to be viable, and adjacent to the much larger and older Cape Colony. Consequently, it was annexed to the Cape Colony in 1866.

Chief Commissioners

1847-1852 George Henry Mackinnon
1852-1860 John Maclean

Lieutenant Governors

1860-1864 John Maclean
1864-1866 Robert Graham

Walker, p. xix.

106 BRITISH NEW GUINEA

British New Guinea is that part (the northeastern) of the islands formerly controlled by Germany (v. German New Guinea, 72). In 1914, on the outbreak of World War I, the area was occupied by Australia. Between 1920 and 1942 Australia governed the area under a League of Nations mandate. New Guinea was occupied by the Japanese from 1942 to 1945. Australian rule was restored in 1945. Since then, New Guinea and Papua (q.v.), the southeastern section of the island, have been administered jointly.

Administrators

1914-1915 William Holmes
1915-1917 Samuel Augustus Pethebridge
1917-1918 Seaforth Simpson Mackenzie
1918-1920 George Jameson Johnston
1920-1921 Thomas Griffiths (1)
1921-1933 Evan Alexander Wisdom
1933-1934 Thomas Griffiths (2)

1934-1942 Walter Ramsay McNicoll
1942-1945 (under Japan)

Papua-New Guinea

Administrators

1945-1952 Jack Keith Murray
1952-1967 Donald Mackinnon Cleland
1967—   David Osborne Hay

Australian Encyclopaedia, 6:480; Rowley, passim.

107 BRITISH NORTH BORNEO

In 1877 and 1879 the territory later to comprise British North Borneo was ceded to a British syndicate by its nominal ruler, the sultan of Brunei (q.v.). In 1882 the British North Borneo Company acquired the rights over the territory. Six years later the British government assumed a formal protectorate although under this agreement the company would continue to administer the area. From 1942 to 1945 British North Borneo was occupied by the Japanese. After World War II North Borneo, instead of being returned to company control, was erected into a crown colony, with Labuan (q.v.) attached to it. In 1963 British North Borneo became a member of the Federation of Malaysia as Sahab.

Governors

1881-1887	William Hodd Treacher	1925-1926	Aylmer Cavendish Pearson (2)
1888-1895	Charles Vandeleur Creagh	1926-1929	John Lisseter Humphreys
1895-1900	Leicester Paul Beaufort	1929-1933	Arthur Frederick Richards
1900-1901	Hugh Clifford	1933-1937	Douglas James Jardine
1901-1904	Ernest Woodford Birch	1937-1942	Charles Robert Smith
1904-1912	Edward Peregrine Gueritz	1942-1945	(under Japan)
1912-1915	Cecil William Chase Parr	1946-1949	Edward Francis Twining
1915-1922	Aylmer Cavendish Pearson (1)	1949-1954	Herbert Ralph Hone
1922-1925	William Henry Rycroft	1954-1960	Roland Evelyn Turnbull
		1960-1963	William Allmond Codrington Goode

Tregonning, passim.

108 BRITISH SOLOMON ISLANDS PROTECTORATE

The Solomon Islands were discovered by Spaniards in 1567. After 1845 they were the scene of French missionary activity and later of recruitment of labor for the plantations of Fiji and Queensland (qq.v.). In 1893 Great Britain assumed a protectorate over the southern islands, and in 1899 Germany ceded the northern islands to Britain in exchange for abandonment of British interests in Samoa (v. German Samoa, 73). A few of the westerly Solomon Islands are administered by Australia through British New Guinea (q.v.). From 1942 to 1945 most of the Solomon Islands were occupied by the Japanese and the area became one of the main combat zones of the war. On January 1, 1953, the office of the Western Pacific High Commission (q.v.) was removed from Fiji to the British Solomon Islands Protectorate and the office of resident commissioner was abolished.

Resident Commissioners

1896-1915	Charles Morris Woodford	1929-1939	Francis Noel Ashley
1915-1917	Frederick Joshua Barnett	1939-1943	William Sydney Marchant
1917-1921	Charles Rufus Marshall Workman	1943-1950	Owen Cyril Noel
1921-1929	Richard Rutledge Kane	1950-1953	Henry Graham Gregory-Smith

Pacific Islands Year Book and Who's Who, p. 435.

109 BRITISH SOMALILAND

The part of the Somali coast opposite Aden had been occupied by Egyptian troops from about 1870 to 1884 when they withdrew. Great Britain then established a protectorate over part of th coast and a resident/political agent was appointed from Aden. In 1898 Somaliland was transferred from the Government of India to the Foreign Office and the political agent became consu general. In 1905 the Colonial Office assumed control and an administrator was appointed. In 1914 the administrator was replaced by a commissioner. After 1919 Somaliland, although rema ing nominally a protectorate, was placed under a governor. British Somaliland was briefly occ pied by Italian troops in 1940/41. In 1960 British Somaliland became independent and immediately united with Italian Somaliland (255) to form the Republic of Somalia.

Residents/Political Agents
1884-1888	Frederick Mercer Hunter
1889-1893	Edward Vincent Stace
1893-1896	Charles William Henry Sealy
1896-1897	William Butler Ferris
1897-1898	James Hayes Sadler

Consuls-General
1898-1901	James Hayes Sadler
1902-1905	Eric John Eagles Swayne

Administrators
1905-1910	Harry Edward Spiller Cordeaux
1910-1911	William Henry Manning
1911-1914	Horace Archer Byatt

Commissioner
1914-1919	Geoffrey Francis Archer

Governors
1919-1922	Geoffrey Francis Archer
1922-1926	Gerald Henry Summers
1926-1932	Harold Baxter Kittermaster
1932-1939	Arthur Salisbury Lawrance
1939-1941	Vincent Goncalves Glenday
1941-1943	Arthur Reginald Chater
1943-1948	Gerald Thomas Fisher
1948-1954	Gerald Reece
1954-1959	Theodore Ousley Pike
1959-1960	Douglas Basil Hall

Colonial Office List, 1905–40; *India Office List*, 1884–99; *Statesman's Year Book*, 1940–60.

110 BRITISH VIRGIN ISLANDS

Tortola, the most important of the British Virgin Islands, was occupied by the Dutch in 1648 an by the British from 1672 when they expelled the Dutch. They were included in the government the Leeward Islands (q.v.) until 1960. On the dissolution of the Leeward Islands government i 1960 the British Virgin Islands were erected into a separate administration. For the islands of Saint Croix, Saint John's, and Saint Thomas see the Danish West Indies (4) and the American Virgin Islands (412).

Presidents[1]
1741	John Pickering
1742-1750	John Hunt
1750-1751	James Purcell
1751-1775	John Purcell
1775-1782	John Nugent
1811-	Richard Hetherington
1839-1850	Edward Hay Drummond Hay
1852-1854	John Cornell Chads
1854-1857	Cornelius Hendricksen Kortwright
1859-1861	Thomas Price

1861-1864	James Robert Longden
1866-1869	Carlo Arthur Henry Rumbold
1869-1872	Alexander Wilson Muir
1873-1879	Richard Mahoney Hickson
1879-1882	John Kemys Spencer Churchill
1882-1884	Richard H. Dyett
1884-1887	Frederick Augustus Pickering

Administrators
1887-1894	Edward John Cameron
1894-1896	Alexander R. Mackay

896–1903	Nathaniel George Cookman	1934–1946	Donald Percy Wailling
903–1910	Robert Stephen Earl	1946–1954	John Augustus Cockburn Cruikshank
910–1919	Thomas Leslie Hardtman Jarvis	1954–1956	Henry Anthony Camilio Howard
919–1922	Herbert Walter Peebles	1956–1959	Geoffrey Pole Allesbrook
922–1923	R. Hargrove	1959–1962	Gerald Jackson Bryan
923–1926	Otho Lewis Hancock	1962–1967	Martin Samuel Staveley
926–1934	Frank Cecil Clarkson	1967——	John Sutherland Thomson

1. Before 1887 the administrators of the British Virgin Islands were most often styled President, although some were simply termed Officer administering the government, while at least two, John Purcell and John Nugent, carried the title of Lieutenant Governor.

nformation from V. Scatliffe, for the Administrator of the Virgin Islands, Road Town, Tortola, and rom J. S. Thomson, Administrator of B.V.I., Road Town, Tortola, British Virgin Islands.

111 BRUNEI

n 1888 the sultan of Brunei surrendered the control of his external affairs to Great Britain and accepted a British protectorate. After 1906 a British resident was appointed to Brunei, although until 1915 he resided at Labuan (q.v.). In 1959 the resident became high commissioner. Brunei declined to accede to the Federation of Malaysia and remains in a state of subsidiary alliance with Great Britain.

Residents

1906–1907	Malcolm Stewart Hannibal McArthur (1)	1931–1934	Thomas Falkland Carey
		1934–1937	Roland Evelyn Turnbull
1907–1908	Harvey Chevallier (1)	1937–1940	John Graham Black
1908	Malcolm Stewart Hannibal McArthur (2)	1940–1941	Ernest Edgar Pengilly
		1941–1945	(under Japan)
1908–1909	John Fortescue Owen	1946–1948	William John Peel
1909–1913	Harvey Chevallier (2)	1948–1951	Eric Ernest Falk Pretty (3)
1913–1915	Francis William Douglas	1951–1954	John Coleraine Hanbury Barcroft
1915–1916	Ernest Barton Maundrell	1954–1958	John Orman Gilbert
1916–1921	Geoffrey Edmund Cator	1958–1959	Dennis Charles White
1921–1923	Lucien Arthur Allen		
1923–1926	Eric Ernest Falk Pretty (1)	*High Commissioners*	
1926–1927	Oswald Eric Venables	1959–1963	Dennis Charles White
1927–1928	Eric Ernest Falk Pretty (2)	1963	Angus McKay Mackintosh
1928–1931	Patrick Alexander Bruce McKerron	1963–1965	Edward Ord Laird
		1965–1967	Fernley Douglas Webber
		1967——	Arthur Robin Adair

Colonial Office List, 1906–40; *Statesman's Year Book*, 1940 to date.

112 BURMA

During the 19th century the British engaged in a series of wars with the kingdom of Burma and progressively occupied its territory. Arakan in the northwest and Tenasserim in the south were annexed as a result of the First Burmese War of 1824—26. Pegu to the north of Tenasserim was retained as a result of the Second Burmese War, 1852—53. In 1862 the three provinces were united to form Lower Burma. Finally, in 1885, the core of the kingdom, called Upper Burma by the British, was annexed and the whole called Burma. Burma was part of British India (v. India) until 1937 when it was separated and made a crown colony. From 1942 to 1945 most of Burma was occupied by Japanese forces. In 1948 Burma became independent and chose not to become a member of the Commonwealth.

Arakan
Commissioners
1826-1829 George Hunter
1829-1830 Charles Paton
1830-1837 Thomas Dickinson
1837-1849 Archibald Bogle
1849-1852 Arthur Purves Phayre
1852-1862 (not separately administered)

Tenasserim
Commissioners
1826-1828 Archibald Campbell
1828-1833 Anthony De la Combe Maingy
1833-1843 Edmund Augustus Blundell
1843-1844 George Broadfoot
1844-1846 Henry Marion Durand
1846-1849 John Russell Colvin
1849-1858 Archibald Bogle
1858-1862 Albert Fytche

Pegu
Chief Commissioner
1852-1862 Arthur Purves Phayre

Lower Burma
Chief Commissioners
1862-1867 Arthur Purves Phayre
1867-1871 Albert Fytche
1871-1875 Ashley Eden

1875-1878 Augustus Rivers Thompson
1878-1880 Charles Umpherston Aitchison
1880-1885 Charles Edward Bernard

Burma
Chief Commissioners
1885-1887 Charles Edward Bernard
1887-1890 Charles Haukes Todd Crosthwait
1890-1895 Alexander Mackenzie
1895-1897 Frederic William Richards Fryer

Lieutenant Governors
1897-1903 Frederic William Richards Fryer
1903-1905 Hugh Shakespear Barnes
1905-1910 Herbert Thirkell White
1910-1915 Harvey Adamson
1915-1918 Spencer Harcourt Butler (1)
1918-1923 Reginald Henry Craddock

Governors
1923-1927 Spencer Harcourt Butler (2)
1927-1933 Charles Alexander Innes
1933-1936 Hugh Lansdown Stephenson
1936-1941 Archibald Cochrane Douglas
1941-1942 Reginald Hugh Dorman-Smith
1942-1945 (under Japan)
1945-1946 Reginald Hugh Dorman-Smith
1946 Henry Foley Knight
1946-1948 Hubert Elvin Rance

Cambridge History of India, 6:441; *India Office List and Burma Office List*, 1940, pp. 186—8

113 CANADA

Until 1758 the area of what was to become Canada was predominantly under the control of France (v. Acadia, 6, Île Royale, 32, Montreal, 46, New France, 49, and Plaisance, 53), or under no European control whatever, although some areas around Hudson's Bay were susceptible to the influence exercised by the Hudson's Bay Company (q.v.). Nonetheless British interest in the area was manifested almost as early as that of the French and during the middle part of the 17th century Great Britain, with some success, contended for control of the area settled by the French (see especially Acadia and New France). In 1710, with the conquest and annexation of Acadia (v. Nova Scotia), permanent British control began. During the Seven Years' War Great Britain conquered all of the French possessions and retained them by the Peace of Paris in 1763. In 1729 the British began to administer Newfoundland on a regular basis. The nucleus of the British possessions in Canada, that is, the area roughly congruent with the former New France, was divided after 1791 into Upper and Lower Canada. In 1841 the two colonies were united. The eastern provinces were governed as separate colonies; these were Nova Scotia, Prince Edward Island, Cape Breton (until it was absorbed into Nova Scotia in 1820), New Brunswick, and New-foundland (qq.v.). Interest in a union (or "confederation") of all these colonies was manifested by the integration of Lower Canada and Upper Canada in 1841. This interest was crystallized in 1867 with the confederation of Upper and Lower Canada with New Brunswick and Nova Scotia. In 1869 the Hudson's Bay Company sold its territorial rights to Canada, and in 1871 British Columbia (q.v.) joined and Canada became transcontinental. In 1873 Prince Edward Island ac-ceded to the confederation; Newfoundland, although an original province, did not join until 1949. From the area acquired from the Hudson's Bay Company Manitoba was created in 1870 and Alberta and Saskatchewan in 1905. The Northwest Territory and Yukon Territory, in northwestern Canada, although part of Canada since the Hudson's Bay Company cession of 1869, have never become provinces. Canada, the model dominion, remains within the British Commonwealth. The crown is represented by an appointed governor-general, whose role is symbolic and ceremonial only.

Quebec

Governors

1760-1763	Jeffrey Amherst, Baron Amherst
1763-1768	James Murray
1768-1778	Guy Carleton
1778-1786	Frederick Haldimand
1786-1791	Guy Carleton, Baron Dorchester

Lower Canada

Governors

1791-1796	Guy Carleton, Baron Dorchester
1796-1799	Robert Prescott
1799-1805	Robert Shore Milnes
1805-1807	Thomas Dunn
1807-1811	James Henry Craig
1811-1815	George Prevost
1815-1816	Gordon Drummond
1816-1818	John Coape Sherbrooke
1818-1819	Charles Gordon Lennox, Duke of Richmond
1820-1828	George Ramsay, Earl of Dalhousie
1828-1830	James Kempt
1830-1835	Matthew Whitworth-Aylmer, Baron Aylmer
1835-1838	Archibald Acheson, Earl of Gosford
1838	John George Lambton, Earl of Durham
1838-1839	John Colborne
1839-1841	Charles Edward Poulett Thomson, Baron Sydenham

Upper Canada

Lieutenant Governors

1791-1796	John Graves Simcoe
1796-1799	Peter Russell
1799-1805	Peter Hunter
1805-1806	Alexander Grant
1806-1817	Francis Gore
1817-1818	Samuel Smith
1818-1828	Peregrine Maitland
1829-1836	John Colborne
1836-1838	Francis Bond Head
1838-1841	George Arthur

Upper and Lower Canada

Governors

1841	Charles Edward Poulett Thomson, Baron Sydenham
1842-1843	Charles Bagot
1843-1845	Charles Theophilus Metcalfe, Baron Metcalfe
1845-1847	Charles Murray Cathcart, Baron Cathcart
1847-1854	James Bruce, Baron Elgin
1854-1861	Edmund Walker Head
1861-1867	Charles Stanley Monck, Viscount Monck

Canada

Governors-General

1867-1868	Charles Stanley Monck, Viscount Monck
1868-1872	John Young, Baron Lisgar
1872-1878	Frederick Temple Hamilton-Temple-Blackwood, Marquess of Dufferin
1878-1883	John Douglas Campbell, Marquess of Lorne
1883-1888	Henry Charles Keith Petty Fitz-maurice, Marquess of Lansdowne
1888-1893	Frederick Arthur Stanley, Earl of Derby
1893-1898	John Campbell Hamilton-Gordon, Marquess of Aberdeen

Great Britain

1898-1904	Gilbert John Elliot-Murray-Kynynmond, Earl of Minto	1931-1935	Vere Brabazon Ponsonby, Earl of Bessborough
1904-1911	Albert Henry George Grey, Earl Grey	1935-1940	John Buchan, Baron Tweedsmuir
1911-1916	Arthur William Patrick Albert, Duke of Connaught	1940-1946	Alexander Augustus Cambridge, Earl of Athlone
1916-1921	Victor Christian Cavendish, Duke of Devonshire	1946-1952	Harold Rupert Leofric George Alexander, Viscount Alexander
1921-1926	Julian Hedworth George Byng, Baron Byng	1952-1959	Vincent Massey
1926-1931	Freeman Freeman-Thomas, Marquess of Willingdon	1959-1967	George Philias Vanier
		1967—	Daniel Roland Michener

Audet, pp. 86–108; *Encyclopedia Canadiana*, under individual names; Lemieux, pp. 85–325; Read, pp. 19–203.

114 CAPE BRETON

The Cape Breton portion of Nova Scotia (q.v.) was the site of the earlier French colony of Île Royale (33). After the British occupation of Île Royale in 1758 settlement was discouraged and i was only in 1784 that Loyalists from the former American colonies to the south were allowed to settle there. At this time Cape Breton was created a separate government, being detached from Nova Scotia. However, this arrangement proved impractical and in 1820 Cape Breton was re-united to Nova Scotia.

Lieutenant Governors
1784-1787   Joseph Frederick Wallet DesBarres
1787-1795   William McCormick

Administrators
1795-1798   David Matthews
1798-1799   James Ogilvie

1799-1800   John Murray
1800-1807   John Despard
1807-1812   Nicholas Nepean
1812-1816   Hugh Swayne

Lieutenant Governor
1816-1820   George Robert Ainslie

Audet, p. 58; Brown, pp. 386–443.

115 CAPE COLONY

The Cape Colony, settled by the Dutch in 1652 (see Cape Colony, 261), was seized by the Britis in 1795, but returned in 1803. In 1806 it was seized once again and retained permanently by the British. During the course of the 19th century the areas east and north of Capetown were brough under administrative control of the Cape. Partly as a result of this extension of British authority the Dutch Boers in the colony emigrated northwards, seeking to escape British control, and founded the Orange Free State and Transvaal. In 1843 the British established Natal (q.v.) on the eastern coast of South Africa. In 1872 parliamentary government was introduced into the Cape Colony. From 1847 to 1901 the governor of the Cape Colony was also high commissioner for

South Africa (q.v.), being responsible in this role primarily for the government of the indigenous peoples. In this capacity, but not as governor of the Cape Colony, the high commissioner exercised authority over the resident commissioners of Basutoland, Bechuanaland, and Swaziland (qq.v.). In 1910 the Cape Colony joined with Natal and with the Orange River Colony and Transvaal (q.v.), both annexed as a result of the Anglo-Boer War of 1899–1902, to form the Union of South Africa (q.v.).

Governors
1795-1797	James Henry Craig
1797-1798	George Macartney, Earl Macartney
1798-1799	Francis Dundas (1)
1799-1801	George Yonge
1801-1803	Francis Dundas (2)
1803-1806	(under the Netherlands)
1806-1807	David Baird
1807-1811	DuPre Alexander, Earl of Caledon
1811-1813	John Francis Cradock
1814-1826	Charles Henry Somerset
1826-1828	Richard Bourke
1828-1833	Galbraith Lowry Cole
1834-1838	Benjamin D'Urban
1838-1844	George Thomas Napier
1844-1847	Peregrine Maitland

Governors/High Commissioners
1847	Henry Eldred Pottinger
1847-1852	Henry Wakelyn Smith
1852-1854	George Cathcart
1854-1861	George Grey
1862-1870	Philip Edmond Wodehouse
1870-1877	Henry Barkly
1877-1880	Henry Bartle Edward Frere
1881-1889	Hercules George Robert Robinson (1)
1889	Henry Augustus Smyth
1889-1895	Henry Brougham Loch
1895-1897	Hercules George Robert Robinson, Baron Rosmead (2)
1897-1900	Alfred Milner, Viscount Milner

Governors
1900-1901	Alfred Milner, Viscount Milner
1901-1910	Walter Francis Hely-Hutchinson

Walker, pp. xvii–xix.

116 CAYMAN ISLANDS

The Cayman Islands, consisting of Grand Cayman, Little Cayman, and Cayman Brac, are located about 200 miles northwest of Jamaica. They were ceded by Spain, which claimed but did not occupy them, to Great Britain in 1670. Beginning in 1734 they were settled from Jamaica. Until 1900 they were locally governed by justices of the peace. From 1900 to 1962 they were governed by commissioners and administrators subject to Jamaica. Since 1962 the Cayman Islands have been administered as a separate colony.

Commissioners
1900-1906	Fred Shedden Sanguinetti
1906-1907	Charles Henry Yorke Slader
1907-1913	George Stephenson Shirt Hirst
1913-1916	Aubrey Charles Robinson
1916-1919	Cecil Everard Mellish
1919-1929	Hugh Houston Hutchings
1929-1931	Geoffrey Hammond Frith
1931-1934	Ernest Arthur Weston
1934-1941	Alan Wolsey Cardinall
1941-1946	John Penry Jones
1946-1952	Ivor Otterbein Smith
1952-1956	Andrew Morris Gerrard
1956-1958	Alan Hilliard Donald

Administrators
1958-1960	Alan Hilliard Donald
1960-1964	Jack Rose
1964-1968	John Alfred Cumber
1968—	Athelstan Charles Ethelwold Long

Information from J. Rose, Administrator of the Cayman Islands, Cayman Islands. Also, Hirst, passim.

117 CENTRAL PROVINCES AND BERAR

In 1853 the Maratha kingdom of Nagpur was annexed to British India (v. India). Initially it was attached to Bengal (q.v.), but the remoteness of the new area led to the creation of a new province, known as the Central Provinces, in 1861. The Berar province of Hyderabad was administered as part of the Central Provinces until 1901 when it was purchased from the nizam and added to the Central Provinces. In 1947 the Central Provinces and Berar became part of India.

Chief Commissioners

1861-1864	Edward King Elliot
1864-1867	Richard Temple
1867-1868	George Campbell
1868-1883	John Henry Morris
1883-1884	William Bence Jones
1884-1885	Charles Haukes Todd Crosthwaite
1885-1887	Dennis Fitzpatrick
1887-1890	Alexander Mackenzie
1891-1893	Anthony Patrick McDonnell
1893-1895	John Woodburn
1895-1898	Charles James Lyall
1898-1902	Denzil Charles Jelf Ibbetson
1902	Andrew Henderson Leith Fraser
1902-1904	John Prescott Hewett
1904-1905	Frederic Styles Philpin Lely
1905-1906	John Ontario Miller
1906-1907	Stanley Ismay
1907-1912	Reginald Henry Craddock
1912-1919	Benjamin Robertson
1919-1921	Frank George Sly

Lieutenant Governors

1921-1925	Frank George Sly
1925-1933	Montagu Sherard Dawes Butler
1933-1938	Hyde Clarendon Gowan
1938	Hugh Bomford
1938-1940	Francis Verner Wylie
1940-1946	Henry Joseph Twynam
1946-1947	Frederick Chalmers Bourne

India Office List and Burma Office List, 1940, pp. 119—20.

118 CEYLON

From 1518 to 1796 parts of Ceylon had been held by both the Portuguese (291) and the Dutch (26 In 1796 the British seized the Dutch possessions in Ceylon as they had those in India and elsewhere in the East. Ceylon was retained by the British under the Treaty of Amiens. Until 1798 Ceylon was under military rule and administered as a part of the presidency of Madras (q.v.). Ir 1798 it was agreed that a governor should be appointed by the crown but that he would be subjec to the East India Company. This arrangement was terminated in 1802 when Ceylon became a crown colony. In 1815 the inland kingdom of Kandy was conquered and the entire island came under European control for the first time. Ceylon remained a crown colony until 1948 when it became an independent dominion within the British Commonwealth.

Military Governors

1796	James Stuart
1796-1797	Welborne Ellis Doyle
1797-1798	Pierre-Frédéric de Meuron

Governors

1798-1805	Frederick North
1805-1812	Thomas Maitland
1812-1820	Robert Brownrigg
1822	Edward Paget
1824-1831	Edward Barnes
1831-1837	Robert Wilmot-Horton
1837-1841	James Alexander Stewart Mackenz
1841-1847	Colin Campbell
1847-1850	George Byng, Viscount Torrington
1850-1855	George William Anderson
1855-1860	Henry George Ward
1860-1864	Charles Justin McCarthy
1865-1872	Hercules George Robert Robinson
1872-1877	William Henry Gregory
1877-1883	James Robert Longden
1883-1890	Arthur Charles Hamilton-Gordon, Baron Stanmore
1890-1895	Arthur Elibank Havelock

1895-1903	Joseph West Ridgeway	1937-1944	Andrew Caldecott
1903-1907	Henry Arthur Blake	1944-1948	Henry Monck-Mason Moore
1907-1913	Henry Edward McCallum		
1913-1916	Robert Chalmers	*Governors-General*	
1916-1918	John Anderson	1948-1949	Henry Monck-Mason Moore
1918-1925	William Henry Manning	1949-1955	Herwald Ramsbotham, Viscount
1925-1927	Hugh Clifford		Soulbury
1927-1931	Herbert James Stanley	1955-1962	Oliver Ernest Goonetilleke
1931-1933	Graeme Thomson	1962——	William Gopallawa
1933-1937	Reginald Edward Stubbs		

Hulugalle, passim; Turner, pp. 41—42.

119 CONNECTICUT

Connecticut was founded in 1639 by settlers from Massachusetts Bay (q.v.) who regarded with distaste the excessively puritanical and theocratic approach adopted by the leaders of Massachusetts Bay. In 1662 Connecticut was granted a charter according it an unusual degree of self-government, and it remained governed in accordance with this charter even after its break with Great Britain in 1776. In 1664 Connecticut absorbed its smaller neighbor, New Haven (q.v.). From 1687 to 1690 it was part of the Dominion of New England. In 1776 Connecticut, like Britain's other North American colonies between Florida and Canada, severed its connection with Great Britain.

Governors

1639	John Haynes (1)	1654	Edward Hopkins (7)
1640	Edward Hopkins (1)	1655-1656	Thomas Welles (1)
1641	John Haynes (2)	1656-1657	John Webster
1642	George Wyllys	1657-1658	John Winthrop (1)
1643	John Haynes (3)	1658-1659	Thomas Welles (2)
1644	Edward Hopkins (2)	1659-1676	John Winthrop (2)
1645	John Haynes (4)	1676-1683	William Leete
1646	Edward Hopkins (3)	1683-1698	Robert Treat
1647	John Haynes (5)	1698-1708	FitzJohn Winthrop
1648	Edward Hopkins (4)	1708-1725	Gordon Saltonstall
1649	John Haynes (6)	1725-1742	Joseph Talcott
1650	Edward Hopkins (5)	1742-1751	Jonathan Law
1651	John Haynes (7)	1751-1754	Roger Wolcott
1652	Edward Hopkins (6)	1754-1766	Thomas Fitch
1653	John Haynes (8)	1766-1769	William Pitkin
		1769-1776	Jonathan Trumbull

Norton, pp. 1—104.

120 COOK ISLANDS

The Cook Islands, a group of some fifteen islands in the South Pacific, were discovered by Spaniards in 1595 but named for the English navigator James Cook. As in most of the Pacific islands, early 19th century European interest took the form of missionary activity, but in 1888 a protectorate was proclaimed, and residents were appointed from New Zealand (q.v.). In 1901 the Cook Islands were made a dependency of New Zealand and the residents were replaced by resident commissioners. Internal self-government was granted in 1965 and the resident commissioner replaced by a high commissioner who controls the islands' foreign affairs, defense, and finance.

Residents
1888-1891	Richard Exham
1891-1898	Frederick Joseph Moss
1898-1901	Walter Edward Gudgeon

Resident Commissioners
1901-1909	Walter Edward Gudgeon
1909-1913	James Eman Smith
1913-1916	Henry William Northcroft
1916-1921	Frederick William Platts
1921-1923	John George Lewis Hewitt
1923-1937	Hugh Fraser Ayson (1)
1937-1938	Stephen John Smith
1938-1943	Hugh Fraser Ayson (2)
1943-1951	William Tailby
1951-1960	Geoffrey Nevill
1960-1965	Albert Oliver Dare

High Commissioners
1965	Albert Oliver Dare
1965—	Leslie James Davis

Information from Department of Island Territories, Wellington, New Zealand. Also, Gilson, passim.

121 COORG

In 1834 the kingdom of Coorg was annexed to British India (v. India) on the grounds of misgove ment. From 1834 to 1869 the commissioner of Mysore served also as commissioner of Coorg. 1869 Coorg was created a chief commissioner's province and the commissioner (after 1881, resi dent) of Mysore continued to serve as chief commissioner of Coorg until 1940. In 1947 Coorg acceded to the Union of India.

Chief Commissioners
1869-1870	Lewin Bentham Bowring
1870-1876	Richard John Meade
1876-1878	Charles Burslem Saunders
1878-1883	James Davidson Gordon
1883-1887	James Broadwood Lyall
1887	Dennis Fitzpatrick
1887-1889	Harry North Dalrymple Prendergast (1)
1889-1891	Oliver Beauchamp Coventry St. John
1891-1892	Harry North Dalrymple Prendergast (2)
1892-1895	Philip Durham Henderson
1895	William Lee-Warner
1895-1896	William Mackworth Young
1896-1903	Donald Robertson
1903-1905	James Austin Bourdillon
1905-1910	Stuart Mitford Fraser
1910-1916	Hugh Daly
1916-1920	Henry Venn Cobb
1920-1925	William Pell Barton
1925-1930	Steuart Edmund Pears
1930-1933	Richard John Charles Burke
1933-1937	Charles Terence Chichele Plowc
1937-1940	John de la Hay Gordon
1940-1943	Joseph William Pritchard
1943-1947	Bahadur Chengappa

India Office List and Burma Office List, 1940, p. 125; Rao, 2, pt. 4:3110.

122 CURAÇAO

For the British governors of Curaçao from 1800 to 1803 and 1807 to 1816, see the Dutch colony, Curaçao, 265.

123 CYPRUS

The island of Cyprus in the eastern Mediterranean was, until 1878, a part of the Ottoman Empire. In that year it was handed over to Great Britain for administrative purposes, although not formally ceded. However, on the outbreak of World War I in 1914 Cyprus was annexed to the British Empire, and in 1925 it was constituted a crown colony and the high commissioner became governor. In 1960 Cyprus became an independent nation inside the British Commonwealth.

High Commissioners
1878-1879	Garnet Joseph Wolseley
1879-1886	Robert Biddulph
1886-1892	Henry Ernest Gascoyne Bulwer
1892-1898	Walter Joseph Sendall
1898-1904	William Frederick Haynes Smith
1904-1911	Charles Anthony King-Harman
1911-1915	Hamilton John Goold-Adams
1915-1920	John Eugene Clauson
1920-1925	Malcolm Stevenson

Governors
1925-1926	Malcolm Stevenson

1926-1932	Ronald Storrs
1932-1933	Reginald Edward Stubbs
1933-1939	Herbert Richmond Palmer
1939-1941	William Denis Battershill
1941-1946	Charles Campbell Woolley
1946-1949	Reginald Thomas Herbert Fletcher, Baron Winster
1949-1953	Andrew Barkworth Wright
1953-1955	Robert Perceval Armitage
1955-1958	John Harding
1958-1960	Hugh Mackintosh Foot

Hill, 4:641.

124 DELHI

Delhi was the capital of the Mughal kingdom until its abolition in 1857. From 1857 to 1859 the area was under the North-West Provinces (v. United Provinces of Agra and Oudh) and from 1859 it was under the Punjab (q.v.). In 1912 the capital of British India was transferred from Calcutta to Delhi and the area surrounding the new capital was removed from the jurisdiction of the Punjab and created a separate chief commissioner's province. It remained so until 1947 when it joined the new Union of India (v. India).

Chief Commissioners
1912-1918	William Malcolm Hailey
1918-1924	Claud Alexander Barron
1924-1926	Evelyn Robins Abbott
1926-1928	Alexander Montague Stow

1928-1932	John Perronet Thompson
1932-1937	John Nesbitt Gordon Johnson
1937-1940	Evan Meredith Jenkins
1940-1945	Arthur Vivian Askwith
1945-1947	William Christie

India Office and Burma Office List, 1940, p. 125.

125 DOMINICA

Dominica is an island in the Lesser Antilles and like most of the West Indies islands it led a checkered existence in the 17th and 18th centuries. It was settled by the French after 1632 from nearby Martinique and Guadeloupe (qq.v.), but captured by the British in 1761 and made a part of the Windward Islands (q.v.) government until 1771 when it became a separate colony. It was retaken by the French in 1778 but ceded to Great Britain at the peace of 1783. In 1833 it became a part of the Leeward Islands (q.v.) and remained so until 1940 when it was transferred to the Windward Islands (q.v.). At the dissolution of the Windward Islands government in 1960 Dominica again became a separate colony. In 1967 Dominica joined the Associated States of th West Indies.

Governors

1768–1771	William Young
1771–1775	William Stewart
1775–1778	Thomas Shirley
1778–1784	(under France)
1784–1789	John Orde
1789–1794	Thomas Bruce
1794–1796	Henry Hamilton
1797–1802	Andrew James Cochrane Johnstone
1802–1805	George Prevost
1805–1808	George Metcalfe[1]
1808–1809	James Montgomery
1809–1812	Edward Barnes
1813–1815	George Robert Ainslie
1816–1819	Charles William Maxwell
1819–1821	Samuel Ford Whittingham
1822–1824	Hans Francis Hastings, Earl of Huntingdon
1824–1831	William Nicolay
1831–1833	Evan John Murray McGregor

Lieutenant Governors

1833–1834	Charles Marsh Schomberg
1834–1837	J. P. Lockhart[1]
1837–1838	Henry Light
1838	John Longley
1839–1843	John McPhail
1843–1845	D. S. Laidlaw[1]
1845–1851	George McDonald
1851–1857	Samuel Wensley Blackall

1857–1860	Harry St. George Ord
1861–1864	Thomas Price
1864–1867	James Robert Longden
1869	Henry Gascoyne Ernest Bulwer
1869–1871	Sanford Freeling

Presidents

1872–1873	Alexander Wilson Moir
1873–1882	Charles Monroe Eldridge
1882–1887	James Meade
1887–1894	Charles Ruthven LeHunte

Administrators

1895–1899	Philip Arthur Templer
1899–1905	Henry Hesketh Joudou Bell
1905–1913	William Douglas Young
1914	Edward Rawle Drayton
1915–1919	Arthur William Mahaffy
1919–1923	Robert Walter
1923–1930	Edward Carlyon Eliot
1931–1933	Walter Andrew Bowring
1933–1937	Henry Bradshaw Popham
1938–1945	James Scott Neill
1946–1952	Edwin Porter Arrowsmith
1952–1959	Henry Laurence Lindo
1959–1967	Alec Lovelace

Governors

1967–1968	Geoffrey Colin Guy
1968——	Louis Cools-Lartigue

1. President.

Information from Alec Lovelace, Administrator of Dominica, Roseau, Dominica. Also, Andrews, pp. 438–39.

126 EGYPT

In 1876 British and French controllers were appointed in Egypt to stabilize the chaotic financial situation there. In the following years the authority of these officials gradually increased. Following the inevitable Egyptian reaction, British and French troops invaded the country, ostensibly to protect their financial interests. France withdrew the following year, but the British remained and a resident/consul-general was appointed, although the fiction was officially maintained that Egypt was an integral part of the Ottoman Empire. With the entry of the Ottoman Empire into World War I on the side of the Central Powers, Great Britain proclaimed a protectorate over Egypt and the resident/consul-general was replaced by a high commissioner. Eight years later the protectorate was withdrawn and Egypt became independent of official British control.

Residents/Consuls-General
1883-1907 Evelyn Baring, Baron Cromer
1907-1911 John Eldon Gorst
1911-1914 Horatio Herbert Kitchener, Earl
          Kitchener

1914-1916 Arthur Henry MacMahon
1916-1919 Francis Reginald Wingate
1919-1922 Edmund Henry Hynman Allenby,
          Viscount Allenby

High Commissioners
1914   Milne Chatham

Statesman's Year Book, 1883–1922.

127 FALKLAND ISLANDS

The Falkland Islands consists of two large and over a hundred small islands in the South Atlantic Ocean, and the colony includes the dependencies of South Georgia, South Sandwich, and South Shetland. The British planted a small garrison on West Falkland Island in 1766 but abandoned possession in 1774 after a dispute with the Spaniards who took possession of both East and West Falkland which they called the Malvinas Islands (353). After a brief Argentinian occupation the British reclaimed the islands in 1832 for the purpose of protecting whalers in the area. Until 1841 the administration was conducted by a naval officer-in-charge, but a formal civil administration was established in 1841 under a lieutenant governor, whose title was changed to governor in 1843. The Falkland Islands remains a crown colony, although Argentina has never abandoned its claims.

West Falkland
Naval Officers-in-Charge
1766-1767 John McBride
1767-1770 Anthony Hunt
1770   George Farmer
1770-1773 John Burr
1773-1774 Samuel Wittewrong Clayton
1774   (abandoned)

Falkland Islands and dependencies
Naval Officers-in-Charge
1834-1838 Henry Smith
1838-1839 Robert Lowcay
1839-1841 John Tyssen

Lieutenant Governor
1841-1843 Richard Clement Moore

Governors
1843-1848 Richard Clement Moore
1848-1855 George Rennie
1855-1862 Thomas Edward Laws Moore
1862-1866 James George Mackenzie
1866-1870 William Francis Cleaver
          Robinson
1870-1876 George Abbas Kooli D'Arcy
1876-1880 Jeremiah Thomas Fitzgerald
          Callaghan
1880-1891 Thomas Kerr

Great Britain

1891-1897	Roger Tuckfield Goldsworthy	1935-1941	Herbert Henniker Heaton
1897-1904	William Grey-Wilson	1941-1946	Allan Wolsey Cardinall
1904-1915	William Lamond Allardyce	1946-1954	Geoffrey Miles Clifford
1915-1920	William Douglas Young	1954-1957	Oswald Raynor Arthur
1920-1927	John Middleton	1957-1964	Edwin Porter Arrowsmith
1927-1931	Arnold Meinholt Hodson	1964——	Cosmo Dugal Thomas Haskard
1931-1935	James O'Grady		

Boyson, pp. 188—89 and passim; *Statesman's Year Book*, 1924 to date.

128 FEDERATED MALAY STATES

British control of the several states of the Malay Peninsula spread after 1826 from their colony of the Straits Settlements (q.v.). In the end, this control became duoform. The states of Pahang, Perak, Selangor, and Negri Sembilan became known as the Federated Malay States; the remaining states were called the Unfederated Malay States. British residents were introduced into Pahang, Perak, and Selangor in 1874, and into Negri Sembilan in 1889. In 1895 the four states formed a federation at the head of which was a resident-general. In 1911 new procedures resulted in a change of title to chief secretary. In 1936 the title was changed to Federal Secretary, and the status and functions of the office were curtailed. In each instance these individuals were under the authority of the governor of the Straits Settlements. In 1941—42 all of Malaya was occupied by the Japanese, and with the British reoccupation in 1945 the Federated Malay States was not revived. However, each of the four states joined the new Union of Malaya (v. Malaya).

Residents-General

1896-1904	Frank Athelstane Swettenham
1904-1910	William Thomas Taylor
1910-1911	Arthur Henderson Young

Chief Secretaries

1911-1920	Edward Lewis Brockman
1920-1926	William George Maxwell
1926-1930	William Peel

1930-1932	Charles Walter Hamilton Cochrane
1932-1934	Andrew Caldecott
1934-1935	Malcolm Bond Shelley
1935-1936	Marcus Rex

Federal Secretaries

1936-1939	Christopher Dominic Ahearne
1939-1942	Hugh Fraser

Colonial Office List, 1896—1940.

129 FIJI

The colony of Fiji comprises more than three hundred islands located in the Pacific Ocean between latitude 15° and 22° south and longitude 177° west and 175° east. However, two main islands, Viti Levu and Vanua Levu, comprise sixth/sevenths of the total land area. During the first half of the 19th century these two islands were torn by internal strife. Cakobau, ruler of Bau, and perhaps the most powerful of the Fijian rulers, claimed, but was unable to exercise, paramountcy over the islands. He had offered the islands to Great Britain in 1858 and to Germany in 1872, but without success. A second tender to Great Britain in 1874 was, however, accepted. Fiji was proclaimed a crown colony. Fiji is the most important British possession in the Pacific, and from 1877 to 1952 the governor of Fiji was also high commissioner for the Western Pacific (v. Western Pacific High Commission). Ministerial government was introduced in 1967, but Fiji still remains a crown colony.

Governors

1875-1880	Arthur Charles Hamilton-Gordon, Baron Stanmore	1925-1929	Eyre Hutson
1880-1887	George William DesVoeux	1929-1935	Arthur Murchison Fletcher
1887-1888	Charles Bullen Hugh Mitchell	1936-1938	Arthur Frederick Richards
1888-1897	John Bates Thurston	1938-1942	Harry Charles Joseph Luke
1897-1902	George Thomas Mackey O'Brien	1942-1945	Philip Euen Mitchell
1902-1904	Henry Moore Jackson	1945-1948	Alexander William Grantham
1904-1911	Everard Ferdinand Im Thurn	1948-1952	Leslie Brian Freeston
1911-1912	Francis Henry May	1952-1958	Ronald Herbert Garvey
1912-1918	Ernest Bickham Sweet-Escott	1958-1963	Kenneth Phipson Maddocks
1918-1925	Cecil Hunter Rodwell	1963-1968	Francis Derek Jakeway
		1968——	Robert Sidney Foster

Tudor, p. 216.

130 FLORIDAS

The Spanish colony of Florida (339), at the southern flank of Britain's North American colonies, was ceded to England by Spain at the end of the Seven Years' War in 1763. Great Britain divided the colony into West Florida and East Florida. Secured for strategic purposes and never settled by any large numbers of English settlers, the Floridas were the only English colony in what was to become the United States that did not directly participate in the American Revolution against England. However, at the Treaty of Paris in 1783 the two Floridas retroceded to Spain which had, in fact, already occupied West Florida in 1780—81.

East Florida

Governors

1764-1771	James Grant
1771-1773	James Moultrie
1773-1783	Patrick Tonyn

West Florida

Governors

1763-1767	George Johnstone
1767-1769	Montfort Browne
1769	John Eliot
1769-1770	Elias Durnford
1770-1781	Peter Chester

Johnson, passim; Mowat, p. 162.

131 FORT WILLIAM

English trading interests in the Bengal area dated from 1633. In 1690 a British factory was established on the site of Calcutta, and ten years later this post was raised to a presidency known as Fort William. Friction with the Mughal subahdar (governor) of Bengal led to greatly increased British interest in and control of the area. After defeating the subahdar in 1757, Great Britain gained effective control of the whole province of Bengal and soon thereafter of Bihar (qq.v.). These were used as springboards for the eventual conquest of the entire Indian subcontinent. For the governors of Bengal after 1758, see India.

Presidents			
1700–1701	Charles Eyre	1728–1732	John Deane (2)
1701–1705	John Beard	1732–1739	John Stackhouse
1705–1710	(none)	1739–1745	Thomas Braddyll
1710–1711	Andrew Weltden	1746–1748	John Forster
1711–1713	John Russell	1748–1749	William Barwell
1713–1718	Robert Hedges	1749–1752	Adam Dawson
1718–1723	Samuel Feake	1752	William Fytche
1723–1726	John Deane (1)	1752–1756	Roger Drake (1)
1726–1728	Henry Frankland	1756–1757	John Zephaniah Holwell
1728	Edward Stephenson	1757–1758	Roger Drake (2)

Birney; Datta, 1:41; *India Office List*, 1918, p. 129; Wilson.

132 THE GAMBIA

English traders had begun to explore the area of the Gambia River in western Africa in the early 17th century, but had not permanently established themselves there. In 1651 the Duke of Kurland built a post at the mouth of the river. Ten years later this post was seized by the English who then built their own post, called James Fort, on an island in the river. Until 1766 this post was under the jurisdiction of various chartered companies, including the Gambia Adventurers and the Royal African Company. In 1766 the British establishments on the Gambia fell under the new colony of Senegambia (q.v.). The French captured the British posts in the Senegambian area in 1779 and no further settlement was made there until 1816, although the area was under the nominal control of the Company of Merchants trading to Africa. A small fort was established in 1816. Give years later the Gambia became part of Sierra Leone (q.v.), and in 1829 a lieutenant governor was appointed. From 1843 to 1866 the Gambia was a separate colony. From 1866 to 1888 it was part of the government called the West Africa Settlements, centered at Sierra Leone, which also included Lagos (v. Nigeria) and the Gold Coast (q.v.). From 1888 the Gambia was once again a separate colony. The upriver area, known as the Protectorate, has been administered as part of the Gambia since 1894. In 1965 the Gambia became an independent republic within the British Commonwealth.

James Fort			
Agents[1]		1677–1680	Thomas Thurloe
1661	Francis Kerby	1680–1681	Thomas Forde
1661–1662	Morgan Facey	1681–1684	John Kastell
1662–1664	Stephen Ustick	1684–1688	Alexander Cleeve
1664–1666	John Ladd	1688–1693	John Booker
1672–1674	Rice Wight	1693–1695	William Heath
		1695	John Hanbury

1695-1699	(abandoned)
1699-1700	Thomas Corker
1700	Paul Pindar
1700-1701	Thomas Gresham
1702-1703	Humphrey Chishull
1703-1704	Thomas Weaver
1704-1706	John Chidley
1706	John Tozer
1706-1709	John Snow
1709-1713	(abandoned)
1713-1714	William Cooke
1714-1717	David Francis
1717-1721	Charles Orfeur (1)
1721	Thomas Whitney
1721-1723	Henry Glynne
1723	Joseph Willey
1723-1725	Robert Plunkett
1725-1728	Anthony Rogers (1)
1728	Richard Hull (1)
1728-1729	Charles Cornewall
1729-1733	Anthony Rogers (2)
1733-1737	Richard Hull (2)
1737-1745	Charles Orfeur (2)
-1750	John Gootheridge
1750-1752	James Alison
1752-1754	James Skinner
1754-1755	Robert Lawrie
1755-_1758_	Tobias Lisle
_1760_-1766	Joseph Debat

The Gambia
Lieutenant Governors

1829-1830	Alexander Findlay
1830-1837	George Rendall
1837-1838	Thomas Lewis Ingram (1)
1838-1839	William Mackie
1839-1840	Thomas Lewis Ingram (2)
1840-1841	Henry Vere Huntley
1841-1843	Thomas Lewis Ingram (3)

Governors

1843	Henry Froude Seegram

1843-1844	Edmund Norcott
1844-1847	Charles Fitzgerald
1847-1852	Richard Graves McDonnell
1852-1859	Luke Smythe O'Connor
1859-1866	George Abbas Kooli D'Arcy

Administrators

1866-1869	Charles George Edward Patey
1869-1871	Alexander Bravo
1871-1873	Jeremiah Thomas Fitzgerald Callaghan
1873-1875	Cornelius Hendricksen Kortright
1875-1877	Samuel Rowe
1877-1884	Valesius Skipton Gouldsbury
1884-1886	Cornelius Alfred Moloney
1886-1888	James Shaw Hay
1888-1891	Gilbert Thomas Carter
1891-1900	Robert Baxter Llewelyn
1900-1901	George Chardin Denton

Governors

1901-1911	George Chardin Denton
1911-1914	Henry Lionel Gallwey
1914-1920	Edward John Cameron
1920-1927	Cecil Hamilton Armitage
1927-1928	John Middleton
1928-1930	Edward Brandis Denham
1930-1933	Herbert Richmond Palmer
1933-1936	Arthur Frederick Richards
1936-1942	Wilfred Thomas Southorn
1942-1947	Hilary Rudolph Blood
1947-1949	Andrew Barkworth Wright
1949-1958	Percy Wyn-Harris
1958-1962	Edward Henry Windley
1962-1965	John Warburton Paul

Governors-General

1965-1966	John Warburton Paul
1966—	Farimang Mamadi Singhateh

1. Some agents in the 18th century held the title of governor.

Gailey, pp. 210–11; Gray, passim.

133 GEORGIA

Of England's colonies in North America, Georgia was the last to be settled. It was founded to provide a buffer between the other English colonies and the Spaniards in Florida (339) and as an experiment in debtor rehabilitation. The first colonists arrived in 1733. Until 1754 Georgia was a proprietary colony. From 1754 it was a royal colony. Insulated from the agitation against

England of its northern neighbors, Georgia nonetheless expelled the royal governor in 1776. In 1779 the British were able to reoccupy most of Georgia, but in 1782 they were finally forced to abandon the colony.

Governors			
1733-1750	James Edward Oglethorpe	1757-1760	Henry Ellis
1750	William Stephens	1760-1776	James Wright (1)
1750-1754	Henry Parker	1776-1779	(no British governor)
1754-1757	John Reynolds	1779-1782	James Wright (2)

Abbot, passim; McCain, passim.

134 GIBRALTAR

The fortress of Gibraltar, located at the end of a promontory at the western entrance to the Mediterranean Sea, was captured by the British in 1704 during the War of the Spanish Succession, and retained by Great Britain at the Treaty of Utrecht in 1713. During the 18th century, while Britain held Minorca (q.v.), Gibraltar was less highly regarded as a strategic necessity, although it was tenaciously held during a lengthy siege lasting from 1779 to 1783. After the final loss of Minorca in 1802, Gibraltar assumed a greater role in Great Britain's imperial strategy. Until 1969 the governor of Gibraltar was invariably a senior general in the British army and he served simultaneously as commander of the garrison stationed in Gibraltar.

Governors			
1704-1706	Georg von Hessen-Darmstadt	1806	Hew Whitefoord Dalrymple
1707-1711	Roger Elliott	1806-1809	Gordon Drummond
1711-1713	Thomas Stanwix	1809-1810	John Francis Cradock (Caradoc)
1713-1720	David Colyear, Earl of Portmore	1810-1814	Colin Campbell
1720-1727	Richard Kane	1814-1820	George Don
1727-1730	Jasper Clayton	1820-1835	John Pitt, Earl of Chatham
1730-1738	Joseph Sabine	1835-1842	Alexander George Woodford
1738-1739	Francis Columbine	1842-1848	Robert Thomas Wilson
1739-1749	William Hargrave	1848-1855	Robert William Gardiner
1749-1752	Humphry Bland	1855-1859	James Fergusson
1752-1756	Thomas Fowke	1859-1865	William John Codrington
1756	James O'Hara, Earl of Tyrawley	1865-1870	Richard Airey
1756-1758	William Maule, Earl of Panmure	1870-1876	William Fenwick Williams
1758-1761	William, Earl Home	1876-1883	Robert Cornelis Napier, Baron Napier
1761-1762	John Parslow	1883-1886	John Miller Adye
1762-1770	Edward Cornwallis	1886-1890	Arthur Edward Hardinge
1770-1775	Robert Boyd (1)	1890-1891	Leicester Smyth
1775-1790	George Augustus Eliott, Baron Heathfield	1891-1893	Lothian Nicholson
		1893-1900	Robert Biddulph
1790-1794	Robert Boyd (2)	1900-1905	George Stuart White
1794-1795	Henry Clinton	1905-1910	Frederick William Edward Forestier-Walker
1795-1802	Charles O'Hara		
1802	Thomas Trigge	1910-1913	Archibald Hunter
1802-1820	Edward Augustus, Duke of Strathearn and Kent	1913-1918	Herbert Scott Gould Miles
		1918-1923	Herbert Lockwood Smith-Dorrien
1802-1804	Charles Barnet[1]	1923-1928	Charles Carmichael Monro
1804-1806	Henry Edward Fox	1928-1933	Alexander John Godley

1933-1938	Charles Harington Harington	1947-1952	Kenneth Arthur Anderson
1938-1939	Edmund Ironside	1952-1955	Gordon Holmes MacMillan
1939-1941	Clive Liddell	1955-1958	Harold Redman
1941-1942	John Standish Surtees Prendergast	1958-1962	Charles Frederic Keightley
	Vereker, Viscount Gort	1962-1965	Alfred Dudley Ward
1942-1944	Noel Mason-Macfarlane	1965-1969	Gerald William Lathbury
1944-1947	Ralph Eastwood	1969 ——	Varyl Cargill Begg

1. During the incumbency of the Duke of Stratheam and Kent, 1802-1820, the administration was carried out by resident lieutenant governors.

Dalton, ed., *English Army Lists*, under individual names.

135 GILBERT AND ELLICE ISLANDS

The Gilbert and Ellice Islands group consists of twenty-five atolls in the South Pacific. Some of these atolls were discovered by Spaniards in the 16th century, and the islands became a center of British and American missionary activity after the 1840's. In 1877 the Gilbert and Ellice Islands came under the general supervision of the Western Pacific High Commission (q.v.) and were formally made a protectorate in 1892. In 1915, at the request of the native rulers, the islands were annexed as a crown colony. From 1941 to 1943 the Gilbert Islands were occupied by the Japanese. After the war, the administration was entrusted to a resident commissioner under the authority of the high commissioner for the Western Pacific.

Resident Commissioners		1933-1941	Jack Charles Barley
1892-1901	Charles Richard Swayne	1941-1946	Vivian Fox-Strangways
1901-1909	W. Telfer Campbell	1946-1949	Henry Evans Maude
1909-1913	John Quayle Dickson	1949-1952	William John Peel
1913-1921	Edward Carlyon Eliot	1952-1961	Michael Louis Bernacchi
1921-1926	Herbert Reginald McClure	1961 ——	Valdemar Jens Andersen
1926-1933	Arthur Francis Grimble		

Information from A. R. Robinson, Colonial Office, London.

136 GOLD COAST

The English, like the Dutch, French, Portuguese, Danish, and others, established trading forts along the Guinea coast of West Africa. From 1632 to 1665 the chief post of the English was Kormantin; afterwards it was moved to Cape Coast Castle. These posts from 1632 to 1821 were under the following administrations:

    1632-1651 Company of Merchants trading to Guinea
    1651-1658 Company of London Merchants
    1658-1663 East India Company
    1663-1672 Company of Royal Adventurers

Great Britain

1672-1751   Royal African Company
1751-1821   Company of Merchants trading to Africa

Until 1751 the government was usually collegial, with the chief factor presiding, and the following list begins only with 1751. In 1821 the crown assumed direct control for the settlements along the Gold Coast, placing them under the control of Sierra Leone (q.v.). In 1850 the nearby Danish settlements (Danish Gold Coast, 3) were purchased and the combined colony ceased to remain under Sierra Leone. From 1866 to 1874, however, the Gold Coast settlements were part of the West Africa Settlements, centered at Sierra Leone. In 1874 the colony of the Gold Coast was erected, with Lagos (v. Nigeria) subordinate to it until 1886. From 1874 to 1906 the colony expanded northwards, annexing Ashanti (q.v.) and the area known as the Northern Territories. In 1906 the limits of the colony were defined. The Gold Coast became the most politically advanced of Britain's African colonies, and in 1951 it was granted a large degree of self-government. Six years later the Gold Coast became the first independent African member of the British Commonwealth as Ghana. In 1960 Ghana became a republic but remained within the Commonwealth.

Chief Agents
1751-1756	Thomas Melvil
1756	William Tymewell
1756-1757	Charles Bell (1)
1757-1761	Nassau Senior
1761-1763	Charles Bell (2)
1763-1766	William Mutter
1766	John Hippisley
1766-1769	Gilbert Petrie
1769-1770	John Grossle
1770-1777	David Mill
1777-1780	Richard Miles (1)
1780-1781	John Roberts
1781-1782	John Bernard Weuves
1782-1784	Richard Miles (2)
1784-1787	James Mourgan
1787	Thomas Price
1787-1789	Thomas Norris
1789-1791	William Fielde
1791-1792	John Gordon (1)
1792-1798	Archibald Dalzel (1)
1798-1799	Jacob Mould (1)
1799-1800	John Gordon (2)
1800-1802	Archibald Dalzel (2)
1802-1805	Jacob Mould (2)
1805-1807	George Torrane
1807-1816	Edward William White
1816-1817	Joseph Dawson
1817-1822	John Hope Smith

Governors
1822-1824	Charles MacCarthy
1824	James Chisholm
1824-1825	Edward Purdon
1825	Charles Turner
1825-1826	Neil Campbell
1826-1827	Henry John Ricketts (1)
1827-1828	Hugh Lumley
1828	George Hingston
1828	Henry John Ricketts (2)

1828-1830	John Jackson
1830-1836	George Maclean (1)
1836-1838	William Topp
1838-1843	George Maclean (2)
1843-1845	Henry Worsley Hill
1845-1846	James Lilley
1846-1849	William Winniett (1)
1849-1850	James Coleman Fitzpatrick
1850	William Winniett (2)
1850-1851	James Bannerman
1851-1854	Stephen John Hill
1854-1857	Henry Connor
1857-1860	Benjamin Chilley Campbell Pine
1860-1862	Edward Bullock Andrews
1862-1866	Richard Pine

Administrators
1867-1872	Herbert Taylor Ussher (1)
1872	John Pope Hennessey
1872-1873	Robert William Harley
1873-1874	Garnet Joseph Wolseley
1874	George Cumine Strahan

Governors
1874-1876	George Cumine Strahan
1876-1879	Stanford Freeling
1879-1880	Herbert Taylor Ussher (2)
1881-1884	Samuel Rowe
1884-1885	William Alexander George Young
1885-1895	William Brandford Griffith
1895-1897	William Edward Maxwell
1897-1900	Frederic Mitchell Hodgson
1900-1904	Matthew Nathan
1904-1910	John Pickersgill Rodger
1910-1912	James Jamieson Thorburn
1912-1919	Hugh Clifford
1919-1927	Frederick Gordon Guggisberg
1927-1932	Alexander Ransford Slater
1932-1934	Thomas Shenton Whitelegge Thomas

1934-1941   Arnold Weinholt Hodson

1941-1948   Alan Cuthbert Maxwell Burns

1948-1949   Gerald Hallen Creasy

1949-1957   Charles Noble Arden-Clarke

Ghana

Governor-General

1957-1960   William Francis Hare, Earl of Listowel

Claridge, 2:582—86. For administrators of the English Gold Coast settlements before 1751, see R. Porter, pp. 199—209.

137 GOLD COAST, NORTHERN TERRITORIES

The area of the Gold Coast north of Ashanti (q.v.) began to be occupied and administratively organized in 1899 and was fully organized by 1906. It represented the rather conglomerate area left to British expansion after the conquest of the kingdom of Ashanti. Much of it had been subject to Ashanti during the 19th century. In 1953 the chief commissioner was replaced by a regional officer. On the independence of the Gold Coast in 1957 the office was abolished.

Chief Commissioners

1899-1904   Arthur Henry Morris

1905-1910   Alan Edward Garrard Watherston

1910-1920   Cecil Hamilton Armitage

1921-1924   Arthur James Philbrick

1924-1930   Arthur Henry Camberlain Walker-Leigh

1930-1933   Francis Walter Fitton Jackson

1933-1942   William John Andrew Jones

1942-1946   George Howard Gibbs

1947-1948   William Harold Ingrams

1948-1950   Edward Norton Jones

1950-1953   Geoffrey Noel Burden

Regional Officers

1953-1954   Arthur John Loveridge

1954-1957   Sydney MacDonald-Smith

Statesman's Year Book, 1899—1957.

138 GOLD COAST COLONY

The Gold Coast Colony is that part of the Gold Coast lying along the coast south of Ashanti (q.v.). In other words, it approximates the area held by Great Britain before the annexation of Ashanti in 1896. It was created a separate region, analogous to those of Ashanti and the Gold Coast, Northern Territories (qq.v.), under a chief commissioner in 1945, but was abolished eight years later.

Chief Commissioners

1945-1950   Thorleif Rattray Orde Mangin

1950-1953   Arthur John Loveridge

Statesman's Year Book, 1945—53.

139 GRENADA

Grenada, one of the Lesser Antilles, was discovered by Columbus in 1498. It was settled by the French in 1650 (v. 30) and remained under France until its capture by the British in 1762. A previous British attempt at a settlement had failed in 1609. Grenada was a member of the Southern Caribbee Islands government until 1779 when it was captured by the French. It was returned to Great Britain in 1783. From 1833 to 1885 Grenada was included in the Windward Islands government centered at Barbados (q.v.). When Barbados was created a separate colony in 1885 Grenada became the seat of the governor of the Windward Islands (q.v.) and the colonial secretary of the Windward Islands government served as administrator of Grenada until 1944. Grenada remained in the Windward Islands government until its dissolution in 1960 when it became a separate colony. In 1967 Grenada became a member of the Associated States of the West Indies.

Governors

1762-1764	George Scott
1764	Robert Melville (1)
1764-1770	Ulysses FitzMaurice (1)
1770-1771	Robert Melville (2)
1771	Ulysses FitzMaurice (2)
1771-1775	William Leybourne Leybourne
1776-1776	William Young
1776-1779	George Macartney, Earl Macartney
1779-1783	(under France)
1784-1785	Edward Mathew
1785-1787	William Lucas[1]
1787-1788	Samuel Williams[1] (1)
1788-1789	James Campbell[1]
1789-1793	Samuel Williams[1] (2)
1793-1795	Ninian Home
1795	Kenneth Francis Mackenzie[1]
1795-1796	Samuel Mitchell[1]
1796-1797	Alexander Houstoun
1797-1801	Charles Green
1801-1802	Samuel Dent[1]

Lieutenant Governors

1802-1803	George Vere Hobart
1803-1804	Thomas Hislop
1804-1805	William Douglas McLean Clephane
1805-1811	Frederick Maitland
1811-1812	Abraham Charles Adye
1812-1813	George Robert Ainslie
1813-1815	Charles Shipley[1]
1815-1816	George Paterson[1] (1)
1816-1823	Phineas Riall
1823-1826	George Paterson[1] (2)

1826-1833	James Campbell
1833-1835	George Middlemore
1835-1836	John Hastings Mair
1836-1846	Carlo Joseph Doyle
1846-1853	Ker Baillie Hamilton
1853-1857	Robert William Keate
1857-1864	Cornelius Hendricksen Kortright
1864-1871	Robert Miller Mundy
1871-1875	Sanford Freeling
1875-1877	Cyril Clerke Graham
1877-1882	Robert William Harley

Administrators

1882	Irwin Charles Maling (1)
1882-1883	Roger Tuckfield Goldsworthy
1883-1886	Edward Daniel Laborde (1)
1886-1887	Irwin Charles Maling (2)
1887-1888	Henry Rawlins Pipon Schooles
1889	Edward Daniel Laborde (2)
1889-1892	John Elliott
1892-1915	Edward Rawle Drayton
1915-1930	Herbert Ferguson
1930-1935	Hilary Rudolph Robert Blood
1935-1940	William Leslie Heape
1940-1942	Charles Harry Vincent Talbot
1942-1951	George Conrad Green
1951-1957	Wallace Macmillan
1957-1962	James Montieth Lloyd
1962-1964	Lionel Achille Pinard
1964-1967	Ian Graham Turbott

Governors

1967-1968	Ian Graham Turbott
1968——	Hilda Louisa Bynoe

1. Presidents.

Information from the Secretary to the Government of Grenada, St. George's, Grenada.

140 GRIQUALAND WEST

Griqualand West assumed importance as a result of the discovery of diamonds there in 1867. The area was hotly disputed between the Cape Colony (q.v.) and the Boer Republic of Transvaal. Most of the area was awarded to the former by arbitration in 1871 and the governor of the Cape Colony became ex officio governor of Griqualand West. However, because of disputes within the Cape Colony the area of Griqualand remained in an administrative limbo until 1880 when it was finally annexed to the Cape Colony.

Lieutenant Governor
1873-1875   Richard Southey

Administrator
1875-1879   Owen William Lanyon

Walker, p. xx.

141 GUADELOUPE

For the British governors of Guadeloupe from 1759 to 1763 and 1810 to 1814, see the French colony, Guadeloupe, 31.

142 HELIGOLAND

Heligoland is a very small (1/4 square mile) island in the North Sea off the northwestern coast of Germany. It was seized from Denmark by Great Britain in 1807 and formally ceded seven years later. The island remained a colony of Great Britain until 1890 when it was ceded to Germany in return for a free hand in Zanzibar (q.v.) and other concessions in Africa.

Lieutenant Governors
1807-1814   Corbet James D'Auvergne
1814-1817   Charles Hamilton
1817-1839   Henry King
1839-1857   John Hindmarsh
1857-1863   Richard Pattinson
1863-1868   Henry Fitzhardinge Berkeley
                     Maxse

Governors
1868-1881   Henry Fitzhardinge Berkeley
                     Maxse
1881-1888   John Terence Nicolls O'Brien
1888-1890   Arthur Cecil Stuart Barkly

Information from N. Jenkins, Colonial Office, London.

143 HONG KONG

Early British interest in the China trade was manifested by the establishment of a factory at Amoy in 1670 but this was shortly afterwards abandoned and trade carried on through the south-western Chinese port of Canton. In 1841 the island of Hong Kong, off the Chinese coast near Canton, was seized by the British and subsequently ceded by China. In 1860 the neighboring Kowloon Peninsula was also ceded to Great Britain as a result of the "Arrow" War. From 1941 to 1945 Hong Kong was occupied by the Japanese. Hong Kong remains a crown colony of Great Britain.

Administrators
1841   Charles Elliot
1841-1843   Henry Eldred Pottinger

Governors
1843-1844   Henry Eldred Pottinger
1844-1848   John Francis Davis
1848-1854   Samuel George Bonham
1854-1859   John Bowring
1859-1865   Hercules George Robert Robinson
1865-1872   Richard Graves MacDonnell
1872-1877   Arthur Edward Kennedy
1877-1882   John Pope Hennessey
1882-1887   George Ferguson Bowen
1887-1891   George William DesVoeux
1891-1898   William Robinson
1898-1903   Henry Arthur Blake
1904-1907   Matthew Nathan
1907-1912   Frederick John Dealtry Lugard
1912-1919   Francis Henry May

1919-1925   Reginald Edward Stubbs
1925-1930   Cecil Clementi
1930-1935   William Peel
1935-1937   Andrew Caldecott
1937-1940   Geoffrey Alexander Northcote
1940-1941   Edward Felix Norton
1941   Mark Aitchison Young

under Japan

Governor
1941-1945   Rensuka Isogai

under Great Britain

Governors
1945-1947   Mark Aitchison Young
1948-1958   Alexander William Grantham
1958-1964   Robert Brown Black
1964—   David Clive Crosbie Trench

Endacott, p. 313.

144 HUDSON'S BAY COMPANY

The Hudson's Bay Company was formed in 1670 to seek a northwest passage to the Orient and to exploit the lucrative fur trade of Canada by flanking the French, already established in the Saint Lawrence valley. The company was granted all rights to lands draining into Hudson's Bay, but initially only established a few posts around the littoral of the bay. (For a more detailed history of these posts v. Rupert's Land.) The company was often forced to fight its French rivals before 1763, and when the French competition was removed it was replaced by that of the "pedlars" or interlopers from British Canada. This competition proved much more serious than that of the French, especially after the formation of the North West Company in 1776. The success of the North West Company nearly caused the Hudson's Bay Company to withdraw completely from the fur trade in 1808. But in the next decade the Hudson's Bay Company began to compete more vigorously. The resulting hostilities benefited no one and in 1821 the two companies merged, retaining the name of the Hudson's Bay Company. A governor-in-chief was soon thereafter appointed over its lands. In 1869 the Hudson's Bay Company sold rights of all its lands to the new Dominion of Canada (q.v.) and after that it existed as a commercial corporation only.

The following list is of the governors of the Hudson's Bay company residing in England. For information on the administration of the company's posts and possessions in Canada, see Rupert's Land.

Governors

1670-1683	Prince Rupert
1683-1685	James Stuart
1685-1691	John Churchill
1691-1696	Stephen Evance (1)
1696-1700	William Trumbull
1700-1712	Stephen Evance (2)
1712-1743	Bibye Lake
1743-1746	Benjamin Pitt
1746-1750	Thomas Knapp
1750-1760	Atwell Lake
1760-1770	William Baker

1770-1782	Bibye Lake, Jr.
1782-1799	Samuel Wegg
1799-1807	James Winter Lake
1807-1812	William Mainwaring
1812-1822	Joseph Berens
1822-1852	John Henry Pelly
1852-1856	Andrew Wedderburn Colvile
1856-1858	John Shepherd
1858-1863	Henry Hulse Berens
1863-1868	Edmund Walker Head
1868-1869	John Wodehouse, Earl of Kimberley
1869-1874	Stafford Henry Northcote

Rich, passim; Willson, p. 531 and passim.

145 INDIA

British interest in India began early in the 17th century when the East India Company established several posts along the various coasts of India. For the history of these posts before 1757, see Bombay, Fort William, Madras, and Surat. As a result of the Seven Years' War and a dispute with the ruler of Bengal, British involvement intensified in 1757. Between 1757 and 1765 all of Bengal and Bihar (qq.v.) came under British control, and Great Britain had become the greatest power in northern India. In 1774 the governor of Bengal was given authority, as governor-general, over all British possessions in India. Once territorially involved in the complex affairs of India, Great Britain soon began to extend its influence throughout the subcontinent. By 1818 all of India except the area of the Punjab was controlled by Great Britain, or rather by the East India Company. In 1846 and 1849 the Punjab (q.v.) was added. In 1858, as an aftermath of the rebellion known as the Sepoy Mutiny, the British crown took over the administration of India. Between 1860 and 1900 the British possessions in India were rounded out by the addition of the Andaman and Nicobar Islands, Baluchistan, Burma, and the area of the North-West Frontier Provinces (qq.v.). Conversely, in 1867 the Straits Settlements (q.v.) was detached from India and created a separate colony. Although there were several hundred "Native States" in subsidiary alliance with the government of British India, the vast proportion of India was under its direct rule. For the administrative provinces into which India was ultimately divided by 1947, see Ajmer-Merwara, the Andaman and Nicobar Islands, Assam, Baluchistan, Bengal, Bihar, Bombay, Burma (to 1937), the Central Provinces and Berar, Coorg, Delhi, Madras, North-West Frontier Provinces, Orissa, Oudh (to 1877), Punjab, Sind, and the United Provinces of Agra and Oudh. These provinces were governed by governors, lieutenant governors, or chief commissioners—their status in the official hierarchy changing over time. India was separately administered by the India Office and was therefore distinct from other British possessions, normally administered by the Colonial Office. In 1947, after a long period of "decolonization," British India became independent. It was divided into two new nations. Most of the predominantly Hindu areas became India, while the predominantly Muslim areas, at the western and eastern extremities of British India, became Pakistan.

Bengal

Governors

1758-1760	Robert Clive (1)
1760-1764	Henry Vansittart
1764-1767	Robert Clive, Baron Clive (2)
1767-1769	Harry Verelst
1769-1772	John Cartier
1772-1774	Warren Hastings

Governors-General

1774-1785	Warren Hastings
1785-1786	John Macpherson
1786-1793	Charles Mann Cornwallis, Marquess Cornwallis (1)
1793-1798	John Shore, Baron Teignmouth
1798-1805	Richard Colley Wellesley, Earl of Mornington

Great Britain

1805	Charles Mann Cornwallis, Marquess Cornwallis (2)	1876–1880	Edward Robert Bulwer-Lytton, Earl of Lytton
1805–1807	George Hilaro Barlow	1880–1884	George Frederick Samuel Robinson, Marquess of Ripon
1807–1813	Gilbert Elliot-Murray-Kynynmond, Earl of Minto	1884–1888	Frederick Temple Hamilton-Temple-Blackwood, Marquess of Dufferin
1813–1823	Francis Rawdon-Hastings, Earl of Moira	1888–1894	Henry Charles Keith Petty-Fitzmaurice, Marquess of Lansdowne
1823–1828	William Pitt Amherst, Earl Amherst	1894–1899	Victor Alexander Bruce, Earl of Elgin and Kincardine
1828–1833	William Cavendish Bentinck	1899–1905	George Nathaniel Curzon, Marquess Curzon

India

Governors-General

1833–1835	William Cavendish Bentinck	1905–1910	Gilbert John Elliot-Murray-Kynynmond, Earl of Minto
1835–1836	Charles Theophilus Metcalfe, Baron Metcalfe	1910–1916	Charles Hardinge, Baron Hardinge
1836–1842	George Eden, Earl of Auckland	1916–1921	Frederick John Napier Thesiger, Baron Chelmsford
1842–1844	Edward Law, Earl of Ellenborough	1921–1926	Rufus Daniel Isaacs, Marquess of Reading
1844–1848	Henry Hardinge, Viscount Hardinge	1926–1931	Edward Frederick Lindley Wood-Halifax, Baron Irwin
1848–1856	James Andrew Broun Ramsay, Marquess of Dalhousie	1931–1936	Freeman Freeman-Thomas, Marquess of Willingdon
1856–1858	Charles John Canning, Earl Canning	1936–1943	Victor Alexander Hope, Marquess of Linlithgow
		1943–1947	Archibald Percival Wavell, Viscount Wavell

Viceroys

1858–1862	Charles John Canning, Earl Canning	1947	Louis Francis Mountbatten, Earl Mountbatten
1862–1863	James Bruce, Earl of Elgin and Kincardine		
1864–1869	John Laird Mair Lawrence, Baron Lawrence	*Governors-General*	
1869–1872	Richard Southwell Bourke, Earl of Mayo	1947–1948	Louis Francis Mountbatten, Earl Mountbatten
1872–1876	Thomas George Baring, Earl of Northbrook	1948–1950	Chakravarti Rajagopalachari

Mersey, passim.

146 IONIAN ISLANDS

The islands of Cephalonia, Cerigo, Corfu, Ithaca, Leucas, Paxo, and Zante, located in the Ionian Sea off the coast of western Greece, were occupied by Venice until 1797 when they were ceded to France. In 1799 Russia occupied the islands and created in 1800 the Septinsular Republic under its protection. Surrendered to France by the Treaty of Tilsit, they were occupied in 1809 by Great Britain. Britain, like Russia, established a protectorate over the islands. Finally, in 1864, in response to demands from the inhabitants of the islands, they were ceded to Greece.

Lord High Commissioners

1815–1824	Thomas Maitland	1832–1835	George Nugent Grenville, Baron Nugent
1824–1832	Frederick Adam	1835–1841	Howard Douglas

1841-1843	James Alexander Stuart Mackenzie	1855-1859	John Young
1843-1849	John Colborne, Baron Seaton	1859	William Ewart Gladstone
1849-1855	Henry George Ward	1859-1864	Henry Knight Storks

Kirkwall, 1:75-288.

147 IRAQ

The area of Mesopotamia came under British control as a result of several campaigns during World War I. After the war the area, thereafter known as Iraq, was, like the other Asian possessions of the Ottoman Empire, granted as a mandate by the League of Nations, in this case to Great Britain. Iraq was virtually independent during this period although a high commissioner was appointed who "advised" the king, and British advisors were attached to the various ministries. Finally in 1932 the mandate was terminated and Iraq became fully independent.

Mesopotamia
Civil Commissioners

1914-1917	Percy Zachariah Cox (1)
1917-1920	Arnold Talbot Wilson

Iraq
High Commissioners

1920-1923	Percy Zachariah Cox (2)
1923-1928	Henry Robert Conway Dobbs
1928-1929	Gilbert Falkingham Clayton
1929-1932	Francis Henry Humphrys

Longrigg, passim.

148 IRISH FREE STATE

Part of Ireland came under English control in 1171 and by the beginning of the 17th century the entire island had been conquered. However, the Irish never accepted British control with equanimity and centuries of tension culminated in the Easter Rebellion of 1916. The resulting civil war was only ended by treaty in 1921 by which Ireland (the Ulster counties excepted) was granted dominion status as the Irish Free State. This proved to be a wholly unsuitable arrangement which solved nothing and satisfied no one. The nominal relationship with Great Britain was largely ignored in the Irish Free State, and the office of governor-general, always held by Irishmen, was abolished in 1936. Although the concept of a republic within the British Commonwealth had not yet been mooted, Ireland (now known as Eire) was in fact a republic in all but name, with a president replacing the governor-general, and any allegiance to the British monarch forgotten in fact, if not yet in form. In 1949 Eire formally withdrew from the Commonwealth and proclaimed itself a republic.

127

Great Britain

Governors-General
1922-1928   Timothy Michael Healy
1928-1932   James McNeill
1932-1936   Domhnall Ua Buachalla (Donald
            Buckley)

Statesman's Year Book, 1922-37.

149 JAMAICA

Jamaica is the largest British possession in the West Indies. Until 1655 it was a Spanish colony (350), but it was then occupied by the English. During the rest of the century it served as a headquarters for English raids on Spanish possessions around the Caribbean Sea. Until 1866 Jamaica possessed representative government but it was withdrawn from 1866 to 1944. The governor of Jamaica was ex officio governor of the Bay Islands (q.v.) from 1852 to 1861. The Cayman Islands (q.v.) from 1734 to 1962, and the Turks and Caicos Islands (q.v.) from 1874 to 1962 were dependencies of Jamaica. From 1958 to 1961 Jamaica was the principal member of the West Indie Federation (q.v.). In 1962 Jamaica became an independent member of the British Commonwealth.

Governors

1655-1656	Edward D'Oyley (1)
1656-1657	William Brayne
1657-1662	Edward D'Oyley (2)
1662-1663	Thomas Hickman Windsor
1663	Charles Lyttleton[1]
1663-1664	Thomas Lynch[1] (1)
1664-1671	Thomas Modyford
1671-1675	Thomas Lynch[1] (2)
1675-1678	John Vaughan
1678-1680	Charles Howard, Earl of Carlisle
1680-1682	Henry Morgan[1]
1682-1684	Thomas Lynch (3)
1684-1687	Hender Molesworth
1687-1688	Christopher Monck, Duke of Albemarle
1688-1690	Francis Watson[2]
1690-1691	William O'Brien, Earl of Inchiquin
1691-1692	John White[2]
1692-1693	John Bourden[2]
1693-1702	William Beeston[1]
1702	William Selwyn
1702	Peter Beckford[1]
1702-1711	Thomas Handasyde
1711-1716	Archibald Hamilton
1716-1718	Peter Heywood
1718-1722	Nicholas Lawes
1722-1726	Henry Bentinck, Duke of Portland
1726-1728	John Ayscough[2] (1)
1728-1734	Robert Hunter
1734-1735	John Ayscough[2] (2)
1735-1736	Henry Cunninghame
1736-1738	John Gregory[2]

1738-1752	Edward Trelawney
1752-1756	Charles Knowles
1756-1759	Henry Moore[1] (1)
1759	George Haldane
1759-1762	Henry Moore[1] (2)
1762-1766	William Henry Lyttelton, Baron Westcote
1766-1767	Roger Hope Elletson[1]
1767-1772	William Trelawney
1772-1774	John Dalling[1] (1)
1774-1777	Basil Keith
1777-1781	John Dalling[1] (2)
1781-1784	Archibald Campbell
1784-1790	Alured Clarke[1]
1790-1791	Thomas Howard, Earl of Effingham
1791-1795	Adam Williamson[1]
1795-1801	Alexander Lindsay, Earl of Balcarres
1801-1806	George Nugent
1806-1808	Eyre Coote
1808-1827	William Montagu, Duke of Manchester
1827-1829	John Keane[1]
1829-1832	Somerset Lowry-Corry, Earl Belmore
1832-1834	Constantine Henry Phipps, Earl of Mulgrave
1834-1836	Howe Peter Browne, Marquess of Sligo
1836-1839	Lionel Smith
1839-1842	Charles Theophilus Metcalfe
1842-1846	James Bruce, Earl of Elgin and Kincardine

1846-1847	George Henry Frederick Berkeley	1907-1913	Sydney Haldane Olivier
1847-1853	Charles Edward Grey	1913-1918	William Henry Manning
1853-1856	Henry Barkly	1918-1924	Leslie Probyn
1856-1857	Edward Wells Bell[1]	1924-1926	Samuel Herbert Wilson
1857-1862	Charles Henry Darling	1926-1932	Reginald Edward Stubbs
1862-1866	Edward John Eyre	1932-1934	Alexander Ransford Slater
1866	Henry Knight Storks	1934-1938	Edward Brandis Denham
1866-1874	John Peter Grant	1938-1943	Arthur Frederick Richards
1874-1877	William Grey	1943-1951	John Huggins
1877-1879	Edward Everard Rushworth	1951-1957	Hugh Mackintosh Foot
1879-1883	Anthony Musgrave	1957-1962	Kenneth William Blackburne
1883-1889	Henry Wylie Norman		
1889-1898	Henry Arthur Blake	*Governors-General*	
1898-1904	Augustus William Lawson Hemming	1962	Kenneth William Blackburne
1904-1907	James Alexander Swettenham	1962—	Clifford Clarence Campbell

1. Lieutenant Governor.
2. President.

Andrews, pp. 445–57; Burns, pp. 252–61; 314–24, 326–37, 379–83, 444–52, 492–96, 510–13, 550–52, 598–600, 641–43; Cundall, *The Governors of Jamaica in the Seventeenth Century*, pp. xiii-xvi and passim; idem, *The Governors of Jamaica in the First Half of the Eighteenth Century*, pp. xv-xvii and passim.

150 JAVA

For the British governors of Java from 1811 to 1816, see Netherlands East Indies, 275.

151 KENYA

The Anglo-German Agreement of 1886 designated the area later known as Kenya to be within the projected British sphere of influence under the terms of the Berlin Conference of 1884/85. Great Britain had already acquired a preponderant influence in Zanzibar (q.v.), the sultan of which claimed a vague hegemony over the mainland opposite. In 1887 the sultan "conceded" to the Imperial British East Africa Company the administration of whatever mainland claims remained to him after the creation of German East Africa (71). In 1890 a British protectorate was proclaimed over the sultanate of Witu. The main efforts of the I.B.E.A. were directed toward Buganda, of reputed strategic and commercial importance, and the intervening area was regarded almost solely as a means of access to Buganda. The effort required to control Buganda ruined the I.B.E.A. financially, and a British protectorate was proclaimed there in 1894 (v. Uganda). In the following year the Foreign Office similarly assumed control of the company's possessions in East Africa known as the East Africa Protectorate, and a commissioner was appointed who was also, until 1904, the consul-general in Zanzibar. In 1906 control was transferred to the Colonial Office and a governor appointed. In 1920 the area of the East Africa Protectorate, with the exception of the coastal strip originally leased from Zanzibar, was created a crown colony with the name Kenya. Kenya acquired a large white settler population after 1920, thereby exacerbating relations with the African peoples. Nationalistic impulses in the 1950's, marked by the so-called Mau Mau Rebellion, created a decade of mutual distrust. In 1963 Kenya became independent within the British Commonwealth and one year later it proclaimed itself a republic.

British East Africa		*Kenya*	
Commissioners[1]		*Governors*	
1888-1890	George Sutherland Mackenzie (1)	1920-1922	Edward Northey
1890-1891	Francis Walter de Winton	1922-1925	Robert Thorne Coryndon
1891	George Sutherland Mackenzie (2)	1925-1931	Edward Macleay Grigg
1891-1892	Ernest James Lennox Berkeley	1931-1937	Joseph Aloysius Byrne
1892-1895	John Robert Wilson Pigott	1937-1940	Henry Robert Brooke-Popham
1896-1900	Arthur Henry Hardinge	1940-1944	Henry Monck-Mason Moore
1900-1904	Charles Norton Edgecumbe Eliot	1944-1952	Philip Euen Mitchell
1904-1905	Donald William Stewart	1952-1957	Evelyn Baring
1905-1906	James Hayes Sadler	1957-1959	Frederick Crawford
		1959-1963	Patrick Muir Renison
Governors		1963	Malcolm John MacDonald
1906-1909	James Hayes Sadler		
1909-1912	Edward Percy Cranwill Girouard		
1912-1919	Henry Conway Belfield	1963-1964	Malcolm John MacDonald
1919-1920	Edward Northey		

1. To 1895 the commissioners were appointed by the Imperial British East Africa Company.

Colonial Office List, 1906 to 1963; Mungeam, p. 289; Vere-Hodge, p. v.

152 KUWAIT

The sheikhdom of Kuwait was situated at the western end of the Persian Gulf. During the 19th century it was nominally under the jurisdiction of the Ottoman authorities at Basra. In 1904, in order to free himself of Ottoman constraints, the sheikh recognized the protection of the British, who had longstanding interests in the Persian Gulf (q.v.) area and a political agent was appointe. The political agents were subject to the authority of the British chief political resident of the Pe sian Gulf. The protected status of Kuwait was terminated in 1961 and it became fully independe

Political Agents		1936-1939	Gerald S. H. DeGaury
1904-1909	Stuart George Knox	1939-1941	Arnold Crawshaw Galloway (1)
1909-1915	William Henry Irvine Shakespear	1941-1943	Tom Hickinbotham
1915-1916	William George Grey	1943-1945	Maurice O'Connor Tandy
1916-1918	Robert Edward Archibald	1945-1947	Arnold Crawshaw Galloway (2)
	Hamilton	1947-1951	Herbert George Jakins
1918	Percy Gordon Loch	1951-1955	Cornelius James Pelly
1918-1920	D. V. MacCollum	1955-1957	Gawain Westray Bell
1920-1930	James Carmichael More	1957-1959	Aubrey Seymour Halford
1930-1936	Harold Richard Patrick Dickson	1959-1961	John Christopher Blake Richmond

Information from M. I. Moir, Indian Office Records, London.

153 LABUAN

Labuan is a small island (28.6 sq. mi.) situated off the north coast of Borneo. The British first attempted to settle it in 1775 but failed. In 1846 it was ceded to Britain by the sultan of Brunei (q.v.). Great Britain needed the previously uninhabited island because it was "desirable that British ships shall have some port where they may careen and fit and deposit such stores and merchandise as shall be necessary for the carrying on of trade" with Brunei. In return the British navy undertook to suppress piracy in the area. In 1848 Labuan became a crown colony. Financial difficulties led to its being entrusted to the control of the British North Borneo Company in 1890. In 1905 the governor of the Straits Settlements (q.v.) became ex officio governor of Labuan and two years later the island was annexed to the Straits Settlements.

Lieutenant Governors
1847-1848   James Brooke
1848-1850   William Napier
1850-1856   John Scott

Governors
1856-1861   George Warren Edwardes
1861-1866   Jeremiah Thomas Fitzgerald
              Callaghan

1866-1867   Hugh Low
1867-1871   John Pope Hennessey
1871-1875   Henry Ernest Gascoyne Bulwer
1875-1879   Herbert Taylor Ussher
1879-1881   Charles Cameron Lees
1881-1888   Peter Leys
1888-1890   Arthur Shirley Hamilton

Colonial Office List, 1890.

154 LEEWARD ISLANDS

The scattered British possessions in the Lesser Antilles were organized into the Leeward Islands government in 1671. These included Antigua, Montserrat, British Virgin Islands, Saint Kitts, Nevis (qq.v.), Barbuda, and Anguilla. From 1816 to 1833 the Leeward Islands were divided into two separate administrative units, but they were united again in 1833 at which time Dominica (q.v.) acquired in 1761, was added. From 1871 the Leeward Islands was a federal colony. The seat of the government remained on the island of Antigua. In 1960 the Leeward Islands government, along with its counterpart the Windward Islands government (q.v.) was abolished and its constituent parts became separate colonies.

Governors
1671-1672   Charles Wheler
1672-1685   William Stapleton
1685-1689   Nathaniel Johnson
1689-1698   Christopher Codrington
1698-1699   Edward Fox
1699-1704   Christopher Codrington II
1704   William Mathew
1704-1706   John Johnson
1706-1710   Daniel Parke
1710-1711   Walter Hamilton (1)
1711-1714   Walter Douglas
1714-1715   William Mathew, Jr. (1)
1715-1721   Walter Hamilton (2)
1721-1727   John Hart

1727-1729   Thomas Pitt, Earl of Londonderry
1729-1752   William Mathew, Jr. (2)
1753-1766   George Thomas
1766-1768   James Verchild
1768-1771   William Woodley
1771-1776   Ralph Payne (1)
1776-1781   William Mathew Burt
1781-1788   Thomas Shirley (1)
1788-1790   John Nugent
1790-1791   Thomas Shirley (2)
1791-1794   William Woodley
1795-1799   Charles Leigh
1799-1808   Ralph Payne, Baron Lavington (2)
1808-1813   Hugh Elliot
1814-1816   James Leith

Great Britain

Antigua-Montserrat-Barbuda
Governors
1816-1820 George William Ramsay
1820-1826 Benjamin D'Urban
1826-1832 Patrick Ross
1832-1833 Evan John Murray McGregor

Saint Kitts-Nevis-Anguilla-British Virgin Islands
Governor
1816-1833 Charles William Maxwell

Leeward Islands
Governors
1833-1837 Evan John Murray McGregor
1837-1842 William McBean George Colebrooke
1842-1846 Charles Augustus Fitzroy
1846-1850 James Macaulay Higginson
1850-1855 Robert James Mackintosh
1855-1862 Ker Baillie Hamilton
1862-1869 Stephen John Hill
1869-1873 Benjamin Chilley Campbell Pine
1873-1875 Henry Turner Irving

1875-1881 George Berkeley
1881-1884 John Hawley Glover
1884-1885 Charles Cameron Lees
1885-1888 Jenico William Joseph Preston, Viscount Gormanston
1888   Charles Bullen Hugh Mitchell
1888-1895 William Frederick Haynes Smith
1895-1901 Francis Fleming
1901-1902 Henry Moore Jackson
1902-1904 Gerald Strickland
1904-1906 Clement Courtenay Knollys
1906-1912 Ernest Bickham Sweet-Escott
1912-1916 Henry Hesketh Joudou Bell
1916-1921 Edward Marsh Merewether
1921-1929 Eustace Edward Twisleton-Wykeham-Fiennes
1929-1936 Thomas Reginald St. Johnston
1936-1941 Gordon James Lethem
1941-1943 Douglas James Jardine
1943-1948 Leslie Brian Freeston
1948-1950 Oliver Ridsdale Baldwin, Earl Baldwin
1950-1957 Kenneth William Blackburne
1957-1960 Alexander Thomas Williams

Burns, pp. 338—51, 374—79, 413—25, 457—62, 498—99, 508—10, 544—48, 602—4, 655; Harper, pp. 4—18.

155 MADRAS

The headquarters of English commercial interests along India's Coromandel coast was Masulipatam from 1611 until 1641 when it was moved to Madras. Until 1652 Madras was under Bantam (q.v.) in Java, where the main English factory was located at that time. In 1652 Madras was raised to the rank of a presidency but it lapsed to agency status in 1655. In 1684 it again became a presidency. From 1746 to 1749 the French occupied Madras and the presidency was removed to Fort St. David near Cuddalore down the coast from Madras. In 1947 Madras acceded to the Indian Union (v. India) in which it became a state.

Governors
1641-1643 Andrew Cogan
1643-1644 Francis Day
1644-1648 Thomas Ivie
1648-1652 Henry Greenhill (1)
1652-1655 Aaron Baker
1655-1658 Henry Greenhill (2)
1659-1661 Thomas Chamber
1661-1665 Edward Winter (1)
1665   George Foxcroft (1)
1665-1668 Edward Winter (2)
1668-1670 George Foxcroft (2)
1670-1678 William Langhorne
1678-1681 Streynsham Master

1681-1687 William Gyfford
1687-1692 Elihu Yale
1692-1698 Nathaniel Higginson
1698-1709 Thomas Pitt
1709   Gulston Addison
1709-1711 William Fraser
1711-1717 Edward Harrison
1717-1720 Joseph Collet
1720-1721 Francis Hastings
1721-1725 Nathaniel Elwich
1725-1730 James Macrae
1730-1735 George Morton Pitt
1735-1743 Richard Benyon
1743-1746 Nicholas Morse

1746-1747	John Hinde	1854-1859	George Francis Robert Harris, Baron Harris
1747-1750	Charles Floyer	1859-1860	Charles Edward Trevelyan
1750-1755	Thomas Saunders	1861-1866	William Thomas Denison
1755-1763	George Pigot (1)	1866-1872	Francis Napier, Baron Ettrick
1763-1767	Robert Palk	1872-1875	Vere Henry Hobart
1767-1770	Charles Bourchier	1875-1880	Richard Plantagenet Campbell Temple-Nugent-Brydges-Chandos-Grenville, Duke of Buckingham and Chandos
1770-1773	Josias Dupré		
1773-1775	Alexander Wynch		
1775-1776	George Pigot (2)		
1776-1777	George Stratton	1880-1881	William Patrick Adam
1777-1778	John Whitehill	1881-1886	Montstuart Elphinstone Grant-Duff
1778-1780	Thomas Rumbold		
1781-1785	George Macartney	1886-1891	Robert Bourke, Baron Connemara
1786-1789	Archibald Campbell	1891-1896	Beilby Lawley, Baron Wenlock
1789-1790	John Hollond	1896-1901	Arthur Elibank Havelock
1790-1792	William Medows	1901-1906	Oliver Arthur Villiers Russell, Baron Ampthill
1792-1794	Charles Oakley		
1794-1798	Robert Hobart, Earl of Buckinghamshire	1906-1911	Arthur Lawley
		1911-1912	Thomas David Gibson-Carmichael, Baron Carmichael
1798	George Harris		
1798-1803	Edward Clive, Baron Powis	1912-1919	John Sinclair, Baron Pentland
1803-1807	William Cavendish Bentinck	1919-1924	Freeman Freeman-Thomas, Marquess of Willingdon
1807-1814	George Hilaro Barlow		
1814-1820	Hugh Elliot	1924-1929	George Joachim Goschen, Viscount Goschen
1820-1827	Thomas Munro		
1827-1832	Stephen Rumbold Lushington	1929-1934	George Frederick Stanley
1832-1837	Frederick Adam	1934-1940	Thomas Wilfred Erskine, Viscount Erskine
1837-1842	John Elphinstone, Baron Elphinstone		
1842-1848	George Hay, Marquess of Tweeddale	1940-1946	Arthur Oswald James Hope, Baron Rankeillour
1848-1854	Henry Eldred Pottinger	1946-1947	Archibald Edward Nye

India Office List and Burma Office List, 1947, pp. 23—24; Love, 3:543—46.

156 MALAYA

Before 1942 the British possessions in Malaya were governed by the governor of the Straits Settlements (q.v.) who served as high commissioner to the Unfederated Malay States as well as having jurisdiction over the chief secretaries of the Federated Malay States (q.v.). After World War II these governments were abolished and replaced by the Union of Malaya, which encompassed them all except Singapore, which was made a separate colony. Simultaneously, from 1946 to 1948 the office of governor-general of Malaya existed with jurisdiction over Malaya, Singapore, British North Borneo, Sarawak, and Brunei (qq.v.). In 1948 the Union of Malaya was replaced by the Federation of Malaya and the governor became high commissioner. The office of governor-general was abolished and replaced by that of commissioner-general whose jurisdiction was all of Southeast Asia. In 1957 Malaya became a self-governing dominion. In 1963 Malaya, together with other former British colonies in Southeast Asia, united to form Malaysia. Malaysia remains in the Commonwealth as one of its three monarchies.

Great Britain

High Commissioners
1946-1948 Gerard Edward James Gent
1948-1951 Henry Lovell Goldsworthy Gurney
1952-1954 Gerald Walter Robert Templer

1954-1957 Donald Charles McGillivray

Governor-General
1946-1948 Malcolm John McDonald

Statesman's Year Book, 1946 to 1957.

157 MALTA

The colony of Malta consisted of the islands of Malta, Gozo, and Comino, situated in the Mediterranean Sea directly south of Sicily. Until 1798 Malta was occupied by the Knights of Jerusalem. In that year it was conquered by Napoleon. In 1799–1800 the British occupied the islands. The Treaty of Amiens of 1802 had provided for the return of Malta to the Knights, but this provision was never implemented and they were permanently annexed by Great Britain in 1814 by terms of the Treaty of Paris. In 1813 the civil commissioner gave way to a military governor who was in turn replaced by a civil governor in 1847. In deference to the islands' population the governors were Roman Catholic. Malta remained a crown colony until 1921 when it was given representative government. In 1933 it reverted to crown colony status. In 1964 Malta became an independent member of the British Commonwealth.

Civil Commissioners
1799-1801 Alexander John Ball (1)
1801   Henry Pigot
1801-1802 Charles Cameron
1802-1809 Alexander John Ball (2)
1810-1813 Hildebrand Oakes

Governors
1813-1824 Thomas Maitland
1824-1826 Francis Rawdon-Hastings, Earl
             of Moira
1827-1836 Frederick Cavendish Ponsonby
1836-1843 Henry Frederick Bouverie
1843-1847 Patrick Stuart
1847-1851 Richard More O'Farrell
1851-1858 William Reid
1858-1864 John Gaspard LeMarchant
1864-1866 Henry Knight Storks
1867-1872 Patrick Grant
1872-1878 Charles Thomas Van Straubenzee
1878-1884 Arthur Borton
1884-1888 John Lintorn Arabin Simmons
1888-1890 Henry D'Oyley Torrens
1890-1893 Henry Augustus Smyth
1893-1899 Arthur James Lyon Fremantle

1899-1903 Francis Wallace Grenfell, Baron
             Grenfell
1903-1907 Charles Mansfield Clarke
1907-1909 Henry Fane Grant
1909-1915 Henry Macleod Leslie Rundle
1915-1919 Paul Sanford Methuen, Baron
             Methuen
1919-1924 Herbert Charles Plumer, Baron
             Plumer
1924-1927 Walter Norris Congreve
1927-1931 John Philip DuCane
1931-1936 David Graham Campbell
1936-1940 Charles Bonham-Carter
1940-1942 William George Dobbie
1942-1944 John Standish Surtees Prendergast
             Vereker, Viscount Gort
1944-1946 Edmond Charles Screiber
1946-1949 Francis Campbell Douglas
1949-1954 Gerald Hallen Creasy
1954-1959 Robert Edward Laycock
1959-1962 Guy Grantham
1962-1964 Maurice Henry Dorman

Governors-General
1964—   Maurice Henry Dorman

Luke, pp. 195–96.

158 MARTINIQUE

For the British governors of Martinique from 1762 to 1763, 1794 to 1802, and 1809 to 1814, see the French colony, Martinique, 41.

159 MARYLAND

The area of Maryland was granted to George Calvert in 1632 and created from part of the area granted Virginia (q.v.) earlier. It was colonized in 1634. Maryland was the first English colony in North America officially to establish freedom of worship. Part of Maryland was lost when the colony of Pennsylvania (q.v.) was created in 1681. Maryland was a proprietary colony from 1632 to 1691, and again from 1716 to 1776. During the latter period, however, the rights of the proprietor were confined to receiving the revenues of the colony. In 1776 Maryland expelled its governor and terminated its status as a British colony.

Governors

1634–1647	Leonard Calvert	1698–1701	Nathaniel Blackistone
1647–1648	Thomas Green	1703–1709	John Seymour
1648–1654	William Stone	1709–1714	Edward Lloyd
1654–1657	Richard Bennett	1714–1720	John Hart
1657–1660	Josias Fendall	1720–1726	Charles Calvert (1)
1660–1661	Philip Calvert	1726–1731	Benedict Leonard Calvert
1661–1676	Charles Calvert (1)	1731–1732	Samuel Ogle (1)
1676–1681	Thomas Noltey	1732–1735	Charles Calvert (2)
1681–1684	Charles Calvert (2)	1735–1742	Samuel Ogle (2)
1684–1688	William Joseph	1742–1747	Thomas Bladen
1691–1693	Lionel Copley	1747–1752	Samuel Ogle (3)
1693–1694	Thomas Lawrence	1752–1753	Benjamin Taskar
1694–1698	Francis Nicholson	1753–1769	Horatio Sharpe
		1769–1776	Robert Eden

Kummer, 1:313–14.

160 MASSACHUSETTS BAY

Massachusetts Bay was colonized in 1629 under the auspices of the Massachusetts Bay Company. The colony was the most successful in New England. After 1668 it governed Maine. New Hampshire (q.v.) was under Massachusetts until 1680, and from 1692 to 1741. In 1684 the charter of the company was revoked and Massachusetts Bay became a royal colony. From 1686 to 1689 it was part of the Dominion of New England. In 1692 Massachusetts Bay absorbed its neighbor New Plymouth (q.v.) and became known as Massachusetts. After 1750 Massachusetts became the most outspoken of the American colonies in opposing the policies of Great Britain regarding its colonies. In 1775 Massachusetts expelled the last of its royal governors.

Great Britain

Hart, 1:607, and 2:591; Whitmore, pp. 16–17, 43–44.

161 MAURITIUS

The island of Mauritius in the western Indian Ocean had previously been occupied by the Dutch (272) and the French (42). During the Napoleonic Wars it served as a base for privateering raids on English shipping in the Indian Ocean. Consequently the British seized the island in 1810, and they retained it after the peace of 1814. From 1810 to 1903 the Seychelles (q.v.) were a dependency of Mauritius. In 1968 Mauritius became an independent member of the British Commonwealth.

1942-1949	Henry Charles Donald Cleveland Mackenzie-Kennedy	1962-1968	John Shaw Rennie
1949-1953	Hilary Rudolph Robert Blood	*Governors-General*	
1953-1959	Robert Scott	1968	John Shaw Rennie
1959-1962	Colville Montgomery Deverell	1968—	Arthur Leonard Williams

Toussaint, under individual names.

162 MINORCA

Minorca, the most easterly of the Balearic Islands in the western Mediterranean, was seized from Spain by Great Britain in 1708, and retained by the Treaty of Utrecht five years later. It was captured by the French in 1756 but returned to Great Britain in 1763. The island was surrendered to the Spanish in 1782, recovered in 1798, and finally ceded to Spain in 1802. During the 18th century Minorca was more highly regarded for its strategic value by the British than Gibraltar (q.v.), but the results of sieges of both in the 1780's proved that Gibraltar would be the more valuable, if only because it was more easily defended. The administration of Minorca, like that of Gibraltar at the same time, was rather ill-defined. There might be either a governor or a lieutenant governor, or both simultaneously, at Port Mahon, and occasionally an additional lieutenant governor at Fort Saint Philip, of inferior status to his counterpart at Port Mahon. The office of governor tended in some instances to be a sinecure, with the governor remaining at home or attending to duties elsewhere in the Mediterranean. In certain cases (e.g., Kane and Murray), a lieutenant governor would be raised to the rank of governor. Kane was lieutenant governor of Gibraltar at the same time he was serving in Minorca. This situation is reflected in many of the secondary sources, which fail adequately to distinguish the precise office held by individuals administering the island. The following list is itself incomplete, although perhaps the nature of the British administration of Minorca was such that this is inevitable. None of the lieutenant governors at Fort Saint Philip is included.

Governors

1708-1711	James Stanhope
1711-1713	John Campbell, Duke of Argyll (1)
1713-1714	Charles Mordaunt, Earl of Peterborough
1714-1716	John Campbell, Duke of Argyll (2)
1716-1718	George Carpenter
1718-1719	George Forbes
1730-1737	Richard Kane
1737-1742	Algernon Seymour, Earl of Hertford
1742-1747	John Dalrymple, Earl of Stair
1747-1756	James O'Hara, Earl of Tyrawley

Lieutenant Governors

1711-1712	John Fermor
1712-1729	Richard Kane
1737-	William Pinfold
-1742	Richard Offarell (or D'Offarell)
1742-1743	Philip Anstruther
1743-1745	Roger Handasyde
1745-1748	John Wynyard
1748-1756	William Blakeney

under France

Governors

1756-1758	Hyacinthe-Cajetan de Lannion (1)
1758-1759	Jean-Toussaint de la Pierre de Frémeur
1759-1760	Louis-Félicien de Boffin d'Argenson et Pusignieu (1)
1760-1762	Hyacinthe-Cajetan de Lannion (2)
1762-1763	Louis-Félicien de Boffin d'Argenson et Pusignieu (2)

under Great Britain

Governors

1763-1766	Richard Lyttelton
1766-1768	George Howard
1768-1778	John Mostyn
1779-1782	James Murray
1782-1798	(under Spain)
1798-1800	Charles Stuart
1801-1802	Henry Edward Fox

Great Britain

Colonial Office: "Minorca Correspondence" (C.O. 174/1—21, in Public Record Office, London. Also, Dalton, *George the First's Army*, under individual names; idem, *English Army Lists*, under individual names; Guillon, passim.

163 MONTSERRAT

The island of Montserrat in the Lesser Antilles was discovered by Columbus in 1493 and named for the famous Spanish monastery of that name. It was settled by the English from Saint Kitts (q.v.) in 1632, and became part of the Leeward Islands (q.v.) government in 1671. The practice of appointing deputy or lieutenant governors for Montserrat fell into disuse in the 18th century, and although a few were appointed later, the office was a sinecure with the appointee remaining in England. In 1667, and from 1782 to 1784, Montserrat was occupied by the French. Each time it was returned to Great Britain by treaty. From 1854 administrators, and later, commissioners, governed the island. Montserrat remained a member of the Leeward Islands until the dissolution of that government in 1960. Since then it has remained a separate colony. To date it has not joined the Associated States of the West Indies.

Information from the office of the Administrator of Montserrat, Plymouth, Montserrat. Also, Public Record Office, *C.S.P.*, *Colonial*, *1661—68* to *1737*, passim; idem, *Journal of the Commissioners for Trade and Plantations, 1704—8/1709* to *1734—41*, passim.

164 MOSKITO COAST

The area known as the Moskito (or Mosquito) Coast is situated along the eastern coast of what is now Nicaragua. As a result of a treaty by which a native ruler ceded his lands to Great Britain a superintendent was appointed in 1740 to supervise the logging settlements. In 1782 the office was abolished as British interests in Central America focused at Belize (in British Honduras, q.v.) to the north. However, a shadowy protectorate was maintained by Great Britain over the area until 1860 when these rights were transferred to Nicaragua (358).

Superintendents			
1740-1759	Robert Hodgson	1768-1776	Robert Hodgson, Jr.
1759-1768	Joseph Otway	1776	John Ferguson
		1776-1782	James Lawrie

Floyd, p. 214.

165 NATAL

The colony of Natal was established in 1843 to prevent the trekking Boers from securing an outlet on the Indian Ocean and thereby lessening their dependence on the Cape Colony (q.v.). The colony never prospered and was granted responsible government only in 1893. Zululand (q.v.) and Tongaland were incorporated into the colony in 1897. Natal, with the Orange River Colony, Transvaal, and the Cape Colony (qq.v.) united in 1910 to form the Union of South Africa (q.v.).

Lieutenant Governors		*Governors*	
1843-1844	Henry Cloete	1880-1881	George Pomeroy Colley
1845-1849	Martin Thomas West	1881-1882	Charles Bullen Hugh Mitchell (1)
1849-1855	Benjamin Chilley Campbell Pine (1)	1882-1885	Henry Gascoyne Ernest Bulwer (2)
1856-1864	John Scott	1885-1889	Arthur Elibank Havelock
1864-1865	John Maclean	1889-1893	Charles Bullen Hugh Mitchell (2)
1865-1867	John Jarvis Besset	1893-1901	Walter Francis Hely-Hutchinson
1867-1872	Robert William Keate	1901-1907	Henry Edward McCallum
1872-1873	Anthony Musgrave	1907-1909	Matthew Nathan
1873-1875	Benjamin Chilley Campbell Pine (2)	1909-1910	Paul Sanford Methuen, Baron
1875	Garnet Joseph Wolseley		Methuen
1875-1880	Henry Gascoyne Ernest Bulwer (1)		

Brookes and Webb, p. 305; Walker, pp. xix-xx.

166 NAURU

The phosphate-rich atoll of Nauru, located in the South Pacific east of New Guinea, was administered by Germany as part of the Marshall Islands under German New Guinea (72) from 1888 to 1914. In 1914 it was seized by Australian forces. Until 1921 it was under the administration of the Western Pacific High Commission (q.v.). In 1921 it was granted as a League of Nations mandate jointly to Great Britain, New Zealand, and Australia, although it was administered solely by Australia. From 1942 to 1945 it was occupied by the Japanese. From 1947 to 1968 Australia administered Nauru as a United Nations trusteeship. In 1968 Nauru became independent.

Administrators			
1921-1927	Thomas Griffiths	1949	Harold Hastings Reeve
1927-1933	William Augustus Newman	1949-1953	Robert Stanley Richards
1933-1938	Rupert Clare Garsia	1953-1954	John Keith Lawrence
1938-1942	Frederick Roydon Chalmers	1954-1958	Reginald Sylvester Leydin (1)
1942-1945	(under Japan)	1958-1962	John Preston White
1945-1949	Mark Ridgway	1962-1966	Reginald Sylvester Leydin (2)
		1966-1968	Leslie Dudley King

Information from H. L. White, National Librarian, National Library of Australia, Canberra.

167 NEVIS

Nevis, in the Lesser Antilles, is immediately adjacent to the somewhat larger island of Saint Kitts (q.v.). It was discovered by Columbus in 1493 and settled by the English from Saint Kitts in 1628. In 1671 it became part of the Leeward Islands (q.v.) government and was administered by deputy or lieutenant governors who, until 1733, normally served as acting-governors of the Leeward Islands during the absence or incapacity of the substantive governors. The proximity of Nevis to Saint Kitts rendered a completely autonomous administration unnecessary, and in 1733 the rank of its administrator was reduced to president and later to that of president administering the government. Nevis was briefly occupied by the French in 1706 and from 1782 to 1784. Nevis continued to remain nominally separated from Saint Kitts until 1882 when it was united with the latter to form the government of Saint Kitts-Nevis-Anguilla (q.v.).

Governors		1692-1699	Samuel Gardner
1628-1629	Anthony Hilton (1)	1699-1702	Roger Elrington
1629-1630	George Hay	1703-1706	John Johnson
1630-	Anthony Hilton (2)	1706-1712	Walter Hamilton
-1634	Thomas Littleton	1712-1722	Daniel Smith
1634-	Luke Stoakes (1)	1722-1732	Charles Sibourg
-	Thomas Spurrow	1733-<u>1737</u>	William Hanmer
<u>1638</u>	Henry Huncks		
-	James Jennings	*Presidents*	
-	Jenkins Lloyd	1731-1744	Michael Smith
-	John Meakem	1745-1756	James Symonds
-1641	John Kettleby	1756-	William Maynard
1641-1651	Jacob Lake	1761-<u>1771</u>	James Johnston[1]
1651-1657	Luke Stoakes (2)	1762-1766	Joseph Herbert (1)
1657-<u>1668</u>	James Russell (1)	1766	Charles Pym Burt
		1766-1767	Joseph Herbert (2)
Deputy or Lieutenant Governors		1767-1782	John Richardson Herbert (1)
1671-	James Russell	1782-1784	(under France)
<u>1672</u>-1678	Randall Russell	1784-1793	John Richardson Herbert (2)
1678-1685	(none?)	1793-1807	(information lacking)
1685	William Burt	1807-1841	James Daniell
1685-1687	James Russell (2)	1841-1842	Josiah Webbe Maynard
1687-1691	John Netheway	1842-1844	Lawrence Graeme

1845-1854	Willoughby Shortland		1872-1873	Charles Monroe Eldridge
1854-1857	Frederick Seymour		1873-1876	Alexander Augustus Melfort Campbell
1857-1860	Carlo Arthur Edward Rumbold			
1860-1864	George Cavell Webbe		1876-1877	Roger Tuckfield Goldsworthy
1864-1866	James Watson Sheriff		1877-1878	Arthur Elibank Havelock
1866-1872	(none?)		1879-1882	Charles Spencer Salmon

1. Lieutenant Governor.

Colonial Office: "Nevis Acts, 1664–1772" (C.O. 185/1–15); "Nevis Sessional Papers, 1721–1882" (C.O. 186/1–22); "Minutes, Board of Trade and Plantations, 1675–1782" (C.O. 391/1–120). All housed in Public Record Office, London.

168 NEW BRUNSWICK

New Brunswick was part of the French colony of Acadia (6) until 1710 and thereafter of Nova Scotia (q.v.). The area was colonized from New England in 1762, and a large immigration of Loyalists occurred during and after the American Revolution. In 1784 New Brunswick was detached from Nova Scotia and erected into a separate colony. In 1867 it became a charter member of the Confederation of Canada (q.v.).

Governors				
1784-1803	Thomas Carleton		1837-1841	John Harvey
1803-1808	Gabriel George Ludlow		1841-1848	William Macbean George Colebrooke
1808	Edward Winslow			
1808-1812	Martin Hunter		1848-1854	Edmund Walker Head
1812-1823	George Stracey Smyth		1854-1861	John Henry Thomas Manners-Sutton, Viscount Canterbury
1823-1824	Ward Chipman			
1824-1831	Howard Douglas		1861-1866	Arthur Charles Hamilton-Gordon, Baron Stanmore
1831-1837	Archibald Campbell			

Audet, pp. 59–63; *Encyclopedia Canadiana*, 7:270; McNutt, passim.

169 NEWFOUNDLAND

The fishing banks of Newfoundland had been frequented by Portuguese, Spanish, French, and English fishermen from the end of the 15th century. An English attempt to colonize the island in 1583 failed, but in 1610 the Company of Adventurers and Planters of London and Bristol for the Colony or Plantations of Newfoundland was formed, and a small colony was established the following year. Several other small settlements were established in the following years but they all languished and in 1675 it was decided to remove all the colonists. However, the establishment of a French colony at Plaisance (q.v.) or Placentia led to the rescinding of this decision, since it was deemed desirable by the Royal Navy that British influence be maintained in the area. From 1675 the Newfoundland settlements were supervised by the commodores of the annual fishing convoys. The commodore remained only during the fishing season, and during the rest of the year the settlements were governed by their own leaders, or "fishing admirals." The French we[re] expelled from Plaisance during the War of the Spanish Succession. After 1700 there were resi- dent lieutenant governors, first at Saint Johns and then at Placentia, who exercised military fun[c]- tions and were latterly appointed from Nova Scotia. This state of affairs was ameliorated after 1729 when civil government was instituted and a royal governor appointed. These governors continued to be naval officers whose main responsibility remained the protection of the convoy[s.] Only in 1818 was the first resident governor appointed and Newfoundland raised to full colonia[l] status. In 1763 Labrador, ceded by France by the Treaty of Paris, was included in the governme[nt] of Newfoundland. Responsible government was instituted in 1855. Unlike the other Canadian colonies, Newfoundland did not confederate in 1867 but remained a separate colony. In 1918 Newfoundland acquired dominion status, but in 1934 this status was held to be "in suspension" and a commission replaced the cabinet. Cabinet government was not restored until 1949 when Newfoundland became Canada's tenth province.

Governors

Cuper's Cove
1611-1614 John Guy
1615-1621 John Mason

Bristol's Hope
1618-1628 Robert Hayman

Trepassey
1618-1620 Richard Whitbourne

South Falkland
1623-1625 Francis Tanfield

Avalon
1621-1625 Edward Wynne
1626-1627 Arthur Aston
1627-1629 George Calvert, Baron Baltimore
1629-1634 (unknown)
1634-1638 William Hill

all settlements
1638-1651 David Kirke
1652-1660 John Treworgie

Commodores of the fishing convoys
1675 John Berry
1676 Edward Russell
1677 William Poole
1678
1679 Charles Talbot (1)
1680 Robert Robinson
1681 James Story (?)
1682 Daniel Jones
1683 Charles Talbot (2)
1684 Francis Wheler
1685
1686
1687
1688
1689 Thomas Perry (?)
1690
1691 Charles Hawkins
1692 Thomas Crawley
1693

1694
1695
1696 Samuel Whetstone
1697-1698 John Norris
1699 Andrew Leake
1700 Stafford Fairborne
1701 John Graydon
1702 John Leake
1703
1704-1705 Timothy Bridge
1706-1707 John Underdown
1708 John Mitchell
1709 Joseph Taylour
1710 John Aldred
1711 Josias Crowe
1712 Nicholas Trevanion
1713 Robert Leake
1714 Charles Fotherby
1715 William Kempthorn
1716 John Hagar
1717 William Passenger
1718 Thomas Scott
1719 Chaloner Ogle
1720 Francis Percy
1721 James Stuart
1722-1727 Edward Bowler
1728 Vere Beauclerk

Commodore-Governors
1729-1730 Henry Osborn
1731 George Clinton
1732 Edward Falkingham
1733-1734 Robert MacCarty, Viscount Muskerry
1735-1737 FitzRoy Henry Lee
1738 Philip Vanbrugh
1739-1740 Henry Medley
1740 George Grahame
1741 Thomas Smith (1)
1742 John Byng
1743 Thomas Smith (2)
1744 Charles Hardy
1745 Richard Edwards (1)
1746-1747 (none)
1748 Charles Watson

1749	George Brydges Rodney		1825-1834	Thomas John Cochrane
1750-1752	Francis William Drake		1834-1841	Henry Prescott
1753-1754	Hugh Bonfoy		1841-1846	John Harvey
1755-1756	Richard Dorrill		1846-1847	John Law
1757-1759	Richard Edwards (2)		1847-1852	John LeMarchant Gaspard
1760	James Webb		1852-1855	Ker Baillie Hamilton
1761-1763	Thomas Graves		1855-1857	Charles Henry Darling
1764-1768	Hugh Palliser		1857-1863	Alexander Bannerman
1769-1771	John Byron		1864-1869	Anthony Musgrave
1772-1774	Molyneux Shuldham		1869-1876	Stephen John Hill
1775	Richard Duff		1876-1881	John Hawley Glover (1)
1776-1778	John Montagu		1881-1883	Henry Fitzhardinge Berkeley
1779-1781	Richard Edwards			Maxse
1782-1785	John Campbell		1883-1885	John Hawley Glover (2)
1786-1788	John Elliott		1886-1887	George William DesVoeux
1789-1791	Mark Milbanke		1887-1888	Henry Arthur Blake
1792-1793	Richard King		1889-1895	John Terence Nicolls O'Brien
1794-1796	James Wallace		1895-1898	Herbert Harley Murray
1797-1799	William Waldegrave		1898-1901	Henry Edward McCallum
1800-1801	Charles Morice Pole		1901-1904	Cavendish Boyle
1802-1803	James Gambier		1904-1909	William Macgregor
1804-1806	Erasmus Gower		1909-1913	Ralph Champneys Williams
1807-1809	John Holloway		1913-1917	Walter Edward Davidson
1810-1812	John Thomas Duckworth		1917-1922	Charles Alexander Harris
1813-1816	Richard Godwin Keats		1922-1928	William Lamond Allardyce
1817-1818	Francis Pickmore		1928-1932	John Middleton
			1933-1935	David Murray Anderson
Governors			1936-1946	Humphrey Thomas Walwyn
1818-1824	Charles Hamilton		1946-1949	Gordon Macdonald

1. There may have been two commodores in 1708. Peter Chamberlain was appointed early in the year, but John Mitchell answered the inquiries submitted to each commodore at the end of the year and he obviously served all or part of the season as commodore. It is possible that Chamberlain gave up the post early for some reason, or that he never took up his commission at all.

2. The lieutenant governors at Saint John's and later at Placentia during part of the 18th century were:

1700-1702	Michael Richards
1703-1704	Thomas Lloyd (1)
1704-1705	John Moody (1)
1705-1708	Thomas Lloyd (2)
1709-1712	John Collins
1712-1719	John Moody (2)
1719-1735	Samuel Gledhill
1737-1770	Otho Hamilton
1770-1774	Joseph Gorham

Colonial Office, Public Record Office, London: "Colonial Papers, General Series" (C.O. 1); "Newfoundland. Original Correspondence" (C.O. 194); "Newfoundland. Entry Books" (C.O. 195); *Colonial Office List*, 1915—49. Also, Andrews, pp. 477—82; Audet, pp. 75—77 (the list is worthless for the 18th century); Charnock, under individual names; Lounsbury, passim; Prowse, pp. 552—61; Scisco.

170 NEW HAMPSHIRE

Settlers began coming into what is now New Hampshire from Massachusetts Bay (q.v.) in about 1630. Until 1680, and again from 1692 to 1741, New Hampshire was governed from Massachusetts—after 1699 the governor of Massachusetts serving also as governor of New Hampshire. Between 1680 and 1692, and between 1741 and 1776, New Hampshire was a separate colony of Great Britain, its governor appointed by the crown.

Presidents of the Council
1680-1681 John Cutt
1681-1682 Richard Waldron
1682-1685 Edward Cranfield
1685-1868 Walter Barefoot
1686   Joseph Dudley

Lieutenant Governors
1692-1697 John Usher (1)
1697-1699 William Partridge

1699-1703 (office vacant)
1703-1715 John Usher (2)
1715-1717 George Vaughan
1717-1730 John Wentworth
1730-1741 David Dunbar

Governors
1741-1767 Benning Wentworth
1767-1776 John Wentworth

Fry, passim; Pillsbury, 4:1244—45.

171 NEW HAVEN

The colony of New Haven was settled in 1638 from Massachusetts Bay (q.v.). A separate colonial government was established in 1643. Controversies with New York (q.v.) and the small size of the colony led to its absorption into Connecticut (q.v.) in 1664.

Governors
1643-1658 Theophilus Eaton

1658-1660 Francis Newman
1660-1664 William Leete

Jacobus, under individual names.

172 NEW HEBRIDES CONDOMINIUM

The New Hebrides Island group in the southwestern Pacific Ocean was discovered by Spanish mariners in 1606. The group consists of about eighty islands. During the 19th century the islands were the locale of heavy labor recruiting for the plantations of Fiji (q.v.), New Caledonia, and Queensland (q.v.). Both France and Great Britain had designs on the islands, and their inability to resolve this issue led to the formation of a joint Anglo-French Naval Commission in 1887, which governed the islands until 1902. After further negotiations a formal condominium was established in 1906. Under the condominium the British resident commissioner is appointed by the high commissioner for the Western Pacific region (v. Western Pacific High Commission), while the French resident commissioner is appointed by the French high commissioner at New

Caledonia (48). The New Hebrides government is the only true example of a condominium established by the various European colonial powers. For the French resident commissioners, see New Hebrides, 50.

Resident Commissioners		1940-1950	Richard Denis Blandy
1902-1907	Ernest Goldfinch Rason	1950-1955	Hubert James Marlowe Flaxman
1907-1924	Merton King	1955-1962	John Shaw Rennie
1924-1927	Geoffrey Whistler Bingham Smith-Rewse	1962-1966	Alexander Mair Wilkie
		1966—	Colin Hamilton Allan
1927-1940	George Andrew Joy		

Information from Office of the British Resident Commissioner, Vila, New Hebrides.

173 NEW JERSEY

The area of New Jersey was included in the grant given to James, Duke of York, in 1664 (v. New York). Previously there had been some Dutch and Swedish settlement in the area (v. New Netherlands, 277, and New Sweden, 403). West Jersey was held by William Penn from 1676 to 1702, while East Jersey was granted as a proprietary colony to Philip Carteret. In 1702 proprietary government was abolished and the two provinces were united under royal authority. Until 1736 the governor of New York served also as governor of New Jersey, although New Jersey retained its own assembly. In 1776 the last royal governor was expelled.

East Jersey		1708-1709	John Lovelace
Governors		1709-1710	Richard Ingoldsby
1667-1682	Philip Carteret	1710-1719	Robert Hunter
1682-1684	Thomas Rudyard	1719-1720	Lewis Morris (1)
1684-1686	Gawen Lawrie	1720-1728	William Burnet
1686-1687	Neil Campbell	1728-1731	John Montgomerie
1687-1697	Andrew Hamilton (1)	1731-1732	Lewis Morris (2)
1698-1699	Jeremiah Basse	1732-1736	William Cosby
1699-1703	Andrew Hamilton (2)	1736-1738	John Hamilton (1)
		1738-1746	Lewis Morris (3)
West Jersey		1746-1747	John Hamilton (2)
Governors		1747-1757	Jonathan Belcher
1680-1684	Samuel Jennings	1757	Thomas Pownall
1684	Thomas Ollive	1757-1758	John Reading
1684-1692	John Skene	1758-1760	Francis Bernard
1692-1697	Andrew Hamilton (1)	1760-1761	Thomas Boone
1697-1699	Jeremiah Basse	1761-1763	Josiah Hardy
1699-1703	Andrew Hamilton (2)	1763-1776	William Franklin

East and West (New) Jersey
Governors
1703-1708 Edward Hyde, Baron Cornbury

Pomfret, *New Jersey Proprietors*, pp. 121–23; idem, *Province of East New Jersey*, passim; idem, *Province of West New Jersey*, passim.

174 NEW MUNSTER

In 1848 New Zealand (q.v.) was divided administratively into New Munster, which included part of North Island, and New Ulster (q.v.) which included the remainder of North Island and all of South Island. This experiment proved unsuccessful and in 1853 the two provinces were abolished.

Lieutenant Governor
1848-1853   Edward John Eyre

McLintock.

175 NEW PLYMOUTH

New Plymouth, in Massachusetts, was settled in 1620 by English Puritans seeking to escape the religious intolerance of the period. Although its settlement antedated that of Massachusetts Bay (q.v.), the location of the colony had been poorly chosen and lacked good harbors. As a result it atrophied and was eventually absorbed into Massachusetts in 1692.

Governors			
1620-1621	John Carver	1639-1644	William Bradford (4)
1621-1633	William Bradford (1)	1644-1645	Edward Winslow (3)
1633-1634	Edward Winslow (1)	1645-1657	William Bradford (5)
1634-1635	Thomas Prence (1)	1657-1672	Thomas Prence (3)
1635-1636	William Bradford (2)	1673-1680	Josias Winslow
1636-1637	Edward Winslow (2)	1680-1686	Thomas Hinckley (1)
1637-1638	William Bradford (3)	1686-1689	Edmond Andros
1638-1639	Thomas Prence (2)	1689-1692	Thomas Hinckley (2)

Langdon, passim; Whitmore, p. 35.

176 NEW SOUTH WALES

New South Wales, in the southeastern corner of the Australian continent, was discovered and named by James Cook in 1770. In 1788 it became the site of the first British colony in Australia– which was, in fact, a penal colony established at Botany Bay. Effective settlement took place only after 1810. Originally, New South Wales included the whole continent, except Western Australia, and New Zealand (qq.v.). However, as settlement became more extensive new colonie were created. Tasmania (q.v.) was detached in 1825, South Australia (q.v.) in 1836, New Zealand in 1841, Victoria (q.v.) in 1851, Queensland (q.v.) in 1859, and Northern Australia (q.v.), which was placed under South Australia, in 1863. New South Wales was thereby reduced to about 10 per cent of the continent. In 1901 New South Wales joined the Commonwealth of Australia (v. Australia). In 1911 the Australian National Capital Territory was carved from New South Wales.

Governors

1788-1792	Arthur Phillip
1792-1794	Francis Grose
1794-1795	William Paterson (1)
1795-1800	John Hunter
1800-1806	Philip Gidley King
1806-1808	William Bligh
1808-1809	Joseph Foveaux
1809	William Paterson (2)
1809-1821	Lachlan Macquarie
1821-1825	Thomas Makdougall Brisbane
1825-1831	Ralph Darling
1831-1837	Richard Bourke
1838-1846	George Gipps
1846-1855	Charles Augustus FitzRoy

1855-1861	William Thomas Denison
1861-1867	John Young
1867-1872	Somerset Richard Lowry-Corry, Earl Belmore
1872-1879	Hercules George Robert Robinson
1879-1885	Augustus William Frederick Spencer Loftus
1885-1890	Charles Robert Wynn-Carrington
1890-1893	Victor Alfred George Child Villiers, Earl of Jersey
1893-1895	Robert William Duff
1895-1899	Henry Robert Brand, Viscount Hampden
1899-1901	William Lygon, Earl Beauchamp

Australian Encyclopaedia, 4:352—53.

177 NEW ULSTER

See New Munster.

Lieutenant Governors

1848-1851	George Dean Pitt
1851-1853	Robert Henry Wynward

McLintock.

178 NEW YORK

The Dutch colony of New Netherlands (277) along the Hudson River was seized by the British in 1664 and retained at the Peace of Breda, by which the English surrendered their rights in Surinam (q.v.) to the Dutch (v. 281). In 1673—74 the Dutch briefly reoccupied their former colony. The conquered colony was granted to James, Duke of York, the brother of Charles II, in 1664. The grant included also the areas of what were to become New Jersey and Pennsylvania (qq.v.). From 1688 to 1689 New York formed part of the Dominion of New England. This was an effort to consolidate several of England's North American colonies in the interest of administrative efficiency. It was established in 1686 and then included Connecticut, Massachusetts Bay, New Plymouth, and Rhode Island (qq.v.), together with New Hampshire (q.v.) and Maine. It was expanded to include New Jersey (q.v.) and New York in 1688, but was dissolved after the deposition of James II in 1688. New York fell under royal control in 1689. During the 18th century the colony rapidly expanded north and west from the nucleus along the Hudson and became one of the most prosperous North American colonies. The British retained control of part of New York longer than they did of the other colonies in North America. New York City was not surrendered to the Americans until 1783.

Great Britain

Governors

1664-1668	Richard Nichols
1668-1673	Francis Lovelace
1673-1674	(under the Netherlands)
1674-1677	Edmund Andros (1)
1677-1678	Anthony Brockholls (1)
1678-1681	Edmund Andros (2)
1681-1683	Anthony Brockholls (2)
1683-1688	Thomas Dongan
1688	Edmund Andros (3)
1688-1689	Francis Nicholson
1689-1691	Jacob Leisler
1691	Henry Sloughter
1691-1692	Richard Ingoldsby (1)
1692-1698	Benjamin Fletcher
1698-1701	Richard Coote, Earl of Bellomont
1701-1702	John Nanfan
1702-1708	Edward Hyde, Baron Cornbury
1708-1709	John Lovelace
1709-1710	Richard Ingoldsby (2)
1710-1719	Robert Hunter

1719-1720	Peter Schuyler
1720-1728	William Burnet
1728-1731	John Montgomerie
1731-1732	Rip Van Dam
1732-1736	William Cosby
1736-1743	George Clarke
1743-1753	George Clinton
1753-1755	James De Lancey (1)
1755-1757	Charles Hardy
1757-1760	James De Lancey (2)
1760-1762	Cadwallader Colden (1)
1762-1763	Robert Monckton
1763-1765	Cadwallader Colden (2)
1765-1769	Henry Moore
1769-1770	Cadwallader Colden (3)
1770-1771	John Murray, Earl of Dunmore
1771-1774	William Tryon
1774-1775	Cadwallader Colden (4)
1775-1780	William Tyron
1780-1783	James Robertson

Lincoln, pp. 46—59.

---

179 NEW ZEALAND

The two large islands of what was to become New Zealand were annexed by James Cook in 1769, but his action was disregarded by British authorities. Traders from New South Wales (q.v.) began to frequent the islands as early as 1791, and French and British missionaries were active after 1814. An effort at settlement from New South Wales failed in 1826. In 1837 Edward Gibbon Wakefield formed the New Zealand Association with the intention of applying his principles of scientific settlement to New Zealand. Pressure from Wakefield and other hopeful colonizers, as well as from the missionaries, prompted the British government to dispatch a governor who in 1840 signed the Treaty of Waitingi with several Maori chiefs under which they acknowledged the sovereignty of the British crown. In 1841 New Zealand was proclaimed a crown colony. Subsequently both North and South Island were rapidly settled. Beginning in 1843 a series of wars with the Maoris expanded the area of the colony until it included the entire area of both islands. From 1848 to 1853 New Zealand was briefly divided into New Munster and New Ulster (qq.v.). In 1907 New Zealand, after the examples of Canada and Australia (qq.v.), received dominion status. New Zealand began administering the Cook Islands (q.v.) in 1888, and Niue (q.v.) in 1901. In addition New Zealand was granted a League of Nations mandate, and later a United Nations trusteeship, over Western Samoa (q.v.).

Governors

1840-1842	William Hobson
1843-1845	Robert Fitzroy
1845-1855	George Grey (1)
1855-1861	Thomas Gore Browne
1861-1868	George Grey (2)
1868-1872	George Ferguson Bowen
1873-1874	James Fergusson

1874-1879	George Augustus Constantine Phipps, Marquess of Normanby
1879-1880	Hercules George Robert Robinson
1880-1882	Arthur Charles Hamilton-Gordon, Baron Stanmore
1883-1889	William Francis Drummond Jervois
1889-1892	William Hillier Onslow, Earl of Onslow

1892-1897	David Boyle, Earl of Glascow	1924-1930	Charles Fergusson
1897-1904	Uchter Mark John Knox, Earl of Ranfurly	1930-1935	Charles Bathurst, Viscount Bledisloe
1904-1910	William Lee Plunket, Baron Plunket	1935-1941	George Vere Arundell Monckton-Arundell, Viscount Galway
1910-1912	John Poynder Dickson-Poynder, Baron Islington	1941-1945	Cyril Louis Norton Newall, Viscount Newall
1912-1917	Arthur William de Brito Savile Foljambe, Earl of Liverpool	1945-1952	Bernard Cyril Freyberg
		1952-1957	Charles Willoughby Moke Norrie, Baron Norrie

Governors-General

1917-1920	Arthur William de Brito Savile Foljambe, Earl of Liverpool	1957-1962	Charles John Lyttelton, Viscount Cobham
1920-1924	John Rushworth Jellicoe, Earl Jellicoe	1962-1967	Bernard Edward Fergusson
		1967—	Arthur Espie Porritt

McLintock, 1:867 and under individual names.

180 NIGERIA

No permanent European trading posts were established along the coast of what was to become Nigeria, although the Portuguese had reached the kingdom of Benin there at least as early as 1486. Latent British interest was aroused in the early 19th century with the abolition of the slave trade and the consequent desire to secure alternative trade items. Until 1849 British interest in such goods was unofficial and was maintained by and under the responsibility of the anti-slavery patrols of Great Britain's West African Squadron, operating from Fernando Po (v. Spanish Guinea, 389). In 1849 a consul was appointed for the Bight of Biafra, or the eastern part of Nigeria's coast. Two years later, on grounds of suppressing the slave trade there, a protectorate was established over the coastal state of Lagos, and in 1852 another consul was appointed for the Bight of Benin with headquarters at Lagos. In 1862 Lagos was annexed as a crown colony and the governor of Lagos acted as consul for the Bight of Benin until 1867 when the consul for the Bight of Biafra added it to his charge. These consuls resided at Fernando Po until 1873, then at Old Calabar on the coast to 1875, then at Fernando Po again, to 1882, and again at Old Calabar after 1882.

From 1866 to 1874 Lagos was part of the West Africa Settlements (v. Sierra Leone), and from 1874 to 1886 it was subordinate to the Gold Coast (q.v.). In 1885 the Bights of Biafra and Benin became the Oil Rivers Protectorate, and in 1891 the consul there became commissioner. In 1893 this protectorate was extended inland and its name was changed to the Niger Coast Protectorate. Meanwhile, in 1886 the Royal Niger Company had been granted a charter and rights to govern territory up the Niger River. In 1900 the company's charter was revoked, its coastal territory was added to the Niger Coast Protectorate, and the combined government was called the Protectorate of Southern Nigeria. In 1906 Lagos was added to this and the result was termed the Colony and Protectorate of Southern Nigeria. Meanwhile, the interior lands of the Royal Niger Company were formed into the Protectorate of Northern Nigeria in 1900, and during the next decade the many small Hausa and Fulani states of the north were conquered and added to this protectorate. In 1914 the two areas of Southern Nigeria and Northern Nigeria were amalgamated into the Colony and Protectorate of Nigeria. The two former areas were entrusted to lieutenant governors, and later to commissioners. In 1939 Southern Nigeria was divided into an eastern and a western region. Thereby, after 1939, Nigeria was administratively divided into three areas, constructed more or less on ethnic lines. These regions remained bases of administration until and after 1960 when Nigeria became an independent member of the British Commonwealth. Three years later Nigeria became a republic within the Commonwealth. A small part of the German colony of Kamerun (75) had been mandated to Great Britain after World War I and was attached to Nigeria for administrative purposes. In 1961 this area voted to remain part of the now independent Nigeria.

Bight of Biafra
Consuls
1849–1854 John Beecroft
1855–1861 Thomas Joseph Hutchinson
1861–1864 Richard Francis Burton
1864–1867 Charles Livingstone

Bight of Benin (Lagos)
Consuls
1852–1853 Louis Fraser
1853–1859 Benjamin Campbell
1859–1860 George Brand
1860   Henry Grant Foote
1860–1861 Henry Hand

Bights of Biafra and Benin
Consuls
1867–1873 Charles Livingstone
1873–1878 George Hartley
1878–1879 David Hopkins
1880–1885 Edward Hyde Hewett

Lagos
Administrators
1862–1865 Henry Stanhope Freeman
1865–1872 John Hawley Glover
1872–1873 George Berkeley
1873–1874 George Cumine Strahan
1874–1880 Charles Cameron Lees
1880–1886 William Brandford Griffith

Governors
1886–1891 Cornelius Alfred Moloney
1891–1897 Gilbert Thomas Carter
1897–1899 Henry Edward McCallum
1899–1904 William Macgregor
1904–1906 Walter Egerton

Oil Rivers Protectorate
Consul
1885–1891 Edward Hyde Hewett

Commissioner
1891–1893 Claude Maxwell Macdonald

Niger Coast Protectorate
Commissioners
1893–1896 Claude Maxwell Macdonald
1896–1900 Ralph Denham Rayment Moor

Southern Nigeria
High Commissioners
1900–1904 Ralph Denham Rayment Moor
1904–1912 Walter Egerton
1912–1914 Frederick John Dealtry Lugard

Northern Nigeria
High Commissioners
1900–1907 Frederick John Dealtry Lugard (1)
1907–1909 Edward Percy Cranwill Girouard
1909–1912 Henry Hesketh Joudou Bell
1912–1914 Frederick John Dealtry Lugard (2)

Nigeria
Governors
1914–1919 Frederick John Dealtry Lugard
1919–1925 Hugh Clifford
1925–1931 Graeme Thomson
1931–1935 Donald Charles Cameron
1935–1942 Bernard Henry Bourdillon
1942–1943 Alan Cuthbert Maxwell Burns
1943–1948 Arthur Frederick Richards
1948–1954 John Stewart Macpherson

Governors-General
1954–1955 John Stewart Macpherson
1955–1960 James Robertson

Nigeria, Southern Provinces
Lieutenant Governors
1914–1920 Alexander George Boyle
1920–1925 Harry Claude Moorhouse
1925–1929 Upton FitzHerbert Ruxton
1929–1930 Cyril Wilson Alexander
1930–1935 Walter Buchanan-Smith

Chief Commissioner
1935–1939 William Edgar Hunt

Nigeria, Northern Region
Lieutenant Governors
1914–1917 Charles Lindsay Temple
1917–1921 Herbert Symonds Goldsmith
1921–1925 William Frederick Gowers
1925–1930 Herbert Richmond Palmer
1930–1932 Cyril Wilson Alexander

Chief Commissioners
1933–1937 George Sinclair Browne
1937–1943 Theodore Samuel Adams
1943–1947 John Robert Patterson
1948–1951 Eric Westbury Thompstone

Lieutenant Governors
1951–1952 Eric Westbury Thompstone
1952–1954 Bryan Evars Sharwood-Smith

Governors
1954–1957 Bryan Evars Sharwood-Smith
1957–1962 Gawain Westray Bell

Nigeria, Eastern Region	*Nigeria, Western Region*

Chief Commissioners

1939-1943 George Gay Shute
1943-1948 Frederick Bernard Carr
1948-1951 James Grenville Pyke-Nott

Lieutenant Governors

1951-1952 James Grenville Pyke-Nott
1952-1954 Clement John Pleass

Governors

1954-1956 Clement John Pleass
1956-1960 Robert deStapledon Stapledon

Chief Commissioners

1939-1946 Gerald Charles Whiteley
1946-1951 Theodore Chandos Hoskyns-
           Abrahall

Lieutenant Governors

1951 Theodore Chandos Hoskyns-
      Abrahall
1951-1954 Hugo Frank Marshall

Governor

1954-1960 John Dalzell Rankine

Anene, p. 336 (though this list implies that David Hopkins was consul to 1882, whereas he died in 1879, and that John Beecroft was consul to 1855, whereas he died in 1854); Biobaku, p. 100; Bouchaud, pp. 19–37; Egharevba, pp. 97–100.

181 NIUE

Niue Island lies in the South Pacific about 300 miles east of Tonga (q.v.). It was discovered by James Cook in 1774, and from 1861 was the scene of British missionary activities. In 1887 and subsequently the inhabitants requested British protection, and in 1900 a protectorate was proclaimed. In 1901 the island was annexed to New Zealand (q.v.) and a resident commissioner appointed.

Resident Commissioners

1901-1902 Stephenson Percy Smith
1902-1907 Christopher Freke Maxwell
1907-1918 Henry Greyshott Cornwall
1918-1920 Guy Norman Morris (1)
1920-1922 John Crouchley Murray Evison
1922-1926 Guy Norman Morris (2)
1926-1931 Albert Arthur Luckham

1931-1942 William Moody Bell
1942-1943 Joseph Patrick McMahon-Box
1943-1953 Cecil Hector Watson Larsen
1953-1956 Jock Malcolm McEwen
1956-1958 Albert Oliver Dare
1958-1962 David Walter Reginald Heatley
1962-1968 Lyle Allen Shanks
1968—   Selwyn Digby Wilson

Information from C. A. J. McRae, Department of Island Territories, Wellington, New Zealand.

182 NORFOLK ISLAND

Norfolk Island lies in the South Pacific between New Zealand (q.v.) and New Caledonia. It was discovered by James Cook in 1774. It was used as a convict settlement by New South Wales (q.v.) from 1788 to 1844, and by Tasmania (q.v.) from 1844 to 1856 (except in 1853 when it was abandoned). In 1856 the administration of the island reverted to New South Wales, the convict settlement was dissolved, and the island was resettled from Pitcairn Island (q.v.). Since 1914 it has been a national territory of Australia (q.v.).

Great Britain

Information on annual magistrates from H. L. White, National Librarian, National Library of Australia, Canberra, Australia. See also *Australian Encyclopaedia*, 6:353.

183 NORTH CAROLINA

In 1585 Roanoke Island, off the coast of North Carolina, became the site of the first English colony in North America, but it was soon abandoned. In 1663 Charles II granted Carolina, which included both North Carolina and South Carolina (q.v.) to eight lords proprietors. The northern part of this grant, that is, North Carolina, was sparsely settled and in 1691 it fell under South Carolina and was ruled by deputy governors until 1712. In 1729 proprietary control was revoked, because of the indifference of the proprietors to the colony's affairs, and royal government was substituted. In 1775 the last royal governor was expelled.

Governors

1664-1667	William Drummond
1667-1670	Samuel Stephens
1670-1672	Peter Carteret
1672-1677	John Jenkins (1)
1677	Thomas Miller
1678	Seth Sothel (1)
1678-1679	John Harvey (1)
1680-1681	John Jenkins (2)
1682-1689	Seth Sothel (2)
1689-1691	Philip Ludwell
1691-1694	Thomas Jarvis
1694-1696	John Archdale
1696-1699	John Harvey (2)
1699-1704	Henderson Walker
1704-1705	Robert Daniel
1705-1706	Thomas Cary (1)
1706-1708	William Glover
1708-1711	Thomas Cary (2)
1711-1712	Edward Hyde
1712-1714	Thomas Pollock (1)
1714-1722	Charles Eden
1722	Thomas Pollock (2)
1722-1724	William Reed
1724-1725	George Burrington (1)
1725-1729	Richard Everard
1729-1731	Richard Everard
1731-1734	George Burrington (2)
1734-1752	Gabriel Johnston
1752-1753	Nathaniel Rice
1753-1754	Matthew Rowan
1754-1765	Arthur Dobbs
1765-1771	William Tryon
1771	James Hasell
1771-1775	Josiah Martin

Butler, p. 299; Crabtree, pp. 3–45.

184 NORTHERN AUSTRALIA

The first settlement in the area that became known as Northern Australia took place in 1824 but was abandoned in 1829. New and more permanent settlement occurred after 1838. A territorial government was created in 1863 and Northern Australia, which had hitherto been under New South Wales (q.v.), was placed under South Australia (q.v.), where it remained until 1910 when it became a national territory of the Commonwealth of Australia (v. Australia).

Melville Island (Fort Dundas)
Commandants

1824-1826	Maurice Barlow
1826-1828	John Campbell
1828-1829	Humphrey Robert Hartley

Raffles Bay (Fort Wellington)
Commandants

1827	James Stirling
1827-1828	Henry Smyth
1828	George Sleeman
1828-1829	Collet Barker

Port Essington
Commandants

1838-1839	James John Gordon Bremer
1839-1849	John McArthur

Northern Australia
Administrators

1864-1866	Boyle Travers Finniss
1866-1867	John Thomas Manton
1869-1870	Goerge Woodroffe Goyder
1870	John Stokes Milner (1)
1870-1873	Bloomfield Douglas
1873	John Stokes Milner (2)
1873-1876	George Byng Scott
1876-1883	Edward William Price
1883-1884	Gilbert Rothersdale McMinn
1884-1890	John Langdon Parsons
1890-1892	John George Knight
1892-1901	Charles James Dashwood

Australia, *Historical Records*, 5:737–824, and 6:643–845; *Australian Encyclopaedia*, 6:369.

185 NORTHERN RHODESIA

Northern Rhodesia, which lies north of the Zambezi River, fell within the territory included in the charter of the British South African Company. Until 1911 the area was divided into North-Eastern Rhodesia and North-Western Rhodesia, but in 1911 the two were combined to form Northern Rhodesia. The British South African Company continued to administer Northern Rhodesia until 1924 when it became a crown colony. From 1953 to 1963 Northern Rhodesia formed, with Southern Rhodesia and Nyasaland (qq.v.), the Federation of Rhodesia and Nyasaland (v. Rhodesia and Nyasaland). After the dissolution of the federation, Northern Rhodesia became independent as Zambia. Zambia is a republic within the Commonwealth.

North-Eastern Rhodesia
Administrators
1895–1897 Patrick William Forbes
1897–1898 Henry Lawrence Daly
1898–1907 Robert Edward Codrington
1907–1909 Lawrence Aubrey Wallace
1909–1911 Leicester Paul Beaufort

North-Western Rhodesia
Administrators
1897–1907 Robert Thomas Coryndon
1907–1908 Robert Edward Codrington
1909–1911 Lawrence Aubrey Wallace

Northern Rhodesia
Administrators
1911–1921 Lawrence Aubrey Wallace

1921–1923 Drummond Percy Chaplin
1923–1924 Richard Allmond Jeffrey Goode

Governors
1924–1927 Herbert James Stanley
1927–1932 James Crawford Maxwell
1932–1934 Ronald Storrs
1934–1938 Hubert Winthrop Young
1938–1941 John Alexander Maybin
1941–1947 Eubule John Waddington
1948–1954 Gilbert McCall Rennie
1954–1958 Arthur Edward Trevor Benson
1958–1964 Evelyn Dennison Hone

Walker, pp. xxi–xxii, xxiv.

186 NORTH-WEST FRONTIER PROVINCE

The northwestern area of India, traditionally the invasion route to the subcontinent, became a matter of growing concern to the British government of India (q.v.) after the 1830's. Finally, the necessity of preserving a stable frontier prompted the creation of a separate province, the North-West Frontier Province, in 1901. In 1932 the NWFP became a governor's province. In 1947 it became a part of Pakistan.

Chief Commissioners
1901–1908 Harold Arthur Deane
1908–1919 George Olof Roos-Keppel
1919–1921 Alfred Hamilton Grant
1921–1924 John Loader Maffey
1924–1930 Horatio Norman Bolton
1930–1931 Steuart Edmund Pears
1931–1932 Ralph Edwin Hotchkin Griffith

Governors
1932–1937 Ralph Edwin Hotchkin Griffith
1937–1946 George Cunningham (1)
1946–1947 Olaf Kirkpatrick Caroe
1947–1948 George Cunningham (2)
1948–1949 Ambrose Dundas Flux Dundas

Caroe, p. 467.

187 NOVA SCOTIA

Nova Scotia, at the eastern tip of Canada, was discovered by John Cabot in 1497. From 1604 to 1710 the French colony of Acadia (6) was located there, although the English occupied the colony from 1629 to 1632, and again from 1654 to 1670. After the British conquest of Acadia in 1710 the area began to be settled by the English. Until 1749, however, it was only informally administered. From 1763 to 1769 Prince Edward Island (q.v.) was part of Nova Scotia and from 1763 to 1784 and again from 1820 Cape Breton (q.v.) was likewise attached to Nova Scotia. In 1848 Nova Scotia achieved responsible government, the first British colony to do so. In 1867 it became an original member of the Confederation of Canada.

Governors

1710–1712	Samuel Vetch (1)
1712–1715	Francis Nicholson
1715–1717	Samuel Vetch (2)
1717–1749	Richard Philipps[1]
1749–1752	Edward Cornwallis
1752–1756	Peregrine Thomas Hopson
1756–1760	Charles Lawrence
1760–1763	Jonathan Belcher
1763–1766	Montague Wilmot
1766–1773	William Campbell
1773–1782	Francis Legge
1782–1791	John Parr
1792–1808	John Wentworth
1808–1811	George Prevost
1811–1816	John Coape Sherbrooke
1816–1820	George Ramsay, Earl of Dalhousie
1820–1828	James Kempt
1828–1834	Peregrine Maitland
1834–1840	Colin Campbell
1840–1846	Lucius Bentinck Cary, Viscount Falkland
1846–1852	John Harvey
1852–1858	John Gaspard LeMarchant
1858–1863	George Augustus Constantine Phipps, Earl of Musgrave
1864–1865	Richard Graves MacDonnell
1865–1867	William Fenwick Williams

1. During the term of Governor Philipps, who spent only four years in Nova Scotia, the following lieutenant governors administered the government:

1717–1725	John Doucett
1725–1739	Lawrence Armstrong
1740–1749	Paul Mascarene

Andrews, pp. 501–7; Audet, pp. 52–57 (but confusing for the period before 1749); Beck, pp. 340, 347–48; Macmechan, passim.

188 NYASALAND

British interests in the area around Lake Nyasa in southeastern Africa began with missionary activities after 1874. A consul was appointed in 1883, and a protectorate was proclaimed over a limited area in 1889. In 1891 this protectorate was expanded to include the entire western shore of Lake Nyasa. The name of the colony was changed to the British Central African Protectorate in 1893, but reverted to its former name of Nyasaland in 1907 when the consul-general was replaced by a governor. In theory Nyasaland remained a protectorate. From 1953 to 1963 it joined with Northern Rhodesia and Southern Rhodesia (qq.v.) to form the Federation of Rhodesia and Nyasaland (v. Rhodesia and Nyasaland). After the dissolution of the federation, Nyasaland became an independent member of the Commonwealth as Malawi in 1964. Two years later it became a republic, while remaining in the Commonwealth.

Great Britain

Statesman's Year Book, 1891–1966; Walker, pp. xxii, xxiv.

189 ORANGE RIVER COLONY

In 1848 the area north of the Orange River occupied by the Boers was annexed by the governor of Cape Colony (q.v.) and administered by a resident appointed from Capetown. This annexation proved abortive and British sovereignty was transferred, in 1854, to the Boers, who established the Orange Free State. This state was occupied and annexed as a result of the Anglo-Boer War of 1899–1902 and was renamed the Orange River Colony. Until 1907 the high commissioner for South Africa (q.v.), who was also governor of the Cape Colony, served as governor of the Orange River Colony, while a lieutenant governor administered the area. In 1907 responsible government was granted and the lieutenant governor became governor. In 1910 the Orange River Colony, together with the Cape Colony, Natal (q.v.), and Transvaal (q.v.), united to form the Union of South Africa (q.v.).

Walker, pp. xix, xxi.

190 ORISSA

The area of Orissa, southwest of Bengal, was occupied by the British after 1803. Until 1912 it was part of Bengal (q.v.), and then, until 1936, of Bihar (q.v.). In 1936 it became a separate province, and eleven years later Orissa became a state of the Union of India (v. India).

India Office List and Burma Office List, 1947, p. 28.

191 OUDH

The kingdom of Oudh (or Awadh) in northern India was annexed to the British crown in 1856 on charges of misgovernment, and a chief commissioner was appointed to administer the area. Oudh remained a separate province until 1877 when it was amalgamated with Agra (v. United Provinces of Agra and Oudh).

Chief Commissioners

1856-1857	James Outram (1)	1859-1866	Charles John Wingfield
1857	Henry Montgomery Lawrence	1866-1867	John Strachey
1857	John Sherbrooke Banks	1867-1871	Richard Henry Davies
1857-1858	James Outram (2)	1871	Lousada Barrow
1858-1859	Robert Montgomery	1871-1876	George Ebenezer Wilson Couper
		1876-1877	John Forbes David Inglis

India List and India Office List, 1902, p. 129.

192 PALESTINE

At the end of World War I, at the parcelling out of the non-Anatolian Asian portion of the Ottoman Empire as mandates, Palestine fell to Britain's lot. It was projected as a future Jewish homeland, although little was done before World War II in this respect. However, immigration to Palestine increased markedly after 1945, and in 1948 the Republic of Israel was proclaimed and the British high commissioner departed.

High Commissioners

1920-1925	Herbert Louis Samuel	1938-1944	Harold Alfred MacMichael
1925-1928	Herbert Charles Onslow Plumer	1944-1946	John Standish Surtees Prendergast
1928-1931	John Robert Chancellor		Vereker, Viscount Gort
1931-1938	Arthur Grenfell Wauchope	1946-1948	Alan Gordon Cunningham

Statesman's Year Book, 1920–48.

193 PAPUA

Papua, the southeastern part of New Guinea, was annexed to the Australian colony of Queensland (q.v.) in 1883. Five years later it was annexed to Great Britain under the name British New Guinea. In 1906 it was made a territory of Australia and renamed Papua. Papua was occupied by the Japanese from 1942 to 1945. After the war Papua and the area immediately to the north, British New Guinea (q.v.) were administratively combined, and since 1949 the entire area has been known as Papua and New Guinea.

Great Britain

Australian Encyclopaedia, 6:480; *Pacific Islands Year Book and Who's Who*, p. 393.

194 PENANG

In search of a port east of India the British secured, in 1786, by cession from the sultan of Kedah, the small island of Penang oft the northwestern coast of the Malay Peninsula. During its early existence Penang was called Prince of Wales Island. In 1800 the mainland territory opposite, called Province Wellesley, was purchased. In 1805 Penang was raised to the status of a presidency. Nonetheless, Penang proved unsuitable because of widespread piracy in the area and because of its inferior harbor facilities. Consequently the British secured Singapore (q.v.) in 1824, and two years later Penang, Singapore, and Malacca were united to form the Straits Settlements (q.v.).

Cowan.

195 PENNSYLVANIA

Parts of Pennsylvania were settled before the middle of the 17th century by both the Swedes (v. New Sweden, 402) and the Dutch (v. New Netherlands, 277). Pennsylvania was included in the charter given to James, Duke of York, in 1664 (v. New York). However, in 1681 the area was detached from New York and granted as a proprietary to William Penn who began bringing in settlers immediately. Pennsylvania remained a proprietary province under the Penn family until 1776 and was ordinarily ruled by deputy governors appointed by the proprietors. In 1776 the last proprietary governor was expelled.

Governors

1681–1682	William Markham (1)	1726–1736	Patrick Gordon
1682–1684	William Penn (1)	1736–1738	James Logan
1684–1688	Thomas Lloyd (1)	1738–1747	George Thomas
1688–1690	John Blackwell	1747–1748	Anthony Palmer
1690–1693	Thomas Lloyd (2)	1748–1754	James Hamilton (1)
1693–1699	William Markham (2)	1754–1756	Robert Hunter Morris
1699–1701	William Penn (2)	1756–1759	William Denny
1701–1703	Andrew Hamilton	1759–1763	James Hamilton (2)
1703–1704	Edward Shippen	1763–1771	John Penn (1)
1704–1709	John Evans	1771	James Hamilton (3)
1709–1717	Charles Gookin	1771–1773	Richard Penn
1717–1726	William Keith	1773–1776	John Penn

Greene, pp. 25–47; "Officers of the Province of Pennsylvania," pp. 621–23.

196 PERSIAN GULF

European interest in the Persian Gulf began in 1515 when the Portuguese occupied Hormuz (q.v.). The East India Company began trading after 1614 and soon acquired the dominant position among the European nations trading there. In 1763 a residency was established at Bushir and later another at Basra. In 1822 these were amalgamated to form the Persian Gulf residency. In 1820, and again in 1853, Great Britain imposed truces on the neighboring sheikhdoms, designed to suppress the piracy endemic to the Gulf. Until 1873 the resident was subordinate to the governor of Bombay (q.v.), and from 1873 to 1947 to the viceroy of India (q.v.). He resided at Bushir, on the Persian mainland until 1946 when the headquarters of the residency was moved to Bahrain. Early in this century the states of Bahrain and Kuwait (qq.v.) were taken under British protection and political agents appointed. British representatives in Qatar, the trucial sheikhdoms, and Omen are also subordinate to the chief resident.

Chief Political Residents

1822–1823	John Macleod	1900–1904	Charles Arnold Kemball
1823–1827	Ephraim Gerrish Stannus	1904–1920	Percy Zachariah Cox
1827–1831	David Wilson	1920–1924	Arthur Prescott Trevor
1831–1835	David Alexander Blane	1924–1927	Francis Beville Prideaux
1835–1838	James Morison	1927–1929	Lionel Berkeley Holt Haworth
1838–1852	Samuel Hennell	1929	Cyril Charles Johnson Barrett
1852–1856	Arnold Borrowes Kemball	1929–1932	Hugh Vincent Biscoe
1856–1862	Felix Jones	1932–1939	Trenchard Craven William Fowle
1862–1872	Lewis Pelly	1939–1946	Charles Geoffrey Prior
1872–1891	Edward Charles Ross	1946–1953	William Rupert Hay
1891–1894	Adelbert Cecil Talbot	1953–1958	Bernard Alexander Brocas Burrows
1894–1897	Frederick Alexander Wilson	1958–1961	George Humphrey Middleton
1897–1900	Malcolm John Meade	1961–1966	William Henry Tucker Luce
		1966—	Robert Stewart Crawford

Kelly, passim; Lorimer, 2:2674–75; *Statesman's Year Book*, 1900 to date.

197 PITCAIRN ISLAND

Pitcairn Island, in the east-central Pacific Ocean, was discovered by an English navigator in 176
In 1790 it was settled by mutineers from the *Bounty*. Pitcairn Island was governed by annually
elected chief magistrates whose names are known, with a few exceptions, from 1838. In 1856 the
inhabitants removed to Norfolk Island (q.v.), but seven years later some returned to Pitcairn, and
today both islands remain inhabited by descendants of the mutineers. The chief magistrates
were replaced by the president of the council from 1897 to 1904. In 1904 the office of chief
magistrate was reinstituted. Since 1953 the chief magistrate has been elected triennially. An
unofficial British protectorate was instituted over Pitcairn Island in the early 19th century. In
1898 the island was formally brought within the jurisdiction of the Western Pacific High Commission (q.v.). In 1952 responsibility was transferred to the governor of Fiji (q.v.).

Chief Magistrates

1838-1839	Edward Quintal
1840-1841	Arthur Quintal I
1842	Fletcher Christian II
1843	Matthew McCoy
1844	Thursday October Christian II (1)
1845-1846	Arthur Quintal II (1)
1847	Charles Christian III
1848	George Adams
1849	Simon Young
1850	Arthur Quintal II (2)
1851	Thursday October Christian II (2)
1852	Abraham Blatchly Quintal
1853	Matthew McCoy
1854	Arthur Quintal II (3)
1855-1856	George Henry Frederick Young
1857-1863	(abandoned, see Norfolk Island)
1864	Thursday October Christian II (3)
1865-1866	Moses Young (1)
1867	Thursday October Christian II (4)
1868	Robert Pitcairn Buffett
1869	Moses Young (2)
1870-1872	James Russell McCoy (1)
1873	Thursday October Christian II (5)
1874	(unknown)
1875	Moses Young (3)
1876	Thursday October Christian II (6)
1877	(unknown)
1878-1879	James Russell McCoy (2)
1880	Thursday October Christian II (7)
1881	Moses Young (4)
1882	Thursday October Christian II (8)
1883	James Russell McCoy (3)
1884-1885	Benjamin Stanley Young (1)
1886-1889	James Russell McCoy (4)
1890-1891	Charles Carleton Vieder Young
1892	Benjamin Stanley Young (2)

Presidents of the Council

1893-1896	James Russell McCoy (5)
1897	William Alfred Young (1)
1898-1904	James Russell McCoy (6)
1904	William Alfred Young (2)

Chief Magistrates

1904-1906	James Russell McCoy (7)
1907	Arthur Herbert Young
1908	William Alfred Young (3)
1909	Edmund McCoy
1910-1919	Gerard Bromley Christian
1920	Charles R. Parkin Christian (1)
1921	Fred Christian
1922	Charles R. Parkin Christian (2)
1923-1924	Edgar Allen Christian (1)
1925	Charles R. Parkin Christian (3)
1926-1929	Edgar Allen Christian (2)
1930-1931	Arthur Herbert Young
1932	Edgar Allen Christian (3)
1933-1934	Charles R. Parkin Christian (4)
1935-1939	Edgar Allen Christian (4)
1940	Andrew David Young
1941	Frederick Martin Christian (1)
1942	Charles R. Parkin Christian (5)
1943	Frederick Martin Christian (2)
1944	Charles R. Parkin Christian (6)
1945-1948	Henry Norris Young
1949	Charles R. Parkin Christian (7)
1950-1951	Warren C. Christian (1)
1952-1954	John Lorenzo Christian (1)
1955-1957	Charles R. Parkin Christian (8)
1958-1960	Warren C. Christian (2)
1961-1966	John Lorenzo Christian (2)
1967—	Purvis Young

Nicolson, pp. 208-9. The names of the early chief magistrates are recorded in the Pitcairn Island Register Book and in a register kept by John Buffett, Chief Magistrate of Norfolk Island,
from 1867 to 1870 and 1881 to 1882.

198 PRINCE EDWARD ISLAND

Prince Edward Island, off the coast of Nova Scotia, was occupied by the French (v. Île Saint-Jean, 34) until its seizure by the English in 1758. Until 1769 it was part of Nova Scotia (q.v.) but in that year it was created a separate colony. In 1851 Prince Edward Island was granted responsible government. It did not join the Confederation of Canada until 1873, six years after its formation.

Governors

1770-1775	Walter Patterson (1)	1836-1837	John Harvey
1775-1780	Phillips Callbeck	1837-1841	Charles Augustus FitzRoy
1780-1786	Walter Patterson (2)	1841-1847	Henry Vere Huntley
1786-1804	Edmund Fanning	1847-1850	Donald Campbell
1804-1813	Joseph Frederick Wallet DesBarres	1851-1854	Alexander Bannerman
		1854-1859	Dominick Daly
1813-1824	Charles Douglass Smith	1859	Charles Young
1824-1831	John Ready	1859-1868	George Dundas
1831-1835	Aretas William Young	1868-1870	Archibald Edward Harbord Anson
		1870-1873	William Cleaver Francis Robinson

Audet, pp. 64–66; Callbeck, passim.

199 PROVIDENCE

The island of Providence was located in the southwestern Caribbean some 100 miles off the coast of Nicaragua. It was settled by the Providence Company, an offshoot of the Somers Islands Company (v. Bermuda) in 1630. In spite of its strategic location astride the shipping routes to the Isthmus of Panama, the colony remained under company rule and was weakened by internal strife. In 1641 it was captured by a Spanish expedition from Cartagena (328). In 1665 Providence was briefly recaptured by English buccaneers, but it was retaken by Spain within a year (v. Santa Catalina, 385).

Governors

1630-1636	Philip Bell	1638-1640	Nathaniel Butler
1636-1638	Robert Hunt	1640-1641	Andrew Carter

Newton, passim.

200 PUNJAB

Most of the Punjab area of western India was occupied by the Sikh kingdom in the early 19th century. As a result of the First Sikh War the eastern part was annexed to British India (v. India) in 1846, and three years later the remainder was likewise annexed. Until 1856 the Punjab was ruled by a Board of Administration, then by chief commissioners to 1859 when a lieutenant governor was appointed on the transfer of the old Mughal capital of Delhi to its jurisdiction. Delhi (q.v.) was created a separate province in 1912. In 1921 the Punjab was raised to a governor's province. In 1947 the province of the Punjab was divided between the new states of India and Pakistan.

Chief Commissioner
1856-1859   John Laird Mair Lawrence

Lieutenant Governors
1859-1865   Robert Montgomery
1865-1870   Donald Friell Macleod
1870-1871   Henry Marion Durand
1871-1877   Robert Henry Davies
1877-1882   Robert Eyles Egerton
1882-1887   Charles Umpherston Aitchison
1887-1892   James Broadwood Lyall
1892-1897   Dennis Fitzpatrick
1897-1902   William Mackworth Young
1902-1907   Charles Montgomery Rivaz
1907-1908   Denzil Charles Jelf Ibbetson

1908-1911   Louis William Dane
1911-1913   James McCrone Douie
1913-1919   Michael Francis O'Dwyer
1919-1921   Edward Douglas Maclagan

Governors
1921-1924   Edward Douglas Maclagan
1924-1928   William Malcolm Hailey
1928-1933   Geoffrey Fitzhervey de
              Montmorency
1933-1938   Herbert William Emerson
1938-1941   Henry Duffield Craik
1941-1946   Bertrand James Glancy
1946-1947   Evan Meredith Jenkins

India Office List and Burma Office List, 1940, p. 118.

201 QUEENSLAND

The first settlement in Queensland, located in northeastern Australia, was a penal colony established from New South Wales (q.v.) in 1824. In 1842 the area was opened to free settlement. Seventeen years later it was detached from New South Wales, granted responsible government, and constituted a separate colony under a governor. In 1901 Queensland joined the newly established Commonwealth of Australia (q.v.).

Governors
1859-1868   George Ferguson Bowen
1868-1871   Samuel Wensley Blackall
1871-1875   George Augustus Constantine
              Phipps, Marquess of Normanby
1875-1877   William Wellington Cairns

1877-1883   Arthur Edward Kennedy
1883-1889   Anthony Musgrave
1889-1896   Henry Wylie Norman
1896-1901   Charles Wallace Alexander
              Napier Cochrane-Baillie, Baron
              Lamington

Australian Encyclopaedia, 4:354—55.

202 RÉUNION

For the British governors of Réunion from 1810 to 1815, see the Frency colony, Réunion, 54.

203 RHODE ISLAND

Rhode Island was settled by religious dissidents from Massachusetts Bay (q.v.) in 1638. The colony consisted originally of four towns—Newport, Portsmouth, Providence, and Warwick— each separately governed. After 1647 these towns began a process of amalgamation which was completed in 1654. In 1663 the colony was granted a charter as Rhode Island. From 1686 to 1689 Rhode Island was part of the short-lived Dominion of New England. In 1775 the colony ceased allegiance to Great Britain.

Governors

Portsmouth
1638-1639	William Coddington
1639-1640	William Hutchinson

Newport
1639-1640	William Coddington

Newport and Portsmouth
1640-1647	William Coddington (1)

Newport, Portsmouth, Providence, Warwick
1647-1648	John Coggeshall
1648-1649	Jeremy Clarke
1649-1650	John Smith
1650-1651	Nicholas Easton

Newport and Portsmouth
1651-1653	William Coddington (2)
1653-1654	John Sanford

Providence and Warwick
1651-1652	Samuel Gorton
1652-1653	John Smith
1653-1654	Gregory Dexter

Newport, Portsmouth, Providence, Warwick
1654	Nicholas Easton (1)
1654-1657	Roger Williams
1657-1660	Benedict Arnold (1)
1660-1662	William Brenton (1)
1662-1663	Benedict Arnold (2)

Rhode Island
1663-1666	Benedict Arnold
1666-1669	William Brenton (2)

1669-1672	Benedict Arnold (3)
1672-1674	Nicholas Easton (2)
1674-1676	William Coddington (1)
1676-1677	Walter Clarke (1)
1677-1678	Benedict Arnold (4)
1678	William Coddington (2)
1678-1680	John Cranston
1680-1683	Peleg Sanford
1683-1685	William Coddington, Jr.
1685-1686	Henry Bull (1)
1686	Walter Clarke (2)
1686-1689	Edmond Andros
1689-1690	John Coggeshall
1690	Henry Bull (2)
1690-1695	John Easton
1695	Caleb Carr
1696-1698	Walter Clarke (3)
1698-1727	Samuel Cranston
1727-1732	Joseph Jencks
1732-1733	William Wanton
1734-1740	John Wanton
1740-1743	Richard Ward
1743-1745	William Greene (1)
1745-1746	Gideon Wanton (1)
1746-1747	William Greene (2)
1747-1748	Gideon Wanton (2)
1748-1755	William Greene (3)
1755-1757	Stephen Hopkins (1)
1757-1758	William Greene (4)
1758-1762	Stephen Hopkins (2)
1762-1763	Samuel Ward (1)
1763-1765	Stephen Hopkins (3)
1765-1767	Samuel Ward (2)
1767-1768	Stephen Hopkins (4)
1768-1769	Josias Lyndon
1769-1775	Joseph Wanton

Mohr, pp. 49−51.

204 RHODESIA AND NYASALAND

In 1953 Nyasaland, Northern Rhodesia, and Southern Rhodesia (qq.v.) united to form the Federation of Rhodesia and Nyasaland, and a governor-general was appointed. The many differences in policy between the African-dominated Northern Rhodesia and Nyasaland, and Southern Rhodesia led to the dissolution of the federation in 1963.

Governors-General
1953-1957   John Jestyn Llewellin, Baron
            Llewellin
1957-1963   Simon Ramsay, Earl of Dalhousie

Statesman's Year Book, 1953—63.

205 RUPERT'S LAND

Rupert's Land was the name given to the area granted to the Hudson's Bay Company (q.v.) in 1670. Broadly, it included all lands draining into Hudson's Bay. Between 1672 and 1719 posts were established at York Fort, Albany, and Churchill, all on the shores of the bay, to serve as entrepots for the fur trade. During the 18th century other posts were established inland. The English traders competed first with the French *coureurs de bois* and later with the interlopers from British Canada (q.v.). These last formed in 1776, the North West Company, which was able to compete very successfully with the Hudson's Bay Company. Hudson's Bay Company rule, such as it was, was carried out by the governors or chief factors of the various posts. Of these, those three established early, as mentioned above, were considered the most important. This decentralization unquestionably contributed to the success of the North West Company, so in 1810 the Hudson's Bay Company's territories were divided into a Northern Department (including York, Churchill, and the Saskatchewan and Winnipeg posts) and a Southern Department (including, Albany, Moose, and Eastmain)—each under a superintendent. In 1815 a governor-in-chief was appointed who, significantly, had never been engaged in the fur trade. With the amalgamation of the Hudson's Bay and North West Companies in 1821, the office of governor-in-chief was temporarily abolished, but it was revived, in practice, five years later (although formally only in 1839). The colony of Assiniboia (q.v.) was administratively separate from Rupert's Land, although the governor-in-chief of Rupert's Land took precedence over the governor of Assiniboia. The territorial rights of the Hudson's Bay Company were sold to Canada in 1869, and were transferred a year later. Four Canadian provinces and the Northwest and Yukon Territories were eventually created from them.

York Fort (Fort Nelson)

Chiefs			
1672-1674	Charles Bayly (1)	1697-1714	(under France)
1674-1675	William Lydall	1714-1718	James Knight
1675-1679	Charles Bayly (2)	1718-1722	Henry Kelsey
1679-1682	John Nixon	1722-1726	Thomas McCliesh (Macklish) (1)
1682-1683	John Bridgar	1726-1727	Anthony Beale
1683-1686	Thomas Phipps	1727-1734	Thomas McCliesh (2)
1686-1693	George Geyer	1734-1737	Thomas White (1)
1693-1694	Thomas Walsh	1737-1741	James Isham (1)
1694-1696	(under France)	1741-1746	Thomas White (2)
1696-1697	Henry Baley	1746-1748	James Isham (2)
		1748-1750	John Newton
		1750-1761	James Isham (3)

1761	Andrew Graham		1723-1727	Richard Norton (1)
1761-1762	Humphrey Marten (1)		1727-1731	Anthony Beale
1762-1775	Ferdinand Jacobs		1731-1735	Richard Norton (2)
1775-1781	Humphrey Marten (2)		1735-1736	James Napper
1781-1782	Matthew Cocking		1736-1741	Richard Norton (3)
1782-1783	(abandoned)		1741-1745	James Isham
1783-1786	Humphrey Marten (3)		1745-1749	Robert Pilgrim
1786-1798	Joseph Colen[1]		1749-1752	Joseph Isbister
1798-1802	John Ballanden[1]		1752-1759	Ferdinand Jacobs (1)
1802-1809	John MacNab		1759-1760	Moses Norton (1)
1809-1810	William Hemmings Cook		1760-1762	Ferdinand Jacobs (2)

1761   Andrew Graham
1761-1762   Humphrey Marten (1)
1762-1775   Ferdinand Jacobs
1775-1781   Humphrey Marten (2)
1781-1782   Matthew Cocking
1782-1783   (abandoned)
1783-1786   Humphrey Marten (3)
1786-1798   Joseph Colen[1]
1798-1802   John Ballanden[1]
1802-1809   John MacNab
1809-1810   William Hemmings Cook

Albany
Chiefs
1679-1681   John Bridgar
1681-1683   James Knight (1)
1683-1686   Henry Sergeant
1686-1693   (under France)
1693-1697   James Knight (2)
1697-1698   John Fullartine (1)
1698-1700   James Knight (3)
1700-1705   John Fullartine (2)
1705-1708   Anthony Beale (1)
1708-1711   John Fullartine (3)
1711-1714   Anthony Beale (2)
1714-1715   Richard Staunton (1)
1715-1721   Thomas McCliesh (Macklish)
1721-1723   Joseph Myatt (1)
1723-1726   Richard Staunton (2)
1726-1730   Joseph Myatt (2)
1730-1737   Joseph Adams
1737-1739   Thomas Bird
1739-1740   Rowland Waggoner
1740-1741   George Spence (1)
1741-1748   Joseph Isbister (1)
1748-1753   George Spence (2)
1753-1756   Joseph Isbister (2)
1756-1764   Robert Temple
1764-1768   Humphrey Marten (1)
1768-1769   Thomas Hopkins
1769-1774   Humphrey Marten (2)
1774-1782   Thomas Hutchins
1782-1789   Edward Jarvis (1)
1789-1790   John MacNab (1)
1790-1792   Edward Jarvis (2)
1792-1800   John MacNab (2)
1800-1807   John Hodgson (1)
1807-1808   Thomas Vincent
1808-1810   John Hodgson (2)

Fort Churchill (Fort Prince of Wales)
Chiefs
1719-1722   Richard Staunton
1722-1723   Nathaniel Bishop

1723-1727   Richard Norton (1)
1727-1731   Anthony Beale
1731-1735   Richard Norton (2)
1735-1736   James Napper
1736-1741   Richard Norton (3)
1741-1745   James Isham
1745-1749   Robert Pilgrim
1749-1752   Joseph Isbister
1752-1759   Ferdinand Jacobs (1)
1759-1760   Moses Norton (1)
1760-1762   Ferdinand Jacobs (2)
1762-1773   Moses Norton (2)
1775-1782   Samuel Hearne (1)
1782-1783   (abandoned)
1783-1787   Samuel Hearne (2)
1787-1792   William Jefferson
1792-1797   Thomas Stayner (1)
1797-1798   William Auld (1)
1798-1800   Thomas Stayner (2)
1800-1802   John MacNab
1802-1804   William Auld (2)
1804-1805   Thomas Topping (1)
1805-1808   William Auld (3)
1808-1809   Thomas Topping (2)
1809-1810   William Auld (4)

Northern Department
Superintendents
1810-1814   William Auld
1814-1815   Thomas Thomas

Southern Department
Superintendent
1810-1814   Thomas Thomas

Rupert's Land
Governors-in-Chief
1815-1816   George Semple
1816-1818   James Bird
1818-1821   William Williams

Northern Department
Governor
1821-1826   George Simpson

Southern Department
Governor
1821-1826   William Williams

Rupert's Land
Governors-in-Chief
1826-1860   George Simpson
1862-1864   Alexander Grant Dallas
1864-1870   William Mactavish

1. Colen and Ballanden were entitled residents and were subordinate to chiefs who resided at the now more important inland posts. These were William Tomison, from 1786 to 1804, and James Bird, from 1804 to 1810.

Davies, pp. 331-32; Rich, passim.

206 SAINT EUSTATIUS

For the British governors of Saint Eustatius from 1672 to after 1674, 1690 to 1693, 1781, and 1810 to 1816, see the Dutch colony, Saint Eustatius, 280.

207 SAINT HELENA

Saint Helena is a small island in the South Atlantic Ocean, 1,200 miles west of Africa. It was discovered and named by the Portuguese in 1502. The island was occupied by the Dutch in 1645 but abandoned in 1651. It was then occupied by the East India Company for use as a way-station on the trip from England to India. Saint Helena remained under the administration of the East India Company until 1834 except for the period of Napoleon's exile there from 1815 to 1821 when it was directly administered by the crown. In 1834 the British government assumed direct and permanent control of the island. Ascension Island, from 1922, and Tristan da Cunha, from 1938, have formed dependencies of Saint Helena, which remains a crown colony.

Governors

1659–1661	John Dutton	1801–1808	Robert Patton
1661–1671	Robert Stringer	1808–1813	Alexander Beatson
1671–1672	Richard Coney	1813–1816	Mark Wilks
1672–1673	Anthony Beale	1816–1823	Hudson Lowe
1673	Richard Munden	1823–1828	Alexander Walker
1673–1674	Richard Kedgwin	1828–1836	Charles Dallas
1674–1678	Gregory Field	1836–1842	George Middlemore
1678–1690	John Blackmore	1842–1846	Hamelin Trelawney
1690–1693	Joshua Johnson	1846–1851	Patrick Ross
1693–1697	Richard Kelinge	1851–1856	Thomas Gore Browne
1697–1707	Stephen Poirier	1856–1863	Edward Hay Drummond Hay
1707–1708	Thomas Goodwin	1863–1870	Charles Elliot
1708–1711	John Roberts	1870–1873	Charles George Edward Patey
1711–1714	Benjamin Boucher	1873–1884	Hudson Ralph Janisch
1714–1719	Isaac Pyke (1)	1884–1887	Grant Blunt
1719–1723	Edward Johnson	1887–1897	William Grey-Wilson
1723–1727	John Smith	1897–1903	Robert Armitage Sterndale
1727–1731	Edward Byfield	1903–1911	Henry Lionel Gallwey
1731–1738	Isaac Pyke (2)	1912–1920	Harry Edward Spiller Cordeaux
1738–1739	John Goodwin	1920–1925	Robert Francis Peel
1740–1741	Robert Jenkins	1925–1932	Charles Henry Harper
1741	Thomas Lambert	1932–1938	Steuart Spencer Davis
1741–1743	George Gabriel Powel	1938–1941	Henry Guy Pilling
1743–1747	David Dunbar	1941–1947	William Bain Gray
1747–1764	Charles Hutchison	1947–1954	George Andrew Joy
1764–1782	John Skottowe	1954–1958	James Dundas Harford
1782–1788	Daniel Corneille	1958–1962	Robert Edmund Alford
1788–1800	Robert Brooke	1962–1968	John Osbaldiston Field
1800–1801	Francis Robson	1968——	Dermot Art Pelly Murphy

Information from Acting Government Secretary, Jamestown, Saint Helena. Also, Brooke, passim.

208 SAINT KITTS-NEVIS-ANGUILLA

Saint Kitts (or Saint Christopher) in the Lesser Antilles was settled by the English in 1623. During most of the 17th century the island was shared with the French, who occupied both ends while the British held the center (v. Saint-Christophe, 55). In 1702 the French were finally expelled from the island, which has remained British since. In 1882 the neighboring island of Nevis (q.v.), which had heretofore been governed separately, was, along with Anguilla, united with Saint Kitts in a single colony. Saint Kitts was a member of the Leeward Islands (q.v.) government from 1671 to 1960 and has since been a separate colony. It was a member of the West Indies Federation (q.v.) from 1958 to 1962, and became a member of the Associated States of the West Indies in 1967.

Saint Kitts

Governors

1623-1649	Thomas Warner
1649-1651	Rowland Rich (Redge)
1651-1660	Clement Everard
1660-1666	William Watts
1666-1671	(under France)

Deputy or Lieutenant Governors

1671-1681	Abednego Mathew
1682-1697	Thomas Hill
1697-1701	James Norton
1704-1706	Walter Hamilton
1706-1715	Michael Lambert
1715-1733	William Mathew, Jr.
1733-1769	Gilbert Fleming

Governors

1816	Stedman Rawlins
1816-1821	Thomas Probyn
1821-1832	Charles William Maxwell
1832-1833	William Nicolay

Lieutenant Governors

1834-1836	James Lyons Nixon
1836-1839	Henry George Macleod
1839-1847	Charles Cunningham
1847-1850	Robert James Mackintosh
1850-1855	Edward Hay Drummond Hay
1855-1859	Hercules George Robert Robinson
1860-1866	Benjamin Chilley Campbell Pine
1867-1869	James George Mackenzie
1869-1870	William Wellington Cairns

Presidents

1870-1872	Francis Spencer Wigley (1)
1872-1873	James Samuel Berridge
1873-1882	Alexander Wilson Moir

Saint Kitts-Nevis-Anguilla[1]

Presidents

1882-1883	Alexander Wilson Moir
1883-1885	Charles Monroe Eldridge
1885-1888	Francis Spencer Wigley (2)

Commissioner

1889-1895	John Kemys Spencer Churchill

Administrators

1895-1899	Thomas Risely Griffith
1899-1904	Charles Thomas Cox
1904-1906	Robert Bromley
1906-1916	Thomas Laurence Roxburgh
1916-1925	John Alder Burdon
1925-1929	Thomas Reginald St. Johnston
1929-1931	Terence Charles Macnaghten
1931-1940	Douglas Roy Stewart
1940-1947	James Dundas Harford
1947-1949	Leslie Stuart Greening
1949	Frederick Mitchell Noad
1949-1956	Hugh Burrowes
1956-1966	Henry Anthony Camilio Howard
1966-1967	Frederick Albert Phillips

Governors

1967—	Frederick Albert Phillips

1. Since 1969 Anguilla has been detached from Saint Kitts and Nevis and has been administered by commissioners. These have been:

1969	Anthony Lee
1969	John Alfred Cumber
1969—	Willoughby Harry Thompson

Information from H. Versailles, Acting Information Officer, Basseterre, Saint Kitts. Also, Public Record Office, *C.S.P.*, *Colonial*, *1661-68* to *1737*, passim; idem, *Journal of the Commissioner for Trade and Plantations*, *1704-8/1709* to *1768-75*, passim.

209 SAINT LUCIA

Saint Lucia, the largest of the Windward Islands in the Lesser Antilles, led a peculiarly checkered administrative existence before 1781. It was held by the French six times, and by the British three times, and was declared neutral twice. After 1781 it remained English except for
periods from 1783 to 1794, 1795 to 1796, and 1802 to 1803 when it was occupied by the French
(v. Sainte Lucie, 57). Until 1838 Saint Lucia was a separate colony. In 1838 it joined the
Windward Islands government under Barbados (q.v.). After the separation of Barbados, Saint
Lucia became a member of the Windward Islands (q.v.) government until its dissolution in 1960,
when it again became a separate colony. Since 1967 Saint Lucia has been a member of the Associated States of the West Indies.

Lieutenant Governors

1781-1783	Arthur St. Leger
1783-1794	(under France)
1794-1795	Charles Gordon
1795	James Stewart
1795-1796	(under France)
1796-1797	John Moore
1797-1798	James Drummond
1798-1802	George Prevost
1802	George Henry Vansittart
1802-1803	(under France)

Governors

1803-1807	Robert Brereton
1807-1814	Alexander Wood
1814-1815	Francis Delaval
1815-1816	Edward Stehelin
1816	Robert Douglass
1816-1817	Richard Augustus Seymour
1817-1818	Edward O'Hara
1818-1819	John Keane
1819-1821	John Joseph Winkler
1821-1824	John Montagu Mainwaring (1)
1824-1826	Nathaniel Shepherd Blackwell
1826-1827	John Montagu Mainwaring (2)
1827-1829	Lorenzo Moore
1829	David Stewart
1829-1830	Francis Power
1830-1831	James Alexander Farquharson (1)
1831	George Mackie
1831-1832	Mark Anthony Bozon
1832-1834	James Alexander Farquharson

Lieutenant Governors

1834-1837	Dudley St. Leger Hill
1837-1838	Thomas Bunbury
1838-1839	John Alexander Mein
1839-1841	Mathias Everard
1841-1843	George Graydon

1843-1844	Andrew Clarke
1844-1848	Arthur Wellesley Torrens
1848-1852	Charles Henry Darling
1852	Henry Clermont Cobbe
1852-1857	Maurice Power

Administrators

1857-1862	Henry Hegart Breen
1862-1869	James Mayer Grant
1869-1878	George William DesVoeux
1878-1879	Arthur Elibank Havelock
1881-1884	Roger Tuckfield Goldsworthy
1885-1889	Edward Daniel Laborde

Commissioners

1889-1891	Robert Baxter Llewelyn
1891-1897	Valesius Skipton Gouldsbury
1897-1899	Charles Anthony King-Harman
1900-1902	Harry Langhorne Thompson
1902-1905	George Melville
1905-1909	Philip Clarke Cork
1909-1914	Edward John Cameron
1914-1915	William Douglas Young
1915-1918	Charles Gideon Murray
1918-1927	Wilfred Bennett Davidson-Houston
1928-1935	Charles William Doorly
1935-1938	Edward William Baynes
1938-1944	Arthur Alban Wright
1944-1946	Edward Francis Twining
1947-1953	John Montague Stow
1953-1958	John Kingsmill Thorp

Administrators

1958-1962	Julian Edward Asquith, Earl of Oxford and Asquith
1962-1967	Gerald Jackson Bryan

Governors

1967—	Frederick Joseph Clarke

Information from the Office of the Administrator of Saint Lucia, Castries, Saint Lucia. Also,
Breen, pp. 97–113, 119–20, 420–21.

210 SAINT VINCENT

Saint Vincent, one of the Lesser Antilles, remained a refuge of the Caribs long after the settlement of its neighbors. Although granted by Charles I to the Earl of Carlisle in 1627, it remained unoccupied by Europeans until well into the 18th century. It was occupied by the British in 1762 and ceded to them by the Treaty of Paris in 1763. Except for a brief interval from 1779 to 1783 it has since remained a British colony. From 1833 to 1885 it was, together with the other Windward Islands, under Barbados (q.v.). From 1885 to 1960 it was part of the Windward Islands (q.v.) government. Since 1960 it has been a separate colony.

Lieutenant Governors
1763-1764   George Maddison
1764-1766   Joseph Higginson
1766   Lauchlin McLean
1766-1772   Ulysses FitzMaurice
1772-1776   Valentine Morris

Governors
1776-1779   Valentine Morris
1779-1783   (under France)
1783-1787   Edmund Lincoln
1787-1798   James Seton
1798-1802   William Bentinck
1802-1806   Henry William Bentinck
1806-1808   George Beckwith
1808-1829   Charles Brisbane
1829-1831   William John Struth[1]
1831-1833   George Fitzgerald Hill

Lieutenant Governors
1833-1842   George Tyler
1842-1845   Richard Doherty
1845-1853   John Campbell
1853-1854   Richard Graves MacDonell
1854-1861   Edward John Eyre
1861-1864   Anthony Musgrave

1864-1871   George Berkeley
1871-1875   William Hepburn Rennie
1875-1880   George Dundas
1880-1886   Augustus Frederick Gore

Administrators
1888-1889   Robert Baxter Llewelyn
1889-1893   Irwin Charles Maling
1893-1895   John Hartley Sandwith
1895-1901   Harry Langhorne Thompson
1901-1909   Edward John Cameron
1909-1915   Charles Gideon Murray
1915-1923   Reginald Popham Lobb
1923-1929   Robert Walter
1929-1933   Herbert Walter Peebles
1933-1936   Arthur Francis Grimble
1936-1938   Arthur Alban Wright
1938-1941   William Bain Gray
1941-1944   Alexander Elder Beattie
1944-1948   Ronald Herbert Garvey
1948-1955   Walter Fleming Coutts
1955-1961   Alexander Falconer Giles
1961-1966   Samuel Horatio Graham
1966-1967   John Lionel Chapman
1967——   Hywel George

1. President.

Information from the Administrator of Saint Vincent, Kingstown, Saint Vincent. Also, Shepard, passim.

211 SARAWAK

Sarawak in northern Borneo was ceded to James Brooke, an Englishman, by the sultan of Brunei (q.v.) in 1841. From 1841 to 1946, except for a period of occupation by Japanese troops from 1942 to 1945, Sarawak remained a possession of the Brooke family. In 1888 it officially came under British protection. In 1946 the last ruler of Sarawak, Charles Vyner Brooke, ceded his rights to Sarawak to the British crown and Sarawak became a crown colony. In 1963 Sarawak acceded to the newly formed Federation of Malaysia.

Great Britain

Governors
1946-1949   Charles Noble Arden-Clarke
1949   Duncan George Stewart

1949-1959   Anthony Foster Abell
1959-1963   Alexander Nicol Waddell

Colonial Office List, 1946-63.

212 SENEGAL

For the British governors of Senegal from 1758 to 1763 and 1809 to 1816, see the French colony, Senegal, 61.

213 SENEGAMBIA

The British had occupied the French colony of Senegal (61) in 1758 and had only returned the islet of Gorée (28) in 1763. The remainder, with the British posts on the Gambia River, was incorporated into the colony of Senegambia that was formed in 1765—the first British crown colony in Africa. Jurisdictional disputes among the British administrators of the colony facilitated the French recapture of Senegal in 1778, and by the Treaty of Paris in 1783 Great Britain retained only her former posts on the Gambia. These posts were put under the authority of the Company of Merchants trading to Africa (v. Gambia) and the colony of Senegambia officially came to an end, although in practical terms it had already ended in 1779 since no governors were appointed after that time.

Governors
1765-1775   Charles O'Hara[1]
1775-1777   Matthias MacNamara

1777-1778   John Clarke
1778-1779   William Lacy

1. From 1763 to 1765 John Barnes was governor, under the Royal African Company, of Britain's Senegalese possessions.

Gray, pp. 234—75; Martin, passim.

214 SEYCHELLES ISLANDS

The Seychelles Islands, in the western Indian Ocean, were discovered by the Portuguese in 1505. In 1743 the French claimed the islands and shortly thereafter began to settle them from Île de France (32). In 1794 the Seychelles were captured by the British, but they were treated as a French colony until 1810 when they were formally annexed and put under Mauritius (q.v.). The

Seychelles remained under Mauritius until 1903 when they were erected into a separate crown colony. Since 1965 the governors of the Seychelles have been ex officio high commissioners of the British Indian Ocean Territory (q.v.).

under France

Commandants

1788-1792	Louis-Jean-Baptiste-Philogène de Malavois
1792-1794	Charles-Joseph Esnouf
1794-1810	Jean-Baptiste Quéau de Quincy

under Great Britain

Civil Agents/Commissioners

1810-1811	Jean-Baptiste Quéau de Quincy
1811-1812	Bartholomew Sullivan
1812-1815	Bibye Lesage
1815-1822	Edward Henry Madge

Civil Agents

1822-1837	George Harrison
1837-1839	Arthur Wilson

Civil Commissioners

1839-1850	Charles Augustus Etienne Mylius
1850-1852	Robert William Keate
1852-1862	George Thompson Wade
1862-1868	Swinburne Ward

Chief Civil Commissioners

1868-1874	William Hales Franklyn
1874-1879	Charles Spencer Salmon

1879-1880	Arthur Elibank Havelock
1880-1882	Francis Theophilus Blunt
1882-1888	Arthur Cecil Stuart Barkly

Administrators

1889-1895	Thomas Risely Griffith
1895-1899	Henry Cockburn Stewart
1899-1903	Ernest Bickham Sweet-Escott

Governors

1903-1904	Ernest Bickham Sweet-Escott
1904-1912	Walter Edward Davidson
1912-1918	Charles Richard Mackey O'Brien
1918-1921	Eustace Edward Twisleton-Wykeham-Fiennes
1922-1927	Joseph Aloysius Byrne
1927	Malcolm Stevenson
1928-1934	DeSymons Montagu George Honey
1934-1936	Gordon James Lethem
1936-1942	Arthur Francis Grimble
1942-1947	William Marston Logan
1947-1951	Percy Selwyn Selwyn-Clarke
1951-1953	Frederick Crawford
1953-1958	William Addis
1958-1961	John Kingsmill Thorp
1961-1967	Julian Edward Asquith, Earl of Oxford and Asquith
1967-1969	Hugh Selby Norman-Walker
1969——	Bruce Greatbatch

Information from the Private Secretary, Government of Seychelles, Victoria, and from the Government Archivist, Victoria, Seychelles Is.

215 SIERRA LEONE

The province of Freedom, established in 1787 on the Sierra Leone coast of West Africa, was settled mainly by freed slaves from the former American colonies. Freedom was self-governing and not under direct British control. However, beginning in 1792 further settlers, again primarily freed slaves, arrived under the aegis of the Sierra Leone Company. These settlers were later supplemented by Maroons from Jamaica (q.v.) and by "recaptives," or Negroes taken by the British Navy from ships engaged in the slave trade after Great Britain's unilateral prohibition of the trade in 1807. Until 1808 the colony was governed by the Sierra Leone Company. In that year it became a crown colony. From 1821 to 1850 the governor of Sierra Leone exercised jurisdiction over the Gold Coast (q.v.), and from 1821 to 1843 over the Gambia (q.v.) as well. From 1866 to 1888 the governor of Sierra Leone was also governor-in-chief of the West Africa Settlements, which included Lagos and the Gold Coast until 1874, and the Gambia until 1888. With the separation of all the subordinate governments the West Africa Settlements government was abolished in 1888. In 1896 the interior of Sierra Leone, called the Protectorate, was annexed.

Great Britain

In 1961 Sierra Leone became an independent member of the British Commonwealth, and it is expected soon to become a republic within the Commonwealth.

Governors

1792	John Clarkson
1792–1796	William Dawes (1)
1796–1798	Zachary Macaulay
1798–1801	Thomas Ludlam (1)
1801–1803	William Dawes (2)
1803–1805	William Day
1805–1808	Thomas Ludlam (2)
1808–1810	Thomas Perronet Thompson
1810–1811	Edward Henry Columbine
1811–1815	Charles William Maxwell
1815–1824	Charles MacCarthy
1824–1825	Daniel Molloy Hamilton
1825–1826	Charles Turner
1826	Kenneth Macaulay
1826	Samuel Smart
1826–1827	Neil Campbell

Lieutenant Governors

1827–1828	Hugh Lumley (1)
1828	Dixon Denham
1828	Hugh Lumley (2)
1828	Samuel Smart
1828–1829	Henry John Ricketts
1829–1830	Alexander Maclean Fraser
1830–1833	Alexander Findlay
1833	Michael Melville
1833–1834	Octavius Temple
1834–1835	Thomas Cole
1835–1837	Henry Dundas Campbell

Governors

1837–1840	Richard Doherty
1840–1841	John Jeremie
1842–1844	George Macdonald
1844–1846	William Fergusson
1846–1852	Norman William Macdonald
1852–1854	Arthur Edward Kennedy (1)
1855–1862	Stephen John Hill
1862–1866	Samuel Wensley Blackall

West African Settlements

Governors

1866–1868	Samuel Wensley Blackall
1868–1872	Arthur Edward Kennedy (2)
1872–1873	John Pope Hennessey
1873	Robert William Keate
1873–1875	George Berkeley
1875–1877	Cornelius Hendricksen Kortright
1877–1881	Samuel Rowe (1)
1881–1885	Arthur Elibank Havelock
1885–1888	Samuel Rowe (2)

Sierra Leone

Governors

1888–1892	James Shaw Hay
1892–1894	Francis Fleming
1894–1900	Frederic Cardew
1900–1904	Charles Anthony King-Harman
1904–1911	Leslie Probyn
1911–1916	Edward Marsh Merewether
1916–1922	Richard James Wilkinson
1922–1927	Alexander Ransford Slater
1927–1931	Joseph Aloysius Byrne
1931–1934	Arnold Meinholt Hodson
1934–1937	Henry Monck-Mason Moore
1937–1941	Douglas James Jardine
1941–1948	Hubert Craddock Stevenson
1948–1953	George Beresford Stooke
1953–1956	Robert de Zouche Hall
1956–1961	Maurice Henry Dorman

Governors-General

1961–1962	Maurice Henry Dorman
1962–1968	Henry Josiah Lightfoot Boston
1968——	Banja Tejan-Sie

Colonial Office List, 1900–1961; Crooks, pp. 366–69; Fyfe, passim.

216 SIND

Sind, in southwestern India, was annexed to British India in 1843 and placed under a commissioner subject to the governor of Bombay (q.v.). In 1936 it became a separate province of India (q.v.) under a governor. In 1947 Sind became a part of Pakistan.

Commissioners

1843-1847	Charles James Napier
1847-1851	Richard Keith Pringle
1851-1859	Henry Edward Bartle Frere
1859-1862	Jonathan Duncan Inverarity
1862-1867	Samuel Mansfield
1867-1868	William Henry Havelock
1868-1877	William Lockyer Merewether
1877-1879	Francis Dawes Melvill
1879-1887	Henry Napier Bruce Erskine
1887-1889	Charles Bradley Pritchard
1889-1891	Arthur Charles Trevor
1891-1900	Henry Evan Murchison James
1900-1902	Robert Giles
1902-1903	Alexander Cumine
1903-1904	Horace Charles Mules

1904-1905	John William Pitt Muir-Mackenzie
1905-1912	Arthur Delaval Younghusband
1912-1916	William Henry Lucas
1916-1920	Henry Staveley Lawrence
1920-1925	Jean Louis Rieu
1925-1926	Patrick Robert Cadell
1926-1929	Walter Frank Hudson
1929-1931	George Arthur Thomas
1931-1935	Raymond Evelyn Gibson
1935-1936	Godfrey Ferdinando Stratford Collins

Governors

1936-1941	Lancelot Graham
1941-1946	Hugh Dow
1946-1947	Robert Francis Mudie

Gazetteer of the Province of Sind, pp. 145–53; *India Office List*, 1905–37; *India Office List and Burma Office List*, 1938–47.

217 SINGAPORE

Singapore, at the southern tip of the Malay Peninsula, was purchased in 1819 from the sultan of Johore to replace Penang (q.v.) as the main British port in Southeast Asia. From 1819 to 1826 it was governed by residents. In 1826 it joined Penang and Malacca (271), acquired from the Dutch in 1825, to form the Straits Settlements (q.v.). After the end of the Japanese occupation in 1945 the government of the Straits Settlements was not reconstituted. Instead, all its components except Singapore joined together in the Union of Malaya (v. Malaya). Singapore, because of its particular value to British imperial strategy, was separated and created a crown colony. In 1959 Singapore became independent, and three years later it joined the Federation of Malaysia, only to withdraw in 1965 and join the Commonwealth as an independent republic.

Governors

1946-1952	Franklin Charles Gimson
1952-1955	John Fearns Nicoll

1955-1957	Robert Brown Black
1957-1959	William Allmond Codrington Goode

Buckley, passim; *Statesman's Year Book*, 1946–59.

218 SOUTH AFRICA (HIGH COMMISSION)

Before 1931 the governors of the Cape Colony (q.v.) and then the governors-general of the Union of South Africa (q.v.) served ex officio as high commissioners for South Africa (q.v.) and in that role they were responsible for the protectorates of Basutoland, Bechuanaland, and Swaziland (qq.v.) which were administered by resident commissioners. In 1931 the offices of governor-general and high commissioner were separated and the high commissioner was thenceforth responsible only for the protectorates. In 1964, as the three territories evolved toward independence, the office of high commissioner was abolished.

High Commissioners

1901-1905	Alfred Milner, Viscount Milner
1905-1910	William Waldegrave Palmer, Earl of Selborne
1910-1931	(under Union of South Africa)
1931-1935	Herbert James Stanley
1935-1940	William Henry Clark
1940-1941	Walter Clarence Huggard (1)
1941-1944	William George Arthur Ormsby-Gore, Baron Harlech
1944	Walter Clarence Huggard (2)
1944-1951	Evelyn Baring
1951-1955	John Helier le Rougetel
1955-1958	Percivale Liesching
1959-1963	John Primatt Ratcliffe Maud
1963-1964	Hugh Southern Stephenson

Walker, p. xxiii.

219 SOUTH ARABIAN FEDERATION

Until 1959 the government of Aden had been responsible for the so-called Eastern and Western Protectorates, encompassing some twenty emirates, sheikhdoms, and sultanates in subsidiary treaty alliance with Great Britain. In 1959 five of these formed the Federation of Arab Emirates of the South, and by 1963 most of the other states had joined. In 1962 the name was changed to Federation of South Arabia. In 1963 Aden itself joined and ceased to be a crown colony. In 1967 the Federation of South Arabia became independent as the Republic of South Yemen.

High Commissioners

1959-1960	William Henry Tucker Luce
1960-1963	Charles Hepburn Johnston
1963-1965	Gerald Kennedy Nicholas Trevaski
1965-1967	Richard Gordon Turnbull
1967—	Humphrey Trevelyan

Statesman's Year Book, 1959—67.

220 SOUTH AUSTRALIA

The area of South Australia was under New South Wales (q.v.) until 1836, although unsettled. In that year settlement began under the aegis of the South Australia Company, operating under the principles of controlled colonization formulated by Edward Gibbon Wakefield. From 1836 to 1845 and 1855 to 1901 South Australia was under governors; from 1845 to 1855 under lieutenant governors. From 1863 to 1910 Northern Australia (q.v.), also known as the Northern Territory, was under the jurisdiction of South Australia. In 1901 South Australia joined the new Commonwealth of Australia (v. Australia).

Governors

1836-1838	John Hindmarsh
1838-1841	George Gawler
1841-1845	George Grey
1845-1848	Frederick Holt Robe
1848-1854	Henry Edward Fox Young

1855–1862	Richard Graves MacDonell	1883–1889	William Cleaver Francis Robinson
1862–1869	Dominick Daly	1889–1895	Algernon Hawkins Thomond Keith-Falconer, Earl of Kintore
1869–1873	James Fergusson	1895–1899	Thomas Fowell Buxton
1873–1877	Anthony Musgrave	1899–1901	Hallam Tennyson, Baron Tennyson
1877–1883	William Francis Drummond Jervois		

Australian Encyclopaedia, 4:355–56.

221 SOUTH CAROLINA

The first attempt at settlement in what became South Carolina was made by French Huguenots in 1562, but it failed. Carolina, including both South Carolina and North Carolina (q.v.), was granted by Charles II to a group of proprietors in 1663 but settlement was planted only in 1670. Until 1719 governors were appointed by the proprietors. After 1719 the crown appointed South Carolina's governors although proprietary rights to the colony were only officially transferred to the crown in 1729. From 1691 to 1712 North Carolina was ruled by governors appointed from South Carolina. South Carolina remained a royal province until 1775 when, at the outbreak of the American Revolution, royal government ended.

Governors

1670–1671	William Sayle	1710–1711	Robert Gibbes
1671–1672	Joseph West (1)	1711–1717	Charles Craven
1672–1674	John Yeamans	1717–1719	Robert Johnson (1)
1674–1682	Joseph West (2)	1719–1721	James Moore (2)
1682–1684	Joseph Morton	1721–1724	Francis Nicholson
1684	Richard Kyrle	1724–1729	Arthur Middleton
1684–1685	Joseph West (3)	1729–1735	Robert Johnson (2)
1685	Robert Quary	1735–1737	Thomas Broughton
1685–1686	Joseph Morton	1737–1743	William Bull (1)
1686–1690	James Colleton	1743–1756	James Glen
1690–1692	Seth Sothel	1756–1760	William Henry Lyttelton
1692–1693	Philip Ludwell	1760–1761	William Bull (2)
1693–1694	Thomas Smith	1761–1764	Thomas Boone
1694–1695	Joseph Blake (1)	1764–1766	William Bull, Jr. (1)
1695–1696	John Archdale	1766–1769	Charles Greville Montagu (1)
1696–1700	Joseph Blake (2)	1769–1771	William Bull, Jr. (2)
1700–1703	James Moore (1)	1771–1774	Charles Greville Montagu (2)
1703–1709	Nathaniel Johnson	1774–1775	William Bull, Jr. (3)
1709–1710	Edward Tynte	1775	William Campbell

McCrady, *History of South Carolina under Proprietary Government*, p. 719; idem, *History of South Carolina under the Royal Governors*, pp. 799–800.

222 SOUTHERN RHODESIA

In 1889 the British South African Company was conceded the right to settle and administer the territory north of the British possessions in South Africa (q.v.). In 1893 the major African kingdom of the area, that of the Ndebele, was subjugated. Until 1894 the colony was known as Mashonaland and was governed by a resident commissioner. In that year it was renamed Southern Rhodesia. Southern Rhodesia was governed by the British South African Company until 1923 when it became a crown colony with self-government. From 1953 to 1963 it was the dominant member of the Federation of Rhodesia and Nyasaland (v. Rhodesia and Nyasaland). Over the years Southern Rhodesia acquired a large immigrant white settler population, and the fear that political control of the colony would eventually fall to the majority African population led the white leaders of Southern Rhodesia to proclaim its independence in 1965. While Great Britain has refused to recognize this act, Rhodesia has nonetheless been effectively independent since that time.

Mashonaland

Resident Commissioners

1890-1891	Archibald Ross Colquhoun
1891-1894	Leander Starr Jameson

Southern Rhodesia

Administrators

1894-1896	Leander Starr Jameson
1896-1897	Albert Henry George Grey, Earl Grey
1897-1914	William Henry Milton
1914-1923	Francis Drummond Percy Chaplin

Governors

1923-1928	John Robert Chancellor
1928-1934	Cecil Hunter Rodwell
1934-1942	Herbert James Stanley
1942-1944	Evelyn Baring
1944-1946	William Campbell Tait
1947-1953	John Noble Kennedy
1954-1959	Peveril Barton Reiby Wallop William-Powlett
1959-1965	Humphrey Vicary Gibbs

Walker, pp. xxi, xxiii.

223 STRAITS SETTLEMENTS

Britain's control over the Malayan peninsula began with the establishment of Penang (q.v.) in 1786. In 1819 Singapore (q.v.) was acquired and in 1825 Malacca (271) was ceded by the Dutch. These three enclaves were united to form the Straits Settlements in 1826. Until 1867 the Straits Settlements colony was a part of British India (v. India) but it became a crown colony in that year. From about this time British control began to spread rapidly throughout the peninsula. The governor of the Straits Settlements became high commissioner to the Unfederated Malay States in 1909. Earlier, in 1895, four other states had formed the Federated Malay States (q.v.), also under the control of the Straits Settlements government. The Cocos and Keeling Islands were placed under the Straits Settlements in 1886 and Christmas Island in 1900—both remaining so until 1946. In 1942 the Straits Settlements were occupied by the Japanese. After the Japanese withdrawal in 1945 the Straits Settlements colony was not reconstituted but rather was replaced by the Union of Malaya (v. Malaya) and by Singapore.

Governors

1826-1827	Robert Fullerton		1843-1855	William John Butterworth
1827-1833	Robert Ibbetson		1855-1861	Edmund Augustus Blundell
1833-1837	Kenneth Murchison		1861-1867	Orfeur Cavenagh
1837-1843	Samuel George Bonham		1867-1873	Harry St. George Ord
			1873-1875	Andrew Clarke

1875-1877	William Francis Drummond Jervois	1904-1911	John Anderson
1877-1879	William Cleaver Francis Robinson	1911-1919	Arthur Henderson Young
1880-1887	Frederick Aloysius Weld	1919-1928	Laurence Nunns Guillemard
1887-1893	Cecil Clementi Smith	1928-1930	Hugh Clifford
1893-1899	Charles Bullen Hugh Mitchell	1930-1936	Cecil Clementi
1899-1901	James Alexander Swettenham	1936-1942	Thomas Shenton Whitelegge Thomas
1901-1904	Frank Athelstane Swettenham	1942-1945	(under Japan)

Information from the Embassy of the Federation of Malaya, Washington. Also, Buckley, passim.

224 SURAT

Surat, on India's west coast, was the site of the first English factory in India, built in 1612. In 1616 Surat became the chief British factory in western India. In 1668 Surat was replaced by Bombay (q.v.) as the English headquarters, but the presidency remained in Surat to 1687, with the governors of Bombay serving as presidents and governing Bombay itself through deputies. In 1687 it came under the government of Bombay and remained part of the province of Bombay until 1947.

Governors

1616-1621	Thomas Kerridge (1)	1649-1652	Thomas Merry
1621-1625	Thomas Rastell (1)	1652-1654	Jeremy Blackman
1625-1628	Thomas Kerridge (2)	1654-1655	John Spiller (1)
1628-1630	Richard Wylde	1655-1656	Edward Pearce
1630	John Skibbow	1656-1657	John Spiller (2)
1630-1631	Thomas Rastell (2)	1657-1658	Thomas Revington
1631-1633	John Hopkinson	1659-1662	Matthew Andrews
1633-1638	William Methwold	1662-1669	George Oxinden
1638-1644	William Fremlen	1669-1677	Gerald Aungier
1644-1649	Francis Breton	1677-1682	Thomas Rolt
		1682-1687	John Child

Fawcett, 1:v—xxi, and 3:xxvii—xxxv; Foster, passim.

225 SURINAM

For the British governors of Surinam from 1804 to 1815, see the Dutch colony, Surinam, 281.

226 SWAZILAND

The area ruled by the Swazi had become dependent on the Transvaal in 1895. After the Anglo-Boer War of 1899—1902 it was placed under the now British colony of Transvaal (q.v.), but in 1906 it was made directly dependent on the high commissioner for South Africa, as were also Basutoland and Bechuanaland (qq.v.). In 1907 a resident commissioner was appointed. Swaziland remained a protectorate until 1968 when it became independent, remaining within the Commonwealth as a monarchy.

Resident Commissioners

1907-1916	Robert Thorne Coryndon	1942-1946	Eric Kellett Featherstone
1917-1928	deSymons Montagu George Honey	1946-1950	Edward Betham Beetham
1928-1935	Thomas Ainsworth Dickson	1950-1956	David Loftus Morgan
1935-1937	Allan Graham Marwick	1956-1963	Brian Allan Marwick
1937-1942	Charles Lamb Bruton	1963-1968	Francis Alfred Loyd

Information from A. E. H. Sammons, Colonial Office, London.

227 TANGANYIKA

Tanganyika is the former colony of German East Africa (71). It was conquered by the British and Belgians after an arduous campaign extending from 1914 to 1918. In 1920 the area, except for Ruanda-Urundi (v. 2 under Belgium) was awarded by the League of Nations as a mandate to Great Britain. The mandate became a United Nations trusteeship in 1947. In 1961 Tanganyika was made an independent dominion within the British Commonwealth; a year later it became the independent Republic of Tanganyika; and in 1964 it combined with Zanzibar (q.v.) to become Tanzania. Tanzania is a member of the Commonwealth.

Governors

1916-1924	Horace Archer Byatt	1938-1942	Mark Aitchison Young
1924-1931	Donald Charles Cameron	1942-1945	Wilfrid Edward Jackson
1931-1933	George Stewart Symes	1945-1949	William Denis Battershill
1933-1938	Harold Alfred MacMichael	1949-1958	Edward Francis Twining
		1958-1961	Richard Gordon Turnbull

Statesman's Year Book, 1920—61.

228 TANGIER

The town and fortress of Tangier, on the northwest tip of Africa at the entrance to the Strait of Gibraltar, was seized by the Portuguese in 1471. In 1661 it, like Bombay (q.v.), was included in the dowry of Catarina of Bragança, wife of Charles II. The English occupied Tangier only until 1684 when it was abandoned in the face of a long siege by the ruler of Morocco.

Governors

1661-1663	Henry Mordaunt, Earl of Peterborough
1663-1664	Andrew Rutherford, Earl of Teviot
1664-1665	John Fitzgerald
1665-1666	John, Baron Belasyse
1666-1669	Henry Norwood
1669-1674	John Middleton, Earl of Middleton
1675-1680	William O'Brien, Earl of Inchiquin
1680	Palmes Fairbourne
1680-1681	Edward Sackville
1681-1683	Piercy Kirke
1683-1684	George Legge, Baron Dartmouth

Routh, passim.

229 TASMANIA

A large island off the southeastern coast of Australia, Tasmania was discovered in 1642 by the Dutch navigator Abel Janszoon Tasman and named Van Diemen's Land. Great Britain annexed it to New South Wales (q.v.) in 1803 for use an auxiliary penal colony. It was separated from New South Wales in 1825 and made a separate colony. In 1855 the island was renamed Tasmania. It was ruled by lieutenant governors until 1855, by governors thereafter. In 1901 Tasmania became a state in the new Commonwealth of Australia (v. Australia).

Governors[1]

1803-1804	John Bowen
1804-1810	David Collins
1810	Edward Lord
1810-1812	John Murray
1812-1813	Andrew Geils
1813-1817	Thomas Davey
1817-1824	William Sorell
1824-1836	George Arthur
1837-1843	John Franklin
1843-1846	John Eardley Wilmot
1847-1855	William Thomas Denison
1855-1861	Henry Edward Fox Young
1861-1868	Thomas Gore Browne
1868-1874	Charles DuCane
1874-1880	Frederick Aloysius Weld
1880-1881	John Henry Lefroy
1881-1886	George Cumine Strahan
1886-1892	Robert George Crookshank Hamilton
1893-1899	Jenico William Joseph Preston, Viscount Gormanston
1899-1901	John Dodds

1. From 1804 to 1812 the settlement at Port Dalrymple in the north of the island was separately governed. Its commandants were:

1804-1808	William Paterson
1808-1810	John Brabyn
1810-1812	George Alexander Gordon.

Australia, *Historical Records*, 1:605–728; *Australian Encyclopaedia*, 4:357–58.

230 TOBAGO

Tobago, a smaller neighbor of Trinidad off the coast of Venezuela, was settled by the English briefly in 1616, by the Dutch from 1658 to 1677, and by the British and French variously from 1677 to 1762. From 1763 to 1781 it was part of the Southern Caribbee Islands. It was held by the French from 1781 to 1793 and from 1802 to 1803. Tobago was part of the Windward Islands government under Barbados (q.v.) from 1833 to 1885 and of the separate Windward Islands (q.v.) government from 1885 to 1889. In 1889 it was transferred to Trinidad (q.v.). Finally in 1899 it was merged with Trinidad.

Governors
1764-1766	Alexander Brown
1766-1767	William Hill
1767-1769	Roderick Gwynne
1769-1770	William Stewart
1770-1777	William Young
1777-1779	Peter Campbell
1779-1781	John Graham
1781	George Ferguson

under France

Governors
1781-1784	Philibert-François Rouxel de Blanchelande
1784-1786	René-Marie d'Arrot
1786-1789	Arthur Dillon
1789-1792	Antoine de Jobal de Poigny
1792-1793	Philippe-Marie de Marguenat

under Great Britain

Governors
1793-1794	William Myers
1794-1795	George Poyntz Rickets
1795-1796	William Lindsay
1796-1799	Stephen DeLancy
1799-1800	Richard Master
1800-1802	Joseph Robley
1802	Hugh Lyle Carmichael

under France

Governors
1802	Jean-Joseph-François-Léonard Damarzit de Laroche Sahuguet
1802-1803	Louis-César-Gabriel Berthier

under Great Britain

Governors
1803	Thomas Picton
1803	Donald McDonald
1803-1804	Andrew James Cochrane Johnstone
1804-1805	John Halkett
1805-1806	Robert Mitchell
1806-1807	John Balfour (1)
1807-1815	William Young
1815-1816	John Balfour (2)
1816-1827	Frederick Phillips Robinson
1827-1828	Elphinstone Piggott
1828-1833	Nathaniel Shepherd Blackwell
1833	Lionel Smith
1833-1845	Charles Henry Darling
1845-1851	Lawrence H. Graeme
1851	David Robert Ross
1852-1854	Dominick Daly
1854-1857	Willoughby Shortland
1857-1865	James Vickery Drysdale
1865-1872	Cornelius Hendricksen Kortright
1872-1875	Herbert Taylor Ussher
1875-1877	Robert William Harley

Administrators
1877-1880	Augustus Frederick Gore
1880-1883	Edward Daniel Laborde
1883-1885	John Worrell Carrington
1885-1888	Robert Baxter Llewelyn
1888-1889	Loraine Gedded Hay

Commissioners
1889-1892	Loraine Gedded Hay
1892	Thomas Crossley Rayner
1892-1899	William Low

Information from the Librarian, Central Library, Port-of-Spain, Trinidad. Also, Carmichael, pp. 306–17, 434–35; Nardin, p. 72.

231 TONGA

The Tonga Islands, located in the southwest Pacific, contain three main island groups, Tongatapu Ha'apai, and Vava'u. These groups were united by Jiaoji Tupou I in 1843. His government was stable and efficient, and Tonga remained free of overt European influence until 1900 when Great Britain received "rights" to Tonga as a result of negotiations regarding Samoa (v. Western

Samoa). A treaty of protection was promptly negotiated with Jiaoji Tupou II and a consul appointed. Tonga was under the Western Pacific High Commission (q.v.) until 1952, and under Fiji (q.v.) to 1965. Since 1965 it has been directly under the British Commonwealth Relations Office. The agent/consul became, in 1959, the commissioner/consul. It is anticipated that Tonga will become completely and formally independent in the very near future.

Consuls		1943-1949	Charles Walter Trevor Johnson
1901-1909	Hamilton Hunter	1949-1954	James Edward Windrum
1909-1913	W. Telfer Campbell	1954-1957	Charles Robert Harley Nott
1913-1917	Henry Eugene Walter Grant	1957-1959	Archibald Cameron Reid (1)
1917-1926	Islay McOwan	1959-1965	Edward James Coode
1926-1937	James Scott Neill	1965—	Archibald Cameron Reid (2)
1937-1943	Arthur Leopold Armstrong		

Colonial Office List, 1901–60; *Statesman's Year Book*, 1960 to date.

232 TRANSJORDAN

The area known as Transjordan was given to Great Britain as a mandate after World War I and in 1923 a kingdom was established there. Transjordan was administered by the high commissioner for Palestine (q.v.) who became ex officio high commissioner for Transjordan in 1928. He was represented in Transjordan by a resident. This office was abolished in 1946 when Transjordan became formally independent and adopted the name the Hashimite Kingdom of Jordan.

Residents		1924-1939	Charles Henry Fortrom Cox
1921-1924	Harry St. George Bridger Philby	1939-1946	Alec Seath Kirkbride

Statesman's Year Book, 1921–46.

233 TRANSVAAL

In 1877 British forces invaded and occupied the Boer Republic of Transvaal and it was annexed to the British crown. Adverse public reaction, and the persistant resistance of the Boers, led to British withdrawal from the Transvaal in 1881. In the Anglo-Boer War of 1899–1902, however, the territory was reoccupied by the British, who erected it into the colony of the Transvaal, with the high commissioner for South Africa as governor. Until 1906 the Transvaal was locally administered by a lieutenant governor. The Transvaal was granted responsible government, and in 1910 was joined with the Cape Colony, Natal, and the Orange River Colony (qq.v.) to form the Union of South Africa (q.v.).

Great Britain

234 TRINIDAD AND TOBAGO

The large island of Trinidad in the Lesser Antilles off the coast of Venezuela was a Spanish colony until 1797 (v. 395). In 1797 Trinidad was seized by Great Britain, and it was retained under the provisions of the Treaty of Amiens in 1802. In 1889 the neighboring island of Tobago (q.v.) was detached from the Windward Islands (q.v.) government and added to Trinidad, and the crown colony was thenceforth called Trinidad and Tobago. From 1958 to 1962 the colony of Trinidad and Tobago was part of the West Indies Federation (q.v.). On the dissolution of the federation Trinidad and Tobago became independent within the British Commonwealth.

Information from S. Chan-Pong, Acting Governor's Secretary, Port-of-Spain, Trinidad. Also, Carmichael, passim.

235 TURKS AND CAICOS ISLANDS

The Turks and Caicos Islands are two groups of islands at the southern end of the Bahamas (q.v.). They were used by the inhabitants of Bermuda (q.v.) as sources of salt and began attracting settlers from Bermuda in 1678, although the first permanent settlement did not occur until late in the 18th century. The islands were part of the Bahamas from 1799 to 1848. From 1848 to 1874, when they were made dependencies of Jamaica (q.v.), they were a separate colony. Since 1962 they have again been a separate colony, although maintaining an unofficial relationship with the Bahamas.

Presidents of the Council
1848-1854 Frederick Henry Alexander Forth
1854-1862 William Robert Inglis
1862-1869 Alexander Wilson Moir
1869-1872 Alexander Augustus Melfort
          Campbell
1872-1874 Daniel Thomas Smith

Commissioners
1874-1878 Daniel Thomas Smith
1878 Edward Noel Walker
1878-1883 Robert Baxter Llewelyn
1883-1885 Fred Shedden Sanguinetti
1885-1888 Henry Moore Jackson
1888-1891 Alexis Wynns Harriott
1891-1893 Henry Huggins
1893-1899 Edward John Cameron
1899-1901 Geoffrey Peter St. Aubyn

1901-1905 William Douglas Young
1905-1914 Frederick Henry Watkins
1914-1923 George Whitfield Smith
1923-1932 Harold Ernest Phillips
1933-1934 Hugh Houston Hutchings
1934-1936 Frank Cecil Clarkson
1936-1940 Hugh Charles Norwood Hill
1940-1946 Edwin Porter Arrowsmith
1947-1952 Cyril Eric Wool-Lewis
1952-1955 Peter Bleackley
1955-1958 I. Ernest Gordon Lewis
1958-1959 Geoffrey Colin Guy

Administrators
1959-1965 Geoffrey Colin Guy
1965 Robert Everard Wainwright (1)
1965-1967 John Anthony Golding
1967—— Robert Everard Wainwright (2)

Information from the Administrator's Deputy, Grand Turk, and from the Administrator, Grand Turk.

236 UGANDA

In the latter half of the 18th century British interest was drawn to the lakes region of East Africa as the source of the White Nile. What was to become Uganda was then divided among several states, of which the most powerful was Buganda. During the 1880's Buganda was weakened by dynastic and religious dissension. In 1890 the Imperial British East Africa Company began to extend its control over the area, reserved to Great Britain by the British–German Agreement of 1890 (v. Heligoland and Zanzibar). In 1894 Buganda was declared a protectorate, and similar proclamations followed for the other states of the area. Under the Uganda Protectorate, Buganda retained a privileged status. In 1962 Uganda became independent within the Commonwealth, and the following year it became the Republic of Uganda while remaining within the Commonwealth.

Commissioners
1893 Gerald Portal
1893-1895 Henry Edward Colville
1895-1899 Ernest James Lennox Berkeley
1899-1902 Harry Hamilton Johnston
1902-1905 James Hayes Sadler

Governors
1905-1910 Henry Hesketh Joudou Bell
1910-1911 Harry Edward Spiller Cordeaux
1911-1918 Frederick John Jackson
1918-1922 Robert Thorne Coryndon
1922-1925 Geoffrey Francis Archer

Great Britain

1925-1932	William Frederick Gowers	1952-1957	Andrew Benjamin Cohen
1932-1935	Bernard Henry Bourdillon	1957-1961	Frederick Crawford
1935-1940	Philip Euen Mitchell	1961-1962	Walter Fleming Coutts
1940-1944	Charles Cecil Farquharson Dundas		
1944-1952	John Hathorn Hall		

Governor-General
1962-1963   Walter Fleming Coutts

Colonial Office List, 1894–1962.

237 UNION OF SOUTH AFRICA

In 1910 the Cape Colony, Natal, the Orange River Colony and the Transvaal (qq.v.) united to form the Union of South Africa. The governors-general of the Union were ex officio high commissioners for South Africa and as such were responsible for the administration of the so-called High Commission Territories of Basutoland, Bechuanaland, and Swaziland (qq.v.), which were locally administered by resident commissioners. The growing dissatisfaction of the predominantly Afrikaner population of the Union with British policies led to the withdrawal of the Union from the British Commonwealth in 1961 and the establishment of the Republic of South Africa.

Governors-General

1910-1914	Herbert John Gladstone, Viscount Gladstone	1931-1937	George Herbert Villiers, Earl of Clarendon
1914-1920	Sydney Charles Buxton, Earl Buxton	1937-1943	Patrick Duncan
1920-1923	Arthur Frederick Patrick Albert, Prince of Connaught	1943-1946	Nikolaas Jacobus de Wet
		1946-1951	Gideon Brand van Zyl
		1951-1959	Ernest Jansen
1924-1930	Alexander Augustus Cambridge, Earl of Athlone	1959-1961	Charles Robberts Swart

Walker, pp. xxii-xxiii.

238 UNITED PROVINCES OF AGRA AND OUDH

As British control in India expanded, the nuclear province of Bengal (q.v.) became too large (v. India). In 1833 the presidency of Agra was created but not implemented. Rather, in 1836 the North-West Provinces was created under a lieutenant governor. In 1871 Ajmer-Merwara (q.v.) was taken from the North-West Provinces and created a chief commissionership. However, in 1877 Oudh (q.v.) was added and the lieutenant governor of the North-West Provinces became chief commissioner of Oudh as well. In 1902 the name was changed to United Provinces of Agra and Oudh. In 1921 it was raised to a governor's province. In 1947 the United Provinces became the state of Uttar Pradesh in India.

North-West Provinces

Lieutenant Governors

1836-1838	Charles Theophilus Metcalfe
1838-1840	(Governor-General of India)
1840-1842	Thomas Campbell Robertson
1842-1843	(Governor-General of India)
1843-1853	James Thomason
1853-1857	John Russell Colvin
1857-1858	Hugh Fraser
1859-1863	George Frederick Edmondstone
1863-1868	Edward Drummond
1868-1874	William Muir
1874-1876	John Strachey
1876-1877	George Ebenezer Wilson Couper

Lieutenant Governors, North-West Provinces, and Chief Commissioners, Oudh

1877-1882	George Ebenezer Wilson Couper
1882-1887	Alfred Comyns Lyall
1887-1892	Auckland Colvin
1892-1895	Charles Haukes Todd Crosthwaite
1895-1901	Anthony Patrick McDonnell
1901-1902	John James Digges LaTouche

United Provinces of Agra and Oudh

Lieutenant Governors

1902-1907	John James Digges LaTouche
1907-1912	John Prescott Hewett
1912-1917	James Scorgie Meston
1917-1921	Spencer Harcourt Butler

Governors

1921-1922	Spencer Harcourt Butler
1922-1927	William Sinclair Marris
1927-1928	Alexander Philipps Muddiman
1928-1933	William Malcolm Hailey
1934-1939	Harry Graham Haig
1939-1945	Maurice Garnier Hallett
1945-1947	Francis Verner Wylie

Bhanu, passim; *India Office and Burma Office List*, 1940, pp. 116, 117—18.

239 VICTORIA

The colony of Victoria occupied the extreme southeast corner of the Australian continent. The first attempt at settlement, made from New South Wales (q.v.) in 1803, was unsuccessful. It was not until 1834 that the first permanent settlement was established. Five years later a superintendent was appointed. In 1851 Victoria was separated from New South Wales and the superintendent became lieutenant governor. In 1855 responsible government was granted and the lieutenant governor became governor. In 1901 Victoria became a state in the newly established Commonwealth of Australia (v. Australia).

Superintendent

1839-1851	Charles Joseph LaTrobe

Lieutenant Governors

1851-1854	Charles Joseph LaTrobe
1854-1855	Charles Hotham

Governors

1855-1856	Charles Hotham
1856-1863	Henry Barkly
1863-1866	Charles Henry Darling
1866-1873	John Henry Thomas Manners-Sutton, Viscount Canterbury
1873-1879	George Ferguson Bowen
1879-1884	George Augustus Constantine Phipps, Marquess of Normanby
1884-1889	Henry Brougham Loch
1889-1895	John Adrian Louis Hope, Earl of Hopetoun
1895-1900	Thomas Brassey, Baron Brassey

Australian Encyclopaedia, 4:353—54.

240 VIRGINIA

Virginia was the first permanent English settlement on the North American continent. It was established in 1607 under the auspices of the Virginia Company of London. The company governed the colony until 1624 when it was brought under royal control. In 1632 Maryland (q.v.) was created from territory granted to Virginia under its charter. From 1697 to 1768 Virginia was nominally ruled by a series of governors-in-chief who, however, never were resident in the colony, and who ruled through a lieutenant governor. In 1775 the last royal governor was forced to flee.

Governors

1607	Edward Maria Wingfield[1]	1678-1680	Henry Chichele[2] (1)
1607-1608	John Ratcliffe[1]	1680	Thomas Culpeper, Baron Thorsway
1608-1609	John Smith[1]	1680-1682	Henry Chichele[2] (2)
1609-1610	George Percy[1]	1682-1683	Thomas Culpeper, Baron Thorsway
1610	Thomas Gates[2] (1)	1683-1684	Nicholas Spencer[1]
1610-1611	Thomas West, Lord de la Warr	1684-1688	Francis Howard, Baron Effingham[3]
1611	Thomas Dale (1)	1688-1690	Nathaniel Bacon[1]
1611-1614	Thomas Gates (2)	1690-1692	Francis Nicholson[3] (1)
1614-1616	Thomas Dale (2)	1692-1698	Edmund Andros[5]
1616-1617	George Yeardley[3] (1)	1698-1705	Francis Nicholson[3] (2)
1617-1619	Samuel Argall[3]	1705-1706	Edward Nott[3]
1619-1621	George Yeardley (2)	1706-1710	Edmund Jennings[1]
1621-1626	Francis Wyatt (1)	1710-1722	Alexander Spotswood[3]
1626-1627	George Yeardley (3)	1722-1726	Hugh Drysdale[3]
1627-1629	Francis West[1]	1726-1727	Robert Carter[1]
1629-1630	John Pott[1]	1727-1740	William Gooch[3] (1)
1630-1635	John Harvey (1)	1740-1741	James Blair[1]
1635-1636	John West[2]	1741-1749	William Gooch[3] (2)
1636-1639	John Harvey (2)	1749-1751	Thomas Lee[1]
1639-1642	Francis Wyatt (2)	1751	Lewis Burwell[1]
1642-1652	William Berkeley (1)	1751-1758	Robert Dinwiddie[3]
1652-1655	Richard Bennett	1758-1768	Francis Fauquier[3]
1655-1658	Edward Digges[1]	1768-1770	Norborne Berkeley, Baron de
1658-1660	Samuel Mathews[1]		Botetourt[4]
1660-1677	William Berkeley (2)	1770-1771	William Nelson[3]
1677-1678	Herbert Jeffries[3]	1771-1775	John Murray, Earl Dunmore[4]

1. President of the Council.   2. Deputy Governor.   3. Lieutenant Governor.
4. Governor-in-Chief.
5. Between 1697 and 1768 the following held the title Governor-in-Chief, but were resident in England and exercised no actual authority:

   1697-1737 George Hamilton Douglas, Earl of Orkney
   1737-1754 William Anne Keppel, Earl of Albemarle
   1756-1763 John Campbell, Earl of Loudoun
   1763-1768 Jeffrey Amherst

Squires, pp. 43–309.

241 WEIHAIWEI

The port of Weihaiwei, in the province of Shantung, was leased by the British from China on July 1, 1898. An order-in-council of July 24, 1901, provided for the appointment of a commissioner to represent British interests in the area. On October 1, 1930, Great Britain relinquished control of the port to the Republic of China.

Commissioners
1902-1921	James Haldane Stewart Lockhart
1921-1923	Arthur Powlett Blunt

1923-1927	Walter Russell Brown
1927-1930	Reginald Fleming Johnston

Statesman's Year Book, 1899–1931.

242 WESTERN AUSTRALIA

The coast of western Australia was discovered by the Dutch in 1616 but remained unsettled until 1826 when a small group of convicts was dispatched from New South Wales (q.v.). Two years later a lieutenant governor was appointed, to be replaced by a governor in 1832. Settlement languished and a penal colony was established in 1850 to supplement the population. Responsible government was granted to Western Australia only in 1890, long after the other Australian colonies had received it. In 1901 Western Australia joined the Commonwealth of Australia (v. Australia).

Lieutenant Governor
1828-1832	James Stirling (1)

Governors
1832-1833	Frederick Chidley Irwin (1)
1833-1834	Richard Daniell
1834-1839	James Stirling
1839-1846	John Hutt
1846-1847	Andrew Clarke
1847-1848	Frederick Chidley Irwin (2)
1848-1855	Charles Fitzgerald
1855-1862	Arthur Edward Kennedy

1862-1868	John Stephen Hampton
1869-1875	Frederick Aloysius Weld
1875-1877	William Cleaver Francis Robinson (1)
1877-1880	Harry St. George Ord
1880-1883	William Cleaver Francis Robinson (2)
1883-1890	Frederick Napier Broome
1890-1895	William Cleaver Francis Robinson (3)
1895-1901	Gerard Smith

Australian Encyclopaedia, 4:354–55.

243 WESTERN PACIFIC HIGH COMMISSION

Great Britain's growing but scattered interests in the Pacific Ocean led to the creation of the Western Pacific High Commission in 1877. From 1877 to 1952 the governor of Fiji (q.v.) acted as high commissioner and came to exercise jurisdiction over the Gilbert and Ellice Islands, the

British Solomon Islands Protectorate, the New Hebrides Condominium, Tonga, and Pitcairn Island (qq.v.) as well as Fiji. In 1953 the High Commission office was moved to Honiara in the British Solomon Islands and the governor of Fiji ceased to be high commissioner. Since 1952 the high commissioner has not had responsibility for Tonga, Pitcairn Island, and Fiji.

High Commissioners
1877-1952 (see Fiji)
1952-1955 Robert Christopher Stanley
1955-1961 John Gutch

1961-1964 David Clive Crosbie Trench
1964-1968 Robert Sidney Foster
1968——— Michael David Irving Gass

Statesman's Year Book, 1952 to date.

244 WESTERN SAMOA

Western Samoa was the former German colony of Samoa (73). It was occupied by New Zealand troops in 1914. In 1920 a League of Nations mandate was granted to New Zealand (q.v.) for Western Samoa, and in 1946 it became a United Nations trusteeship of New Zealand. The resident administrator (high commissioner after 1948) was appointed by the governor-general of New Zealand. In 1962 Western Samoa became independent and chose not to remain within the Commonwealth.

Administrators
1914-1919 Robert Logan
1920-1923 Robert Ward Tate
1923-1928 George Spafford Richardson
1928-1931 Stephen Shepherd Allen
1931-1935 Herbert Ernest Hart
1935-1946 Alfred Clarke Turnbull

1946-1948 Francis William Voelcker

High Commissioners
1948-1949 Francis William Voelcker
1949-1960 Guy Richardson Powles
1960-1962 John Bird Wright

Pacific Islands Year Book and Who's Who, p. 100.

245 WEST INDIES FEDERATION

In 1958 all of the British West Indian colonies with the exception of the Bahamas and the British Virgin Islands (qq.v.) united to form the West Indies Federation, with its capital on Trinidad (q.v.). The stresses created by the disparity of interests between the large colonies of Jamaica (q.v.) and Trinidad and the many very small colonies led to the dissolution of the federation in 1962. Jamaica had already withdrawn a year earlier.

Governor-General
1958-1962 Patrick George Thomas Buchan-
          Hepburn, Baron Hailes

Statesman's Year Book, 1958—62.

246 WILLOUGHBY

A colony was planted at the mouth of the Surinam River in 1651 under the auspices of Francis Willoughby, Proprietary of Barbados (q.v.). This small settlement lasted only until 1667 when it was captured by the Dutch. By the terms of the Treaty of Breda in 1670 the Dutch retained Surinam (281) in exchange for New Netherlands (277), which had been occupied by the British in 1664.

Governors
1651-1652	Anthony Rowse	1654-1657	(none)
1652-1654	Richard Holdip	1657-1667	William Byam

Williamson, pp. 150—84.

247 WINDWARD ISLANDS

The Windward Islands government, composing Saint Lucia, Saint Vincent, Tobago, Grenada and the Grenadines, was organized into a separate colony in 1885. Previously these islands had been governed by the governor of Barbados (q.v.). In 1889 Tobago was detached and united with Trinidad to form the colony of Trinidad and Tobago (q.v.). With the exception of the Grenadines each of the component islands was governed by an administrator subject to the governor of the Windward Islands. In 1960 the Windward Islands government, like that of the Leeward Islands (q.v.), was dissolved.

Governors
1885-1889	Walter Joseph Sendall	1923-1930	Frederick Seton James
1889-1893	Walter Francis Hely-Hutchinson	1930-1935	Thomas Alexander Best
1893-1897	Charles Bruce	1935-1937	Selwyn Macgregor Grier
1897-1900	Cornelius Alfred Moloney	1937-1942	Henry Bradshaw Popham
1900-1906	Robert Baxter Llewelyn	1942-1948	Arthur Francis Grimble
1906-1909	Ralph Champneys Williams	1948-1953	Robert Duncan Arundell
1909-1914	James Hayes Sadler	1953-1955	Edward Betham Beetham
1914-1923	George Basil Haddon-Smith	1955-1960	Colville Montgomery Deverell

Burns, pp. 795—96.

248 ZANZIBAR

British interests in the island of Zanzibar off the east coast of Africa were maintained, after 1840, by consuls. In 1890 the supremacy of British interests was recognized by France and Germany. In return Great Britain renounced claims to Madagascar (40) in favor of France and ceded Heligoland (q.v.) to Germany. For other aspects of these conventions see German East Africa (71), German Southwest Africa (74), Uganda, and Tonga (qq.v.). A protectorate was established in 1891 under a consul-general subject to the British Foreign Office. In 1913 the Colonial Office assumed control, although the form of the protectorate remained, and a resident was appointed. In 1963 Zanzibar became independent, and in 1964 it joined neighboring Tanganyika (q.v.) to form Tanzania.

Consuls
1840–1857 Atkins Hamerton
1858–1860 Christopher Palmer Rigby
1861–1862 Lewis Pelly
1862–1865 Robert Lambert Playfair
1865–1870 Henry Adrian Churchill
1870–1873 John Kirk

Consuls-General
1873–1886 John Kirk
1887–1888 Claude Maxwell Macdonald
1888–1891 Charles Bean Euan Smith
1891–1893 Gerald Portal
1893–1894 James Rennell Rodd
1894–1900 Arthur Henry Hardinge

1900–1904 Charles Norton Edgecumbe Eliot
1904–1909 Basil Shillito Cave
1909–1913 Edward Clarke

Residents
1914–1922 Francis Barrow Pearce
1922–1924 John Houston Sinclair
1924–1930 Alfred Claud Hollis
1930–1937 Richard Sims Donkin Rankine
1937–1940 John Hathorn Hall
1941–1946 Henry Guy Pilling
1946–1951 Vincent Goncalves Glenday
1952–1954 John Dalzell Rankine
1954–1960 Henry Steven Potter
1960–1963 George Rixson Mooring

Colonial Office List, 1900–1940; *Statesman's Year Book*, 1940–63; Wills and Barrett, p. 230.

249 ZULULAND

The Zulu were the most powerful people in southern Africa during the first three-quarters of the 19th century. However, their proximity to the colony of Natal (q.v.) made conflict with the British inevitable. As a result of the Zulu War of 1879 a resident was appointed at the court of the Zulu king. In 1887 Zululand was annexed and the resident commissioner was made responsible to the governor of Natal. Zululand was separately administered only until 1897 when it was incorporated into Natal.

Residents
1879–1880 William Douglas Wheelwright
1880–1887 Melmoth Osborn

Resident Commissioners
1887–1893 Melmoth Osborn
1893–1897 Marshall James Clarke

Colonial Office List, 1879–97.

Bibliography: Great Britain

Abbot, William Wright. *The Royal Governors of Georgia 1754–1775.* Chapel Hill: University of North Carolina Press, 1959.

Andrews, Charles McLean, ed. "List of Commissions, Instructions and Additional Instructions Issued to the Royal Governors and Others in America." *Annual Report of the American Historical Association for 1911,* 1:393–528.

Anene, Joseph C. *Southern Nigeria in Transition, 1885–1906: Theory and Practice in a Colonial Protectorate.* Cambridge: Cambridge University Press, 1966.

Audet, François Joseph. *Canadian Historical Dates and Events, 1492–1915.* Ottawa: G. Beauregard, 1917.

——. "Gouverneurs, lieutenants-gouverneurs et administrateurs de la province de Québec, des Bas et Haut Canada sous l'union et de la puissance du Canada, 1763–1908." *Mémoires et comptes-rendus de la Société royale du Canada,*3d ser. 2 (1908): sec. 1, 85–124.

Australia. Parliament. Joint Library Committee. *Historical Records of Australia, 3d series, Despatches and Papers relating to the Settlement of the States.* 6 vols. Canberra: Library Committee of Commonwealth Parliament, 1921–23.

Australian Dictionary of Biography. General editor, Douglas Pike. 2 vols. to date. Melbourne: University of Melbourne Press, 1966-.

Australian Encyclopaedia. 10 vols. East Lansing: Michigan State University Press, 1958.

Bastin, John Sturgus, ed. *The British in West Sumatra, 1685–1825.* Kuala Lumpur: University of Malaysia Press, 1965.

Beck, James Murray. *The Government of Nova Scotia.* Toronto: University of Toronto Press, 1957.

Bhanu, Dharma. "History and Administration of the Province of Agra, 1803–1858." *Uttara Bharati* 3 (1956):147–56.

Biobaku, Saburi O. *The Egba and their Neighbours, 1842–72.* Oxford: Clarendon Press, 1957.

Birney, William S. "Forgotten Governors in the 'Bay of Bengal' and at 'Fort William' in Calcutta (1713–52)." *Bengal Past and Present* 63, nos. 1 and 2 (1940):53–56.

Boase, Frederic. *Modern English Biography.* 6 vols. New York: Barnes and Noble, 1965.

Bouchaud, Joseph. "Les consuls anglais de la baie de Biafre." *Bulletin de la Société d'études camerounaises,* no. 25 (1949), pp. 19–37.

Boyson, V. F. *The Falkland Islands.* Oxford: Clarendon Press, 1924.

Brebner, John Bartlett. *New England's Outpost: Acadia before the conquest of Canada.* Columbia University Studies in History, Economics and Public Law, no. 293. New York: Columbia University Press, 1927.

Breen, Henry Hegart. *St. Lucia: Historical, Statistical and Descriptive.* London: Longmans, Browne, Green & Longmans, 1844.

Brooke, Thomas H. *A History of the Island of St. Helena from its Discovery by the Portuguese to the year 1806.* London: Black, Parry & Kingsbury, 1808.

Brookes, Edgar H. and Webb, Colin deB. *A History of Natal.* Pietermaritzburg: University of Natal Press, 1965.

Brown, Richard A. *A History of the Island of Cape Breton with Some Account of the Discovery and Settlement of Canada, Nova Scotia and Newfoundland.* London: Sampson, Low, Son & Marston, 1869.

Buckland, Charles Edward. *Bengal under the Lieutenant-Governors: being a Narrative of the Principal Events and Public Measures Undertaken during Their Periods of Office from 1854 to 1898.* 2 vols. Calcutta: S. K. Lahiri, 1901–2.

——. *Dictionary of Indian Biography.* London: Swan Sonnenschein & Co., 1906.

Buckley, Charles Burton. *An Anecdotal History of Old Times in Singapore from the Foundation of the Settlement under the Honourable the East India Company on February 6, 1819, to the Transfer to the Colonial Office as part of the Colonial Possessions of the Crown on April 1st, 1867.* Kuala Lumpur: University of Malaysia Press, 1965.

Burdon, John Alder, ed. *Archives of British Honduras.*3 vols. London: Sifton, Praed & Co., 1935.

Burns, Alan C. M. *A History of the British West Indies.* London: George Allen & Unwin, 1954.

Butler, Lindley S. "The Governors of Albemarle County, 1663–1689." *North Carolina Historical Review* 66, no. 3 (1969):281–99.

Callbeck, Lorne Clayton. *The Cradle of Confederation: A Brief History of Prince Edward Island from its Discovery in 1534 to the Present Time.* Frederictown, New Brunswick: Brunswick Press, 1964.

Cambridge History of India. 5 vols. Delhi: S. Chand, 1958.

Carmichael, Gertrude. *The History of the West Indian Islands of Trinidad and Tobago, 1498–1900.* London: Alvin Redman, 1961.

Caroe, Olaf Kirkpatrick. *The Pathans, 550 B.C.-A.D. 1957.* London: Macmillan & Co., 1958.

Charnock, John. *Biographia navalis: or Impartial Memoirs of the Lives and Characters of Officers of the Navy of Great Britain from the Year 1660 to the Present Time, Drawn from the Most Authentic Sources, and Disposed in a Chronological Arrangement.* 6 vols. London: R. Faulder, 1794–98.

Chaudhuri, K. N. *The English East India Company: The Study of an Early Joint-Stock Company, 1600–1640.* London: Frank Cass & Co., 1965.

Claridge, William Walton. *History of the Gold Coast and Ashanti.* 2 vols. New York: Barnes & Noble, 1964.

Colonial Office List. See under Great Britain.

Cowan, C. D. "Early Penang and the Rise of Singapore, 1805–1832." *Journal of the Malayan Branch of the Royal Asiatic Society* 23, no. 2 (1950):1–210.

Crabtree, Elizabeth G. *North Carolina Governors, 1585–1958.* Raleigh: North Carolina Department of Archives and History, 1958.

Crooks, John Joseph. *A History of the Colony of Sierra Leone, Western Africa.* Dublin: Browne & Nolan, 1903.

Cundall, Frank. *The Governors of Jamaica in the First Half of the Eighteenth Century.* London: West India Committee, 1937.

——. *The Governors of Jamaica in the Seventeenth Century.* London: West India Committee, 1926.

Dalton, Charles, ed. *English Army Lists and Commission Registers, 1661–1714.* 6 vols. London: Eyre and Spottiswoode, 1892, Francis Edwards, 1960.

——. *George the First's Army, 1714–1727.* 2 vols. London: Eyre and Spottiswoode, 1910–12.

Datta, Kalikinkar, ed. *Fort William-India House Correspondence and Other Contemporary Documents Relating Thereto.* 21 vols. Delhi: Manager of Government Printing, 1949–.

Davies, Kenneth Gordon, ed. *Letters from Hudson's Bay, 1703–1740.* Hudson's Bay Record Society Publications, no. 25. London: Hudson's Bay Record Society, 1965.

Details of the Principal Military Events of the Last Century, or the Royal Military Calendar, containing the services and progress of promotions of the Generals, Lieutenant-Generals, Major-Generals, Colonels, Lieutenant-Colonels, and Majors of the Army, according to Seniority. Edited by John Philippart. 5 vols. London [1820].

Dictionary of Canadian Biography. One vol. to date. Toronto: University of Toronto Press, 1966–.

Egharevba, Jacob U. *A Short History of Benin.* 3d ed. Ibadan: University Press, 1960.

Encyclopedia Canadiana. Editor-in-chief, John E. Robbins. 10 vols. Ottawa: Canadiana Co., 1957–58.

Endacott, G. B. *A History of Hong Kong.* London: Oxford University Press, 1958.

Fawcett, Charles, ed. *The English Factories in India.* New series, 4 vols. Oxford: Clarendon Press, 1955.

Floyd, Troy S. *The Anglo-Spanish Struggle for Mosquitia.* Albuquerque: University of New Mexico Press, 1967.

Foster, William, ed. *The English Factors in India, 1618–1669.* 13 vols. Oxford: Clarendon Press, 1906–27.

Fry, William Henry. *New Hampshire as a Royal Province.* New York: Columbia University Press, 1908.

Fyfe, Christopher. *A History of Sierra Leone.* London: Oxford University Press, 1962.

Gailey, Harry A. *A History of the Gambia.* London: Routledge & Kegan Paul, 1964.

Gazetteer of the Province of Sind. Compiled by E. H. Aitken. Karachi: Government Printer, 1907.

Gilson, R. P. "Administration of the Cook Islands (Rarotonga)." M.Sc. thesis. University of London, 1952.

Gray, John Milner. *A History of the Gambia.* Cambridge: Cambridge University Press, 1940.

Great Britain, Colonial Office. *Colonial Office List: Comprising Historical and Statistical Information Respecting the Colonial Dependencies of Great Britain.* Compiled from official records, 1862–1966. London: H.M.S.O., 1862–1966.

——, India Office. *East India Register and Directory,* 1803–44; *East India Register and Army List,* 1845–60; *Indian Army and Civil Service List,* 1861–76; *India List, Civil and Military,* 1877–85; *India Office List,* 1886–95; *India List and India Office List,* 1896–1906; *India Office List,* 1907–37; *India Office List and Burma Office List,* 1938–47.

——, Public Record Office. *Calendar of State Papers: Colonial, America and the West Indies, 1661–1737.* 37 vols. London: H.M.S.O., 1880–1963.

——, Public Record Office. *Journal of the Commissioners for Trade and Plantations from April 1704 to May 1782.* 14 vols. London: H.M.S.O., 1920–38.

Greene, LeRoy. *Shelter for His Excellency: The Story of Pennsylvania's Executive Mansion and the One Hundred Governors of the Commonwealth.* Harrisburg, Pa.: Stackpole Books, 1951.

Guillon, E. *La France à Minorca sous Louis XV, 1756–1763.* Paris: E. Leroux, 1894.

Harper, Bessie. *A Short History of the Heads of Government of the Island of Antigua.* Antigua: Government Printing Office, 1962.

Hart, Alfred Bushnell, ed. *Commonwealth History of Massachusetts.* 5 vols. New York: States Historical Co., 1928–30.

Higham, Charles Strachan Sanders. *The Development of the Leeward Islands under the Restoration, 1660–1688: A Study of the Foundations of the Old Colonial System.* Cambridge: Cambridge University Press, 1921.

Hill, George Francis. *History of Cyprus.* 4 vols. Cambridge: Cambridge University Press, 1940–52.

Hirst, George S. S. *History of the Cayman Islands.* Kingston, Jamaica: P. A. Benjamin Mfg. Co., 1910.

"Historical Tables concerning the Presidency of Fort St. George." *Madras Journal of Literature and Science,* 1879, pp. 103–34.

Hodson, Vernon Charles Paget. *List of the Officers of the Bengal Army, 1758–1834.* 4 vols. London: Constable & Co., 1927–47.

Hulugalle, H. A. J. *British Governors of Ceylon.* Colombo: Associated Newspapers of Ceylon, 1963.

India List. See under Great Britain.

India Office List. See under Great Britain.

Jacobus, Donald Lines. *List of Officers, Civil, Military and Ecclesiastical of Connecticut Colony from March 1636 through 11 October 1677 and of New Haven Colony throughout its Separate Existence.* New Haven: R. M. Mooker, 1935.

Johnson, Cecil. *British West Florida, 1763–1783.* New Haven: Yale University Press, 1943.

Kelly, John Barrett. *Britain and the Persian Gulf, 1795–1880.* London: Oxford University Press, 1968.

Khadduri, Majid. *Independent Iraq.* London: Oxford University Press, 1951.

Kirkwall, George William Hamilton Fitzmaurice, Viscount. *Four Years in the Ionian Islands: Their Political and Social Condition, with a History of the British Protectorate.* 2 vols. London: Chapman & Hall, 1864.

Kummer, Frederic Arnold. *The Free State of Maryland: A History of the State and Its People, 1634–1941.* 4 vols. Baltimore: Historical Records Association, 1941.

Lagden, Godfrey Yeatman. *The Basutos: The Mountaineers and Their Country.* 2 vols. London: Hutchinson & Co., 1909.

Langdon, George D., Jr. *Pilgrim Colony: A History of New Plymouth, 1620–1691.* New Haven: Yale University Press, 1966.

Lemieux, Louis Joseph. *The Governors-General of Canada, 1608–1931.* London: Lake & Bell, 1931.

Lincoln, Charles Z. "The Governors of New York." *Proceedings of the New York State Historical Association* 9 (1910):33–98b.

Longrigg, Stephen Hemsley. *Iraq, 1900 to 1950: A Political, Social and Economic History.* London: Oxford University Press, 1953.

Lorimer, John Gordon. *Geographical and Historical Gazetteer of the Persian Gulf, Oman and Central Arabia.* 2 vols. in 5. Bombay: Supt. of Government Printing, 1907–15.

Lounsbury, Ralph Greenlee. *The British Fishery at Newfoundland, 1634–1763.* New Haven: Yale University Press, 1934.

Love, Henry Davison. *Vestiges of Old Madras.* 3 vols. London: John Murray, 1913.

Luke, Harry Charles Joseph. *Malta: An Account and an Appreciation.* London: G. G. Harrap, 1949.

McCain, James Ross. *Georgia as a Proprietary Province: The Execution of a Trust.* Boston: Richard G. Badger, 1917.

McCrady, Edward. *The History of South Carolina under Proprietary Government.* New York: Macmillan Co., 1897.

——. *The History of South Carolina under the Royal Governors, 1719-1776.* New York: Macmillan Co., 1899.

McLintock, Alexander H., ed. *An Encyclopaedia of New Zealand.* 3 vols. Wellington: R. E. Owen, Government Printer, 1966.

Macmechan, Archibald M. *A Calendar of Two Letter Books and One Commission-Book in the Possession of the Government of Nova Scotia, 1713–1741.* Halifax, n.p., 1902.

McNutt, William Stewart. *New Brunswick, A History: 1784–1867.* Toronto: Macmillan & Co., 1963.

Martin, Eveline Christiana. *The British West Africa Settlements, 1750–1821: A Study in Local Administration.* London: Longmans, Green & Co., 1927.

Mersey, Clive Bingham, Viscount. *The Viceroys and Governors-General of India, 1757–1947.* London: John Murray, 1949.

Mohr, Ralph S. *Governors for Three Hundred Years, 1638–1959. Rhode Island and Providence Plantations.* Providence: Oxford Press, 1959.

Mowat, Charles Loch. *East Florida as a British Province, 1763–1784.* Berkeley: University of California Press, 1943.

Mungeam, E. H. *British Rule in Kenya, 1895–1912. The Establishment of Administration in the East Africa Protectorate.* Oxford: Clarendon Press, 1966.

Nardin, J. C. "Tabago, Antille française, 1781–1793." *Annales des Antilles,* no. 14 (1966), pp. 9–104.

Newton, Arthur Percival. *The Colonising Activities of the English Puritans: The Last Phase of the Elizabethan Struggle against Spain.* New Haven: Yale University Press, 1914.

Nicolson, Robert B. *The Pitcairners.* Sydney: Angus & Robertson, 1965.

Norton, Frederick Calvin. *The Governors of Connecticut.* Hartford: The Connecticut Magazine, 1905.

O'Byrne, William R. *A Naval Biographical Dictionary, Comprising the Life and Services of Every Living Officer in Her Majesty's Navy, from the Rank of Admiral of the Fleet to that of Lieutenant, Inclusive.* London: John Murray, 1849.

"Officers of the Province of Pennsylvania, 1681–1776." *Pennsylvania Archives,* 2d ser. 9 (1880):619–39.

Pacific Islands Year Book and Who's Who. Edited by Judy Tudor. 10th ed. Sydney: Pacific Publications Pty, 1968.

Pillsbury, Hobart. *New Hampshire, Resources, Attractions, and Its People: A History.* 5 vols. New York: Lewis Historical Publishing Co., 1927–30.

Pomfret, John Edwin. *The New Jersey Proprietors and Their Lands.* Princeton: Van Nostrand, 1964.

——. *The Province of East New Jersey, 1609–1702: The Rebellious Proprietary.* Princeton: Princeton University Press, 1962.

——. *The Province of West New Jersey.* Princeton: Princeton University Press, 1956.

Porter, R. "English Chief Factors on the Gold Coast, 1632–1753." *African Historical Studies* 1, no. 2 (1968):199–209.

Portman, M. V. *A History of our Relations with the Andamanese Compiled from Histories and Travels and from the Records of the Government of India.* 2 vols. Calcutta: Supt. of Government Printing, 1897.

Prinsep, Charles Campbell. *Record of Services of the Honourable East India Company's Civil Servants in the Madras Presidency from 1741 to 1858.* London: Trübner & Co., 1885.

Prowse, Daniel Woodley. *A History of Newfoundland, from the English, Colonial and Foreign Records.* London: Macmillan & Co., 1895.

Rao, C. Hayavadana, ed. *Mysore Gazetteer.* 5 vols. in 8. Bangalore: Government Press, 1927–30.

Read, David Breckenridge. *The Lieutenant-Governors of Upper Canada and Ontario, 1792–1899.* Toronto: William Briggs, 1900.

Rich, Edwin Ernest. *The History of the Hudson's Bay Company, 1670–1870.* 2 vols. Hudson's Bay Record Society Publications, nos. 21, 22. London: Hudson's Bay Record Society, 1958–59.

Routh, Enid M. G. *Tangier, England's Lost Atlantic Outpost, 1661–1684.* London: John Murray, 1912.

Rowley, Charles Dunford. *The Australians in German New Guinea.* Melbourne: Melbourne University Press, 1958.

Schomburgk, Robert H. *The History of Barbados, Comprising a Geographical and Statistical Description of the Island, a Sketch of Historical Events since the Settlement and an Account of its Geology and Natural Products.* London: Longmans, Brown, Green & Longmans, 1848.

Scisco, L. D. "Calvert's Proceeding against Kirke." *Canadian Historical Review* 8(1927): 132–36.

Shepard, Charles. *An Historical Account of the Island of Saint Vincent.* London: W. Nicol, 1831.

Squires, William Henry Tappey. *Through Centuries Three: A Short History of the People of Virginia.* Portsmouth, Va.: Printcraft Press, 1929.

Statesman's Year Book: Statistical and Historical Annual of the States of the World. London: Macmillan & Co., 1864 to date.

Toussaint, A., dir. *Dictionary of Mauritian Biography.* Port-Louis: Standard Printing Establishment, 1941 to date (issued in fascicles).

Tregonning, Kenneth G. *Under Chartered Company Rule: North Borneo, 1881–1946.* Singapore: University of Malaya Press, 1958.

Tudor, Judy, ed. *Handbook of Fiji.* Sydney: Pacific Publication Pty., 1962.

Turner, L. J. B. "The Madras Administration of the Maritime Provinces of Ceylon, 1795–1798." *Ceylon Antiquarian and Literary Register* 4(1918/19):36–53.

Vere-Hodge, Edward Reginald. *Imperial British East Africa Company.* London: Macmillan & Co., 1960.

Waddell, David A. G. "Great Britain and the Bay Islands, 1821–1861." *Historical Journal* 2, pt. 1(1959):59–77.

Walker, Eric A. *A History of Southern Africa.* 2d ed. London: Longmans, 1957.

Whitmore, William Henry. *The Massachusetts Civil List for the Colonial and Provincial Periods, 1630–1774, being a list of the names and dates of appointment of all the civil officers constituted by the authority of the charters, or local government.* Albany, N.Y.: J. Munsell, 1870.

Who's Who, an Annual Biographical Dictionary. London: A. & C. Black, etc., 1849 to date.

Wilkinson, Henry C. *Bermuda in the Old Empire: A History of the Island from the Dissolution oft the Somers Island Company until the End of the American Revolution, 1684–1784.* London: Oxford University Press, 1950.

Williamson, James A. *The Caribbee Islands under Proprietary Patents.* London: Oxford University Press, 1926.

——. *English Colonies in Guiana and on the Amazon, 1604–1668.* Oxford: Clarendon Press, 1923.

Wills, Walter H., and Barrett, R. J., eds. *Anglo-African Who's Who and Biographical Sketch-Book.* London: George Routledge & Sons, 1905.

Willson, Henry Beckles. *The Great Company: A History of the Honourable Company of Merchants-Adventurers Trading into Hudson's Bay.* Toronto: Copp, Clark Co., 1899.

Wilson, C. R. "An Unrecorded Governor of Fort William in Bengal." *Journal of the Asiatic Society of Bengal* 67(1898):167–77.

Wink, P. "De Onderafdeeling Lais in de Residentie Bengkoeloe." *Verhandelingen van het Koninklijk Bataviaasch Genootschap van Kunsten en Wettenschappen* 66(1926):1–131.

Italy

Italy only became a nation in 1871, and it was slow to participate in the late 19th-century contest for colonies. Its ventures in Eritrea and Somaliland were not interfered with because Great Britain regarded them as a desirable alternative to French expansion in the same areas. The effort to use Eritrea as a beachhead for expansion into Ethiopia was signally defeated at Adua in 1896, and Italy had the ignominious experience of being the only European nation to suffer a major defeat, in the late 19th century, at the hands of an African nation.

By a series of agreements—with Germany in 1887, Great Britain in 1890, and France in 1900—Italy obtained recognition of its prime interest in the Libyan area, then a part of the Ottoman Empire, but only in 1911–12, during the Italo-Turkish War, did it move to implement this understanding. During this war Libya and the Dodecanese Islands in the Aegean Sea were annexed. Involvement in World War I prevented Italy from organizing these new conquests until after the war.

The memory of Adua lingered long in the Italian official mind and the expansionist tendencies of the Mussolini regime quite naturally found a first outlet in East Africa. Ethiopia was conquered in 1935—the last gasp of western colonialism—and all Italian possessions in East Africa were grouped together into an imposing unit known as Italian East Africa. But its existence was brief. Early in World War II all of Italian East Africa was conquered by British forces, and later Libya and the Dodecanese were likewise occupied.

As Germany had lost its colonial possessions after World War I, so also were Italy's lost after World War II. Until disposition was made of them the Italian colonies were under British military organization. By 1951 all except Italian Somaliland had been "decolonized." Italian Somaliland was, almost by default due to the lack of interest of other European powers, given as a trusteeship to Italy in 1950, the only example of a defeated colonial power's being accorded this distinction. In 1960 Somalia became independent.

Italy's role in colonial history was unimportant. It consisted primarily of filling in the empty spaces which the other European powers could not otherwise conveniently and amicably fill.

250 DODECANESE ISLANDS

Despite its name the group known as the Dodecanese Islands consists of about fifty islands— of which Rhodes, Kos, and Karpathos are the most important—in the southern Aegean Sea off the southwestern coast of Turkey. The group was occupied by Italy in 1912 during the Italo-Turkish War. In 1915 the islands were formally recognized by the Allies as Italian possessions. Italian sovereignty was acknowledged by the Ottoman government in the Treaty of Sèvres (1920), and subsequently by the Turkish Republic in the Treaty of Lausanne (1923). During World War II, the islands were progressively occupied by Great Britain. Until 1947 they remained under British military control. In 1947 they were ceded to Greece.

Governors		<u>under Great Britain</u>	
1923-1936	Mario Fago		
1936-1940	Cesare Maria de Vecchi di Val	*Chief Administrators*	
	Cismon	1945	Peter Bevil Edward Acland
1940-1941	Ettore Bastico	1945-1946	Charles Henry Gormley
1941-1943	Inigo Campione	1946-1947	Arthur Stanley Parker

Rennell, passim; *Statesman's Year Book*, 1923-43.

251 ERITREA

The area of Eritrea, along the western coast of the Red Sea, was historically a part of Ethiopia until much of it was occupied by the Ottoman Turks in the 16th century. Early in the 19th century the Egyptians replaced the Turks. In 1870 the Italians established themselves at Assab, and at the withdrawal of the Egyptians in 1882 Italy proclaimed its sovereignty over Assab. Massawa was added three years later. A protectorate was soon proclaimed over the Danakil area, and in 1890 this expanded area was proclaimed the colony of Eritrea. By the Treaty of Uccialli in 1889 Ethiopia had, according to the Italian interpretation, accepted Italian rule in the Eritrean area. Conflicts over the validity of this interpretation led to an attempt by the Italians to expand into Ethiopia, but this effort was frustrated by the Ethiopians at Aduwa in 1896. Nearly forty years later, in 1935, Italy successfully occupied Ethiopia and reorganized its possessions in the area as Italian East Africa (q.v.), of which Eritrea was a part. In 1941 British troops occupied Eritrea, and it remained under British administration until 1952 when it was federally united with Ethiopia.

Assab		1890-1892	Antonio Gandolfi
Commandant		1892-1896	Oreste Baratieri
1882-1885	Guilio Pestalozza	1896-1897	Antonio Baldissera (2)
		1897-1907	Ferdinando Martini
Massawa		1907-1915	Giuseppe Salvago-Raggi
Commandants		1916-1919	Nobile Giacomo di Martino
1885	Tancredi Saletta	1919-1923	Giovanni Cerrina-Feroni
1885-1887	Carlo Genè	1923-1928	Jacopo Gasparini
1887-1888	Alessandro Asinardi di San Marzano	1928-1930	Corrado Zoli
1888-1889	Antonio Baldissera (1)	1930-1935	Riccardo Astuto dei Duchi di Lucchesi
Eritrea		1936-1937	Alfredo Guzzoni
Governors		1937	Vincenzo de Feo
1889-1890	Baldassare Orero	1937-1940	Guiseppe Daodiace

under Great Britain	1942-1944	Stephen Hemsley Longrigg
	1944-1945	C. D. McCarthy
Eritrea	1945-1946	John Meredith Benoy
Chief Administrators	1946-1951	Francis Greville Drew
1941-1942 Brian Kennedy-Cooke	1951-1952	Duncan Cameron Cumming

Italy, Ministerio degli Affari Esteri, pp. 417–18, 428; Trevaskis, passim.

252 ITALIAN EAST AFRICA

From the time of the establishment of Eritrea (q.v.) in 1890 Italy had had designs on the neighboring kingdom of Ethiopia. An attack in 1896 had been frustrated, but another in 1935 ended in the conquest and annexation of Ethiopia. Ethiopia itself was divided into the provinces of Amhara, Galla e Sidama, Harar, and Scioa and, together with Italy's older colonies of Eritrea and Italian Somaliland (q.v.), was formed into Italian East Africa. Italian East Africa was governed by a high commissioner to 1936 and then by a governor-general, or viceroy. Italy's East African empire was of short duration, for in 1941 all its various parts were occupied by Allied troops. Ethiopia was reconstituted as an independent state—the other colonies coming under British military administration.

High Commissioners		*Governors-General*	
1935	Emilio de Bono	1936-1937	Rodolfo Graziani
1935-1936	Pietro Badoglio	1937-1941	Amedeo di Savoia, Duca d'Aosta

Italy, Ministerio degli Affari Esteri, pp. 426–27.

253 ITALIAN SOMALILAND

The Somali area of northeastern Africa, although visited by the Portuguese around 1500, was one of the last areas in Africa to be subjected to European penetration. In the 1880's Great Britain and France established themselves in the northernmost Somali areas (v. French Somaliland, 23, and British Somaliland, 109). In 1889 Italy proclaimed a protectorate over the Mijerstein sultanates of Alula and Obbia. The area south of this was leased from Zanzibar from 1889 to 1905, first by the Filonardi Company (1893–96) and then by the Benadir Company (1896–1905). After 1905 it was directly ruled as an Italian colony. Jubaland in the extreme south was ceded by Great Britain in 1925, and the following year the two northern sultanates were incorporated directly into Italian Somaliland. In 1935 Italian Somaliland became a part of Italian East Africa (q.v.) and remained so until the British military occupation in 1941. British rule continued until 1950 when Italy, almost through default, was granted a United Nations trusteeship over its former colony. In 1960 the former Italian Somaliland and the former British Somaliland united to form the independent Republic of Somalia.

Italy

Governors		under Great Britain	
1893-1897	Vincenzo Filonardi		
1897-1903	Emilio Dulio	Governors	
1903-1905	Alessandro Sapelli (1)	1941	Reginald Hopkinson Smith
1905-1906	Luigi Mercatelli	1941-1943	William Eric Halstead Scupham
1906	Alessandro Sapelli (2)	1943-	Denis Henry Wickham
1906-1907	Giovanni Cerrina-Feroni (1)	1948	Eric Armar Vully de Candole
1907-1908	Tommaso Carletti	1948-1950	Geoffrey Massey Gamble
1908-1910	Gino Macchioro		
1910-1916	Nobile Giacomo de Martino	under Italy	
1916-1920	Giovanni Cerrina-Feroni (2)		
1920-1923	Carlo Riveri	Somalia	
1923-1928	Cesare Maria de Vecchi di Val	Administrators	
	Cismon	1950-1953	Giovanni Fornari
1928-1931	Guido Corni	1953-1955	Enrico Martino
1931-1935	Maurizio Rava	1955-1958	Enrico Anzilotti
1935-1936	Rodolfo Graziani	1958-1960	Mario di Stefani
1936-1937	Ruggiero Santini		
1937-1940	Francesco Saverio Caroselli		
1940	Gustavo Pesenti		
1940-1941	Carlo De Simone		

Hess, p. 212; Italy, Ministerio degli Affari Esteri, pp. 420—22, 428; Rennell, passim.

254 LIBYA

Libya, the last area of northern Africa to fall under European control, was partially occupied by Italy during the Italo-Turkish War of 1911—12. The area was divided into two administrative areas, Cirenaica and Tripolitania. In 1919 the two were made separate colonies, only to be reunited in 1928 under a governor-general. Libya was the scene of heavy fighting during the year 1940—43. By 1943, however, the Italians had been driven from Libya. Cirenaica and Tripolitania were administered by Great Britain while the south, or Fezzan, was administered by France. In 1949 Cyrenaica was granted autonomy, and two years later all three areas were federally united to form the kingdom of Libya.

Cirenaica		Tripolitania	
Governors		Governors	
1912-1913	Ottavio Briccola	1911	Raffaele Borea Ricci d'Olmo
1913-1918	Giovanni Batista Ameglio	1911-1912	Carlo Caneva
1918-1919	Vincenzo Garioni	1912-1913	Ottavio Ragni
1919-1921	Nobile Giacomo de Martino	1913-1914	Vincenzo Garioni
1921-1922	Luigi Pintor	1914-1915	Luigi Druetti
1922	Eduardo Baccari	1915	Guilio Cesare Tassoni
1922-1924	Luigi Bongiovanni	1915-1918	Giovanni Batista Ameglio
1924-1926	Ernesto Mombelli	1918-1919	Vincenzo Garioni
1926-1928	Attilio Teruzzi	1919-1920	Vittorio Menzinger
		1920-1921	Luigi Mercatelli
Vice-Governors		1921-1925	Guiseppe Volpi di Misurata
1929-1930	Domenico Siciliani	1925-1928	Emilio de Bono
1930-1934	Rodolfo Graziani		
1934-1935	Guglielmo Nasi		

Libya

Governors-General

1928-1933 Pietro Badoglio
1933-1940 Italo Balbo
1940-1941 Rodolfo Graziani, Marchese di
           Neghelli
1941   Italo Gariboldi
1941-1943 Ettore Bastico

under Great Britain

Cirenaica

Chief Administrators

1942-1945 Duncan Cameron Cumming
1945-1946 Peter Bevil Edward Acland
1946-1948 James William Norris Haugh
1948-1951 Eric Armar Vully de Candole

Tripolitania

Chief Administrator

1943-1951 Travers Robert Blackley

Italy, Ministerio degli Affari Esteri, pp. 423—25; Rennell, passim.

Bibliography: Italy

Hess, Robert L. *Italian Colonialism in Somalia*. Chicago: University of Chicago Press, 1966.

Italy, Ministerio degli affari esteri. *Il governo dei territori oltremare, 1869—1955*. L'Italia in Africa, vol. 2. Rome: Istituto Poligrafico dello Stato, 1963.

Khadduri, Majid. *Modern Libya: A Study in Political Development*. Baltimore: Johns Hopkins University Press, 1963.

Rennell, Francis James Rennell Rodd, Baron. *British Military Administration of Occupied Territories in Africa during the Years 1941—1947*. London: H.M.S.O., 1948.

Statesman's Year Book: Statistical and Historical Annual of the States of the World. London: Macmillan & Co., 1864 to date.

Trevaskis, Gerald Kennedy Nicholas. *Eritrea: A Colony in Transition, 1941—52*. London: Oxford University Press, 1960.

Japan

Japan, as a result of the rapid adaptation of western technology to its own conditions after 1868, and its subsequent industrialization, was soon in a position vis-à-vis its neighbors in East Asia not unlike that of Europe to the rest of the world. In this restricted sense Japan became a microcosm of Europe and felt the same need to expand into less-favored areas. Japan's colonial empire may be said to begin with the occupation of the Ryukyu Islands in 1879, a step recognized by China, the islands' former ruler, in 1881. Japan's subsequent colonial possessions were almost solely acquired in war. China's weak position, already manifested in 1881, was accentuated by the Sino-Japanese War of 1894—95 from which Japan emerged with Formosa as the prize. The Russo-Japanese War of 1904—5 added Kwantung Leased Territory and southern Sakhalin (Karafuto) to her growing empire. Japan's preeminent position in Korea, although of long standing, was materially fostered, and the annexation of Korea made possible by the result of this war. The Pacific islands formerly belonging to Germany were mandated to Japan for her participation in World War I on the Allies' side.

The Japanese Empire was greatly expanded in the decade before World War II and in the early years of the War. Between 1931 and 1945 Japan occupied Manchuria (Manchukuo), large parts of China, all of Southeast Asia—namely, Indochina, Thailand, Burma, Malaya, and Indonesia—and many of the islands in the Pacific Ocean not hitherto under its control. This huge area was called the Greater East Asia Co-Prosperity Sphere, reflecting Japan's view of itself as the protector of Asian interests against western imperialism. The Japanese Empire began to collapse during the last stages of the war, and with the surrender of Japan in 1945 all its imperial possessions were lost. The British reoccupied Burma and Malaya; the French and Dutch competed with powerful nationalist movements to regain their former colonies of Indochina and Indonesia; and the United States kept all the Pacific islands formerly occupied by Japan.

255 CHOSEN (KOREA)

Japanese interest in the Korean peninsula was of long standing. From the 4th to the 6th centuries A.D. a part of the south was under Japanese control. From 1592 to 1598 Japanese forces overran most of the peninsula, but Chinese intervention, and internal dissension in Japan, led to withdrawal. Interest was revived in 1876 with a trade agreement with the Korean kingdom. As a result of the Sino-Japanese War of 1894–95 Japan secured effective control of the government of Korea and was ceded Formosa (q.v.). This control progressively intensified and a resident-general was appointed in 1906. In 1910 the Korean monarchy was abolished and Korea, renamed Chosen, was formally annexed to Japan. Chosen remained under Japan until the end of World War II. In 1945 it was divided, the north coming under Russian control, the south under American.

Residents-General		1919-1927	Saitō Makoto (1)
1906-1909	Ito Hirobumi	1927	Ugaki Kazushige (1)
1909-1910	Sone Arasuke	1927-1929	Yamanashi Hanzo
1910	Terauchi Masakata	1929-1931	Saitō Makoto (2)
		1931-1936	Ugaki Kazushige (2)
Governors-General		1936-1942	Minami Jirō
1910-1916	Terauchi Masakata	1942-1944	Koiso Kuniteru
1916-1919	Hasagawa Yoshimichi	1944-1945	Abe Nobuyuki

Kim and Kim, passim; *Korean Studies Guide*, p. 185.

256 FORMOSA (TAIWAN)

The island of Formosa, off the east coast of China, had been ruled by the Dutch and Spaniards during the 17th century (v. Tayowan, 282) and reverted to Chinese rule after the Koxinga interlude in 1683. It was ceded to Japan as a result of the Treaty of Shimonoseki in 1895 and forthwith conquered and occupied by Japan. Formosa was thus Japan's first colonial possession, and it remained in Japanese hands until the end of World War II in 1945 when it was returned to China. In 1949 it became the seat of the Chinese Nationalist government.

Governors		1924-1926	Izawa Takio
1895-1896	Kabayama Sukenori	1926-1928	Ueyama Mitsonushin
1896	Katsura Taro	1928-1929	Kawamura Takeji
1896-1898	Nogi Norisuke	1929-1931	Ishizuka Eizō
1898-1905	Kodama Gentaro	1931-1932	Ōta Masahiro
1905-1915	Sakuma Samata	1932	Minami Hiroshi
1915-1918	Andō Sadayoshi	1932-1936	Nagakawa Kenzo
1918-1919	Akashi Motojiro	1936-1940	Kobayashi Seizo
1919-1923	Den Kenjiro	1940-1944	Hasegawa Kiyoshi
1923-1924	Ushida Yoshikichi	1944-1945	Andō Rikichi

Information from Chiang Fu-tsung, Director, National Central Library, Taipei, Taiwan.

257 KARAFUTO

The southern part of Sakhalin, an island directly north of Japan belonging to Russia, was ceded to Japan by Russia under the terms of the Treaty of Portsmouth in 1905 which ended the Russo-Japanese War. In 1907 Japan established a military administration over its part of Sakhalin, which was termed Karafuto. Karafuto remained under Japanese control until 1945, at the end of World War II, when it was occupied by Russian troops.

Governors-General			
1907-1908	Kususe Sachihiko	1926-1927	Toyoda Katsuzō
1908	Tokonami Takejirō	1927-1929	Kita Kōji
1908-1914	Hiraoka Sadatarō	1929-1931	Agata Shinobu
1914-1916	Okada Bunji	1931-1932	Kishimoto Masao
1916-1919	Sakaya Akira (1)	1932-1938	Imamura Takeshi
1919-1924	Nagai Kinjirō	1938-1940	Munesue Shun'ichi
1924-1926	Sakaya Akira (2)	1940-1943	Ogawa Seigi
		1943-1945	Ōtsu Toshio

Information from Y. Sakai, Director, Division of Interlibrary Services, National Diet Library, Tokyo.

258 KWANTUNG LEASED TERRITORY

Kwantung is located at the southern end of the Liaotung peninsula in northeastern China, or Manchuria. In 1898 it, like other enclaves along the Chinese coast (v. Kouang-Tchéou-Wan, 37, France; Kiaochow, 76, Germany; and Weihaiwei, 241, Great Britain), was leased by China to a European power—in this case Russia. Russian occupancy was short, for Kwantung fell to Japan, which assumed Russia's lease, as part of the spoils of the Russo-Japanese War of 1904–5. Port Arthur (Ryojun) became an important Japanese naval base and the terminus of the Southern Manchuria Railway. Until 1919 Kwantung Leased Territory was under military administration. In 1932 Japanese influence in Manchuria was greatly expanded and the puppet state of Manchukuo was created. After 1934 the Japanese ambassador to Manchukuo was also in charge of Kwantung Leased Territory. In 1945 the area was occupied by the Russians and the Soviet Union renewed its dormant lease. In 1955 the area of Kwantung Leased Territory reverted to Chinese authority.

Governors-General			
1905-1912	Ōshima Yoshimasa	1929-1931	Ōta Masahirō
1912-1914	Fukushima Yasumasa	1931-1932	Tsukamoto Seiji
1914-1917	Nakamura Satoru	1932	Yamaoka Mannosuke
1917-1919	Nakamura Yujirō	1932-1933	Mutō Nobuyoshi
1919-1920	Hayashi Gonsuke	1933-1934	Hishikari Takashi
1920-1922	Yamagata Isaburō	1934-1936	Minami Jirō
1922-1923	Ijuin Hikokichi	1936-1939	Ueda Kenkichi
1923-1927	Kodama Hideo	1939-1944	Umezu Yoshijirō
1928-1929	Kinoshita Kenjirō	1944-1945	Yamada Otozō

Information provided by Y. Sakai, Director, Division of Interlibrary Services, National Diet Library, Tokyo. Also, *Japan Year Book*, 1906–31; *Who's Who in Japan*, 1912–40.

259 PACIFIC ISLANDS MANDATE

In 1914 Japan occupied the Marshall, Mariana, and Caroline islands, hitherto part of German New Guinea (72). An agreement with Great Britain in 1917 stipulated that the island groups which were north of the equator would be administered by Japan, while the southern portions of German New Guinea, that is, New Guinea, the Bismarck Archipelago, Nauru, and scattered other islands would be administered by Great Britain or a Commonwealth member (v. British New Guinea, 106, and Nauru, 166). In fact Japan was awarded a League of Nations mandate for the three island groups in 1919. From 1914 to 1921 the islands were under military administration. Civil rule was introduced in 1921. In 1944–45 the islands of the Pacific Islands Mandate were occupied by American forces.

Governors			
1921–1923	Tezuka Toshiro	1932–1933	Matsuda Masayuki
1923–1931	Yokota Gosuke	1933–1936	Hayashi Hisao
1931	Horiguchi Mitsusada	1936–1940	Kitajima Kenjiro
1931–1932	Tawara Kazuo	1940–1943	Kondo Shunsuke
		1943–1944	Hosokaya Ishiro

Clyde, p. 80n; *Japan Year Book*, 1934–39.

Bibliography: Japan

Clyde, Paul Hibbert. *Japan's Pacific Mandate*. New York: Macmillan Co., 1935.

Japan Year Book: Complete Cyclopaedia of General Information and Statistics on Japan and Japanese Territories, 1905–31. Tokyo: Japan Year Book Office, 1905–31.

Kim, C. I. Eugene, and Kim, H-K. *Korea and the Politics of Imperialism, 1876–1910*. Berkeley: University of California Press, 1968.

Korean Studies Guide. University of California, Institute of East Asiatic Studies. Berkeley: University of California Press, 1954.

The Netherlands

In 1568 the Low Countries rebelled against Spain and initiated a long and bitter struggle for independence. Not until the Treaty of Westphalia in 1648 did Spain recognize this independence, although it was substantially won by 1609. One aspect of the Dutch Republic's efforts was a worldwide assault on Spain's overseas possessions, including those of Portugal, then (1580—1640) united with Spain. In 1602 the Vereenigde Oost-Indische Compagnie, or V.O.C. (United East India Company) was established, and in 1621 its counterpart, the West-Indische Compagnie (West India Company), was formed.

The years from 1620 to 1650 marked the acme of Dutch success in this endeavor. Ironically, it was against the Portuguese colonies—enclaves more susceptible to seizure than the larger Spanish settlement colonies—that the Dutch had the greatest success. In 1641 Malacca was captured, and shortly thereafter the Portuguese were driven from Ceylon and from their posts in the East Indies. Portuguese control of the lucrative East Indian spice trade was shattered forever.

In the Atlantic area large parts of Brazil were seized, as well as the coast of Angola, hobbling the Portuguese economic systems in these areas, which were largely mutually supportive. Here, however, Dutch success was ephemeral. Between 1645 and 1654 the Portuguese were able to win back all they had lost, at least in terms of territory. The Dutch had, however, taken the knowledge of sugar technology from Brazil to the West Indies, and Brazil soon lost its commanding position as a sugar producer. After 1667 the Dutch were left with only a few islands in the West Indies and some settlements on the Guiana coast of South America.

In the East, Dutch power continued to wax. Dutch control over the spice trade reached as close as was possible to monopolistic status. In the 17th, 18th, and early 19th centuries the Dutch were able to exercise a true monopoly of the Japanese trade, albeit on the sufferance of the Japanese. Likewise the Dutch began, after the middle of the 17th century, to become, necessarily if not enthusiastically, territorially involved in Java and other areas of the East Indies.

Decentralization was the dominant characteristic of the administration of the Dutch colonies, as in fact it was of the administration in the metropolis. The Dutch government, weak in the Netherlands, exercised no control over the Dutch possessions. The colonies in the East remained under the V.O.C. until 1795 and those left in the western hemisphere continued to be governed by the West India Company until 1791. Even in the case of the companies themselves, the government was decentralized. Each was ruled by a large council, dominated by the Chambers of Amsterdam and Zeeland. The ruling council of the V.O.C. was known as the Heeren XVII and that of the West India Company as the Heeren XIX. Throughout the period, basic policies within broad outlines were determined and implemented by the "men on the spot."

During the period of the Napoleonic Wars from 1795 to 1816—18 all of the Dutch overseas possessions were occupied by the British, except Surinam wh fell to the Portuguese from Brazil. At the peace of 1814—15 the Netherlands lost the Cape Colony, Ceylon, and some of its possessions in Guiana. In 18. Malacca and all Dutch possessions in India were ceded to the British in retu for Bencoolen and a free hand in the East Indies. Finally, in 1872 the Nether lands sold the few scattered Dutch posts on the Gold Coast to Great Britain.

The Netherlands took no part in the colonial efflorescence of the 19th cen tury but rather concentrated on developing its control in the East Indies, for t spice trade no longer sufficed and revenue had to be raised from sources re- quiring greater exploitation of land and human resources. In 1830 the Cultuu. stelsel (Culture System) was introduced into the East Indies. This soon evol into an efficient and highly profitable form of taxation based on payment in k Regrettably, it was profitable because it imposed harsh and unreasonable de- mands on those being taxed, and the outcry both from within and from without the Netherlands resulted in its virtual abandonment by 1877. Meanwhile, the Dutch had spent much of the 19th century extending, often with great difficul its control over Sumatra, Borneo, and the other islands in the East Indies, mo of which had lain beyond the pale of effective control in 1815. It was only i 1914 that the Dutch government could claim to exercise sovereignty over the entire archipelago.

Dutch administration of the East Indies was only mildly benevolent and ce tainly grossly myopic. Nationalist expression met with indifference and ther repression. Not surprisingly, then, the Japanese were welcomed as liberator in 1941, and Dutch authority collapsed with little resistance by the Dutch an less assistance from the Indonesians. Although Japanese rule quickly outliv its welcome, the interlude was of sufficient duration and impact to affect per nently the relationship between the Dutch and the governed peoples of the Ea Indies. Shortly before the end of Japanese control in 1945, the Republic of Ir donesia, then largely a paper creation, was formed. The Dutch on their retur proved unable to stifle the growing nationalist sentiment. Quixotically they expected to be able to govern on the same basis as they had before the war, and they displayed a singular incapacity to recognize the altered circumstan Their unwillingness to compromise led to full-scale civil war between the na tionalist and Dutch forces. In the post-World War II ambience, bald force as a means of perpetuating colonialism was clearly disconsonant with internatic opinion. Furthermore the Dutch lacked the resources, and later the desire, to reimpose their sovereignty over the East Indies. In 1949 sovereignty over th East Indies, with the exception of western New Guinea, was transferred to th Republic of Indonesia. The New Guinea enclave, having little purpose beyor that of a memento of bygone times, was given up by the Dutch in 1962 and th United Nations assumed control. Six months later it was transferred to Indo nesia.

The Dutch colonial experience in the West Indies and Surinam was more halcyon. An attempt in 1828 to unite all the Dutch colonies into a single administrative unit proved abortive, but in 1845 all the West Indian possessions were united into the Netherlands Antilles. In 1954 Surinam and the Netherlands Antilles were granted internal autonomy and became overseas provinces of the Netherlands, thus ending their colonial status in the same way as neighboring Guadeloupe and Martinique ended theirs by becoming departments of France.

260 BERBICE

Berbice was the easternmost of the four Dutch settlements on the coast of western Guiana. A concession in the area was granted in 1627 to the house of van Pere and the settlement was privately administered by this group from 1666 to 1714. From 1720 it was governed by the Berbice Association. Along with the other Dutch colonies in this area, Berbice was occupied by the English in 1803 and retained by them thereafter (v. British Guiana, 102).

Governors

1666	Matthijs Bergenaar	1760-1764	Wolfert Simon van Hoogenheim
1671	Cornelis Marinus	1764-1767	Johan Heijliger
1683	Gideon Bourse	1768-1773	Stephen Hendrik de la Sabloniere
1684	Lucas Coudrie	1773-1774	Johan Christoffel de Winter
1687	Matthijs de Feer	1774-1777	Isaac Kaecks
1712	Steven de Waterman	1778-1781	Pieter Hendrik Koppiers (1)
1714-1733	Antony Tierens	1781-1782	(under Great Britain)
1733-1740	Bernhardt Waterham	1782-1784	(under France)
1740-1749	Jan Andries Lossner	1784-1789	Pieter Hendrik Koppiers (2)
1749-1755	Jan Frederik Colier	1789-1802	Abraham Jacob van Imbijze van
1755-1759	Hendrik Jan van Rijswijck		Batenburg

Information from H. R. Persaud, Archivist of British Guiana, Georgetown, British Guiana.

261 CAPE COLONY

Capetown, at the southern tip of Africa, was established by the Dutch East India Company in 1652 to serve as a way-station on voyages to the East Indies. Although the company desired that the colony remain only a victualling point, it rapidly became a colony of settlement, spreading its boundaries eastward along the cape. Eventually the colony outgrew its original purpose and became resentful of the company's efforts to control its growth. Company rule ended in 1794, and in the following year the British first occupied Cape Colony. It was returned to the Dutch under terms of the Treaty of Amiens in 1803, but again, and finally, reoccupied by the British in 1806 (v. Cape Colony, 115).

Commanders

1652-1662	Jan Anthonie van Riebeeck	1708-1711	Lodewijk van Assenburgh
1662-1666	Zacharias Wagenaar	1711-1714	Willem Helot
1666-1668	Cornelis van Quaelberg	1714-1724	Maurits Pasques de Chavonnes
1668-1670	Jakob Borghorst	1724-1727	Jean de la Fontaine (1)
1670-1671	Pieter Hackius	1727-1729	Pieter Gysbert Noodt
1672	Albert van Breughel	1729-1737	Jean de la Fontaine (2)
1672-1676	Isbrand Goske	1737	Adriaan van Kervel
1676-1678	Johan Bacx	1737-1739	Daniel van den Henghel
1678-1679	Hendrik Crudorp	1739-1751	Hendrik Swellengrebel
1679-1691	Simon van der Stel	1751-1771	Ryk Tulbagh
		1771-1785	Joachim van Plettenberg
		1785-1791	Cornelis Jakobus van der Graaff
Governors		1791-1792	Johan Isaak Rhenius
1691-1699	Simon van der Stel	1792-1793	Sebastiaan Cornelis Nederburgh
1699-1707	Willem Adriaan van der Stel	1793-1795	Simon Hendrik Frykenius
1707-1708	Johan Cornelis d'Ableing	1793-1795	Abraham Josias Sluysken

1795-1803 (under Great Britain)
1803-1804 Jakobus Abraham de Mist

1804-1806 Jan Willem Janssens

Walker, pp. xvii—xviii.

262 CEARÁ

For the Dutch commanders of Ceará from 1637 to 1654, see the Portuguese colony, Ceará, 289.

263 CEYLON

The Dutch came to Ceylon in 1640 at the invitation of the ruler of Kandy who hoped to use them to drive the Portuguese from the island (v. 291). By 1658 the Portuguese had been expelled, but the Dutch remained and in course of time increased greatly the territory which had been held by the Portuguese. By 1765 the Dutch controlled the entire coastline, reducing the kingdom of Kandy to an isolated inland kingdom in the highlands although they were unable to subjugate it completely. In 1796 the British occupied the Dutch possessions in Ceylon (v. 118) and retained the island permanently thereafter, although the other Dutch possessions in and around the Indian Ocean were returned either after the Treaty of Amiens (1802) or after the end of the Napoleonic Wars.

Governors
1640	Willem Jacobszoon Coster
1640-1646	Jan Thyssen Payart
1646-1650	Jan Maetsuycker
1650-1653	Jacob van Kittensteijn
1653-1662	Adriaan van der Meijden
1662-1663	Rijklof van Goens (1)
1663-1664	Jacob Hustaert
1665-1675	Rijklof van Goens (2)
1675-1679	Rijklof van Goens, Jr.
1679-1692	Laurens Pijl
1692-1697	Thomas van Rhee
1697-1702	Gerrit de Heere
1703-1707	Cornelis Jan Simonszoon
1707-1716	Hendrik Bekker
1716-1723	Isaak Augustijn Rumph
1723-1726	Johannes Hertenberg
1726-1729	Pieter Vuijst
1729-1731	Stephanus Versluijs
1731-1732	Wouter Hendriks
1733-1736	Diederik van Domburch
1736-1740	Gustaaf Willem van Imhoff
1740-1742	Willem Maurits Bruininck
1742-1743	Daniel Overbeek
1743-1751	Julius Valentijn Steijn van Gollonesse
1751-1752	Gerard Johan Vreelandt
1752-1756	Joan Gideon Loten
1756-1761	Jan Schreuder
1761-1765	Lubbert Jan van Eck
1765-1785	Iman William Falck
1785-1794	Willem Jacob van de Graaff
1794-1796	Johan Gerard van Angelbeek

Information from A. E. M. Ribberink, Deputy Director, Algemeen Rijksarchief, The Hague. See also Wijnaendts van Resandt, pp. 54—86.

264 COROMANDEL COAST

The Dutch early established themselves along the Coromandel coast to exploit the textile trade there for use in their intercoastal Asian trade. During the 17th century these posts were prosperous, but the advent of the English and French during the last quarter of the century caused Dutch trade to decline. In 1690 the center of Dutch power was shifted from Pulicat to Negapatam. From 1693 to 1699 the Dutch were able to occupy the French posts in the area (v. French India, 21), but in the 18th century they were no longer a serious factor. From 1795 to 1818 the Dutch posts on the Coromandel coast, like those elsewhere in India, were occupied by the British. In 1825 they were definitely ceded to Great Britain in return for concessions elsewhere (v. Malacca and Bencoolen, 96).

Governors

1608-1610	Pieter Isaacx Eyloff
1610-1612	Jan van Wesicke
1612-1615	Wemmer van Berchem
1615-1616	Hans de Haze (1)
1616-1617	Samuel Kint
1617-1619	Adolp Thomassen
1619-1620	Hans de Haze (2)
1620-1622	Andries Soury (1)
1622-1624	Abraham van Uffelen
1625-1626	Andries Soury (2)
1626-1632	Maarten Isbrantsz (1)
1632-1633	David Pietersz
1633-1636	Maarten Isbrantsz (2)
1636-1638	Carel Reijniersz
1638-1643	Arent Gardenijs
1643-1650	Arnout Heussen
1650-1651	Laurens Pit (1)
1651	Jacob de With
1652-1663	Laurens Pit (2)
1663-1665	Cornelis Speelman
1665-1676	Anthonie Paviljoen
1676-1679	Jacques Caulier
1679-1681	Willem Carel Hartsinck
1681-1686	Jacob Joriszoon Pits
1687-1698	Laurens Pits, Jr.
1698-1705	Dirk Comans
1705-1710	Johannes van Steelandt
1710-1716	Daniel Bernard Guilliams
1716-1719	Adriaan de Visscher
1719-1723	Gerard van Westrenen
1723-1730	Dirk van Cloon
1730-1733	Adriaan Pla
1733-1737	Elias Guillot
1738-1743	Jacob Mossel
1743-1747	Galenus Mersen
1747-1753	Librecht Hooreman
1753-1758	Steven Vermont
1758-1761	Lubbert Jan van Eck
1761-1765	Christiaan van Teylingen
1765-1773	Pieter Haksteen
1773-1780	Reinier van Vlissingen
1780-1784	(under Great Britain)
1785-1789	Willem Blauwkamer
1790-1795	Jacob Eilbracht
1795-1816	(under Great Britain)
1818-1824	F. C. Regel
1824-1825	Henry François von Söhsten

Raychaudhuri, pp. 217—18; Wijnaendts van Resandt, pp. 88—119.

265 CURAÇAO

Until 1634 the island of Curaçao was occupied by Spaniards but it was conquered by the Dutch in that year. Soon afterwards the smaller neighboring islands of Aruba and Bonaire were occupied and made administratively dependent on Curaçao. The islands were administered by the first West India Company to 1674 and by the second West India Company to 1792 when they came under direct state control. They were occupied by the British from 1800 to 1803, and again from 1807 to 1816. From 1828 to 1845 Curaçao, Aruba, and Bonaire were subordinated to the short-lived government-general of the Dutch West Indies headquartered at Surinam. In 1845 this government was dissolved and Curaçao became administratively independent. In the same year Saint Eustatius (q.v.), Saint Martin, and Saba were added, and the colony came to be known, with this addition, as the Netherlands Antilles (q.v.).

Governors			
1634-1638	Johannes van Walbeeck		
1638-1641	Jacob Pieterszoon Tolck		
1641-1642	Jan Claeszoon van Campen		
1642-1647	Pieter Stuijvesant[1]		
1647-1657	Lucas Rodenburch		
1657-1668	Matthias Beck		
1668-1669	Willem Beck (1)		
1669-1670	Lodewijk Boudewijn van Berlicum		
1670	Willem Beck (2)		
1670-1673	Dirk Otterinck		
1673-1679	Jan Doncker		
1679-1682	Nikolaas van Liebergen		
1682-1683	Apero van der Hoeven (1)		
1683-1685	Jan van Erpecum		
1685-1686	Apero van der Hoeven (2)		
1685-1686	Willibrord van Engelen		
1686-1692	Willem Kerckrinck		
1692-1700	Bastiaan Bernagie		
1700-1701	Coenraad Bergh		
1701-1704	Nikolaas van Beck		
1704-1708	Jacob Beck		
1708-1710	Abraham Beck		
1710-1715	Jeremias van Collen		
1715-1720	Jonathan van Beuningen		
1720	Jan van Beuningen		
1721-1731	Jan Noach du Faij		
1731-1738	Juan Pedro van Collen		
1738-1740	Jan Gales		
1740-1758	Isaäc Faesch		
1758-1761	Jean Isai Claris Rodier de la Brugière (1)		
1761-1762	Jacob van Bosveld		
1762-1781	Jean Isai Claris Rodier de la Brugière (2)		
1782-1796	Johannes Abrahamszoon de Veer		
1796-1800	Johan Rudolf Lauffer		

under Great Britain

Governors	
1800	Hugh Seymour
1800	Johan Rudolf Lauffer
1800-1801	Walter Tremenheere
1801	William Carlyon Hughes (1)
1801-1802	Arthur Whetham
1802-1803	William Carlyon Hughes (2)

under the Netherlands

Governors	
1803-1804	Cornelis Berch
1803-1804	Abraham de Veer
1804-1807	Pierre Jean Changuion

under Great Britain

Governors	
1807	Charles Brisbane
1807-1808	Micaiah Malbon
1808	Robert Nicholas
1808-1809	James Cockburn
1809-1811	John Thomas Layard
1811-1814	John Hodgson
1814-1816	John Le Couteur

under the Netherlands

Governors	
1816-1819	Albert Kikkert
1819-1820	Petrus Bernardus van Starkenborgh
1820-1828	Paulus Roelof Cantz'laar
1828-1836	Isaäk Johannes Rammelman Elsevier
1836-1845	Reinier Frederik van Raders

1. Stuijvesant's next post was as governor of New Netherlands (q.v.), and he held simultaneously the post of director-general of Curaço. Thus the actual title of Rodenburch, and of Beck until 1664, the resident administrators in Curaçao, was Vice-Director.

Gaay Fortman; Hartog, 2:1136–40; Krafft, pp. 383–84.

266 DEMERARA

The settlement of Demerara was developed from Essequibo (q.v.) in 1750 and remained subject to the latter until 1781 when it was captured by the British. The French occupied the colony from 1782 to 1784 when it was returned to the Dutch. From 1784 it replaced Essequibo as the headquarters of the Dutch administration in western Guiana. Occupied by the British from 1796 to 1802, it was returned to the Dutch, only to be finally occupied in 1803 (v. British Guiana, 102).

The Netherlands

Governors	
1750-1761	Jonathan Samuel Storm van 's Gravesende
1761-1764	Laurens Lodewijk van Bercheijk
1765-1770	Jan Cornelis van der Heuvel
1772-1781	Paulus van Schuylenburgh

under Great Britain

Demerara, Essequibo, and Berbice
Governors

1781-1782	Robert Kingston

under France

Demerara, Essequibo, and Berbice
Governors

1782	Louis-Antoine Dazemard de Lusignan

1782	Armand-Gui Coetnempren de Kergrist
1782-1784	Georges Manganon de la Perrière

under the Netherlands

Demerara and Essequibo
Directors-General

1784	Joseph Bourda
1784-1789	Jan L'Éspinasse
1789-1793	Albertus Backer
1793-1795	Willem August van Sirtema van Grovestins
1795-1796	Antony Beaujon
1796-1802	(under Great Britain)
1802-1803	Antony Meertens

Information from H. R. Persaud, Archivist of British Guiana, Georgetown, British Guiana.

267 ESSEQUIBO

The area at the mouth of the Essequibo River in western Guiana was settled by the Dutch West India Company in 1624. It was briefly captured by the English in 1666, but retaken. In 1750 the Demerara area was settled from Essequibo, and in 1784, after brief British and French occupations, Essequibo became subordinate to Demerara. In 1803 the British occupied the colony as well as the other Dutch possessions in western Guiana (v. British Guiana, 102).

Governors

1624-1627	Jacob Conijn
1627-1638	Jan van der Goes
1638-1641	Cornelis Pieterszoon Hose
1641-1644	Adriaen van der Woestijne
1644-	Adriaen Janszoon[1]
1657-1664	Aert Adriaenszoon Groenewegel[1]
1666	Adriaen Groenewegel
1667-1670	Baerland
1670-1676	Hendrik Bol
1676-1678	Jacob Hars
1678-1690	Abraham Beekman
1690-1707	Samuel Beekman
1707-1719	Pieter van der Heyden Resen
1719-1729	Laurens de Heere
1729-1742	Hermanus Gelskerke
1742-1750	Laurens Storm van 's Gravesende

Essequibo and Demerara
Directors-General

1750-1772	Laurens Storm van 's Gravesende
1772-1781	George Hendrik Trotz (1)
1781-1782	(under Great Britain)
1782-1784	(under France)

Essequibo
Commanders

1784	Albert Siraut des Touches
1784-1787	Johannes Cornelis Bert
1787-1789	Albertus Backer (1)
1789-1791	Gustaaf Eduard Meijerhelm
1791-1793	Matthijs Thierens
1793-1796	Albertus Backer (2)
1796-1802	Antony Beaujon
1802-1803	George Hendrik Trotz (2)

1. These two may be identical. See Harris and de Villiers, 1:150—51.

Information from H. R. Persaud, Archivist of British Guiana, Georgetown, British Guiana.

268 GOLD COAST

Several European nations began to challenge the Portuguese monopoly along the western coast of Africa in the early 17th century, but the Dutch were initially the most successful. In 1637 they captured the main Portuguese fort at Elmina (v. São Jorge da Mina, 314) and by 1642 they had driven the Portuguese from the coast entirely. The major forts controlled by the Dutch on the Guinea coast were Axim, Kormantin, Takoradi, Elmina, and Accra. They also partook of the extensive trade at Ouidah (v. Dahomey, 14, France). The changing situation in the 19th century rendered isolated posts such as these useless and the Dutch, like the Danes, found it expedient to divest themselves of them. In 1867 the eastern posts were sold to the British and five years later the remaining posts were likewise sold to the British for cash and for concessions in Sumatra where the Dutch were entering their last expansionist stage.

Directors-General

1638-1639	Nikolaas van Iperen
1639-1641	Arend Jacobszen Montfort
1641-1645	Jacob Ruyghaver (1)
1645-1650	Jacob van der Well
1650	Hendrik Doedens
1650-1651	Arent Cocq
1651-1656	Jacob Ruyghaver (2)
1656-1659	Jan Valkenburg (1)
1659-1662	Caspar van Houssen
1662-1663	Dirk Wilré (1)
1663-1667	Jan Valkenburg (2)
1667-1669	Huybert van Ongerdonk
1669-1674	Dirk Wilré (2)
1674-1675	Joan Boot
1675-1679	Abraham Meermans
1679-1682	Daniël Verhoutert
1682-1684	Thomas Ernsthius
1684-1690	Nicolaas Sweerts
1690-1694	Joel Smits
1694-1696	Jan Staphorst
1696-1702	Jan van Sevenhuysen
1702-1705	Willem de la Palma
1705-1708	Pieter Nuyts
1708-1709	Henrikus van Weesel
1709-1711	Adriaan Schoonheidt
1711-1716	Hieronimus Haring
1716-1718	Robberts Abraham Engelgraef
1718-1722	Willem Bullier
1722-1723	Abraham Houtman
1723	Mattheus de Kraane
1723-1727	Pieter Valkenier
1727-1730	Robbert Norri
1730-1734	Jan Pranger
1734-1736	Anthonie van Overbeek
1736-1740	Martinus François des Bordes
1740-1741	François Barbrius
1741-1747	Jacob de Petersen
1747-1754	Jan van Voorst
1754-1755	Nikolaas Mattheus van der Nood de Gieterre
1755-1758	Roelof Ulsen
1758-1759	Lambert Jacob van Tets
1759-1760	Jan Pieter Theodoor Huydecoper (1)
1760-1763	David Pieter Erasmi
1763-1764	Hendrik Walmbeek
1764-1767	Jan Pieter Theodoor Huydecoper (2)
1767-1780	Pieter Woortman
1780	Jacobus van der Puye
1780-1784	Pieter Volkmar
1784-1785	Gilles Servaas Gallé (1)
1785-1786	Adolp Thierens
1786-1787	Gilles Servaas Gallé (2)
1787-1790	Lieven van Bergen van der Grijp (1)
1790-1794	Jacobus de Veer
1794-1795	Lieven van Bergen van der Grijp (2)
1795-1796	Otto Arnoldus Duim
1796-1798	Gerhardus Hubertus van Hamel
1798-1801	Cornelis Ludewich Bartels

Governors-General

1801-1804	Cornelis Ludewich Bartels
1804-1805	Izaak de Roever
1805-1807	Pieter Linthorst
1807-1808	Johannes Petrus Hoogenboom
1808-1810	Jan Frederik Koning

Commandant-General

1810-1816	Abraham de Veer

Governors-General

1816-1818	Herman Willem Daendels
1818-1820	Frans Christiaan Eberhard Oldenburg

Commanders

1820-1821	Johannes Oosthout
1821-1822	Frederich Frans Ludewich Ulrich Last (1)
1822	Librecht Jan Temmink
1822-1823	Willem Poolman
1823-1824	Hendrik Adriaan Mouwe, Jr.
1824	Johan David Carel Pagenstecher
1824-1826	Frederich Frans Ludewich Ulrich Last (2)
1826-1827	Jacobus Cornelis van der Breggen Paauw
1827-1832	Frederich Frans Ludewich Ulrich Last (3)
1832	Jan Thieleman Jacobus Cremer

The Netherlands

1832-1833	Eduard Daniel Leopold van Ingen	1857	Jules Félicien Romain Stanislas van den Bossche
1833	Martinus Swarte		
1833-1836	Christiaan Ernst Lans	1858-1862	Cornelis Johannes Marius Nagtglas (1)
1836-1837	Hendrikus Jacobus Tonneboeijer		
1837-1838	Anthony van der Eb (1)	1862-1865	Henry Alexander Elias
		1865-1867	Willem Hendrik Johan van Idzinga
Governors			
1838-1840	Hendrik Bosch	1867-1869	Georg Pieter Willem Boers
1840-1846	Anthony van der Eb (2)	1869-1871	Cornelius Johannes Marius Nagtglas (2)
1846-1847	Willem George Frederik Derx		
1847-1852	Anthony van der Eb (3)	1871	Jan Albert Hendrik Hugenholz
1852-1856	Hero Schomerus	1871-1872	Jan Helenus Ferguson

Information from A. E. M. Ribberink, Deputy Director, Algemeen Rijksarchief, The Hague.

269 LUANDA

As part of their broad offensive against the Portuguese possessions in the 17th century, the Dutch, in 1641, captured Luanda, Benguela, and the other coastal towns of Angola (284), driving the Portuguese into the interior. The Dutch used these ports to ship slaves to their newly acquired possessions in Brazil (v. Netherlands Brazil), also wrested from the Portuguese. The Dutch interlude in Angola was brief, for in 1648 they were expelled by the Portuguese, as they were soon also to be driven from Brazil.

Directors
1641-1642 Pieter Moorthamer
1642-1648 Cornelis Hendrikszoon Ouman

Information from Mrs. Dr. M. A. P. Meilink-Roelofsz, Algemeen Rijksarchief, The Hague.

270 MALABAR COAST

Seeking to participate in the pepper trade, then in the hands of the Portuguese, the Dutch appeared on the Malabar coast in 1656. In 1663 they captured Cochin, which was to remain their headquarters. After the beginning of the 18th century the competition of the French and British caused a decline in Dutch commerce. In 1795 the remaining Dutch posts were taken by the British and, like Ceylon, they were retained by the British in 1818 when the Dutch posts at Malacca and on the Coromandel coast (qq.v.) were returned to the Netherlands.

Commanders		1669-1677	Hendrik Adriaan van Reede van Drakenstein
1663-1666	Ludolph van Coulster		
1666-1667	Isband Godske[n]	1677-1678	Jacob Lobs
1667-1669	Lucas van der Dussen	1678-1683	Martin Huysman

1683–1687	Gelmer Vosberg		1742–1747	Reinierus Siersma
1688–1693	Isaäc van Dielen		1747–1751	Corijn Stevens
1693–1694	Alexander Wigman		1751	Abraham Cornelis de la Haye
1694–1697	Adriaan van Ommen		1751–1756	Frederik Cunes
1697–1701	Magnus Wichelmann		1756–1761	Casparus de Jong
1701–1704	Abraham Vink		1761–1765	Godefrid Weyerman
1704–1708	Willem Moerman		1765–1768	Cornelis Breekpot
1708–1709	Adam van der Duijn		1768–1770	Christiaan Lodewijk Senff
1709–1716	Barend Ketel		1770–1781	Adriaan Moens
1716–1723	Johannes Hertenberg		1781–1793	Johan Gerard van Angelbeek
1723–1731	Jacob de Jong		1793–1795	Jan Lambertus van Spall
1731–1734	Adriaan Maten			
1734–1742	Julius Valentijn Steijn von Gollonesse			

Wijnaendts van Resandt, pp. 179–99.

271 MALACCA

The strategic post of Malacca was captured from the Portuguese in 1641 (v. 298). While it failed to prosper commercially, it became the most important Dutch post on the Malay Peninsula because of its strategic value. In 1795 Malacca, like all Dutch possessions outside the East Indies, was occupied by the British, who retained it until 1818. Seven years later it was ceded to the English in return for Bencoolen (96) as a result of the agreement of 1824 which demarcated Malaya as a British sphere of influence and yielded the East Indies to the Dutch. Soon thereafter Malacca was integrated into the British Straits Settlements (223).

Governors			1707–1709	Pieter Rooselaar
1641–1642	Jan van Twist		1709–1711	Willem Six
1642–1645	Jeremias van Vliet		1711–1717	Willem Moerman
1645–1646	Arnout de Vlamingh van Oudtshoon		1717–1726	Herman van Suchtelen
1646–1662	Jan Thyszoon Payart		1726–1730	Johan Frederik Gobius
1662–1665	Jan Anthonie van Riebeeck		1730–1735	Pieter Rochus Pasques de Chavonnes
1665–1679	Balthasar Bort		1735–1741	Rogier de Lavez
1679–1680	Jacob Joriszoon Pits		1741–1748	Willem Bernard Albinus
1680–1684	Cornelis van Quaelberg		1748–1753	Pieter van Heemskerk
1684–1686	Nikolaas Schaghen		1753–1758	Willem Dekker
1686	Dirk Komans (1)		1758–1764	David Boelen
1686–1691	Thomas Slicher		1764–1771	Thomas Schippers
1691–1692	Dirk Komans (2)		1771–1775	Jan Crans
1692–1697	Gelmer Vosberg		1775–1788	Pieter Gerardus de Bruijn
1697–1700	Govert van Hoorn		1788–1795	Abraham Couperus
1700–1704	Bernard Phoonsen		1795–1818	(under Great Britain)
1704	Johan Grootenhuis		1818–1823	Jan Samuel Timmerman Thijssen
1704–1707	Karel Bolner		1823–1825	Hendrik Stephanus van Son

Boelen; Coolhaas; Wijnaendts van Resandt, pp. 200–31.

272 MAURITIUS

Mauritius, named after Maurits van Nassau, stadholder of Holland, was occupied by the Dutch in 1638 to serve as a way-station on the route to the East Indies. The Cape Colony, settled in 1652, proved to be superior in this respect and Mauritius was abandoned in 1658. Partially resettled in 1664, it was finally abandoned in 1710. Twelve years later it was occupied by the French (v. Île de France, 32).

Commanders

1638-1639	Cornelis Simonszoon Goyer
1639-1645	Adriaan van der Stel
1645-1648	Jacob van der Meersch[en]
1648-1653	Reinier Por
1653-1654	Joost van der Woutbeek[1]
1653-1656	Maximiliaan de Jongh[1]
1656-1658	Abraham Evertszoon
1658-1664	(abandoned)
1664	Jacobus Nieuwland
1665-1667	Georg Frederik Wreede (1)
1667-1668	Jan van Laar
1668-1669	Dirk Janszoon Smient
1669-1672	Georg Frederik Wreede (2)
1672-1673	Pieter Philippe Col
1673-1677	Hubert Hugo
1677-1692	Isaäc Johannes Lamotius
1692-1703	Roelof Di[e]odati
1703-1710	Abraham Momber van de Velde

1. Van der Woutbeek and de Jongh governed jointly until the death of the former.

Information from A. E. M. Ribberink, Deputy Director, Algemeen Rijksarchief, The Hague. Also *Suid-Afrikaanse argiefstukke*, 1:48n, 372; 2:55n, 105–7, 191–97; 3:226n.

273 NETHERLANDS ANTILLES

In 1845 the colony of Curaçao (q.v.) with its dependencies of Aruba and Bonaire, and the colony of Saint Eustatius (q.v.) and its dependencies of Saint Martin and Saba, were united, with the seat of the government on Curaçao. From this date the colony may be termed Netherlands Antilles. In 1954 Netherlands Antilles, like Surinam (q.v.), became an autonomous and equal province within the kingdom of the Netherlands.

Governors

1845-1848	Rutgerus Hermanus Esser
1848-1854	Isaäk Johannes Rammelman Elsevier, Jr.
1854-1856	Jacob Bennebroek Gravenhorst
1856-1859	Reinhart Frans Cornelis van Lansberge
1859-1866	Johannes Didericus Crol
1866-1870	Abraham Matthieu de Rouville
1870-1877	Herman François Gerardus Wagner
1877-1880	Hendrik Bernardus Kip
1880-1882	Johannes Herbert August Willem van Heerdt 'tot Eversberg
1882-1890	Nikolaas van den Brandhof
1890-1901	Charles Augustinus Henry Barge
1901-1909	Jan Olphert de Jong van Beek en Donk
1909-1919	Theodorus Isaäk Andreas Nuyens
1919-1921	Oscar Louis Helfrich
1921-1928	Nikolaas Johannes Laurentius Brantjes
1928-1929	Leonard Albert Fruytier
1929-1936	Bartholomaeus Wouther Theodorus van Slobbe
1936-1942	Gielliam Johannes Josephus Wouters
1942-1948	Petrus Albert Kasteel
1948-1951	Leonard Antoon Hubert Peters
1951-1954	Anton Arnold Maria Struycken

Hartog, 2:1138–40.

274 NETHERLANDS BRAZIL

Dutch efforts to supplant the Portuguese in Brazil began with the brief occupation of the Portuguese capital Bahia (286) in 1624. In 1630 the Dutch began to encroach on Portuguese colonies in the northeastern corner of Brazil. By 1641 several of the Portuguese captaincies there had been occupied by the Dutch. After the departure of Johan Maurits van Nassau-Siegen in 1644, however, the Dutch effort stagnated, and by 1654 the Portuguese had completely driven the Dutch from Brazil. The Dutch possessions were officially known as New Holland.

Governor
1630–1632   Diedrik van Waerdenburgh

Councillors
1632–1634   Mathias van Ceulen
1632–1634   Johan Gijsselingh

Governor
1634–1637   Sigismund van Schoppe

Governor-General
1637–1644   Johan Maurits van Nassau-Siegen

Councillors
1644–1647   Hendrik Hamel
1644–1647   Pieter Bas
1644   Dirk Codde van der Burgh
1644–1647   Adriaan Bullestrate
1647–1654   Walter van Schonenburgh
1647–1653   Michiel van Goch
1647–1649   Simon van Beaumont
1647   Abraham Trouwers
1647–1654   Hendrik Haecxs

Boxer, passim.

275 NETHERLANDS EAST INDIES

The Spice Islands were the cynosures for the European trading nations after the first Portuguese ventures there in the early 16th century. The first Dutch expedition to them took place in 1595, and thereafter they began to establish scattered posts. In 1602 the Veerinigde Oost-Indische Compagnie, or V.O.C. (United East India Company), was established, and in 1609 a governor-general over the company's "forts, places, factories, persons and business" was appointed, his headquarters at Bantam in Java until 1619 when Batavia was founded. The 17th century was one of growth for the V.O.C. Gradually the Portuguese, English, and Spaniards were eliminated as commercial rivals, the Moluccas (the true Spice Islands) and Macassar were subdued, and the conquest of Java had begun. By 1755, by adroitly taking advantage of civil wars in Mataram, the Dutch were firmly in control of Java. The V.O.C. declined after the middle of the 18th century and was abolished in 1799, the East Indies coming under the control of the Dutch government. During its height the V.O.C. controlled, outside the East Indies, areas in Ceylon, the Coromandel Coast, the Malabar Coast, Malacca, and Tayowan (qq.v.) and had established trading posts from Japan to Mocha in the Yemen. From 1811 to 1816 Java and most of the rest of the East Indies came under the control of the British. By the agreement of 1824 the Dutch were left with a free hand in the East Indies. They proceeded, during the course of the 19th century, to round out their control of the archipelago (except Portuguese Timor, 320) by the conquest of Sumatra and various outlying islands.

During World War II the Japanese occupied the East Indies and suppressed Dutch rule. In attempting to reassert their control after 1945 the Dutch found themselves faced with a nationalist government formed during the last days of the Japanese occupation. Unable to suppress this government militarily, and unwilling to agree to a mutually acceptable compromise, the Dutch government was forced to agree to a transfer of sovereignty over the islands to the Republic of Indonesia in 1949.

The Netherlands

Governors-General

1609-1614	Pieter Both
1614-1616	Gerrit Reijnst
1616-1618	Laurens Reaals
1618-1623	Jan Pieterszoon Coen (1)
1623-1627	Pieter de Carpentier
1627-1629	Jan Pieterszoon Coen (2)
1629-1632	Jakob Specx
1632-1636	Hendrik Brouwer
1636-1645	Anthonie van Diemen
1645-1650	Cornelis van der Lijn
1650-1653	Carel Reijniersz
1653-1678	Jan Maetsuycker
1678-1681	Rijklof van Goens
1681-1684	Cornelis Speelman
1684-1691	Jan Camphuijs
1691-1704	Willem van Outhoorn
1704-1709	Johan van Hoorn
1709-1713	Abraham van Riebeeck
1713-1718	Christoffel van Swoll
1718-1725	Hendrik Zwardeekroon
1725-1729	Matthijs de Haan
1729-1732	Dirk Durven
1732-1735	Dirk van Kloon
1735-1737	Abraham Patras
1737-1741	Adriaan Valckenier
1741-1743	Johannes Thedens
1743-1750	Gustaaf Willem van Imhoff
1750-1761	Jakob Mossel
1761-1775	Pieter Albertus van der Parra
1775-1777	Jeremias van Riemsdijk
1777-1780	Pieter de Klerk
1780-1796	Willem Arnold Alting
1796-1801	Pieter Gerrit van Overstraten
1801-1805	Johannes Siberg
1805-1808	Albertus Hendricus Wiese
1808-1811	Herman Willem Daendels
1811	Jan Willem Janssens

under Great Britain

Lieutenant Governors

1811-1816	Thomas Stamford Raffles
1816	John Fendall

under the Netherlands

Governors

1816-1826	Godert Alexander Gerard Philip van der Capellen
1826-1830	Leonard Pieter Joseph du Bus de Ghisignies
1830-1833	Johannes van den Bosch
1833-1836	Jean Chretien Baud
1836-1840	Dominique Jacques de Eerens
1840-1841	Carel Sirardus Willem van Hogendorp
1841-1844	Pieter Merkus
1844-1845	Joan Cornelis Reijnst
1845-1851	Jakob Johannes Rochussen
1851-1856	Albert Joan Duijmaer van Twist
1856-1861	Charles Ferdinand Pahud
1861-1866	Ludolf Anne Jan Wilt Sloet van de Beele
1866-1872	Pieter Mijer
1872-1875	James Loudon
1875-1881	Johannes Wilhelm van Lansberg
1881-1884	Frederik 's Jacob
1884-1888	Otto van Rees
1888-1893	Cornelis Pijnacker Hordijk
1893-1899	Carel Hermann Aart van der Wijck
1899-1904	Willem Rooseboom
1904-1909	Johannes Benedictus van Heutsz
1909-1916	Alexander Willem Frederik van Idenburg
1916-1921	Johannes Paul van Limburg-Styrum
1921-1926	Dirk Fock
1926-1931	Andries Cornelis Dirk de Graeff
1931-1936	Bonifacius Cornelis de Lange
1936-1942	Alidius Warmoldus Lambertus Tjarda van Starckenbourgh Stachower
1942-1945	(under Japan)
1945-1949	Hubertus Johannes van Mook

Lists of the governors-general of the East Indies are plentiful. For the most detailed treatment of the governors-general, see Stapel, passim.

276 NETHERLANDS NEW GUINEA

The western portion of New Guinea was a part of the Netherlands East Indies (q.v.), and was retained by the Dutch after their loss of the East Indies. The colony had little real value and the constant agitation by the new Indonesian government to acquire it led to the Netherlands' turning it over to the control of the United Nations in 1962. In 1963 the United Nations turned it over to the Republic of Indonesia, which created it the province of West Irian.

Governors
1949-1953 Simon Lodewijk Johan van
              Waardenburg
1953-1958 Jan van Baal
1958-1962 Pieter Johannes Platteel

Statesman's Year Book, 1949—62.

277 NEW NETHERLANDS

The Dutch Republic wanted a settlement along the Hudson River to exploit the profitable North American fur trade. The West India Company established a settlement upriver at Albany in 1624 and another two years later at the mouth of the river. Directors-general were appointed from 1626, and Pieter Stuijvesant, the last of these, was simultaneously director-general of Curaçao, thereby temporarily uniting the two governments. New Netherlands was taken by the English in 1664, but briefly recaptured by the Dutch nine years later. In 1674 it was surrendered to England in return for English acceptance of Dutch rule in Surinam (q.v.)

Governors
1624-1625 Cornelis Jacobsen May (or Mey)
1625-1626 Willem Verhulst
1626-1632 Pieter Minuit
1633-1638 Wouter van Twiller
1638-1647 Willem Kieft
1647-1664 Pieter Stuijvesant
1664-1673 (under England)
1673-1674 Anthonie Colve

Folsom, pp. 449—56; Raesly, pp. 56—76 and passim.

278 PARAÍBA

For the Dutch governors of Paraíba from 1635 to 1645 see the Portuguese colony, Paraíba, 305.

279 POMEROON

Pomeroon in western Guiana was settled by fugitives from Netherlands Brazil (q.v.), and in 1657 it was created a separate post subordinated to the main Dutch settlement in the area at Essequibo (q.v.). The English briefly occupied it in 1666 and it was not resettled until 1679. Ten years later a French-Carib attack devastated the colony and it subsequently existed only as a frontier post under Essequibo.

Commanders		
1657-1661	Cornelis Goliat	
1661-1666	François de Fijne	
1667-1670	Sael	

1670-1676	Hendrik Rol	
1676-1676	Jacob Hars	
1678-1686	Abraham Beekman	
1686-1689	Jacob Pieterszoon de Jonge	

Information from H. R. Persaud, Archivist of British Guiana, Georgetown, British Guiana.

280 SAINT EUSTATIUS

Saint Eustatius, at the northern end of the Lesser Antilles, was settled under the Dutch West India Company after 1636. The nearby islands of Saint Martin and Saba (southwest of Saint Thomas) were settled about the same time and were attached to Saint Eustatius administratively. Saint Eustatius was occupied by the English from 1665 to 1668, 1672 to after 1674, 1690 to 1696, 1781, 1801 to 1802, and 1810 to 1816, and by the French from 1689 to 1690 and 1781 to 1784. Saint Martin and Saba were also occupied at various times; in fact, part of Saint Martin became permanently French at the beginning of the 18th century. From 1828 to 1845 Saint Eustatius and its dependencies were part of the government-general of the Dutch West Indies (v. Surinam). Upon the dissolution of the government-general in 1845 Saint Eustatius was attached to Curaçao (v. Netherlands Antilles) and ceased to exist as a separate colony.

Commanders

1636	Pieter van Corselles
1639-1641	Pieter Gardijn
1641-1644	Abraham Adriaenszoon (1)
1644-1645	Pieter van de Woestijne
1648	Abraham Adriaenszoon (2)
-1665	Pieter Adriaenszoon (1)
1665-1668	(under England)
1668-1671	Pieter Adriaenszoon (2)
1671-1672	Lucas Jacobsen

under England

Governors

1672-	John Pogson
1674-	Peter Batterie

under the Netherlands

Commanders

1682-1686	Louis Houtkoper
1686-1689	Lucas Schorer

under England

Governor

1690-1693	Timothy Thornhill

under the Netherlands

Commanders

1696-1700	Johannes Salomonszoon
1700-1701	Jan Simonszoon Doncker (1)
1701-1704	Isaac Lamont (1)
1704-1709	Jan Simonszoon Doncker (2)
1709	Isaac Lamont (2)
1709-1717	Jan Simonszoon Doncker (3)
1717	Gerard de Mepsche
1717-1719	Johan Heijliger (1)
1719-1720	Jacob Stalpert
1720-1721	Johan Heijliger (2)
1721-1722	Jacobus Stevens
1722-1728	Johan Lindesaij
1728-1733	Everard Raecx
1733-1736	Johan Heijliger (3)
1736-1737	Johan Markoe
1737-1740	Isaac Faesch
1740-1741	Hendrik Coesveldt
1741-1743	Jasper Ellis
1743-1752	Johannes Heijliger Pzn.
1752-1775	Jan de Windt, Jr.
1775-1776	Abraham Heijliger (1)
1776-1781	Johannes de Graaff

under Great Britain

Governor
1781 David Ogilvy

under France

Governors
1781-1784 Charles Chabert
1784   Thomas de FitzMaurice

under the Netherlands

Governors
1784-1785 Olivier Oijen
1785   Abraham Heijliger (2)
1785-1789 Johannes Runnels (1)
1789-1792 Pieter Anthony Godin
1792-1795 Johannes Runnels (2)
1795-1801 Daniel Roda

1801-1802 (under Great Britain)
1802-1809 Albertus van Heyningen, Jr.
1809-1810 William Charles Mussenden

under Great Britain

Governor
1810-1816 Charles Barrow

under the Netherlands

Governors
1816-1817 Reinier 't Hoen
1817-1822 Abraham de Veer
1822-1823 Diederik Johannes van Romondt
1823-1828 Willem Albert van Spengler
1828-1836 Willem Johan Leendert van Raders
1836-1837 Theophilus Georg Groebe
1837-1845 Johannes de Veer

Information from Mrs. Dr. M. A. P. Meilink-Roelofsz, Algemeen Rijksarchief, The Hague. See also Knappert, p. 293 and passim.

281 SURINAM

The Dutch captured the English colony of Willoughby (246) in 1667 and retained it at the Peace of Breda in the same year in return for the cession of New Netherlands (q.v.). Surinam was occupied by the British from 1804 to 1815 and was the only Dutch possession in Guiana which was returned after the Napoleonic Wars. From 1828 to 1845 the governor of Surinam was also governor-general of the Dutch West Indies. In 1954 Surinam, like the Netherlands Antilles (q.v.), became autonomous and an equal partner with the other provinces in the kingdom of the Netherlands.

Governors

1665-1667	Maurits de Rama	1716-1717	Johan de Mahony
1667-1669	Abrahaam Krijnssen	1717-1718	François Anthonie de Raineval (3)
1669-1671	Philip Julius Lichtenberg	1718-1721	Jan Coetier
1671-1677	Pierre Versterre	1721-1722	François Anthonie de Raineval (4)
1677	Abel Thisse	1722-1727	Hendrik Temminck
1677-1678	Tobias Adriaensen	1727-1728	Johan Bley
1678-1680	Johannes Heinsius	1728-1734	Carel Emilius Henry de Cheusses
1680	Everhard van Hemert	1734-1735	Jacobus Alexander Henry de Cheusses
1680-1683	Laurens Verboom	1735	Johan François Cornelis de Vries
1683-1688	Cornelis van Aersen van Sommelsdijk	1735-1737	Johan Raije van Breuelerwaard
		1737-1742	Gerrit van de Schepper
1688-1689	Abrahaam van Vridenburgh	1742-1751	Johan Jacob Mauritius
1689-1696	Johan van Scharphuizen	1751-1752	Hendrik Ernst van Spoercke
1696-1707	Paulus van der Veere	1752-1754	Wigbold Crommelin (1)
1707	Willem de Gruyter	1754-1756	Pieter Albert van der Meer
1707-1710	François Anthonie de Raineval (1)	1756-1757	Jan Nepveu (1)
1710-1715	Johan de Goyer	1757-1768	Wigbold Crommelin (2)
1715-1716	François Anthonie de Raineval (2)	1768-1779	Jan Nepveu (2)

The Netherlands

1779-1783	Bernhard Texier		1852-1855	Johan Georg Otto Stuart von Schmidt auf Altenstadt
1783-1784	Wolphus Johan Beeldsnijder Matroos		1855-1859	Charles Pierre Schimpf
1784-1790	Jan Gerhard Wichers		1859-1867	Reinhart Frans Comelis van Lansberge
1790-1802	Jurriaan François de Frederici		1867-1873	Willem Hendrik Johan van Idzinga
1802-1803	Willem Otto Bloys van Treslong		1873-1882	Cornelis Ascanius van Sypesteyn
1803-1804	Pierre Berrangier		1882-1885	Johannes Herbert August Willem van Heerdt 'tot Eversberg

under Great Britain

Governors

			1885-1888	Hendrik Jan Smidt
1804-1805	Charles Green		1888-1889	Warmolt Tonckens (1)
1805-1808	William Carlyon Hughes		1889-1891	Maurits Adriaan de Savornin Lohman
1808-1809	John Wardlau		1891-1896	Titus Antonius Jacob van Asch van Wijk
1809-1811	Charles Bentinck			
1811-1815	Pinson Bonham		1896-1902	Warmolt Tonckens (2)
			1902-1905	Cornelis Lely

under the Netherlands

Governors

			1905-1908	Alexander Willem Frederik Idenburg
1816	Willem Benjamin van Panhuijs		1908-1911	Dirk Fock
1816-1822	Cornelis Reinhard Vaillant		1911-1916	Willem Dirk Hendrik van Asbeck
1822-1827	Abraham de Veer		1916-1921	Gerard Johan Staal
1827-1828	Johannes van den Bosch		1921-1928	Arnoud Jan Anna Aleid van Heemstra
1828-1831	Paulus Roelof Cantz'laar		1928-1933	Abrahaam Arnoud Lodewijk Rutgers
1831-1838	Evart Ludolph van Heeckeren		1933-1944	Johannes Coenraad Kielstra
1839-1842	Julius Constantijn Rijk		1944-1948	Johannes Cornelius Brons
1842-1845	Burkhard Jean Elias		1948-1949	Willem Huender
1845-1852	Reinier Frederik van Raders		1949-1954	Jan Klaasesz

Oudschans Dentz, pp. 112—21.

282 TAYOWAN (FORMOSA)

In 1624 the Dutch occupied the southern part of Formosa (now Taiwan) after being driven from the Pescadores Islands by the Chinese. In 1626 the Spanish founded a small colony in the northern part of the island, but they abandoned it in 1642, after which the Dutch controlled the entire island. Formosa was valuable to the Dutch in the East as an entrepot for the Chinese and Japanese trade as well as for its camphor. In 1662, however, the large Chinese immigrant population, led by Cheng Ch'eng-kung (Koxinga) drove the Dutch from the island completely. The Dutch called Formosa, Tayowan, probably after the small island of the same name where Zeelandia, the first Dutch capital, was built.

Governors

1624-1625	Maarten Sonck		1643-1644	Maximiliaan le Maire
1625-1627	Gerard Frederikszoon de With		1644-1648	François Caron
1627-1629	Pieter Nuyts		1648-1649	Pieter Anthoniszoon Overtwater
1629-1636	Hans Putmans		1649-1653	Nikolaas Verburg
1636-1640	Johan van der Burch		1653-1656	Comelis Caesar
1640-1643	Paulus Traudenius		1656-1662	Frederik Coyett

Winaendts van Resandt, pp. 120—35; Zeeuw, passim.

224

Bibliography: Netherlands

Boelen, H. J. "Iets over Malaka." *Nederlandsch-Indië oud en nieuw* 5 (1920/21):366—79.
Boxer, Charles R. *The Dutch in Brazil, 1624—1654.* London: Oxford University Press, 1957.
Coolhaas, Willem Philip. "Malacca under Jan van Riebeeck." *Journal of the Malayan Branch of the Royal Asiatic Society* 38, no. 2 (1965):173—82.
Folsom, George. "A Few Particulars Concerning the Directors General or Governors of New-Netherlands." *Collections of the New-York Historical Society*, n.s. 1 (1841):449—56.
Gaay Fortman, B. de. "De kolonie Curacao onder Engelsch bestuur van 1807 tot 1815." *De West Indische Gids*, 1944/45, pp. 229—46.
Harris, C. A., and de Villiers, J. A. J., eds. *Storm van 's Gravesende: The Rise of British Guiana.* 2 vols. Hakluyt Society Works, 2d ser., nos. 26, 27. London: for the Hakluyt Society, 1911.
Hartog, Johannes. *Curacao, van kolonie tot autonomie.* 2 vols. Oranjestad, Aruba: D. J. de Wit, 1961.
Knappert, Laurentius. *De geschiedenis van de Nederlandse bovenwindsche eilanden in de 18de eeuw.* The Hague: M. Nijhoff, 1932.
Krafft, A. J. C. *Historie en oude families van de Nederlandsche Antillen.* The Hague: M. Nijhoff, 1951.
Oudschans Dentz, Frederik. *Geschiedkundige tijdtafel van Suriname.* Amsterdam: J. H. de Bussy, 1949.
Raesly, Ellis Lawrence. *Portrait of New Netherlands.* New York: Columbia University Press, 1945.
Raychaudhuri, Tanpankumar. *Jan Compagnie in Coromandel.* The Hague: M. Nijhoff, 1962.
Stapel, Frederik Willem. *De gouverneurs-generaal van Nederlandsch-Indië in beeld en woord.* The Hague: W. P. van Stockum, 1941.
Suid-Afrikaanse argiefstukke, Kaap. 5 vols to date. Kaapstad: The Cape Times, 1957-.
Van der Marck, J. P. C. "Lijst der Nederlandsche landvoogden van Ceylon." *Tijdschrift voor Indische taal-, land- en volkenkunde van het Bataviaasch genootschap* 14, no. 2 (1865):184—86.
———. "Lijst der Nederlandsche landvoogden van Tayoewan (Formosa)." *Tijdschrift voor Indische taal-, land- en volkenkunde van het Bataviaasch genootschap* 16, no. 3 (1867):259.
Walker, Eric Anderson. *A History of Southern Africa.* 3d ed. London: Longmans, 1957.
Wijnaendts van Resandt, Willem. *De gezaghebbers der Oost-Indische Compagnie op hare buiten-comptoiren in Azië.* Amsterdam: Uitgeverij Liebaert, 1944.
Zeeuw, P. de. *De Hollanders op Formosa, 1624—1662: Een bladzijde uit onze koloniale en zendengsgeschiedenis.* Amsterdam: W. Kirchner, 1924.

Portugal

The period of modern colonialism began with the Portuguese seizure of Ceuta, across the Strait of Gibraltar, in 1415. The acquisition of Ceuta was at once a logical extension of the *Reconquista* in the Iberian peninsula and an impetus for further Portuguese expansion—expansion which could be considered an aspect of the war on Islam only insofar as one of its declared objectives was to reach India and thereby deprive the Muslim states of the Middle East of their roles in the spice trade. Free, unlike Spain, of the presence of any Muslim political entity on its soil, and isolated from the interstate politics of Europe, Portugal looked to the sea as a natural outlet for its expansive energies.

During the rest of the 15th century Portuguese explorers inched their way down the western coast of Africa and out into the Atlantic where Madeira and the Azores were occupied. In 1498 the southern tip of Africa was rounded and the first Portuguese navigator reached India. It was in this area that Portugal's primary interests lay, and within half a century Portugal had established a network of posts around the littoral of the Indian Ocean. These posts were designed to control both the trade from the Orient to Europe and the coastal trade within Asia itself. The Portuguese were not able, nor did they desire, to establish any form of territorial empire in the East. Like the Dutch in the next century they were content to create a commercial empire based on a minimal investment in men and material. The Portuguese preoccupation with this aspect of overseas expansion, quite legitimate given the circumstances, and quite profitable to the Portuguese state, caused Manuel I (1495—1521) to be derisively labelled "le roi épicier" or "the grocer king" by his contemporary, Francis I.

For much of the 16th century the Portuguese were in fact able to monopolize a significant part of the East-West trade in spices. Yet this control was fragile and based on naval superiority vis-à-vis the predominantly land-oriented states of Asia. Toward the end of the century several factors combined to destroy the Portuguese commercial empire in the East. Portugal had never been able to provide large numbers of its population for overseas activities and a century of combat had inevitably erosive effects. The Ottoman conquest of the Middle East after 1517, and the entrance of Ottoman naval forces into the Indian Ocean and its various arms presented a challenge more severe than any the Portuguese had previously faced, for the Ottomans were able to divert an increasing share of the spice trade overland, thereby robbing the Portuguese of lucrative revenues. Portugal's enforced union with Spain (1580—1640) further diminished its resources and made it the joint legatee of the hostility of Spain's principal enemy, the Dutch Republic. The great Dutch onslaught against the Spanish colonies in

the first half of the 16th century meant, in effect, that it would be the expose
and weakened Portuguese colonies which would suffer most heavily, and so i
was, particularly in the East. The Portuguese were driven from point after po.
by the Dutch and the English, and by 1658 nothing was left to the now indepe
ent Portuguese crown but Macao and three enclaves on the western coast of
India. Gone were the spice trade of the Indies, the rich trade with Japan (Ma
raison d'être), and the cinnamon of Ceylon. Portugal's adventure in the East
ended. Henceforth Portugal took no part in the colonial activities of Asia—w
Timor a minor exception—and its colonies there remained relics suitable for
calling to mind past achievements but of dubious economic or strategic value
the mother country.

While Portugal was concentrating on the eastern route to the Indies, Spain
was looking westward. Rid of the last Muslim state on Spanish soil, the Spar
ish monarchy sponsored Columbus's trips westward to discover what was init
ally thought to be the Indies. Portugal, chagrined to see its nearly century-lc
efforts apparently come to naught, managed to salvage more than might logica
have been expected by the Treaty of Tordesillas, arranged by the Pope, in 149
Under the treaty the line of demarcation between the respective areas of futur
Spanish and Portuguese expansion—no other European nation was thought wo
of consideration—was drawn at a point 370 leagues west of the Cape Verde i.
lands, or approximately latitude 46° west. This line, rather whimsically draw
and apparently of little value to the Portuguese, included, in the Portuguese
sphere, Brazil, only discovered six years later. Portugal made no serious effc
to settle its windfall colony until 1530, and then partly as a response to Frenc
interests in the area. From 1534 to 1536 the whole of Brazil's coast was divi
into a series of *donatárias* extending indefinitely inland. The donatária was a
area granted to an individual on a quasi-feudal basis in return for his bearing
the expense of settling it. The *donatário*, or landlord, was seldom resident, a
governed his donatária through a *capitão-mor* (lit. captain-major) appointed f
fixed term, typically three years. This system had been adopted in Madeira, t
Azores, and São Tomé and Príncipe. The donatária system was a Portuguese a
logue of the chartered company method adopted by France, Great Britain, and t
Netherlands during the 16th and 17th centuries. It enabled the Portuguese cro
to settle and administer overseas areas with minimal expense and inconvenier
to itself. The donatária system was neither as successful nor as enduring in t
Portuguese colonial system as the chartered companies were in other systems
Many of the donatários showed little disposition to implement their agreement
and most of the donatárias lapsed to crown control. As early as 1549 a royal
governor was sent to Brazil to maintain royal interests and a sense of unity in
the colony. By the middle of the 17th century all of the important Brazilian
donatárias were administered by royally-appointed governors.

Until the 18th century Portuguese settlement in Brazil was sparse and confined to the coastal areas except in the northeast. There the cultivation of
sugar was introduced from Madeira, and this area rapidly developed into the
prototype of the New World plantation system. Supplied with slaves shipped
through the Portuguese posts in West Africa—posts specifically established
for this purpose—the sugar plantations flourished in the 17th century and Braz
became the world's largest sugar producer. Brazil did not escape the Dutch

assault in the 17th century. Most of northeast Brazil, that is, the sugar-producing area, was occupied by the Dutch from 1630 to 1654. Although the Brazilian colonists managed ultimately to expel the Dutch, the economic implications of the Dutch occupation were longlasting, for the Dutch took with them to the West Indies the knowledge of Brazilian sugar technology. By the end of the 17th century, due to the planters' improvements on Brazilian techniques, the West Indian islands had replaced Brazil as the most important sugar producer.

Fortuitously, at this critical stage, gold and diamonds, long sought by the Portuguese, were discovered in large quantities in the interior of Brazil. These deposits provided the basis of the Brazilian (and thus Portuguese) economy in the 18th century, just as sugar had done in the previous century. But the minerals discovered fulfilled an even more important function, for they created a demographic revolution in Brazil by drawing the seaboard population away from its coastal orientation and spreading it over a much greater area of the colony, thereby legitimizing Portuguese claims to an area much broader than that included in the terms of the Treaty of Tordesillas or established by previous settlement. Portugal and Spain had long disputed the location of the Tordesillas line, Portugal professing to believe it lay west of the Plate estuary and Spain claiming large parts of Amazonia under its terms. These disputes were settled in 1750 and 1777 by treaties in which the boundaries between Portuguese and Spanish South America were demarcated. The spread of Portuguese settlement enabled Portugal to retain the Amazon basin and the interior of Brazil. In fact, Brazil, though sparsely settled in comparison with the Spanish colonies, emerged with an area very nearly equal to that of all the Spanish colonies combined.

Brazil was easily the most important Portuguese colony after 1600 and surpassed Portugal itself in natural wealth and population. In 1808 Brazil became temporarily the center of the Portuguese Empire when the royal court, fleeing Lisbon before the advancing French armies, established itself in Brazil. In 1815 Brazil was raised to the status of a kingdom nominally equal to that of Portugal. In 1821 the Portuguese king, João VI, returned to Portugal leaving his son as regent in Brazil. The Portuguese Cortes foolishly and unrealistically sought to reduce Brazil to its former colonial status. The result was Brazil's declaration of independence in 1822.

The loss of Brazil, Portugal's only important colony, marked the end of what might be termed Portugal's old empire. Until this time Portugal's attention had been directed to Asia and to Brazil. Its African possessions were considered to be of marginal interest, valuable for the slaves that could be sent to Brazil but for little else. With the abolition of the slave trade in the Portuguese colonies in 1836 Portuguese interest languished further. In fact Portugal's lack of interest in expanding its Angolan holdings along the Congo River provided the opportunity for Leopold II of Belgium to create his Congo Free State. Nonetheless Portugal clung to its African possessions during this period and the "scramble" of the 1880's brought a reward for this tenacity, for Portugal could point to its holdings in Africa as legitimation for its joining in the partition of the continent. During the scramble Portugal made no attempt to stake out claims in other parts of Africa but confined itself to enlarging its present holdings. In this effort it benefitted from its position as a weak European power and thus as

an acceptable alternative to one or another major European power. Thus, a "wi
to survive" and "the forbearance of others" enabled Portugal to construct a sec
ond colonial empire, based on, but distinct from, its earlier possessions.[1] In
the decades after 1880, in a process not fully completed until the mid-1930's,
Portugal expanded its control over some 800,000 square miles of African territc
Portugal was never able to exploit its colonies profitably despite the introduction of chartered companies for this purpose. Politically and administratively
Portuguese colonial practices, unlike those of most of the other European colonial powers, showed almost no evolution. The Portuguese administrative syste
compared most closely with that of France. It was highly centralized and there
were no local legislative bodies—all decisions emanated from Lisbon. In 193
the Estado Nôvo was inaugurated and under this system deputies, always Portu
guese, were elected from the colonies to the Portuguese National Assembly. I
Portuguese political theory the Portuguese colonies are considered an integral
part of metropolitan Portugal and on this basis they were transformed into over
seas territories in 1951. Consonant with this theory there could be no questic
of decolonization and eventual independence for the Portuguese overseas terri
tories since this would represent secession from a unified body politic. Because of this attitude, the Portuguese African overseas territories in the 1960'
have been described as "in roughly the position other African colonies had
reached some twenty years earlier."[2] There is no serious indication that the
Portuguese government will alter its position in this matter in the foreseeable
future. The unrealistic and intransigent position of Portugal has produced sev
eral nationalist revolts in its African possessions since 1961. Although these
revolts have little chance of success, they do give the lie to the Portuguese
position that its African possessions are multiracial Portuguese societies.

Thus Portugal remains the only true colonial power left in the world today.
Despite juridical legerdemain its colonial system has changed little in essen
during this century. Except for the loss of Portuguese India the Portuguese Er
pire remains in extent what it was in 1900. But there is reason to believe tha
it is incapable of justifying and maintaining its existence for an indefinite
period in the future.

---

1. R. J. Hammond, *Portugal and Africa, 1815–1910* (Stanford: Stanford Ur
versity Press, 1966), p. 2.

2. David K. Fieldhouse, *The Colonial Empires: A Comparative Survey
from the Eighteenth Century* (London: Weidenfeld and Nicolson, 1966), p. 35

283 ALAGÔAS

Until 1817 Alagôas was a district of Pernambuco (q.v.). It existed as a separate captaincy only four years, only two years with its own governor, before it became a province of the empire of Brazil.

Governor
1819-1821   Sebastião Francisco de Melo e Póvoas

Varnhagen, 5:376.

284 ANGOLA

The coast of Angola was discovered in 1482 by Diogo Cão. In 1491 Portuguese missionaries baptized the ruler of the kingdom of Kongo, near the Congo estuary. What began as a genuine missionary effort soon degenerated into Portuguese military control of this state, which, however, remained nominally independent until 1883. In 1575 Paulo Dias de Novais was granted an area along the coast south of the Congo as a donatária. At his death in 1589 this territory, the beginning of the colony of Angola, retroceded to the Portuguese crown. In 1617 Benguela, along the coast farther south, was colonized. From 1641 to 1648 the Dutch occupied all the Portuguese settlements along the coast (v. Luanda, 269), forcing the Portuguese inland. During the 17th century the kingdom of Ndongo, ruled by the Ngola after whom the colony was named, was reduced, and over the next two centuries most of the interior was gradually occupied, including the Ovimbundu states and those in the southern highlands. In 1837 the governor was raised to the rank of governor-general, and in 1920 the governor-general became high commissioner as well. Since 1951 Angola has been an overseas territory of Portugal.

Donatário
1575-1589   Paulo Dias de Novais

Governors
1589-1591   Luís Serrão
1591-1592   André Ferreira Pereira
1592-1593   Francisco de Almeida
1593-1594   Jerónimo de Almeida
1594-1602   João Furtado de Mendonça
1602-1603   João Rodrigues Coutinho
1603-1606   Manuel Cerveira Pereira (1)
1607-1611   Manuel Pereira Forjaz
1611-1615   Bento Banha Cardoso
1615-1617   Manuel Cerveira Pereira (2)
1617-1621   Luís Mendes de Vasconcelos
1621-1623   João Correia de Soúsa
1623   Pedro de Sousa Coelho
1623-1624   Simão de Mascarenhas
1624-1630   Fernão de Sousa
1630-1635   Manuel Pereira Coutinho
1635-1639   Francisco de Vasconcelos da
            Cunha

1639-1645   Pedro César de Meneses
1645-1646   Francisco de Souto-Maior
1646-1648   (junta)
1648-1651   Salvador Correia de Sá e
            Benevides
1651-1653   Rodrigo de Miranda Henriques
1653-1655   Bartolomeu de Vasconcelos da
            Cunha
1655-1658   Luís Mendes de Sousa Chicorro
1658-1661   João Fernandes Vieira
1661-1666   André Vidal de Negreiros
1666-1667   Tristão da Cunha
1667-1669   (juntas)
1669-1676   Francisco de Távora
1676-1680   Aires de Saldanha de Sousa e
            Meneses
1680-1684   João da Silva e Sousa
1684-1688   Luís Lobo da Silva
1688-1691   João de Lencastre
1691-1694   Gonçalo da Costa de Alcáçova
            Carneiro de Meneses
1694-1697   Henrique Jacques de Magalhães

Portugal

1697-1701	Luís César de Meneses	1854-1860	José Rodrigues Coelho do Amaral (1)
1701-1703	Bernardino de Távora de Sousa Tavares	1860-1861	Carlos Augusto Franco
1703-1705	(junta)	1861-1862	Sebastião Lopes de Calheiros e Meneses
1705-1709	Lourenço de Almada		
1709-1713	António de Saldanha de Albuquerque Castro e Ribafria	1862-1865	José Baptista de Andrade (1)
		1866-1868	Francisco António Gonçalves Cardoso
1713-1717	João Manuel de Noronha		
1717-1722	Henrique de Figueiredo e Alarcão	1869-1870	José Rodrigues Coelho do Amaral (2)
1722-1725	António de Albuquerque Coelho de Carvalho	1870-1873	José Maria da Ponte e Horta
1725-1726	José Carvalho da Costa	1873-1876	José Baptista de Andrade (2)
1726-1732	Paulo Caetano de Albuquerque	1876-1878	Caetano Alexandre de Almeida e Albuquerque
1733-1738	Rodrigo César de Meneses		
1738-1748	João Jacques de Magalhães	1878-1880	Vasco Guedes de Carvalho e Meneses
1749-1753	António de Almeida Soares Portugal de Alarção Eça e Melo, Marquês do Lavradio	1880-1882	António Eleutério Dantas
		1882-1886	Francisco Joaquim Ferreira do Amaral
1753-1758	António Álvares da Cunha		
1758-1764	António de Vasconcelos	1886-1891	Guilherme Augusto de Brito Capelo (1)
1764-1772	Francisco Inocéncio de Sousa Coutinho	1891-1893	Jaime Lôbo Brito Godins
		1893-1896	Álvaro da Costa Ferreira
1772-1779	António de Lencastre	1896-1897	Guilherme Augusto de Brito Capelo (2)
1779-1782	João Gonçalo da Câmara		
1782-1784	(juntas)	1897-1900	António Duarte Ramada Curto (1)
1784-1790	José de Almeida e Vasconcelos Soveral Carvalho e Albergaria, Barão de Moçâmedes	1900-1903	Francisco Xavier Cabral de Oliveira Moncada
		1903-1904	Eduardo Augusto Ferreira da Costa (1)
1790-1797	Manuel de Almeida Vasconcelos		
1797-1802	Miguel António de Melo	1904	Custódio Miguel de Borja
1802-1806	Fernando António de Noronha	1904-1906	António Duarte Ramada Curto (2)
1807-1810	António de Saldanha da Gama	1906-1907	Eduardo Augusto Ferreira da Costa (2)
1810-1816	José de Oliveira Barbosa		
1816-1819	Luís da Mota Fêo e Torres	1907-1909	Henrique Mitchel de Paiva Couceiro
1819-1821	Manuel Vieira Tovar de Albuquerque		
		1909	Álvaro Antonio da Costa Ferreira
1821-1822	Joaquim Inácio de Lima	1909-1910	José Augusto Alves Roçadas
1822-1823	(junta)	1910-1911	Caetano Francisco Cláudio Eugénio Gonçalves
1823	Cristóvão Avelino Dias		
1824-1829	Nicolau de Abreu Castelo Branco	1911-1912	Manuel Maria Coelho
1829-1834	José Maria de Sousa Macedo Almeida e Vasconcelos, Barão de Santa Comba Dão	1912-1915	José Mendes Ribeiro Norton de Matos (1)
		1915-1916	António Júlio da Costa Pereira de Eça
1834-1836	(junta)		
1836	Domingos de Saldanha de Oliveira Daun	1916-1917	Pedro Francisco Massano do Amorim
		1917-1918	Jaime Alberto de Castro Morais
		1918-1919	Filomeno da Câmara Melo Cabral (1)

Governors-General

1837-1839	Manuel Bernardo Vidal	1919-1920	Francisco Carlos do Amaral Reis
1839	Antonio Manuel de Noronha		
1839-1842	Manuel Eleutério Malheiro		
1842-1843	José Xavier Bressane Leite		

Governors-General/High Commissioners

1844-1845	Lourenço Germack Possolo	1921-1924	José Mendes Ribeiro Norton de Matos (2)
1845-1848	Pedro Alexandrino da Cunha		
1848-1851	Adrião da Silveira Pinto	1924	João Augusto Crispiniano Soares
1851-1853	António Sérgio de Sousa	1924-1925	Antero Tavares de Carvalho
1853	António Ricardo Graça	1925-1926	Francisco Cunha Rêgo Chaves
1853-1854	Miguel Ximenes Rodrigues Sandoval de Castro e Viegas, Visconde de Pinheiro	1926-1928	António Vicente Ferreira
		1928-1929	António Damas Mora

1929-1930	Filomeno da Câmara Melo Cabral (2)	1943-1947	Vasco Lopes Alves
1930-1931	José Dionísio Carneiro Sousa Faro	1947	Fernando Falcão Pacheco Mena
1931-1934	Eduardo Ferreira Viana	1947-1955	José Agapito da Silva Carvalho
1934-1935	Júlio Garcês Lencastre	1956-1959	Horácio de Sá Viana Rebêlo
1935-1939	António Lopes Mateus	1960-1961	Álvaro Rodrigues da Silva Tavares
1939-1941	Manuel da Cunha e Costa Marquês Mano	1961-1962	Venâncio Augusto Deslandes
1941-1942	Abel de Abreu Souto-Maior	1962-1966	Jaime Silvério Marquês
1942-1943	Álvaro de Freitas Morna	1966 —	Camilo Augusto de Miranda Rebocho Vaz
1943	Manuel Pereira Figueira		

Information from Carlos da Costa Gomes Bersa, Chefe de Gabinete de Governador Geral de Angola, and from Manuel Santos Estevens, Biblioteca Nacional de Lisboa, Nôva Lisboa, Angola.

285 AZORES

The Azores are a group of islands, including Corvo, Faial, Flores, Graçiosa, Pico, Santa Maria, São Jorge, São Miguel, and Terceira, which lie in the Atlantic Ocean 800 miles west of Portugal. These islands was known in Europe in the 14th century. They were discovered by the Portuguese in 1427, and settlement began in 1432. As each of the islands became settled it was created a donatária, and this system of government remained in effect until 1766 when the islands were united under a single government. In 1831 the islands were administratively re-grouped into three metropolitan districts of Portugal.

Captains-General

1766-1776	Antão de Almada	1806-1810	Miguel António de Melo, Conde de Murça
1776-1793	Dinís Gregório de Melo Castro e Mendonça	1810-1816	Aires Pinto de Sousa
1793-1795	José d'Ave Maria Leite da Costa e Silva	1817-1819	Francisco António de Araújo
		1819-1824	Francisco de Borja Garção Stockler, Barão da Vila da Praia
1795-1798	Luís de Moura Furtado		
1798-1803	Lourenço de Almada	1824-1828	Manuel Vieira Touvar de Albuquerque
1803-1806	José António da Silva César de Meneses, Marquês de Sabugosa	1828-1831	Henrique de Sousa Prego

Archivo dos Açores, 5:528. For the donatários of the various islands, see the following: Angra da Terceira, Cordeiro, 2:17—20; Fayal and Pico, *Archivo dos Açores*, 1:152—57, and Cordeiro, 2:274—77; Flores and Corvo, *Archivo dos Açores*, 5:526—27; Graçiosa, Cordeiro, 2: 250—61; Praia, Cordeiro, 2:14—17; Santa Maria, *Archivo dos Açores*, 4:195—206, and Cordeiro, 1:148—74; São Miguel, Cordeiro, 1:221—36.

286 BAHIA

In 1534 Bahia (Baía de Todos os Santos, or Bay of All Saints) in Brazil had been granted as a donatária but soon thereafter it was sold to the crown. In 1549 a governor (after 1578 called governor-general) was appointed at Bahia. Much of the east coast of Brazil had already been parcelled out as donatárias and settlement had begun. The governor-general at Bahia did not replace or supersede the donatários but rather supplemented them and provided coherence and security to the scattered Portuguese possessions in Brazil (q.v.). From 1574 to 1578 and 1608 to 1612 the southern captaincies were detached from Bahia and administered separately (v. Rio de Janeiro). With the settlement of the "east-west" coast of Brazil early in the 17th century this area was administered completely independently of the older settlements of the south as the Estado do Maranhão (q.v.), while the rest of the Portuguese colonies were denoted the Estado do Brasil and were administered by the governor-general at Bahia. Philip IV of Spain created the office of viceroy but not the viceroyalty itself, and during the 17th and 18th centuries several of the administrators held the title of viceroy. As the economic focus of Brazil shifted southward Bahia became a backwater and in 1763 the seat of the viceroy was transferred to Rio de Janeiro. Bahia remained the seat of a captain-general until 1822 when it became a province of the empire of Brazil.

Governors

1549-1553	Tomé de Sousa
1553-1558	Duarte da Costa
1558-1572	Mem de Sá
1572-1578	Luís de Brito de Almeida

Governors-General

1578-1582	Lourenço da Veiga
1582-1584	(council)
1584-1588	Manuel Teles Barreto
1588-1591	(council)
1591-1602	Francisco de Sousa
1602-1608	Diogo Botelho
1608-1612	Diogo de Meneses e Siqueira
1613-1617	Gaspar de Sousa
1618-1621	Luís de Sousa, Conde do Prado
1621-1624	Diogo de Mendonça Furtado
1624-1627	Matias de Albuquerque[1]
1627-1635	Diogo Luís de Oliveira
1635-1638	Pedro da Silva, Conde de São Lourenço
1639	Fernando de Mascarenhas, Conde da Tôrre
1639-1640	Vasco de Mascarenhas, Conde de Óbidos
1640-1641	Jorge de Mascarenhas, Marquês de Montalvão[2]
1642-1647	António Teles da Silva
1647-1650	António Teles de Meneses, Conde de Vila Pouca de Aguiar
1650-1654	João Rodrigues de Vascancelos e Sousa, Conde de Castelo Melhor
1654-1657	Jerónimo de Ataíde, Conde de Atouguia
1657-1663	Francisco Barreto de Meneses
1663-1667	Vasco de Mascarenhas, Conde de Óbidos[2]
1667-1671	Alexandre de Sousa Freire
1671-1675	Afonso Furtado de Castro do Rio de Mendonça, Visconde de Barbacena
1675-1678	(council)
1678-1682	Roque da Costa Barreto
1682-1684	António de Sousa de Meneses
1684-1687	António Luís de Sousa Telo de Meneses, Marquês das Minas
1687-1688	Matias da Cunha
1688-1690	(council)
1690-1694	António Luís Gonçalves da Câmara Coutinho
1694-1702	João de Lencastre
1702-1705	Rodrigo da Costa
1705-1710	Luís César de Meneses
1710-1711	Lourenço de Almada
1711-1714	Pedro de Vasconcelos e Sousa, Conde de Castelo Melhor
1714-1718	Pedro António de Noronha Albuquerque e Sousa, Marquês de Angeja[2]
1718-1719	Sancho de Faro e Sousa, Conde de Vimeiro
1720-1735	Vasco Fernandes César de Meneses, Conde de Sabugosa[2]
1735-1749	André de Melo e Castro, Conde das Galveias[2]
1749-1754	Luís Pedro Peregrino de Carvalho de Meneses e Ataíde, Conde de Atouguia[2]
1755-1760	Marcos José de Noronha e Brito, Conde dos Arcos[2]
1760	António de Almeida Soares e Portugal de Alarção Eça e Melo, Marquês do Lavradio[2]
1760-1766	(council)
1766-1767	António Rolim de Moura Tavares, Conde de Azambuja
1768-1769	Luís de Almeida Portugal Soares de Alarcão Eça e Melo Silva e Mascarenhas, Marquês do Lavradio
1769-1774	Luís José da Cunha Grã Ataíde e Melo, Conde de Povolide
1774-1779	Manuel da Cunha e Meneses
1779-1783	Afonso Miguel de Portugal e Castro, Marquês de Valença
1784-1788	Rodrigo José de Meneses e Castro
1788-1801	Fernando José de Portugal e Castro

1802-1805 Francisco da Cunha e Meneses
1805-1809 João de Saldanha da Gama Melo
        Tôrres Guedes de Brito, Conde
        da Ponte

1810-1818 Marcos de Noronha e Brito, Conde
        dos Arcos
1818-1821 Francisco de Assis Mascarenhas,
        Conde da Palma

1. Albuquerque, who was capitão-mor of Pernambuco (q.v.), seems to have served as governor-general during this period, although he remained in Pernambuco. Most historians list Francisco de Moura as governor-general although he seems in fact to have been only capitão-mor of the Recôncavo (the hinterland of the city of Bahia) during the Dutch occupation of that city from 1624-1625. On this, see Viana, "Acrésimos," pp. 45—46, and idem, *Estudios*, pp. 207—11.
2. Viceroy.

Campo Belo, pp. 31—140; Varnhagen, 5:302—10.

287 BRAZIL

As an administrative unit congruent with its geographic connotation, Brazil only came into existence in 1775 with the incorporation of the Estado do Maranhão (q.v.) into the viceroyalty at Rio de Janeiro (q.v.), but the following list begins with the transfer of the viceroyalty from Bahia (q.v.) to Rio de Janeiro in 1763. Until 1775 the area south of a line running roughly northeast-southwest from a point on the coast north of the northeastern tip of Brazil was called the Estado do Brasil in contradistinction to the Estado do Maranhão. Since this area comprised a large number of royal captaincies and a larger number of donatárias and yet lacked a distinctive administrative unit, it might be well to give here a brief outline of the growth of the Estado do Brasil, at least in administrative terms. Following is a list of the donatárias within the boundaries of the Estado do Brasil and the dates of their creation:[1]

1504	Fernão de Noronha	1534-36	Santo Amaro
1534-36	Ceará (q.v.)	1534-36	Santana
1534-36	Rio Grande do Norte (q.v.)	1539	Ilha da Trindade
1534-36	Itamaracá	1566	Itaparica
1534-36	Pernambuco (q.v.)	ca. 1570	Paraguaçu (Recôncavo
1534-36	Bahia de Todos os Santos		da Bahia)
1534-36	Ilhéus	1624	Itanhaêm (q.v.)
1534-36	Pôrto Seguro	1657	Paranaguá
1534-36	Espíritu Santo (q.v.)	1664	Santa Catarina (q.v.)
1534-36	São Tomé (q.v.)	ca. 1670	Campos dos Goitacases
1534-36	São Vicente (q.v.)		

Many of these donatárias were never effectively occupied and claims to them were abandoned. Others remained in existence into the 18th century. The areas of lapsed donatárias were eventually settled and became royal captaincies from the very beginning of their settlement. These (qq.v.) included Bahia, Ceará, Goiás, Mato Grosso, Minas Gerais, Paraíba, Rio de Janeiro, Rio Grande do Norte, Rio Grande do Sul, São Paulo, Nova Colônia do Sacramento, Sergipe d'el Rei. For the areas included in the Estado do Maranhão, see Maranhão.

The viceroyalty of Brazil ended in 1808 when the Portuguese Prince Regent João VI fled to Brazil and became in effect his own viceroy.

Viceroys
1763-1767 António Álvares da Cunha, Conde da Cunha
1767-1769 António Rolim de Moura Tavares, Conde de Azambuja
1769-1779 Lufs de Almeida Soares Portugal de Alarçao Eça e Melo Silva e Mascarenhas,
        Marquês do Lavradio

Portugal

1779-1790	Luís de Vasconcelos e Sousa, Conde de Figueiró
1790-1801	José Luís de Castro, Conde de Resende
1801-1806	Fernando José de Portugal e Castro, Conde de Aguiar
1806-1808	Marcos de Noronha e Brito, Conde dos Arcos

1. The number and identity of some of the donatárias have not been universally agreed upon. The information here is based on Viana, *História do Brasil*, 1:62—78, 267—68, 346—49, and idem "Liquidação das donatárias."

Campo Belo, pp. 141—53; Varnhagen, 5:323—24.

288 CAPE VERDE ISLANDS

The Cape Verde Islands are situated in the Atlantic Ocean 320 miles west of Cape Verde, the westernmost point of Africa. The group consists of ten inhabited islands, of which the most important are São Tiago, São Antão, and São Vicente. The archipelago was discovered, possibly in 1456 but more probably in 1460, by Portuguese navigators, and settlement began in 1462. Until 1495 the islands were granted as appanages to members of the Portuguese royal family. In 1495 they were taken over by the Portuguese crown and parcelled out as donatárias. These donatárias reverted to the crown in 1564 and 1586.[1] But already in 1550 the *corregedores* (magistrates) began to exercise the functions of capitães-mores in Ribeira Grande, the most important donatária, because of the incompetence of its donatário. In 1587 the Spanish rulers of Portugal, seeking to centralize control, appointed a single governor over all the islands, as they were to do a little later in Madeira (q.v.). The coast of Africa in what was later to become Portuguese Guinea (q.v.) was settled from the Cape Verde Islands and settlements were established at Cacheu and Bissau. These posts remained under the government of the Cape Verde Islands until 1879 when Portuguese Guinea became a separate province. In 1951 Cape Verde Islands were constituted an overseas territory of Portugal.

Ribeira Grande
Corregedors/Capitães-Mores

1550-1555	Jorge Pimentel
1555-1558	Manuel de Andrade (1)
1558-1562	Luís Martins de Evangelho
1562-1565	Bernardo de Alpoim
1565-1569	Manuel de Andrade (2)
1569-1578	António Velho Tinoco
1578-1583	Gaspar de Andrade
1583-1587	Diogo Dias Magro

Cape Verde
Governors

1587-1591	Duarte Lôbo da Gama
1591-1595	Brás Soares de Melo
1595-1596	Amador Lopes Raposo
1596-1603	Francisco Lôbo da Gama
1603-1606	Fernão de Mesquita de Brito
1606-1611	Francisco Correia da Silva
1611-1614	Francisco Martins de Sequeira
1614-1618	Nicolau de Castilho
1618-1622	Francisco de Moura
1622	Francisco Rolim

1622-1624	Manuel Afonso de Guerra
1624-1628	Francisco Vasconcelos da Cunha
1628-1632	João Pereira Corte-Real
1632-1636	Cristóvão de Cabral
1636-1639	Jorge de Castilho
1639-1640	Jerónimo de Cavalcanti e Albuquerque
1640-1645	João Serrão da Cunha
1645-1646	Lourenço Garro
1646-1648	Jorge de Araújo
1648	Roque de Barros do Rêgo
1648-1650	(council)
1650	Gonçalo de Gambôa Ayala
1650-1651	Pedro Semedo Cardoso
1651-1653	Jorge de Mesquita Castelo Branco
1653-1658	Pedro Ferreira Barreto
1658-1663	Francisco de Figueroa
1663-1667	António Galvão
1667-1671	Manuel da Costa Pessôa (1)
1671-1676	Manuel Pacheco de Melo
1676	João Cardoso Pássaro
1678-1683	Manuel da Costa Pessôa (2)
1683-1687	Inácio de Franca Barbosa

1687-1688	Veríssimo Carvalho da Costa	1858-1860	Sebastião Lopes de Calheiros Meneses
1688-1690	Vítoriano da Costa		
1690	Diogo Ramires Esquivel	1860-1861	Januário Correia de Almeida
1692-1696	Manuel António Pinheiro da Câmara	1861-1864	Carlos Augusto Franco
1696	António Gomes Mena	1864-1869	José Guedes de Carvalho e Meneses
1698-1702	António Salgado		
1702-1707	Gonçalo de Lemos Mascarenhas	1869-1876	Caetano Alexandre de Almeida e Albuquerque
1707-1711	Rodrigo de Oliveira da Fonseca		
1711-1715	José Pinheiro da Câmara	1876-1878	Vasco Guedes de Carvalho e Meneses
1715	Manuel Pereira Calheiros de Araújo		
1716-1720	Serafim Teixeira Sarmento de Sá	1878-1881	António do Nascimento Pereira de Sampaio
1720-1725	António Vieira		
1726-1728	Francisco Miguel de Nóbrega Vasconcelos	1881-1886	João Pais de Vasconcelos
		1886-1889	João Cesário de Lacerda (1)
1728-1733	Francisco de Oliveira Grans	1889-1890	Augusto César Carlos de Carvalho
1733-1737	Bento Gomes Coelho	1890-1893	José Guedes Brandão de Melo
1737-1738	José da Fonseca Barbosa	1893-1894	Fernando de Magalhães e Meneses
1738-1741	(Senado da Câmara)	1894-1898	Alexandre Alberto da Rocha Serpa Pinto
1741-1752	João Zuzarte de Santa Maria		
1752	António José d'Eça de Faria	1898-1900	João Cesário de Lacerda (2)
1752-1757	Luís António da Cunha d'Eça	1900-1902	Arnaldo de Novais Guedes de Rebêlo
1757-1761	Manuel Antonio de Sousa e Meneses		
		1902-1903	Francisco de Paula Cid
1761	Marcelino Pereira de Ávila	1903-1904	António Alfredo Barjona de Freitas
1761-1764	António de Barros Bezerra		
1764-1766	Bartolomeu de Sousa Tigre	1904-1907	Amâncio de Alpoim de Cerqueira Borges Cabral
1766-1767	João Jácome Barena Henriques		
1768-1777	Joaquim Salema Saldanha Lôbo	1907-1909	Bernardo António da Costa de Sousa de Mecedo
1777-1781	António do Vale de Sousa e Meneses		
		1909-1910	Martinho Pinto de Queirós Montenegro
1781-1782	Duarte de Melo da Silva Castro de Almeida		
		1910-1911	António de Macedo Ramalho Ortigão
1782-1783	Francisco de São Simão		
1785-1790	António Machado de Faria e Maia	1911	Artur Marinha de Campos
1790-1795	Francisco José Teixeira Carneiro	1911-1915	Joaquim Pedro Vieira Júdice Biker
1795-1796	José da Silva Maldonaldo d'Eça	1915-1918	Abel Fontoura da Costa
1796-1802	Marcelino António Bastos	1918-1919	Teófilo Duarte
1803-1818	António Coutinho de Lencastre	1919-1921	Manuel Firmino de Almeida da Maia Magalhães
1818-1822	António Pussich		
1822-1826	João da Mata Chapuzet	1921-1922	Filipe Carlos Dias de Carvalho
1826-1830	Caetano Procópio Godinho de Vasconcelos	1924-1926	Júlio Henriques de Abreu
		1927-1931	António Álvares Guedes Vaz
1830-1833	Duarte da Costa de Sousa Macedo[2]	1931-1941	Amadeu Gomes de Figueiredo
1833-1835	Manuel António Martins	1941-1943	José Diogo Ferreira Martins
1835-1836	Joaquim Pereira Marinho (1)	1943-1949	João de Figueiredo
1836-1837	Domingos Correia Arouca	1949-1953	Carlos Alberto Garcia Alves Roçadas
1837-1839	Joaquim Pereira Marinho (2)		
1839-1842	João de Fontes Pereira de Melo (1)	1953-1957	Manuel Marques de Abrantes Amaral
1842-1845	Francisco de Bastos Paula		
1845-1847	José Miguel de Noronha	1957-1958	António Augusto Peixoto Correia
1848-1851	João de Fontes Pereira de Melo (2)	1958-1963	Silvino Silvério Marques
1851-1854	Fortunato José Barreiros	1963—	Leão Maria de Tavares Rosado do Sacramento Monteiro
1854-1858	António Maria Barreiros Arrobas		

1. For the donatários of Ribeira Grande and Alcatraz, see Melo Barreto, pp. 66—67n.
2. Some sources give Duarte de Mesquitela.

Information from José Manuel Fradinho da Costa, Director da Direcção da Imprensa Nacional, Divisão da Propaganda e Informação, Praia, Cape Verde Islands. Also, Melo Barreto, pp. 260—73; Senna Barcellos, 1:128—55, and 2 to 6: passim.

289 CEARÁ

Ceará, in northeastern Brazil, was created a donatária in 1534 but the area was not settled and the donation lapsed. In 1603 Ceará was settled from neighboring Pernambuco (q.v.). In 1619 Ceará was erected into a royal captaincy. From 1621 to 1656 the capitães-mores were subject to Maranhão (q.v.). Between 1637 and 1654 Ceará was occupied by the Dutch. Portuguese capitães-mores appointed during the period were unable to assume their post. In 1656 Ceará was removed from the jurisdiction of Maranhão and placed under Pernambuco where it remained until 1799, when it was detached and became a separate captaincy. In 1822 it became a provinc of the empire of Brazil.

Capitães-Mores

1612-1613	Martim Soares Moreno (1)
1613-1614	Estêvão de Campos
1614-1617	Manuel de Brito Freire
1617-1619	Domingos Lopes Lôbo
1619-1631	Martim Soares Moreno (2)
1631-	Domingos da Veiga Cabral
-1637	Bartolome de Brito

under the Netherlands

Commanders

1637-1640	Hendrik van Ham
1640-1643	Gedeon Maurits de Jongh
1643-1649	(abandoned)
1649-1654	Mathias Beck

under Portugal

Capitães-Mores

1654-1655	Álvaro de Azevedo Barreto
1655-1659	Domingos de Sá Barbosa
1659-1660	António Fernandes Mouxica
1660-1663	Diogo Coelho de Albuquerque
1663-1666	João de Melo Gusmão
1666-1670	João Tavares de Almeida (1)
1670-1673	Jorge Correia da Silva
1673-1677	João Tavares de Almeida (2)
1677-1678	Manuel Pereira da Silva
1678-1682	Sebastião de Sá (1)
1682-1684	Bento de Macedo de Faria
1684-1688	Sebastião de Sá (2)
1688-	Tomás Cabral de Olival
1693	Pedro Lelou
1694-1696	Fernão Carrilho (1)
1696-1699	João de Freitas da Cunha

1699	Fernão Carrilho (2)
1699-1703	Francisco Gil Ribeiro
1703-1704	Jorge de Barros Leite
1704-1705	João da Mota
1705-1709	Gabriel da Silva Lago
1709-1713	Francisco Duarte de Vasconcelos
1713-1715	Plácido de Azevedo Falcão
1715-1718	Manuel da Fonseca Jaime
1718-1721	Salvador Álvares da Silva
1721-1727	Manuel Francês
1727-1731	João Baptista Furtado
1731-1735	Leonel de Abreu Lima
1735-1739	Domingos Simões Jordão
1739-1743	Francisco Ximenes do Aragão
1743-1746	João de Teive Barreto e Meneses
1746-1748	Francisco de Miranda Costa
1748-1751	Pedro de Morais Magalhães
1751-1755	Luís Quaresma Dourado
1755-1759	Francisco Xavier de Miranda Henriques
1759-1765	João Baltasar de Quesedo Homem de Magalhães
1765-1781	António José Vítoriano Borges da Fonseca
1782-1789	João Baptista de Azevedo Coutinh de Montauri
1790-1799	Luís da Mota Fêo e Tôrres

Governors

1799-1802	Bernardo Manuel de Vasconcelos
1803-1807	João Carlos Augusto de Oeynhausen e Gravenburg
1808-1812	Luís Barba Alardo de Meneses
1812-1820	Manuel Inácio de Sampaio e Pina Freire
1820-1821	Francisco Alberto Rubim

Girão, pp. 133–40; Studart, 37:234–335.

290 CEUTA

Ceuta, on the North African coast just across the Straits of Gibraltar from the Iberian peninsula, was captured by the Portuguese in 1415. In a large sense this seizure was merely a logical extension of the *Reconquista* in Spain and Portugal—a process already several hundred years old. In retrospect, though, it may also be seen as the first small step in what was to become a worldwide occupation of non-European areas by the various European colonial powers. Ceuta remained a Portuguese possession until 1640. During the period of Spanish rule in Portugal (1580–1640), Ceuta, like the other Portuguese possessions, continued to be administered by Portuguese. But whereas Portugal retained control of her other possessions after expelling the Spaniards, Ceuta remained in Spanish possession, and in fact continues at the present to be governed by Spain.

Captains-General

1415-1430	Pedro de Meneses, Conde de Viana (1)
1430-1434	Duarte de Meneses, Conde de Viana (1)
1434-1437	Pedro de Meneses, Conde de Viana (2)
1437-1438	Duarte de Meneses, Conde de Viana (2)
1438-1445	Fernão de Noronha, Conde de Vila Real
1445-1447	António Pacheco
1447-1450	Fernão de Bragança, Duque de Bragança
1450-1460	Sancho de Noronha, Conde de Odemira
1461-1464	Pedro de Meneses, Conde Vila Real
1464-1479	João Rodrigues de Vasconcelos Ribeiro
1479-1481	Rui Mendes de Vasconcelos Ribeiro
1481-1487	João de Noronha
1487-1491	António de Noronha, Conde de Linhares
1491-1509	Fernão de Meneses, Conde de Alcoutim
1509-1512	Pedro Barbo Alardo
1512-1517	Pedro de Meneses, Conde de Alcoutim (1)
1518	João da Silva, Conde de Portalegre
1519-1521	Gomes da Silva de Vasconcelos (1)
1522-1524	João de Noronha
1524	Pedro de Meneses, Conde de Alcoutim (2)
1525-1529	Gomes da Silva de Vasconcelos (2)
1529-1539	Nunho Álvares Pereira de Noronha
1540-1549	Afonso de Noronha
1549	Antão de Noronha
1549-1550	Martim Correia da Silva (1)
1550-1553	Pedro de Meneses
1553	Pedro da Cunha (1)

1553	João Rodrigues Pereira
1553-1555	Martim Correia da Silva (2)
1555-1557	Jorge Vieira
1557-1562	Fernão de Meneses (1)
1562-1563	Miguel de Meneses, Conde de Vila Real
1563-1564	Fernão de Meneses (2)
1564-1565	Pedro da Cunha (2)
1566-1567	Francisco Pereira
1567-1574	Manuel de Meneses e Noronha, Duque de Vila Real (1)
1574-1577	Diogo Lopes da França
1577-1578	Manuel de Meneses e Noronha, Duque de Vila Real (2)
1578-1580	Leonís (or Dionísio) Pereira
1580-1586	Jorge Pessanha
1586-1591	Gil Annes da Costa
1591-1592	Francisco de Andrade
1592-1594	Miguel de Meneses, Duque de Caminha (1)
1594-1597	Mendo Rodrigues de Ledesma
1597-1601	Miguel de Meneses, Duque de Caminha (2)
1602-1605	Afonso de Noronha
1605-1616	Miguel de Meneses, Duque de Caminha (3)
1616-1622	Luís de Noronha e Meneses, Conde de Vila Real
1623	Miguel de Meneses, Duque de Caminha (4)
1623-1624	António da Costa Albuquerque
1624-1625	Fernão de Mascarenhas, Conde da Tôrre
1625	Gonçalo Correia Alcoforado
1625-1626	Miguel de Meneses, Duque de Caminha (5)
1627	Dinís de Mascarenhas de Lencastre
1627-1634	Jorge de Mendonça Pessanha
1634-1636	Brás Teles de Meneses
1637	Fernão Teles de Meneses
1637-1641	Francisco de Almeida

Dornellas, 4:21–160.

291 CEYLON

In the early 16th century Ceylon was divided into three warring states. The ruler of Kotte, one of these states, solicited the assistance of the Portuguese, then the dominant power in the Indian Ocean. The Portuguese came to stay. In 1518 a captain was appointed to Colombo, center of the Kotte kingdom. By 1550 the Portuguese were masters of the southwest coastal area of Ceylon. Finally, the Catholicized ruler of Kotte ceded his kingdom to the Portuguese and a governor/captain-general was appointed in 1594. In 1619 the Portuguese annexed the kingdom of Jaffna in the extreme north and soon controlled most of Ceylon's coastal area, though little of the interior. Meanwhile, the kingdom of Kandy arose in the interior highlands and in 1638 its rulers called upon the Dutch, by then successor to the Portuguese in the Indian Ocean, to assist them in expelling the Portuguese. This effort, begun in 1639, was completed in 1658 with the capture of Colombo. But, like the Portuguese, the Dutch, once in Ceylon, were to remain (v. 263).

Capitães-Mores		*Governors*	
1518	João da Silveira	1594	Pedro Lopes de Sousa
-1522	Lopo de Brito	1594-1612	Jerónimo de Azevedo
1522-1524	Fernão Gomes de Lemos	1613-1614	Francisco de Meneses
1524-1551	(office abolished)	1614-1616	Manuel Mascarenhas Homem
1551-1552	João Henriques	1616-1618	Nuno Álvares Pereira
1552	Diogo de Melo Coutinho (1)	1618-1622	Costantino de Sá de Noronha (1)
1552-1553	Duarte de Eça	1622-1623	Jorge de Albuquerque
1553-1555	Fernão Carvalho	1623-1630	Costantino de Sá de Noronha (2)
1555-1559	Afonso Pereira de Lacerda	1630-1631	Filipe Mascarenhas (1)
1559-1560	Jorge de Meneses Baroche	1631-1633	Jorge de Almeida (1)
1560-1564	Baltasar Guedes de Sousa	1633-1635	Diogo de Melo e Castro (1)
1564-1565	Pedro de Ataíde Inferno	1635-1636	Jorge de Almeida (2)
1565-1568	Diogo de Melo	1636-1638	Diogo de Melo e Castro (2)
1568-1570	Fernando de Monroy	1638-1640	António Mascarenhas
1570-1572	Diogo de Melo Coutinho (2)	1640-1645	Filipe Mascarenhas (2)
1572-	António de Noronha	1645-1653	Manuel Mascarenhas Homem
1575-1578	Fernando de Albuquerque	1653-1655	Francisco de Melo e Castro
1578-1583	Manuel de Sousa Coutinho	1655-1656	António de Sousa Coutinho
1583-1590	João Correia de Brito	1656-1658	António do Amaral de Meneses
1590-1591	Simão de Brito		
1591-1594	Pedro Homem Pereira		

Ferguson, pp. 28, 122, 168, 223, 260, 388, and passim; Pieris, passim.

292 ESPÍRITU SANTO

Espíritu Santo on the southeast coast of Brazil was created a donatária in 1535. It remained under donatários, who later appointed capitães-mores, until 1718 when it lapsed to the Portuguese crown and was placed under Bahia (q.v.) as a royal captaincy. In 1822 Espíritu Santo became a province of the empire of Brazil.

Capitães-Mores			
1535-1560	Vasco Fernandes Coutinho[1] (I)	1564-1589	Vasco Fernandes Coutinho[1] (II)
1560-1564	Belchior de Azeredo	1589-1593	Luisa Grinalda[1]
		1593-1605	Miguel de Azeredo

1605-1627	Francisco de Aguiar Coutinho[1]		1716-1721	João de Velasco de Molina (2)
1627-	Manuel de Escobar Cabral		1721-1724	António de Oliveira Madail
-1635	Francisco Alemão de Cisneiros		1724-1726	Dionísio Carvalho de Abreu
1635-1636	Domingos Barbosa de Araújo		1726-1731	António Pires Forsas
1636-1640	António do Couto de Almeida (1)		1732-1741	Silvestre Cirne da Veiga
1640-	João Dias Guedes		1741-1745	Domingos de Morais Navarro
1643-1648	António do Couto de Almeida (2)		1745-1748	Estêvão de Faria Delgado (1)
1648-	João Ferrão de Castelo Branco		1748-1749	Martinho da Gama Pereira
-1650	Feliciano Salgado		1749-1751	Estêvão de Faria Delgado (2)
1650-	Manuel da Rocha de Almeida		1751-	José Gomes Borges
1651-1655	Simão de Carvalho		1759-1761	Gonçalo da Costa Barbalho
1655-1656	Francisco Luís de Oliveira		1761-1762	Baltasar da Costa Silva
1656-1657	Gaspar Pacheco e Contreiras		1762-1768	Anastásio Joaquim da Moita
1657-1659	João de Almeida Rios			Furtado (1)
1661-1662	Dinís Lôbo (1)		1768-1770	Raimundo da Costa Vieira
1662	José Rabelo Leite		1770-1775	José Ramos dos Santos
1662-1663	Dinís Lôbo (2)		1775-1779	Álvaro Correia de Morais (1)
1663	José Lopes		1779-1781	Anastásio Joaquim da Moita
1663-1664	Brás do Couto de Aguiar			Furtado (2)
1664-1667	Diogo de Seixas Barraca		1781-1782	Álvaro Correia de Morais (2)
1667-1671	António Mendes de Figuieredo		1782-1798	Inácio João Monjardim (1)
1671-1674	Inácio de Lercar(o)		1798-1799	Manuel Fernandes da Silveira
1674-1682	Francisco Gil de Araújo			
1682-1688	Manuel de Morais		*Governors*	
1688-1690	Manuel Peixoto da Mota		1800-1804	António Pires da Silva Pontes
1690-1694	João de Velasco de Molina (1)			Pais Leme e Camargo
1694-1699	José Pinheiro de Barbuda		1804-1811	Manuel Vieira de Albuquerque e
1699-	Francisco Monteiro de Morais			Tovar
1702-1705	Francisco Ribeiro de Miranda		1811-1812	Inácio João Monjardim (2)
1705-1709	Álvaro Lôbo de Contreiras		1812-1819	Francisco Alberto Rubim
1709-1710	Francisco de Albuquerque Teles		1819-1822	Baltasar de Sousa Botelho e
1710-1716	Manuel Correia de Lemos			Vasconcelos

1. Donatários.

Assis, [pp. 91–93]; Carvalho Daemon, pp. 152–201; Oliveira, passim.

293 GOIÁS

As the mineral and ranching frontier moved away from the coast of Brazil into the interior high-lands, the province of São Paulo (q.v.) became too large to administer effectively. First Minas Gerais (q.v.), then Goiás, and finally Mato Grasso (q.v.) were detached and created separate provinces. In 1822 Goiás became a province of the empire of Brazil.

Governors				
1749-1755	Marcos José de Noronha e Brito,		1772-1778	José de Almeida Vasconcelos
	Conde dos Arcos			Soveral e Carvalho
1755-1759	Alvaro José Xavier Botelho de		1778-1783	Luís da Cunha e Meneses
	Távora		1783-1800	Tristão da Cunha e Meneses
1759-1770	João Manuel de Melo		1800-1804	João Manuel de Meneses
1770-1772	António Carlos Furtado de		1804-1809	Francisco de Assis Mascarenhas
	Mendonça		1809-1820	Fernão Delgado Freire de Castilho
			1820-1821	Manuel Inácio de Sampaio e Pina

Varnhagen, 5:368–70.

294 GRÃO-PARÁ

Grão-Pará, extending inland from the mouth of the Amazon, was settled at the same time as neighboring Maranhão, and from 1615 to 1737 Grão-Pará was ruled by capitães-mores under Maranhão (q.v.). From 1737 to 1775 Maranhão and Grão-Pará were still administratively united but the increasing importance of Belém, the capital of Grão-Pará, resulted in the transfer of the governor-general to Grão-Pará in 1753 while Maranhão itself was governed by capitães-mores. In 1775 Maranhão and Grão-Pará were given separate administrations. In 1757 the vast interior of the Amazon hinterland, hitherto part of Grão-Pará, was erected into the province of São José do Rio Negro (q.v.), which, however, remained under Grão-Pará. In 1822, as Pará, Grão-Pará became a province of the empire of Brazil.

Grão-Pará

Capitães-Mores

1615-1618	Francisco Caldeira Castelo Branco
1618-1619	Baltasar Rodrigues de Melo
1619	Jerónimo Fragoso de Albuquerque
1619	Matias de Albuquerque
1620-1621	Pedro Teixeira (1)
1621-1626	Bento Maciel Parente
1626-1629	Manuel de Sousa d'Eça
1629-1630	Luís Aranha de Vasconcelos
1630	Jácome Raimundo de Noronha
1630-1633	Antônio Cavalcanti de Albuquerque
1633-1636	Luís do Rêgo Barros
1636-1637	Francisco de Azevedo
1637-1638	Aires de Sousa Chicorro (1)
1638	Feliciano de Sousa e Meneses
1638-1639	Aires de Sousa Chicorro (2)
1639-1640	Manuel Madeira
1640-1641	Pedro Teixeira (2)
1641-1642	Francisco Cordovil Camacho
1642-1646	(municipal government)
1646-1647	Paulo Soares de Avelar
1647-1648	Sebastião de Lucena e Azevedo
1648-1649	Aires de Sousa Chicorro (3)
1649-1650	Inácio do Rêgo Barreto (1)
1650-1652	Aires de Sousa Chicorro (4)
1652-1654	Inácio do Rêgo Barreto (2)
1654	Pedro Correia de Bittencourt
1654-1655	Aires de Sousa Chicorro (5)
1655-1656	Luís Pimenta de Morais
1656-1658	Feliciano Correia (1)
1658-1662	Marçal Nunes da Costa (1)
1662-1665	Francisco de Seixas Pinto
1665-1666	Feliciano Correia (2)
1666-1667	Antônio Pinto da Gaia (1)
1667-1668	Manuel Guedes Aranha
1668-1669	Paulo Martins Garro
1669-1670	Feliciano Correia (3)
1670-1674	Antônio Pinto da Gaia (2)
1674-1685	Marçal Nunes da Costa (2)

1685-1690	Antônio de Albuquerque Coelho de Carvalho
1690-1697	Hilário de Sousa de Azevedo
1698-1707	João Velasco de Molina
1707-1710	Pedro Mendes Tomás
1710-1716	João de Barros Guerra
1716-1719	José Velho de Azevedo
1719-1728	Manuel de Machado Lôbo
1728-1732	Antônio Marreiros
1732-1737	Antônio Duarte de Barros
1737-1747	João de Abreu Castelo Branco
1747-1751	Francisco Pedro de Mendonça Gurjão
1751-1753	Francisco Xavier de Mendonça Furtado

Grão-Pará and Maranhão

Governors-General

1753-1759	Francisco Xavier de Mendonça Furtado
1759-1763	Manuel Bernardo de Melo e Castro
1763-1772	Fernão da Costa de Ataíde Teive Sousa Coutinho

Grão-Pará and Rio Negro

Governors-General

1772-1780	João Pereira Caldas
1780-1783	José Nápoles Telo de Meneses

Governors

1783-1790	Martinho de Sousa e Albuquerque
1790-1803	Francisco Maurício de Sousa Coutinho
1803-1806	Marcos de Noronha e Brito, Conde dos Arcos
1806-1810	José Narciso de Magalhães de Meneses
1810-1817	(juntas)
1817-1820	Antônio José de Sousa Manuel de Meneses Severim e Noronha, Conde de Vila Flór

Braga, pp. 293—98; Cruz, 2:745—51.

295 HORMUZ

The island of Hormuz, whose location at the entrance to the Persian Gulf rendered it ideal for controlling the extensive trade up the Gulf through the Ottoman Empire to Europe, was occupied by the Portuguese in 1515. The Portuguese position at Hormuz was subjected in the 16th century to attacks by the Turks and by the forces of the shah of Persia, and after 1600 the Dutch and English competed with the Portuguese for control of the trade of the area. Finally in 1622 Persian forces, supported by the English East India Company, expelled the Portuguese from Hormuz, which became a part of the Safavid kingdom. Hormuz was governed by a capitão-mor subject to the authority of the Portuguese viceroy at Goa (v. Portuguese India). The following list is incomplete and probably inaccurate as well. For Hormuz, as for Malacca (q.v.), we are almost entirely dependent on the Portuguese chroniclers of the 16th and 17th centuries and it is not always possible to resolve the ambiguities or fill the gaps in their accounts.

Capitães-Mores

1515-1518	Pero de Albuquerque	1564-1566	Pedro de Sousa (2?)
1518-1521	Garcia Coutinho	1566-1569	Luís de Melo
1521-1523	João Rodrigues de Noronha (or	1569-1572	Francisco Mascarenhas
	da Câmara)	1572-1574	Fernão Teles
1523-1527	Diogo de Melo	1574-	Diogo de Melo
1527-1532	Cristóvão de Mendonça	-1577	Diogo de Meneses
1532	Belchior de Sousa	1580-1583	Gonçalo de Meneses
1532-1536	António da Silveira de Meneses	1584-1587	Matias de Albuquerque
1536-1538	Pedro de Castelo Branco	1587-	João Gomes da Silva
1539	Fernão de Lima	1594-	Diogo Lopes Coutinho
1540-1544	Martim Afonso de Melo Zuzarte	-1597	António de Azevedo
1544-1547	Luís Falcão	1597-1599	António de Lima
1547	Manuel da Silveira	1599-	Luís de Gama (1)
1547-1550	Manuel de Lima	-	(unknown)
1550-1552	Álvaro de Noronha	1605-	Luís da Gama (2)
1554-	Fernão Gomes de Sousa	1610	Henrique de Noronha
-1556	Bernaldim de Sousa	-1612	Jorge de Castelo Branco
1556-1558	João de Ataíde (1)	1612-1613	Pedro de Brito de Lima
1558-1561	Antão de Noronha	1613-1619	Luís da Gama (3)
1561	Francisco Mascarenhas Palha	1619-1620	Luís de Sousa
1561-	Pedro de Sousa (1)	1620-1622	Francisco de Sousa
-	João de Ataíde (2)[1]	1622	Simão de Melo

1. Ataíde was capitão-mor during the viceroyalty of Francisco Countinho at Goa (1561–64). It would therefore appear that he was in office between the two incumbencies of Pedro de Sousa.

Barros, passim; Botelho de Sousa, passim; Correa, passim; Silva Rêgo, 1:443–48.

296 MACAO

Macao is located on the coast of Kwangtung province in southwest China. The Portuguese began to visit the area in 1516, and in 1557 Macao was leased from China. From 1557 to 1623 (except for the periods 1563–65 and 1616–17) Macao was governed by the captain of the annual Japan voyage (cf. Newfoundland, 169). After 1623 Macao was governed by a resident governor who was, until 1844, subordinate to the viceroy or governor-general of Portuguese India (q.v.). In 1849 Portugal proclaimed its sovereignty over Macao and ceased paying an annual rent to China. This unilateral action was only recognized by China in 1887. From 1844 to 1896 Timor (q.v.) was administratively subject to Macao. After the erection of the British colony at nearby Hong Kong (143) in 1841, Macao's prosperity declined noticeably. In 1951 Macao became an overseas territory of Portugal.

Capitães-Mores

1557-1558	Francisco Martins
1558-1559	Lionel de Sousa
1559-1560	Rui Barreto
1560-1561	Manuel de Mendonça
1561-1562	Fernão de Sousa
1562-1563	Pero Barreto Rolim
1563-1565	Diogo Pereira
1565-1566	João Pedro Pereira
1566-1567	Simão de Mendonça (1)
1567-1568	Tristão Vaz da Veiga (1)
1568-1569	António de Sousa
1569-1571	Manuel Travassos
1571-1572	Tristão Vaz da Veiga (2)
1572-1573	João de Almeida (1)
1573-1574	António de Vilhena
1574-1575	Simão de Mendonça (2)
1575-1576	Vasco Pereira
1576-1579	Domingos Monteiro (1)
1579-1580	Lionel de Brito
1580-1581	Miguel da Gama
1581-1582	Inácio de Lima
1582-1583	João de Almeida (2)
1583-1585	Airès Gonçalves de Miranda
1585-1586	Francisco Pais
1586-1587	Domingos Monteiro (2)
1587-1589	Jerónimo Pereira
1589-1590	(unknown)[1]
1590-1951	Anrique (or António) da Costa
1591-1592	Roque de Melo Pereira
1592-1593	Domingos Monteiro (3)
1593-1594	Gaspar Pinto da Rocha
1594-1595	(uncertain)
1595-1596	Manuel de Miranda
1596-1597	Rui Mendes de Figuieredo
1597-1598	(unknown)[1]
1598-1599	Nunho de Mendonça
1599-1603	Paulo de Portugal
1603-1604	Gonçalo Rodrigues de Sousa
1604-1605	João Caiado de Gambôa
1605-1607	Diogo de Vasconcelos de Meneses
1607-1609	André Pessôa
1609-1611	(unknown)[1]
1611-1612	Pedro Martin Gaio
1612-1614	Miguel de Sousa Pimentel
1614-1615	João Serrão da Cunha
1615-1616	Martim da Cunha
1616-1617	Francisco Lopes Carrasco
1617-1618	Lopo Sarmento de Carvalho (1)
1618-1619	António de Oliveira de Morais
1619-1621	Jerónimo de Macedo de Carvalho
1621-1622	Lopo Sarmento de Carvalho (2)

Governors

1623-1626	Francisco Mascarenhas
1626-1629	Filipe Lôbo
1630	Jerónimo da Silveira
1631-1636	Manuel da Câmara de Noronha
1636-1638	Domingos da Câmara de Noronha
1638-1644	Sebastião Lôbo de Silveira
1644-1646	Luís de Carvalho de Sousa
1646	Diogo Coutinho Doçem
1647-1650	João Pereira
1650-1654	João de Sousa Pereira
1654-1664	(uncertain)
1664-1666	Manuel Coelho da Silva
1667-1670	Álvaro da Silva
1670-1672	Manuel Borges da Silva
1672-1677	António Barbosa Lôbo
1678-1679	António de Castro Sande
1679-1682	Luís de Melo Sampaio
1682-1685	Belchior do Amaral de Meneses
1685-1688	António de Mesquita Pimentel
1688-1691	André Coelho Vieira
1691-1693	Francisco da Costa
1693-1694	António da Silva Melo
1694-1697	Gil Vaz Lôbo Freire
1697	Cosme Rodrigues de Carvalho e Sousa
1698-1700	Pedro Vaz de Sequeira (1)
1700-1702	Diogo de Melo Sampaio
1702-1703	Pedro Vaz de Sequeira (2)
1703-1706	José da Gama Machado
1706-1710	Diogo do Pinho Teixeira
1710-1711	Francisco de Melo e Castro
1711-1714	António de Sequeira de Noronha
1714-1718	Francisco de Alarcão de Souto-Maior
1718-1719	António de Albuquerque Coelho
1719-1722	António da Silva Telo e Meneses
1722-1724	Cristóvão de Severim Manuel
1724-1727	António Carneiro de Alcáçova
1727-1732	António Muniz Barreto
1732-1735	António do Amaral Meneses
1735	João do Casal
1735-1738	Cosme Damião Pinto Pereira (1)
1738-1743	Manuel Pereira Coutinho
1743-1747	Cosme Damião Pinto Pereira (2)
1747-1749	António José Teles de Meneses
1749-1752	João Manuel de Melo
1752-1755	Rodrigo de Castro (1)
1755-1758	Francisco António Pereira Coutinho
1758-1761	Diogo Pereira
1761-1764	António de Mendonça Corte-Real
1764-1767	José Plácido de Matos Saraiva

1767-1770	Diogo Fernandes Salema e Saldanha (1)
1770-1771	Rodrigo de Castro (2)
1771-1777	Diogo Fernandes Salema e Saldanha (2)
1777-1778	Alexandre da Silva Pedrosa Guimarães
1778-1780	João Vicente da Silveira e Meneses
1780-1781	António José da Costa
1781-1783	Francisco de Castro
1783-1788	Bernardo Aleixo de Lemos Faria (1)
1788-1789	Francisco Xavier de Mendonça Corte-Real
1789-1790	Lázaro da Silva Ferreira
1790-1793	Vasco Luís Carneiro de Sousa Faro
1793-1797	José Manuel Pinto (1)
1797-1800	Cristóvão Pereira de Castro
1800-1803	José Manuel Pinto (2)
1803-1806	Caetano de Sousa Pereira
1806-1808	Bernardo Aleixo de Lemos Faira (2)
1808-1810	Lucas José de Alvarenga
1810-1817	Bernardo Aleixo de Lemos Faria (3)
1817-1822	José Onório de Castro e Albuquerque
1822-1825	(council)
1825-1827	Joaquim Mourão Garcês Palha
1827-1830	(council)
1830-1833	João Cabral de Estefique
1833-1837	Bernardo José de Sousa Soares de Andrea
1837-1843	Adrião Acácio da Silveira Pinto
1843-1846	José Gregório Pegado
1846-1849	João Maria Ferreira do Amaral
1850	Pedro Alexandrino da Cunha
1851	Francisco António Gonçalves Cardoso
1851-1863	Isidoro Francisco Guimarães
1863-1866	José Rodrigues Coelho do Amaral
1866-1868	José Maria da Ponte e Horta
1868-1872	António Sérgio de Sousa
1872-1874	Januário Correia de Almeida, Visconde de São Januário
1874-1876	José Maria Lôbo de Ávila
1876-1879	Carlos Eugénio Correia da Silva
1879-1883	Joaquim José Graça
1883-1886	Tomás de Sousa Rósa
1886-1888	Firmino José da Costa
1889-1890	Francisco Teixeira da Silva
1890-1894	Custódio Miguel de Borja
1894-1897	José Maria de Sousa Horta e Costa (1)
1897-1900	Eduardo Augusto Rodrigues Galhardo
1900-1902	José Maria de Sousa Horta e Costa (2)
1902-1903	Arnaldo Novais Guedes Rebêlo
1904-1907	Martinho Pinto de Quierós Montenegro
1907-1908	Pedro de Azevedo Coutinho
1908-1909	José Augusto Alves Roçadas
1909-1910	Eduardo Augusto Marquês
1910-1912	Álvaro de Melo Machado
1912-1914	Aníbal Augusto Sanches de Miranda
1914-1916	José Carlos da Maia
1917-1918	Fernando Augusto Vieira de Matos
1918-1919	Artur Tamagnini de Sousa Barbosa (1)
1919-1922	Henrique Monteiro Correia da Silva
1922-1923	Luís António de Magalhães Correia
1923-1924	Rodrigo José Rodrigues
1924-1925	Joaquim Augusto dos Santos
1925-1926	Manuel Firmino de Almeida Maia Magalhães
1926-1929	Artur Tamagnini de Sousa Barbosa (2)
1929-1931	João Pereira de Magalhães (1)
1931	Joaquim Anselmo da Mata e Oliveira
1931-1932	João Pereira de Magalhães (2)
1932-1935	António José Bernardes de Miranda
1935-1936	João Pereira Barbosa
1936-1937	António Joaquim Ferreira da Silva Júnior
1937-1940	Artur Tamagnini de Sousa Barbosa (3)
1940-1946	Gabriel Maurício Teixeira
1947-1951	Albano Rodrigues de Oliveira
1951-1957	Joaquim Marquês Esparteiro
1957-1958	Pedro Correia Barros
1958-1959	Manuel Peixoto Nunes
1959-1962	Jaime Silvério Marquês
1962-1966	António Adriano Faria Lopes dos Santos
1966—	José Manuel de Sousa e Faro Nobre de Carvalho

1. In this year there was no Japan voyage.

Information from António Herculano de Miranda Dias, Chefe de Gabinete, Macao. Also, Boxer, *Fidalgos*, pp. 272–76.

297 MADEIRA

The Madeira archipelago is located 360 miles off the northwest coast of Africa. It consists of two inhabited islands, Madeira and Pôrto Santo, and a number of islets. Madeira was evidently known to the Genoese by the 14th century, but permanent settlement began with the Portuguese discovery in 1418–20. The two islands were granted as donatárias. Madeira was divided into the donatárias of Funchal and Machico, while the smaller island of Pôrto Santo was a single donatária.[1] After the Spanish occupation of Portugal in 1580 the islands were united under a governor-general, later a governor, and remained so governed until 1834, when Madeira became a metropolitan district of Portugal. English influence in the islands was great and Madeira was occupied by them in 1801–2 and from 1807 to 1814, although nominal Portuguese control was maintained.

Governors-General

1581–1585	João Leitão
1585–1591	Tristão Vaz da Veiga
1591–1595	António Pereira de Barredo
1595–1600	Diogo de Azambuja e Melo
1600–1603	Cristóvão Falcão de Sousa
1603–1609	João Fogaça d'Eça
1609–1614	Manuel Pereira Coutinho
1614–1618	Jorge da Câmara
1618–1622	Pedro da Silva
1622–1624	Francisco Henriques
1625–1626	Fernão de Saldanha
1626–1628	Jerónimo Fernando
1628–1634	Francisco de Sousa
1634–1636	João de Meneses
1636–1640	Luís de Miranda de Henriques Pinto

Governors

1642–1645	Nunho Pereira Freire
1645–1648	Manuel de Sousa Mascarenhas
1648–1651	Manuel Lôbo da Silva
1651–1655	Bartolomeu de Vasconcelos
1655–1660	Pedro da Silva da Cunha
1660–1665	Diogo de Mendonça Furtado
1665–1668	Francisco de Mascarenhas
1669–1672	Aires de Saldanha de Sousa e Meneses
1672–1676	João de Saldanha e Albuquerque
1676–1680	Alexandre de Moura e Albuquerque
1680–1684	João da Costa de Brito
1684–1688	Pedro de Lima Brandão
1688–1690	Lourenço de Almada
1690–1694	Rodrigo da Costa
1694–1698	Pantaleão de Sá e Melo

1698–1701	António Jorge de Melo
1701–1704	João da Costa de Ataíde e Azevedo
1704–1712	Duarte Sodré Pereira
1712–1715	Pedro Álvares da Cunha
1715–1718	João de Saldanha da Gama
1718–1724	Jorge Martins de Sousa e Meneses
1724–1727	Francisco da Costa Freire
1727–1734	Filipe de Alarção Mascarenhas
1734–1737	João de Abreu Castelo Branco
1737–1747	Francisco Pedro de Meneses Gurjão
1747–1751	João do Nascimento
1751–1754	Álvaro José Xavier Botelho de Távora
1754–1757	Manuel de Saldanha e Albuquerque
1757–1759	Gaspar Afonso da Costa Brandão
1759–1767	José Correia de Sá
1767–1777	João Antonio de Sá Pereira
1777–1781	João Gonçalves da Câmara Coutinho
1781–1798	Diogo Pereira Forjaz Coutinho
1800–1803	José Manuel da Câmara
1803–1807	Ascenso de Sequeira Freire
1807–1813	Pedro Facundes Bacelar de Antas e Meneses
1813–1814	Luís Beltrão de Gouveia e Almeida
1815–1819	Floréncio José Correia de Melo
1819–1821	Sebastião Xavier Botelho
1821–1822	Rodrigo António de Melo
1822–1823	António Manuel de Noronha
1823–1827	Manuel de Portugal e Castro
1827–1828	José Lúcio Travassos Valdês
1828–1830	José Maria Monteiro
1830–1834	Álvaro da Costa de Sousa e Macedo

1. For donatários of Funchal, see Silva and Meneses, 1:378; for Machico, ibid., 1:378–79; for Pôrto Santo, ibid., 1:379 and 3:116–17.

Silva and Meneses, under individual names. Note that lists at 2:98–100 are incomplete and inaccurate.

298 MALACCA

Malacca, on the western coast of the Malay Peninsula, dominated the western entrance to the Straits of Malacca leading from the Indian Ocean to the South China Sea. From about 1400 it had been the seat of a Malay sultanate. In 1511 the Portuguese, newly arrived in the Indian Ocean and seeking to secure strategic posts around its perimeter, seized Malacca. Malacca remained the most important Portuguese post in the Eastern seas until its capture by the Dutch in 1641 (v. 271). It was governed by a capitão-mor subject to the viceroy at Goa (v. Portuguese India).

Capitães-Mores

1512-1514	Rui de Brito Patalim
1514-1516	Jorge de Albuquerque (1)
1516-1517	Jorge de Brito
1517-1518	Nuno Vaz Pereira
1518-1519	Afonso Lopes da Costa
1519-1521	Garcia de Sá (1)
1521-1525	Jorge de Albuquerque (2)
1525-1526	Pero de Mascarenhas
1526-1528	Jorge Cabral
1528-1529	Pedro de Faria (1)
1529-1533	Garcia de Sá (2)
1533-1534	Paulo da Gama
1534-1538	Estêvão da Gama
1539-1542	Pedro de Faria (2)
1543-1544	Rui Vaz Pereira Marramoque
1544-1545	Simão Botelho de Andrade
1545	Garcia de Sá (3)
1545-1548	Simão de Melo
1548-1552	Pedro da Silva da Gama
1552	Francisco Álvares
1552-1554	Álvaro de Ataíde
1554-1556	António de Noronha
1556-1557	João Pereira
1557-1560	João de Mendonça
1560-1564	Francisco de Eça
1564-1567	Diogo de Meneses
1567-1570	Leonís Pereira (1)
1570-1571	Francisco da Costa
1571-1573	António Moniz Barreto
1573	Miguel de Castro
1573-1574	Leonís Pereira (2)
1574-1575	Tristão Vaz da Veiga

1575-1577	Miguel de Castro
1577-1579	Aires de Saldanha
1581-1582	João da Gama
1582-1584	Roque de Melo
1584-1587	João da Silva
1587	João Ribeiro Gaio
1587-	Nuno Velho Pereira
-	Diogo Lôbo
-1594	Pedro Lopes de Sousa
1597-1598	Francisco da Silva Meneses
1598-1599	Martim Afonso de Melo Coutinho
1599-1603	Fernão de Albuquerque
1603-1606	André Furtado de Mendonça
1606-1607	António de Meneses
1610-1613	Francisco Henriques
1613-1615	Gaspar Afonso de Melo
1615	João Caiado de Gambôa
1615-1616	António Pinto da Fonseca
1616-1617	João da Silveira
1619	Lopes de Sousa
1624	Filipe de Sousa
-1626	Luís de Melo
-1634	Gaspar de Melo Sampaio
1634-1635	Álvaro de Castro
-1636	Francisco de Sousa de Castro
1636-1638	Diogo Coutinho Doçem
1638-1641	Manuel de Sousa Coutinho

Captains-General[1]

1616-1635	António Pinto da Fonseca
1636-1637	Francisco Coutinho Doçem
1637-1641	Luís Martins de Sousa Chichorro

1. The captains-general exercised general supervision over Malacca and surrounding waters under Portuguese control during the struggles with the Dutch.

Information from Fr. M. J. Pintado, St. Peter's Church, Malacca, Malaysia. Also, Macgregor, p. 42.

299 MARANHÃO

The area of Maranhão, on the north coast of Brazil east of the Amazon estuary, was granted in two donatárias in 1534, but these lapsed and no settlement was made until early in the 17th century. This initial settlement was made in response to a French effort at colonization of the Maranhão area. Because the "east-west" coastline of Brazil, including Maranhão, was more accessible to Portugal itself than to the "north-south" coastline settled the century before, a sep arate Estado do Maranhão was created in 1621 (effective 1626), which included Grão-Pará (q.v.) as well. The Estado was abolished in 1652 but quickly revived two years later. During the 17th century several donatárias were created in Maranhão. These were

Cametá	1633-1754
Cumã (or Tapuitapera)	1633-1754
Caeté (or Gurupi)	1634-1753
Cabo Norte	1637-ca. 1695
Ilha Grande de Joanes (or Marajó)	1665-1754
Xingu	1685-?

Each of these was eventually sold or ceded to the Portuguese crown and absorbed into the Estado do Maranhão. After 1737 the center of government was removed to Belém in Grão Pará; after 1745 Maranhão was governed by capitães-mores. In 1775 the Estado do Maranhão was abolished and the entire area came under the jurisdiction of the viceroy at Rio de Janeiro (v. Brazil). At its abolition in 1775 the Estado do Maranhão was divided into Grão-Pará, São José do Rio Negro, Piauí (qq.v.), and a truncated province of Maranhão. In 1822 Maranhão became a province of the empire of Brazil.

Capitães-mores

1616-1618	Jerónimo de Albuquerque Maranhão
1618-1619	António de Albuquerque
1619-1622	Diogo da Costa Machado
1622-1626	António Muniz Barreiros Filho

Maranhão and Grão-Pará

Governors

1626-1636	Francisco de Albuquerque Coelho de Carvalho
1636-1638	Jácome Raimundo de Noronha
1638-1641	Bento Maciel Parente
1641-1643	(under the Netherlands)
1643-1644	Pedro de Albuquerque
1644-1646	António Teixeira de Melo
1646-1648	Francisco Coelho de Carvalho
1648-1649	Manuel Pita da Veiga
1649-1652	Luís de Magalhães

São Luís

Governor

1652-1655	Baltasar de Sousa Pereira

Maranhão, Grão Pará, and Rio Negro

Governors

1655-1656	André Vidal de Negreiros
1656-1658	Agostinho Correia
1658-1662	Pedro de Melo
1662-1667	Rui Vaz de Sequeira
1667-1671	António de Albuquerque Coelho de Carvalho (I)
1671-1678	Pedro César de Meneses

1678-1682	Inácio Coelho da Silva
1682-1684	Francisco de Sá e Meneses
1685-1687	Gomes Freire de Andrade
1687-1690	Artur de Sá e Meneses
1690-1701	António de Albuquerque Coelho de Carvalho (II)
1701-1702	Fernão Carrilho
1702-1705	Manuel Rolim de Moura Tavares
1705-1707	João Velasco de Molina
1707-1718	Cristóvão da Costa Freire
1718-1722	Bernardo Pereira de Berredo e Castro

Maranhão

Governors

1722-1728	João da Maia da Gama
1728-1732	Alexandre de Sousa Freire
1732-1736	José da Serra
1736-1737	João Alves de Carvalho
1737-1745	João de Abreu Castelo Branco

Capitães-Mores

1745-1751	Domingos Duarte Sardinha
1751-1752	Luís de Vasconcelos Lôbo
1752-1753	Severino de Faria
1753-1761	Gonçalo Pereira Lobato e Sousa
1761-1775	Joaquim de Melo e Póvoas

Governors

1775-1779	Joaquim de Melo e Póvoas
1779-1784	António de Sales e Noronha
1784-1787	José Teles da Silva

1787-1792 Fernando Pereira Leite de Foios
1792-1798 Fernando António de Noronha
1798-1804 Diogo de Sousa
1804-1806 António de Saldanha da Gama
1806-1809 Francisco de Melo Manuel de
　　　　　 Câmara

1809-1811 José Tomás de Meneses
1811-1819 Paulo José da Silva Gama
1819-1821 Bernardo da Silveira Pinto da
　　　　　 Fonseca

Meireles, pp. 55—207. For the donatários, see Studart Filho, passim.

300 MATO GRASSO

Like Goiás and Minas Gerais (qq.v.), the province of Mato Grasso was created because the influx of settlers into the Brazilian interior highlands had extended the boundaries of São Paulo (q.v.) to the point where São Paulo was too large to be governed efficiently as a unit. Mato Grasso became a province of the empire of Brazil in 1822.

Governors
1751-1762 António Rolim de Moura Tavares,
　　　　　 Conde de Azambuja
1765-1769 João Pedro da Câmara
1769-1772 Luís Pinto de Sousa Coutinho
1772-1789 Luís de Albuquerque de Melo
　　　　　 Pereira e Cáceres
1789-1796 João de Albuquerque de Melo
　　　　　 Pereira e Cáceres

1796-1803 Caetano Pinto de Miranda
　　　　　 Montenegro
1804-1805 Manuel Carlos de Abreu e
　　　　　 Meneses
1805-1807 (juntas)
1807-1817 João Carlos Augusto de Oeyn-
　　　　　 hausen e Gravenburg
1817-1821 Francisco de Paula Magesi
　　　　　 Tavares de Carvalho

Varnhagen, 5:370—72.

301 MINAS GERAIS

As its name implies, the area of Minas Gerais was rich in mineral wealth, particularly gold and diamonds. Before 1710 the area was part of São Vicente (q.v.) and then, until 1720, of São Paulo (q.v.). Already in 1710 the growing importance of Minas Gerais was recognized when the new captaincy of São Paulo e Minas do Ouro was created. Within a decade this arrangement proved unwieldy and Minas Gerais was constituted a separate province or captaincy. In like fashion Goiás and Mato Grasso (qq.v.) were later formed. Minas Gerais remained a separate province until 1822 when it became a part of the empire of Brazil, in which it continued to retain its administrative individuality.

Governors
1720-1732 Lourenço de Almeida
1732-1735 André de Melo e Castro, Conde
　　　　　 das Galveias

1735-1736 Gomes Freire de Andrade (1)
1736-1737 Martinho de Mendonça de Pina e
　　　　　 Proença
1737-1752 Gomes Freire de Andrade (2)

Portugal

1752-1758	José Antonio Freire de Andrade	1780-1783	Rodrigo José de Meneses e Castro
1758-1763	Gomes Freire de Andrade, Conde de Bobadela (3)	1783-1788	Luís da Cunha e Meneses, Conde de Lumiares
1763	António Álvares da Cunha	1788-1797	Luís António Furtado de Mendonça, Visconde de Barbacena
1763-1768	Luís Diogo Lôbo da Silva		
1768-1773	José Luís de Meneses Abranches Castelo Branco, Conde de Valadares	1797-1803	Bernardo José da Silveira e Lorena
		1803-1810	Pedro Maria Xavier de Ataíde e Melo, Conde de Condeixa
1773-1775	António Carlos Furtado de Mendonça	1810-1814	Francisco de Assis Mascarenhas
1775	Pedro António da Gama Freitas	1814-1821	Manuel Francisco Zacharias de Portugal e Castro
1775-1780	António de Noronha		

Oliveira Tôrres, 5:1489—92.

302 MOMBASA

Mombasa, located on the east coast of Africa 1300 miles north of Sofala (v. Mozambique), was occupied by the Portuguese in 1593, presumably to prevent the Ottomans from doing likewise. Earlier the Portuguese had held Kilwa (1505—1512) and the island of Socotra (1507—1511) in the same area. Mombasa never proved to be an important link in Portugal's chain of posts around the Indian Ocean (v. Mozambique, Portuguese India, Ceylon, and Malacca) and was consequently given little attention. It was captured by the Omanis in 1698. The Portuguese regained Mombasa in 1728—29 but abandoned it in the face of a siege by Omani forces.

Capitães-Mores

1593-1596	Mateus Mendes de Vasoncelos	1658-1663	José Botelho da Silva
1596-1598	António Godinho de Andrade	1663-1667	Manuel de Campos
—	Rui Soares de Melo	1667-1670	João Santos Cota
1606-1609	Gaspar Pereira	1671-1673	José Homem da Costa
1609-1610	Pedro Gomes de Abreu	1673-1676	Manuel de Campos Mergulhão
1610-1614	Manuel de Melo Pereira	1676-1679	Francisco Morais de Faria
1614-1620	Simão de Melo Pereira	1679-	Manuel Teixeira Franco
1620-1625	Francisco de Sousa Pereira	-1682	Pedro Taveira Henriques
1625-1626	João Pereira Semedo	1682-1686	Leonardo da Costa
1626-1629	Marçal de Macedo	1686-1688	João Antunes Portugal
1629-1631	Pedro Leitão de Gambôa	1688-1693	Duarte Figueiredo de Melo
1632-1635	Pedro Rodrigues Botelho	1693-1694	Pascual de Abreu Sarmento
1635-1639	Francisco de Seixas Cabreira (1)	1694-1696	João Rodrigues Leão
1639-1642	Martim Afonso Manuel	1696-1697	António Mogo de Melo
1643-1646	Manuel de Sousa Coutinho	1697-1698	Dau (Prince of Faza)
1646-1648	Diogo de Barros da Silva	1698	Leonardo Barbosa Souto-Maior
1648-1651	António da Silva de Meneses	1698-1728	(under Arab rule)
1651-1653	Francisco de Seixas Cabreira (2)	1728-1729	Álvaro Caetano de Melo e Castro

Boxer and de Azevedo, p. 118.

303 MOZAMBIQUE

The coast of Mozambique in southeast Africa was first sighted by Vasco da Gama in 1498 on his voyage to India. In 1505 a fort was built at Sofala to exploit the gold trade from the interior. Later in the 16th century, posts were established at Sena and Tete, up the Zambezi River. Until the early 19th century whatever prosperity Mozambique attained was based on the extensive slave trade of the area. Until 1752 Mozambique was subject to the viceroy at Goa (v. Portuguese India); in that year it was created a separate province under a governor/captain-general. In 1951 Mozambique became an overseas territory of Portugal, although this change has had no effect on its colonial status.

Sofala
Capitães-Mores
1501-1505	Sancho de Tovar (1)
1505-1506	Pedro da Naia
1506	Manuel Fernandes
1506-1507	Nunho Vaz Pereira

Sofala and Mozambique
Capitães-Mores
1507-1508	Vasco Gomes de Abreu
1508-1509	Rui de Brito Patalim
1509-1512	António de Saldanha
1512-1515	Simão de Miranda de Azevedo
1515-1518	Cristóvão de Távora
1518-1520	Sancho de Tovar (2)
1521-1524	Diogo de Sepúlveda
1525-1528	Lopo de Almeida
1528-1531	António da Silveira de Meneses
1531-1538	Vicente Pegado
1538-1541	Aleixo de Sousa Chicorro
1541-1548	João de Sepúlveda
1548-1551	Fernão de Sousa de Távora
1552-1553	Diogo de Mesquita
1554-1557	Diogo de Sousa
1558-1560	Sebastião de Sá
1560-1564	Pantaleão de Sá
1564-1567	Jerónimo Barreto
1567-1569	Pedro Barreto Rolim

Mozambique
Captains-General
1569-1573	Francisco Barreto
1573-1577	Vasco Fernandes Homem
1577-1582	Pedro de Castro
1583-1586	Nunho Velho Pereira
1586-1589	Jorge Telo de Meneses
1589-1590	Lourenço de Brito
1591-1595	Pedro de Sousa
1595-1598	Nunho da Cunha e Ataíde
1598-1601	Álvaro Abranches
1601-1604	Vasco de Mascarenhas
1604-1607	Sebastião de Macedo
1607-1609	Estêvão de Ataíde (1)

Mozambique, Sofala, Rios de Cuama, and Monomotapa
Governors
1609-1611	Nunho Alvares Pereira (1)
1611-1612	Estêvão de Ataíde (2)
1612	Diogo Simões de Madeira
1612-1614	João de Azevedo
1614-1618	Rui de Melo Sampaio
1619-1623	Nunho Álvares Pereira (2)
1623	Nunho da Cunha
1623-1624	Lopo de Almeida
1624-1627	Diogo de Sousa de Meneses (1)
1628-1631	Nunho Álvares Pereira (3)
1631-1632	Cristóvão de Brito e Vasconcelos
1632-1633	Diogo de Sousa de Meneses (2)
1633-1634	Filipe de Mascarenhas
1635-1639	Lourenço de Souto-Maior
1639-1640	Diogo de Vasconcelos
1640-1641	António de Brito Pacheco
1641-1642	Francisco da Silveira
1643-1646	Júlio Moniz da Silva
1646-	Fernão Dias Baião
1649-1651	Álvaro de Sousa de Távora
1652	Francisco de Mascarenhas
1653-1657	Francisco de Lima
1657-1661	Manuel Corte-Real de Sampaio
1661-1664	Manuel de Mascarenhas
1664-1667	António de Melo e Castro
1667-1670	Inácio Sarmento de Carvalho
1670-1673	João de Sousa Freire (1)
1673-1674	Simão Gomes da Silva
1674	André Pinto da Fonseca
1674-1676	Manuel da Silva
1676-1682	João de Sousa Freire (2)
1682-1686	Caetano de Melo e Castro
1686-1689	Miguel de Almeida
1689-1692	Manuel dos Santos Pinto
1692-1693	Tomé de Sousa Correia
1694	Francisco Correia de Mesquita
1694-1695	Estêvão José da Costa
1696	Francisco da Costa
1696-1699	Luís de Melo Sampaio
1699-1703	Jácome de Morais Sarmento

Portugal

1703-1706	João Fernandes de Almeida (1)
1706-1707	Luís de Brito Freire
1708-1712	Luís Gonçalves de Câmara
1712-1714	João Fernandes de Almeida (2)
1714-1715	Francisco de Mascarenhas
1716-1719	Francisco de Souto-Maior
1719-1721	Francisco de Alarção e Souto-Maior
1722-1723	Álvaro Caetano de Melo e Castro
1723-1726	António João Sequeira e Faria
1726-1730	António Cardim Fróis
1730-1733	António Casco de Melo
1733-1736	José Barbosa Leal
1736-1739	Nicolau Tolentino de Almeida
1740-1743	Lourenço de Noronha
1743-1746	Pedro do Rêgo Barreto da Gama e Castro
1746-1750	Caetano Correia de Sá

Mozambique, the Zambesi, and Sofala
Governors/Captains-General

1752-1758	Francisco de Melo e Castro
1758	João Manuel de Melo
1758	David Marques Pereira
1758-1763	Pedro de Saldanha e Albuquerque (1)
1763-1765	João Pereira da Silva Barba
1765-1779	Baltasar Manuel Pereira do Lago
1779-1780	José de Vasconcelos e Almeida
1781-1782	Vicente Caetano da Maia e Vasconcelos
1782-1783	Pedro de Saldanha e Albuquerque (2)
1783-1786	(junta)
1786-1793	António Manuel de Melo e Castro
1793-1797	Diogo de Sousa Coutinho
1797-1801	Francisco Guedes de Carvalho Meneses da Costa
1801-1805	Isidro de Almeida Sousa e Sá
1805-1807	Francisco de Paula de Albuquerque do Amaral Cardoso
1807-1809	(junta)
1809-1812	António Manuel de Melo e Castro de Mendonça
1812-1817	Marcos Caetano de Abreu e Meneses
1817-1818	José Francisco de Paula Cavalcanti de Albuquerque
1819-1821	João da Costa Brito Sanches
1821-1824	(juntas)
1824-1825	João Manuel da Silva
1825-1829	Sebastião Xavier Botelho
1829-1832	Paulo José Miguel de Brito
1832-1834	(junta)
1834-1836	José Gregório Pegado

Mozambique
Governors-General

| 1837 | António José de Melo |

1837-1838	João Carlos Augusto de Oeynhausen e Gravenburg, Marquês de Aracaty
1838-1840	(council)
1840-1841	Joaquim Pereira Marinho
1841-1843	João da Costa Xavier
1843-1847	Rodrigo Luciano de Abreu e Lima
1847-1851	Domingos Fortunato do Vale
1851-1854	Joaquim Pinto de Magalhães
1854-1857	Vasco Guedes de Carvalho e Meneses
1857-1864	João Tavares de Almeida
1864-1867	António do Canto e Castro
1867-1868	António Augusto de Almeida Portugal Correia de Lacerda
1869	António Tavares de Almeida
1869	Fernão da Costa Leal
1870-1873	José Rodrigues Coelho do Amaral
1874-1877	José Guedes de Carvalho e Meneses
1877-1880	Francisco Maria da Cunha
1880-1881	Augusto César Rodrigues Sarmento
1881-1882	Carlos Eugénio Correia da Silva, Visconde de Paço de Arcos
1882-1885	Agostinho Coelho
1885-1889	Augusto Vidal de Castilho Barreto e Noronha
1889-1890	José António de Brissac das Neves Ferreira
1890-1891	Joaquim José Machado (1)
1891-1893	Rafael Jácome Lopes de Andrade
1893-1894	Francisco Teixeira da Silva
1894-1895	Fernão de Magalhães e Meneses
1895-1896	António José Enes
1896-1897	Joaquim Augusto Mousinho de Albuquerque
1897-1898	Baltasar Freire Cabral
1898	Carlos Alberto Schultz Xavier
1898-1900	Álvaro António da Costa Ferreira
1900	Júlio José Marques da Costa
1900	Joaquim José Machado (2)
1900-1902	Manuel Rafael Gorjão
1902-1905	Tomás António Garcia Rosado
1905-1906	João António de Azevedo Coutinho Fragoso de Sequeira
1906-1910	Alfredo Augusto Freire de Andrade
1910-1911	José de Freitas Ribeiro
1911-1912	José Francisco de Azevedo e Silva
1912-1913	José Afonso Mendes de Magalhães
1913-1914	Augusto Ferreira dos Santos
1914-1915	Joaquim José Machado (3)
1915	Alfredo Baptista Coelho
1915-1918	Álvaro Xavier de Castro
1918-1919	Pedro Francisco Massano do Amorim
1919-1921	Manuel Moreira da Fonseca (1)
1921-1923	Manuel de Brito Camacho
1923-1924	Manuel Moreira da Fonseca (2)
1924-1926	Vítor Hugo de Azevedo Coutinho

1926-1938	José Ricardo Pereira Cabral	1958-1961	Pedro Correia de Barros
1938-1940	José Nunes de Oliveira	1961-1964	Manuel Maria Sarmento Rodrigues
1940-1947	José Tristão de Bettencourt	1964-1968	José Augusto da Costa Almeida
1947-1958	Gabriel Maurício Teixeira	1968—	Baltasar Rebêlo de Sousa

Information from Manuel Estevens, Biblioteca Nacional de Lisboa, Lisbon, Portugal. Also, Alcântara Guerreiro, pp. 3−17; Lopes de Lima, 4:103−35.

304 NOVA COLÔNIA DO SACRAMENTO

In 1680 the Portuguese placed a colony on the north bank of the Plate estuary directly opposite the Spanish colony of Buenos Aires (325), but it was immediately occupied by the Spaniards and only returned in 1683. From 1705 to 1715 Sacramento was again occupied by the Spaniards, but it was returned by terms of the Treaty of Utrecht. To counteract Sacramento the Spaniards established the post of Montevideo (356) in 1724, while the Portuguese, as a supportive measure, occupied and settled Santa Catarina and Rio Grando do Sul (qq.v.). Nonetheless Sacramento remained an exposed outpost, and although it flourished and expanded the Portuguese agreed by the Treaty of Madrid, 1750, to abandon the colony. This proposal was not implemented, however, until 1777 when by the Treaty of San Ildefonso Portugal abandoned Sacramento in return for renewed Spanish acceptance of Portuguese sovereignty in the Amazon hinterland, already previously granted by the Treaty of Madrid (v. São José do Rio Negro).

Governors

1683-1689	Cristóvão Dornelas de Abreu	1721-1749	António Pedro de Vasconcelos
1689-1699	Francisco Naper Lencastre	1749-1760	Luís Garcia de Bivar
1699-1705	Sebastião da Veiga Cabral	1760-1762	Vicente da Silva Fonseca
1705-1715	(abandoned)	1763-1775	Pedro José Soares de Figueiredo Sarmento
1715-1721	Manuel Gomes Barbosa	1775-1777	Francisco José da Rocha

Monteiro, 1:passim.

305 PARAÍBA

The area of Paraíba was settled from Pernambuco (q.v.) and was a captaincy subject to Pernambuco. From 1635 to 1645 Paraíba was occupied by the Dutch. Paraíba remained under Pernambuco until 1799 when, like Ceará (q.v.), it was removed and created an autonomous captaincy.

Capitães-Mores

1582-	Frutuoso Barbosa (1)	1607-1608	André de Albuquerque Maranhão
1586	João Tavares	1608-1612	Francisco de Albuquerque Coelho de Carvalho
1587-	Frutuoso Barbosa (2)	1612-1616	João Rebêlo de Lima
1595-1596	Feliciano Coelho de Carvalho	1616-1618	João de Brito Correia
1600-1603	Francisco de Sousa Pereira	1618-1625	Afonso de França
1603-1607	Francisco Nunes Marinho de Sá	1628-1633	António de Albuquerque Maranhão

Portugal

under the Netherlands

Directors
1635-1636	Servan Carpentier
1636	Ippo Eisen
1636-1644	Elias Herckman
1644-1645	Gijsbert Wilt
1645	Paul Linge

under Portugal

Capitães-Mores
1645-	(junta)
1655-1657	João Fernandes Vieira
1657-1663	Matias de Albuquerque Maranhão
1663-1670	João do Rêgo Barros
1670-1673	Luís Nunes de Carvalho
1673-1675	Inácio Coelho da Silva
1675-1678	Manuel Pereira de Lacerda
1678-1684	Alexandre de Sousa de Azevedo
1684-1687	António da Silva Barbosa
1687-1692	Amaro Velho Cerqueira
1692-1697	Manuel Nunes Leitão
1697-1700	Manuel Soares de Albuquerque
1700-1703	Francisco de Alves Pereira

1703-1708	Fernão de Barros de Vasconcelos
1708-1717	João da Maia da Gama
1717-1719	António Velho Coelho
1720-1722	António Fernão de Castelo Branco
1722-1729	João de Abreu Castelo Branco
1729-1734	Francisco Pedro de Mendonça Gurjão
1734-1744	Pedro Monteiro de Macedo
1744-1745	João Lôbo de Lacerda
1745-1753	António Borges da Fonseca
1753-1757	Luís António de Brito de Lemos
1757-1761	José Henriques de Carvalho
1761-1764	Francisco Xavier de Miranda Henriques
1764-1797	Jerónimo José de Melo e Castro

Governors
1798-1802	Fernão Delgado Freire de Castilho
1802-1805	Luís da Mota Fêo e Torres
1805-1809	Amaro Joaquim Raposo de Albuquerque
1809-1815	António Caetano Pereira
1815-1817	(juntas)
1817-1819	Tomás de Sousa Mafra
1819-1821	Joaquim Rebêlo da Fonseca Rosado

Nóbrega, pp. 128–31.

306 PERNAMBUCO

Pernambuco, in northeast Brazil, was granted as a donatária in 1534 by the king of Portugal. Un-like most of these early donatárias (v. Brazil), Pernambuco, known as Nôva Lusitania throughout much of the 16th century, flourished and was in fact the most important captaincy in Brazil at this time. Until 1576 Pernambuco was governed by its donatários, who were resident in the captaincy. Thereafter it was ruled by capitães-mores. Until 1637 these were appointed by the donatários. From 1637 to 1654 Pernambuco was under the Netherlands and was the center of Dutch control in Brazil (v. 274). With the restoration of Portuguese rule Pernambuco came under control of the Portuguese crown, although it nominally remained a donatária until 1716 when the last donatário sold his rights to the crown. Ceará (q.v.) was subordinate to Pernambuco from 1656 to 1799, Paraíba (q.v.) from 1582 to 1799, Rio Grande do Norte (q.v.) from 1701 to 1808, and the area of Alagôas (q.v.) until 1817.

Resident Donatários
1534-1554	Duarte Coelho
1554-1560	Dona Brites
1560-1572	Duarte Coelho de Albuquerque
1572-1576	Jorge de Albuquerque Coelho

Capitães-Mores
1576-1580	Jerónimo de Albuquerque
1584-1595	Filipe de Moura
1596	Pedro Homem de Castro

1598-1603	Manuel Mascarenhas Homem
1605-1617	Alexandre de Moura
1619-	Martim de Sousa Sampaio
1620-1626	Matias de Albuquerque (1)
1626-1629	André Dias da França
1629-1635	Matias de Albuquerque (2)
1635-1636	Luis de Rojas y Borja, Duque de Ganja
1636-1637	Duarte de Albuquerque Coelho[1]
1637-1654	(under the Netherlands)

Governors

1654–1657	Francisco Barreto de Meneses
1657–1661	André Vidal de Negreiros (1)
1661–1664	Francisco de Brito Freire
1664–1666	Jerónimo de Mendonça Furtado
1667	André Vidal de Negreiros (2)
1667–1670	Bernardo de Miranda Henriques
1670–1674	Fernando de Sousa Coutinho
1674–1678	Pedro de Almeida
1678–1682	Aires de Sousa de Castro
1682–1685	João de Sousa de Castro
1685–1688	João da Cunha Souto-Maior
1688	Fernão Cabral
1688–1689	Matias Figueiredo de Melo
1689–1690	António Luís Gonçalves da Câmara Coutinho
1690–1693	António Félix Machado da Silva e Castro, Marquês de Montebelo
1693–1699	Caetano de Melo e Castro
1699–1703	Fernão Martins Mascarenhas de Lencastre
1703–1707	Francisco de Castro Morais
1707–1710	Sebastião de Castro e Caldas
1710–1711	Manuel Álvares da Costa

1711–1715	Félix José Machado de Mendonça Eça Castro e Vasconcelos
1715–1718	Lourenço de Almeida
1718–1721	Manuel de Sousa Tavares e Távora
1721–1722	Francisco de Sousa
1722–1727	Manuel Rolim de Moura
1727–1737	Duarte Sodré Pereira Tibão
1737–1746	Henrique Luís Pereira Freire de Andrada
1746–1749	Marcos José de Noronha e Brito, Conde dos Arcos
1749–1756	Luís Correia de Sá
1756–1763	Luís Diogo Lôbo da Silva
1763–1768	António de Sousa Manuel de Meneses, Conde de Vila Flór
1768–1769	Luís José da Cunha Grã Ataíde e Melo, Conde de Povolide
1769–1774	Manuel da Cunha e Meneses
1774–1787	José César de Meneses
1787–1798	Tomás José de Melo
1798–1804	(juntas)
1804–1817	Caetano Pinto de Miranda Montenegro
1817–1821	Luís do Rêgo Barreto

1. Resident donatário.

Costa, passim; João Fernando de Almeida Prado, passim; Varnhagen, 5:310–16.

307 PIAUÍ

Piauí in northeast Brazil was occupied, pacified, and settled from Bahia (q.v.) in 1682. In 1715 the area was transferred to the control of Maranhão (q.v.) but only in 1759 was Piauí erected into a captaincy, still remaining under the jurisdiction of Maranhão. In 1811 it was detached from Maranhão and became a separate province.

Capitães-Mores

1759–1769	João Pereira Caldas
1769–1775	Gonçalo Pereira Botelho de Castro
1775–1777	(juntas)
1777–	Manuel Pinheiro
–	Fernão José Veloso de Miranda
–	José Estêves Falcão
–	José Rodrigues de Azevedo
–	Domingos Barreira de Macedo
–	Manuel Pacheco Taveira
–	António Teixeira de Novais
–	José Pereira de Brito
–	João Pereira de Carvalho
–	Caetano da Cea de Figueiredo
–	Inácio Rodrigues de Miranda
–	António Gomes da Cruz

	António Gameiro da Cruz
–1797	Agostinho de Sousa Monteiro
1797–1799	João do Amorim Pereira (1)
1799–1803	Francisco Diogo de Morais
1803	João do Amorim Pereira (2)
1803–1805	Pedro César de Meneses
1805–1806	Luís António Sarmento da Maia
1806–1810	Carlos César Burlamaque
1810–1811	Francisco da Costa Rabêlo

Governors

1811–1814	Amaro Joaquim Raposo de Albuquerque
1814–1819	Baltasar de Sousa Botelho de Vasconcelos
1819–1821	Elias José Ribeiro de Carvalho

Alencastre, pp. 5–13.

308 PORTUGUESE GUINEA

The area which became Portuguese Guinea on the west coast of Africa was probably discovered by the Portuguese Nuno Tristão in 1446 and was settled from the Cape Verde Islands (q.v.) in the 16th century. Initially the few settlers were traders but as settlement increased a capitão-mor was appointed at Cacheu in 1641, subject to the governor of the Cape Verde Islands. In 1687 Bissau was established and a capitão-mor was appointed there five years later. From 1707 to 1753 the captaincy of Bissau was suppressed. By the early 19th century Bissau had surpassed Cacheu in importance, and after 1852 the administration at Cacheu was suppressed. In 1879 the area was detached from the government of the Cape Verde Islands and erected into the colony of Portuguese Guinea. From 1890 to 1915 the interior was occupied and Portuguese control coincided with the colony's boundaries. In 1951 Portuguese Guinea became an overseas territory.

Cacheu
Capitães-Mores

1614	João Tavares de Sousa
1615-1616	Baltasar Pereira de Castelo Branco
1622	Francisco de Távora
1625-	Francisco Sodré Pereira
-1634	Francisco Nunes de Andrade
1634	Domingos Lôbo Reimão
1634-	Paulo Barradas da Silva
-	Manuel da Silva Botelho
-1641	Luís de Magalhães
1644-1649	Gonçalo de Gamboa Avala
1649-1650	Gaspar Vogado
1650-1654	João Correia Fidalgo
1655-	Francisco Pereira da Cunha
1658-1662	Manuel Dias Contrim
1662-1664	António da Fonseca Ornelas
1664-	João Carvalho Moutinho
-	Manuel de Almeida
-	Ambrósio Gomes
1674	Sebastião Vidigal da Rosa
1676-1682	António Barros Bezerra (1)
1682-1685	Gaspar da Fonseca Pacheco
1685-1686	João Gonçalves de Oliveira
1687-1688	António Barros Bezerra (2)
1688-1689	Rodrigo Oliveira da Fonseca
1689-1690	José Pinheiro da Câmara
1690-1691	Domingos Monteiro de Carvalho
1691-1707	Santos de Vidigal Castanho
1707-	Paulo Gomes de Abreu e Lima
1715-1718	António Barros Bezerra Júnior (1)
1718-	Inácio Lopes Ferreira
1721	António Barros Bezerra Júnior (2)
1723	Pedro de Barros
1726-	Manuel Lopes Lôbo
1729-1731	João Perestrelo
1731-	António Barros Bezerra Júnior (3)
1733-1734	João Pereira de Carvalho
1737	Damião de Bastos
1741	Nicolau Pino de Araújo
1748-1751	João de Távora
1751-1755	Francisco Roque Souto-Maior
1765-1770	Sebastião da Cunha Souto-Maior
1775-	António Vaz de Araújo
-1785	António Teles de Meneses

1785-	João Pereira Barreto
1786-	Luís de Araújo e Silva
1798-	Lopo Almeida Henriques
1800-	Manuel Pinto de Gouveia
1802-1803	José Joaquim de Sousa Torvão
1803-	João António Pinto
1811-1814	Joaquim José Rebêlo de Figueiredo e Góis
1815-	João Cabral da Cunha Goodolfim (1)
-1819	João Teles de Meneses
	Drumont (1)
1820	José Correia de Barros
1821-	João de Araújo Gomes
1823-1825	João Cabral de Cunha Goodofilm (2)
1826	António Tavares da Veiga Santos
1835	José António Ferreira
1838-	Delfim José dos Santos
1842-1844	António dos Santos Chaves
1844-1846	José Xavier do Crato (1)
1846-1847	Honório Pereira Barreto (1)
1847-1849	José Xavier do Crato (2)
1852	Honório Pereira Barreto (2)

Bissau
Capitães-Mores

1696-1699	José Pinheiro da Câmara
1699-1707	Rodrigo Oliveira da Fonseca
1707-1753	(abandoned)
1753-	Nicolau Pino de Araújo
1757-1759	Manuel Pires
1759-	Duarte José Róis
1763	Filipe José de Souto-Maior
1770-1775	Sebastião da Cunha Souto-Maior
1777	Inácio Xavier Baião
1793-1796	José António Pinto
1799-	João das Neves Leão
1803	António Cardoso Faria
1805-1811	Manuel Pinto de Gouveia
1811-	António Cardoso Figueiredo
1820-1821	João Higino Curvo Semedo
1822-	Joaquim António de Matos (1)
-1825	Domingos Alves de Abreu Picaluga
1825-1827	Joaquim António de Matos (2)
1827-	Francisco José Muacho

1829-1830   Caetano José Nozolini (1)
1830-   Joaquim António de Matos (3)
   -1834   Caetano José Nozolini (2)
1834-   Joaquim António de Matos (4)
1836   José Eleutério Rocha Vieira
1836-1839   Honório Pereira Barreto (1)
1839-1840   José Gonçalves Barbosa
1840-1841   Honório Pereira Barreto (2)
1841-1842   José Paulo Machado
1842   António Tavares da Veiga Santos
1842-1843   António José Tôrres
1843-1844   José Maria Coelho
1844-1845   Alois da Rôla Dziezaski (1)
1845-1847   Joaquim de Azevedo Alpoim
1847-1848   Carlos Maximiliano de Sousa
1848-1850   Caetano José Nozolini (3)
1851   Alois da Rôla Dziezaski (2)
1852   Libanio Evangelista dos Santos
1852-1853   José Maria Lôbo de Ávila
1853-1854   José Maria Correia da Silva
1854   Pedro Henriques Romão Ferreira
1855-1858   Honório Pereira Barreto (3)
1858   António Pereira Mousinho de
                 Albuquerque Cota Falcão
1858-1859   Honório Pereira Barreto (4)
1860-1862   António Cândido Zagalo
1863-   Joaquim Alberto Marquês (1)
1867-1868   Bernardo José Moreira
1868-1869   Manuel Fortunato Meira
1869-1871   Álvaro Teles Caldeira
1871   José Xavier do Crato
1871-   Joaquim Alberto Marquês (2)
1877-1879   António José Cabral Vieira

                 Portuguese Guinea
Governors
1879-1881   Agostinho Coelho
1881-1884   Pedro Inácio de Gouveia (1)
1885-1886   Francisco Paula Gomes Barbosa
1886-1887   José Eduardo de Brito

1887-1888   Eusébio Castella do Vale
1888   Francisco Teixeira da Silva
1888-1890   Joaquim da Graça Correia e Lança
1890-1891   Augusto Rogério Gonçalves dos
                 Santos
1891-1895   Luís Augusto de Vasconcelos e Sá
1895-1897   Pedro Inácio de Gouveia (2)
1897-1900   Álvaro Herculano da Cunha
1901-1903   Joaquim Pedro Vieira Júdice Biker
1903-1904   Alfredo Cardoso de Soveral Martins
1904   João Mateus Lapa Valente
1904-1906   Carlos de Almeida Pessanha
1906-1909   João Augusto de Oliveira Muzanty
1909-1910   Francelino Pimentel
1910-1913   Carlos de Almeida Pereira
1913   José António de Andrade
                 Sequeira (1)
1914-1915   José de Oliveira Duque (1)
1915-1917   José António de Andrade
                 Sequeira (2)
1917   Manuel Maria Coelho
1917-1918   Carlos Ivo de Sá Ferreira
1918-1919   José de Oliveira Duque (2)
1919   José Luís Teixeira Marinho
1919-1920   Henrique Alberto de Sousa Guerra
1921-1926   Jorge Frederico Veles Caroço
1927-1931   António Leite de Magalhães
1931-1932   João José Soares Zilhão
1932-1940   Luís António de Carvalho Viegas
1941-1945   Ricardo Vaz Monteiro
1945-1949   Manuel Maria Sarmento Rodrigues
1949-1953   Raimundo António Rodrigues Serrão
1953-1956   Diogo António José Leite Pereira
                 de Melo e Alvim
1956-1958   Álvaro Rodrigues da Silva Tavares
1958-1962   António Augusto Peixoto Correia
1962-1965   Vasco António Martins Rodrigues
1965-1968   Arnaldo Schultz
1968——   António Sebastião Ribeiro de
                 Spínola

Information from António Augusto Peixoto Correia, Capitão da Fragata, Governador de Guiné
Português, Bissau, Portuguese Guinea. Also, Melo Barreto, pp. 273—79; Carreira, pp. 79—86;
Duarte, "Capitães-Mores," pp. 199—220; idem, "Cartas," pp. 961—84; Faro, pp. 100—102;
Teixeira, pp. 97, 104, 117, 118.

309 PORTUGUESE INDIA

Goa, on the western coast of India, was seized by the Portuguese from the ruler of Bijapur in
1510. Diu and Damão, several hundred miles to the north, were occupied in 1535 and 1538
respectively. These three enclaves formed Portuguese India. The viceroy or governor-general
of Portuguese India at Goa was the supreme Portuguese authority in the East, governing, at
various times Mozambique, Mombasa, Hormuz, Ceylon, Malacca, Timor, and Macao (qq.v.), and

other scattered Portuguese possessions in the Indian Ocean and eastward. Portugal retained these enclaves after the other European powers had withdrawn from India. However, in 1961 the Republic of India militarily occupied each of the three areas, putting an end to Portuguese sovereignty.

Governors-General

1505-1509	Francisco de Almeida[1]
1509-1515	Afonso de Albuquerque
1515-1518	Lopo Soares de Albergaria
1518-1522	Diogo Lopes de Sequeira
1522-1524	Duarte de Meneses
1524	Vasco da Gama, Conde de Vidigueira[1]
1524-1526	Henrique de Meneses
1526-1529	Lopo Vaz de Sampaio
1529-1538	Nunho da Cunha
1538-1540	Garcia de Noronha[1]
1540-1542	Estêvão da Gama
1542-1545	Martim Afonso de Sousa
1545-1548	João de Castro[1]
1548-1549	Garcia de Sá
1549-1550	Jorge Cabral
1550-1554	Afonso de Noronha[1]
1554-1555	Pedro Mascarenhas[1]
1555-1558	Francisco Barreto
1558-1561	Costantino de Bragança[1]
1561-1564	Francisco Coutinho, Conde do Redondo[1]
1564	João de Mendonça
1564-1568	Antão de Noronha[1]
1568-1571	Luís de Ataíde, Conde de Atouguia[1] (1)
1571-1573	António de Noronha[1]
1573-1576	António Moniz Barreto
1576-1578	Diogo de Meneses
1578-1580	Luís de Ataíde, Conde de Atouguia[1] (2)
1581	Fernão Teles de Meneses, Conde de Vilar Maior
1581-1584	Francisco Mascarenhas, Conde da Orta[1]
1584-1588	Duarte de Meneses, Conde de Tarouca[1]
1588-1591	Manuel de Sousa Coutinho
1591-1597	Matias de Albuquerque[1]
1597-1600	Francisco da Gama, Conde de Vidigueira[1] (1)
1600-1605	Aires de Saldanha[1]
1605-1607	Martim Afonso de Castro[1]
1607-1609	Aleixo de Meneses
1609	André Furtado de Mendonça
1609-1612	Rui Lourenço de Távora[1]
1612-1617	Jerónimo de Azevedo[1]
1617-1619	João Coutinho, Conde do Redondo[1]
1619-1622	Fernão de Albuquerque
1622-1628	Francisco da Gama, Conde de Vidigueira[1] (2)
1628-1629	Luís de Brito
1629-1635	Miguel de Noronha, Conde de Linhares[1]
1635-1639	Pedro da Silva[1]
1639-1640	António Teles de Meneses
1640-1645	João da Silva Telo de Meneses, Conde de Aveiras[1]
1645-1651	Filipe Mascarenhas[1]
1652-1653	Vasco Mascarenhas, Conde de Óbidos[1]
1653-1655	Brás de Castro
1655-1656	Rodrigo da Silveira, Conde de Sarzedas[1]
1656	Manuel Mascarenhas Homem
1656-1662	(juntas)
1662-1666	António de Melo e Castro[1]
1666-1668	João Nunes da Costa, Conde de São Vicente[1]
1668-1671	(junta)
1671-1677	Luís de Mendonca Furtado e Albuquerque, Conde do Lavradio[1]
1677-1678	Pedro de Almeida, Conde de Assumar[1]
1678-1681	(junta)
1681-1686	Francisco de Távora, Conde de Alvor[1]
1686-1690	Rodrigo da Costa (1)
1690-1691	Miguel de Almeida
1691-1693	(junta)
1693-1698	Pedro António de Noronha de Albuquerque, Conde de Vila Verde[1]
1698-1701	António Luís Gonçalves da Câmara Coutinho[1]
1702-1707	Caetano de Melo e Castro[1]
1707-1712	Rodrigo da Costa[1] (2)
1712-1717	Vasco Femandes César de Meneses[1]
1717	Sebastião de Andrade Pessanha
1717-1720	Luís Carlos Inácio Xavier de Meneses, Conde de Ericeira[1] (1)
1720-1723	Francisco José de Sampaio e Castro[1]
1723	Cristóvão de Melo
1723-1725	(junta)
1725-1732	João de Saldanha da Gama[1]
1732-1741	Pedro Mascarenhas, Conde de Sandomil[1]
1741-1742	Luís Carlos Inácio Xavier de Meneses, Marquês de Louriçal (2)
1742-1744	(junta)

1744–1750	Pedro Miguel de Almeida e Portugal, Marquês de Alorna[1]	1878–1882	Caetano Alexandre de Almeida e Albuquerque
1750–1754	Francisco de Assis de Távora, Marquês de Távora[1]	1882–1885	Carlos Eugénio Correia da Silva, Conde de Paço de Arcos
1754–1756	Luís de Mascarenhas, Conde de Alva[1]	1886	Francisco Joaquim Ferreira do Amaral
1756–1758	(junta)	1886–1889	Augusto César Cardoso de Carvalho
1758–1765	Manuel de Saldanha de Albuquerque, Conde de Ega[1]	1889–1891	Vasco Guedes de Carvalho e Meneses
1765–1768	(junta)		
1768–1774	João José de Melo	1891–1892	Francisco Maria da Cunha
1774	Filipe de Valadares Souto-Maior	1892–1893	Francisco Teixeira da Silva
1774–1779	José Pedro da Câmara	1893–1894	Rafael Jácome Lopes de Andrade (1)
1779–1786	Frederico Guilherme de Sousa		
1786–1794	Francisco da Cunha e Meneses	1894–1895	Elesbão Bettencourt Lapa, Visconde de Vila Nova de Ourém
1794–1807	Francisco António da Veiga Cabral da Câmara Pimentel	1895–1896	Rafael Jácome Lopes de Andrade (2)
1807–1816	Bernardo José da Silveira e Lorena, Conde de Sarzedas[1]	1896	Afonso Henriques, Duque de Pôrto[1]
1816–1821	Diogo de Sousa, Conde de Rio Pardo[1]	1896–1897	João António de Brissac das Neves Ferreira
1822–1825	Manuel da Câmara	1897–1900	Joaquim José Machado
1826–1835	Manuel de Portugal e Castro[1]	1900–1905	Eduardo Augusto Rodrigues Galhardo
1835	Bernardo Peres da Silva		
1835–1837	(junta)	1905–1907	Arnaldo de Novais Guedes Rebêlo
1837–1838	Simão Infante de Lacerda de Sousa Tavares, Barão de Sabroso	1907–1910	José Maria de Sousa Horta e Costa
1839	José António Vieira da Fonseca	1910–1917	Francisco Manuel Couceiro da Costa
1839–1840	Manuel José Mendes, Barão de Candal		
1840–1842	José Joaquim Lopes de Lima	1917–1919	José de Freitas Ribeiro
1842–1843	Francisco Xavier da Silva Pereira, Conde das Antas	1919	Augusto de Paiva Bobela Mota
		1919–1925	Jaime Alberto da Costa Morais
1843–1844	Joaquim Mourão Garcês Palha	1925–1926	Mariano Martins
1844–1851	José Ferreira Pestana (1)	1926–1929	Pedro Francisco Massano de Amorim
1851–1855	José Joaquim Januário Lapa, Visconde de Vila Nova de Ourém	1929	Artur Alfredo Pedro de Almeida
1855–1864	António César de Vasconcelos Correia, Conde de Torres Novas	1929–1936	João Carlos Craveiro Lopes
		1936–1938	Francisco Higino Craveiro Lopes
1864–1870	José Ferreira Pestana (2)	1938–1945	José Ricardo Pereira Cabral
1870–1871	Januário Correia de Almeida, Visconde de São Januário	1945–1946	Paulo Bénard Guedes (1)
		1946–1948	José Silvestre Ferreira Bossa
1871–1875	Joaquim José Macedo e Couto	1948–1952	Fernando de Quintanilha Mendonça e Dias
1875–1877	João Tavares de Almeida		
1877–1878	António Sérgio de Sousa, Visconde Sérgio de Sousa	1952–1958	Paulo Bénard Guedes (2)
		1958–1961	Manuel António Vasalo e Silva

1. Viceroy.

Information from António dos Mártires Lopes, Director, Centro de Informação e Turismo, Goa, in July 1960. Also, Ferreira Martins, pp. 268–76; Sales; Zuquete, passim.

310 RIO DE JANEIRO

The area of Rio de Janeiro was the site of a French settlement, grandiloquently termed Antarctic France, from 1555 to 1560, when the French were expelled by the Portuguese. In 1563–65 the Portuguese settled the area and a captaincy was created. Rio de Janeiro was under the governor general at Bahia (q.v.) until 1763, except for the periods 1574–78 and 1608–12 when it was briefly removed from the control of Bahia. During the late 17th century the discovery of great mineral wealth in the south of Brazil led to the increasing importance of Rio de Janeiro and the resulting decline of the northern areas of Bahia. Consequently in 1763 the seat of the viceroy was shifted from Bahia to Rio de Janeiro and with the suppression of the Estado do Maranhão in 1775 Brazil was for the first time united under a single administration. After 1763, however, Rio de Janeiro ceased to be a separate province.

Governors

1565-1567	Estácio de Sá
1567-1571	Salvador Correia de Sá (1)
1571-1573	Cristóvão de Barros
1574-1578	António de Salema
1578-1598	Salvador Correia de Sá (2)
1598-1602	Francisco de Mendonça e Vasconcelos
1602-1608	Martim de Sá (1)
1608-1614	Afonso de Albuquerque
1614-1617	Costantino de Menelau
1617-1620	Rui Vaz Pinto
1620-1623	Francisco de Fajardo
1623-1632	Martim de Sá (2)
1633-1637	Rodrigo de Miranda Henriques
1637-1643	Salvador Correia de Sá e Benevides (1)
1643-1644	Luís Barbalho Bezerra
1644-1645	Francisco de Souto-Maior
1645-1648	Duarte Correia Vasqueanes (1)
1648	Salvador Correia de Sá e Benevides (2)
1648	Duarte Correia Vasqueanes (2)
1648-1649	Luís de Almeida, Conde de Avintes (1)
1649-1651	Salvador de Brito Pereira
1651-1652	António Galvão
1652-1657	Luís de Almeida, Conde de Avintes (2)
1657-1659	Tomás Correia de Alvarenga
1659-1662	Salvador Correia de Sá e Benevides (3)

1662-1666	Pedro de Melo
1666-1669	Pedro de Mascarenhas
1669-1675	João da Silva e Sousa
1675-1679	Matias da Cunha
1679-1681	João Tavares Roldão
1681-1682	Pedro Gomes
1682-1686	Duarte Teixeira Chaves
1686-1689	João Furtado de Mendonça
1689-1690	Francisco Naper de Lencastre
1690-1693	Luís César de Meneses
1693-1694	António Pais de Sande
1694-1695	André Cusaco
1695-1697	Sebastião de Castro e Caldas
1697-1702	Artur de Sá e Meneses
1702-1704	Álvaro da Silveira e Albuquerque
1705-1709	Femão Martins Mascarenhas e Lencastre
1709-1710	António de Albuquerque Coelho de Carvalho (1)
1710-1711	Francisco de Castro Morais
1711-1713	António de Albuquerque Coelho de Carvalho (2)
1713-1716	Francisco Xavier de Távora
1716-1717	Manuel de Almeida Castelo Branco
1717-1719	António de Brito Freire de Meneses
1719-1725	Aires de Saldanha de Albuquerque Coutinho Matos e Noronha
1725-1732	Luís Vahia Monteiro
1732-1733	Manuel de Freitas da Fonseca
1733-1763	Gomes Freire de Andrade

Coaracy, 3:481–506.

311 RIO GRANDE DO NORTE

Rio Grande (do Norte)[1] was one of the fourteen donatárias created between 1534 and 1536 (v. Brazil) but efforts to settle the area failed and its donatário sold his rights to the Portuguese crown. After 1597 the area was settled from Pernambuco (q.v.) and governed by capitães-mores (except for the period of Dutch rule, 1633–54) until 1701 when these were replaced by governors, still under the authority, however, of Pernambuco. In 1822 Rio Grande do Norte became a province of the empire of Brazil.

Capitães-Mores

1598–	Jerónimo de Albuquerque (1)
1599–1603	João Rodrigues Colaço
1603–1610	Jerónimo de Albuquerque (2)
1610–1613	Lourenço Peixoto Cirne
1613–1615	Francisco Caldeira de Castelo Branco
1615–1617	Estêvão Soares de Albergaria
1617–1621	Ambrósio Machado de Carvalho
1621–1624	André Pereira Temudo
1624–	Francisco Gomes de Melo
–	Bernardo da Mota
–1631	Domingos da Veiga Cabral
1631–1633	Cipriano Portocarreiro
1633	Pedro Mendes de Gouveia
1633–1654	(under the Netherlands)
1654–1663	António Vaz Gondim (1)
1663–1670	Valentim Tavares Cabral
1670–1673	António de Barros Rêgo e Catanho
1673–1677	António Vaz Gondim (2)
1677–1678	Francisco Pereira Guimarães
1679–1681	Geraldo de Suni
1681–1682	António da Silva Barbosa
1682–1685	Manuel Muniz
1685–1688	Pascoal Gonçalves de Carvalho
1688–1692	Agostinho César de Andrade (1)
1692–1693	Sebastião Pimentel
1694–1695	Agostinho César de Andrade (2)

1697–1701	Bernardo Vieira de Melo

Governors

1701–1705	António de Carvalho e Almeida
1705–1708	Sebastião Nunes Colares
1708–1711	André Nogueira da Costa
1711–1715	Salvador Álvares da Silva
1715–1718	Domingos Amado
1718–1722	Luís Ferreira Freire
1722–1728	João Pereira da Fonseca
1728–1731	Domingos de Morais Navarro
1731–1734	João de Barros Braga
1734–1739	João de Teive Barreto e Meneses
1739–1751	Francisco Xavier de Miranda Henriques
1751–1757	Pedro de Albuquerque e Melo
1757–1760	João Coutinho de Bragança
1760–1774	Joaquim Félix de Lima
1774–1791	(Senado da Câmara)[2]
1791–1800	Caetano da Silva Sanches
1800–1802	(junta)
1802–1805	Lopo Joaquim de Almeida Henriques
1806–1811	José Francisco de Paula Cavalcanti de Albuquerque
1812–1816	Sebastião Francisco de Melo e Póvoas
1816–1821	José Inácio Borges

1. Initially this captaincy was called simply Rio Grande, but the creation of Rio Grande de São Pedro, or Rio Grande do Sul (q.v.), necessitated the adding of "do Norte" to distinguish this Rio Grande from its southern counterpart.

2. For details of the administrators during this period, see Varnhagen, 5:331–32.

Cascudo, pp. 441–46; Lira, pp. 159–210.

312 RIO GRANDE DO SUL

The area of Rio Grande do Sul in southern Brazil was settled by gaucho elements early in the 18th century. This settlement was countenanced by the Portuguese government as it was thought imperative that the area south of São Paulo (q.v.) be occupied to connect up with Nova Colônia do Sacramento (q.v.) on the Rio de la Plata estuary. From 1737 to 1761 Rio Grande do Sul was governed by military commandants since the area was subject to constant intrusions from Spanish territory to the west (v. Paraguay, 370). The colony was under Rio de Janeiro until 1807, when it was erected into a separate captaincy-general. During its colonial existence Rio Grande do Sul was known as Rio Grande do São Pedro. Gradually it came to be distinguished from and contrasted with Rio Grande do Norte and began to be called Rio Grande do Sul.

Military Commandants

1737	João da Silva Pais
1737-1739	André Ribeiro Coutinho
1739-1752	Diogo Osório Cardosa
1752-1761	Pascual de Azevedo

Governors

1761-1763	Inácio Elói de Madureira
1763-1764	Luís Manuel da Silva Pais
1764-1769	José Custódio de Sá e Faria
1769-1771	José Marcelino de Figueiredo[1] (1)
1771-1773	António da Veiga de Andrade
1773-1780	José. Marcelino de Figueiredo (2)

1780-1801	Sebastião Xavier da Veiga Cabral da Câmara
1801-1803	Francisco João Rossio
1803-1809	Paulo José da Silva Gama
1809-1814	Diogo de Sousa
1814-1818	Luís Teles da Silva Caminha e Meneses, Marquês de Alegrete
1818-1820	José Maria Rita de Castelo Branco Correia da Cunha Vasconcelos e Sousa, Conde de Figueira
1821	João Carlos Gregório Domingues Vicente Francisco de Saldanha Oliveira e Daun

1. His real name was Manuel Jorge Gomes de Sepúlveda. He used the alias of José Marcelino de Figueiredo in Brazil to avoid prosecution for the murder of an English officer in Portugal. Later he returned to Portugal and resumed his true name. See Florência de Abreu, "Govêrno de José Marcelino de Figueiredo no govêrno de São Pedro—1769 a 1780," *Congresso sulriograndense de história e geográfia, Anais* (1937), 2, no. 3:177—204.

Information from Ney Brito, Chefe da Casa Civil, Gabinete do Governador de Rio Grande do Sul, Pôrto Alegre, Rio Grande do Sul. Also, Spalding, pp. 85—87.

313 SANTA CATARINA

The creation of Nova Colônia do Sacramento (q.v.) necessitated the settlement and administrative organization of the territory south of São Paulo (q.v.) in order to provide logistical support to the isolated Sacramento. The island of Santa Catarina had been granted as a donatária in 1664 but this was never implemented. A settlement established in 1662 was likewise soon abandoned. However, in 1739 Santa Catarina, like its neighbor Rio Grande do Sul (q.v.), was organized and in the next decade the island and the adjacent area inland from the coast were systematically settled from the Azores (q.v.). In this way a continuous settlement was created as far as Sacramento. Santa Catarina remained subordinate to Rio de Janeiro (q.v.). In 1822 it became a provin of the empire of Brazil.

Governors

1739-1749	José da Silva Pais
1749-1753	Manuel Escudeiro Ferreira de Sousa
1753-1762	José de Melo Manuel
1762-1765	Francisco António Cardoso de Meneses e Sousa
1765-1775	Francisco de Sousa Meneses

1775-1777	Pedro António da Gama Freitas
1777-1779	Francisco António da Veiga Cabral da Câmara
1779-1786	Francisco de Barros de Morais Araújo Teixeira Homem
1786-1791	José Pereira Pinto
1791-1793	Manuel Soares Coimbra
1793-1800	João Alberto de Miranda Ribeiro

1800-1805   Joaquim Xavier Curado   1817-1821   João Vieira Tovar de Albuquerque
1805-1817   Luís Maurício da Silveira   1821-1822   Tomé Joaquim Pereira Valente

Cabral, pp. 74—106; Varnhagen, 5:362—64.

314 SÃO JORGE DA MINA

In 1482 the Portuguese established a post on the Gold coast of West Africa, optimistically naming it São Jorge da Mina in the hope of utilizing it to exploit the putatively large trade in gold. This hope was never realized, and after 1530 São Jorge da Mina declined in prosperity. The advent of French and Dutch competition later in the 16th century accelerated this decline. In 1596 the Dutch attacked but failed to capture São Jorge. Finally, in 1637 the Dutch did seize São Jorge da Mina, and five years later the neighboring Portuguese post at Axim (v. Gold Coast, 268). With this the Portuguese disappeared from the Gold Coast, confining their activities in the area to their colony of São Tomé and Príncipe (q.v.) and the Niger delta area, and later at Ouidah (v. Dahomey). The following list must be considered incomplete.

Capitães-Mores

1482-1484	Diogo de Azambuja	1550-1552	Diogo Soares de Albergaria (2)
1486	Álvaro Vaz Pestano	1552-1555	Rui de Melo
1487	João Fogaça	1557	Afonso Gonçalves Botafogo
1493	Lopo Soares de Albergaria	-1562	Rui Gomes de Azevedo
1502	Nuno Vaz de Castelo Branco	1562-	Manuel de Mesquita Perestrelo
1504	António de Miranda de Azevedo	1564-	Martim Afonso
1504-1505	Diogo Lopes de Sequeira	1570-	António de Sá
1505-	Martinho da Silva	1574	Mendo da Mota
1508-1509	Bobadilha	1579	Vasco Fernandes Pimentel
1509-1510	Manuel de Góis	-1584	João Rodrigues Peçanha
-1513	Afonso Caldeira	1584-	Bernardino Ribeiro Pacheco
1517-1519	Fernão Lopes Correia	1586-1595	João Róis Coutinho
1519-1522	Duarte Pacheco Pereira	-	Duarte Lôbo da Gama
1522-1524	Afonso de Albuquerque	1597-1608	Cristóvão da Gama
1524-1525	João de Barros	1608-1613	Duarte de Lima
1529-	Estêvão da Gama	1613	João do Crasto
1536-1539	Manuel de Albuquerque	1613-1615	Pero da Silva
1539-1541	António de Miranda	1616-1624	Manuel da Cunha e Teive
-	Fernão Cardoso	1624-1625	Francisco de Souto-Maior
1541-	Lopo de Sousa Coutinho (1)	-	Luís Tomé de Castro
1545-	Diogo Soares de Albergaria (1)	-1629	João da Sera de Morais
1548-1550	Lopo de Sousa Coutinho (2)	1632-1634	Pedro de Mascarenhas
		1634-	António da Rocha Magalhães

Brásio, vols. 1–3, 5–8, passim; Furley, "Notes"; idem, "Provisional List." For the directors of the post at Ouidah, see Akinjogbin, pp. 217, and Verger, passim.

315 SÃO JOSÉ DO RIO NEGRO

Until 1750 the area of the upper Amazon was contested between Portugal and Spain. By the
Treaty of Madrid in that year boundaries between the two countries' possessions were tenta-
tively demarcated. Heretofore the area claimed by Portugal had been administered as part of
Grão-Pará. In the hope of stabilizing control of the area a new province was created in 1757,
that of São José do Rio Negro, with its capital at Manaus. São José do Rio Negro remained
subordinate to Grão-Pará until 1822. The province was suppressed in that year, the only one in
Brazil not retained as a province under the empire. However, in 1850—52 the province of
Amazonas, substantially representing the old captaincy of São José do Rio Negro, was created.

Governors			
1758-1760	Joaquim de Melo e Póvoas	1783	João Baptista Mardel
1760-1761	Gabriel de Sousa Filgueiras	1784	Sebastião Eusébio de Matos
1761-1763	Valério Correia Botelho de Andrade	1785	António Francisco Mendes
1763-1779	Joaquim Tinoco Valente	1786	José Gomes da Silva
1779	António Nunes	1786-1799	Manuel da Gama Lôbo de Almada
1780	Domingos Franco de Carvalho	1799-1804	José António Salgado
1781	Filipe Serrão de Castro	1804-1805	José Simões de Carvalho
1782	Bento José do Rêgo	1806-1818	José Joaquim Vitório da Costa
		1818-1821	Manuel Joaquim do Paço

Ferreira, "Diário," 49:269—72; Varnhagen, 5:372—74.

316 SÃO PAULO

In 1681 the capital of the captaincy of São Vicente (q.v.) was moved from Santos to São Paulo.
In 1710 the donatárias of São Vicente, Santo Amaro, and Itanhaêm were sold to the Portuguese
crown and these areas, together with the vast area in the interior recently settled, were formed
into the new province of São Paulo e Minas do Ouro. The expansion into the interior proved to
be so great that by 1750 Minas Gerais, Goiás, and Mato Grosso (qq.v.) had been separated from
São Paulo. In 1822 São Paulo became a province of the empire of Brazil.

São Paulo e Minas do Ouro
Governors

1710-1713	António de Albuquerque Coelho de Carvalho	1732-1737	António Luís de Távora, Conde de Sarzedas
1713-1717	Brás Baltasar da Silveira	1737-1739	Gomes Freire de Andrade
1717-1721	Pedro (or João) de Almeida e Portugal, Conde de Assumar	1739-1748	Luís de Mascarenhas
		1748-1763	(under Rio de Janeiro)
		1763-1765	António Álvares da Cunha, Conde da Cunha

São Paulo
Governors

1721-1726	Rodrigo César de Meneses	1765-1775	Luís António de Sousa Botelho e Mourão
1726-1727	Domingos Rodrigues da Fonseca Leme	1775-1782	Martim Lopes Lôbo de Saldanha
		1782-1786	Francisco da Cunha Meneses
1727-1732	António da Silva Caldeira Pimentel	1786-1788	José Raimundo Chicorro da Gama Lôbo
		1788-1797	Bernardo José da Silveira Lorena, Conde de Sarzedas

1797–1802	António Manuel de Melo Castro e Mendonça	1814–1817	Francisco de Assis Mascarenhas, Conde da Palma
1802–1811	António José da Fonseca e Horta	1817–1819	(council)
1811–1813	Luís Teles da Silva Caminha e Meneses, Marquês de Alegrete	1819–1821	João Carlos Augusto de Oeynhausen e Gravenburg

Varnhagen, 5:356–59.

317 SÃO TOMÉ AND PRÍNCIPE

The islands of São Tomé and Príncipe are located in the Gulf of Guinea near the coast of Africa. They were discovered by the Portuguese in 1470. São Tomé, much the larger of the two islands, was granted as a donatária in 1485, but reverted to the control of the crown in 1522. Príncipe was a donatária from 1500 to 1753.[1] Before 1586 São Tomé was ruled by capitães-mores. In that year a governor was appointed to replace the capitão-mor. From 1641 to 1644 the Dutch, intent on replacing the Portuguese along the West African coast (v. São Jorge da Mina and Angola, and the Dutch Gold Coast, 268), occupied São Tomé, but not Príncipe. Since 1648 São Tomé and Príncipe have remained Portuguese possessions. In 1951 the colony was constituted an overseas territory.

São Tomé

Capitães-Mores

1485–1490	João da Paiva
1490–1493	João Pereira
1493–1499	Álvaro da Caminha Souto-Maior
1499–1510	Fernão de Melo
1516	Diogo de Alcáçova
1517–1522	João de Melo
1522–	Vasco Estevens
1531–1535	Henrique Pereira
1541–1545	Diogo Botelho Pereira
1546–1554	Francisco de Barros de Paiva
1558	Pedro Botelho
1560–1564	Cristóvão Dória de Sousa
1564–1569	Francisco de Gouveia
1569–1571	Francisco de Paiva Teles
1571–1575	Diogo Salema
1575–1582	António Monteiro Maciel
1584	Francisco Fernandes de Figueiredo

Governors

1586–1587	Francisco Fernandes de Figueiredo
1587–1591	Miguel Teles de Moura
1591–1592	Duarte Peixoto da Silva
1592–1593	Francisco de Vila Nova
1593–1597	Fernando de Meneses
1597–1598	Vasco de Carvalho
1598–1601	João Barbosa da Cunha (1)
1601–1604	António Maciel Monteiro
1604–	Pedro Botelho de Andrade
–1609	João Barbosa da Cunha (2)
1609	Fernando de Noronha

1609	João Barbosa da Cunha (3)
1609–1611	Costantino Lôbo Tavares
1611	João Barbosa da Cunha (4)
1611	Francisco Teles de Meneses
1611–1613	Luís Dias de Abreu (1)
1613–1614	Feliciano Coelho Carvalho
1614–1616	Luís Dias de Abreu (2)
1616–1620	Miguel Correia Baharem
1620–1621	Pedro da Cunha
1621–1623	Félix Pereira
1623–1627	Jerónimo de Melo Fernando
1627–1628	André Gonçalves Maracote
1628–1632	Lourenço Pires de Távora (1)
1632	Francisco Barreto de Meneses
1632–1636	Lourenço Pires de Távora (2)
1636	António de Sousa de Carvalho
1636–1640	Lourenço Pires de Távora (3)
1640	Manuel Quaresma Carneiro
1640–1641	Miguel Pereira de Melo e Albuquerque
1641–1642	Paulo da Ponte
1642–1650	Lourenço Pires de Távora (4)
1656–1657	Cristóvão de Barros do Rêgo
1661	Pedro da Silva
1669–1671	Paulo Ferreira de Noronha
1671–1673	(Senado da Câmara)
1673–1677	Julião de Campos Barreto
1677–1680	Bernardim Freire de Andrade
1680–1683	Jacinto de Figueiredo e Abreu
1683–1686	João Álvares da Cunha
1686	António Pereira de Brito Lemos
1686–1689	Bento de Sousa Lima

Portugal

1689-1693	António Pereira de Lacerda
1693-1694	António Pereira de Barredo
1695-1696	José Pereira Sodré
1696-1697	João da Costa Matos
1697-1702	Manuel António Pinheiro da Câmara
1702-1709	José Correia de Castro
1709-1710	Vicente Dinís Pinheiro
1710-1715	(junta)
1715-1716	Bartolomeu da Costa Ponte
1717-1720	António Furtado Mendonça
1720-1722	(junta)
1722-1727	José Pinheiro da Câmara
1727-1734	Serafim Teixeira Sarmento
1734-1736	Lope de Sousa Coutinho (1)
1736-1741	José Caetano Souto-Maior
1741	António Ferrão de Castelo Branco
1741-1744	(Senado da Câmara)
1744	Francisco Luís da Conceição
1744-1745	Francisco de Alva Brandão
1745-1747	(Senado da Câmara)
1747-1748	Francisco Luís das Chagas
1748-1751	(Senado da Câmara)
1751	António Rodrigues Neves
1751-1753	(Senado da Câmara)

São Tomé and Príncipe

Governors

1753-1755	(Senado de Câmara)
1755	Lopo de Sousa Coutinho (2)
1755-1758	(Senado da Câmara)
1758-1761	Luís Henrique da Mota e Melo
1761-1767	(Senado da Câmara)
1767-1768	Lourenço Lôbo de Almeida Garcês Palha
1768-1770	(Senado da Câmara)
1770-1778	Vicente Gomes Ferreira
1778-1782	João Manuel de Azambuja
1782-1788	Cristóvão Xavier de Sá
1788-1797	João Resende Tavares Leote
1797	Inácio Francisco de Nóbrega Sousa Coutinho
1797-1799	(juntas)
1799-1802	João Baptista da Silva
1802-1805	Gabriel António Franco de Castro
1805-1817	Luís Joaquim Lisboa
1817-1824	Filipe de Freitas
1824-1830	João Maria Xavier de Borto
1830-1834	Joaquim Bento da Fonseca
1836-1837	Fernando Correia Henriques de Noronha
1837-1838	Leandro José da Costa (1)
1838-1839	José Joaquim de Urbanski
1839-1843	José Fernandes da Costa
1839-1843	Bernardo José de Sousa Soares de Andréa
1843	Leandro José da Costa (2)
1843-1846	José Maria Marques (1)
1847	Leandro José da Costa (3)

1847	Carlos Augusto de Morais e Almeida
1848-1849	José Caetano René Vimont Pessôa
1849-1851	Leandro José da Costa (4)
1851-1853	José Maria Marques (2)
1853-1855	Francisco José de Pina Rolo
1855-1857	Adriano Maria Passalaqua
1858	Francisco António Correia
1859-1860	Luís José Pereira e Horta
1860-1862	José Pedro de Melo
1862-1863	José Eduardo da Costa Moura
1863-1864	João Baptista Brunachy (1)
1864-1865	Estanislau Xavier de Assunção e Almeida (1)
1865-1867	João Baptista Brunachy (2)
1867	António Joaquim da Fonseca
1867-1869	Estanislau Xavier de Assunção e Almeida (2)
1869-1872	Pedro Carlos de Aguiar Craveiro Lopes
1872-1873	João Clímaco de Carvalho
1873-1876	Gregório Jose Ribeiro
1876-1879	Estanislau Xavier de Assunção e Almeida (3)
1879	Francisco Joaquim Ferreira do Amaral
1879-1880	Custódio Miguel de Borja (1)
1880-1881	Vicente Pinheiro Lôbo Machado de Melo e Almada
1881-1882	Augusto Maria Leão
1882-1884	Francisco Teixeira da Silva
1884-1886	Custódio Miguel de Borja (2)
1886-1890	Augusto César Rodrigues Sarmento
1890-1891	Firmeno José da Costa
1891-1894	Francisco Eugénio Pereira de Miranda
1895-1897	Cipriano Leite Pereira Jardim
1897-1899	Joaquim da Graça Correia e Lança
1899-1901	Amâncio de Alpoim Cerqueira Borges Cabral
1901-1902	Joaquim Xavier de Brito
1902-1903	João Abel Antunes Mesquita Guimarães
1903	João Gregório Duarte Ferreira (1)
1903-1907	Francisco de Paula Cid
1907-1908	Pedro Berquó
1909-1910	José Augusto Vieira da Fonseca
1910	Jaime Daniel Leite do Rêgo (1)
1910	Henrique Alberto de Oliveira
1910	Carlos de Mendonça Pimentel e Melo
1910-1911	António Pinto Miranda Guedes
1911	Jaime Daniel Leite do Rêgo (2)
1911-1913	Mariano Martins
1913-1917	Pedro do Amaral Boto Machado
1917-1918	Rafael dos Santos Oliveira
1918-1919	José Gregório Duarte Ferreira (2)
1919-1920	Avelino Augusto de Oliveira Leite
1920-1921	Eduardo Nogueira de Lemos

1921–1924	António José Pereira	1941–1945	Amadeu Gomes de Figueiredo
1924–1926	Eugénio de Barros Soares Branco	1945–1953	Carlos de Sousa Gorgulho
1926–1928	José Duarte Junqueira Rato	1953–1957	Francisco António Pires Barata
1928–1929	Sebastião José Barbosa	1957–1963	Manuel Marques de Abrantes
1929–1933	Luís António Vieira Fernandes		Amaral
1933–1941	Ricardo Vaz Monteiro	1963—	António Jorge da Silva Sebastião

1. For the donatários, see Lopes de Lima, 2, pt. 1:39, and 2, pt. 2:3—7, 23—25.

Information from Manuel Santos Estevens, Biblioteca Nacional de Lisboa, Lisbon, Portugal. Also, "Alguns dados estatísticos sôbres S. Tomé e Príncipe"; Brásio, vols. 1, 2, and 3, passim; Lopes de Lima, 2, pt. 1:39—40.

318 SÃO VICENTE AND ITANHAÊM

São Vicente, established in 1532, was the first permanent Portuguese settlement in Brazil. Two years later it was created a donatária. The neighboring donatárias of Santo Amaro, Santana, and Itamaracá were usually held by the donatário of São Vicente. In 1624 a dispute over succession rights to these donatárias led to a century of litigation and much confusion in the administrative history of São Vicente. The donatária of Itanhaêm was created, while São Vicente, however improperly, came to be called Santo Amaro as well as São Vicente. Itanhaêm, or more properly Nossa Senhora da Conceição de Itanhaêm, was largely a paper donatária and its history is inextricably bound up with that of São Vicente. It was often carelessly referred to as São Vicente. The capitães-mores were appointed by donatários and often served in both provinces simultaneously by default. These factors make it impossible to completely distinguish the capitães-mores of São Vicente from those of Itanhaêm and the following lists should be viewed with this in mind. In 1657 Paranaguá was separated from Itanhaêm and created a separate donatária. In 1710 the donatários de São Vicente (with Santo Amaro and Santana) sold their holdings to the Portuguese crown and these donatárias were integrated into the new royal province of São Paulo e Minas do Ouro (q.v.). Itanhaêm remained a donatário until 1755 when the crown purchased the rights to it and it was annexed to São Paulo.

	São Vicente	1595–1598	João Pereira de Sousa
Capitães-Mores		1598	Roque Barreto (1)
1533–1538	Gonçalo Monteiro	1598–1602	Diogo Arias Aguirre
1538–1542	António de Oliveira (1)	1602	Pedro Vaz de Barros (1)
1542–1545	Cristóvão de Aguiar de Altero	1602–1605	Roque Barreto (2)
1545–1549	Brás Cubas (1)	1605	Pedro Vaz de Barros (2)
1549–1552	António de Oliveira (2)	1605–1607	Pedro Cubas
1552–1554	Brás Cubas (2)	1607–1608	António Pedroso de Barros
1554–1556	Gonçalo Afonso	1608–1612	Gaspar Coqueiro
1556–1557	Jorge Ferreira (1)	1612	Luís de Freitas Matoso
1557–1559	António Rodrigues de Almeida (1)	1612–1613	Nuno Pereira Freire
1559–1563	Francisco de Morais Barreto	1613	Roque Barreto (3)
1563–1567	Pedro Ferraz Barreto	1613–1614	Francisco de Sá Souto-Maior
1567–1569	Jorge Ferreira (2)	1614	Domingos Pereira Jácome
1569–1571	António Rodrigues de Almeida (2)	1614–1615	Paulo da Rocha e Sequeira
1571–1573	Pedro Colaço Villela	1615–1617	Baltasar de Seixas Rabêlo (1)
1573–1580	Jerónimo Leitão (1)	1617–1618	Gonçalo Correia de Sá (1)
1580–1583	António de Proença	1618–1619	Martim Correia de Sá
1583–1592	Jerónimo Leitão (2)	1619–1620	Baltasar de Seixas Rabêlo (2)
1592–1595	Jorge Correia	1620–1622	Manuel Rodrigues de Morais

Portugal

1622	João de Moura Fogaça (1)	1690-1691	Manuel Peixoto da Mota (1)
1622-1624	Fernão Vieira Tavares	1691-1692	Manuel Pereira da Silva
1624-1626	Álvaro Luís do Vale (1)	1692-1694	Manuel Peixoto da Mota (2)
1626	João de Moura Fogaça (2)	1694-1695	Manuel Garcia
1626-1632	Gonçalo Correia de Sá (2)	1695	Simão de Toledo Piza
1632	Pedro da Mota Leite	1695-1698	Pedro Rodrigues Sanches
1632-1635	Francisco da Costa	1698-1702	Gaspar Teixeira de Azevedo
1635-1638	Francisco da Rocha	1702-1703	Tomás da Costa Barbosa
1638-1639	António de Aguiar Barriga	1703-1704	António Correia de Lemos
1639-1640	Vasco da Mota	1704-1707	José de Godói Moreira
1640	João Luís Mafra	1707-1709	João de Campos e Matos
1640-1641	Calixto da Mota	1709-1710	Francisco do Amaral Coutinho
1641-1642	Gonçalo Correia de Sá (3)		
1642	Gaspar de Sousa Ulhôa		*Itanhaêm*
1642	Francisco da Fonseca Falcão	*Capitães-Mores*	
1642-1644	António Ribeiro de Morais	1624-1626	João de Moura Fogaça
1644	Jacques Félix	1626-1630	Gonçalo Correia de Sá
1644-1647	António Lopes da Costa	1630-1633	João Luís Mafra
1647-1649	Manuel Carvalho	1633-1636	Francisco da Rocha
1649	Manuel Pereira Lôbo	1636-1639	Vasco da Mota
1649-1650	Dionísio da Costa	1640-1646	António Barbosa de Morais (or de
1650-1652	Álvaro Luís do Vale (2)		Aguiar)
1652	Francisco Álvaro Marinho	1646-1648	Valério de Carvalho
1652-1653	Gonçalo Couraça de Mesquita (1)	1649-1651	Dionísio da Costa (1)
1653	Valério Carvalho	1651-1652	António Lopes da Costa
1653-1654	Jorge Fernandes da Fonseca (1)	1652-1653	Jorge Fernandes da Fonseca
1654-1656	Gonçalo Couraça de Mesquita (2)	1653-1654	Dionísio da Costa (2)
1656	Simão Dias da Fonseca	1654-1656	Diogo Vaz de Escobar
1656-1657	Manuel de Sousa da Silva	1656-1660	Simão Dias de Moura
1657-1658	Manuel de Quevedo e Vasconcelos	1660-1662	António Barbosa Souto-Maior
1658-1660	Jerónimo Pantojo Leitão	1662-1666	João Blan
1660-1662	Jorge Fernandes da Fonseca (2)	1667-1670	Roque Leitão Roballo
1662-1665	António Raposo da Silveira	1670-1677	Henrique Roballo Leitão
1665	Cipriano Tavares	–	Sebastião de Moura Pereira
1665-1666	Tomás Fernandes de Oliveira (1)	–	Jordão Homem da Costa
1666-1668	Agostinho de Figueiredo	1679-1685	Luís Lopes de Carvalho
1668-1669	Jorge Bron	1685-	Filipe Carneiro de Alcáçova
1669-1670	Henrique Leitão Robalo	1691-1697	Martim Garcia Lumbria
1670-1675	Atanásio da Mota	1697-1699	Carlos Pedroso da Silveira (1)
1675-1678	Tomás Fernandes de Oliveira (2)	1699-1701	Tomé Monteiro de Faria
1678-1679	Diogo Pinto do Rêgo (1)	1701-1702	Carlos Pedroso da Silveira (2)
1679-1681	Luís Lopes Carvalho	1702-1705	Miguel Teles da Costa
1681-1684	Diogo Pinto do Rêgo (2)	1705-	Carlos Pedroso da Silveira (3)
1684	Diogo Arias de Araújo	–	João Pimenta de Carvalho
1684-1687	Pedro Taques de Almeida	1720-1721	Francisco Cordeiro de Carvalho
1687-1690	Filipe de Carvalho	1721-	António Caetano Pinto Coelho

For São Vicente, Calixto, "Capitanias Paulistas," pp. 282—98, and Martins dos Santos, 1:219—2?
for Itanhaêm, Calixto, "Capitania de Itanhaen," pp. 426—85.

319 SERGIPE D'EL REI

The area of Sergipe, in northeast Brazil, was settled from Bahia (q.v.) in 1590. From 1637 to 1648 Sergipe, like all of northeastern Brazil, was disputed by the Portuguese and the Dutch and no organized government existed in the area. Until 1821 Sergipe was governed by capitães-mores who were subordinate to the governor-general (later governor) at Bahia. In 1821 it became a separate province, the last one to be created in Brazil. However, its separate existence was very brief for in 1822 it became a province of the empire of Brazil.

Capitães-Mores

1590–1591	Cristóvão de Barros
1591–1595	Tomé da Rocha (1)
1595–1600	Diogo de Quadros
1600–1602	Manuel Miranda Barbosa
1602–1603	Cosme Barbosa
1603–1606	Tomé da Rocha (2)
1606–	Nicolão Faleiro de Vasconcelos
–1611	António Pinheiro de Carvalho
1611–1614	João Mendes (1)
1614–	Amaro da Cruz Portocarreiro (1)
1621–1623	João Mendes (2)
1626–1630	Amaro da Cruz Portocarreiro (2)
1630–1636	Pedro Barbosa
1636–1637	João Rodrigues Molenar
1637–1640	(under the Netherlands)
1640–1645	(Portuguese)
1645–1648	(under the Netherlands)
1648–1651	Baltasar de Quierós de Sequeira
1651–1654	João Ribeiro Vila Franca (1)
1654–1655	Manuel Pestana de Brito
1655–1656	João Ribeiro Vila Franca (2)
1656–1657	Baltasar dos Reis Barrenhos
1657	Manuel de Barros
1657–1659	Jerónimo de Albuquerque
1659–1662	Francisco de Brás
1663–1664	Ambrósio Luís de Lapenha
1664–1666	Álvaro Correia de Freitas
1666–1669	António de Alemão
1669–1671	José Rabelo Leite
1671–1678	João Munhós
1678–1681	António Prégo de Castro
1681–1682	Manuel de Abreu Soares

1682–1687	Brás da Rocha Cardoso
1687–1690	Jorge de Barros Leite (1)
1690–1692	Brás Soares dos Passos
1692–1695	Gonçalo de Lemos Mascarenhas
1696–1704	Sebastião Nunes Colares
1704–1708	Fernando Lôbo de Sousa
1708–1712	Salvador da Silva Bragança
1712–1713	Jorge de Barros Leite (2)
1713–1717	António Vieira
1717–1724	Custódio Rabelo Pereira
1727	José Pereira de Araújo
1732	António Martins Fronte
1733–1737	Francisco da Costa (1)
1737–1741	Estêvão de Faria Delgado
1741–1747	Francisco da Costa (2)
1747–1751	Manuel Francisco
1751–1755	Manuel da Cruz Silva
1755	Duarte Fernandes Lôbo Pontes
1755–1759	José de Matos Henrique
1759–1765	(unknown)
1765–1766	Francisco Álves da Silva
1766–1776	José Gomes da Cruz
1776–1782	Bento José de Oliveira
1782–1790	José Caetano da Silva Loureiro
1790–1793	António Pereira Marinho
1793–1797	Valério dos Santos
1797	Joaquim José Monteiro
1797–1800	Manuel Fernandes da Silveira
1800–	(unknown)
1817–1821	António Luís da Fonseca Machado

Governor

1821	Carlos César Burlamaque

Freire, passim; Ivo do Prado, pp. 88–90.

320 TIMOR

Timor is the largest of the Lesser Sunda Islands of Indonesia. Portuguese traders frequented the area as early as 1520. From 1566 to 1613 the nearby island of Solor served as the main Portuguese base in the area.[1] Solor and the western part of Timor were seized by the Dutch early in the 17th century (v. Netherlands East Indies, 275), and the Portuguese have since occupied only

Portugal

the eastern part of the island and a small enclave on the northwest coast. Longstanding disputes regarding demarcation of the respective spheres were finally settled by treaty in 1904.

Chaotic conditions in the island prevented any successful attempt at organized administration before 1702, although governors were sporadically appointed before this.[1] Until 1844 Timor was under Portuguese India (q.v.) and from 1844 to 1896 it was subordinated to Macao (q.v.). After 1896 it was a separate colony. Like the other Portuguese colonies, Timor became an overseas territory in 1951. It was occupied by the Japanese from 1942 to 1945.

Governors

1702–1705	António Coelho Guerreiro
1705–1706	Lourenço Lopes
1706–1708	Manuel Ferreira de Almeida (1)
1708–1709	Jácome de Morais Sarmento
1709–1714	Manuel de Souto-Maior
1714	Manuel Ferreira de Almeida (2)
1714–1718	Domingos da Costa
1718–1719	Francisco de Melo e Castro
1719–1722	Manuel de Santo António
1722–1725	António de Albuquerque Coelho
1725–1729	António Moniz de Macedo (1)
1729–1731	Pedro de Melo
1731–1734	Pedro do Rêgo Barreto da Gama e Castro
1734–1739	António Moniz de Macedo (2)
1741–1745	Manuel Leonís de Castro
1745–1748	Francisco Xavier Doutel
1748–1751	Manuel Correia de Lacerda
1751–1759	Manuel Doutel de Figueiredo Sarmento
1759–1760	Sebastião de Azevedo e Brito
1760–1763	(council)
1763–1765	Dionísio Gonçalves Rebêlo Galvão
1765–1768	(council)
1768–1776	António José Teles de Meneses
1776–1779	Caetano de Lemos Telo de Meneses
1779–1782	Lourenço de Brito Correia
1782–1785	João Anselmo de Almeida Soares
1785–1788	João Baptista Vieira Godinho
1788–1790	Feliciano António Nogueira Lisboa
1790–1794	Joaquim Xavier de Morais Sarmento
1794–1800	João Baptista Verquaim
1800–1804	José Joaquim de Sousa
1804–1807	João Vicente Soares da Veiga
1807–1810	António de Mendonça Corte-Real
1810	António Botelho Homem Bernardes Pessôa
1812–1815	Vítorino Freire da Cunha Gusmão
1815–1819	José Pinto Alcoforado de Azevedo e Sousa
1821–1832	Manuel Joaquim de Matos Góis
1832	Miguel da Silveira Lorena

1834–1839	José Maria Marques
1839–1844	Frederico Leão Cabreira
1844–1848	Julião José da Silva Vieira
1848–1851	António Olavo Monteiro Tôrres
1851–1852	José Joaquim Lopes de Lima
1852–1856	Manuel de Saldanha da Gama
1856–1859	Luís Augusto de Almeida Macedo
1859–1863	Afonso de Castro
1863–1864	José Manuel Pereira de Almeida
1864–1866	José Eduardo da Costa Meneses
1866–1869	Francisco Teixeira da Silva
1870–1871	João Clímaco de Carvalho
1873–1876	Hugo Goodair de Lacerda Castelo Branco (1)
1876–1878	Joaquim António da Silva Ferrão
1878–1880	Hugo Goodair de Lacerda Castelo Branco (2)
1880–1881	Augusto César Cardoso de Carvalho
1882–1883	Bento da França Pinto de Oliveira
1883–1885	João Maria Pereira
1885–1887	Alfredo de Lacerda Maia
1887–1888	António Francisco da Costa
1888–1890	Rafael Jácome Lopes de Andrade
1891–1894	Cipriano Forjaz
1894–1908	José Celestino da Silva
1908–1909	Eduardo Augusto Marquês
1910	Alfredo Augusto Soveral Martins
1911–1917	Filomeno da Câmara Melo Cabral
1919–1921	Manuel Paulo de Sousa Gentil
1924–1926	Raimundo Enes Meira
1926–1928	Teófilo Duarte
1929–1930	Cesário Augusto de Almeida Viana
1930–1933	António Baptista Justo
1933–1936	Raúl de Antas Manso Preto Mende Cruz
1937–1939	Álvaro Eugénio Neves de Fontoura
1940–1942	Manuel de Abreu Ferreira de Carvalho
1942–1945	(under Japan)
1946–1950	Óscar Freire de Vasconcelos Rua
1950–1958	César Maria de Serpa Rosa
1959–1963	Filipe José Freire Temudo Barata
1963–1968	José Alberty Correia
1968–	José Nogueira Valente Pires

1. For information on the capitães-mores on Solor and Timor before 1702, see Leitão, *Os Portugueses*, passim.

Information from Amândio M. Raposo, Intendente Administrativo, Repartição Provincial dos Servi de Administração Civil, Deli, Timor. Also, Cabreira, 427–39; Leitão, *Vinte e oito aros de história de Timor*, pp. 343–46.

Bibliography: Portugal

Akinjogbin, Isaac Adeagbo. *Dahomey and its Neighbours, 1708–1818*. Cambridge: Cambridge University Press, 1967.

Alcântara Guerreiro. *Quadro sinóptico da governaçao civil e eclesiástica de Moçambique e chronologia provável desde a descoverta*. Lourenço Marques: Imprensa Nacional de Moçambique, 1954.

Alencastre, José Martins Pereira de. "Memória chronológica, histórica e corográfica da provincia do Piauhy." *Revista do Instituto histórico e geográfico brasileiro* 20(1857):5–59.

"Alguns dados estatísticos sôbre Cabo Verde." *Boletim da Agencia geral das colónias*, no. 45 (1929), pp. 221–26.

"Alguns dados estatísticos sôbre S. Tomé e Príncipe." *Boletim da Agencia geral das colónias*, no. 43(1929), pp. 159–70.

Andrade, Antônio Alberto de. *Relações de Moçambique setecentista*. Lisbon: Agencia Geral do Ultramar, 1955.

Archivo dos Açores: Publicação destinada á vulgarisação dos elementos indispensaveis para todos os ramos da história açoriana. 14 vols., nos. 1–80. Terceira: n.p., 1878–[1927].

Assis, Eugênio de. "Governos do Espírito Santo." *Revista do Instituto histórico e geográfico do Espíritu Santo*, no. 12(1939), [pp. 86–93].

Barros, João de. Continued by Diogo do Couto. *Da Asia de João de Barros e de Diogo do Couto*. 21 vols. Lisbon: Na Regia officina typografica, 1777–88.

Botelho de Sousa, Alfredo. *Subsidios para a história militar marítima da India, 1585–1669*. 4 vols. Lisbon: Imprensa da Armada and União Gráfica, 1950–56.

Boxer, Charles Ralph. *Fidalgos in the Far East (1550–1770): Fact and Fancy in the History of Macao*. The Hague: 'M. Nijhoff, 1948.

———. *Salvador de Sá and the Struggle for Brazil and Angola, 1602–1686*. London: University of London Press, 1952.

———. *Subsidios para a história dos capitães gerais e governadores de Macau (1557–1770)*. Macau: n.p., 1944.

———, and Azevedo, Carlos de. *Fort Jesus and the Portuguese in Mombasa, 1593–1729*. London: Hollis and Carter, 1960.

Braga, Teodoro. "Historia do Pará (mais dois capitães-mores no governo de capitania)." *Revista do Instituto histórico e geográfico do Pará* 3, no. 3(1920):293–98.

Brásio, António [Duarte]. *Monumenta missionaria africana: Africa ocidental*. 19 vols. to date. Lisbon: Agencia Geral do Ultramar, 1958–.

Cabral, Oswaldo R. *Santa Catharina (historia-evolução)*. São Paulo: Companhia editôra nacional, 1937.

Cabreira, António. "Um subsídio para a história de Timor." *Boletim da Sociedade de geografia de Lisboa* 60(1942):427–39.

Calixto, Benedicto. "Capitania de Itanhaen." *Revista do Instituto histórico e geográfico de São Paulo* 20(1915):401–742.

———. "Capitanias Paulistas." *Revista do Instituto histórico e geográfico de São Paulo* 21 (1916–21):89–302.

Campo Belo, Henrique Leite Pereira de Paiva de Faira Távora e Cernache, Conde de. *Governadores gerais e vice-reis do Brasil*. Lisbon: Agencia Geral do Ultramar, 1935.

Carreira, Antonio. "As Companhias Pombalinas de navegação, comércio e tráfico de escravatura entre a costa africana e o nordeste brasileiro." *Boletim cultural da Guiné Portuguesa*, nos. 89/90 (1968), pp. 5–88, and nos. 81/82(1968), pp. 301–454.

Carvalho Daemon, Bazilio. *A provincia de Espíritu-Santo, sua descoberta, história cronológica, synopsis e estatística*. Victória: Typo. do Espíritu-Santense, 1879.

Cascudo, Luís da Câmara. *História do Rio Grande do Norte*. Rio de Janeiro: Ministerio da Educação e Cultura, 1955.

Coaracy, Vivaldo. *Memórias da cidade do Rio de Janeiro*. 3 vols. Rio de Janeiro: Livraria José Olympio Editôra, 1965.

Cordeiro, Antônio. *História insulana das ilhas a Portugal sugeitas no oceano occidental*. 2 vols. Lisbon: Typographia do Panorama, 1866.

Correa, Gaspar. *Lendas da India*. 4 vols. Lisbon: Typographia da Academia Real das Sciencas, 1858–64.

Costa, F. A. Pereira da. "Governadores e capitães generaes de Pernambuco, 1654–1821." *Revista do Instituto archeológico, histórico e geográfico pernambucano*, no. 55 (1901), pp. 153–200; no. 56 (1902), pp. 97–123; no. 57 (1903), pp. 271–89; no. 58 (1903), pp. 446–59; no. 59 (1903), pp. 566–75; no. 62 (1904), pp. 546–58.

Cruz, Ernesto. *História do Pará*. 2 vols. Belém: Universidade do Pará, [1963].

Dornellas, Affonso de. *História e genealogia*. 14 vols. Lisbon: Livreria Ferin-Casa Português 1913–22.

Duarte, Fausto. "Os capitães-mores das praças da Guiné." *Boletim cultural da Guiné Portuguesa*, no. 21 (1951), pp. 173–220.

——. "Cartas de capitães-mores, feitores, bispos, visitadores e assistentes das praças e presidios da Guiné." *Boletim cultural da Guiné Portuguesa*, no. 24 (1951), pp. 761–84.

Faro, Jorge. "A organização administrativa da Guiné de 1615 a 1676." *Boletim cultural da Guiné Portuguesa*, no. 53 (1959), pp. 97–122.

Ferguson, Donald, ed. "The History of Ceylon, from the Earliest Times to 1600 A.D. as related by João de Barros and Diogo do Couto." *Journal of the Royal Asiatic Society, Ceylon Branc* 20 (1908):1–445.

Ferreira, Alexandre Rodrigues, ed. "Diário da Viagem philosophica pela capitania de São José d Rio-Negro." *Revista do Instituto histórico e geográfico brasileiro* 48, no. 1 (1885):1–234; 49, no. 1 (1886):123–288; 50, no. 2 (1887):11–141.

——. "Noticia histórica de ilha de Joanes ou Marajó." *Revista do Livro* 7, no. 26 (1964):137–64.

Ferreira Martins, José Frederico. *Crónica dos vice-reis e governadores da India*. Nôva Goa: Imprensa Nacional, 1919.

Freire, Felisbello Firmo de Oliveira. *História de Sergipe (1575–1855)*. Rio de Janeiro: Typographia Perseverança, 1891.

Furley, J.T. "Notes on Some Portuguese Governors of the Captaincy da Mina." *Transactions o, the Historical Society of Ghana* 3, no. 3 (1958):194–214.

——. "Provisional List of Some Portuguese Governors of the Captaincy da Mina." *Transactio of the Gold Coast and Togoland Historical Society* 2, no. 2 (1956):53–62.

Girão, Raimundo. *Pequena história do Ceará*. Fortaleza: Editôra Instituto do Ceará, 1962.

Lamego, Alberto. "A capitania de São Tomé sob o dominio dos donatários." *Revista do Institut histórico e geográfico brasileiro* 198 (1947):63–105.

Leitão, Humberto. *Os Portugueses em Solor e Timor de 1515 a 1702*. Lisbon: Tip. da Liga dos Combatentes da Grande Guerra, 1948.

——. *Vinte e oito anos de história de Timor (1698 a 1725)*. Lisbon: Agencia Geral do Ultram 1952.

Lemos, Vicente de. "Catálogo dos governadores geraes do Brasil." *Revista do Instituto histór e geográfico do Rio Grande do Norte* 7 (1909):183–96.

Lira, A. Tavares de. "Sinopse histórica da capitania do Rio Grande do Norte." *Anais do IV Congresso de história nacional* (1949) 2:159–210.

Lopes, António. "A capitania do Cumã." *Anais do IV Congresso de história nacional* (1949) 4:7–68.

Lopes de Lima, José Joaquim. *Ensaios sobre a estatística das possessões Portuguezas na Africa occidental e oriental, na Asia occidental, na China e na Oceania*. 5 vols. Lisbon: Imprensa Nacional, 1844–62.

Macgregor, Ian A. "The Portuguese in Malacca." *Journal of the Royal Asiatic Society, Malay Branch* 28, no. 2 (1955):5–47.

Martins dos Santos, Francisco. *História de Santos, 1532–1936*. 2 vols. São Paulo: Empreza Graphica da "Revista dos tribunães," 1937.

Medeiros, João Rodrigues Coriolano de. "Parahyba." *Revista do Instituto histórico e geográfi de São Paulo* 20 (1915):57–93.

Meireles, Mario Martins. *História do Maranhão*. Rio de Janeiro: DASP Serviço de Documentaç 1960.

Melo Barreto, João Carlos. *História da Guiné, 1418–1918*. Lisbon: Edição do Autor, 1938.

Minas Gerais, Departamento estadual de estatística. *Representação politica*. Belo Horizonte: Dep. Estadual da Estatística, 1962.

Monteiro, Jonathas da Costa Rêgo. *A colônia do Sacramento, 1680–1777*. 2 vols. Porto Alegr Livraria do globo, 1937.

Nóbrega, Apolônio. "Chefes do executivo paraibano." *Revista do Instituto histórico e geográfico brasileiro* 249 (1960):45–145.

Nobreza de Portugal: Bibliografia, biografia, cronologia, filatelia, genealogia, heráldica, historia, nobiliarquia, numismática. 3 vols. Lisbon: Editorial enciclopédia, 1960—61.

Oliveira, José Teixeira de. *História do estado do Espíritu Santo.* Rio de Janeiro: n.p., 1951.

Oliveira Tôrres, João Camillo de. *História de Minas Gerais.* 5 vols. n.p.: Difusão Pan-Americano do Libro, [1962].

Pieris, Paulus E. *Ceylon and the Portuguese, 1505—1658.* Tellippalai: American Ceylon Mission Press, 1920.

Pinto, Luiz. *Sintese histôrica da Paraiba (1501—1960).* n.p.: Gráfica Ouvidor Editôra, 1960.

Prado, Ivo do. *A capitania de Sergipe e suas ouvidorias: Memórias sobre questões de limites.* Rio de Janeiro: Papelaria Brazil, 1919.

Prado, João Fernando de Almeida. *Pernambuco e as capitanias do norte do Brasil (1530—1630).* São Paulo: Companhia Editôra Nacional, 1939.

Sales, Ernest. "Vice-Reis e governadores da India portuguesa, desde 1505 a 1910." *Revista de história* (Lisbon) 10 (1921):209—16.

Senna Barcellos, José Christiano de. *Subsidios para a história de Cabo Verde e Guiné.* 7 vols. Lisbon: Academia das Ciencas, 1898—1900.

Silva, Fernando Augusto da, and Meneses, Carlos Azevedo de. *Elucidário madeirense.* 3 vols. 2d ed. Funchal: Typographia Esperança, 1940—46.

Silva Rêgo, António da. *História das missões do padroado portuguêsa do oriente.* 1 vol. to date. Lisbon: Agência Geral das Colonias, Divisão de Publicações e Biblioteca, 1949—.

Spalding, Walter. "Governadores do Rio Grande do Sul, 1737—1963." *Revista do Instituto histórico e geográfico de Santa Maria* 2, no. 2 (1963):85—90.

Studart, Guilherme, Barão. "Geografia do Ceará." *Revista do Instituto do Ceará* 37 (1923):160—384; 38 (1924):3—124.

Studart Filho, Carlos. *O antigo estado do Maranhão e suas capitanias feudais.* Fortaleza: Imprensa Universitária do Ceará, 1960.

Teixeira, Cândido da Silva. "Companhia de Cacheu, Rios e Comercio da Guiné. Documentos para a sua história." *Boletim do Arquivo histórico colonial* 1 (1950):85—132.

Varnhagen, Francisco Adolpho de, Visconde de Pôrto Seguro. *História geral do Brasil antes da sua separação e independencia de Portugal.* 5 vols. São Paulo: Cia Melhoramentos de São Paulo, n.d.

Verger, Pierre. "Le fort portugais de Ouidah." *Études dahoméennes*, n.s., no. 4 (1965), pp. 5—50; no. 6 (1965), pp. 5—50; nos. 6/7 (1966), pp. 5—46.

Viana, Hélio. "Acrésimos a biografia de Matias de Albuquerque." *Revista do Instituto histórico e geográfico brasileiro* 151 (1961):39—55.

———. *Estudios de história colonial.* Brasiliana, vol. 261. São Paulo: Companhia Editôra Nacional, 1948.

———. *História do Brasil.* 2 vols. São Paulo: Edições Melhoramentos, 1961.

———. "Liquidação das donatárias." *Revista do Instituto histórico e geográfico brasileiro* 273 (1966):147—58.

Zuquete, Afonso. *Tratado de todos os vice-reis e governadores da India.* Lisbon: n.p., 1962.

Russia

The status of Russia as an imperial power has been summed up as "a problem of distinguishing colonies from metropolis."[1] Russia's expansion was almost entirely overland, analogous to the westward expansion of the United States after 1783, and one must decide whether occupied territory became a colony or was merely an extension of the metropolitan area. If colonialism were defined as the imposition of political and economic control over an essentially alien cultural area, then Russian imperialism would be said to have begun in the 16th century with the conquest of the Tatar khanates of Astrakhan and Kazan, and expansion eastward would in every case have to be considered a form of colonialism or colonization. For instance, Russia used Siberia as Great Britain used Australia and France used French Guiana, and Russian control over the area was achieved in a fashion reminiscent of French and later British occupation of Canada, or of Portuguese penetration into the Brazilian interior. But the areas of the Russian Empire perhaps most closely conforming to any widely accepted definition of imperialism would be Alaska and Turkestan. The khanates in Turkestan were absorbed in the latter part of the 19th century, that is, about the same time Alaska was sold to the United States. They were absorbed either as directly administered areas (Khokand) or as protectorates (Bukhara and Khiva). The area was administered by two governors-general with powers similar to colonial governors in other European imperial systems.[2] Under the Soviet regime these areas became more closely, perhaps even fully, integrated into the Soviet Union and the protectorates were abolished and replaced by Union Republics, nominally equal to those in other parts of the Soviet Union. This integration has not proceeded as far as that in the United States, where large-scale settlement and sparse previous occupation made the western areas reflections of the eastern seaboard in culture, language, and general life style, but these areas of the Soviet Union have nonetheless become progressively less distinct.

---

1. David K. Fieldhouse, *The Colonial Empires. A Comparative Survey from the Eighteenth Century* (London: Weidenfeld and Nicolson, 1966), p. 334.

2. For the governors-general of Turkestan and of the steppe, see Richard A. Pierce, *Russian Central Asia, 1867–1917: A Study in Colonial Rule* (Berkeley: University of California Press, 1960), p. 307.

321 RUSSIAN AMERICA

The coasts of Russian America, or Alaska, were explored in 1741 by the Russian navigator Vitus Bering. In 1784 the Shelekhov-Golikov Company established a post on Kodiak Island to exploit the fur trade. This was succeeded in 1799 by the Russian-American Company. Posts were established along the coast as far south as California, but the Russians began to explore the interior of Alaska only after 1833. After 1821 the Russian posts were ruled by a naval governor, although the Russian-American Company continued to administer the area until 1861 when its charter was not renewed and ownership was assumed by the state. The Crimean War had emphasized the vulnerability of this remote possession of the Russian Empire. In 1867 Russian rights to the area were sold to the United States.

Governors

1790-1818	Aleksandr Andreyevich Baranof
1818	Leontiy Adrianovich Gagemeyster
1818-1820	Semen Ivanovich Yanovskiy
1820-1825	Matvey Ivanovich Muravyev
1825-1830	Petr Togorovich Chistyakov
1830-1835	Ferdinand Petrovich von Wrangell
1835-1840	Ivan Antonovich Kupriyanov
1840-1845	Adolp Karlovich Etolin
1845-1850	Mikhail Dmitriyevich Tebenkov
1850-1853	Nikolai Yakovlevich Rosenberg
1853-1854	Aleksandr Ilyich Rudakov
1854-1859	Stefan Vasiliyevich Voyevodskiy
1859-1863	Ivan Vasiliyevich Furuhelm
1863-1867	Dmitriy Maksoutof

Michael, p. 305.

Bibliography: Russia

Michael, Henry N., ed. *Lieutenant Zagoskin's Travels in Russian America, 1842–1844. The First Ethnographic and Geographic Investigations in the Yukon and Kuskokwim Valleys of Alaska.* Arctic Institute of North America. Translations, no. 7. Toronto: University of Toronto Press, 1967.

Spain

In the 14th century the kingdom of Aragon initiated Spanish overseas expansion by conquering Sardinia. At the same time, the energies of Castile, the other major Spanish kingdom, were absorbed in the *Reconquista* . The union of the two kingdoms in 1479 and the conquest of the last Muslim state in Spain allowed the Spanish monarchy to follow the course already charted by Portugal. But although Spain had already begun the occupation of the Canary Islands and had established a post on the African coast opposite these islands, it chose not to follow the Portuguese down the western coast of Africa. Rather, the Spanish rulers accepted the proposal of Christopher Columbus, a Genoese navigator, to sail directly westward in seeking the Indies. Columbus, on his voyages from 1492 to 1504, discovered for Spain, not the East Indies, but a new continental land mass. Under terms of the Treaty of Tordesillas of 1494 Spain was granted exclusive rights to all territories discovered beyond a line drawn 370 leagues west of the Cape Verde Islands, or approximately longitude 46° west, an area which included all of North and South America except part of Brazil. In subsequent voyages, Columbus explored the West Indian islands and the coasts of Central America and of northern South America.

The true beginning of the Spanish Empire began with the conquest of the Aztec kingdom in Mexico in 1519–21. In the first years of exploration and settlement the Spaniards quickly realized that they had not in fact reached the spice-rich islands of the East Indies. The barren civilizations of the Arawaks and Caribs of the West Indian islands offered no hope of the kind of profit the Portuguese were realizing from their participation in the spice trade. Spanish chagrin and disappointment disappeared with the entry into Mexico. The astonishing ease of the conquest and the enormous wealth accruing from it radically altered the Spanish perspective and emboldened the conquistadores to further similar adventures. In 1532 the Inca kingdom in Peru, mightier than that of the Aztecs, was even more easily overthrown.

The nature of the conquest and the type of wealth available to the Spaniards necessitated heavy settlement—a commitment not required of the Portuguese. In 1535 and 1542 the viceroyalties of Nueva España and Peru were created from the territories of the conquered Aztec and Inca kingdoms. The expansion of Spanish control from these nuclear areas was rapid. By the end of the 16th century most of Mexico and Central America had been brought under the viceroyalty of Nueva España, while large areas of northern and western South America and the area of the Plate estuary and its hinterland were added to the viceroyalty of Peru. Additionally, Florida on the North American continent and parts of the

Philippine Islands had been occupied. Much of this rapid expansion can be attributed to the feeble resistance of the indigenous societies. Only in the extremities of northern Nueva España and southern Chile was Spanish control and settlement deterred by prolonged resistance. Although the Spanish colonies all received sizeable emigrations from the mother country, at least in contemporary terms, dense settlement occurred only in the areas of Peru and Nueva España, the two areas most favored with mineral wealth, the backbone of the Spanish colonial economy.

The Spanish Empire in America was the most hierarchically organized of the colonial empires. The administration was designed to reflect that already in existence in Spain to as great a degree as was possible given the intrusion of circumstances not present in the mother country. Each of the two viceroyalties was at the apex of an administrative pyramid. In theory these viceroyalties, and the various *audiencias*, were regarded as being *reinos* (kingdoms) having the same relationship with the Spanish crown as the Spanish kingdoms of Valencia, Catalonia, Aragon, León, and Castile had. That is, the tie was a dynastic one expressed through the person of the Spanish king. Pursuant to this the Spanish monarch was usually referred to as *rey de las Españas y de las Indias*, or King of the Spains and the Indies, and the Spanish Empire in the aggregate was termed *estos reinos y esos reinos*—these [peninsular] kingdoms and those [American] kingdoms. In practice this equality disappeared and Nueva España or Peru were no more equal to Castile, the premier kingdom, than was, say, Valencia.

Within and under the viceroyalties were a number of *audiencias*. The audiencia was an appellate tribunal with administrative functions. The audiencias, administered by an official called a *presidente*, were not all of equal status. The viceregal audiencias, in which the viceroy served as president, were naturally highest in rank. Next came those audiencias whose presidents held the additional military title of captain-general. These audiencias were practically independent of viceregal control and corresponded directly with Spain. Finally, there was the lowest rank of audiencia, that presided over by a *letrado*, or lawyer, who lacked any additional prestigial rank. During the 16th and 17th centuries the Spanish administrative system remained rather ossified, and it may be useful to present here schematically the audiencial structure within the viceroyalties during this period:

Viceroyalty of Nueva España
    1. Viceregal audiencia of Mexico (1529)
    2. Audiencia of Santo Domingo (1511)
       Audiencia of Panama (1538)
       Audiencia of Guatemala[1] (1544)
       Audiencia of Manila (the Philippines) (1583)
    3. Audiencia of Guadalajara (Nueva Galicia) (1549)
Viceroyalty of Peru
    1. Viceregal audiencia of Lima (1542)

---

1. Initially called *Audiencia de los Confines*.

2. Audiencia of Santa Fé de Bogotá (Nueva Granada) (1549)
    Audiencia of Chile (1609)
    Audiencia of Buenos Aires (1661—71)
3. Audiencia of Charcas (1559)
    Audiencia of Quito (1564)

Under the audiencias were a number of *gobiernos*, or provinces. Each province had a governor, and in judicial and some administrative matters it was subject to the jurisdiction of one of the audiencias, as noted in the introductions to the provinces. In civil and military matters they were autonomous and in cases where a province was also a captaincy-general its governor could be of a higher rank than the president of his audiencia.[2]

Each province was divided into a large number of smaller districts comprising a town and its surrounding hinterland. In the viceroyalty of Nueva España these units were called *alcaldia mayores*, and in the viceroyalty of Peru, *corregimientos*. Occasionally a group of these would be united, when circumstances warranted, to form a new province. The *corregidor*, or *alcalde mayor*, was regarded as the key official in the Spanish colonial administration. Certainly it was he who had the greatest impact on the population. The towns themselves were governed by *cabildos*, or municipal corporations. Only in the cabildos did the *criollos*, or colony-born Spanish, have any control. The higher offices were almost exclusively granted to *peninsulares*, or those Spaniards born in Spain.[3] The Indian populations were organized into their own *cabildo* system in Nueva España and Peru with their own *caciques*, who were often, especially in Nueva España, descendants of the preconquest Indian nobility.

After 1524 all colonial matters came under the jurisdiction of a body called the *Real y Supremo Consejo de las Indias*. The Council of the Indies was an advisory body similar to the Council of Castile. It made nominations for colonial offices and offered suggestions regarding Indian policy, territorial reorganization, economic policies, etc. Its main function was advisory, however. The crown made the decisions and the Council of the Indies implemented them. Membership on the council was considered the pinnacle of Spanish colonial service and many of the colonial viceroys, governors, and presidents closed their careers with service on the council. The Council of the Indies lingered on until 1834, but after 1714 most of its important functions were assumed by the new Ministry of Marine and the Indies.

---

2. This brief account does not include the provinces created in the first stages of Spanish expansion and given for a period of several generations, or in perpetuity, to the conquerors as *adelantados*. The adelantado, often granted unusually extensive powers, was similar to the Portuguese *donatário*, although the analogy must not be overdrawn. These provinces were invariably of brief duration, principally because the Spanish crown, jealous of the prerogatives of the adelantados, would manage to abrogate the agreements at the first opportunity.

3. Lucas Alamán, *Historia de México*, 5 vols. (Mexico City: Impr. de V. Agüeros, 1883—85), 1:57n., estimates that scarcely 2 percent of the officials of the rank of governor or higher were criollos.

In the 18th century the entire Spanish colonial administrative system underwent a radical transformation, much of which was economically induced. Like
all other European imperial powers of this time, Spain's commercial system was
based on strictly mercantilist principles. But, given the size of the Spanish
colonial empire and its lack of real compactness, the measures adopted by the
Spanish crown were unrealistically inflexible. From the colonies, all goods
destined for Spain were transported overland to specified entrepots. Each year
two convoys of ships would leave Seville. One, bound for Vera Cruz and called
the *flota*, would deliver the goods for, and collect those from, the viceroyalty of
Nueva España. The other, called the *galeones*, would proceed to Portobello or
Cartagena de Indias in the viceroyalty of Peru for the same purposes. The two
fleets were then to unite at Havana in Cuba and return to Spain. Until 1720
these fleets could sail from and return only to Seville; after 1720 Cádiz replaced Seville as the home port for the colonial trade. Intercolonial trade was
forbidden for any goods competitive with those shipped from Spain.

While enabling Spain to keep firm control of the trade to and from its colonies, this system had numerous and obvious drawbacks. The collection of
great quantities of goods, including gold and silver bullion, in one place at one
time proved tempting to Spain's enemies, and numerous raids were conducted
against these entrepots. The convoys travelling across the Atlantic also proved
choice targets. More important, such a procrustean channelization of commerce
created unnecessary and much-resented hardships for the colonists. The cost
of goods shipped to Panama and then transshipped overland as far as Río de la
Plata would be exorbitant, and artificially so. The result was an increasingly
large contraband trade, particularly in areas like Río de la Plata which were
both distant from the designated entrepots and located where accessible to the
merchants of other European nations, particularly of Great Britain. After 1700
the use of the convoy system fell into desuetude, although it was not officially
abandoned until 1789.

Having no African colonies other than a few enclaves in the north, the Spanish crown found it necessary to let contracts for the importation of slaves. An
asiento, or license, would be granted to an individual or group to provide a
specified number of slaves at a specified price over a given number of years.
The asiento system, introduced in 1518, endured until the end of the 18th century. The asiento rights came to be regarded as important enough to be ex-
torted as spoils of war by being written into treaties. Spain thereby found
itself in the unenviable position of relying on its enemies to provide it with
slaves, and at a non-competitive price unilaterally agreed upon.

The failure of Spain's administrative and commercial policies to adjust to
changing exigencies became so manifest by the middle of the 18th century that
even the Spanish crown became cognizant of it and widespread changes were
effected. Two new viceroyalties, Nueva Granada and Río de la Plata, were
created from the cumbrous viceroyalty of Peru. The mercantilist policies of the
previous two centuries were replaced by a modified form of free trade—a
change in policy which amounted to sanctifying reality, but with the hope that
some of the revenue from the contraband trade would now be diverted to Spanish
coffers. From an administrative perspective the most important innovation was
the introduction of the *intendencia* system, borrowed from that in use in France.

The intendencia was experimentally introduced into Cuba in 1765, and in the 1780's it was expanded into the viceroyalties of Nueva España, Peru, and Río de la Plata. The basic purpose of the intendencia was to increase royal revenues by increasing administrative efficiency and eliminating corruption. The numerous corregimientos and alcaldias mayores, the centers of much of the colonial corruption, were abolished and replaced by a much smaller number of intendencias. The *intendentes*, or intendants, were invariably peninsulares and, unlike the corregidores and alcaldes mayores, could serve for very long terms.

The new efficiency and purposefulness in the Spanish colonial system came too late to be given a proper test. In the event, the intendencia system was attacked on all sides. The viceroys and other conservative elements resented the intrusion of the intendants into the system. The criollos resented the fact that the intendants were peninsulares, whereas the corregidores and alcalde mayors had often been drawn from criollo ranks. The American Revolution, followed by the overthrow of the French monarchy, undoubtedly had a cumulative effect on the perspectives of the inhabitants of the Spanish colonies. The reorganization and expansion of the colonial militia after 1764 created a potential tool for revolt against Spain, and the success of this militia against the British in the Río de la Plata in 1806 confirmed its utility in this regard. The French invasion of Spain in 1808 and the unedifying collapse of the Spanish monarchy provided both opportunity and reason for the repudiation of Spanish royal authority and ushered in a period of nearly twenty years of struggle. The Spanish military efforts to recover their former possession were unsuccessful and were hampered by the intransigently reactionary position of the Spanish king. These two factors encouraged the spread of the revolt, and by 1825 all of the colonies in America had been lost except Cuba, Puerto Rico, the Philippines, and the Marianas.

Spain's subsequent imperial experience deserves only brief notice. During the 19th century Spain rather unenthusiastically acquired Spanish Guinea and Spanish West Africa. This was more than counterbalanced by the loss of the rest of its old possessions during the Spanish-American War of 1898. Thus, at the turn of this century Spain's colonial empire included Ceuta and Melilla on the Moroccan coast and Spanish Guinea and Spanish West Africa, consisting of Spanish Sahara and Ifni. Spain added the Spanish zone of Morocco in 1913, but this was just an hors d'oeuvre at the Moroccan banquet and represented an extension of the Ceuta and Melilla enclaves. The disintegration of the Spanish overseas possessions began in 1956 when the Spanish zone, like its counterpart the French zone, was returned to Moroccan sovereignty, and Ceuta and Melilla were attached to Spanish provinces. In 1968 Spanish Guinea, now Equatorial Guinea, became independent, and the enclave of Ifni was retroceded to Morocco. At this writing only Spanish Sahara remains as a Spanish overseas possession.

322 ANTIOQUIA

The region of Antioquia in northwestern Colombia immediately south of Panama was first penetrated in 1537 by Spaniards in search of a fabled treasure. Settlement followed soon after. Until 1579 Antioquia was part of the province of Popayán (q.v.) to the south. In that year it was erected into a separate province subject to the audiencia at Santa Fé (v. Nueva Granada). Antioquia remained under the audiencia and later the viceroyalty of Nueva Granada until, as a result of the wars of independence in the early 19th century, it became part of Gran Colombia.

Governors

1579-1592	Gaspar de Rodas
1592-1614	Bartolomé Alarcón y Villanueva
1615-1617	Luis Enríquez de Monroy
1617-1624	Francisco de Berrío y Quesada
1624-1627	García Tello de Sandoval
1627	Pedro Pérez de Aristizábal
1628-1629	Juan Clemente de Cháves
1629-1630	Luis de Angulo Velarde
1630	Juan Vélez de Guevara y Salamanca (1)
1630-1634	Alonso Turrillo de Yebra
1634-1643	Juan Vélez de Guevara y Salamanca (2)
1643-1646	Antonio Portocarrero y Monroy
1646-1648	José de Viedma y Labastida
1648-1649	Pedro Pablo Zapata de Heredia
1649-1651	Mateo de Castrillón y Heredia
1651-1653	Fernando Lozano Infante Paniagua
1653-1658	Manuel de Benavides y Ayala Calderón
1658-1664	Juan Gómez de Salazar
1664-1669	Luis Francisco de Berrío y Guzmán
1669-1675	Francisco de Montoya y Salazar
1675-1679	Miguel de Aguinaga y Mendigoitía
1679-1685	Diego Radillo de Arce
1685-1690	Francisco Carrillo de Albornoz
1690-1698	Pedro Eusebio Correa
1698-1707	Francisco Fernández de Heredia y Ocampo
1707-1712	José López de Carvajal
1712-1717	José de Yarza
1717-1721	Gaspar de Guiral y Urriolagoitía
1721-1727	Facundo Guerra Calderón
1727-1734	José Joaquín de la Rocha y Labarcés
1734-1735	Salvador de Monforte
1736-1737	Juan de Ortega y Urdanegui
1737-1740	Juan Alonso de Manzaneda
1742-1752	Francisco Antonio Osorio de Velasco
1752-1755	Manuel López de Castilla (or Castrillón)
1755-1769	José Barón de Chaves
1769-1775	Juan Jerónimo de Enciso
1775-1776	Francisco Silvestre y Sánchez (1)
1776-1782	Cayetano Buelta Lorenzana
1782-1785	Francisco Silvestre y Sánchez (2)
1785-1788	Juan Antonio Mon y Velarde Pardo y Cienfuegos
1788-1793	Francisco Baraya y la Campa
1793-1795	Juan Pablo Pérez de Rublas
1795-1796	José Felipe de Inciarte
1796-1804	Victor de Salcedo y Somodevila
1804-1805	Antonio Viana y Ceballos
1805-1811	Francisco de Ayala Gudino Medina y Calderón

Restrepo Sáenz, passim.

323 AREQUIPA

Arequipa, in southern Peru, became one of the intendencias in the viceroyalty of Peru (q.v.). It was one of the last areas in South America to be evacuated by Spanish troops and only became a part of the Republic of Peru in 1825.

Intendants		1812-1814	José Gabriel Moscoso y Peralta
1784-1785	José Menéndez y Escalada	1815-1817	Pío de Tristán y Moscoso
1785-1796	Antonio Álvarez y Jiménez	1817-1825	Juan Bautista de Lavalle y
1796-1812	Bartolomé María Rodríguez de		Sagasti
	Salamanca		

Deustua Pimentel, pp. 59—84; Martínez, *Gobernadores*, pp. 189—208; Mendiburú, 8:415.

324 BARINAS

The province of Barinas was created in the captaincy-general of Venezuela (q.v.) in 1782. It was the last separate province to be created in Venezuela. After 1810 Spanish control was spasmodic. In 1819 it became a part of Gran Colombia, and later of the Republic of Venezuela.

Governors
1786-1798   Fernando Miyares y González
1798-1810   Miguel de Ungaro y Dusmet

Tosta, pp. 53—80.

325 BUENOS AIRES

In 1618 the province of Río de la Plata (q.v., 380) was divided into the provinces of Paraguay (q.v.) and Buenos Aires (also called Río de la Plata). An audiencia was established at Buenos Aires in 1661, but it was abolished in 1671. For other than this decade, Buenos Aires was under the jurisdiction of the audiencia of Charcas (q.v.). Throughout the period Buenos Aires, considered by Spain to be a frontier area since the Spanish commercial scheme called for the trade routes to run north through Peru to the Caribbean and then across the Atlantic, continued to flourish and expand because of its participation in the large-scale contraband trade made so obvious and enticing by its location. The increasing economic importance of the Argentine area and the new commercial policies adopted by Spain in the middle of the 18th century led to the creation of the viceroyalty of Río de la Plata (q.v., 381) in 1-777. This included Buenos Aires, as well as Paraguay, Tucumán (q.v.) and areas detached from the viceroyalty of Peru (q.v.).

Governors		1660-1663	Alonso de Mercado y Villacorte
1618-1620	Diego de Góngora y Elizalde	1663-1674	Jose Martínez de Salazar
1623-1624	Alonso Pérez de Salazar	1674-1678	Andrés de Robles y Gómez
1624-1631	Francisco de Céspedes	1678-1682	José de Garro Senei y Artola
1631-1637	Pedro Esteban de Ávila	1682-1691	José de Herrera y Sotomayor
1637-1640	Mendo de la Cueva y Benavides	1691-1700	Agustín de Robles Lorenzana
1640-1641	Ventura Mújica	1700-1702	Manuel de Prado y Maldonado
1641-1645	Jerónimo Luis de Cabrera	1702-1708	Alonso José de Valdés y Inclán
1645-1653	Jacinto de Lariz	1708-1712	Manuel de Velasco y Tejada
1653-1660	Pedro de Ruíz Baygorri	1712-1714	Alonso Arce y Soria

Spain

1715-1717	Baltasar García Ros	1756-1766	Pedro Antonio de Ceballos Cortés y Calderón (1)
1717-1734	Bruno Mauricio de Zavala y Cortázar	1766-1770	Francisco de Paula Bucareli y Ursúa
1734-1742	Miguel de Salcedo y Sierra Alta	1770-1777	Juan José Vértiz y Salcedo
1742-1745	Domingo Ortiz de Rosas García de Villasuso, Marqués de Poblaciones	1777-1778	Pedro Antonio de Ceballos Cortés y Calderón (2)
1745-1756	José de Andonaegui y la Plaza		

Sierra, vols. 2 and 3, passim; Torre Revello, pp. 293—332.

326 CALIFORNIA

The peninsula later known as Baja California was discovered by the Spaniards in 1533. By 1543 the entire coast of both Baja and Alta California had been explored, although no settlement took place until 1697 when several missions were erected in Baja California and local officials appointed. Serious Spanish occupation began in 1767 and was a response to the possibility of British or Russian encroachment in the area. The two provinces were excluded from the control of the commandant-general of the Provincias Internas (q.v.). Until 1804 they were ruled jointly, but they were then separated into two parts. In 1822 they became part of the Republic of Mexico. Alta California fell into the hands of the United States in 1846, while Baja California continues to be a state of Mexico.

Baja and Alta California

Governors
1767-1769	Gaspar de Portolá
1769-1770	Matías de Armona
1770-1775	Felipe Barri
1775-1782	Felipe de Neve
1782-1791	Pedro Fages
1791-1792	José Antonio de Roméu
1792-1794	José Joaquín de Arrillaga (1)
1794-1800	Diego de Borica
1800-1802	Pedro de Alberni
1802-1804	José Joaquín de Arrillaga (2)

Alta California

Governors
1804-1814	José Joaquín de Arrillaga
1814-1815	José Darío Argüello
1815-1822	Pablo Vicente de Solá

Baja California

Governors
1804-1805	José Joaquín de Arrillaga
1806-1814	Felipe de Goycoechea
1814-1822	José Darío Argüello

Bolton, pp. 474—75; Richman, pp. 520—23.

327 CANARY ISLANDS

The existence of the Canary Islands, off the northwest coast of Africa, was known in antiquity when they were called the Fortunate Isles. In the tenth century Arab traders frequented the islands. In 1402 a Frenchman, Jean de Bethencourt, effected settlements on some of the islands, especially Fuerteventura, but recognized the suzerainty of Castile over them. After his death the islands were sold several times and inevitably conflicting claims arose. Furthermore, the

284

Portuguese began to dispute the rights of Castile. However, Spanish sovereignty was recognized by the Treaty of Alcáçovas in 1479, and immediately thereafter settlement began. The most important islands were Gran Canaria and Tenerife (qq.v.), but the islands of La Palma, Gomera, Hierro, Lanzarote, and Fuerteventura were also settled. The aboriginal inhabitants, the Guanches, fiercely resisted the Spanish occupation and were nearly exterminated for their troubles. Until 1589 the islands were governed individually, mainly on a seigneurial basis. However, military exigencies necessitated the appointment, in 1589, of a captain-general, who possessed jurisdiction over the entire archipelago. He was appointed directly by the crown. The islands were favorite targets of French and English attacks from the 16th to the early 19th centuries. In 1821 the administration of the Canaries was reconstructed and it became a metropolitan province of Spain. After 1841 no substantive captains-general were appointed.

Captains-General

1589-1591	Luis de la Cueva y Benavides, Marqués de Bedmar
1593-1625	(islands individually governed)
1625-1626	Francisco González de Andía Irarrazábal y Zárate
1629-1634	Juan de Rivera y Zambrana
1634-1638	Iñigo de Brizuela y Urbina
1638-1644	Luis Fernández de Córdoba y Arce
1644-1650	Pedro Carrillo de Guzmán
1650-1659	Alfonso Dávila y Guzmán
1659-1661	Sebastián Hurtado de Corcuera y Gaviría
1661-1665	Jerónimo de Benavente de Quiñones
1665-1666	Juan de Toledo
1666-1671	Gabriel Lasso de la Vega y Licques de Recourt Figueroa y de Merode, Conde de Puertollano
1671-1676	Juan de Balboa Mogrobejo
1677-1681	Jerónimo de Velasco
1681-1685	Félix Nieto de Silva, Conde de Guaro
1685-1689	Francisco Bernardo Varona (or Barahona)
1689-1697	Antonio de Eril Vicentelo y Toledo, Marqués de Fuensagrada
1697-1701	Pedro de Ponte y Llarena Hoyo y Calderón, Conde del Palmar
1701-1705	Miguel González de Otazo
1705-1709	Agustín de Robles Laurenzana
1709-1713	Francisco Chacón Medina y Salazar
1713-1718	Ventura de Landaeta y Horna
1718-1719	José Antonio de Chaves y Osorio
1719-1722	Juan de Mur Aguirre y Argaiz
1723-1735	Lorenzo Fernández de Vilavicencio, Marqués de Valhermoso
1735-1741	Francisco José Emparán
1741-1744	Andrés Bonito Pignately
1744-1745	José Masones de Lima
1745-1746	Luis Mayone Salazar
1747-1764	Juan de Urbina
1764	Pedro Rodríguez Moreno y Pérez de Oteyro
1764-1768	Domingo Bernardí Gómez
1768-1775	Miguel López Fernández de Heredia
1775-1779	Enrique Fernández de Alvarado y Perales Hurtado y Colomo, Marqués de los Tabalosos
1779-1784	Joaquín Ibáñez y Valero de Bernabé, Marqués de la Cañada Ibáñez
1784-1789	Miguel de la Grúa Talamanca y Branciforte, Marqués de Branciforte
1789-1791	José de Avellaneda
1791-1799	Antonio Gutiérrez de Otero y Santallana
1799-1803	José de Perlasca
1803-1809	Fernando Cagigal de la Vega y Martínez Niño de San Miguel y Pacheco, Marqués de Casa Cagigal
1809-1810	Carlos Luján
1810	Diego de Cañas y Portocarrero, Duque del Parque
1810-1811	Ramón Carvajal
1811-1820	Pedro Rodríguez de la Buría

Blanco, passim; Martínez de Campos y Serrano, pp. 387–94.

328 CARTAGENA DE INDIAS

The city of Cartagena was founded on the northern coast of Colombia in 1533 and became, like Santa Marta (q.v.), a major entrepot for the mineral riches of the viceroyalty of Peru (q.v.). As a result it was several times sacked by the other European powers in the Caribbean area. Cartagena was under the audiencia of Santa Fé (v. Nueva Granada) after its creation in 1549. Later it became a part of the viceroyalty of Nueva Granada. In 1811 Cartagena became independent, only to fall again under Spanish control from 1816 to 1821 when it became part of Gran Colombia.

Information on the governors of Cartagena de Indias is·particularly scanty and confusing. The succession was marred by many disputes and an excessively large number of acting governors. The following list can be considered accurate only for the 18th century. The sources for the period prior to 1700 are so contradictory that some arbitrariness was necessary in forming this list.

Governors	
1618-1625	García Girón de Loaysa
1625-1628	Diego de Escobar
1628-1629	Francisco de Berrío
1629-1636	Francisco de Murga
1637-1638	Gonzalo de Herrera
1638	Vicente de los Reyes Villalobos
1638-1641	Melchor de Aguilera
1641-1643	Hortuño de Aldape
1643-1646	Luis Fernández de Córdoba
1646-1647	Juan Díez Flórez
1647-1648	Clemente Soriano
1648-1659	Pedro de Zapata y Mendoza
1659	Benito de Figueroa y Barrantes (1)
1659-1662	Lope de Ceballos Borceda
1663-1664	Martín Manuel Palomeque
1664-1665	Fernando de Prado y Plaza
1666-1669	Benito de Figueroa y Barrantes (2)
1670-1671	Pedro de Ulloa Rivedineira
1671-1672	Francisco Ramírez de Lescano
1672-1674	Juan del Pando y Estrada (1)
1675-1677	Juan Daza y Guzmán
1677	Francisco de Castro (1)
1677-1679	Domingo de la Rocha Ferrer
1679-1680	Rafael Capsir y Sanz
1680-1681	Manuel Antonio de Flórez y Bedguín
1681-1682	Juan del Pando y Estrada (2)
1682-1685	Gregorio Lasso de la Vega
1686-1687	Francisco de Castro (2)
1687	Eugenio de la Escalera
1687-1690	Martín de Ceballos y la Cerda (1)
1690-1691	Pedro Martín de Montoya
1691-1694	Martín de Ceballos y la Cerda (2)

1694-1695	Sancho Jimeno
1695-1699	Diego de los Ríos
1699-1705	Juan Díaz Pimienta
1706	Lázaro de Herrera y Leyva
1706-1713	José de Zúñiga y la Cerda
1713-1716	Jerónimo Badillo (1)
1716-1717	Francisco Baloco Leigrave
1717-1719	Jerónimo Badillo (2)
1719-1720	Carlos de Sucre
1720-1724	Alberto de Bertodano y Navarra
1724-1727	Luis de Aponte
1728-1730	Juan José de Andía Vivero Urbina y Velasco, Marqués de Villahermosa
1731-1737	Antonio de Salas
1737-1739	Pedro José Fidalgo
1739-1743	Melchor de Navarrete
1743-1749	Basilio de Gante
1749-1753	Ignacio Sala y Garrigó
1753-1761	Diego Tavares Haumada y Barríos
1761-1766	José Antonio Bravo de Sobremonte Castillo y Díaz de Carranceja, Marqués de Sobremonte
1766-1770	Fernando Morillo Velarde
1770-1772	Gregorio de la Sierra
1772-1774	Roque de Quiroga (1)
1774-1782	Juan de Torrezal Díaz Pimienta
1782-1785	Roque de Quiroga (2)
1785-1789	José Carrión y Andrade
1789-1796	Joaquín de Cañaveral y Ponce
1796-1808	Anastasio Zejudo
1808-1809	Blas de Soria y Santa Cruz
1809-1811	Francisco de Montes

Academia Colombiana de la Historia, 3, no. 1:68, 288—91; 3, no. 2:58—67, 224—40, 317—22; 3, no. 3:369—70; Restrepo Sáenz, "Gobernadores de Cartagena," passim. The list in Vargas, pp. 67—75, is hopelessly confusing.

329 CEUTA AND MELILLA

Ceuta, conquered by the Portuguese in 1415, had remained, like the other Portuguese possessions, under Portuguese control during Portugal's union with Spain from 1580 to 1640. When Portugal rebelled in 1640 Ceuta remained loyal to the Spanish crown, and the treaty of 1668, recognizing Portuguese independence, confirmed the Spanish possession of Ceuta.

The neighboring *plaza* of Melilla had been occupied by the Duke of Medina Sidonia in 1497 and was transferred to the Spanish crown in 1556. During the 16th and 17th centuries the islands of Peñón de Vélez de la Gomera and Alhucemas came under Spanish control and were subjected to Melilla. Ceuta and Melilla were governed separately until 1847 when the captaincy-general of North Africa was created. This included all the Spanish enclaves in the area and the governor of Ceuta became captain-general. With the formation of the Spanish zone of Morocco in 1913, Ceuta and Melilla, together with the smaller plazas, became part of the zone and lost their administrative identity. Since the end of the protectorate in 1956 Ceuta and Melilla have been governed by mayors and are attached to the Spanish provinces of Cádiz and Malaga respectively. Throughout their separate administrative existence both Ceuta and Melilla were under military government because of their exposed locations.

Melilla		1719	Francisco Ibáñez y Rubalcava
Governors		1719-1730	Alonso de Guevara y Vasconcellos
1556-1559	Alonso de Urrea	1730-1732	Juan Andrés del Thoso
1561-1568	Pedro Venegas de Córdoba	1732-1757	Antonio Villalba y Angulo
1568-1571	Francisco Sánchez de Córdoba	1757-1758	Francisco de Alba
1571-1595	Antonio de Tejada	1758-1767	Narciso Vázquez y Nicuesa
1595-1596	Jerónimo de los Barrios	1767-1772	Miguel Fernández de Saavedra
1596-1601	Martín Dávalos y Padilla	1772-1777	José Carrión y Andrade
1603-1611	Pedro de Heredia	1777-1779	Bernardo Tortosa
1612-1617	Domingo de Dieguez	1780-1782	Antonio Manso
1617	Gaspar de Mondragón	1782-1786	José Granados
1618	Domingo de Ochoa	1786-1788	José Naranjo
1619-1620	Diego de Leyva	1788-1798	José Rivera
1620-1622	Francisco Rodríguez de Sanabria	1798-1800	Fernando Moyano
1622-1624	Francisco Ruíz	1800-1814	Ramón Conti
1625-1632	Luis de Sotomayor	1814-1821	Jacinto Díaz Capilla
1632-1633	Pedro Moreo	1821-1823	Antonio Mateos y Malpartida
1633-1635	Tomás Mejía de Escobedo	1823-1824	Juan José Pérez del Hacho y
1637-1648	Gabriel de Peñalosa y Estrada		Oliván
1649	Luis de Sotomayor	1824-1826	Luis Cappa y Rioseco (1)
1649-1650	Jordán Jerez	1826-1829	Manuel García
1651-1655	Pedro Palacio y Guevara	1829-1830	Juan Serrano y Reyna
1655-1656	Diego de Arce (1)	1830-1835	Luis Cappa y Rioseco (2)
1656-1669	Luis de Velázquez y Angulo	1835-1838	Rafael Delgado y Moreno
1669-1672	Francisco Osorio y Astorga	1839-1847	Demetrio María de Benito y
1672-1674	Diego de Arce (2)		Hernández
1675-1680	José Frias	1847-1848	Manuel Arcaya
1680-1683	Diego Toscano y Brito	1848-1850	Ignacio Chacón
1684-1686	Diego Pacheco y Arce	1850-1854	José Eustaquio de Castro y
1687	Francisco López Moreno		Méndez
1687-1688	Antonio Domínguez de Durán	1854-1856	Manuel Buceta del Villar (1)
1688-1691	Bernabé Ramos y Miranda	1856-1858	José Morcillo Ezquerra
1692-1697	Antonio de Zúñiga y la Cerda	1858-1860	Manuel Buceta del Villar (2)
1697-1703	Domingo Canal y Soldevila	1860-1861	Luis Lemni Demandre de la Breche
1704-1707	Blas de Trincheria	1861-1862	Felipe Ginovés del Espinar
1707-1711	Diego de Flores	1862-1863	Manuel Álvarez Maldonaldo
1711-1714	Juan Jerónimo Ungo de Velasco	1863-1864	Tomás O'Ryan y Vázquez
1714-1715	Patricio Gómez de la Hoz	1864-1866	Bartolomé Benavides y Campuzano
1715-1716	Pedro Sansón, Conde de Desallois	1866-1868	José Salcedo y González
1716-1719	Pedro Borrás	1868-1871	Pedro Beaumont y Peralta

1871–1873	Bernardo Alemañy y Perote
1873–1879	Andrés Cuadra y Bourman
1879–1880	Manuel Macias y Casado (1)
1880	Angel Navascués
1880–1881	Evaristo García y Reyna
1881–1886	Manuel Macias y Casado (2)
1886–1887	Teodoro Camino y Alcobendas
1887–1888	Mariano de la Iglesia y Guillén
1888	Juan Villalonga y Soler
1888–1889	Rafael Assin y Bazán
1889–1891	José Mirelis y González
1891–1893	Juan García y Margallo
1893–1894	Manuel Macias y Casado (3)
1894	Juan Arolas y Esplugues
1894–1895	Rafael Cerero
1895–1898	José Alcántara Pérez
1898–1899	Fernando Alameda y Liancourt
1899–1904	Venancio Hernández y Fernández
1904	Manuel Serrano y Ruíz
1905	Enrique Segura y Campoy
1905–1910	José Marina Vega
1910–1913	José García Aldave

Ceuta

Governors

1641–1644	Juan Fernández Córdoba y Coalla, Marqués de Miranda de Auta
1645–1646	Luis de Lencastre, Marqués de Malagón
1646–1653	Juan Suárez de Aragón y Melo, Marqués de Torcifal
1653–1661	José Fernández de Sotomayor y Lima, Marqués de Tenorio
1662–1665	Jerónimo de Noronha, Marqués de Castelo Mendo
1665–1672	Pedro da Cunha, Marquês de Sentar
1672–1677	Francisco Suárez de Alarcón, Conde de Torres Vedras
1677	Antonio de Medina Chacón y Ponce de León (1)
1677–1678	Diego de Portugal
1678–1679	Antonio de Medina Chacón y Ponce de León (2)
1679–1681	Juan Arias y Pacheco Dávila y Bobadilla Girón de Mendoza, Conde de Puñonrostro
1681–1689	Francisco de Velasco y Tovar
1689–1692	Francisco Bernardo Varona
1692–1695	Sebastián González de Andía y Irarrazábal Álvarez de Toledo Enríquez de Guzmán, Marqués de Valparaiso
1695–1698	Melchor de Avellaneda Sandoval y Rojas, Marqués de Valdecañas
1698–1702	Francisco del Castillo Fajardo, Marqués de Villadarias
1702–1704	José de Agulló y Pinós, Marqués de Gironella
1705–1709	Juan Francisco Manrique de Araña (1)
1709–1715	Gonzalo Chacón y Arellano Mendoza Toledo Sandoval y Rojas
1715–1719	Francisco Fernández y Rivadeo (1)
1719	Francisco Pérez Mancheño
1719–1720	Luis Rigio, Principe de Campo Florido
1720	Juan Francisco Manrique de Araña (2)
1720–1725	Francisco Fernández y Rivadeo (2)
1725–1731	Emmanuel d'Orléans, Comte de Charny
1731–1738	Álvaro de Navia Osorio y Vigil, Marqués de Santa Cruz de Marcenado
1738–1739	Antonio Manso Maldonaldo
1739–1745	Pedro de Vargas Maldonaldo, Marqués de Campofuerte
1745	Juan Antonio Tineo y Fuertes
1745–1746	Juan José de Palafox y Centurión
1746–1751	José Horcasitas y Oleaga
1751	Pedro de Loaysa, Marqués de la Matilla
1751–1755	Carlos Francisco de Croix, Marqués de Croix
1755–1760	Miguel Agustín Carreño
1760–1763	Juan Warmarch Lumen de la Vice, Marqués de Warmarch
1763–1776	Diego María Osorio
1776–1783	Francisco Tineo, Marqués de Casa Tremañes
1783–1784	Domingo Joaquín de Salcedo
1784–1791	Miguel Porcel y Manrique de Araña Menchaca y Zaldívar
1791–1792	José de Sotomayor
1792–1794	José de Urrutia y las Casas
1794–1795	Miguel Álvarez de Sotomayor y Flores, Conde de Santa Clara
1795	Diego de la Peña
1795–1798	José Vassallo
1798–1801	José Bautista de Castro
1801–1805	Antonio Terrero
1805–1807	Francisco de Horta
1807–1808	Ramón de Carvajal
1808–1809	Carlos Luján
1809–1810	Carlos Gand
1810–1813	José María Alós
1813	José María Lastres
1813	Pedro Grimarest (1)
1813–1814	Fernando Gómez de Buitrón (1)
1814–1815	Pedro Grimarest (2)
1815–1816	Luis Antonio Flores
1816–1818	Juan de Pontons y Mujica
1818–1820	José de Miranda (1)
1820	Vicente Rorique
1820–1822	Fernando Gómez de Buitrón (2)
1822–1823	Álvaro María Chacón

1823	Manuel Fernández	1868	Antonio del Rey y Caballero
1823	Antonio Quiroga	1868	Joaquín Cristón y Gasatín
1823-1824	Juan María Muñoz (1)	1870-1872	Enrique Serrano Dolz
1824-1826	José de Miranda (2)	1872-1873	Carlos Sáenz Delcourt
1826	Joaquín Bureau	1873	Manuel Keller y García
1826	Julio O'Neill	1873-1875	Fulgencio Gávila y Solá
1826-1830	Juan María Muñoz (2)	1875-1876	Pedro Sartorius y Tapia
1830-1833	Carlos Ullmann	1876-1877	Fernando del Piño Villamil
1833-1835	Mateo Ramírez	1877	Juan García Torres
1835	Carlos Espinosa	1877-1878	Victoriano López Pinto
1835-1836	Joaquín Gómez Ansa	1878-1879	José María Velasco Postigo
1836-1837	Francisco Sanjuanena	1879-1881	José Aizpuru y Lorriez Fontecha
1837	Bernardo Tacón	1881-1883	José Merello y Calvo
1837-1844	José María Rodríguez Vera	1883	José Pascual de Bonanza
1844-1847	Antonio Ordóñez	1883-1889	Juan López Pinto y Marín Reyna
1847-1851	Antonio Ros de Olano	1889-1891	Narciso de Fuentes y Sánchez
1851-1854	Salvador de la Puente Pita	1891-1894	Miguel Correa y García
1854-1857	Mariano Rebigliato	1894-1898	Rafael Correa y García
1857-1858	Carlos Tobía	1898-1901	Jacinto de León y Barreda
1858	Manuel Gasset Mercader	1901-1903	Manuel de Aguilar y Diosdado
1858-1864	Ramón Gómez Pulido (1)	1903-1907	Francisco Fernández Bernal
1864-1865	Manuel Álvarez Maldonaldo	1907-1908	Fernando Álvarez de Sotomayor y
1865-1866	Ramón Gómez Pulido (2)		Flórez
1866	Antonio Peláez Compomanes	1908-1910	José García Aldave
1866-1868	José Oribe Sans	1910-1913	Felipe Alfau y Mendoza

For Ceuta, see Dornellas, 4:169–89. For Melilla, see Morales, pp. 520–24. For Peñón and Alhucemas, see ibid., pp. 525–28, 529–31.

330 CHARCAS

The audiencia de los Charcas was created in 1559 to administer the vast territories of Upper Peru. Except for the period from 1661 to 1671, when an audiencia was created for Río de la Plata (v. Buenos Aires), the audiencia of Charcas embraced most of the territory which later became Bolivia, Paraguay, and Argentina. Charcas was subject to the viceroyalty of Peru (q.v.). The presidents did not exercise the functions of governor and captain-general since these powers belonged to the viceroy. When Río de la Plata (q.v., 381) was made a viceroyalty in 1777, Charcas was transferred to its jurisdiction. The area of the audiencia was occupied by forces of the United Provinces of Río de la Plata in 1810 but was reoccupied by royalist forces in 1816. Eight years later Spanish authority was terminated and the audiencia, much reduced in size after 1776, became the nucleus of the Republic of Bolivia.

The following list is incomplete for it includes, with very few exceptions, only substantive presidents. Italicized dates are those when the decree of appointment was issued. It was often several years before an appointee assumed his post. Indeed many appointments were, for various reasons, never taken up, and although most such instances have been eliminated from this list, some doubtless remain. The list is therefore presented only as a point of departure.

Presidents

1559-1572	Pedro Ramírez de Quiñones	1611-1627	Diego de Portugal
1573-1577	Lope Díez Aux de Armendáriz	1627-1632	Martín de Egües
1580-1597	Juan López de Cepeda	1633-1642	Juan de Lizárazu y Recain
1602-	Alonso Maldonaldo de Torres	1647-1656	Francisco de Nestares Marín
		1661-1670	Pedro Vázquez de Velasco

Spain

1673-1685	Bartolomé González de Póveda	1769-1776	Ambrosio de Benavides
1695-1698	Francisco Domínguez	*1776*	Jerónimo Manuel de Ruedas
1702	José Boneu	1779-1780	Agustín de Pinedo Fernández de
1704	José Antonio de la Rocha y		Valdivieso
	Carranza, Marqués de Villarocha	1783-1785	Ignacio Flores
1706	Francisco Pimentel y Sotomayor	1785-1790	Vicente de Gálvez
1709	Gabriel Antonio de Matienzo	1790-1797	Joaquín del Pino y Rosas Romero
1712-1725	Francisco de Herboso y Luza		Negrete
1728	José Francisco de Herrera	1797-1809	Ramón García León de Pizarro
1730	Ignacio Antonio de Querazaju y	1809-1810	Vicente Nieto de las Viñas y
	Mollinedo		García Sánchez de Valencia y
1738	José Gabriel de Jáuregui y Aguirre		González
1746-1757	Nicolás Jiménez de Lobatón y	1810-1816	(under United Provinces of Río d
	Azaña, Marqués de Rocafuerte		la Plata)
1757-1766	Juan Francisco Pestaña y	1816-1818	José Pascual de Vivero y
	Chumacero		Salaverria
1767-1769	Juan Martínez de Tineo	1818-1824	Rafael Maroto y Ysern

Information from Archivo General de Indias, Sevilla, Spain. For the period before 1700 one should also refer to Schafer, 2:504–6, who, like the above cited source, includes only dates of appointment of substantive presidents.

331 CHIAPAS

Chiapas, or Ciudad Real, became part of the captaincy-general of Guatemala (q.v.) in the 16th century and remained so until 1821. However, in 1786, with the introduction of the intendencia system, Chiapas was created an intendencia. In 1821, when Spanish authority was cast off, Chiapas, like the rest of Guatemala, joined the newly formed empire of Mexico. The union, lik the empire itself, was brief. At its dissolution in 1823, however, Chiapas, contiguous to Mexic remained as a part of that country. The following list of intendants is incomplete.

Intendants

1786-	Francisco Saavedra y Carvajal		–	(unknown)
1790-	Agustín de la Cuencas Zayas		-1821	Juan Nepomuceno Batres

Navarro García, *Intendencias*, p. 50.

332 CHILE

Chile, the long narrow strip of coastal plain lying between the Andes and the Pacific Ocean south of Peru, was explored and settled from Peru (q.v.) after ca. 1540. It was initially called Nueva Estremadura but this name had little currency and was quickly replaced by that of Chile. Chile was unique among the Spanish conquests south of Mexico in that Spanish occupation in the southern part of the colony was delayed for hundreds of years because of the fierce resista offered by the Indians called Araucanians by the Spaniards. Only in the 18th century did Spani settlement extend to the southern part of Chile. An audiencia was created at Concepción in 1565 but suppressed ten years later. In 1609 it was revived, this time at Santiago. In 1778 the governor of Chile became captain-general as well. Chile remained under the jurisdiction of the viceroyalty of Peru until the end of Spanish colonial dominion. In Chile this came in 1817.

Governors

1540-1547	Pedro de Valdivia (1)
1547-1549	Francisco de Villagrán (1)
1549-1554	Pedro de Valdivia (2)
1554	Rodrigo de Quiroga (1)
1554-1557	(no governor)
1557-1561	García Hurtado de Mendoza
1561	Rodrigo de Quiroga (2)
1561-1563	Francisco de Villagrán (2)
1563-1565	Pedro de Villagrán
1565-1567	Rodrigo de Quiroga (3)
1567-1575	Melchor Bravo de Saravia
1575-1580	Rodrigo de Quiroga (4)
1580-1583	Martín Ruíz de Gamboa
1583-1592	Alonso de Sotomayor y Andía
1593-1598	Martín García Oñez y Loyola
1599-1600	Francisco de Quiñónes y Villapadierna
1600-1601	Alonso García Ramón (1)
1601-1605	Alonso Ribera y Zambrano (1)
1605-1610	Alonso García Ramón (2)
1610	Luis Merlo de la Fuente
1610-1612	Juan de Jaraquemada
1612-1617	Alonso Ribera y Zambrano (2)
1617-1618	Fernando Talaverano Gallegos
1618-1620	Lope de Ulloa y Lemos
1620-1622	Cristóbal de la Cerda y Sotomayor
1622-1624	Pedro Osores y Ulloa
1624-1625	Francisco de Alava y Norueña
1625-1629	Luis Fernández de Córdoba y Arce
1629-1639	Francisco Lasso de la Vega y Alvarado
1639-1646	Francisco López de Zúñiga, Marqués de Baides
1646-1649	Martín de Mújica y Buitrón
1649-1651	Alonso Figueroa y Córdoba
1651-1656	Alonso de Acuña y Cabrera
1656-1661	Diego Pórter de Casanate
1662-1664	Angel de Peredo
1664-1668	Francisco Menese y Brito
1668-1670	Diego Dávila Coello y Pacheco Castilla y Pedrosa, Marqués de Navamorquende
1671-1682	Juan de Enríquez de las Casas
1682-1692	José de Garro Senei y Cutola
1692-1700	Tomás Marín de Poveda
1700-1707	Francisco Ibáñez y Peralta
1709-1716	Juan Andrés de Ustáriz y Vertizberea
1716-1717	José de Santiago Concha y Salvatierra
1717-1733	Gabriel Cano de Aponte
1734-1737	Manuel Silvestre de Salamanca Cano
1737-1745	José Antonio Manso de Velasco y Sánchez de Samaniego
1745-1746	Francisco José de Obando y Solís, Marqués de Obando
1746-1756	Domingo Ortiz de Rosas García de Villasuso, Marqués de Poblaciones
1756-1761	Manuel de Amat Junient Planella Aimeric y Santa Pau
1761-1762	Félix de Berroeta
1762-1768	Antonio de Guill y Gonzaga
1768-1770	Juan de Balmaceda Censano y Beltrán
1770-1773	Francisco Javier de Morales Castejón y Arroyo
1773-1780	Agustín de Jáuregui y Aldecoa
1781-1787	Ambrosio de Benavides
1787-1788	Tomás Álvarez de Acevedo
1788-1795	Ambrosio O'Higgins, Marqués de Osorno
1796-1799	Gabriel de Avilés y del Fierro, Marqués de Avilés
1799-1801	Joaquín del Pino Rosas Romero y Negrete
1802-1808	Luis Antonio Muñoz de Guzmán
1808-1810	Francisco Antonio García Carrasco
1814-1815	Mariano Osorio
1815-1817	Francisco Casimiro Marcó del Pont

Alcázar Molina, pp. 391–412; Fuentes and Cortés, p. 353 and under individual names.

333 COAHUILA

Coahuila in northern Mexico was first settled by the Spaniards in 1575. In 1674 the area was detached from Nueva Vizcaya (q.v.) and erected into a separate province. Until 1716 Coahuila also covered what was to become the province of Texas (q.v.). In 1777 Coahuila fell under the jurisdiction of the Provincias Internas (q.v.) and remained so until 1822, withal maintaining its own local civil administration. After 1822 Coahuila became part of the Republic of Mexico.

Governors

1674-1676	Antonio Balcárel Rivadaneira y Sotomayor
1687-1691	Alonso de León
1691-1698	Diego Ramón
1698-1703	Francisco Cuervo y Valdés
1703-1705	Matías de Aguirre
1705-1708	Martín de Alarcón
1708-1714	Simón de Padilla y Córdova
1714	Pedro Fermín de Echevers y Subiza
1714-1716	Juan de Valdés
1716-1717	José Antonio de Eca y Múzquiz
1717-1719	Martín de Alarcón
1719-1722	José Azlor y Virto de Vera, Marqués de San Miguel de Aguayo
1723-1729	Blas de la Garza Falcón (1)
1729-1733	Manuel de Sandoval
1733-1735	Blas de la Garza Falcón (2)
1735-1739	Clemente de la Garza Falcón
1739-1744	Juan García Pruneda
1744-1754	Pedro de Rábago y Terán
1754-1756	Manuel Antonio Bustillos y Ceballos
1756-1757	Miguel de Sesma y Escudero
1757-1759	Ángel Martos y Navarrette
1759-1762	Jacinto de Barríos y Jáuregui (1)
1762-1764	Lorenzo Cancio Sierra y Cienfuegos
1764-1765	Diego Ortiz Parrilla
1765-1768	Jacinto de Barríos y Jáuregui (2)
1768-1769	José Costilla y Terán
1769-1777	Jacobo de Ugarte y Loyola
1777-1783	Juan de Ugalde
1783-1788	Pedro Fueros
1788-1790	Juan Gutiérrez de la Cueva (1)
1790-1795	Miguel José de Emparán
1795-1797	Juan Gutiérrez de la Cueva (2)
1797-1805	Antonio Cordero y Bustamante (1)
1805-1807	Juan Ignacio de Arizpe
1807-1809	José Joaquín de Ugarte
1809-1817	Antonio Cordero y Bustamante (2)
1817-1818	Antonio García de Tejada
1818-1819	José Franco
1819-1820	Manuel Pardo
1820-1822	Antonio Elosúa

Information from El Secretario General de Gobierno de Coahuila, Saltillo, Coahuila. Also, Alessi Robles, 2:434–37.

334 COCHABAMBA

The intendencia of Cochabamba was created in 1783 within Río de la Plata (q.v., 381). It comprised most of the area of the earlier province of Santa Cruz de la Sierra. Organized Spanish authority ended after 1810 although some Spanish control lingered on for several more years. In 1825 Cochabamba became part of the Republic of Bolivia.

Intendants

1783-1785	José de Ayarga
1785-1809	Francisco de Viedma y Verdejo
1809-1810	José González de Prada

Lynch, p. 291.

335 CÓRDOBA

With the introduction of the intendencia system in the viceroyalty of Río de la Plata (q.v., 381), the province of Tucumán (q.v.) was divided into two parts, Córdoba in the south and Salta (q.v.) in the north. The intendant of Córdoba was deposed in 1810, and eventually the area became part of the Argentine Republic.

Intendants

1783-1797	Rafael de Sobremonte Núñez Castillo Angulo y Bullón Ramírez de Arellano, Marqués de Sobremonte	1797-1803	Nicolás Pérez del Viso
		1803-1805	José González
		1805-1807	Victoriano Rodríguez
		1807-1810	José Gutiérrez de la Concha

Lynch, p. 290; Videla, p. 754.

336 COSTA RICA

Costa Rica, discovered by Columbus in 1502, was the last part of Central America to be settled by the Spaniards. In 1568 it was made a province under the audiencia of Guatemala (q.v.). The area was initially called Nuevo Cartago. Costa Rica was an unimportant colony and was frequently attacked by English, French, and Dutch buccaneers. Unlike the other provinces of Central America, Costa Rica did not become an intendencia in the late 18th century but remained a simple province. Independent in 1821, Costa Rica formed part of the United States of Central America and later became a separate republic.

Governors

1568-1573	Perafán de Ribera	1693-1698	Manuel de Bustamente y Vivero
1574-1577	Alonso de Anguciana y Gamboa	1698-1704	Francisco Serrano de Reina y Lizarde
1577-1590	Diego de Artieda y Chirino	1704-1707	Diego de Herrera y Campuzano
1590-1591	Juan Valásquez Ramiro	1707-1712	Lorenzo Antonio de Granda y Balbín
1591-1592	Bartolomé de Lences	1713-1717	José Antonio Lacayo de Briones y Palacios
1592-1595	Gonzalo de la Palma		
1595-1599	Fernando de la Cueva	1717-1718	Pedro Ruíz de Bustamante
1600-1604	Gonzalo Vázquez de Coronado y Arias de Ávila	1718-1726	Diego de la Haya y Fernández
		1727-1736	Baltasar Francisco de Valderrama y Haro
1604-1613	Juan de Ocón y Trillo	1736	Antonio Vázquez de la Quadra
1613-1619	Juan de Mendoza y Medrano	1736-1739	Francisco Antonio de Carrandi y Menán
1619-1624	Alonso del Castillo y Guzmán		
1624-1630	Juan de Echáuz	1739-1740	Francisco de Olaechea
1630-1634	Juan de Villalta	1740-1747	Juan Gemmir y Lleonart
1634-1636	Juan de Agüero	1747-1750	Luis Díez Navarro
1636-1644	Gregorio de Sandoval y González de Alcalá	1750-1754	Cristóbal Ignacio de Soría
		1754-1755	Francisco Fernández de la Pástora
1644-1650	Juan de Cháves y Mendoza	1756-1757	José Antonio de Oreamuno y Vázquez Meléndez (1)
1650-1655	Juan Fernández de Salinas y de la Cerda		
1655-1661	Andrés Arias Maldonaldo y Mendoza	1757	José González Rancaño
1662-1664	Rodrigo Arias Maldonaldo	1757-1760	Manuel Soler
1664-1665	Juan de Obregón	1760-1762	Francisco Javier de Oreamuno y Vázquez Meléndez
1665-1674	Juan López de la Flor		
1675-1681	Juan Francisco Sáenz Vázquez y Sendín	1762-1764	José Antonio de Oreamuno y Vázquez Meléndez (2)
1681-1693	Miguel Gómez de Lara	1764-1773	José Joaquín de Nava y Cabezudo

Spain

1773-1778	Juan Fernández de Bobadilla (1)
1778-1780	José Perié y Barros (1)
1780-1781	Juan Fernández de Bobadilla (2)
1781-1785	Juan Flores
1785-1789	José Perié y Barros (2)
1789-1790	Juan Esteban Martínez de Pinillos

1790-1797	José Vázquez y Téllez
1797-1810	Tomás de Acosta y Hurtado de Mendoza
1810-1819	Juan de Dios Ayala y Gudiño
1819-1821	Juan Manuel de Cañas y Trujillo

Fernández Guardia, pp. 133–34; Fernández Peralta, pp. 160–64.

337 CUBA

Spain began occupying Cuba in 1511, and eight years later it served as the staging point for the expedition to Mexico (v. Nueva España). Until 1535 Cuba was administered by lieutenant governors, from 1535 to 1577 by governors, and from 1579 by governors/captains-general, all subject to the audiencia of Santo Domingo (q.v.). In 1762 British forces briefly occupied Havana. In 1764 Cuba became a separate captaincy-general with control over the provinces of Louisiana and later of Florida (qq.v.). When the Santo Domingo audiencia was suppressed in 1797 it was transferred to Puerto Príncipe on Cuba. In 1898 Cuba was occupied by American forces.

Governors

1511-1524	Diego Velásquez de Cuéllar
1524-1526	Juan Altamirano
1526-1531	Gonzalo de Guzmán (1)
1531-1532	Juan de Vadillo
1532-1535	Manuel de Rojas
1535-1538	Gonzalo de Guzmán (2)
1538-1544	Hernán de Soto
1544-1546	Juan de Avila
1546-1548	Antonio de Cháves
1549-1555	Gonzalo Pérez de Angulo
1556-1565	Diego de Mazariegos
1565-1567	Francisco García Osorio
1567-1574	Pedro Menéndez de Avilés[1]
1575-1577	Gabriel Montalvo
1577-1579	Francisco Carreño
1579-1584	Gaspar de Torres
1584-1589	Gabriel de Luján
1589-1593	Juan de Tejeda
1593-1602	Juan Maldonaldo Barnuevo
1602-1608	Pedro Valdés
1608-1616	Gaspar Ruíz de Pereda
1616-1619	Sancho de Alquiza
1620-1624	Francisco de Venegas
1624-1626	Damián Velásquez de Contreras
1626-1630	Lorenzo de Cabrera y Corbera
1630-1634	Juan Bitrián de Viamonte y Navarra
1634-1639	Francisco Riaño y Gamboa
1639-1647	Álvaro de Luna y Sarmiento
1647-1653	Diego de Villalba y Toledo, Marqués de Campo
1653-1654	Francisco Jedler (or Xelder)
1654-1656	Juan de Montanos Blázquez
1656-1658	Diego Rangel
1658-1663	Juan de Salamanca

1663-1664	Rodrigo de Flores y Aldana
1664-1670	Francisco Oregón y Gascón
1670-1680	Francisco Rodríguez de Ledesma
1680-1685	José Fernandez Córdoba Ponce de León
1685-1687	Manuel de Murguia y Mena
1687-1689	Diego Antonio de Viana y Hinojosa
1689-1697	Severino de Manzaneda Salinas y Rozas
1697-1702	Diego de Córdoba Lasso de la Vega
1702-1705	Pedro Nicolás Benítez de Lugo
1705-1706	Luis Chirino Vandevall
1706-1708	Pedro Álvarez de Villamarín
1708-1716	Laureano José de Torres Ayala y Quadros Castellanos, Marqués de Casa Torres
1716-1717	Vicente Raja
1717-1724	Gregorio Guazo y Fernández de la Vega
1724-1734	Dionisio Martínez de la Vega
1734-1746	Juan Francisco de Güemes y Horcasitas Gordón y Sáenz de Villamolinedo, Conde de Revillagigedo
1746	Juan Antonio Tineo y Fuertes
1746-1747	Diego Peñalosa
1747-1760	Francisco Antonio Cagigal de la Vega Salinas y Acevedo
1760-1761	Pedro Alonso
1761-1762	Juan de Prado Mayeza Portocarrero y Luna
1763-1765	Ambrosio Funes Villalpando Abarca de Bolea, Conde de Ricla
1765-1766	Diego Manrique

1766-1771	Antonio María de Bucareli y Ursúa Hinostrosa Lasso de la Vega	1862-1866	Domingo Dulce Guerrero Garay y Sáez, Marqués de Castell Florit (1)
1771-1777	Felipe de Fondesviela y Ondeano, Marqués de la Torre	1866-1867	Francisco Lersundi y Ormaechea y Guerrero Zambrano (1)
1777-1780	Diego José Navarro García de Valladares	1867	Joaquín del Manzano y Manzano
1781-1782	Juan Manuel de Cagigal y Montserrat de la Vega y Adames	1867	Blas Villate y de la Hera, Conde de Valmaseda (1)
1782-1785	Luis Unzaga y Amezaga	1867-1869	Francisco Lersundi y Ormaechea y Guerrero Zambrano (2)
1785	Bernardo Vicente Pólinarde de Gálvez y Galardo	1869	Domingo Dulce Guerrero Garay y Sáez, Marqués de Castell Florit (2)
1785-1789	José Manuel Ignacio Timoteo de Ezpeleta Galdeano Dicastillo y del Prado	1869	Felipe Ginovés del Espinar
1789-1790	Domingo Cabello y Robles	1869-1870	Antonio Cabellero Fernández de Rodas
1790-1796	Luis de las Casas y Aragorri	1870-1872	Blas Villate y de la Hera, Conde de Valmaseda (2)
1796-1799	Juan Procopio Bassecourt y Bryas, Conde de Santa Clara	1872-1873	Francisco Ceballos y Vargas
1799-1812	Salvador de Muro y Salazar, Marqués de Someruelos	1873	Cándido Pieltain y Jove-Huelgo
		1873-1874	Joaquín Jovellar y Soler (1)
1812-1816	Juan Ruíz de Apodaca y Eliza López de Letona y Lasquetty	1874-1875	José Gutiérrez de la Concha y Irigoyen (3)
1816-1819	José Cienfuegos y Jovellanos	1875-1876	Blas Villate y de la Hera, Conde de Valmaseda (3)
1819	Juan María Echéverri		
1819-1821	Juan Manuel de Cagigal y Martínez Niño de San Miguel y Pacneco	1876-1878	Joaquín Jovellar y Soler (2)
		1878-1879	Arnseio Martínez de Campos y Antón (1)
1821-1822	Nicolás Mahy y Romo	1879	Caetano Figueroa y Garahondo
1822-1823	Sebastián Kindelán y Oregón	1879-1881	Ramón Blanco y Erenas, Marqués de Peña Plata (1)
1823-1832	Francisco Dionisio Vivés		
1832-1834	Mariano Ricafort Palacín y Abarca	1881-1883	Luis Prendergast y Gordón Sweetman y Archimbauld, Marqués de Victória de las Tunas
1834-1838	Miguel Tacón Rosique Foxá y Rivera, Marqués de la Unión de Cuba	1883-1884	Ignacio María del Castillo y Gil de la Torre, Conde de Bilbao
1838-1840	Joaquín de Ezpeleta y Enrile	1884-1886	Ramón Fajardo y Izquierdo
1840-1841	Pedro Téllez y Girón	1886-1887	Emilio Calleja y Isasi (1)
1841-1843	Gerónimo Valdés y Sierra	1887-1889	Sabas Marín y González (1)
1843-1848	Leopoldo O'Donnell y Jorris	1889-1890	Manuel Salamanca y Negrete
1848-1850	Federico Roncali Ceruti y Martínez de Murcia	1890	José Sánchez Gómez
		1890-1892	Camilio Polavieja y del Castillo
1850-1852	José Gutiérrez de la Concha y Irigoyen (1)	1892-1893	Alejandro Rodríguez Arias
		1893	José Arderius y García
1852-1853	Valentín Cañedo Miranda	1893-1895	Emilio Calleja y Isasi (2)
1853-1854	Juan Manuel González de la Pezuela y Cabello Sánchez de Aragón Capay y Olarria	1895-1896	Arsenio Martínez de Campos y Antón (2)
		1896	Sabas Marín y González (2)
1854-1859	José Gutiérrez de la Concha y Irigoyen (2)	1896-1897	Valeriano Weyler y Nicolau, Marqués de Tenerife
1859-1862	Francisco Serrano y Domínguez Cuenca y Guevara Vasconcellos, Duque de la Torre	1897-1898	Ramón Blanco y Erenas, Marqués de Peña Plata (2)
		1898	Adolfo Jimenez Castellanos

1. Menéndez de Áviles governed through deputies Francisco de Zayas, Diego de Ribera, Pedro Menéndez Márquez, and Sancho Pardo Osorio since he was simultaneously adelantado of Florida (q.v.).

Alcázar Molina, pp. 151–97; Guerra y Sánchez et al, vols. 1 to 4, passim; Nieto y Cortadellas, under individual names; Peraza Sarausa, pp. 23–48.

338 CUZCO

Cuzco, the former Inca capital, became the seat of an intendencia with an audiencia in 1784. A revolt against Spanish authority failed in 1813 but in 1824 Cuzco fell to Peruvian republican forces.

Intendants			
1784-1787	Benito de la Mata Linares	1809-1814	José Manuel de Goyeneche y Barred
1787-1791	José de la Portilla y Gálvez	1814-1815	Martín de Concha y Jara
1791-1793	Carlos del Corral y Aguirre	1815-1816	Mariano Ricafort Palacín y Abarca
1793-1804	Manuel Ruiz y Urríes de Castilla	1816	Pío de Tristán y Moscoso
	y Cavero, Marqués de Ruiz de	1817-1819	Bartolomé Cucalón y Villamayor
	Castilla		Vera y Garzes
1804-1808	Francisco Muñoz de San Clemente	1821-1822	Melchor de Aymerich
		1822-1824	Antonio María Álvarez

Deustua Pimentel, pp. 163–80; Mendiburu, 8:414–15.

339 FLORIDA

The Florida peninsula, jutting into the Caribbean just north of Cuba, offered a logical area for Spanish settlement. Several unsuccessful efforts were made after 1513. A French Huguenot colony, planted on the east coast in 1562, prompted more serious Spanish efforts, and this French colony was destroyed in 1565, with a Spanish settlement planted in its stead. Pedro Menéndez de Avilés, the first governor, or in this case adelantado, was simultaneously governor of Cuba (q.v.). Florida was a frontier colony and settlement was sparse. The contiguity of the English colonies after 1733 (v. Georgia, 133) further isolated Florida. Florida was ceded to Great Britain after the Seven Years' War. During the Wars of the American Revolution Spain occupied British West Florida, and it was ceded East Florida by the Treaty of Paris in 1783. For administrative purposes Spain retained the British division of East and West Florida. The expansion of the United States and the recurring boundary disputes between the two countries led Spain to sell the Floridas to the United States in 1819. During the period from 1784 to 1821 the Floridas were subject to the captain-general of Cuba.

Governors			
1567-1574	Pedro Menéndez de Avilés	1647-1650	Benito Ruíz de Salazar
1574-1577	Hernando de Miranda		Ballecilla (2)
1577-1589	Pedro Menéndez Márquez	1650-1654	Nicolás Ponce de Léon
1589-1592	Gutierre de Miranda	1654-1655	Pedro Horruytiner Benedit (2)
1592-1595	Domingo Martínez de Avendaño	1655-1659	Diego de Rebolledo
1596-1603	Gonzalo Méndez de Canço	1659-1663	Alonso de Aranguiz y Cotes
1603-1609	Pedro de Ibarra	1663-1670	Francisco de la Guerra y de la
1609-1612	Juan Fernández de Olivera		Vega
1613-1618	Juan Treviño de Guillamas	1670-1673	Manuel de Cendoya
1618-1623	Juan de Salinas	1673-1680	Pablo de Hita y Salazar
1623-1629	Luis de Rojas y Borja	1680-1687	Juan Márquez Cabrera
1629-1631	Andrés Rodríguez de Villegas	1687-1693	Diego de Quiroga y Losado
1633-1638	Luis Horruytiner	1693-1699	Laureano José de Torres Ayala y
1639-1645	Damián de Vega Castro y		Quadros Castellanos
	Pardo	1699-1706	José de Zúñiga y la Cerda
1645-1646	Benito Ruíz de Salazar	1706-1716	Francisco de Córcoles y Martínez
	Ballecilla (1)	1716	Pedro de Olivera y Fullana
1646	Nicolás Ponce de León	1716-1718	Juan de Ayala Escobar
1646-1647	Pedro Horruytiner Benedit (1)	1718-1734	Antonio de Benavides
		1734-1737	Francisco del Moral y Sánchez

1737-1749	Manuel de Montiano	1812-1815	Sebastián Kindelán y Oregón
1749-1752	Melchor de Navarrette	1815-1816	Juan José de Estrada (2)
1752-1755	Fulgencio García de Solís	1816-1821	José Coppinger
1755-1758	Alonso Fernández de Heredia		
1758-1761	Lucas Fernando de Palacio y		*West Florida*
	Valenzuela		*Governors*
1761-1762	Alonso de Cárdenas	1781-1793	Arturo O'Neill y O'Kelly
1762-1764	Melchor Feliú	1793-1796	Enrique White
1764-1781	(under Great Britain)	1796	Francisco de Paula Gelabert
		1796-1812	Vicente Folch y Juan
	East Florida	1812-1813	Mauricio de Zúñiga (1)
Governors		1813-1815	Mateo González Manrique
1784-1790	Vicente Manuel de Cespedes y	1815-1816	José de Soto
	Velasco	1816	Mauricio de Zúñiga (2)
1790-1795	Juan Nepumoceno de Quesada	1816	Francisco Maximilano de San
	y Barnuevo		Maxent
1795	Bartolomé Morales	1816-1819	José Fascot
1796-1811	Enrique White	1819-1821	José Maria Callava
1811-1812	Juan José de Estrada (1)		

Connor, 1:xxxiii—iv; Te Paske, p. 231 and passim.

340 GRAN CANARIA

Settlement of the Canary Islands in the early 15th century had not reached the island of Gran Canaria, which began to be occupied only in 1480. For a time after 1496 Gran Canaria was subordinated to the adelantado of Tenerife (q.v.) in his capacity as governor of all the islands. During the 16th century the islands were governed individually, but the constant attacks on the Spanish settlements by the English and French prompted the creation of the office of captain-general of the Canary Islands (q.v.) in 1589. After five years the post was abolished, but in 1625 it was revived permanently and the captain-general ordinarily resided on Gran Canaria.

Governors		1540-1543	Agustín de Zurbarán (2)
1480-1491	Pedro de Vera	1543-1546	Alonso del Corral
1491-1494	Francisco de Maldonaldo	1546-1549	Juan Ruíz de Miranda
1495-1497	Alonso Fajardo	1549-1553	Rodrigo Manrique de Acuña (1)
1498-1502	Lope Sánchez de Valenzuela	1553-1555	Luis Serrano de Vigil
1502	Antonio de Torres	1555-1557	Rodrigo Manrique de Acuña (2)
1503-1505	Alonso Escudero	1557-1558	Francisco Mejía Márquez y
1505-1517	Lope de Sosa y Mesa		Pedrosa
1517-1518	Pedro Suárez de Castilla (1)	1559-1562	Juan Pacheco de Benavides
1518-1520	Fernán Pérez de Guzmán	1562-1565	Diego del Aguila y Toledo
1520-1521	Bernardino de Anaya	1565-1568	(unknown)
1521-1523	Pedro Suárez de Castilla (2)	1568-1571	Pedro Rodríguez de Herrera
1523-1526	Diego de Herro	1571-1575	Juan Alonso de Benavides
1526-1529	Martín Hernández Cerón (I)	1575-1578	Diego de Melgarejo
1529-1531	Bernardo del Nero	1579-1584	Martín de Benavides
1532-1535	Martín Hernández Cerón (II)	1584-1586	Tomás de Cangas
1535-1536	Agustín de Zurbarán (1)	1586-1589	Álvaro de Acosta
1536-1538	Bernardino de Ledesma	1589-1595	(office suppressed)
1538-1540	Juan Ruíz de Legarte	1595-1599	Alonso de Alvarado y Ulloa

Spain

1599–1601	Antonio Pamachamoso	1615–1621	Fernando Osorio
1601–1607	Jerónimo de Valderrama y Tovar	1621–1624	Pedro de Barrionuevo y Melgoza
1607–1612	Luis de Mendoza	1624–1625	Gabriel Frías de Lara
1612–1615	Francisco de la Rúa		

Rumeu de Armas, *España*, passim; idem., *Piraterías*, passim.

341 GUAM

Guam is the largest and southernmost of the Mariana Islands group in the western Pacific. The island was probably discovered by Magellan in 1521, but it was only in 1668 that the Spaniards seriously attempted to occupy the island in order to help safeguard the shipping routes from Mexico (v. Nueva España) to the Philippines (q.v.). Fierce resistance by the native Chamorros delayed full control by the Spaniards for several decades. In theory Guam and the Marianas were subordinate to the government of the Philippines, but their isolation ensured them considerable autonomy. As a result of the Spanish-American War, Guam was ceded to the United States in 1898 (v. 406), while the rest of the Marianas were sold to Germany (v. German New Guinea, 72).

Governors

1668–1672	Juan de Santa Cruz	1786–1794	José Arlegue y León
1672–1674	Juan de Santiago	1794–1802	Manuel Muro
1674–1676	Damián de Esplaña (1)	1802–1806	Vicente Blanco
1676–1678	Francisco de Irrisarri y Viñar	1806–1812	Alejandro Parreño
1678–1680	Juan Antonio de Salas	1812–1822	José de Mendenilla y Pineda (1)
1680–1681	José de Quiroga (1)	1822–1823	José Montilla
1681–1683	Antonio Saravia	1823–1826	José Ganga Herrero
1683–1688	Damián de Esplaña (2)	1826–1831	José de Mendenilla y Pineda (2)
1688–1690	José de Quiroga (2)	1831–1837	Francisco Ramón de Villalobos
1690–1694	Damian de Esplaña (3)	1837–1843	José Casillas Salazar
1694–1696	José de Quiroga (3)	1843–1848	Gregorio Santa Maria
1696–1700	José Madraso	1848	Félix Calvo
1700–1704	Francisco Madraso y Asiam	1848–1855	Pablo Pérez
1704–1709	Antonio Villamor y Vadillo	1855–1866	Felipe María de la Corte
1709–1720	Juan Antonio Pimentel	1866–1871	Francisco Moscoso y Lara
1720–1725	Luis Antonio Sánchez de Tagle	1871–1873	Luis de Ybáñez y García
1725	Juan de Ojeda	1873–1875	Eduardo Beaumont y Calafat
1725–1730	Manuel Arguelles Valda	1875–1880	Manuel Brabo y Barrera
1730–1734	Pedro Lasso de la Vega	1880–1884	Francisco Brochero y Parreño
1734–1740	Francisco Cárdenas Pacheco	1884	Angel de Pazos Vela-Hidalgo
1740–1746	Miguel Fernández de Cárdenas	1884	Antonio Borreda
1746–1749	Domingo Gómez de la Sierra	1884–1885	Francisco Olive y García
1749–1756	Enrique de Olavide y Michelena (1)	1885–1890	Enrique Solano
1756–1759	Andrés del Barrío y Rabago	1890–1891	Joaquín Vara de Rey
1759–1768	José de Soroa	1891–1892	Luis Santos
1768–1771	Enrique de Olavide y Michelena (2)	1892–1893	Vicente Gómez Hernández
1771–1774	Mariano Tobias	1893	Juan Godoy
1774–1776	Antonio Apodaca	1893–1895	Emilio Galisteo Brunenque
1776–1786	Felipe de Cera	1895–1898	Jacobo Marina

Carano and Sanchez, pp. 162–64.

342 GUANAJUATO

Guanajuato in central Mexico was created an intendencia within the viceroyalty of Nueva España (q.v.) in 1787. It remained an intendencia until 1821 when it became part of the empire of Mexico. Later it became a state in the Republic of Mexico.

Intendants

1787–1790	Andrés de Amat y Tortosa	1792–1810	Juan Antonio Riaño y Bárcena de los Cuetos y Velarde
1790–1792	Pedro José Soriano	1810–1821	Fernando Pérez Marañón

Marmolejo, 2:347–405, and 3:1–153.

343 GUATEMALA

The area of Guatemala was an early center of Mayan culture, largely decadent by the arrival of the Spaniards, who penetrated the area from Nueva España (q.v.). From 1527 to 1544 Guatemala was under the audiencia of Nueva España, then under the audiencia of the Confines to 1564, and again under Nueva España to 1570. From 1570 on, Guatemala was the seat of its own audiencia, the successor to that of the Confines. From 1560 on, the president of the audiencia possessed the additional rank of captain-general. The captaincy-general of Guatemala had under its jurisdiction the governments of Honduras, Nicaragua, Costa Rica (qq.v.), and Soconusco. After 1786 the intendencia of San Salvador (q.v.) was added to its jurisdiction. In 1821 Guatemala became free of Spanish rule and for a brief period the areas of the captaincy-general united with Mexico. Thereafter they formed the United States of Central America, and after 1840 each of the former provinces (including San Salvador) became an independent republic. The northern parts of the captaincy-general remained part of Mexico after the rest had dissolved the brief union.

Governors

1524–1526	Pedro de Alvarado y Contreras (1)
1526	Gonzalo de Alvarado y Contreras
1526–1527	Pedro de Portocarrero
1527–1529	Jorge de Alvarado (1)
1529–1530	Agustín Francisco de Orduña
1530–1533	Pedro de Alvarado y Contreras (2)
1533–1535	Jorge de Alvarado (2)
1535–1536	Pedro de Alvarado y Contreras (3)
1536–1539	Alonso de Maldonaldo (1)
1539–1540	Pedro de Alvarado y Contreras (4)
1540–1541	Francisco de la Cueva y Villacreces (1)
1541	Beatriz de Alva de la Cueva
1541–1542	Francisco de la Cueva y Villacreces[1] (2)
1541–1542	Francisco Marroquín[1]
1542–1548	Alonso de Maldonaldo (2)
1548–1554	Alonso López Cerrato
1554–1558	Antonio Rodríguez de Quesada
1558–1559	Pedro Ramírez de Quiñónes
1559–1564	Juan Núñez de Landecho

1564–1570	Francisco Briceño
1570–1573	Antonio González
1573–1578	Pedro de Villalobos
1578–1589	Pedro García de Valverde
1589–1594	Pedro Mallén de Rueda
1594–1596	Francisco de Sande Picón
1596–1598	Álvaro Gómez de Abaunza
1598–1611	Alonso Criado de Castilla
1611–1627	Antonio Peraza Ayala Castilla y Rojas, Conde de La Gomera
1627–1634	Diego de Acuña
1634–1642	Álvaro de Quiñónes y Osorio y Miranda, Marqués de Lorenzana
1642–1649	Diego de Avendaño
1649–1654	Antonio de Lara y Mogrobejo
1654–1657	Fernando de Altamirano y Velasco, Conde de Santiago de Calimaya
1657–1659	(audiencia)
1659–1668	Martín Carlos de Mencos
1668–1670	Sebastián Álvarez Alonso Rosica de Caldas

Spain

1670-1672	Juan de Santa Maria Sáenz Mañosca y Murillo	1748-1752	José Araujo y Río
1672-1678	Fernando Francisco de Escobedo	1752-1753	José Vásquez Prego Montaos y Sotomayor
1678-1681	Lope de Sierra Osorio	1753-1754	Juan de Velarde y Cienfuegos (1)
1681-1683	Juan Miguel Augurto y Alava	1754-1760	Alonso de Arcos y Moreno
1683-1688	Enrique Enríquez de Guzmán	1760-1761	Juan de Velarde y Cienfuegos (2)
1688-1691	Jacinto de Barrios y Leal (1)	1761-1765	Alonso Fernández de Heredia
1691-1694	Fernando Lope de Ursino y Orbaneja	1765-1771	Pedro de Salazar y Herrera Najera y Mendoza
1694-1695	Jacinto de Barrios y Leal (2)	1771-1773	Juan González Bustillo y Villaseñor
1695-1696	(audiencia)		
1696-1702	Gabriel Sánchez de Berrospe	1773-1779	Martín de Mayorga
1702-1703	Alonso de Ceballos y Villagutierre	1779-1783	Matías de Gálvez García Madrid y Cabrera
1703-1706	Juan Jerónimo Duardo	1783-1789	José de Estacherría
1706-1716	Toribio José de Cosío y Campo, Marqués de Torre Campo	1789-1794	Bernardo Troncoso Martínez del Rincón
1716-1724	Francisco Rodríguez de Rivas	1794-1801	José Domás y Valle
1724-1733	Pedro Antonio de Echévers y Subiza	1801-1811	Antonio González Mollinedo y Saravia
1733-1742	Pedro Rivera y Villalón	1811-1818	José de Bustamante y Guerra
1742-1748	Tomás Rivera y Santa Cruz	1818-1821	Carlos de Urrutia y Montoya

1. De la Cueva y Villacreces and Marroquín governed jointly.

Alcázar Molina, pp. 199–212; Villacorta C[alderón], *Capitania General*, pp. 59–78; idem, "Nómina cronológica," passim.

344 GUAYANA

The province of Guayana in eastern Venezuela was formed in 1591. Until 1735 the province included the nearby island of Trinidad which the Spaniards had unsuccessfully attempted to settle in 1531 and which was finally colonized at the turn of the 17th century. In 1735 Trinidad (q.v.) was separated from Guayana and erected into a separate province. During the period before 1735 the governors of Guayana were often indiscriminately called governors of Trinidad and in fact they often resided there. From 1735 to 1762 the province of Guayana was suppressed and placed under the contiguous province of Nueva Andalucía (q.v.). From its creation in 1591 until 1766 Guayana was subordinate to the Spanish authorities in Nueva Granada (q.v.). In 1766 it was transferred to the captaincy-general of Venezuela (q.v.). Guayana remained under Spanish control until 1817 when it was occupied by patriot forces. It subsequently became part of Gran Colombia and later of the Republic of Venezuela. The following list is extremely conjectural for the 17th century since the sources are contradictory for this period. Nueva Andalucía and Guayana are often confused.

Governors		1619-1624	Fernando de Berrío y Oruña (2)
1591-1597	Antonio de Berrío	1624-1630	Luis de Monsalve y Saavedra
1597-1612	Fernando de Berrío y Oruña (1)	1631-	Cristóbal de Aranda
1612-1614	Sancho de Alquiza	1639-1642	Diego López de Escobar
1614-1616	Antonio de Mujica y Buitrón	1642-1656	Martín Mendoza de la Hoz y Berrío
1616-1618	Diego Palomeque de Acuña		
1618	Juan de Lezama	1656-1658	Cristóbal de Vera
1618-1619	Jerónimo de Grados	1658-	Pedro Juan de Viedma y Carvajal

1664-1670	José de Axpe y Zúñiga	1726-1731	Agustín de Arredondo.
1670-1673	Diego Jiménez de Aldana	1731-1733	Bartolomé de Aldunate y Rada
1675-1682	Tiburcio de Axpe y Zúñiga	1735-1762	(under Nueva Andalucía)
1682-1684	Diego Suárez Ponce de León (1)	1762-1766	Joaquín Moreno de Mendoza
1684-1690	Sebastián de Roteta	1766-1776	Manuel Centurión Guerrero de
1691-1693	Francisco de Meneses y Bravo de		Torres
	Saravia	1776-1777	José de Linares
1693-1696	Diego Suárez Ponce de Léon (2)	1778-1784	Antonio de Pereda Lascanótegui
1698-1699	José de Leoz y Echales		y Boulet
1699-1704	Francisco Ruiz de Aguirre	1784-1790	Miguel Marmión
1704-1711	Felipe de Artieda	1790-1797	Luis Antonio Gil
1711-1716	Cristóbal Félix de Guzmán	1797-1810	Felipe de Inciarte
1716-1721	Pedro de Jara	1810-1815	Matías Farreras
1721	Juan de Orvay	1815-1816	Nicolás Ceruti
1721-1726	Martín Pérez de Anda y Salazar	1816-1817	Lorenzo FitzGerald

Morales Padrón, "Trinidad," p. 181; Tavera Acosta, pp. 80, 107–8, 180, 187–88.

345 GUAYAQUIL

The port of Guayaquil was founded in 1535 and was a corregimiento under the audiencia of Quito (q.v.) until 1763 when it was raised to the status of a province. In 1820 Guayaquil fell into the possession of the patriots and was until 1830 part of Gran Colombia. Guayaquil became part of the Republic of Ecuador at its establishment in 1830.

Governors

1763-1771	Juan Antonio Zelaya y Vergara	1796-1803	Juan de Mata y Urbina Gaytán y
1772-1776	Francisco de Ugarte (1)		Ayala
1776-1777	Domingo Guerrero y Marnara	1803-1810	Bartolomé Cucalón y Villamayor
1777-1779	Francisco de Ugarte (2)		Vera y Garzes
1780-1789	Ramón García de León y Pizarro	1810-1811	Francisco Gil y Taboada
1789-1795	José de Aguirre Irisarri	1811-1816	Juan Vasco y Pascual
1795-1796	Victor de Salcedo y Somodevila	1816-1820	Juan Manuel de Mendiburú
		1820	José Pascual Vivero y Salaverría

Castilla, passim.

346 HONDURAS

The coast of Honduras in Central America was discovered by Columbus on his last voyage in 1502. The area, midway between Mexico (v. Nueva España) and Panama (q.v.), was settled from each and its jurisdiction was disputed by the authorities of both. Honduras was subject to the audiencia of Nueva España from 1528 to 1539 and thereafter of the audiencia of the Confines (later Guatemala). In 1786, on the creation of the intendencias, Honduras, often called Comayagua after its chief city even before this, became the intendencia of Comayagua. The intendencia was suppressed in 1812, and until 1821 the province was an alcaldia mayor. In 1821 Honduras freed itself of Spanish control, and together with the other provinces under the captaincy-general of Guatemala (q.v.) it became part of Mexico. This union was most ephemeral, as was the experiment of the United States of Central America. In 1840 Honduras became a separate republic.

Governors

1526-1530	Diego López de Salcedo
1530-1532	Andrés de Cerezeda (1)
1532	Diego Alvítez
1532-1535	Andrés de Cerezeda (2)
1535-1540	Francisco de Montejo (1)
1541-1542	Diego García de Celís
1542-1544	Francisco de Montejo (2)
1544-1552	(corregidores)
1552-1555	Juan Pérez de Cabrera
1555-1562	Pedro de Salvatierra
1563-1567	Alonso Ortiz de Elgueta
1567-1573	Juan de Vargas Carvajal
1573-1577	Diego de Herrera
1577-1582	Alonso de Contreras Guevara
1582-1589	Rodrigo Ponce de León (1)
1589-1594	Jerónimo Sánchez de Carranza
1594-1602	Rodrigo Ponce de León (2)
1602-	Jorge de Alvarado
-1608	Pedro de Castro
1608-1612	Juan Guerra de Ayala
1612-1617	García Garabito de León
1617-1620	Juan Lobato
1620-1625	Juan de Miranda
1625-1632	Pedro del Rosal
1632-1639	Francisco Martínez de la Ribamontán Santander
1639-1641	Francisco de Avila y Lugo
1641-1643	Alonso de Silva Salazar
1643-1644	Juan de Bustamante Herrera
1644-1647	Melchor Alonso Tamayo
1647-1650	Baltasar de la Cruz
1650-1668	Juan de Zuazo
1668-1672	Juan Márquez Cabrera
1673-1676	Pedro de Godoy Ponce de León
1676-1679	Francisco de Castro y Ayala
1679-1682	Lorenzo Ramírez de Guzmán
1682-1687	Antonio de Navia y Bolaños
1689-1693	Sancho Ordóñez
1693-1698	Antonio de Oseguera y Quevedo
1698-1702	Antonio de Ayala
1702-1712	Antonio de Montfort
1712-1715	Enrique Logman
1715-1717	José Rodezno
1717-1727	Diego Gutiérrez de Argüelles
1727-1738	Manuel de Castilla y Portugal
1738-1741	Francisco de Parga
1741-1745	Tomás Hermenegildo de Arana
1745-1746	Luis Machado
1746-1747	Juan de Vera
1747	Alonso Fernández de Heredia
1747-1750	Diego de Tablada
1750-1751	Pedro Trucco
1751-1757	Pantaleón Ibáñez Cuevas
1757-1759	Fulgencio García de Solís
1759-1761	Gabriel Franco
1761-1769	José Sáenz Bahamonde
1769-1770	Juan Antonio González
1770	Antonio Ferrandis
1770-1775	Bartolomé Pérez Quijano
1775-1780	Agustín Pérez Quijano
1780-1783	Francisco Aybar
1783-1786	Juan Nepomuceno de Quesada y Barnuevo

Governors/Intendants

1786-1789	Juan Nepomuceno de Quesada y Barnuevo
1789-1796	Alejo García Conde
1796-1803	Ramón de Anguiano
1803-1810	Antonio Norberto Serrano y Polo
1810-1812	Carlos Castañón

Alcaldes Mayores

1812	Eusebio Silva
1812	José María Piñol y Muñoz
1812-1819	Juan Antonio de Tornos
1819-1821	José Gregorio Tinoco de Contreras

Chamberlain, passim; Durón y Gamero, pp. 17-133.

347 HUAMANGA

Huamanga, in southern Peru, was one of eight intendencias created within the viceroyalty of Peru (q.v.) in 1784. In 1824 the area fell to the patriot forces and Spanish control was terminated. Huamanga became part of the Republic of Peru.

Intendants

1784-1786	Nicolás Próspero Manrique de Lara, Marqués de Lara
1786-1799	José Menéndez y Escalada
1799-1813	Demetrio O'Higgins
1813-1815	Francisco de Paula Pruna y Aguilar
1815-1817	Narciso Basagoitía
1817-1819	Manuel Quimper Benítez del Pino
1819-1821	Francisco José de Recabarren Aguirre Pardo de Figueroa y Argandoña
1821-1823	Gabriel de Herboso y Astoraica
1823-1824	José Montenegro y Ubalde

Deustua Pimentel, pp. 149–62; Mendiburú, 8:415.

348 HUANCAVELICA

The region of Huancavelica in central Peru was the site of rich mercury deposits and had a superintendent of mines. This official was appointed by the viceroy of Peru (q.v.) until 1736 and directly by the Council of the Indies thereafter. In 1784 Huancavelica became one of the intendencias of the viceroyalty of Peru. In 1822–24 the area was occupied by nationalist forces and became part of the Republic of Peru.

Intendants

1784-1789	Fernando Márquez de la Plata
1789-1791	Pedro de Tagle y Bracho
1791-1794	Manuel Ruíz y Urries de Castilla y Cavero, Conde Ruíz de Castilla
1794-1805	Juan María Gálvez y Montes de Oca
1806-1809	Juan Vives y Echeverría (1)
1809-1810	Francisco Javier de Mendizábal
1810-1813	Lázaro de Ribera Espinosa de los Monteros
1813-1814	Juan Vives y Echeverría (2)
1814-1817	Felipe García Eulate
1818-1820	José Montenegro y Ubalde
1821-1822	Agustín Otermín
1822-1823	Gabriel Pérez

Deusta Pimentel, pp. 85–108; Mendiburú, 4:427, and 8:415–16.

349 IFNI

From 1478 to 1524 the Spaniards occupied the post of Santa Cruz de la Mar Pequeña on the Moroccan coast opposite the Canary Islands (q.v.). With this precedent the Spaniards persuaded the sultan of Morocco in 1860 to recognize the right of Spain to reoccupy the area. However, this was not implemented until 1934 when the area, known as Ifni, began to be occupied by Spanish forces. In 1952 Ifni became a part of Spanish West Africa (q.v.). In 1958 Spanish West Africa was divided into Spanish Sahara and Ifni. The small area of Ifni, an enclave in Morocco (q.v.) was retroceded to Morocco early in 1969.

Spain

Governors
1958-1959 Mariano Gómez Zamallos Quirce
1959-1961 Pedro Latorre Alcubierre
1961-1963 Joaquín Agulla Jiménez Coronado

1963-1965 Adolfo Artalejo Campos
1965-1967 Marino Troyo Larrasquito
1967-1969 José Miguel Vega Rodríguez

Information from José Díaz de Villegas, Presidencia del Gobierno, Director General de Plazas y Provincias Africanas, Madrid.

350 JAMAICA

The island of Jamaica in the western Caribbean was discovered by Columbus in 1494 and subsequently granted to him and to his descendants, the Dukes of Verágua. The Spaniards called the island Sant'Jago, but Jamaica, of Carib derivation, predominated as its name even under Spanish rule. Normally the governor of Jamaica was appointed by the Duke of Verágua with the approval of the Spanish monarch. Jamaica, despite its excellent location, never was of more than marginal value to Spain. In 1655 it was attacked by the English, then firmly established in the Lesser Antilles. By 1660 they had driven the Spaniards from the island (v. Jamaica, 149).

Governors
1509-1514 Juan de Esquivel
1514-1523 Francisco de Garay
1523-1526 Pedro de Mazuelo
1526-   Juan de Mendegurren
1533-1534 Gil González Dávila
1536-   Manuel de Rojas
1539   Pedro Cano (1)
1544   Francisco de Pina
1556   Juan González de Hinojosa
1558   Pedro Cano (2)
1565   Blas de Melo
1567-1572 Juan de Gaudiel
1575   Hernán Manrique de Rojas
    -1577 Iñigo Fuentes
1577-1578 Rodrigo Núñez de la Peña
1578-1583 Lucas del Valle Alvarado (1)
1586   Diego Fernández de Mercado
1591   Lucas del Valle Alvarado (2)

1596   García del Valle
1596-1606 Fernando Melgarejo de Córdoba
1607-1611 Alonso de Miranda
1611-1614 Pedro Espejo Barranco
1614-   Andrés González de Vera
1620   Sebastián Lorenzo Romano
1625-1632 Francisco Terril
1632-1637 Juan Martínez Arana
1637-1639 Gabriel Peñalver Angulo
1639-1640 Jacinto Sedeño Albornoz (1)
1640-1643 Francisco Ladrón de Zegama
1643-1645 (alcades)
1645-1646 Sebastián Fernández de Gamboa
1646-1650 Pedro Caballero
1650   Jacinto Sedeño Albornoz (2)
1650-1651 Francisco de Proenza (1)
1651-1655 Juan Ramírez de Arellano
1655-1656 Francisco de Proenza (2)
1656-1660 Cristóbal Arnaldo Isasi

Morales Padrón, pp. 128–52.

351 LA PAZ

The area around Lake Titicaca was organized into the intendencia of La Paz within the viceroyalty of Río de la Plata (q.v., 381) in 1783. After the transfer of Puno (q.v.) to Peru (q.v.) in 1796 La Paz was the most northwesterly intendencia in Río de la Plata. Although the area re-

304

volted against Spain in 1809, Spanish control was not ended until 1825 when La Paz became part of the Republic of Bolivia.

Intendants

1784-1789	José Sebastián de Segurola y Oliden
1789-1790	José Pablo Conti
1790-1791	Agustín de Goyoneta
1791-1793	Juan Manuel Álvarez
1793-1794	Francisco Antonio Dionísio Cuéllar Artucho Carrillo de los Ríos Ronsvi Valdés
1795-1796	Fernando de la Sota Agüero
1797-1805	Juan Antonio de Burgunyó
1805-1809	Tadeo Dávila
1809-1810	Juan Ramírez Orosco
1810-1813	Domingo Tristán y Moscoso
1813-1814	Gregorio Hoyos de Miranda García de Llano, Marqués de Valde Hoyos
1814-1816	José María Laudavere
1816-1817	Mariano Ricafort Palacín y Abarca
1817-1822	Juan Sánchez Lima
1822-1823	Francisco Huarte y Jáuregui
1823-1825	José Ildefonso Mendizábal y Imaz

Lynch, p. 291; Santa Cruz, pp. 325–45.

352 LOUSIANA

France ceded its colony of Louisiana (39) to Spain in 1762 to prevent its falling into British hands. However, Spain did not take over administration of Louisiana until 1765. During its existence as a Spanish colony Louisiana was under the government of Cuba (q.v.). In 1800, by the Treaty of San Ildefonso, Spain retroceded Louisiana to France on the latter's promise of non-alienation. France only took possession in 1803. Meanwhile, the failure of Napoleon's efforts to reconquer Saint-Domingue (56) persuaded him to dispose of Louisiana, potentially of nuisance value only. Consequently, despite the terms of the treaty, he sold the entire province of Louisiana, which extended indefinitely north and west of New Orleans at the mouth of the Mississippi River, to the United States. Three weeks after taking over from the Spaniards, the French agent handed over authority to the United States.

Governors

1765-1768	Antonio de Ulloa y de la Torre Guiral
1768-1770	Alejandro O'Reilly y McDowell Sillon
1770-1777	Luis de Unzaga y Amezaga
1777-1785	Bernardo Vicente Pólinarde de Gálvez y Galardo
1785-1791	Esteban Rodríguez Miró y Sabater
1791-1797	Francisco Luis Hector de Carondelet de Novelles
1797-1799	Manuel Luis Gayoso de Lemos y Amorín y Magallanes
1799-1802	Sebastián Calvo de la Puerta y O'Farril Arango y Arriola, Marqués de Casa Calvo
1802-1803	Manuel José de Salcedo

Holmes, p. 11, and passim.

353 MALVINAS ISLANDS

The Malvinas Islands, in the South Atlantic off the coast of Argentina, were frequented in the 16th century by French sailors from Saint Malo and hence were called Îles Malouines, and by the Spaniards, Islas Malvinas. The islands were discovered by the English in 1592 and a hundred years later were named by them the Falkland Islands (127). The French established a post on East Falkland but abandoned it in 1767. For the next few years the English and Spaniards fought over possession of the islands, until Great Britain abandoned its post in 1774. The islands remained in undisputed Spanish possession until 1810 when the Spanish governor fled. During this period they were part of the viceroyalty of Río de la Plata (q.v., 381).

Governors

1767-1773	Felipe Ruíz Puente	1793-1794	Pedro Pablo Sanguineto (2)
1773-1774	Domingo Chauri	1794-1795	José de Aldana y Ortega (1)
1774-1777	Francisco Gil y Lemos	1795-1796	Pedro Pablo Sanguineto (3)
1777-1779	Ramón Carassa	1796-1797	José de Aldana y Ortega (2)
1779-1781	Salvador de Medina	1797-1798	Luis de Medina y Torres (1)
1781-1783	Jacinto de Altolaguirre	1798-1799	Francisco Javier de Viana (1)
1783-1784	Fulgencio Montemayor	1799-1800	Luis de Medina y Torres (2)
1784-1786	Agustín Figueroa	1800-1801	Francisco Javier de Viana (2)
1786-1787	Pedro de Mesa y Castro (1)	1801-1802	Ramón Fernández de Villegas
1787-1788	Ramón Clairac (1)	1802-1803	Bernardo Bonavia (1)
1788-1789	Pedro de Mesa y Castro (2)	1803-1804	Antonio Leal de Ibarra (1)
1789-1790	Ramón Clairac (2)	1804-1805	Bernardo Bonavia (2)
1790-1791	Juan José de Elizalde (1)	1805-1806	Antonio Leal de Ibarra (2)
1791-1792	Pedro Pablo Sanguineto (1)	1806-1809	Bernardo Bonavia (3)
1792-1793	Juan José de Elizalde (2)	1809-1810	Gerardo Bondas

Gomez Langenheim, vol. 1, passim.

354 MARGARITA

Margarita, a small island off the coast of Venezuela, was granted to the Villalobos family in 1525 and continued to be governed privately until 1600 when it reverted to the Spanish crown. Until 1739 the province of Margarita was subject to the audiencia of Santo Domingo (q.v.). From 1739 to 1777 it was under the audiencia of Santa Fé (v. Nueva Granada). On the creation of the captaincy-general of Venezuela (q.v.), Margarita fell under its jurisdiction. After 1810 continuous and firm royal control of Margarita ceased, although until 1821 it fluctuated between royal and patriot control. Eventually it became part of the Venezuelan state of Nueva Esparta.

Governors

1575-1581	Miguel Maza de Lizana	1614-1619	Juan Rodríguez de las Varillas
1581	Pedro de Arce	1619-1624	Andrés Rodríguez de Villegas
1583-1593	Juan Sarmiento de Villandrando	1626-1628	García Álvarez de Figueroa
1594-1595	Francisco Gutiérrez Flores	1630-1637	Juan de Eulate
1595-1598	Pedro de Salazar	1638-1642	Juan Luis de Camarena
1598-1602	Pedro Fajardo	1643-1649	Francisco de Santillán y Argote
1603-1608	Fadrique Cáncer	1649-1653	Fernando de Mendoza Mate de Luna
1608-1614	Bernardo de Vargas Machuca	1654-1657	Pedro de Rojas Manrique

1658-1661	Juan Marroquín de Montehermoso		1732-1737	Blas de Castro
1661-1668	Carlos Navarro		1738-1746	José Albear y Velasco
1668-1671	Martín de Tellería		1746-1750	José Longar y Cobián
1671-1676	Francisco de Mejía y Alarcón		1750-1756	Joaquín Moreno de Mendoza
1676-1685	Juan Muñoz de Gadea		1757-1764	Alonso del Río y Castro
1686-1688	Martín Cabeza de Vaca		1764-1776	José de Matos y Rabel
1688-1690	Sancho de Zapata de Mendoza		1776-1785	Félix Francisco Bejarano
1692-1699	José Leoz y Echalaz		1785-1792	Miguel González Dávila
1699-1706	Diego Suinaga y Orbea		1793-1796	Juan de Dios Valdés de Yarza
1707-1712	José de Alcántara		1797-1806	Miguel Herrera
1712-1716	Antonio de Molina y Miñano		1806	Gaspar de Cagigal
1718-1724	José de Arias		1807-1808	Antonio Montaña
1725-1730	Juan de Vera y Fajardo		1808-1810	Joaquín de Puelles

Heredia Herrera, pp. 510–12; Salazar, pp. 107–8.

355 MÉRIDA-LA GRITA

In 1575 the province of Espíritu Santo de La Grita was created under the audiencia of Santa Fé de Bogotá (v. Nueva Granada). This province was suppressed in 1608 and La Grita was united with Mérida to form a corregimiento. In 1625 Mérida-La Grita was raised to a province. In 1676 Maracaibo was detached from Venezuela (q.v.) and added to Mérida-La Grita. Two years later the governor and captain-general (from 1625) removed to Maracaibo, which henceforth became the seat of the government of the province although it was only in 1751 that the name of the province was changed to Maracaibo. Until 1740 Mérida was under the jurisdiction of the audiencia of Santo Domingo (q.v.). Then until 1777 the province was under the audiencia of Santa Fé. In that year it was placed under the new captaincy-general of Venezuela. During the wars of independence after 1811 the province had no organized government. In 1819 it became part of Gran Colombia, and later of the Republic of Venezuela.

La Grita
Governors
1574-1589	Francisco de Cáceres
1589-1590	Andrés Calvo de Cáceres
1590-1593	Juan de Velasco Montalvo
1593-1598	Hernando Barrantes Maldonaldo (1)
1598-1600	Luis Enríquez de Monroy
1600-1608	Hernando Barrantes Maldonaldo (2)

Mérida-La Grita
Corregidores
1608-1609	Pedro Venegas Torrijos
1609-1615	Juan de Aguilar y Carrascoso
1615-1620	Fernando López de Arriete
1620-1625	Juan Pacheco de Velasco

Governors
1625-1634	Juan Pacheco Maldonaldo y Graterol
1634-1639	Alonso Fernández Valentín
1639-1644	Félix Fernández de Guzmán
1644-1651	Francisco Martínez de Espinosa
1651-1658	Juan Bravo de Acuña
1658-1663	Tomás de Torre y Ayala
1663-1664	Miguel de Ursúa Arismendi y Egües Beaumont, Conde de Gerona
1664-1666	Gabriel Guerrero de Sandoval
1666-1667	Juan de Mur Soldevilla
1667-1668	Diego de Villalba y Girón
1668-1674	Pedro Juan de Viedma y Carvajal
1674-1676	Jorge de Madueira Ferreira

Mérida, La Grita, and Maracaibo
Governors
1676-1680	Jorge de Madureira Ferreira
1680-1687	Antonio de Vergara Azcárate y Dávila
1687-1694	José de Cerdeno y Monzón
1694-1701	Gaspar Mateo de Acosta

Spain

1701-1702	Manuel Arias de Puga		

1701-1702 Manuel Arias de Puga
1702-1708 Laureano de Escaray
1708-1712 Pedro Esmayle de Lobato y
  Bobadilla
1712-1718 Francisco de la Rocha Ferrer y
  Labarcés
1718-1723 Guillermo Tomás Hendrixen de
  Roo
1723-1724 Cristóbal Alonso de Gámez y
  Co[a]stilla
1724-1729 Manuel Fernández de la Casa
1729-1734 Ignacio Torreiro Montenegro
1734-1738 Juan José Valderrama y Haro
1738-1740 Manuel de Altuve Gavidria y
  Bedoya
1740-1741 Antonio Benito del Casal y
  Montenegro
1741-1746 Francisco Antonio Salcedo
1746-1751 Francisco Miguel Collado (1)

Maracaibo

Governors

1751-1754 Francisco de Ugarte (1)
1754-1755 Antonio Guill y Gonzaga
1755-1758 Francisco de Ugarte (2)
1758-1764 Francisco Javier Moreno de
  Mendoza
1764-1765 Francisco Miguel Collado (2)
1765-1775 Antonio del Río y Castro
1775-1780 Francisco de Santa Cruz
1780-1782 Miguel de Ayala y Tamayo
1782-1786 Francisco de Arce
1786-1787 Salvador Muñoz y Fernández de
  Allegro
1787-1794 Joaquín Primo de Rivera
1794-1799 Juan Ignacio de Armada, Marqués
  de Santa Cruz de Rivadulla
1799-1810 Fernando Miyares y González
1810-1811 Pedro Ruíz de Porras

Information from Dr. Edilberto Moreno, Gobernador de Mérida, Mérida, Venezuela. Also, Martínez Mendoza, pp. 371–82.

356 MONTEVIDEO

Montevideo, on the north side of the Río de la Plata estuary, was founded in 1726 in response to the threat presented by the establishment of the Portuguese Nova Colônia do Sacramento (304). In 1751 Montevideo was raised to the rank of a province, and it remained one after the introduction of the intendencia system some thirty years later. Nova Colônia do Sacramento was ceded to Spain in 1777 and its territory added to that of Montevideo. This region, between the seat of Spanish authority at Buenos Aires (q.v.) and Portuguese Brazil (q.v.), came to be known as the *banda oriental*. After his expulsion from Buenos Aires in 1810 the viceroy of Río de la Plata (q.v., 381) removed to Montevideo, but in 1814 Spanish authority ended there as well. From then until 1830 the area was contested between the new Argentine government in Buenos Aires, the Portuguese, and even the English. Finally, in 1830 the area became independent, as a sort of buffer zone, as the República Oriental del Uruguay, with Montevideo as its capital.

Governors
1751-1764 José Joaquín de Viana (1)
1764-1771 Agustín de la Rosa
1771-1773 José Joaquín de Viana (2)
1773-1790 Joaquín del Pino y Rosas Romero
  Negrete
1790-1797 Antonio Olaguer y Feliú Heredia
  Lopez y Donec
1797-1804 José de Bustamante y Guerra

1804-1807 Pascual Ruíz Huidobro
1807-1810 Francisco Javier Elío y Olondriz
  Robles y Echaide (1)
1810 Fernando de Soria y Santa Cruz
1810-1811 Gaspar de Vigodet (1)
1811-1812 Francisco Javier Elío y Olondriz
  Robles y Echaide (2)
1812-1814 Gaspar de Vigodet (2)

Araujo, 1:xvii; Thomas, pp. 95–145.

357 MOROCCO

Spanish interest in Morocco was of long standing (v. Ifni). After 1640 Spain directly administered the former Portuguese territories of Ceuta and Melilla (q.v. and v. Ceuta, 290). In the
early years of the 20th century France secured the dominant position in Morocco, and in 1912
it proclaimed a protectorate over most of that country (v. Morocco, 47). In the same year a
Franco-Spanish agreement delimited a zone of Spanish control in the northern part of Morocco
along the Mediterranean coast. Subsequent agreements reduced the size of this area. After
1934 the high commissioner for the Spanish zone had jurisdiction over Spanish West Africa (q.v.)
as well. In 1956 after the French withdrawal from Morocco, Spain, too, resigned its rights to
the Spanish zone, although retaining its ancient possessions of Ceuta and Melilla.

High Commissioners		
1913	Felipe Alfau y Mendoza	
1913-1915	José Marina Vega	
1915-1918	Francisco Gómez Jordana	
1919-1922	Damaso Berenguer y Fuste	
1922-1923	Ricardo Burguete Lana	
1923	Luis Silvela Casado	
1923-1924	Luis Aizpuru	
1924-1925	Miguel Primo de Rivera y Orbaneja	
1925-1928	José Sanjurjo Sacanell Buenrostro y Desojo, Marqués de Malmusi (1)	
1928-1931	Francisco Gómez Jordana y Souza, Conde de Jordana	
1931	José Sanjurjo Sacanell Buenrostro y Desojo, Marqués de Malmusi (2)
1931-1933	Luciano López Ferrer
1933-1934	Juan Moles (1)
1934-1936	Manuel Rico Avello
1936-1937	Juan Moles (2)
1937-1940	Juan Beigbeder y Atienza
1940-1941	Carlos Asensio
1941-1945	Luis Orgaz y Yoldi
1945-1951	José Enrique Varela Iglesias
1951-1956	Rafael García Valiño y Marcén

Hernández de Herrera and García Figueras, vol. 1, passim; *Statesman's Year Book*, 1938–56.

358 NICARAGUA

The coast of Nicaragua had been discovered by Columbus in 1502, and settlement of the area
from Panama (q.v.) began in 1522. Until 1538 Nicaragua was subject to the audiencia of Santo
Domingo (q.v.), to that of Panama from 1539 to 1544, and after 1544 to that of the Confines (later
Guatemala). The eastern coast of Nicaragua, known as the Moskito Coast, was never really
under Spanish control during the colonial period. Until 1782 much of it was subject to strong
British influence, if not actual control (v. Moskito Coast, 164). In 1786 the captaincy-general,
of which Nicaragua was a part, was reconstituted as part of the intendencia system and the governor of Nicaragua became the governor/intendant of León. Revolt against Spain began in Nicaragua in 1811 but only in 1821 was Spanish authority definitely expelled. Nicaragua became
first a part of Mexico and then a member of the United States of Central America. In 1839 it became an independent republic.

Governors		*Alcaldes Mayores*	
1522-1524	Gil González Dávila	1552-1553	Alonso Ortiz de Elgueta
1524-1526	Francisco Hernández de Córdoba	1553	Nicolás López de Urraga (1)
1526-1531	Pedro Arias de Ávila	1553-1555	Juan de Cavallón
1531-1535	Francisco de Castañeda	1555	Juan Márquez
1536-1544	Rodrigo de Contreras	1555-1556	Álvaro de Paz
1544	Diego de Herrera	1556-1557	Nicolás López de Urraga (2)
1544-1552	(audiencia)	1558	Andrés López Moraga

Spain

1558-1560	Francisco de Mendoza		1724-1727	Tomás Marcos Duque de Estrada (1)
1561-1564	Juan Vásquez de Coronado		1727	Antonio Póveda y Rivadineira (2)
1564-1566	Hernando Bermejo		1728-1730	Tomás Marcos Duque de Estrada (2)

Governors

1566-1575	Alonso de Casaos		1730-1736	Bartolomé González Fitoria
1575-1576	Francisco del Valle Marroquín		1736-1740	Antonio de Ortiz
1576-1583	Diego de Artieda y Chirino		1740-1745	José Antonio Lacayo de Briones
1583-1589	Hernando de Gasco		1745	Francisco Antonio de Cáceres Molinedo
1589-1592	Carlos de Arellano			
1592-1599	Bartolomé de Lences		1745-1746	Juan de Vera
1599-1603	Bernardino de Obando		1746-1753	Alonso Fernández de Heredia
1603-1622	Alonso Lara de Córdoba		1753-1756	José González Rancaño
1622	Cristóbal de Villagrán		1756-1759	Melchor Vidal de Lorca y Villena (1)
1622-1623	Alonso Lazo			
1623-1625	Santiago de Figueroa		1759-1765	Pantaleón Ibáñez Cuevas
1625-1627	Lázaro de Albizúa		1765-1766	Melchor Vidal de Lorca y Villena (2)
1627-1630	Juan de Agüero			
1630-1634	Francisco de Asagra y Vargas		1766-1776	Domingo Cabello y Robles
1634-1641	Pedro de Velasco		1777-1782	Manuel de Quiroga
1641-1660	Juan de Bracamonte		1782-1783	José de Estacherría
1660-1665	Diego de Castro		1783-1786	Juan de Ayssa y Blancazo Allue y Palacín
1665-1669	Juan Salinas y Cerda			
1669-1673	Antonio Temiño Dávila			
1673-1681	Pablo de Loyola			*León*
1681	Antonio Coello			*Governors/Intendants*
1681-1689	Pedro Álvarez Castrillón		1786-1789	Juan de Ayssa y Blancazo Allue y Palacín
1689-1693	Gabriel Rodríguez Bravo de Hoyos			
			1789-1793	José Mateu y Aranda
1693-1699	Pedro Jerónimo Luis de Colmenares y Camargo		1793-1811	José de Salvador
			1811-1814	Nicolás García Jerez
1699-1705	Miguel de Camargo		1814-1816	Juan Bautista Gual
1705-1721	Sebastián de Arancibia y Sasi		1816-1818	Manuel de Beltranena
1722-1724	Antonio Póveda y Rivadineira (1)		1818-1821	Miguel González Saravia

Gámez, passim; Molina Argüello, pp. 244–47.

359 NUEVA ANDALUCÍA

The area of Nueva Andalucía in eastern Venezuela was settled by the Spaniards after 1521. The town of Cumaná, or Nueva Córdoba, was founded two years later, the first permanent Spanish settlement in South America. The province of Nueva Andalucía was often referred to as Cumaná after its chief town. The province itself was only created in 1569 from several earlier governments. Nueva Andalucía was under the audiencia of Santo Domingo (q.v.) until 1739 when it fell under that of Santa Fé de Bogotá in the newly-created viceroyalty of Nueva Granada (q.v.). Finally, in 1777 it became part of the captaincy-general of Venezuela (q.v.). Between 1810 and 1821 Nueva Andalucía, like all of Venezuela, was the scene of bitter fighting between royalist and nationalist forces and control of the province changed with kaleidoscopic frequency. After 1821 Nueva Andalucía became part of Gran Colombia and later of Venezuela.

Governors

1569-1570	Diego Fernández de Serpa
1570-	García Fernández de Serpa
1585-1586	Rodrigo Núñez Lobo
1586-1596	Francisco de Vides
1597-1598	Marco Antonio Becerra
1598-1605	Pedro Suárez Amaya
1605-1614	Pedro Suárez Coronel
1614-1619	Juan de Haro y Sanvítores
1619-1626	Diego de Arroyo Daza
1626	Cristóbal de Eguino y Mallea
1626-1630	Enrique Enríquez de Sotomayor
1632	Benito Arias Montano
1642-1643	Fernando de la Riva Agüero y Setien
1648-1650	Gregorio de Castellar y Mantilla
1650-1652	Francisco de Rada Alvarado
1652-1656	Pedro de Brizuela
1660-1665	Pedro Juan de Viedma y Carvajal
1665-1667	Juan Bravo de Acuña
1668-1672	Sancho Fernández de Angulo y Sandoval
1672-1677	Francisco Ventura de Palacios y Rada
1677-1681	Francisco de Vivero Galindo y Torralba
1681-	Juan de Padilla Guardiola y Guzmán
1683-1687	Gaspar Mateo de Acosta
1688-1691	Gaspar del Hoyo Solórzano
1691-1703	José Ramírez de Arellano

1712-1715	Mateo Ruíz del Mazo
1715-1718	(alcaldes)
1718-1720	José Carreño
1721-1733	Juan de la Tornera Sota
1733-1740	Carlos de Sucre
1740-1745	Gregorio Espinosa de los Monteros, Marqués de Monte Oliver
1745-1753	Diego Tavares Haumada y Barríos
1753-1757	Mateo Gual y Pueyo (1)
1758-1759	Nicolás de Castro
1759-1765	José Diguja Villagómez
1765-1766	Pedro José de Urrutia Ramírez de Guzmán (1)
1766-1768	Mateo Gual y Pueyo (2)
1768-1775	Pedro José de Urrutia Ramírez de Guzmán (2)
1777-1780	Maximo du Bouchet
1780-1782	Manuel González de Aguilar Torres de Navarra
1782-1784	Miguel Marmión
1784-1789	Antonio de Pereda Lascanótegui y Boulet
1789-1792	Pedro Carbonell Pinto Vigo y Correa
1792-1804	Vicente de Emparán y Orbe
1804-1809	Juan Manuel Cagigal y Martínez Niño de San Miguel y Pacheco
1809	Miguel Correa
1809	Lorenzo Fernández de la Hoz
1809-1810	Eusebio Escudero

Ramos Martínez, pp. 60—80.

360 NUEVA ESPAÑA

Central Mexico in the early 16th century was the locale of several states with advanced civilizations. Of these the most powerful and wealthiest was the loosely organized entity known as the Aztec Empire. The Spaniards, already well entrenched in the Caribbean, explored the coasts of Mexico in 1518. In the following year Hernán Cortés set out from Cuba and invaded the Mexican mainland. With the aid of Indian allies Cortés was able to overthrow the Aztec state. In 1521 he was named governor and captain-general of Nueva España by the Spanish king. Within the next two decades the Spaniards moved north and south from central Mexico and conquered Central America, Yucatan (q.v.), and areas of central and western Mexico. To regulate the government of Nueva España an audiencia was created in 1529 and six years later a viceroy was appointed, the second in Spanish America. The viceroy of Nueva España came to have authority over all the Spanish possessions in Mexico and Central America, the Caribbean, the coasts of Venezuela, and the Philippine Islands. This jurisdiction included the viceregal audiencia at Mexico City together with the audiencias at Guadalajara (Nueva Galicia), Manila (the Philippine Islands), Santo Domingo, and Guatemala (qq.v.). With the administrative reorganization of the 18th century the viceroy of Mexico lost control over Venezuela and to some extent over the Provincias Internas (q.v.) of northern Mexico. During the 17th and 18th centuries Spanish control in Mexico gradually spread northward, meeting with continuous opposition from the nomadic Indians in the area, until it reached well into what later was the United States of America. Revolts against Spanish authority began in Nueva España in 1810 but these had been suppressed by 1815. Nonetheless Spanish authority had been irretrievably weakened and in 1821 the viceroy was deposed, his replacement was powerless, and the independence of Mexico was proclaimed.

Governors/Captains-General

1521-1526	Hernán Cortés, Marqués del Valle
1526	Luis Ponce de León
1526	Marcos de Aguilar
1526-1528	Alonso de Estrada
1528-1530	Nuño Beltrán de Guzmán
1531-1535	Sebastián Ramírez de Fuenleal

Viceroys

1535-1550	Antonio de Mendoza
1550-1564	Luis de Velasco
1564-1566	(audiencia)
1566-1568	Gastón de Peralta, Marqués de Falces
1568-1580	Martín Enríquez de Almansa
1580-1582	Lorenzo Suárez de Mendoza, Conde de la Coruña
1582-1583	Luis de Villanueva y Zapata
1583-1585	Pedro de Moya y Contreras
1585-1590	Álvaro Manrique de Zúñiga, Marqués de Villamanrique
1590-1595	Luis de Velasco, Marqués de Salinas (1)
1595-1603	Gaspar Zúñiga Acevedo y Fonseca, Marques de Monterrey
1603-1607	Juan Manuel Mendoza y Manrique Hurtado y Padilla, Marqués de Montesclaros
1607-1611	Luis de Velasco, Marqués de Salinas (2)
1611-1612	Francisco García Guerra
1612	Pedro de Otálora
1612-1621	Diego Fernández de Córdoba y López de las Roelas Benavides y Melgarejo, Marqués de Guadalcázar
1621-1624	Diego Carrillo de Mendoza y Pimentel, Marqués de Gelves
1624-1635	Rodrigo Pacheco y Osorio, Marqués de Cerralbo
1635-1640	Lope Díez de Armendáriz, Marqués de Cadereyta
1640-1642	Diego López Pacheco Cabrera y Bobadilla, Duque de Escalona
1642	Juan de Palafox y Mendoza
1642-1648	García Sarmiento y Sotomayor Enríquez de Luna, Conde de Salvatierra
1648-1649	Marcos de Torres y Rueda
1649-1650	Matías de Peralta
1650-1653	Luis Enríquez de Guzmán y Coresma, Conde de Alba de Liste
1653-1660	Francisco Fernández de la Cueva, Duque de Albuquerque
1660-1664	Juan de Leyva y de la Cerda, Conde de Bonos
1664	Diego Osorio de Escobar y Llamas
1664-1673	Antonio Sebastián de Toledo Molina y Salazar, Marqués de Mancera
1673	Pedro Núñez Colón de Portugal y Castro, Duque de Veragua
1673-1680	Payo Enríquez de Ribera
1680-1686	Tomás Antonio Manrique de la Cerda y Aragón, Conde de Paredes
1686-1688	Melchor Portocarrero Lasso de la Vega, Conde de Monclova
1688-1696	Gaspar de le Cerda Sandoval Silva y Mendoza, Conde de Galve
1696-1697	Juan de Ortega Montañes (1)
1697-1701	José Sarmiento de Valladares y Arinas, Conde de Moctezuma
1701-1702	Juan de Ortega Montañes (2)
1702-1711	Francisco Fernández de la Cueva Enríquez, Duque de Albuquerque
1711-1716	Francisco de Alencastre Noroña y Silva, Duque de Linares
1716-1722	Baltasar de Zúñiga Guzmán Sotomayor y Mendoza, Marqués de Valero
1722-1734	Juan de Acuña y Bejarano Astudillo y Marquina, Marqués de Casa Fuerte
1734-1740	Juan Antonio de Vizarrón y Eguiarreta
1740-1741	Pedro de Castro y Salazar Figueroa, Duque de la Conquista

1741-1742   Pedro Malo de Vilavicencio
1742-1746   Pedro de Cebrián y Agustín, Conde de Fuenclara
1746-1755   Juan Francisco de Güemes y Horsacitas Gordón y Saenz de Villamolinedo, Conde
            de Revillagigedo
1755-1760   Agustín de Ahumada y Villalón, Marqués de las Amarillas
1760   Francisco de Echévarri
1760-1761   Francisco Antonio Cagigal de la Vega Salinas y Acevedo
1761-1766   Joaquín de Monserrat y Ciurana, Marqués de Cruillas
1766-1771   Carlos Francisco de Croix, Marqués de Croix
1771-1779   Antonio María de Bucareli y Ursúa Hinostrosa Lasso de la Vega
1779-1783   Martín de Mayorga
1783-1784   Matías de Gálvez García Madrid y Cabrera
1784-1785   Vicente de Herrera y Rivero
1785-1786   Bernardo Vicente Pólinarde de Gálvez y Galardo
1786-1787   Eusebio Sánchez Pareja y Beleño
1787   Alonso Núñez de Haro y Peralta
1787-1789   Manuel Antonio Flores Maldonaldo Martínez de Angulo y Bodquín
1789-1794   Juan Vicente de Güemes Pacheco de Padilla y Horcasitas, Conde de Revillagigedo
1794-1798   Miguel de la Grúa Talamanca y Branciforte, Marqués de Branciforte
1798-1800   Miguel José de Azanza
1800-1803   Félix Berenguer de Marquina
1803-1808   José de Iturrigaray y Aróstegui
1808-1809   Pedro Garibay
1809-1810   Francisco Javier de Lizana y Beaumont
1810-1813   Francisco Javier de Venegas
1813-1816   Félix María Calleja del Rey, Marqués de Calderón
1816-1821   Juan Ruíz de Apodaca y Eliza López de Letona y Lasquetty, Conde del Venadito
1821   Francisco Novella Azabal Pérez y Sicardo

Rubio Mañé, *Introducción*, 1:291-97.

361 NUEVA GALICIA

The area of Nueva Galicia, west of Mexico City, was conquered by the Spaniards in the years after 1530. From 1545 to 1549 it was reduced to an alcaldía mayor. In 1549 an audiencia was created for Nueva Galicia, but no president was appointed until 1574 when a governor/president was appointed. The audiencia had jurisdiction over all the mostly unexplored areas of northern Mexico, but as settlement pushed northward new provinces were created (v. Coahuila, Nueva Vizcaya, Nuevo León, Nuevo México, Sinaloa, Sinora, and Texas) with governors of their own, although still dependent on the audiencia of Nueva Vizcaya. In 1708 the governor/president became captain-general as well. In 1787 the intendencia of Guadalajara was created with the governor/president of Nueva Galicia as intendant. In 1821 Guadalajara became a part of the empire of Mexico.

Governors
1531-1536   Nuño Beltrán de Guzmán
1536-1537   Cristóbal de Oñate y González (1)
1537   Diego Pérez de la Torre
1537-1538   Cristóbal de Oñate y González (2)
1538-1540   Francisco Vázquez de Coronado (1)
1540-1544   Cristóbal de Oñate y González (3)
1544-1545   Francisco Vázquez de Coronado (2)

Alcaldes Mayores
1545-1547   Baltasar de Gallegos
1547-1549   Diego de Guevara
1549-1574   (audiencia)

Governor/President
1574-1580   Jerónimo de Orozco
1580-1585   Antonio Maldonaldo

Spain

1586	Francisco Tello de Guzmán	1716-1724	Tomás Terán de los Ríos
1588-1592	Pedro Altamirano	1724-1727	Nicolás Rivera y Santa Cruz
1592-1593	Lorenzo de Castro y Meza	1727-1732	Tomás Rivera y Santa Cruz
1593-1605	Santiago de Vera	1732-1737	José Barragán de Burgos
1606-1608	Francisco de Pareja	1737-1743	Francisco de Aiza, Marqués del
1608-1610	Juan de Villela		Castillo de Aiza
1610-1613	Pedro de Arévalo y Cedeño	1743-1751	Fermín de Echevers y Subiza
1613-1617	Alonso Pérez de Merchán	1751-1760	José de Basarte y Borán
1618-1624	Pedro de Otálora	1760-1761	Francisco Galindo Quiñónes y
1624-1629	Gaspar de Chávez y Sotomayor		Barrientos (1)
1629-1632	Diego Núñez y Morquecho	1761-1764	Pedro Montesinos de Lara
1632-	Damián Gentil de Párraga	1764-1771	Francisco Galindo Quiñónes y
-1636	Antonio de Salazar		Barrientos (2)
1636-1640	Juan Canseco de Quiñones	1771-1776	Eusebio Sánchez Pareja y
1640-1643	Francisco de Medrano y Pacheco		Beleño (1)
1643-1655	Pedro Fernández de Baeza	1776-1777	Ruperto Vicente de Luyando
1655-1661	Antonio de Ulloa y Chávez	1777-1786	Eusebio Sánchez Pareja y
1661-1662	Jerónimo Fernández de Aldaz		Beleño (2)
1662-1670	Antonio Álvarez de Castro		
1670-1672	Francisco Calderón y Romero		*Guadalajara*
1673-1679	Juan Miguel de Augurto y Alava	*Intendants*	
1679-1702	Alonso de Ceballos y Villagutierre	1787-1791	Antonio de Villaurrutia y Salcedo
1702-1703	Antonio Hipólito de Abarca Vidal	1791-1798	Jacobo de Ugarte y Loyola
	y Valda	1800-1804	José Fernando de Abascal y Souza
1704-1708	Juan de Escalante Colombres y	1804-1805	José Ignacio Ortiz de Salinas
	Mendoza	1805-1811	Roque Abarca
1708-1716	Toribio Rodríguez de Solís	1811-1821	José de la Cruz

Iguiniz.

362 NUEVA GRANADA

In 1525 and 1533 Santa Marta and Cartagena de Indias (qq.v.) were founded on the northwest coast of South America. From these bases the interior was explored and occupied, the Chibcha states were conquered, and the province of Nueva Reino de Granada, or simply Nueva Granada, was created. In 1549 an audiencia was established at Santa Fé de Bogotá in Nueva Granada, although a president was not appointed until 1564. The audiencia of Santa Fé was part of the viceroyalty of Peru (q.v.) and in turn held jurisdiction over the provinces of Cartagena de Indias, Santa Marta, and Popayán (q.v.) until 1563 when it was transferred to the audiencia of Quito (q.v.). After 1564 the governor/president was captain-general as well. In 1717 Nueva Granada was raised to a viceroyalty, the first created in nearly two centuries. This viceroyalty had jurisdiction over Nueva Andalucía, Guayana, Venezuela, Mérida-La Grita (previously under Santo) (qq.v.), Popayán, and Quito (which was suppressed), as well as its old territories of Cartagena and Santa Marta. The viceroyalty was suppressed in 1722 and the various provinces returned to their former allegiances. In 1739 the viceroyalty was re-erected with the same jurisdiction as previously plus Panama (q.v.). In 1777 the captaincy-general of Venezuela was created and Guayana, Mérida-La Grita, Nueva Andalucía, and Venezuela were detached from Nueva Granada and placed under Venezuela. The reduced viceroyalty was the scene of extensive fighting between Spanish and patriot forces after 1810 and the viceroy's authority was limited during much of this period to the northern areas of Cartagena, Santa Marta, and Panama. In 1821 the Spanish forces evacuated Nueva Granada. In 1819 Gran Colombia was created, with the old viceroyalty as its core. This collapsed by 1830 and the Republic of New Granada (later Colombia) was created, with the territorial extent of the viceroyalty after 1777 as its basis.

Governors

1538-1539	Gonzalo Jiménez de Quesada
1539-1542	Hernán Pérez de Quesada
1542-1544	Alonso Luis de Lugo
1545	Luis Montalvo de Lugo
1545-1547	Pedro de Ursúa
1547-1550	Miguel Díez de Armendáriz

Governors/Presidents

1550-1564	(audiencia)
1564-1574	Andrés Díaz Venero de Leyva
1575	Gedeón de Hinojosa
1575-1578	(audiencia)
1578-1580	Lope Díez Aux de Armendáriz
1580-1582	Juan Bautista Monzón
1582-1585	Juan Prieto de Orellana
1585-1590	Francisco Javier Chaparro
1590-1597	Antonio González
1597-1602	Francisco de Sande Picón
1603-1605	Nuno Núñez de Villavicencio
1605-1628	Juan de Borja
1628-1630	(audiencia)
1630-1637	Sancho Girón de Narváez, Marqués de Sófraga
1637-1645	Martin Saavedra y Guzmán
1645-1654	Juan Fernández Córdoba y Coalla, Marqués de Miranda de Auta
1654-1662	Dionisio Pérez Manrique y Círía, Marqués de Santiago
1662-1666	Diego de Egües y Beaumont
1666-1667	Diego del Corro Carrascal
1667-1671	Diego de Villalba y Toledo
1671-1674	Melchor de Liñán y Cisneros
1674-1678	(audiencia)
1678-1686	Francisco del Castillo de la Concha
1686-1687	Sebastián Alfonso de Velasco y Vargas
1687-1703	Gil de Cabrera y Dávalos
1703-1710	Diego de Córdoba Lasso de la Vega (1)
1710-1711	Francisco Cosío y Otero
1711-1712	Diego de Córdoba Lasso de la Vega (2)
1713-1715	Francisco de Meneses y Bravo de Saravia
1715-1717	(audiencia)
1717-1718	Francisco del Rincón
1718-1719	Antonio de la Pedrosa y Guerrero[1]

Viceroy

1719-1724	Jorge de Villalonga, Conde de la Cueva

Governors/Presidents

1724-1731	Antonio Manso Maldonaldo
1731-1733	(audiencia)
1733-1737	Rafael de Eslava y Lazaga
1738	Antonio González Manrique
1739-1740	Francisco González Manrique

Viceroys

1740-1748	Sebastián de Eslava y Lazaga
1749-1753	José Alonso Pizarro, Marqués del Villar
1753-1761	José Solís Folch de Cardona
1761-1773	Pedro Mesía de la Cerda, Marqués de la Vega de Armijo
1773-1776	Manuel de Guirior y Portal de Huarte y Edozain
1776-1782	Manuel Antonio Flores Maldonaldo Martínez de Angulo y Bodquín
1782	Juan de Torrezal Díaz Pimienta
1782	Juan Francisco Gutiérrez de Piñeres
1782-1788	Antonio Caballero y Góngora
1789	Francisco Gil de Taboada Lemos y Villamarín
1789-1797	José Manuel Ignacio Timoteo de Ezpeleta y Galdeano Dicastillo y del Prado
1797-1803	Pedro de Mendinueta y Múzquiz
1803-1810	Antonio Amar y Borbón
1810-1811	Manuel Bernardo de Álvarez
1811-1813	Benito Pérez Brito de los Ríos Fernández Valdelomar
1813-1818	Francisco Montalvo y Ambulodi Arriola y Casabante Valdespino
1818-1819	Juan José de Sámano y Urribarri de Rebollar y Mazorra
1819-1821	Juan de la Cruz Mourgeón y Achet

1. Some historians have considered Pedrosa y Guerrero to have been the first viceroy of Nuevo Granada. However, while he governed the colony after it was erected into a viceroyalty, and was given extraordinary powers and authority, he was never granted the title of viceroy. For a discussion of this problem, see Garrido Conde, pp. 28–32.

Academia Colombiana de la Historia, vol. 3, nos. 1, 2, and 3, passim; Alcázar Molina, pp. 259–88; Restrepo Tirado, *Gobernantes*, passim; Tamayo.

363 NUEVA VIZCAYA

The area of Nueva Vizcaya in northcentral Mexico was settled from Nueva Galicia (q.v.) after 1562. The prolonged resistance of the Chichimec Indians delayed large settlement for several decades and Spanish interests were confined to mining. Initially the province of Nueva Vizcaya covered the whole ill-defined area of the northern part of the viceroyalty of Nueva España (q.v.), but as settlement moved north, Nuevo León, Nuevo México, Coahuila, and Sinaloa and Sonora (qq.v.) were established as separate provinces. The governor/captain-general of Sinaloa was under the jurisdiction of the audiencia of Nueva Galicia. In 1777 Nueva Vizcaya became part of the Provincias Internas (q.v.), and upon the creation of the intendencia system in Nueva España, Nueva Vizcaya became the intendencia of Durango. In 1821, when Spanish control ceased in Mexico, Nueva Vizcaya became part of the Republic of Mexico. The Mexican states of Chihuahua and Durango are roughly coextensive with the intendencia of Durango.

Governors

1562-1575	Francisco de Ibarra y Arandía
1575-1583	Hernando de Trejo
1583	Diego de Ibarra y López de Marquiegui
1585-1587	Hernando de Bazán y Albornoz
1587	Antonio de Alcega y Zúñiga
1587-1590	Antonio de Monroy y Portocarrero
1590-1596	Rodrigo del Río de Loza y Gordejuela
1596-1600	Diego Fernández de Velasco y Enríquez de Almansa
1600-1603	Rodrigo de Vivero y Aberrucia Lasso de la Vega y Velasco
1603-1614	Francisco de Urdiñola y Larrumbide
1614-1620	Gaspar de Alvear y Salazar
1620-1626	Mateo de Vesga López
1626-1630	Hipólito de Velasco Ibarra, Marqués de Salinas del Río Pisuerga
1630-1633	Gonzalo Gómez de Cervantes Casaus
1633-1638	Luis de Monsalve y Saavedra
1639-1640	Francisco Bravo de la Serna
1640-1641	Fernando Sosa de Suárez
1641-1648	Luis de Valdés y Rejano
1648-1653	Diego Guajardo y Fajardo
1654-1660	Enrique Dávila y Pacheco
1660-1665	Francisco Gorráez Beamont y Buitrago Liñán y Benedi
1665-1670	Antonio de Oca y Sarmiento
1670-1671	Bartolomé de Estrada y Ramírez (1)
1671-1676	José García de Salcedo y San Juan
1676	Martín Rebollar y Cueva
1676-1678	Lope de Sierra y Osorio
1679-1684	Bartolomé de Estrada y Ramírez (2)
1684-1687	José de Neira Riomol y Quiroga
1687-1693	Juan Isidro de Pardiñas y Villar de Francos
1693-1698	Gabriel del Castillo y Machado
1698-1703	Juan Bautista de Larrea Palomino y Solís
1703-1708	Juan Fernández de Córdoba
1709-1714	Antonio de Deza y Ulloa
1714-1720	Juan Manuel de San Juan y Santa Cruz
1720-1723	Martín de Alday
1723-1727	José Sebastián López de Carvajal
1728-1733	Ignacio Francisco de Barrutia y Aeta Esenagucia
1733-1738	Juan José Vértiz y Ontañón
1738-1743	Juan Bautista de Belaunzarán y Zumeta
1743-1748	José Enrique de Cosío, Marqués de Torre Campo
1748-1752	Juan Francisco de la Puerta y de la Barrera
1752-1753	Alonso de Gastesi
1753-1761	Mateo Antonio de Mendoza Díaz de Arce
1761-1769	José Carlos de Agüero y González de Agüero
1769-1776	José de Fayni y Gálvez
1776-1784	Felipe de Barri
1784-1785	Juan Velásquez
1785	Manuel Muñoz
1785-1786	Manuel Flon y Tejada, Conde de la Cadena

Durango

Governors/Intendants

1786-1791	Felipe Díaz de Ortega Bustillo
1791-1793	Francisco Antonio de Potau y de Colón de Portugal
1793-1796	Francisco José de Urrutia Montoya
1796-1813	Bernardo Bonavia y Zapata
1813-1817	Alejo García Conde
1817-1818	Angel Pinilla y Pérez
1818-1819	Antonio Cordero y Bustamante
1819-1821	Diego García Conde

Information from Sr. Guillermo Porras Muñoz of Mexico City.

364 NUEVO LEÓN

In 1582 the province of Nuevo Reino de León, or simply Nuevo León, was created in northern Mexico from the earlier province of Nueva Vizcaya (q.v.), and placed under the jurisdiction of the audiencia of Nueva Galicia (q.v.). In 1777 Nuevo León became part of the newly-created Provincias Internas (q.v.), but it was detached from this government in 1793. Nuevo León remained a province of the viceroyalty of Nueva España (q.v.) until 1821 when it became part of the Republic of Mexico.

Governors		1723-1725	Juan José de Arriaga y Brambila
1582-1589	Luis de Carvajal y de la Cueva	1725-1730	Pedro de Saravia Cortés
1589-1610	Diego de Montemayor	1730-1731	Bernardino de Meneses Monroy
1610-1611	Diego de Montemayor, Jr.		y Mendoza Bracamonte, Conde
1611-1615	Agustín de Zavala		de Peñalba
1615-1624	Diego Rodríguez	1731-1740	José Antonio Fernández de
1624-1626	Alonso Lucas		Jáuregui y Urrutia
1626-1664	Martín de Zavala	1740-1746	Pedro del Barrío Junco y
1665-1667	León de Arza		Espriella (1)
1667-1676	Nicolás de Azcárraga y Montero	1746-1752	Vicente Bueno de la Borbolla
1676-1681	Domingo de Pruñeda	1752-1757	Pedro del Barrío Junco y
1681	Domingo de Videgaray y Zarza		Espriella (2)
1681-1682	Juan de Echeverría	1757-1759	Domingo Miguel Guajardo
1683-1684	Alonso de León	1759-1762	Juan Manuel Muñoz de
1684-1687	Antonio de Echevers y Subiza		Villavicencio
1687-1688	Francisco Cuervo de Valdés	1762-1764	Carlos de Velasco
1688-1693	Pedro Fernández de la Ventosa	1764-1772	Ignacio Ussel y Guimbarda
1693-1698	Juan Pérez de Merino	1772-1773	Francisco de Echegaray
1698-1703	Juan Francisco de Vergara y	1773-1781	Melchor Vidal de Lorca y Villena
	Mendoza	1781-1785	Vicente González de Santianes
1703-1705	Francisco Báez Treviño (1)	1785-1787	Joaquín de Mier y Noriega
1705-1707	Gregorio de Salinas Verona	1787-1795	Manuel Bahamonde y Villamil
1707-1708	Cipriano García de Pruneda	1795-1805	Simón de Herrera y Leyva
1708-1710	Luis García de Pruneda	1805-1810	Pedro de Herrera y Leyva
1710-1714	Francisco Mier y Torre	1810-1811	Manuel de Santa María
1714-1718	Francisco Báez Treviño (2)	1813	Ramón Díaz Bustamante
1718-1719	Juan Ignacio Flores Mogollón	1813-1817	(alcaldes)
1719-1723	Francisco de Barbadillo y	1817-1818	Bernardo Villareal
	Vitoria	1818-1821	Francisco Bruno Barrera

Covarrubias, pp. 8–30; Morales Gómez, pp. 10–129, 281–82.

365 NUEVO MÉXICO

The area of the upper Rio Grande in the extreme northern portion of the viceroyalty of Nueva España (q.v.) was granted to Juan de Oñate in return for his settling the area, then part of Nueva Vizcaya (q.v.). The settlement began in 1598 but Nuevo México always remained something of a frontier outpost, subject to constant attacks by the Indians in the vicinity. In fact an Indian uprising in 1680 led to the virtual abandonment of the settlements until 1696. The providence of Nuevo México was under the jurisdiction of the audiencia of Nueva Galicia (q.v.) within the viceroyalty of Nueva España. With the formation of the Provincias Internas (q.v.) in

1777 Nuevo México became part of it—indeed Nuevo Mexico, isolated, thinly populated, and subject to incessant attacks from Indians, most accurately reflected the rationale for the creation of the commandancia-general. Spanish authority ended in 1822 when Nuevo México became part of the Republic of Mexico.

Governors

1598-1608	Juan de Oñate y Salazar
1608-1610	Cristóbal de Oñate y Tolosa Cortés
1610-1614	Pedro de Peralta
1614-1618	Bernardino de Ceballos
1618-1625	Juan de Eulate
1625-1629	Felipe Sotelo Osorio
1629-1632	Francisco Manuel de Silva y Nieto
1632-1635	Francisco de la Mora y Ceballos
1635-1637	Francisco Martínez de Baeza
1637-1641	Luis de Rosas
1641	Juan Flores de Sierra y Valdés
1641-1642	(cabildo)
1642-1644	Alonso Pacheco de Heredia
1644-1647	Fernando de Argüello Carvajal
1647-1649	Luis de Guzmán y Figueroa
1649-1653	Hernando de Ugarte y la Concha
1653-1656	Juan de Samaniego y Xaca
1656-1659	Juan Manso de Contreras
1659-1661	Bernardo López de Mendizábal
1661-1664	Diego Dionisio de Peñalosa Briceño y Berdugo
1664-1665	Juan Durán de Miranda
1665-1668	Fernando de Villanueva
1668-1671	Juan de Medrano y Mesía
1671-1675	Juan Durán de Miranda
1675-1677	Juan Francisco de Treviño
1677-1683	Antonio de Otermín
1683-1686	Domingo Jironza Pétriz de Cruzate (1)
1686-1689	Pedro Reneros de Posada
1689-1691	Domingo Jironza Pétriz de Cruzate (2)
1691-1697	Diego de Vargas y Zapata Luján y Ponce de León (1)
1697-1703	Pedro Rodríguez Cubero
1703-1704	Diego de Vargas y Zapata Luján y Ponce de Leon, Marqués de la Nava Barcinas (2)
1704-1705	Juan Páez Hurtado
1705-1707	Francisco Cuervo y Valdés
1707-1712	José Chacón Medina Salazar y Villaseñor, Marqués de la Peñuela
1712-1715	Juan Ignacio Flores Mogollón
1715-1717	Félix Martínez de Torrelaguna
1717	Juan Páez Hurtado
1717-1722	Antonio Valverde y Cossío
1722-1731	Juan Domingo de Bustamante
1731-1736	Gervasio Cruzat y Góngora
1736-1739	Henrique de Olavide y Micheleña
1739-1743	Gaspar Domingo de Mendoza
1743-1749	Joaquín Codallos y Rabál
1749-1754	Tomás Veles Cachupín (1)
1754-1760	Francisco Antonio Marín del Valle
1760-1762	Manuel del Portillo y Urrisola
1762-1767	Tomás Veles Cachupín (2)
1767-1778	Pedro Fermín de Lara y Mendinueta
1778-1788	Juan Bautista de Anza
1788-1794	Fernando de la Concha
1794-1805	Fernando Chacón
1805-1808	Joaquín del Real Alencastre
1808-1814	José Manrique
1814-1816	Alberto Maynez
1816-1818	Pedro María de Allande
1818-1822	Facundo Melgares

Bloom, pp. 154–56.

366 NUEVO SANTANDER

The area of Nueva España, along its northeastern coast south of the Rio Grande, was practically unsettled before the middle of the 18th century. In 1746 occupation was begun and the province of Nuevo Santander created. Nuevo Santander was part of the Provincias Internas (q.v.) until 1793 when it was detached and once again placed directly under the viceroy of Nueva España (q.v.). After 1812 stable Spanish control of the area ceased and Nuevo Santander was directly administered by the commandant-general of the Provincias Internas (q.v.). Upon the formation of the Republic of Mexico, the area became the state of Tamaulipas.

Governors

1746–1770	José de Escandón y Helguera, Conde de Sierra Gorda
1770–1773	Vicente González Santiañes
1773–1779	Francisco de Echegaray
1780–1781	Manuel Ignacio de Escandón y Llera, Conde de Sierra Gorda (1)
1781–1786	Diego Lazaga

1786–1787	Juan Miguel de Sosaya
1788–1789	Melchor Vidal de Lorca
1790–1800	Manuel Ignacio de Escandón y Llera, Conde de Sierra Gorda (2)
1802–1804	Francisco de Ixart
1804–1811	Manuel de Iturbe (or Iraeta)
1811–1812	Juan Fermín de Juanicotena

Covián Martínez, pp. 79–80.

367 OAXACA

The alcaldia mayor of Oaxaca was made an intendencia of the viceroyalty of Nueva España (q.v.) in 1787. Oaxaca remained an intendencia until 1821, when Mexico became independent of Spain. Later it was a state of the Republic of Mexico.

Intendants

1787–1808	Antonio de Mora y Peysal
1809–1810	Antonio María Izquierdo de la Torre

1810–1814	Joseph María Lazo y Nacarino
1814–1816	Francisco Rendón (1)
1816–1818	Antonio Basilio Gutiérrez de Ulloa
1818–1821	Francisco Rendón (2)

The information, taken from the *Gacetas de México* and *Manuals Calendarios y Guía de Forasteros* for the period, was provided by Jorge Ignacio Rubio Mañé, Director, Archivo General de la Nación, Mexico City.

368 ORÁN

Orán, a city on the northern coast of Africa and a refuge for Spanish Muslims after the fall of Granada in 1492, was occupied by Spanish forces in 1509. Except for the period from 1708 to 1732, when it was captured by the Turks, Orán remained a Spanish possession until 1792 when it was abandoned. The territory surrounding the city was never occupied by Spain; it remained in the hands of the Muslims who recognized the suzerainty of the Ottoman Turks.

Governors

1509	Pedro Navarro, Conde de Oliveto
1509–1510	Rui Díaz Álvarez de Rojas
1510–1512	Diego Fernández de Córdoba
1512–1517	Martín de Argote
1517–1522	Diego Fernández de Córdoba y Arellano, Marqués de Comares
1522–1523	Luis Fernández de Córdoba, Marqués de Comares (1)
1523–1525	Luis de Cárdenas
1525–1531	Luis Fernández de Córdoba, Marqués de Comares (2)

Spain

1531-1534	Pedro de Godoy
1534-1558	Martín Alonso Fernández de Córdoba Montemayor y Velasco, Conde de Alcaudete
1558-1564	Alonso de Córdoba y Fernández de Velasco, Conde de Alcaudete
1564-1565	Andrés Ponce de León
1565-1567	Hernán Tello de Guzmán
1567-1571	Pedro Luis Galcerán de Borja y Castropinós, Marqués de Navarrés
1571-1573	Felipe Galcerán de Borja
1573-1574	Diego Fernández de Córdoba, Conde de Comares (1)
1574-1575	Luis de Bocanegra
1575-1585	Martín de Córdoba y Velasco, Marqués de Cortes
1585-1589	Pedro de Padilla
1589-1594	Diego Fernández de Córdoba, Conde de Comares (2)
1594-1596	Gabriel Niño de Zúñiga
1596-1604	Francisco de Córdoba y Velasco, Conde de Alcaudete
1604-1607	Juan Ramírez de Guzmán, Conde de Teba
1607-1608	Diego de Toledo y Guzmán
1608-1616	Felipe Ramírez de Arellano, Conde de Aguilar de Inestrillas
1616-1625	Jorge de Cárdenas Manrique, Duque de Maqueda
1625-1628	Antonio Sancho Dávila y Toledo, Marqués de Velada
1628-1632	Francisco González de Andía y Irarrazábal y Zárate, Visconde de Santa Clara de Avedillo
1632-1639	Antonio de Zúñiga y de la Cueva, Marqués de Flores Dávila (1)
1639-1643	Álvaro de Bazán Manrique de Lara y Benavides, Marqués del Viso
1643-1647	Rodrigo Pimentel Ponce de León, Marqués de Viana
1647-1652	Antonio de Zúñiga y de la Cueva, Marqués de Flores Dávila (2)
1653-1660	Antonio Gómez Dávila Toledo y Osorio, Marqués de San Román
1660-1666	Gaspar Felipe de Guzmán, Duque de San Lúcar
1666-1672	Fernando Joaquín Fajardo de Requeséns y Zúñiga, Marqués de los Vélez
1672-1675	Diego de Portugal
1675-1678	Iñigo de Toledo y Osorio
1678-1681	Pedro Andrés Ramírez de Guzmán y Acuña, Marqués de Algava
1681-1682	Gaspar Portocarrero, Conde de la Monclova
1682-1683	Pedro Félix José de Silva y Meneses, Conde de Cifuentes
1683-1685	Juan de Villalpando, Marqués de Osera
1685-1687	Antonio Paniagua de Loaysa y Zúñiga, Marqués de Santa Cruz de Paniagua
1687	Diego de Bracamonte, Conde de Bracamonte
1687-1691	Félix Nieto de Silva, Conde de Guaro
1691-1692	Jean-Louis d'Orléans, Comte de Charny
1692-1697	Andrés Copola, Duque de Cansano
1697-1701	Gonzalo Arias Dávila Pacheco Coloma y Borja, Marqués de Casasola
1701-1704	Juan Francisco Manrique de Arana
1704-1707	Carlo Carafa
1707-1708	Melchor Avellaneda y Sandoval Rojas y Ramiro, Marqués de Valdecañas
1708-1732	(under Ottoman Empire)
1732	Álvaro de Navia Osorio y Vigil, Marqués de Santa Cruz de Marcenado
1733	Antonio Arias del Castillo, Marqués de Villadarias
1733-1738	José Vallejo
1738-1742	José Basilio de Aramburu
1742-1748	Alexandre de la Mothe
1749-1752	Pedro de Algaín, Marqués de la Real Corona
1752-1758	Juan Antonio de Escoiquiz
1758-1765	Juan Martín Zermeño
1765-1767	Cristóbal de Córdoba
1767-1770	Victorio Alcondolo Bolognino Visconti, Conde de Bolognino
1770-1774	Eugenio Fernández de Alvarado y Perales Hurtado y Colomo
1774-1778	Pedro Martín Zermeño
1778-1779	Luis de Carvajal
1779-1785	Pedro Guelfi
1785-1789	Luis de la Casas y Aragorri

1789-1790   Manuel Pineda de la Torre y Solís, Marqués de Campo Santo
1790-1791   Joaquín Mayone y Ferrari, Conde de Cumbre Hermosa
1791-1792   Juan de Courten

García Figueras, pp. 290–94. Cazenave, although richer in detail, omits several names and employs some rather quaint Gallic spellings of Spanish names.

369 PANAMA

The Isthmus of Panama connecting North and South America was discovered by the Spaniards in 1501. Early efforts to settle failed, although Panama (often called Tierra Firme and Castilla de Oro) was created a province in 1513. Settlement followed both in the isthmus and to the north (v. Costa Rica, Nicaragua, and Honduras). An audiencia was created in Panama in 1538 only to be suppressed four years later. In 1567 this audiencia was revived and placed under the viceroyalty of Peru (q.v.). It was briefly abolished in 1718, restored in 1722, and finally suppressed in 1751. Panama's prosperity was an artificial one, based on its geographical position at the axes of the trade routes as they were established by the Spanish monarchy. When the policies regarding the trade routes were changed so that ships sailed around Cape Horn to reach Peru, Panama's prosperity vanished. Its audiencia was abolished although it remained a separate province. With the re-creation of the viceroyalty of Nueva Granada (q.v.) in 1739 Panama fell under its jurisdiction and remained so until 1821. During the years 1812 to 1814 and 1819 to 1821 the viceroy, expelled from Bogotá by the patriots, resided in Panama. In 1821 Panama became part of Gran Colombia and after 1830 part of the Republic of Colombia. Only in 1903 did Panama become an independent republic.

The following list is tentative. Alba C. admitted that his own list was only "a point of departure" and the following list doubtless contains some gaps and inconsistencies. The government of Panama suffered, particularly during the 16th century, from constant usurpations and other irregularities of succession. For instance, the viceroy-designate of Peru would often govern Panama during his sojourn there on his way to Peru.

Governors

1514-1526	Pedro Arias de Ávila	1565-1569	Manuel Barros de San Millán
1526-1529	Pedro de los Ríos	1569-1573	Diego de Vera
1530-1532	Antonio de la Gama	1573-1578	Gabriel de Loarte
1533-1536	Francisco de Barrionuevo	1580-1585	Pedro Ramírez de Quiñones (3)
1536-1539	Pedro Velásquez de Acuña	1585-1587	Juan del Barrío Sepúlveda
1540	Cristóbal Vaca de Castro	1587-1596	Francisco de Cárdenas
1540-1543	(junta)	1596-1602	Alonso de Sotomayor y Andía
1543-1545	Pedro Ramírez de Quiñones (1)	1604-1605	Hernando de Añazco
1545	Pedro Casaos	1605-1614	Francisco de Valverde y Mercado
1545	Diego de Herrera	1614-1616	Francisco Manso de Contreras
1545-1546	Hernando de Bachicao	1616-1619	Diego Fernández de Velasco
1546-1548	Alonso de Almaráz	1619-1621	Juan de la Cruz Rivadineira y Enríquez de Almansa
1548	Pedro Ramírez de Quiñones (2)	1621	Roque de Chávez
1549-1550	Juan Barba de Vallecillo	1621-1627	Rodrigo Vivero y Velasco
1550-1553	Sancho de Clavijo	1627-1632	Álvaro de Quiñones Osorio y Miranda
1553-1556	Álvaro de Sosa		
1557-1559	Juan Ruíz de Monjaráz	1632-1634	Sebastián Hurtado de Corcuera y Gaviría
1560-1561	Rafael de Figuerola		
1561-1563	Luis de Guzmán	1635-1639	Enrique Enríquez de Sotomayor
1563-1564	Lope García de Castro	1641-1642	Iñigo de la Mota Sarmiento

Spain

1643-1646	Juan de la Vega y Bazán	1710-1711	Juan de la Rañeta y Vera
1650-1651	Juan Bitrián de Viamonte y Navarra	1711	José Antonio de la Rocha y Carranza, Marqués de Villarocha (2)
1652-1657	Pedro Carrillo de Guzmán	1711-1718	José Hurtado y Amezaga
1658-1663	Fernando de la Riva Agüero y Setien	1718	Juan José Llamas y Rivas
1663-1665	Pablo de Figueroa	1718-1723	Jerónimo Badillo
1665-1667	Juan Pérez de Guzmán y Gonzaga (1)	1724-1730	Manuel de Alderete
1667-1669	Agustín de Bracamonte	1730-1735	Juan José Andía Vivero Urbina y Velasco, Marqués de Villahermosa
1669	Diego de Ibarra		
1669-1671	Juan Pérez de Guzmán y Gonzaga (2)	1735-1743	Dionisio Martínez de la Vega
1671	Francisco Miguel de Marichalar (1)	1743-1749	Dionisio de Alcedo Ugarte y Herrera
1671-1673	Antonio Fernández de Córdoba y Mendoza	1749-1758	Manuel de Montiano
		1758-1761	Antonio Guill y Gonzaga
1673-1675	Antonio de León	1761-1764	José Antonio Raón y Gutiérrez
1675-1676	Francisco Miguel de Marichalar (2)	1764-1767	José Blasco y Orozco
		1767-1768	Manuel de Agreda
-1681	Alonso Mercado de Villacorta	1768-1769	Nicolás de Castro
1681-1682	Lucas Fernández de Piedrahita	1770-1772	Vicente de Olaciregui
1682-1690	Pedro de Ponte y Llerena Hoyo y Calderón, Conde del Palmar	1773-1774	Nicolás Quijano
		1774	Francisco Navas
1690-1695	Pedro José de Guzmán Dávalos Ponce de León Santillán y Mesía, Marqués de la Mina	1774-1779	Pedro Carbonell Pinto Vigo y Correa
		1779-1785	Ramón de Carvajal
		1786-1793	José Domás y Valle
1695-1696	Diego Ladrón de Guevara	1793-1803	Antonio de Narváez y Latorre
1696-1702	Pedro Luis Enríquez de Guzmán, Conde de Canillas	1803-1805	Juan de Marcos Urbina
		1805-1812	Juan Antonio de la Mata
1702-1706	Fernando Dávila Bravo de Laguna	1812-1813	Víctor Salcedo y Somodevila
1706	Juan Eustaquio Vicentelo Toledo y Luca, Marqués de Brenes	1813-1815	Carlos Meyner
		1815-1816	Francisco de Ayala Gudiño Medina y Calderón
1706-1708	José Antonio de la Rocha y Carranza, Marqués de Villarocha (1)	1817-1820	Alejandro de Hore
		1820	Francisco Aguilar
1708-1709	Fernando Haro de Monterroso	1821	José de Fábrega
1709-1710	Juan Bautista de Orueta y Irusta		

Alba C., pp. 7–87.

370 PARAGUAY

Under the earlier province of Río de la Plata (q.v., 380), the area of Paraguay initially predominated and Asunción was the capital before the second foundation of Buenos Aires in 1580. In 1618 Buenos Aires (q.v.) and Paraguay were made separate provinces. Paraguay, like Buenos Aires, was under the audiencia of Charcas (q.v.) except for the years from 1661 to 1671 when there was an audiencia at Buenos Aires. In 1607 the eastern part of Paraguay, inhabited by the Guaraní Indians, became the Jesuit province of Paraguay, or the Misiones, and was completely independent of the governor of Paraguay. In the 1760's this province was divided between the Spaniards and the Portuguese (v. Rio Grande do Sul, 312) and the Jesuits were expelled. In 1783 Paraguay became an intendencia within the viceroyalty of Río de la Plata (q.v., 381) and subject

322

to the new audiencia at Buenos Aires. In 1811 the governor/intendant was driven out and Paraguay henceforth was independent both of Spanish control and of the authority of the government which had succeeded the Spaniards in the viceregal capital of Buenos Aires.

Governors

1618–1626	Manuel de Frías
1626–1628	Diego de Rego y Mendoza
1628–1631	Luis de Céspedes Xeria
1631–1633	Francisco Núñez de Avalos
1633–1636	Martín de Ledesma Valderrama
1636–1641	Pedro de Lugo y Navarra
1641–1647	Gregorio de Hinestrosa
1647–1649	Diego de Escobar de Osorio
1649	Bernardino de Cárdenas
1649–1650	Sebastián de León y Zárate
1650–1653	Andrés de León y Garabito
1653–1656	Cristóbal de Garay y Saavedra
1656–1659	Juan Antonio Blásquez de Valverde
1659–1662	Alonso Sarmiento de Sotomayor y Figueroa
1663–1671	Juan Díez de Andino (1)
1671–1681	Francisco Rege Corbalán
1681–1684	Juan Díez de Andino (2)
1684–1685	Antonio de Vera y Mújica
1685–1691	Francisco de Monfort
1691–1696	Sebastián Félix de Mendiola (1)
1696–1702	Juan Rodríguez de Cota
1702–1705	Antonio de Escobar y Gutiérez
1705–1706	Sebastián Félix de Mendiola (2)
1706–1707	Baltasar García Ros

1707–1712	Manuel de Robles Lorenzana
1713–1717	Juan Gregorio Bazán de Pedraza
1717–1721	Diego de los Reyes Balmaceda
1721–1725	José de Antequera Enríquez y Castro
1725–1730	Martín de Barúa
1730–1731	Ignacio Soroeta
1731–1733	Antonio Ruíz de Arellano
1733–1734	Juan de Arregui y Gutiérrez
1735–1741	Martín José de Echáuri
1741–1747	Rafael de la Moneda
1747–1750	Marcos José de Larrazábal
1750–1761	Jaime Sanjust
1761–1764	José Martínez Fontes
1764–1766	Fulgencio de Yegros y Ledesma
1766–1772	Carlos Morphi
1772–1778	Agustín de Pineda Fernánclez de Valdivieso
1778–1783	Pedro de Melo y Portugal Vilhena

Governors/Intendants

1783–1786	Pedro de Melo y Portugal Vilhena
1786–1796	Joaquín Alós y Brú
1796–1805	Lázaro de Ribera y Espinosa de los Monteros
1806–1811	Bernardo de Velasco y Huidobro

Sierra, vols. 3 and 4, passim; Zinny, pp. 60–210.

371 PERU

The Inca Empire in what was to become Peru was the largest and most advanced in the western hemisphere at the beginning of the 16th century. Unlike the loose Aztec confederacy in Mexico it was well organized and centrally controlled. The Spaniards, moving along the coast south from Panama, learned of the existence of the Inca kingdom in 1522. Ten years later the Spaniards under Francisco Pizarro invaded the Inca state and, with a ridiculously small force, were able to capture and execute the Inca monarch and begin the conquest of the kingdom. This conquest was, with the exception of an area of Inca resistance at Vilcabamba, quickly and easily effected. Peru was initially under the audiencia of Panama but dissension among the Spanish leaders in Peru created chaos and threatened the loss of Peru to royal authority. Consequently an audiencia was established for Lima and a viceroy appointed in 1542. In time the viceroyalty of Peru included all of Spanish South America, except the northern coast of Venezuela, and Panama. Included within it were the audiencias of Lima (the viceregal audiencia), Charcas, Chile, Santa Fé (Nueva Granada), Panama, and Quito (qq.v.). Its extensive silver, gold, and mercury deposits rendered Peru, even more than Nueva España (q.v.), the financial cornerstone of Spain's colonial empire. The viceroyalty's extent and wealth meant that the office of viceroy of Peru was the highest and most prized in the Spanish colonial administrative system. Until the 18th century all Spanish trade in South America was channelled through Peru and then Panama on its way to the homeland. The abandonment of pure mercantilist policies in the 18th century resulted in the creation of the viceroyalties of Nueva Granada and Río de la Plata (q.v., 381) in areas formerly under Peru, and the consequent decline of Peru within the newly oriented Spanish imperial system. From 1780 to 1782 occurred the Indian revolt of Tupac Amaru and in 1809 and 1813, there were further uprisings, but Spanish authority in Peru was not seriously threatened until 1820 when patriot forces invaded Peru from Chile and later from Gran Colombia in the north. After several campaigns the viceregal forces were defeated and Spanish authority was ended. In 1821 the independence of Peru was proclaimed, and a republic was established four years later.

Viceroys

1535-1541	Francisco Pizarro
1541-1542	Diego de Almagro
1542-1544	Cristóbal Vaca de Castro
1544	Blasco Núñez Vela
1544-1547	Gonzalo Pizarro
1547-1550	Pedro de la Gasca
1550-1552	Antonio de Mendoza
1552-1556	(audiencia)
1556-1561	Andrés Hurtado de Mendoza, Marqués de Cañete
1561-1564	Diego López de Zúñiga y Velasco, Conde de Nieva
1564-1569	Lope García de Castro
1569-1581	Francisco de Toledo
1581-1583	Martín Enríquez de Almansa
1583-1586	(audiencia)
1586-1589	Fernando Torres de Portugal y Mesía Venegas y Ponce de León, Conde de Villadompardo
1589-1596	García Hurtado de Mendoza y Manrique, Marqués de Cañete
1596-1604	Luis de Velasco, Marqués de Salinas
1604-1607	Gaspar de Zúñiga Acevedo y Fonseca, Conde de Monterrey
1607-1615	Juan Manuel de Mendoza y Manrique Hurtado y Padilla, Marqués de Montesclaros
1615-1621	Francisco de Borja y Aragón, Príncipe de Esquilache
1621-1629	Diego Fernández de Córdoba y López de las Roelas Benavides y Melgarejo, Marqués de Guadalcázar
1629-1639	Luis Jerónimo Fernández de Cabrera Bobadilla Cerda y Mendoza, Conde de Chinchón
1639-1648	Pedro de Toledo y Leyva, Marqués de Mancera
1648-1655	García Sarmiento de Sotomayor Enríquez de Luna, Conde de Salvatierra
1655-1661	Luis Enríquez de Guzmán y Coresma, Conde de Alba de Liste
1661-1666	Diego de Benavides y de la Cueva, Conde de Santisteban
1666-1674	Pedro Antonio Fernández de Castro Andrade y Portugal, Conde de Lemos
1674-1678	Bartolomé de la Cueva Enríquez Arias de Saavedra Pardo Tavera y Ulloa, Conde de Castellar
1678-1681	Melchor Liñán de Cisneros
1681-1689	Melchor de Navarra y Rocaful, Duque de la Plata
1689-1705	Melchor Portocarrero Lasso de la Vega, Conde de Monclova
1705-1710	Manuel Oms de Santa Pau Olim de Semanat y de La Nuza, Marqués de Castell dos Rius
1710-1716	Diego Ladrón de Guevara
1716-1720	Carmine Niccolo Caracciolo, Príncipe de Santo Buono
1720-1724	Diego Morcillo Rubío de Auñón
1724-1736	José de Armendáriz y Perurena Garrués de Usechi y Urquijo, Marqués de Castellfuerte
1736-1745	José Antonio de Mendoza Caamaño y Sotomayor, Marqués de Villagarcí
1745-1761	José Antonio Manso de Velasco y Sánchez de Samaniego, Conde de Superunda
1761-1776	Manuel de Amat y Junient Planella Aimeric y Santa Pau
1776-1780	Manuel de Guirior y Portal de Huarte y Edozain, Marqués de Guirior
1780-1784	Agustín de Jáuregui y Aldecoa
1784-1789	Teodoro Francisco de Croix, Conde de Croix

1790-1796   Francisco Gil de Taboada Lemos y Villamarín
1796-1801   Ambrosio O'Higgins, Marqués de Osorno
1801-1806   Gabriel de Avilés y del Fierro, Marqués de Avilés
1806-1816   José Fernando Abascal y Sousa, Marqués de la Concordia
1816-1821   Joaquín de la Pezuela y Sánchez Muñoz de Velasco
1821-1824   José de la Serna e Hinojosa

Bromley, passim.

372 PHILIPPINE ISLANDS

The Philippine Islands were discovered by Magellan in 1521 and it was there he met his death. During the middle part of the 16th century Spain and Portugal contested for influence in the area, but in 1565 an expedition from Nueva España (q.v.) began the occupation of the islands for Spain. By 1600 all the major islands except Mindanao and the Sulu archipelago in the south were under Spanish control. These were not effectively occupied until the middle of the 19th century. From 1583 to 1589 and after 1595 there was an audiencia at Manila, the capital, although the Philippine Islands were subject to the viceroy of Nueva España (q.v.). The governor became captain-general as well in 1783. British forces occupied Manila, as they did Havana (v. Cuba), in 1762 but returned it at the Treaty of Paris in 1763. The intendencia system was introduced in 1786 and the intendencias of Manila, Ilocos, Camarines, Iloilo, and Cebú were created, but the next year they were suppressed. During the 19th century nationalist sentiment became prominent in the islands, but with no significant reaction by Spain beyond its attempted suppression. In 1898, during the Spanish-American War the Philippines were invaded and occupied by American troops and Spain ceded them to the United States in the same year.

Governors
1565-1572   Miguel López de Legaspi y
            Gurruchategui
1572-1575   Guido de Lavezares
1575-1580   Francisco de Sande Picón
1580-1583   Gonzalo Ronquillo de Peñalosa
1583-1584   Diego Ronquillo
1584-1590   Santiago de Vera
1590-1593   Gomez Pérez Desmariñas
1593-1596   Luis Pérez Desmariñas
1596-1602   Francisco Tello de Guzmán
1602-1606   Pedro Bravo de Acuña
1606-1608   Cristóbal Telles
1608-1609   Rodrigo de Vivero y Aberrucia
            Lasso de la Vega y Velasco
1609-1616   Juan de Silva
1617-1618   Gregorio de Silva
1618-1624   Alonso Fajardo y Tenza
1624-1625   Jerónimo de Silva
1625-1626   Fernando de Silva
1626-1632   Juan Niño de Tavora
1632-1633   Lorenzo de Olaso
1633-1635   Juan Cerezo de Salamanca
1635-1644   Sebastián Hurtado de Corcuera y
            Gaviría

1644-1653   Diego Fajardo
1653-1663   Sabiniano Manrique de Lara
1663-1668   Diego de Salcedo
1668-1669   Juan Manuel de la Peña Bonifaz
1669-1677   Manuel de León y Saravia
1677-1678   Francisco Sotomayor Mansilla
1678-1684   Juan de Vargas Hurtado
1684-1689   Gabriel de Curuzalaegui y Arriola
1689-1690   Alonso Fuertes
1690-1701   Fausto Cruzat y Góngora
1701-1709   Domingo Zabálburu de Echevarri
1709-1715   Martín de Ursúa y Arismendi
            Aguirre y Vicondo, Conde de
            Lizárraga
1715-1717   José de Torralba
1717-1719   Fernando Manuel de Bustillo
            Bustamante y Rueda
1719-1721   Francisco de la Cuesta
1721-1729   Toribio José Cosío y Campo,
            Marqués de Torre Campo
1729-1739   Fernando de Valdés y Tamón
1739-1745   Gaspar de la Torre
1745-1750   Juan de Arrechederra
1750-1754   Francisco José de Obando y Solís,
            Marqués de Obando

Spain

1754-1759	Pedro Manuel de Arandía y Santisteban	1854-1856	Miguel Crespo y Cebrián
1759-1761	Manuel Lino Ezpeleta	1857-1860	Fernando de Norzagaray y Escudero
1761-1762	Manuel Antonio Rojo del Río y Viera	1860	Ramón María Solano y Llanderol
1762-1764	Simón de Anda y Salazar (1)	1860-1861	Juan Herrera Dávila
1764-1765	Francisco Javier de la Torre	1861-1862	José Lemery y Ibarrola Ney y González
1765-1770	José Antonio Raón y Gutiérrez	1862-1865	Rafael de Echague y Bermingham
1770-1776	Simón de Anda y Salazar (2)	1865-1866	Juan de Lara y Irigoyen
1776-1778	Pedro de Sarrío (1)	1866-1869	José de la Gándara y Navarro
1778-1787	José Basco y Vargas	1869-1871	Carlos María de la Torre y Nava Cerrada
1787-1788	Pedro de Sarrío (2)		
1788-1793	Félix Berenguer de Marquina	1871-1873	Rafael de Izquierdo y Gutiérrez
1793-1806	Rafael María de Aguilar y Ponce de León	1873-1874	Juan Alaminos y de Vivar
		1874-1877	José Malcampo y Monje, Marqués de San Rafael
1806-1810	Mariano Fernández de Folgueras (1)	1877-1880	Domingo Moriones y Murillo Zabaleta y Sanz, Marques de Oroquieta
1810-1813	Manuel González de Aguilar		
1813-1816	José Gardoqui de Jaraveitia		
1816-1822	Mariano Fernández de Folgueras (2)	1880-1883	Fernando Primo de Rivera, Marqués de Estella (1)
1822-1825	Juan Antonio Martínez	1883-1885	Joaquín Jovellar y Soler
1825-1830	Mariano Ricafort Palacín y Abarca	1885-1888	Emilio Terrero y Perinat
1830-1835	Pascual Enrile y Alcedo	1888-1891	Valeriano Weyler y Nicolau, Marqués de Tenerife
1835-1837	Pedro Antonio de Salazar Castillo y Varona	1891-1893	Eulogio Despujol y Dusay, Conde de Caspe
1837-1838	Andrés Camba García		
1838-1841	Luis Lardizábal y Montojo	1893-1896	Ramón Blanco y Erenas, Marqués de Peña Plata
1841-1843	Marcelino de Oraá Lecumberri		
1843-1844	Francisco de Paula Alcalá de la Torre	1896-1897	Camilio de Polavieja y del Fierro
1844-1849	Narciso Clavería y Zaldúa	1897-1898	Fernando Primo de Rivera, Marqués de Estella (2)
1849-1850	Antonio María Blanco		
1850-1853	Antonio de Urbiztondo y Eguía	1898	Basilio Augustín
1854	Miguel Pavía Lacy Miralles y Burgunyó, Marqués de Novaliches	1898	Fermín Jáudens y Alvares
		1898	Diego de los Ríos

Blair and Robertson, 17:285—312.

373 POPAYÁN

The area of southwestern Colombia was settled from Peru after 1536 and erected into the provinc
of Popayán in 1541. In 1549 Popayán fell under the jursidiction of the newly created audiencia
of Santa Fé de Bogotá (v. Nueva Granada), but remained so only until 1563 when the audiencia
of Quito (q.v.) was created. In 1717, with the suppression of the Quito audiencia, Popayán became part of the new viceroyalty of Nueva Granada. By 1820 Spanish authority had been eliminated in Popayán, which became part of the new state of Gran Colombia and later of Colombia.

Governors

1536-1538	Sebastián de Belalcázar (1)	1540-1541	Pascual de Andagoya
1538-1539	Francisco García de Tovar	1541-1549	Sebastián de Belalcázar (2)
1539-1540	Lorenzo de Aldana	1549-1553	Francisco Briceño
		1553-1554	Diego Delgado

326

1554	Juan Montaño	1702-1703	Juan de Mier y Ceballos
1554-1556	Pedro Fernández del Busto (1)	1703-1707	Pedro Bolaños y Mendoza
1556-1561	Luis de Guzmán	1707	Manuel García de Salcedo
1562-1564	Pedro de Agreda	1707-1713	Baltasar Carlos de Viveros,
1564	Pedro García de Valverde		Marqués de San Miguel de la
1564-1566	Francisco de Mosquera		Vega
1566-1572	Álvaro de Mendoza y Carvajal	1713-1718	Eugenio de Alvarado y Coloma
1572-1573	Jerónimo de Silva	1718-1719	Nicolás de Ontañón y Lastra,
1574-1575	Pedro Fernández del Busto (2)		Conde de las Lagunas
1575	Francisco de Gamarra	1719-1724	Marcos Antonio Rivera, Marqués
1575-1576	Bartolomé de Mazmela		de San Juan de la Rivera
1576-1583	Sancho García del Espinar	1724-1729	Fernando Pérez Guerrero y
1583-1589	Juan de la Tuesta Salazar		Peñalosa
1589-1591	Diego Ordóñez de Lara	1729-1733	(cabildo)
1591-1594	Cipriano de la Cueva de Montes	1733-1734	Manuel Ahumada
	de Oca	1734-1739	Pablo Fidalgo
1594-1597	Diego de Noguera y Valenzuela	1739-1747	José Francisco Carreño
1597-1598	Francisco de Hoyos y Blanquero	1747-1749	Antonio Mola de Viñacorta
1598-1599	Francisco de Berrío y Quesada	1749-1752	Juan Francisco de Eguizábal
1599-1610	Vasco de Mendoza y Silva	1752-1755	Francisco Damián de Espejo
1610-1615	Francisco de Sarmiento y	1755-1760	Antonio Alcalá Galiano
	Sotomayor	1760-1761	José Ignacio Ortega (1)
1615-1620	Pedro Lasso de la Guerra	1761-1765	Pedro de la Moneda
1620-1627	Juan Méndez Márquez	1766-1771	José Ignacio Ortega (2)
1628-1633	Juan Bermúdez de Castro	1771-1777	Juan Antonio Zelaya y Vergara
1633-1637	Lorenzo de Villaquirán	1777-1789	Pedro Beccaria Espinosa
1637-1644	Juan de Borja y Heredia	1789-1791	José de Castro y Correa
1644-1652	Juan de Salazar	1791-1806	Diego Antonio Nieto
1652-1656	Luis de Valenzuela Fajardo	1806-1811	Miguel Tacón Rosique Foxá y
1656-1667	Luis Antonio de Guzmán y Toledo		Rivera, Vizconde de Bayamo
1667-1674	Gabriel Díaz de la Cuesta	1813-1814	Juan José de Sámano y Urribarri
1674-1679	Miguel García		de Rebollar y Mazorra (1)
1679-1683	Fernando Martínez de Fresneda	1815-1816	Aparicio Vidaurrázaga
1683-1689	Jerónimo de Berrío y Mendoza	1816	Juan José de Sámano y Urribarri
1689-1696	Rodrigo Roque de Mañosca		de Rebollar y Mazorra (2)
1696-1702	Jerónimo José de la Vega y Valdés,	1816-1818	José Solís
	Marqués de Nevares	1818-1820	Pedro Domínguez

Aragón, *Fastos*, 1:72–90; idem, *Popayán*, pp. 65–83; Arroyo, pp. 345–61.

374 POTOSÍ

The area of Potosí, with its rich silver mines, was transferred from the viceroyalty of Peru (q.v.) to the viceroyalty of Río de la Plata (q.v., 381) in 1777. In 1783 it was created an intendencia. In 1810 the intendant was deposed and executed and for the next dozen years the area was disputed between Spanish and nationalist forces. Eventually most of the intendencia became part of the Republic of Bolivia although some of its area was later lost to Chile.

Intendants
1783-1789	Juan del Pino Manrique de Lara
1789-1810	Francisco de Paula Sanz

Lynch, p. 290.

375 PROVINCIAS INTERNAS

As Spanish settlement in Mexico proceeded northward away from the core area around Mexico City, and as it moved into areas inhabited by less docile Indians than the Spaniards were accustomed to, frontier defense became a primary concern of the Spanish government. These military exigencies resulted in the creation, in 1777, of an administrative unit known as the Provincias Internas. It included all the northern provinces of Nueva España (q.v.) except the Californias. This new jurisdiction was headed by a commandant-general and was initially completely independent of the viceroy. Later the Provincias Internas became partially subordinated to the viceroy, and in fact the relationship of the viceroyalty to the Provincias Internas fluctuated according to ambient circumstances, particularly the characters of the respective individuals in charge. From 1788 to 1793 and again from 1813 to 1821 the Provincias Internas was divided, in the interests of efficiency, into an eastern and western part. After 1793 Nuevo León and Nuevo Santander (qq.v.) were removed from them. Each of the constituent provinces had its own civil governor who was subordinate in some areas to the commandant-general, and independent in others. With the creation of the intendencias in 1787 all of some and parts of others were within the boundaries of the Provincias Internas. Despite the jurisdictional and territorial anomalies involved, the Provincias Internas persevered until the end of the Spanish dominion in Mexico in 1821.

Commandants-Generals
1777-1783 Teodoro Francisco de Croix, Conde de Croix
1783-1784 Felipe de Neve
1784-1786 José Antonio Rengel de Alcaraz y Páez
1786-1788 Jacobo Ugarte y Loyola

Poniente (Sonora, Californias, Nueva Vizcaya, Nuevo México)
1788-1790 Jacobo Ugarte y Loyola
1790-1793 Pedro de Nava

Oriente (Coahuila, Texas, Nuevo León, Nuevo Santander)
1788-1791 Juan de Ugalde
1791-1793 Ramón de Castro y Gutiérrez

Provincias Internas (except Californias, Nuevo León, Nuevo Santander)
1793-1802 Pedro de Nava
1802-1813 Nemesio Salcedo y Salcedo

Poniente
1813-1817 Bernardo Bonavia y Zapata
1817-1821 Alejo García Conde

Oriente
1813   Simón Herrera y Leyva
1813-1821 Joaquín de Arredondo y Mioño Pelegrin y Bustamante

Moorhead, p. 278 n. and passim; Navarro García, *Provincias Internas*, passim.

376 PUEBLA

The alcaldia mayor of Puebla in eastern Mexico was created an intendencia in 1787. In 1821 Puebla became part of the empire of Mexico and later a state in the Republic of Mexico.

Intendants
1787-1811 Manuel Flón y Tejada, Conde de la Cadena
1811-1812 García Dávila

1812   Santiago de Irisarri
1812-1813 Prudencio de Guadalfajara y Aguilera, Conde de Castro Terreño

1814	Ramón Díaz Ortega	1815-1816	Joaquín Estévez
1814-1815	José Moreno y Daioz	1816-1821	Ciriaco del Llano

Palacios, pp. 712—13.

377 PUERTO RICO

Puerto Rico, an island in the eastern Caribbean, was discovered by Columbus in 1493. Settlement began in 1509 from Cuba (q.v.). Like Jamaica (q.v.) Puerto Rico was an economic and political backwater in Spain's American empire, being overshadowed by its neighbors Santo Domingo (q.v.) and Cuba. Puerto Rico, along with Cuba, were, after 1825, Spain's only possessions in the western hemisphere. Like Cuba, Puerto Rico was occupied by American troops during the Spanish-American War in 1898 and formally ceded to the United States in the same year. Puerto Rico then became a territory of the United States (v. 410).

Governors

1508-1509	Juan Ponce de León (1)
1509-1510	Juan Cerón (1)
1510-1511	Juan Ponce de León (2)
1511-1512	Juan Cerón (2)
1512-1513	Rodrigo de Moscoso
1513-1515	Cristóbal de Mendoza
1515-1519	Juan Ponce de León (3)
1519-1521	Antonio de la Gama (1)
1521-1523	Pedro Moreno (1)
1523-1524	Alonso Manso
1524-1529	Pedro Moreno (2)
1529-1530	Antonio de la Gama (2)
1530-1536	Francisco Manuel de Lando
1536-1537	Vasco de Tiedra
1537-1544	(alcaldes)
1544	Gerónimo Ledrón de Quinóñes
1545-1546	Iñigo López Cervantes de Loaysa
1546-1548	Diego de Caraza (1)
1548-1549	Alonso de Vargas
1549-1550	Francisco de Aguilar
1550-1555	Luis de Vallejo
1555-1564	Diego de Caraza (2)
1564	Antonio de la Llama Vallejo
1564-1568	Francisco Bahamonde de Lugo
1568-1574	Francisco de Solís
1575-1579	Francisco de Obando y Mejía
1580-1581	Juan de Céspedes
1581-1582	Juan López Melgarejo
1582-1593	Diego Menéndez de Valdés
1593-1597	Pedro Suárez Coronel (1)
1597	Antonio de Mosquera
1597-1599	Pedro Suárez Coronel (2)
1599-1602	Alonso de Mercado
1602-1608	Sancho Ochóa y Castro, Conde de Salvatierra

1608-1614	Gabriel de Rojas Párano
1614-1620	Felipe de Beaumont y Navarra
1620-1625	Juan de Vargas Aselas (or Machuca)
1625-1631	Juan de Haro y Sanvítores
1631-1635	Enrique Enríquez de Sotomayor
1635-1641	Iñigo de la Mota Sarmiento
1641	Agustín de Silva y Figueroa
1642-1643	Juan de Bolaños
1643-1650	Fernando de la Riva Agüero y Setien
1650-1656	Diego de Aguilera y Gamboa
1655-1661	José de Nóvoa y Moscoso Pérez y Buitrón
1661-1664	Juan Pérez de Guzmán y Chagoyen
1664-1670	Jerónimo de Velasco
1670-1674	Gaspar de Arteaga y Aunoavidao
1674-1675	Baltasar de Figueroa y Castilla
1675-1678	Alonso de Campos y Espinosa
1678-1683	Juan de Robles Lorenzana
1683-1690	Gaspar Martínez de Andino
1690-1695	Gaspar de Arredondo y Valle (1)
1695-1698	Juan Fernández Franco de Medina
1698-1699	Antonio de Robles Silva
1699-1700	Gaspar de Arredondo y Valle (2)
1700-1703	Gabriel Gutiérrez de Riva
1703-1705	Francisco Sánchez Calderón
1705-1706	Pedro de Arroyo y Guerrero
1706-1708	Juan Antonio Morla
1708-1714	Francisco Danío Granados
1714-1718	Juan de Rivera
1718	José Carreño
1718-1720	Alberto Bertodano y Navarro
1720-1724	Francisco Danío
1724-1731	José Antonio de Mendizábal y Azcue
1731-1743	Matías de Abadía

Spain

1743-1750	Juan José Colomo	1855	Andrés Camba García
1750-1751	Agustín de Pareja	1855-1857	José Lemery Ibarrola Ney y
1751-1753	Esteban Bravo de Rivera (1)		González ·
1753-1757	Felipe Ramírez de Estenoz	1857-1860	Fernando Cotoner y Chacón
1757-1759	Esteban Bravo de Rivera (2)	1860-1862	Rafael Echagüe y Bermingham
1759-1760	Antonio de Guazo y Calderón de	1862-1863	Rafael Izquierdo y Gutiérrez
	la Torre	1863-1865	Félix María de Messina
1760-1761	Esteban Bravo de Rivera (3)	1865-1867	José María Marchesi y Oleaga
1761-1766	Ambrosio de Benavides	1867-1868	Julián Juan Pavía
1766-1768	Marcos de Vergara	1868-1870	José Laureano Sanz y Posse (1)
1768-1769	José Trentor	1870-1871	Gabriel Baldrich y Palau
1769-1776	Miguel de Muesas	1871-1872	Ramón Gómez Pulido
1776-1783	José Dufresne	1872	Simón de la Torre
1783-1789	Juan Dabán	1873	Juan Martínez Plowes
1789-1792	Miguel Antonio de Ustáriz	1873-1874	Rafael Primo de Rivera y
1792-1795	Francisco Torralbo		Sobremonte
1795-1804	Ramón de Castro y Gutiérrez	1874-1875	José Laureano Sanz y Posse (2)
1804-1809	Toribio de Montes	1875-1877	Segundo de la Portilla (1)
1809-1820	Salvador Meléndez y Ruíz	1877-1878	Manuel de la Serna y Pinzón,
1820	Juan Vasco y Pascual		Marqués de Irún
1820-1822	Gonzalo de Aróstegui y Herrera	1878-1881	Eulogio Despujols y Dusay
1822	Francisco González de Linares	1881-1883	Segundo de la Portilla (2)
1822-1837	Miguel Luciano de la Torre y	1883-1884	Miguel de la Vega Inclán y Palma,
	Pando		Marqués de la Vega Inclán
1837-1838	Francisco Moreda y Prieto	1884-1887	Luis Dabán y Ramírez de
1838-1841	Miguel López de Baños		Arellano
1841-1844	Santiago Méndez de Vigo	1887	Romualdo Palacíos
1844-1847	Rafael de Aristegui y Vélez,	1888-1890	Pedro Ruíz Dana
	Conde de Mirasol	1890-1893	José Lasso y Pérez
1847-1848	Juan Prim Agüero Prats y	1893-1895	Antonio Dabán y Ramírez de
	González, Conde de Reus		Arellano
1848-1851	Juan de la Pezuela y Ceballos	1895-1896	José Gamir
1851-1852	Enrique de España y Taberner,	1896-1898	Sabas Marín y González
	Marqués de España	1898	Andrés González Muñoz
1852-1855	Fernando de Norzágaray y Escudero	1898	Manuel Macías y Casado

Information gathered by Elsa Reyes Pérez and provided by Sr. Luis M. Rodríguez Morales, Director, Archivo General de Puerto Rico, San Juan, Puerto Rico. Also, González García, passim. Coll y Toste has been largely superseded by these sources.

378 PUNO

Puno was created an intendencia within the viceroyalty of Río de la Plata (q.v., 381) in 1783. It was situated in the extreme northwest of the viceroyalty and its great distance from the viceregal capital of Buenos Aires (q.v.) led to its being transferred to the viceroyalty of Peru (q.v.) in 1796. Some Spanish control was retained in Puno until 1824 after which it became part of the Republic of Peru.

Intendants

1784-1788	José Reseguín	1790-1795	Francisco José de Mesa Ponte
1788-1790	José Joaquín Contreras		Pagés y Castilla, Marqués de
			Casa Hermosa

1795-1798	José Antonio Campos	1810	Diego Antonio Nieto
1798-1801	Tomás de Semper	1810-1814	Manuel Quimper Benítez del
1801	Ignacio Maldonaldo		Pino (2)
1801-1806	José González de Navarra y	1814-1815	Martín Rivarola
	Montoya	1815-1816	Francisco de Paula González
1806-1810	Manuel Quimper Benítez del	1816-1817	Narciso Basagoítia
	Pino (1)	1817-1824	Tadeo Joaquín de Garate

Deustua Pimentel, pp. 193–97; Lynch, p. 291; Mendiburú, 8:416–17.

379 QUITO

Quito, the main northern center of the Inca kingdom, was seized by the Spaniards in 1533. Until 1556 it was administered by a series of lieutenant governors. In 1556 it became a province and in 1563 it was erected into an audiencia under the viceroy of Peru (q.v.). In 1767 the governor/president became captain-general as well. In 1718 the audiencia was suppressed and Quito came under the jurisdiction of the viceroyalty of Nueva Granada (q.v.). On the suppression of the viceroyalty in 1722 the audiencia was reconstituted. In 1739 Quito once again fell under the authority of the viceroy of Nueva Granada but this time retained its audiencia. Spanish authority, already challenged in 1809 with the deposition of the governor/president, was ended in 1822. Until 1830 Quito was part of Gran Colombia. In 1830 the Republic of Ecuador, based on but much smaller than the former audiencia of Quito, was established.

Governors

1556-1559	Gil Ramírez Dávalos	1662-1665	Antonio Fernández de Heredia
1559-1563	Melchor Vázquez de Ávila	1665-1670	(audiencia)
1563-1564	Juan Salazar de Villasante	1670-1673	Diego del Corro Carrascal
1564	Alonso Manuel de Amaya	1674-1677	Alonso de la Peña Montenegro
1564-1568	Hernando de Santillán	1678-1689	Lope Antonio de Munive y Axpe
1568-1571	Gabriel de Loarte	1689-1691	(audiencia)
1571-1574	Lope Díez Aux de Armendáriz	1691-1703	Mateo de la Mata Ponce de León
1575-1578	Pedro García de Valverde	1703-1707	Francisco López de Dicastillo
1578-1581	Diego de Narváez	1707-1715	Juan de Sosaya
1581-1587	Pedro Venegas de Cañaveral	1715-1718	Santiago Larraín y Vicuña (1)
1587	Francisco de Auncibay	1718-1722	(audiencia suppressed)
1587-1594	Manuel Barros de San Millán	1722-1723	Santiago Larraín y Vicuña (2)
1594-1600	Esteban Marañón	1723-1736	Dionisio de Alcedo Ugarte y
1600-1608	Miguel de Ibarra		Herrera
1608-1609	Diego de Armenteros	1736-1743	José de Araujo y Río
1609-1612	Juan Fernández de Recalde	1743-1745	Manuel Rubío de Arévalo (1)
1612-1615	Matías de Peralta Cabeza de Vaca	1745-1753	Fernando Félix Sánchez de
1615-1636	Antonio de Morga Sánchez Garay		Orellana, Marqués de Solanda
	y López de Garfias	1753-1761	Juan Pío de Montúfar y Frasso
1636-1637	Antonio Rodríguez de San Isidro (1)		Porras y del Corro, Marqués de
1637-1642	Alonso Pérez de Salazar		Selva Alegre
1643-1644	Juan de Lizárazu	1761-1766	Manuel Rubío de Arévalo (2)
1645-1646	Antonio Rodríguez de San Isidro (2)	1766-1767	Juan Antonio Zelaya y Vergara
1646-1647	Alonso Ferrer de Ayala	1767-1778	José Diguja Villagómez
1647-1652	Martín de Arriola y Balerdi	1778-1784	José García de León y Pizarro
1652-1655	Juan Morales de Aramburu	1784-1790	Juan José de Villalengua y Marfil
1655-1661	Pedro Vázquez de Velasco	1790-1791	Juan Antonio Mon y Velarde Pardo
			y Cienfuegos

Spain

1791-1798	Luis Antonio Muñoz de Guzmán	1812-1817	Toribio Montes
1798-1806	Luis Francisco Héctor de Carondelet de Novelles	1817-1819	Juan Ramírez Orosco
		1819-1822	Melchor de Aymerich
1806-1808	Juan Antonio Nieto		
1808-1811	Manuel Ruiz y Urríes de Castilla y Cavero, Marqués de Ruiz de Castilla		

Pareja y Díez Canseco, 2:476—77; Vivanco, pp. 16—18. Vivanco includes only substantive governors/presidents and not those serving without royal *titulo*.

380 RÍO DE LA PLATA

The estuary of the Río de la Plata was explored by Sebastian Cabot in Spanish service in 1526. In 1535 the first Spanish settlement in the area occurred. Buenos Aires (q.v.) was founded in 1536 but abandoned the following year in favor of Asunción upriver. In 1580 Buenos Aires was refounded and came to be the seat of the governor of Río de la Plata. The province of Río de la Plata comprised all the Spanish settlements in this area and was under the jurisdiction of the audiencia of Charcas (q.v.). However, in 1618 the rivalry between the cities of Asunción and Buenos Aires led to the division of Río de la Plata into the provinces of Buenos Aires and Paraguay (qq.v.).

Governors		1583-1584	Rodrigo Ortiz de Zárate
1536-1537	Pedro de Mendoza	1584-1587	Juan de Torres Navarrette
1537	Juan de Ayolas	1587-1592	Juan Torres de Vera y Aragón
1537-1541	Domingo Martínez de Irala (1)	1592-1593	Hernando Arias de Saavedra (1)
1541-1545	Álvar Núñez Cabeza de Vaca	1593-1594	Hernando de Zárate
1545-1556	Domingo Martínez de Irala (2)	1594-1596	Hernando Arias de Saavedra (2)
1556-1557	Gonzalo de Mendoza	1596-1597	Juan Ramírez de Velasco
1558-1565	Francisco Ortiz de Vergara	1597-1599	Hernando Arias de Saavedra (3)
1565-1566	Juan Ortiz de Zárate (1)	1599-1601	Diego Rodríguez Valdés y de la Banda
1566-1567	Felipe de Cáceres		
1567-1576	Juan Ortiz de Zárate (2)	1602-1609	Hernando Arias de Saavedra (4)
1576-1577	Diego Ortiz de Zárate Mendieta	1609-1613	Diego Marín Negrón
1577-1578	Luis Osorio de Quiñones	1614-1618	Hernando Arias de Saavedra (5)
1578-1583	Juan de Garay		

Sierra, 1:197—285, 315—33, 363—423, 529—43, and 2:31—59, 99—110.

381 RÍO DE LA PLATA

The city and province of Buenos Aires (q.v.) grew rapidly in importance during the 18th century, due primarily to its central role in the widespread contraband trade which was the consequence of Spain's inflexible adherence to strict mercantilist policies. The abandonment of these policies after 1750 plus the military threat created by the southward advance of the Portuguese in Brazil (v. Nova Colônia do Sacramento, 304) resulted in the creation of the viceroyalty of Río de la Plata in 1777. It included the provinces of Buenos Aires, Paraguay, Tucumán, Montevideo, and the Malvinas Islands (qq.v.), together with the presidency of Charcas (q.v.), detached from Peru, and Cuyo, detached from Chile (q.v.). In 1783 a viceregal audiencia was created in Buenos Aires. In the same year the intendencia system was implemented within the viceroyalty, which was divided into the intendencias of Córdoba, Cochabamba, La Paz, Paraguay, Potosí, Salta, Charcas, Buenos Aires, and Puno (transferred to the viceroyalty of Peru in 1796) (qq.v.), and the provinces of Mojos, Chiquitos, Misiones, Montevideo (q.v.), and the Malvinas Islands (q.v.). In political and economic terms the viceroyalty of Río de la Plata was probably the most important in the Spanish Empire at the turn of the 19th century. In 1806 Buenos Aires was briefly occupied by the British. The inability of the Spanish viceroy to repel the invaders led to the selection of a new viceroy by the populace—an act accepted by the Spanish crown. The efforts of the Spanish government to reimpose its now weakened authority led to the ouster of the viceroy from Buenos Aires in 1810. From this date there was no direct Spanish control, although independence was not formally declared until 1816. Eventually the republics of Argentina, Bolivia, Paraguay, and Uruguay were established within the former territorial limits of the viceroyalty of Río de la Plata.

Viceroys

1778–1784	José Juan Vértiz y Salcedo
1784–1789	Francisco Cristóbal del Campo, Marqués de Loreto
1789–1795	Nicolás de Arredondo
1795–1797	Pedro Melo de Portugal y Vilhena
1797–1799	Antonio Olaguer y Feliú Heredia Lopez y Donec
1799–1801	Gabriel de Avilés y del Fierro, Marqués de Avilés
1801–1804	Joaquín del Pino y Rosas Romero Negrete
1804–1807	Rafael de Sobremonte Núñez Castillo Angulo y Bullón Ramirez de Arellano, Marqués de Sobremonte
1807	Pascual Ruíz Huidobro
1807–1809	Santiago Antonio María de Liniers y Bremont
1809–1810	Baltasar Hidalgo y Cisneros y la Torre

Ravignani, pp. 142–92.

382 SALTA

Salta was the northern part of the old province of Tucumán (q.v.), which had been divided with the introduction of the intendencia system into the viceroyalty of Río de la Plata (q.v., 381) in 1783. After 1810 Salta was no longer under Spanish control and later the area became part of the Republic of Argentina.

Intendants

1783–1790	Andrés Mestre
1790–1797	Ramón García de León y Pizarro
1798–1807	Rafael de la Luz
1807–1808	Tomás Arrigunaga y Archondo
1808–1809	José de Medeiros
1809–1810	Nicolás Severo de Isasmendi y Echalar

Lynch, p. 290.

383 SAN LUIS POTOSÍ

The intendencia of San Luis Potosí was created in 1787 within the viceroyalty of Nueva España (q.v.). In 1821 San Luis Potosí became part of the empire of Mexico and later a state in the Republic of Mexico.

Intendants			
1787–1799	Bruno Díaz de Salcedo	1804–1805	Manuel Ampudía
1799–1800	Vicente Bernabeu	1805–1809	José Ignacio Vélez
1801–1804	Onésimo Antonio Durán	1809–1810	José Ruíz de Aguirre
		1810–1821	Manuel Jacinto de Acevedo

Information from Lic. Diana Torres Ariceaga, Oficial Mayor de Gobierno, San Luis Potosí, Mexico. Also, Grimaldo, pp. xix–xx.

384 SAN SALVADOR

The area of San Salvador, a part of the captaincy-general of Guatemala (q.v.), was erected into an intendencia in 1786. It remained an intendencia, although subject to Guatemala, until 1821 when Spanish authority was terminated by revolt. San Salvador became part of the United States of Central America in 1824. At its dissolution in 1839 the area of the former intendencia of San Salvador became the Republic of El Salvador. The following list of intendants is incomplete.

Intendants			
1786–	José Ortiz de la Peña	1811–1812	José Alejandro de Aycinena y Aldecoa Carrillo y Gálvez
–	(unknown)	1812–	José María Peinado
–1811	Antonio Basilio Gutiérrez de Ulloa	–1821	Pedro Barriere

Navarro García, p. 50.

385 SANTA CATALINA

The island of Santa Catalina, in the Caribbean Sea about one hundred miles off the coast of Nicaragua, was held by the English, who called it Providence (v. 199), from 1630 to 1641. The strategic location of the island, astride the shipping routes from Panama to Spain, led the Spanish authorities of Nueva Granada (q.v.) to seize the island in 1641. In 1666 it was briefly occupied by the English, and again in 1670. During the period 1641 to 1670 the island was under the jurisdiction of the audiencia of Panama (q.v.). Spain reoccupied the island in 1688 but it was not constituted a separate province.

Governors
1641-1662 Jerónimo de Ojeda
  -1666 Juan de Ocampo

1666-1667 (under England)
1667-1670 José Sánchez Jiménez

Rowland, passim.

386 SANTA MARTA-RÍO HACHA

The town of Santa Marta in northern Colombia was founded in 1525 and served as a base for the Spanish conquest of the interior (v. Nueva Granada). After 1600 the province was known as Santa Marta-Río Hacha. Santa Marta remained under the audiencia of Santo Domingo (q.v.) until 1740, except for the interval from 1719 to 1723. After 1740 it was part of the viceroyalty of Nueva Granada and its audiencia of Santa Fé de Bogotá. Like its neighbor to the west, Cartagena de Indias (q.v.), Santa Marta served as a point of departure for the galleons carrying bullion from Peru (q.v.) and was rewarded by due attention from the other European powers in the Caribbean area who sacked it several times during the colonial period. Spanish authority continued in Santa Marta even though in 1810 the Spaniards were expelled from most of Nueva Granada. Indeed, during part of the period from 1810 to 1821 Santa Marta served as the seat of the viceroy. After the final expulsion of Spanish forces in 1821 Santa Marta became a province of Gran Colombia and later part of the Republic of Colombia.

Governors

1525-1527	Rodrigo de Bastidas
1527-1528	Rodrigo Álvarez Palomino
1529	Pedro Badillo
1529-1534	García de Lerma
1534-1536	Rodrigo Infante
1536	Pedro Fernández de Lugo
1536-1537	Antonio Bezos
1537-1541	Jerónimo Lebrón de Quiñones
1541-1544	Alonso Luis de Lugo
1544-1551	Miguel Díez de Armendáriz
1551	Juan López
1551-1554	Pedro de Ursúa
1554-	Luis de Villanueva
-	Luis de Manjarrés (1)
-1556	Gregorio Suárez de Deza
1556-1559	Luis de Manjarrés (2)
1559-1560	Rafael de Figuerola
1560-1561	Juan de Otálora
1561-1566	Luis de Manjarrés (3)
1566-1569	Martín de las Alas
1570-1571	Pedro Fernández del Busto
1571-1576	Luis de Rojas y Mendoza
1576-1589	Lope de Orozco
1589-1592	Francisco Marmolejo
1592-1600	Francisco Manso de Contreras
1600-1606	Juan Guiral y Belón
1606-1610	Andrés de Salcedo
1610-1618	Diego Fernández de Argote y Córdoba
1618-1619	Luis de Coronado
1619-1623	Francisco Martínez de Rivamontán Santander
1623-1630	Jerónimo de Quero y Jiménez
1630-1635	Rodrigo de Velasco
1635-1640	Marcos Gedler Calatayud y Toledo
1640-1642	Francisco Martín Vidal Centeno y Neira
1642-1643	Diego de Mendoza y Acevedo
1643-1648	Vicente de los Reyes Villalobos
1648-1649	Jerónimo de Ortega Arellano
1649-1654	Gabriel de Mencos
1654-1658	Ramón de Zagarriga
1658-1663	Marcos del Puerto
1663-1665	Juan Betín y Viñas
1665-1672	Salvador Barranco
1672-1678	Vicente Sebastián Mestre
1678-1679	Francisco Mesía y Alarcón
1680-1681	Ignacio de Espinosa
1681-1692	Pedro Jerónimo Royo de Arce Rojas y Santoyo
1692-1697	Pedro de Olivera y Ordóñez (1)
1697-1698	Ignacio Espinosa de los Monteros
1698	Juan Eusebio Dávalos
1698	Pedro de Olivera y Ordóñez (2)
1699-1700	Francisco García de Labarcés
1700-1701	Fernando Gómez Gallego
1701-1703	Diego de Peredo
1703-1708	Alonso Valera
1708-1709	Vicente de Aramburú y Echave

Spain

1710-1713	Cristóbal Vélez Ladrón de Guevera y Guzmán Lasso de la Vega, Marqués de Quintana de las Torres	1763-1768	Andrés Pérez Ruíz Caldéron (2)
		1768	Manuel de Herrera y Leiva
		1768-1777	Nicolás Díaz de Perea
		1777-1786	Antonio de Narváez y de la Torre
1713-1718	José Mozo de la Torre		
1718-1726	Juan Beltrán de Caicedo	1786-1793	José Ignacio de Astigárraga
1726-1733	José de Andía y Rivero	1793-1805	Antonio de Samper
1733-1743	Juan de Vera Fajardo	1805-1811	Victor de Salcedo y Somodevila
1743-1748	Juan de Aristegui y Avilés	1811-1813	Tomás de Acosta y Hurtado de Mendoza
1748-1753	Antonio de Alcalá Galiano		
1753-1760	Juan Toribio de Herrera y Leiva	1813-1819	Pedro Ruíz de Porras
1760-1761	Andrés Pérez Ruíz Calderón (1)	1819-1821	Latino Fitz Gerald
1761-1763	Gregorio Rosales Troncoso y Osores		

Restreop Tirado, *Historia . . . de Santa Marta*, passim.

387 SANTO DOMINGO

The island of Hispaniola (Española) was discovered by Columbus on his first voyage in 1492 and became the site of the first permanent Spanish settlement in the New World. The city of Santo Domingo was founded in 1496. Initially the island was given to Columbus and governed by his son, but their ineptitude resulted in the imposition of royal control in 1500. An audiencia was established in 1511, suppressed in 1517, and reconstituted in 1520. The audiencia of Santo Domingo had widespread jurisdiction. It had authority over Cuba, Puerto Rico, and Florida, as well as Mérida-La Grita, Margarita, Nueva Andalucía, Santa Marta, Guayana, and Venezuela (qq.v. on the northern coast of South America. All but the first three of these were removed from Santo Domingo's jurisdiction and placed under the viceroyalty of Nueva Granada (q.v.) in 1739. In 1587 the governor/president of Santo Domingo was given the additional dignity of captain-general. As Spanish control extended into Mexico (v. Nueva España) and South America the prosperity of Santo Domingo began to decline. In 1697 the western third of the island was ceded to France by the Treaty of Ryswick (v. Saint-Domingue, 56). While Saint-Domingue prospered, Santo Domingo continued to stagnate. In 1763 Florida (q.v.) was lost to Great Britain (v. 130) and the following year Cuba was erected into an independent captaincy-general. Finally, in 1797 the audiencia was removed to Puerto Principe on Cuba. In 1801 Haitian forces occupied Santo Domingo. In 1809 Spain recovered the colony, only to lose it again in 1821 to revolutionary elements in Santo Domingo itself. The following year, Haiti reoccupied Santo Domingo, which revolted and finally became independent in 1844.

Governors

		1526-1528	Gaspar de Espinosa
1496-1500	Bartolomé Colón	1528-1531	Sebastián Ramírez de Fuenleal
1500-1502	Francisco de Bobadilla	1531-1533	Alonso de Zuazo
1502-1509	Nicolás de Ovando	1533-1544	Alonso de Fuenmayor
1509-1515	Diego Colón (1)	1544-1549	Alonso (or Juan) López Cerrato
1515-1519	(junta)	1549-1558	Alonso de Maldonaldo
1519-1520	Rodrigo de Figueroa	1558	Hernando de Hoyos
1520-1522	(junta)	1558-1560	Juan López de Cepeda
1522-1523	Diego Colón (2)	1560-1562	Juan de Echagoyan
1523-1524	(audiencia)	1562-1565	Alonso Arias de Herrera
1524	Luis de Figueroa	1565-1567	Alonso de Grajeda
1524-1526	(audiencia)	1567-1568	Diego de Vera

1568-1572	Antonio de Mejía		1684-1690	Andrés de Robles y Gomez
1572-1576	Francisco de Vera		1690-1696	Ignacio Pérez Caro (1)
1576-1581	Gregorio González de Cuenca		1696-1698	Gil Correoso Catalán
1581-1583	Pedro de Arceo		1698-1702	Severino de Manzaneda Salinas y Rojas
1583-1587	Cristóbal de Ovalle		1702-1704	Juan del Barranco
1587-1588	Francisco Aliaga y Ortega		1704-1706	Ignacio Pérez Caro (2)
1588	Juan de Tejeda		1706-	Sebastián Cereceda y Girón (1)
1588-1597	Lope de Vega Portocarrero		1708-1711	Guillermo Morfi
1597-1600	Diego de Osorio		-	Sebastián Cereceda y Girón (2)
1603-1608	Antonio de Osorio		-1714	Pedro de Niela Torres
1608-1623	Diego Gómez de Sandoval		1714-1715	Sebastián Cereceda y Girón (3)
1624-1627	Diego de Acuña		1715-1724	Fernando Constanzo Ramírez de San Jago
1627-1634	Gabriel de Cháves y Osorio		1724-1731	Francisco de la Rocha Ferrer y Labarcés
1634-1635	Alonso de Cereceda			
1636-1645	Juan Bitrián de Viamonte y Navarra		1732-1740	Alonso de Castro y Mazo
1645-1649	Nicolás de Velasco Altamirano		1744-1750	Pedro Zorrilla de San Martín, Marqués de la Gándara Real
1649-1650	Juan Melgarejo Ponce de León			
1650-1651	Luis Fernández de Córdoba		1750-1751	Juan José Colomo
1651-1652	Francisco Pantoja de Ayala		1751-1758	Francisco Rubío y Peñaranda
1652-1653	Andrés Pérez Franco		1758-1771	Manuel Azlór y Urríes
1653-1655	Juan Francisco Montemayor Córdoba y Cuenca		1771-1778	José Solano y Bote
			1778-1785	Isidro de Peralta y Rojas
1655-1656	Bernardino de Meneses Brancamonte y Zapata, Conde de Peñalba		1785-1786	Joaquín García y Moreno (1)
			1786-1788	Manuel González de Aguilar Torres de Navarra
1656-1659	Félix de Zúñiga y Avellaneda, Conde de Sacro Imperio		1789-1801	Joaquín García y Moreno (2)
			1801-1809	(under Haiti)
1659-1661	Juan de Balboa y Mogrobejo		1809-1811	Juan Sánchez Ramírez
1661-1670	Pedro de Carvajal y Cobos		1811-1813	(junta)
1670-1677	Ignacio de Zayas Bazán		1813-1817	Carlos de Urrutia y Montoya
1677-1678	Juan de Padilla Guardiola y Guzmán		1818-1821	Sebastián Kindelán y Oregón
			1821	Pascual Real
1678-1684	Francisco de Segura Sandoval y Castilla			

Incháustegui, 1:214—27; Tejera, passim

388 SINALOA and SONORA

The area of Sinaloa and Sonora in northwestern Mexico was explored as early as 1530 but not settled until later in the century. The Sonora region was a center of mining in the viceroyalty of Nueva España (q.v.). In 1732 the territory was separated from Nueva Vizcaya (q.v.) and created a separate province under the audiencia of Nueva Galicia (q.v.). After 1777 Sinaloa and Sinora formed part of the Provincias Internas (q.v.). In 1787 the area became the intendencia of Sonora. In 1821 Sonora became a part of the empire of Mexico and the next year of the Republic of Mexico. The two regions then became separate states of Mexico.

Governors				
1734-1741	Manuel Bernal de Huidobro		1749-1753	Diego Ortiz de Parrilla
1741-1748	Agustín de Vildósola		1753-1755	Pablo de Arce y Arroyo
1748-1749	José Rafael Rodríguez Gallardo		1755-1760	Juan Antonio de Mendoza
			1761-1762	José Tiendra de Cuervo

Spain

1763-1770	Juan Claudio de Pineda	1790-1793	Enrique Grimarest
1770-1772	Pedro de Corbalán (1)	1793-1796	Alonso Tresierra y Cano
1772-1773	Mateo Sastré	1796-1813	Alejo García Conde
1773-1777	Francisco Antonio Crespo	1813-1817	Antonio Cordero y Bustamante (1)
1777-1787	Pedro de Corbalán (2)	1818	Ignacio de Bustamante (1)
		1818	Manuel Fernández Rojo
	Sonora	1818-1819	Ignacio de Bustamante (2)
Intendants		1819	Juan José Lombán
1787-1789	Pedro Garrido y Durán	1819-1821	Antonio Cordero y Bustamante (2)
1789-1790	Agustín de la Cuenta y Zayas		

Almada, *Diccionário*, under individual names and pp. 309–10; González Dávila, pp. 236–37. González Dávila omits, evidently in a printing error, the governors from 1763 to 1773.

389 SPANISH GUINEA

Spanish Guinea consisted of the islands of Fernando Po and Annobón and the small coastal enclave known as Río Muni, all in or around the Gulf of Guinea in western Africa. The islands were discovered by the Portuguese in 1472 and later disputed by the two countries. In 1777 they were definitely ceded to Spain by Portugal by the Treaty of San Ildefonso in return for concessions in South America (v. Nova Colônia do Sacramento, 304). Nevertheless, the Spaniards made no effort to settle the islands but rather leased them to the British in 1827 to be used as a base by the British in their effort to interdict the slave trade (v. Nigeria). Fernando Po was first settled by Spaniards in 1844 although Spain only undertook the administration in 1855. By 1877 the area of Río Muni had been brought under control. In 1959 Spanish Guinea became an overseas province of Spain. Four years later some internal autonomy was granted, the name was changed to Equatorial Guinea and the governor became high commissioner. In 1968 Equatorial Guinea, comprising all the territories of the former Spanish colony, became independent.

Governors			
1855-1858	Domingo Mustrich	1892	Antonio Martínez
1858	Carlos Chacón y Michelena	1892-1893	Eulogio Merchán
1858-1862	José de la Gándara y Navarro	1893-1895	José de la Puente Basseve
1862-1865	Pantaleón López Ayllón	1895-1897	Adolfo de España y Gómez de
1865-1868	José Gómez Barrera		Humarán
1868-1869	Joaquín Souza Gallardo	1897-1898	Manuel Rico
1869	Antonio Maymó	1898-1900	José Rodríguez Vera
1869-1870	Zoilo Sánchez Ocaña	1900-1901	Francisco Dueñas
1871	Frederico Anrich	1901-1905	José de Ibarra Autrán
1872-1874	Ignacio García Tudela	1905-1906	José Gómez de la Serna
1875-1877	Diego Santisteban Chamorro	1906	Diego Saavedra y Magdalena
1877-1879	Alejandro Arias Salgado	1906-1907	Angel Barrera y Luyando (1)
1879-1880	Enrique Santaló	1907-1908	Luis Ramos Izquierdo
1880-1883	José Montes de Oca (1)	1908-1909	José Centeño Anchorena
1883-1885	Antonio Cano	1910-1924	Angel Barrera y Luyando (2)
1885-1887	José Montes de Oca (2)	1924-1926	Carlos Tovar de Revilla
1887-1888	Luis Navarro	1926-1931	Miguel Núñez de Prado
1888-1889	Antonio Moreno Guerra	1931-1932	Gustavo de Sostoa y Sthamer
1889-1890	José de Ibarra	1933-1934	Estanislao Lluesma García
1890	José Gómez Barreda	1934-1935	Angel Manzaneque Feltrer
1890-1892	José de Barrasa	1935-1936	Luis Sánchez Guerra Sáez
		1937	Manuel de Mendívil y Elío

1937-1941	Juan Fontán y Lobé	
1942-1943	Mariano Alonso Alonso	
1943-1949	Juan Marián Bonelli Rubío	
1949-1962	Faustino Ruíz González	
1962-1963	Francisco Núñez Rodríguez	

Equatorial Guinea
High Commissioners

1963-1964	Francisco Núñez Rodríguez
1964-1966	Pedro Latorre Alcubierre
1966-1968	Victor Suances Díaz del Río

Information from El Secretario General del Gobernador del Golfo de Guinea, Santa Isabel, Guinea. Also, Unzueta y Yuste, pp. 336—39.

390 SPANISH SAHARA

In 1958 the governor-generalship of Spanish West Africa (q.v.) was dissolved and divided into the provinces of Ifni (q.v.), an enclave in southern Morocco, and Spanish Sahara, a much larger area directly south of Morocco on the western coast of Africa. Spanish Sahara remains an overseas province of Spain.

Governors

1958	José Hector Vázquez	1964-1965	Joaquín Agulla Jiménez Coronado
1958-1961	Mariano Alonso Alonso	1965-1967	Angel Enríquez Larrondo
1961-1964	Pedro Latorre Alcubierre	1967—	José María Pérez de Lema Tejero

Information from José Díaz de Villegas, Presidencia del Gobierno, Director de Plazas y Provincias Africanas, Madrid.

391 SPANISH WEST AFRICA

The Río de Oro, flowing into the Atlantic south of Morocco, was discovered by the Portuguese early in the 15th century. The island of Arguin, somewhat to the south, was successively occupied by the Portuguese, Spaniards, Dutch, and French from the 16th to the 18th centuries and used as a port for the slave trade. Otherwise no European interest was shown in the area. In 1860 the Spaniards secured vague rights in the area from Morocco, and in 1884 they proclaimed a protectorate over the coast. A year later a factory was constructed, but only in 1903 was effective occupation begun and an administration established. Boundary arrangements were negotiated with the French who occupied the territories on all sides of Spanish West Africa (sometimes also called Río de Oro). In 1934 Spanish West Africa fell under the control of the high commissioner of the Spanish zone of Morocco (q.v.) but it regained its administrative independence a few years later. In 1934 the Ifni (q.v.) enclave was settled but Ifni remained under the governor of Spanish West Africa until 1958 when the latter was divided into the two separate governments of Ifni and Spanish Sahara (q.v.)

Governors

1903-1925	Francisco Bens Argandoña	1932-1933	Eduardo Cañizares Navarro
1925-1932	Guillermo de la Peña Cusi	1933-1934	José González Deleito
		1934-1939	Antonio de Oro Pulido

Spain

1939-1949	José Bermejo López	1954-1957	Ramón Pardo de Santallana
1949-1952	Francisco Rosaleny Burguet	1957-1958	Enrique Gómez Zamallos Quirce
1952-1954	Venancio Tutor Gil		

Information from José Díaz de Villegas, Presidencia del Gobierno, Director de Plazas y Privincias Africanas, Madrid. Also, Lucini, pp. 85—114.

392 TARMA

Tarma was one of eight intendencias created within the viceroyalty of Peru (q.v.) in 1784. It remained an intendencia until 1823 when Spanish authority ended in the area. Tarma became a part of the Republic of Peru two years later.

Intendants
1784-1793   Juan María de Gálvez y Montes de Oca
1793-1795   Francisco Suárez de Castilla y Belcárel
1796-1811   Ramón de Urrutia y las Casas
1811-1823   José González de Prada

Deustua Pimentel, pp. 127—48; Mendiburú, 8:416.

393 TENERIFE

Tenerife, one of the Canary Islands (q.v.), was conquered by the Spaniards in 1495. Tenerife and Gran Canaria (q.v.) constituted the most important settlements in the archipelago. In 1496 the adelantado of Tenerife, Alonso Fernández de Lugo, became governor of all the Canaries, although each island had its own governor of one sort or another. In 1589, in order to protect the islands from constant raiding by the French and English, a captain-general was appointed over all the islands. This experiment lasted only until 1594, but was revived and became permanent in 1625. Tenerife continued to have its own governor after 1625, but he was subordinate to the captain-general of the Canary Islands.

Governors
1496-1525	Alonso Fernández de Lugo	1554-1557	Juan López de Cepeda
1525-1538	Pedro Fernández de Lugo	1558-1559	Hernando de Cañizares
1538-1540	Alfonso Yáñez Dávila	1559-1561	Plaza
1540-1543	Juan Verdugo	1561-1562	Alonso de Llarena
1543-1546	Jerónimo Álvarez de Sotomayor, Señor de Arenalejo	1562-1565	Armenteros de Paz
		1565-1567	Juan Vélez de Guevara
1546-1548	Diego de Figueroa	1567-1570	Eugenio de Salazar
1548-1550	Juan Bautista de Ayora	1570-1573	Juan Gante del Campo
1550-1551	Hernán Duque de Estrada	1573-1577	Juan Álvarez de Fonseca (1)
1551-1554	Juan Ruíz de Miranda	1577-1579	Juan de Leiva
		1579-1582	Juan Álvarez de Fonseca (2)

1582-1584	Lázaro Moreno de Léon	1609-1615	Juan de Espinosa
1584-1589	Juan Núñez de la Fuente	1615-1618	Melchor Ruíz de Pereda
1589-1597	Tomás de Cangas	1618-1621	Diego de Vega Bazán
1597-1601	Pedro Lasso de la Vega	1621-1624	Rodrigo Álvarez de Bohorques
1601-1603	Luis Manuel Gudiel y Ortiz	1624-1625	Diego de Alvarado Bracamonte
1603-1608	Francisco de Benavides		

Rumeu de Armas, *Piraterías*, passim; Viera y Clavijo, 3:327—29.

394 TEXAS

The area north of the Rio Grande was explored several times by the Spaniards beginning in 1528, but its distance from the core area of Mexico precluded its early settlement and occupation. These only came as a response to French encroachments in the later 17th century (v. Louisiana, 39). The first permanent Spanish settlement in Texas occurred in 1682. In 1716 Texas was separated from Coahuila (q.v.) and created a separate province. Like all of the northern provinces of Nueva España (q.v.), Texas was subordinated to the commandant-general of the Provincias Internas (q.v.), although retaining its own local government. In 1821 Texas came under the control of the newly established empire (later Republic) of Mexico.

Governors

		1751-1759	Jacinto de Barrios y Jáuregui
1716-1719	Martín de Alarcón	1759-1766	Angel de Martos y Navarrette
1719-1722	José Azlor y Virto de Vera, Marqués de San Miguel de Aguayo	1766-1770	Hugo Oconór Cunco y Fali
		1770-1778	Juan María de Ripperdá
1722-1726	Fernando Pérez de Almazán	1778-1786	Domingo Cabello y Robles
1727-1730	Melchor de Media Villa y Ascona	1786-1790	Rafael Martínez Pacheco
1730-	Juan Antonio de Bustillo y Ceballos	1790-1799	Manuel Muñoz
		1800-1805	Juan Bautista de Elguézabal
1734-	Manuel de Sandoval	1805-1808	Antonio Cordero y Bustamante
1736-1737	Carlos Benítez Franquis de Lugo	1808-1813	Manuel María de Salcedo y Quiroga
1737-1740	Prudencio de Orobio y Bazterra	1813-1814	Cristóbal Domínguez
1740-1743	Tomás Felipe Wintuisen	1814-1815	Benito de Armiñán
1743-1744	Justo Boneo y Morales	1815-1816	Mariano Varela
1744-1748	Francisco García Larios	1816-1817	Ignacio Pérez
1748-1750	Pedro del Barrío Junco y Espriella	1817-1822	Antonio María Martínez

Bolton, pp. 478—79; Faulk, pp. 22—37.

395 TRINIDAD

The island of Trinidad, off the coast of Venezuela, was discovered by Columbus in 1498. A governor was appointed in 1532 but no settlement was effected until much later. In fact, during the 17th century the island was a bone of contention among Spain, England, France, the Netherlands, and even the Duchy of Kurland. Trinidad was part of the province of Guayana (q.v.) until

1735 when it was created a separate province. Until 1739 it was under Santo Domingo (q.v.).
Then it came under Nueva Granada (q.v.) until 1777 when it became part of the new captaincy-
general of Venezuela (q.v.). In 1797 Trinidad was conquered by British forces, and it was retained
by Great Britain under terms of the Treaty of Amiens in 1802 (v. 182).

Governors			
1735-1745	Esteban Simón de Liñán y Vera	1762-1766	José Antonio Gil
1745-1746	Félix Espinosa de los Monteros	1767-1773	José de Flores
1746-1752	Juan José Salcedo	1773-1776	Juan de Dios Valdés de Yarza
1752-1757	Francisco de Manclares	1776-1779	Manuel Falquez
1757-1760	Pedro de la Moneda	1779-1783	Martín de Salaverría
1760-1762	Jacinto San Juan	1783-1797	José María Chacón

Information from Lynette C. Hutchinson, Reference Librarian, Central Library, Port-of-Spain,
Trinidad. Also, Borde, 2:95–262.

396 TRUJILLO

Trujillo was the most northerly of the intendencias created in the viceroyalty of Peru (q.v.) in
1784. In 1821 Spanish control ended with the occupation of the area by the forces of Simón
Bolívar. Subsequently Trujillo became part of the Republic of Peru.

Intendants
1784-1791 Fernando de Saavedra
1791-1820 Vicente Gil de Taboada
1820-1821 José Bernardo de Tagle y Portocarrero, Marqués de Torre Tagle

Deustua Pimentel, pp. 109–26; Mendiburú, 8:416.

397 TUCUMÁN

The area of Tucumán in northern Argentina was settled from Peru (q.v.), and a province was
erected in 1550. Until the middle of the 17th century Tucumán was the most populous and prosperous area in Argentina, but it came to be surpassed by Buenos Aires (q.v.). Until 1776 Tucumán
was subject to the audiencia of Charcas (q.v.). With the creation of the viceroyalty of Río de la
Plata (q.v., 381), Tucumán fell within its jurisdiction. When the intendencia system was established in Río de la Plata in 1783, Tucumán was divided into Córdoba and Salta (qq.v.) and ceased
to exist as an administrative unit.

Governors			
1550-1553	Juan Núñez del Prado	1554-1557	Juan Gregorio Bazán
1553-1554	Francisco de Aguirre (1)	1557-1562	Juan Pérez de Zorita
		1562	Gregorio de Castañeda

1562-1567	Francisco de Aguirre (2)	1670-1674	Angel de Peredo
1567-1569	Diego Pacheco	1674-1678	José de Garro Senei de Artola
1569-1570	Francisco de Aguirre (3)	1678-1681	Juan Díez de Andino
1570	Pedro de Arana	1681	Antonio de Vera y Mújica
1570-1572	Nicolás Carrizo	1681-1686	Fernando de Mendoza y Mate de
1572-1574	Jerónimo Luis de Cabrera		Luna
1574-1580	Gonzalo de Abreu	1686-1691	Tomás Félix de Argandoña
1580-1584	Hernando de Lerma	1691-1696	Martín de Jáuregui
1584-1586	Alonso de Cepeda	1696-1701	Juan de Zamudio y Telletu Urcullú
1586-1593	Juan Ramírez de Velasco	1701-1707	Gaspar de Barahona
1593-1594	Hernando de Zárate	1707-1724	Esteban de Urizar y
1594-1600	Pedro de Mercado de Peñalosa		Arespacocheaga
1600-1603	Francisco de Leiva	1724-1726	Isidro Ortiz de Haro
1603-1605	Francisco de Barraza y Cárdenas	1726-1727	Alonso de Alfaro
1605-1611	Alonso de Ribera	1727-1730	Baltasar de Abarca y Velasco
1611-1619	Luis de Quiñones Osorio	1730-1732	Belisario Manuel de Arche[1]
1619-1627	Juan Alonso de Vera y Zárate	1732-1735	Juan de Armasa y Arregui
1627-1637	Felipe de Albornoz	1735-1739	Matías Anglés Gortari y Lizárazu
1637-1641	Francisco de Avendaño y Valdivia	1739-1743	Juan de Santiso y Moscoso
1641-1642	Jerónimo Luis de Cabrera (1)	1743-1749	Juan Alonso de Espinosa de los
1642-1643	Miguel de Sesé		Monteros
1643-1644	Baltasar Pardo de Figueroa y	1749-1752	Juan Victoriano Martínez de Tineo
	Guevara	1752-1757	Juan Francisco de Pestaña y
1644-1650	Gutierre de Acosta y Padilla		Chamucero
1650-1651	Francisco Gil de Negrete	1757-1758	José de Cabrera
1651-1655	Roque de Nestares Aguado	1758-1764	Joaquín de Espinosa y Dávalos
1655-1660	Alonso de Mercado y Villacorta (1)	1764-1769	Juan Manuel Fernández Campero
1660-1662	Jerónimo Luis de Cabrera (2)	1769-1775	Jerónimo Matorras
1662-1663	Lucas de Figueroa y Mendoza	1775-1777	Francisco Gabino Arias
1663-1664	Pedro de Montoya	1777-1778	Antonio Arriaga
1664-1670	Alonso de Mercado y Villacorta (2)	1778-1783	Andrés Mestre

1. Called in some documents Manuel Félix de Arache.

Sierra, 1:281−314, 335−61, 451−526; 2:61−73, 179−99, 281−93, 341−83, 399−417, 517−43; 3:131−61, 263−85, 431−37.

398 VALLADOLID

The Michoacán region of central Mexico was formed into the intendencia of Valladolid in 1787. In 1821 it became part of Mexico.

Intendants
1787-1791 Juan Antonio de Riaño y Bárcena de los Cuetos y Velarde
1792-1808 Felipe Díaz de Ortega Bustillo
1810-1821 Manuel Merino y Moreno

Bravo Ugarte, 2:162.

399 VENEZUELA

The coast of Venezuela was explored by the Spaniards in 1499. In 1528 the area was granted to a German banking family, the Welsers, and remained nominally under their control until 1556, although their government was disputed from many quarters. Venezuela grew to be the largest of the several provinces in the area. Until 1717, and from 1723 to 1730, it was under the jurisdiction of the audiencia of Santo Domingo (q.v.). From 1717 to 1723 and from 1739 to 1742 it was under the viceroyalty of Nueva Granada (q.v.). After 1742 Venezuela was under the viceroyalty of Nueva Granada but the audiencia of Santo Domingo. In 1777 Venezuela was raised to a captaincy-general, having the extent and authority of a viceroyalty if not the title. In 1786 Venezuela secured its own audiencia at Caracas. The captaincy-general of Venezuela had jurisdiction over the provinces of Maracaibo (v. Mérida-La Grita), Barinas, Guayana, Trinidad (to 1797), Margarita, and Nueva Andalucía (qq.v.). In 1810 Venezuela expelled the captain-general, and during the next decade control of the area alternated between the Spanish and patriot forces. In 1820 the Spaniards were finally expelled and Venezuela became part of Gran Colombia. On the dissolution of Gran Colombia the provinces which had been part of the captaincy-general of Venezuela united to form the Republic of Venezuela.

Governors

1527–1529	Juan Martínez de Ampies
1529–1531	Ambrose von Alfinger
1531–1533	Bartholomew Sayler (Bartolomé de Santillana)
1534–1535	Rodrigo de Bastidas (1)
1535–1540	Georg Hohemuth (Jorge de Espira)
1540–1542	Rodrigo de Bastidas (2)
1542–1544	Heinrich Rembolt
1545–1546	Juan de Carvajal
1546–1549	Juan Pérez de Tolosa
1549–1553	Juan de Villegas Maldonado
1553–1557	Alonso Arias de Villasinda
1557–1559	Gutierre de la Peña Langayo
1559–1561	Pablo Collado
1562–1563	Alonso Pérez de Manzanedo
1564–1566	Alonso Bernáldez
1566–1569	Pedro Ponce de León y Riquelme
1569–1570	Francisco Hernández de Chaves
1570–1576	Diego de Mazariegos
1576–1583	Juan de Pimentel
1583–1589	Luis de Rojas y Mendoza
1589–1597	Diego de Osorio
1597–1600	Gonzalo de Piña y Ludueña
1600–1602	Alonso Arias Vaca
1602–1603	Alonso Suárez del Castillo
1603–1606	Francisco Mejía de Godoy
1606–1611	Sancho de Alquiza
1611–1616	García Girón de Loaysa
1616–1621	Francisco de la Hoz Berrío
1621–1623	Juan Treviño Guillamas
1623	Diego Gil de la Sierpe
1624–1630	Juan de Meneses y Padilla, Marqués de Marianela
1630–1637	Pedro Núñez Melián
1637–1644	Ruy Fernández de Fuenmayor
1644–1649	Marcos Gedler Calatayud y Toledo
1649–1651	Pedro de León Villaroel
1652–1653	Diego Francisco de Quero y Figueroa
1654–1655	Martín de Roble y Villafañe
1656–1658	Andrés de Vera y Moscoso
1658–1664	Pedro de Porres Toledo y Vozmediano, Conde de Dabois
1664–1669	Félix Garcí-González de León
1669–1673	Fernando de Villegas
1673–1674	Francisco Dávila Orejón y Gastón
1674–1677	(alcaldes)
1677–1682	Francisco de Alberró
1682–1688	Diego de Melo Maldonado
1688–1692	Diego Jiménez de Enciso, Marqués de Casal de los Griegos
1692–1693	Diego Bartolomé Bravo de Anaya
1693–1699	Francisco de Berrotarán y Gainza, Marqués del Valle de Santiago (1)
1699–1704	Nicolás Eugenio de Ponte y Hoyo
1705–1706	Francisco de Berrotarán y Gainza, Marqués del Valle de Santiago (2)
1706–1711	Fernando de Rojas y Mendoza
1711–1714	José Francisco de Cañas y Merino
1715–1716	Alberto Bertodano y Navarra
1716–1720	Marcos Francisco de Betancourt y Castro
1721	Antonio José Álvarez de Abreu
1721–1728	Diego de Portales y Meneses
1728–1730	Lope de Carrillo de Andrade Sotomayor y Pimentel
1730–1732	Sebastián García de la Torre
1732–1737	Martín de Lardizábal
1737–1747	Gabriel José de Zuloaga Moyúa y Barrena
1747–1749	Luis Francisco de Castellanos
1749–1751	Julián de Arriaga y Rivera
1751–1757	Felipe Ricardos de Wasion y Herrera

1757-1763	Felipe Ramírez de Estenoz	1786-1792	Juan Guillelmi
1763-1771	José Solano y Bote	1792-1799	Pedro Carbonell Pinto Vigo y
1772-1777	José Carlos de Agüero y González		Correa
	de Agüero	1799-1807	Manuel de Guevara y Vasconcelos
1777-1782	Luis Unzaga y Amezaga	1807-1809	Juan de Casas y Barrera
1782-1786	Manuel González de Aguilar Torres	1809-1810	Vicente Emparán y Orbe
	de Navarra		

Sucre, passim.

400 VERA CRUZ

Vera Cruz was created an intendencia within the viceroyalty of Nueva España (q.v.) in 1787. It remained part of the viceroyalty until Mexico became independent in 1821, when it became one of the Mexican states.

Intendants		1810-1812	Carlos de Urrutia y Montoya
1787-1790	Pedro de Corbalán	1813-1814	Pedro Telmo Landero
1790-1794	Pedro Fernández de Gorostiza y	1814-1815	José de Quevedo
	Lorea	1816-1818	José Dávila (1)
1794-1796	Pedro Ponce	1818-1819	Pascual Sebastián de Liñán y
1796-1799	Diego García Panes		Dolz de Espejo
1799-1810	García Dávila	1819-1821	José Dávila (2)

The information, taken from the *Gacetas de México* and *Manuals Calendarios y Guías de Forasteros* for the period, was provided by Sr. Jorge Ignacio Rubio Mañé, Director, Archivo General de la Nación, Mexico City.

401 YUCATÁN

The Yucatán peninsula, in extreme southeastern Mexico, was the site of a major Mayan civilization which had, however, declined and degenerated into a number of petty warring states by the middle of the 15th century. The coast of Yucatán was discovered by the Spaniards in 1517, and ten years later settlement and conquest began. Yucatán was under the audiencia of Mexico (v. Nueva España) from 1527 to 1543, then under that of Los Confines (v. Guatemala) to 1549, Mexico to 1550, Guatemala, 1550 to 1560, and after 1560 that of Mexico. The province was ruled by governors except for the period from 1549 to 1565 when alcaldes mayores governed it. In 1617 the governor was given the additional rank of captain-general. With the establishment of the intendencia system in Mexico, Yucatán became known as the intendencia of Mérida and was governed by a governor/intendant. With the independence of Spain's colonies in the area in 1821 Yucatán became a part of Mexico.

Spain

Governors

1526–1540	Francisco Montejo (1)
1540–1546	Francisco Montejo, Jr.
1546–1549	Francisco Montejo (2)
1549–1565	(alcaldes)
1565–1571	Luis de Céspedes y Oviedo
1571–1573	Diego de Santillán
1573–1577	Francisco Velázquez Gijón
1577–1582	Guillén de las Casas
1582–1586	Francisco de Solís
1586–1593	Antonio de Vozmediano
1593–1595	Alonso Ordóñez de Nevares
1595–1596	Pablo Higueras de la Cerda
1596–1597	Carlos de Sámano y Quiñónes
1597–1604	Diego Fernández de Velasco y Enríquez de Almansa
1604–1612	Carlos de Luna y Arellano
1612–1617	Antonio de Figueroa y Bravo
1617–1619	Francisco Ramírez Briceño
1619–1620	(alcaldes)
1620–1621	Arias de Losada y Taboada
1621–1628	Diego de Cárdenas y Balda
1628–1630	Juan de Vargas Machuca
1631–1633	Fernando Centeño Maldonaldo (1)
1633–1635	Jerónimo de Quero y Jiménez
1635–1636	Fernando Centeño Maldonaldo (2)
1636–1643	Diego Zapata de Cárdenas, Marqués de Santo Floro
1643–1644	Francisco Núñez Melián
1644–1645	Enrique de Ávila Pacheco (1)
1645–1648	Esteban de Azcárraga y Veytias
1648–1650	Enrique de Ávila Pacheco (2)
1650–1652	García Valdés de Osorio Dóriga y Tineo, Marqués de Peñalba
1652–1653	Martín de Roble y Villafañe
1653–1655	Pedro Sáenz Izquierdo
1655–1660	Francisco de Bazán
1660–1662	José Campero y Campos
1663–1664	Juan Francisco Esquivel y de la Rosa (1)
1664	Rodrigo de Flores y Aldana (1)
1664–1667	Juan Francisco Esquivel y de la Rosa (2)
1667–1669	Rodrigo de Flores y Aldana (2)
1669–1670	Frutos Delgado
1670–1672	Fernando Francisco de Escobedo
1672–1674	Miguel Codornio de Sola
1674–1677	Sancho Fernández de Angulo y Sandoval
1677–1683	Antonio de Layseca y Alvarado de la Ronda

1683–1688	Juan Bruno Téllez de Guzmán
1688–1693	Juan José de la Bárcena
1693–1699	Roque Soberanis y Centeno
1699–1703	Martín de Ursúa y Arismendi Aguirre y Vizcondo (1)
1703–1706	Álvaro de Rivaguda Enciso y Luyando
1706–1708	Martín de Ursúa y Arismendi Aguirre y Vizcondo, Conde de Lizárraga (2)
1708–1712	Fernando de Meneses y Bravo de Saravia
1712–1715	Alonso de Meneses y Bravo de Saravia
1715–1720	Juan José de Vértiz y Ontañón
1720–1724	Antonio Cortaire y Terreros
1724–1733	Antonio de Figueroa y Silva Lasso de la Vega Ladrón del Niño de Guevara
1733–1734	Juan Fernández de Sabariego
1734–1736	Santiago de Aguirre Negro y Estrada Martínez de Maturana y Estrada
1736–1743	Manuel Ignacio Salcedo y Sierra Alta y Rado y Bedia
1743–1750	Antonio de Benavides
1750–1752	Juan José de Clou, Marqués de Iscar
1752–1758	Melchor de Navarrette
1758–1761	Alonso Fernández de Heredia
1761–1762	José Crespo y Honorato
1762–1763	Antonio Ainz de Ureta
1763	José Álvarez
1763–1764	Felipe Ramírez de Estenoz
1764–1771	Cristóbal de Zayas
1771–1777	Antonio de Oliver
1778–1779	Hugo Oconór Cunco y Fali
1779–1783	Roberto Rivas Betancourt
1783–1789	José Merino y Ceballos

Mérida

Governors/Intendants

1789–1793	Lucas de Gálvez
1793–1800	Arturo O'Neill y O'Kelly
1800–1811	Benito Pérez Brito de los Ríos y Fernández Valdelomar
1812–1815	Manuel Artazo y Torredemer
1815–1820	Miguel Castro y Araoz
1820–1821	Mariano Carrillo y Albornoz
1821	Juan María Echéverri

Enciclopedia Yucatanense, 3:30–169; Rubio Mañé, *Notas y acotaciones*, pp. 460–85.

402 ZACATECAS

The alcaldia mayor of Zacatecas was raised to an intendencia in the viceroyalty of Nueva
España (q.v.) in 1787. It remained so until 1821 when Spanish authority ended in Mexico.
Zacatecas then became a state in the Republic of Mexico.

Intendants

1789–1792	Felipe Cleere	1811	José Manuel de Ochoa
1792–1796	José de Peón y Valdés	1811	Juan José Zambrano
1796–1810	Francisco Rendón	1811–1812	Martín de Medina
1810–1811	Miguel de Rivera, Conde de	1812–1814	Santiago de Irisarri
	Santiago de la Laguna	1814–1816	Diego García Conde
		1816–1820	José de Gayangos

Vidal, pp. 201–210.

Bibliography: Spain

Academia Colombiana de la Historia. *Historia extensa de Colombia*. 19 vols. to date. Bogotá:
Academia Colombiana de la Historia, 1964-.
Academia Nacional de la Historia [Buenos Aires]. *Historia de la nación Argentina desde los
origenes hasta la organización definitiva en 1862.* 11 vols. Buenos Aires: El Ateneo, 1961–63.
Alba C., Manuel María. "Cronologia de los gobernantes de Panamá, 1510–1932." *Boletín de la
Academia panameña de historia* 3 (1935):i–xxii, 1–182.
Alcázar Molina, Cayetano. *Los virreinatos en el siglo XVIII*. Barcelona: Salvat Editores, 1945.
Alessio Robles, Vito. *Coahuila y Texas*. 2 vols. Mexico City: n.p., 1946.
Almada, Francisco R. *Diccionário de historia, geografía y biografía sonorenses* . Chihuahua:
n.p., 1952.
——. *Resumen de historia del estado de Chihuahua*. Mexico City: Libros Mexicanos, 1955.
Aragon, Arcesio. *Fastos payaneses*. 2 vols. Bogota: Imprenta Nacional, 1939–41.
——. *Popayán*. Popayán: Imprensa del Departamento, 1930.
Araujo, Orestes. *Diccionário popular de historia de la república oriental del Uruguay*. 3 vols.
Montevideo: Imprenta Artística, 1901.
Arroyo, Jaime. *Historia de la gobernación de Popayán seguida de la cronologia de los
gobernadores durante la dominación Española.* Popayán: Imprenta del Departamento, 1907.
Blair, Emma, and Robertson, James A., eds. *The Philippine Islands*. 55 vols. Cleveland: A. H.
Clark Co., 1903–9.
Blanco, Joaquín. *Breve noticia histórica de las Islas Canarias*. Las Palmas de Gran Canaria:
Cabildo Insular de Gran Canaria, 1957.
Bloom, Lansing B. "The Governors of New Mexico." *New Mexico Historical Review* 10, no. 2
(1935):152–57.
Bolton, Herbert Eugene. *Guide to Materials for the History of the United States in the Prin-
cipal Archives of Mexico*. Washington: Carnegie Institution of Washington, 1913.
Borde, Pierre-Gustave-Louis. *Histoire de l'île de la Trinidad*. Paris: Maisonneuve, 1876.
Bravo Ugarte, José. *Historia sucinta de Michoacán*. Vol. 2, *Provincia Mayor e Intendencias*.
Mexico City: Editorial Jus, 1963.
Bromley, Juan. "Recibimientos de virreys en Lima." *Revista histórica* [Lima] 20 (1953):5–108.
Carano, Paul, and Sánchez, Pedro C. *A Complete History of Guam*. Rutland, Vt.: Charles E.
Tuttle Co., 1964.

Castillo, Abel-Romero. *Los gobernadores de Guayaquil del siglo XVIII*. Madrid: Imprenta de Galo Saez, 1931.

Cazenave, Jean. "Les gouverneurs d'Oran pendant l'occupation espagnole de cette ville (1509–1792)." *Revue africaine* 71 (1930):257–99.

Chamberlain, Robert Stoner. *The Conquest and Colonization of Honduras, 1502–1550.* Washington: Carnegie Institution of Washington, 1953.

Coll y Toste, Cayetano. "Rectificación histórica: Catálogo de gobernadores de Puerto Rico." *Boletín histórico de Puerto Rico* 8 (1921):135–46.

Connor, Jeanette Thurber, ed. *Colonial Records of Spanish Florida.* 2 vols. Deland: Florida State Historical Society, 1930.

Covarrubias, Ricardo. *Gobernantes de Nuevo León, 1582–1961.* Monterrey: n.p., [1961].

Covián Martínez, Vidal. "Los gobernantes de Tamaulipas." *Cuadernos de historia* 1 (1968): 79–86.

Deustua Pimentel, Carlos. *Las intendencias en el Peru (1790–1796).* Seville: Escuela de Estudios Hispano-Americanos, 1965.

Dornellas, Affonso de. *História e genealogia.* 14 vols. Lisbon: Livreria Ferin-Casa Portuguêsa, 1913–22.

Dousdebés, Pedro Julio. *Cartagena de Indias, plaza fuerte.* Bogota: Imprenta de Ministério de Guerra, 1948.

Durón y Gamero, Romulo Ernesto. *Bosquejo histórico de Honduras, 1502 à 1921.* San Pedro Sula: Tip. del Comercio, 1927.

Enciclopedia Yucatanense. 7 vols. Mexico City: Edición Oficial del Gobierno de Yucatán, 1947-.

Faulk, Odie B. *The Last Years of Spanish Texas, 1778–1821.* The Hague: Mouton & Co., 1964.

Fernández Guardia, Ricardo. *Cartilla histórica de Costa Rica.* San José: Librería y Imprenta Lehmann, 1933.

Fernández Peralta, Ricardo. "Catálogo de los gobernantes de Costa Rica y otros functionarios que ejercieron el mando de la provincia." *Revista de los Archivos nacionales de Costa Rica* 26 (1962):160–64.

Fuentes, Jardi and Cortés, Lia. *Diccionário histórico de Chile.* Santiago: Editorial del Pacifico, 1963.

Gámez, José Dolores. *Historia de Nicaragua.* Managua: Tipografia de 'El Pais,' 1889.

García Caraffa, Alberto. *Enciclopedia heráldica y genealógica hispano-americana.* 88 vols. Madrid: Nueva Imprensa Radio, 1952–63.

García Figueras, Tomás. *Presencia de España en Berberia central y oriental.* Madrid: Editora Nacional, 1943.

Garrido Conde, María Teresa. *La primera creación del virreinato de Nueva Granada (1717–1723).* Seville: Escuela de Estudios Hispano-Americanos, 1965.

Gómez Langenheim, A. *Elementos para la historia de nuestras Islas Malvinas.* 2 vols. Buenos Aires: El Ateneo, 1939.

González Dávila, Amado. *Diccionário geográfico, histórico, biográfico y estadístico del Estado de Sinaloa.* Culiacán: for Gobierno de Estrado de Sinaloa y el H. Ayuntamiento de Mazatlán, 1959.

González García, Sebastián. "Notes sobre el gobierno y los gobernantes de Puerto Rico em el siglo XVII." *Historia* [Puerto Rico], n.s. 1 (1962):1–98.

Grimaldo, Isaac. *Gobernantes potosinos, 1590–1939.* San Luis Potosí: n.p., 1939.

Guerra y Sánchez, Ramiro, et al. *Historia de la nación cubana.* 10 vols. Havana: Editorial Historia de la Nacion Cubana, 1952.

Heredia Herrera, Antonia M. "Las fortificaciones de la Isla de Margarita en los siglos XVI, XVII y XVIII." *Anuario de estudios americanos* 15 (1958):429–514.

Hernández de Herrera, Carlos, and García Figueras, Tomás. *Acción de España en Marruecos.* 2 vols. Madrid: Imprensa Nacional, 1929–30.

Holmes, Jack D. L. *Honor and Fidelity: The Louisiana Infantry Regiment and the Louisiana Militia Companies, 1766–1821.* Louisiana Collection Series of Books and Documents on Colonial Louisiana, vol. 1. Birmingham, Ala.: n.p., 1965.

Iguiniz, Juan B. "Los gobernantes de Nueva Galicia: Datos y documentos para sus biografias." *Memorias de la Academia mexicana de la historia* 7 (1948):296–395.

Incháustegui, J. Marino. *Historia dominicana.* 2 vols. Ciudad Trujillo: Impresora Dominicana, 1955.

Landaeta Rosales, Manuel. *Gran recopilación geográfica, estradística e histórica de Venezuela.* 2 vols. Caracas: Imprenta Bolívar, 1889.

Lohmann Villena, Guillermo. *Los Americanos en las órdenes nobiliarias (1529–1900).* 2 vols. Madrid: Consejo Superior de Investigaciones Cientificas, 1947.

Lucini, Eduardo. "La Factoria de Rio de Oro." *Boletín de la Real sociedad geográfica de Madrid* 33 (1892):85–114.

Lynch, John. *Spanish Colonial Administration, 1782–1810: The Intendant System in the Vice-royalty of Río de la Plata.* London: Athlone Press, 1958.

Marmolejo, Lucio. *Efemérides guanajuatenses: O datos para formar la historia de la Ciudad de Guanajuato.* Edited by Francisco Díaz. 4 vols. Guanajuato, Mexico: Imp. Livreria y Papelaria de Fr. Díaz, 1907–14.

Martínez, Santiago. *Gobernadores de Arequipa colonial.* Arequipa: Tipografia Cuadros, 1930.

Martínez de Campos y Serrano, Carlos, Duque de la Torre. *Canarias en el brecha: Compendio de historia militar.* Las Palmas de Gran Canaria: El Gabinete Literario, 1953.

Martínez Cosío, Leopoldo. *Los caballeros de las órdenes militares en México.* Mexico City: Editorial Santiago, 1946.

Martínez Mendoza, Jerónimo. "Los gobernadores españoles de la antigua provincia de Mérida y Maracaibo." *Boletín de la Academia nacional de la historia* [Caracas] 41 (1958):370–83.

Mendiburú, Manuel de. *Diccionário histórico-biográfico del Peru.* 8 vols. Lima: Imprenta de Torres Aguirre, 1874–90.

Molina Argüello, Carlos. *El gobernador de Nicaragua en el siglo XVI.* Seville: Escuela de Estudios Hispano-Americanos, 1949.

——. "Gobernaciones, alcaldias mayores y corrigimientos en el reino de Guatemala." *Anuario de estudios americanos* 17 (1960):105–32.

Moorhead, Max L. *The Apache Frontier: Jacobo Ugarte and Spanish-Indian Relations in Northern New Spain, 1769–1791.* Norman: University of Oklahoma Press, 1968.

Morales, Gabriel de. *Datos para la historia de Melilla.* Melilla: Tip. de El Telegrama del Rif, 1909.

Morales Goméz, Antonio. *Cronologia de Nuevo León, 1527–1955.* Mexico City: Ed. Benito Juárez, 1955.

Morales Padrón, Francisco. *Jamaica española.* Seville: Escuela de Estudios Hispano-Americanos, 1952.

——. "Trinidad en el siglo XVII." *Anuario de estudios americanos* 17 (1960):133–81.

Navarro García, Luis. "La gobernación y commandancia general de las Provincias Internas del Norte de Nueva España." *Revista del Instituto de historia del Derecho Ricardo Levene,* no. 14 (1963):118–51.

——. *Intendencias en Indias.* Seville: Escuela de Estudios Hispano-Americanos, 1959.

——. *Las Provincias Internas en el siglo XIX.* Seville: Escuela de Estudios Hispano-Americanos, 1965.

Nieto y Cortadellas, Rafael. *Dignidades nobiliarias en Cuba.* Madrid: Ediciones Cultura Hispanica, 1959.

Palacios, Enrique Juan. *Puebla y sus habitantes.* Mexico City: Secretario del Fomento, 1917.

Pareja y Díez Canseco, Alfredo. *Historia del Ecuador.* 2 vols. Quito: Editorial Casa de la Cultura Ecuatoriana, 1958.

Peraza Sarausa, Fermín. *Indice del'Boletín del Archivo nacional'.* Havana: n.p., 1946.

Ramos Martínez, José Antonio. "Gobernadores y capitanes generales de la Nueva Andalucía." *Cultura venezolana* 18 (1923):60–80.

Ravignani, Emilio. "El virreinato del Río de la Plata." In *Historia de la nación Argentina* (cited under Academia Nacional de la Historia [Buenos Aires]), 4, no. 1:33–234.

Restrepo Sáenz, José María. *Gobernadores de Antioquia, 1571–1819.* Bogota: Imprensa nacional, 1931.

——. "Gobernadores de Cartagena en el siglo XVIII." *Boletín de historia y antigüedades de la Academia colombiana de la historia* 35 (1948):57–79.

Restrepo Tirado, Ernesto. *Gobernantes del Nuevo Reino de Granada durante el siglo XVIII.* Buenos Aires: Imprenta de la Universidad, 1934.

——. *Historia de la provincia de Santa Marta.* 2 vols. Bogota: Ministériode Educación Nacional, 1953.

Richman, Irving Berdine. *California under Spain and Mexico, 1535–1857: A Contribution toward the History of the Pacific Coast of the United States.* New York: Cooper Square Publishers, 1965.

Rowland, Donald. "Spanish Occupation of the Island of Old Providence or Santa Catalina, 1641–1670." *Hispanic American Historical Review* 15 (1935):298–312.

Rubio Mañé, Jorge Ignacio. *Introducción al estudio de los virreys de Nueva España, 1535–1746.* 4 vols. Mexico City: Ediciones Selectas, 1955–63.

——. *Notas y acotaciones a la 'Historia de Yucatán' de Fr. Diego López de Cogolludo, O.F.M.* Mexico City: Editorial Academia Literaria, 1957.

Rumeu de Armas, Antonio. *España en el Africa atlántica.* 2 vols. Seville: Enstituto de Estudios Americanos, 1956–57.

——. *Piraterías y ataques navales contra las Islas Canarias.* 3 vols. in 5. Madrid: Consejo Superior de Investigaciones Cientificas, 1947–50.

Salazar, Mario. *Isla, sol y leyenda.* Caracas: Editorial Arte, 1966.

Saldívar, Gabriel. *Historia compendida de Tamaulipas.* Mexico City: Ed. Nuestra Patria, 1945.

Santa Cruz, Victor. *Historia colonial de La Paz.* La Paz: n.p., 1941.

Schäfer, Ernst. *El consejo real y supremo de las Indias.* 2 vols. Seville: Escuela de Estudios Hispano-Americanos, 1947.

Sierra, Vicente D. *Historia de la Argentina.* 5 vols. Buenos Aires: Unión de Editores Latinos, 1956–62.

Sucre, Luis Alberto. *Gobernadores y capitanes generales de Venezuela.* Caracas: Lit. y Tip. del Comercio, 1928.

Tamayo, Joaquín. "Virreys del Nuevo Reino de Granada." *Revista de la Academia nacional* [Bogotá] 3 (1941):341–45.

Tavera Acosta, Bartolomé, ed. *Anales de Guayana.* Caracas: Impresa de España, 1954.

Tejera, Emiliano. "Gobernadores de la Isla de Santo Domingo, siglos XVI–XVII." *Boletín del Archivo general de la nación* [Ciudad Trujillo] 5 (1941):359–75.

TePaske, John Jay. *The Governorship of Spanish Florida, 1700–1763.* Durham: Duke University Press, 1964.

Thomas, Eduardo. *Compendio de historia nacional.* Montevideo: n.p., 1943.

Torre Revello, José. "Los gobernadores de Buenos Aires (1617–1777)." In *Historia de la nación Argentina* (cited under Academia Nacional de la Historia [Buenos Aires]), 3:233–332.

Tosta, Virgilio. *Sucedio en Barinas: Episodios de historia Menuda.* Caracas: Editorial Sucre, 1964.

Unzueta y Yuste, Abelardo de. *Geografía histórica de la Isla de Fernando Poo.* Madrid: Instituto de Estudios Africanos, 1947.

Vargas, Marco Tulio. "Gobernadores de Cartagena, 1533–1947." *Boletín de historia y antigüedades de la Academia colombiana de la historia* 34 (1947):66–79.

Vergara y Velasco, Francisco Javier. *Tratado de metodologia y critica histórica y elementos de cronologia colombiana.* Bogatá: Imprenta Eléctrica, 1907.

Vidal, Santiago. "Corregidores e intendentes de la provincia de Zacatecas." *Memorias de la Academia mexicana de la historia* 23 (1964):183–211.

Videla, Horacio. *Historia de San Juan.* Buenos Aires: Academia del Plata, 1962.

Viera y Clavijo, José. *Noticias de la historia general de las Islas Canarias.* 4 vols. Las Palmas: Imprenta La Provincia, n.d.

Villacorta C[alderon], Juan Antonio. *Historia de la capitania general de Guatemala.* Guatemala: La Tipografia Nacional, 1942.

——. "Nomina cronológica de los gobernantes de Guatemala." *Anales de la Sociedad de geografía e historia de Guatemala* 11 (1935):418–34.

Vivanco, Carlos. "La real audiencia de Quito en el siglo XVI." *Boletín del Archivo nacional de historia* [Quito] 1, no. 1 (1950):7–21.

Zilli, Juan. *Historia sucinta de Veracruz.* Tacubaya, Mexico: Editorial Citlaltepetl, 1962.

Zinny, Antonio. *Historia de los gobernadores del Paraguay, 1535–1887.* Buenos Aires: Imprensa y Libreria de Mayo, 1887.

Sweden

Sweden's two ventures into colonialism were brief and were separated by nearly a century and a half. During the 17th century, besides acquiring the short-lived American colony of New Sweden, Sweden, like almost every nation in Europe, dabbled in the trade of West Africa's Guinea coast. Between 1652 and 1657 there were three Swedish posts along the Gold Coast—Osu, Takoradi, and Cape Coast Castle—but they were all taken over by the Danes in 1657 and became the basis for the Danish Gold Coast colony.

In the 18th century, plans were occasionally advanced in Sweden to secure a colony in the West Indies as a source for sugar, tobacco, and coffee—commodities which Sweden then had to purchase from other nations. Since by that time there were no vacant islands left in the West Indies, diplomatic methods were resorted to and in 1784 an island was secured from France in return for commercial concessions. This was Saint Barthélemy, of little value to France, which in any case felt it useful "to multiply in the Antilles the possessions of neutral powers."[1] For earlier experiences had shown the utility of having a secure haven nearby in the event of war with Great Britain, at that time always a possibility. And in fact Saint Barthélemy served admirably as a neutral port during the French Revolution, but its prosperity vanished with peace, and the island, like the Danish West Indies nearby, proved to be an incessant economic liability. Sweden considered itself fortunate to be able to sell the island to France in 1877 and wash its hands once and for all of colonial enterprises.

---

1. Quoted in Ernst Ekman, "St. Barthélemy and the French Revolution," *Caribbean Studies* 23, no. 4 (1964):19.

403 NEW SWEDEN

New Sweden, on the Delaware River in what became the state of New Jersey, was fostered and initially governed by disaffected Dutchmen who had left the service of the Dutch West India Company's colony of New Netherlands (q.v.). This colony was ephemeral and unsuccessful. It never received adequate support from the Swedish monarchy, then embroiled in the politics and wars of Europe, and was constantly subject to pressures from the nearby Dutch colony at New Netherlands. Finally, in 1655 the Dutch, under Pieter Stuijvesant, captured all of the Swedish posts and put an end to the colony of New Sweden, which had enjoyed a brief existence of but seventeen years.

Governors			
1638	Pieter Minuit	1643-1653	Johan Bjørnsson Printz
1638-1643	Pieter Hollander Ridder	1653-1654	Johan Papegoja
		1654-1655	Johan Classon Rising

Leiby, passim.

404 SAINT BARTHÉLEMY

Saint Barthélemy is one of the Leeward Islands in the northern Lesser Antilles and is located about 200 miles east of Puerto Rico. During the 17th and 18th centuries it was owned, but never occupied, by France. In the latter part of the 18th century Sweden was seeking a West Indian island to provide a source for sugar and tobacco. After protracted negotiations France sold Sweden Saint Barthélemy in 1784 in return for trading concessions in the Swedish port of Goteborg. The island flourished as a neutral port during the wars of the French Revolution but declined thereafter. The cost of the colony induced Sweden to attempt to sell the island to the United States in 1845 and again in 1868 and 1870 without success. Finally, in 1878, France repurchased the island and incorporated it as a dependency of Guadeloupe (31) and its separate administrative existence ceased.

Governors			
1784-1787	Samuel Moritz von Rajalin	1812-1816	Bernt Robert Gustaf Stackelberg
1787-1790	Pehr Herman von Rosenstein	1816-1818	Johan Samuel Rosenvärd
1790-1795	Carl Fredrik Bagge af Söderby	1819-1826	Johan Norderling
1795-1800	Georg Henrik af Trolle	1826-1860	James Harley Haasum
1800-1812	Hans Henrik Anckerheim	1860-1868	Fredrik Carl Ulrich
		1868-1878	Bror Ulrich

Information from C. G. Löwenhielm, Riksarkivet, Stockholm.

Bibliography: Sweden

Högström, E. O. E. *S. Barthelemy under svenkt Välde*. Upsala: Almqvist & Wiksells Boktr.-Aktiebolag, 1888.
Leiby, Adrian Coulter. *The Early Dutch and Swedish Settlements of New Jersey*. New Jersey Historical Series, vol. 10. Princeton: Van Nostrand, 1964.

United States

The expansion of the United States, like that of Russia, was initially overland and into an area occupied by alien and relatively primitive cultures. This area quickly became populated with settlers from the inhabited core and was eventually assimilated into the growing nation on an equal basis with the nuclear areas.

In 1823 the Monroe Doctrine denounced and warned against any further European efforts to recover former colonies or initiate new colonial adventures in the western hemisphere and the United States strenuously opposed the French imperial effort in Mexico in 1862–67. Nonetheless there are sufficient examples of American imperialist tendencies, clothed in the euphemism of "manifest destiny," to argue that this anti-imperial attitude had other than purely ethical bases. Efforts were made to invade and annex Canada in 1812–13. Florida was purchased from Spain in 1819 under circumstances not far removed from extortion. In 1846–48 the northern half of Mexico was invaded, occupied, and secured by cession, and in 1867 Russian America, or Alaska, was purchased from Russia. All of these areas, except Alaska, were assimilated into the United States and in 1898 no distinguishable American "empire" existed. The Spanish-American War of that year altered this situation markedly. The Philippine Islands, Guam, and Cuba, all Spanish possessions, were occupied and retained, together with Puerto Rico, another Spanish colony, at war's end. Cuba soon became an independent republic but the others remained American possessions. Simultaneously the United States acquired other Pacific possessions—Hawaii in 1898, Wake Island in 1899, and part of Samoa in 1900. The completion of the Panama Canal in 1914 called for further strategic consideration, and ultimately further acquisitions. The zone straddling the canal itself was retained under American sovereignty and the Danish West Indies, lying along an important route to the Panama Canal, were purchased in 1917. American commitment in the Pacific Ocean was further strengthened after World War II when the former Japanese Pacific Islands Mandate was granted to the United States as a trusteeship.

The administration of these scattered possessions has undergone numerous changes. Initially the Virgin Islands (the former Danish West Indies), Guam, and Samoa were administered by the Department of the Navy but later, at different periods, they fell under civil control. The Panama Canal Zone has always been administered by the U.S. Army. The Philippine Islands became completely independent in 1946 and Puerto Rico achieved commonwealth (similar to dominion) status in 1952 (but had already elected its own governors since 1947).

The United States has never considered its possessions to be colonies and in many important respects they were not treated in a typically colonial way— full citizenship was early granted to several of them, for instance. But, view from a distant perspective, enough of the features of imperialism are present make the United States, along with Japan, a non-European example of imperia expansion.

405 AMERICAN SAMOA

American Samoa consists of the large islands of Tutuila and Ta'u and a group of smaller islands. The rights to these islands were acquired as a result of the Tripartite Treaty of 1900 between the United States, Great Britain, and Germany. In this agreement it was specified that all islands of the Samoan group situated east of longitude 171° west were to be in the American sphere while those west of this line were to be controlled by Germany (v. German Samoa, 73). Rather anticlimactically, the islands in the American sphere were formally ceded to the United States by the native rulers in 1900 and 1904. Since naval strategic considerations governed the acquisition of the islands by the United States, they were administered by a naval governor under the Department of the Navy until 1951. Since that time they have been governed by a civilian governor, under the authority of the Department of the Interior, as an unincorporated island territory.

Governors

1900-1901	Benjamin Franklin Tilley	1936-1938	MacGillivray Milne
1901-1902	Uriel Sebree	1938-1940	Edward William Hanson
1903-1905	Edmund Beardsley Underwood	1940-1942	Laurence Wild
1905-1908	Charles Brainard Taylor Moore	1942-1944	John Gould Moyer
1908-1910	John Frederick Parker	1944-1945	Allen Hobbs
1910-1913	William Michael Crose	1945	Ralph Waldo Hungerford
1913-1914	Clark Daniel Stearns	1945-1947	Harold Alexander Houser
1915-1919	John Martin Poyer	1947-1949	Vernon Huber
1919-1920	Warren Jay Terhune	1949-1951	Thomas Francis Darden, Jr.
1920-1922	Waldo Evans	1951-1952	Phelps Phelps
1922-1923	Edwin Taylor Pollock	1952-1953	James Arthur Owing
1923-1925	Edward Stanley Kellogg	1953	Lawrence McAuley Judd
1925-1927	Henry Francis Bryan	1953-1956	Richard Barrett Lowe
1927-1929	Stephen Victor Graham	1956-1960	Peter Tali Coleman
1929-1932	Gatewood Sanders Lincoln	1961-1967	Hyrum Rex Lee
1932-1934	George Bertram Landenberger	1967-1969	Owen Stewart Aspinall
1934-1936	Otto Carl Dowling	1969—	John Haydon

Darden, p. 39; *Statesman's Year Book*, 1951 to date.

406 GUAM

Guam is the largest and southernmost of the Marianas, an island group in the western Pacific. It has a total area of 209 square miles. From 1668 to 1898 it was occupied by Spain (341). As a result of the Spanish-American War of 1898 the island fell under the control of the United States, which valued it for its strategic location. Until 1950 it was, like American Samoa (q.v.), governed by a naval governor. From 1941 to 1944 it was occupied by Japanese forces. Since 1950 it has been governed as an unincorporated island territory by the Department of the Interior.

Governors

1898	José Sisto (1)	1899-1900	Richard Phillips Leary
1898-1899	Francisco Portusach	1900-1901	Seaton Schroeder (1)
1899	José Sisto (2)	1901	William Swift
1899	Joaquín Pérez	1901-1903	Seaton Schroeder (2)
1899	William Coe	1903-1904	William Elbridge Sewell
		1904-1906	George Leland Dyer

United States

1906-1907	Templin Morris Potts	1933-1936	George Andrew Alexander
1907	Luke McNamee	1936-1938	Benjamin Vaughan McCandlish
1907-1911	Edward John Dorn	1938-1940	James Thomas Alexander
1911-1912	George Robert Salisbury	1940-1941	George Johnson McMillin
1912-1913	Robert Edward Coontz	1941-1944	(under Japan)
1913-1916	William John Maxwell	1944-1946	Chester William Nimitz
1916-1918	Roy Campbell Smith	1946-1950	Charles Alan Pownall
1918-1920	William Wirt Gilmer	1950-1953	Carlton Skinner
1920-1922	Ivan Cyrus Wettengel	1953-1956	Ford Quint Elvidge
1922-1923	Adelbert Althouse	1956-1960	Richard Barrett Lowe
1923-1926	Henry Bertram Price	1960-1962	Joseph Flores
1926-1929	Lloyd Stowell Shapley	1962-1963	William Patlov Daniel
1929-1931	Willis Winter Bradley	1963-1969	Manuel Flores León Guerrero
1931-1933	Edmund Spence Root	1969—	Carlos Camacho

Carano and Sánchez, pp. 262–63.

407 MICRONESIAN TRUST TERRITORY

The Micronesian Trust Territory, in the western Pacific, consists of approximately 2,250 islands whose area aggregates only 1,100 square miles. It is composed of the Marshall and Caroline island groups, Wake Island, Marcus Island, and the Mariana Islands, except Guam (q.v.) which is governed separately. The trust territory is the former Japanese Pacific Islands Mandate (259) which was granted to the United States as a trusteeship by the United Nations in 1947 as, in fact, Japan had similarly received it from the League of Nations in 1921. Until 1951 the commander-in-chief of the Pacific Fleet stationed in Hawaii was ex officio high commissioner, although until 1949 a deputy high commissioner was stationed at Guam. In 1951 the trust territory fell to the jurisdiction of the Department of the Interior and a civilian high commissioner was appointed who resides at Saipan in the Mariana Islands.

Deputy High Commissioners		1949-1951	Arthur William Radford
1947-1948	Carleton Herbert Wright	1951-1953	Elbert Duncan Thomas
1948-1949	Leon Sangster Fiske	1953-1954	Frank Elbert Midkiff
		1954-1961	Delmas Henry Nucker
High Commissioners		1961-1966	Maurice Wilfrid Goding
1947-1948	Louis Emil Denfeld	1966-1969	William Robert Norwood
1948-1949	DeWitt Clinton Ramsey	1969—	Edward Elliott Johnston

Statesman's Year Book, 1951 to date; U.S., Department of the Navy, *Report*, passim.

408 PANAMA CANAL ZONE

By treaty of November 18, 1903, with the new Republic of Panama the United States was granted in perpetuity a strip of land across the isthmus on which to build an interoceanic canal. During the construction of this canal the civil administration of the Canal Zone was in the hands first of governors and then of civil heads of the administration. Since the completion of the canal in 1914 the administration of the Panama Canal Zone has been entrusted to a general officer of the U.S. Army who serves ex officio as the president of the Panama Canal Company, responsible for the operation of the canal. The Republic of Panama is paid an annuity by the United States government but up to the present time exercises no jurisdiction whatever over the zone.

Governors
1904-1905	George Whitefield Davis
1905-1906	Charles Edward Magoon

Heads of the Civil Administration
1907-1910	Joseph Clay Styles Blackburn
1910-1913	Maurice Hudson Thatcher
1913-1914	Richard Lee Metcalfe

Governors
1914-1917	George Washington Goethals
1917-1921	Chester Harding
1921-1924	Jay Johnson Morrow
1924-1928	Meriwether Lewis Walker
1928-1932	Harry Burgess
1932-1936	Julian Larcombe Schley
1936-1940	Clarence Eugene Ridley
1940-1944	Glen Edgar Edgerton
1944-1948	Joseph Cowles Mehaffey
1948-1952	Francis Cosler Newcomer
1952-1956	John States Seybold
1956-1960	William Everett Potter
1960-1962	William Arnold Carter
1962-1966	Robert John Fleming, Jr.
1966—	Walter Philip Leber

Mack, p. 501 and passim; *Statesman's Year Book*, 1944 to date; *U.S. Army Registers*, 1914 to date.

409 PHILIPPINE ISLANDS

The Philippine Islands were another of the United States' spoils from the Spanish-American War (v. Philippine Islands, 372). From 1898 to 1901 the islands were under military government. From 1901 to 1935 they were governed by a governor-general appointed by the President of the United States. In 1935 the Philippine Islands were declared a commonwealth and the governor-general was replaced by a high commissioner and a president elected by the Filipinos. From 1942 to 1945 the islands were occupied by Japanese forces. On July 4, 1946 the Philippines were made independent, the Republic of the Philippines was proclaimed, and the office of high commissioner was replaced by that of ambassador.

Governors-General
1898	Wesley Merritt
1898-1900	Elwell Stephen Otis
1900-1901	Arthur McArthur
1901-1904	William Howard Taft
1904-1906	Luke Edward Wright
1906	Henry Clay Ide
1906-1909	James Francis Smith
1909-1913	William Cameron Forbes
1913-1921	Francis Burton Harrison
1921-1927	Leonard Wood
1927-1929	Henry Lewis Stimson
1929-1932	Dwight Finley Davis
1932-1933	Theodore Roosevelt II
1933-1935	Frank Murphy

High Commissioners
1935-1937	Frank Murphy
1937-1939	Paul Vories McNutt (1)
1939-1941	Francis Bowes Sayre
1941-1945	(under Japan)
1945-1946	Paul Vories McNutt (2)

Statesman's Year Book, 1901—46.

410 PUERTO RICO

The United States acquired Puerto Rico at the end of the Spanish-American War in 1898 (v. Puerto Rico, 377, in Spanish section). The island was under military government for a transitional period ending in 1901 when it came under civilian rule. Until 1932 the island was officially denominated Porto Rico. In this year the Spanish spelling was adopted. In 1947 Puerto Ricans were granted the right of choosing their own governor and in 1952 Puerto Rico became a commonwealth of the United States, a position held by the Philippine Islands from 1935 to 1946 but not otherwise held by any American possession.

Governors			
1898	John Rutter Brooke	1913-1921	Arthur Yager
1898-1899	Guy Vernor Henry	1921-1923	Edward Montgomery Reily
1899-1900	George Whitefield Davis	1923-1929	Horace Mann Towner
1900-1902	Charles Herbert Allen	1929-1932	Theodore Roosevelt II
1902-1904	William Henry Hunt	1932-1933	James Rumsey Beverley
1904-1907	Beekman Winthrop	1933-1934	Robert Hayes Gore
1907-1909	Regis Henri Post	1934-1939	Blanton Winship
1909-1913	George Radcliff Colton	1939-1941	William Daniel Leahy
		1941-1946	Rexford Guy Tugwell

Todd, passim.

411 RYUKYU ISLANDS

The Ryukyu Islands, situated between Japan and Taiwan, became a prefecture of Japan in 1879. After World War II, in 1945, the islands were occupied by American forces. Initially the Ryukyu were under purely military rule. The commander-in-chief, Far Eastern Command, served ex officio as governor, while the commanding general of the islands' garrison served as deputy governor. In 1952 civil administration was introduced, but until 1962 the civil administrator was a general officer of the U.S. Army. In 1957 a high commissioner was appointed. He, too, has always been a high ranking general officer of the army. The northern group of islands were returned to Japan in 1953 and the remaining islands will be returned in 1972.

High Commissioners		*Civil Administrators*	
1957-1958	James Edward Moore	1962-1964	Shannon Bailey McCune
1958-1960	Donald Prentice Booth	1964-1967	Gerald Warner
1960-1964	Paul Wyatt Caraway	1967-	Stanley Sherman Carpenter
1964-1966	Albert Watson		
1966-1968	Ferdinand Thomas Unger		
1968-	James Benjamin Lampert		

Hewett, passim; *Statesman's Year Book*, 1957 to date.

412 VIRGIN ISLANDS

The Virgin Islands of the United States, not to be confused with the British Virgin Islands (110) were acquired from Denmark in 1917 for $25,000,000. For their previous administrative history see the Danish West Indies (4). American interest in the islands began with the completion of the Panama Canal, for the islands controlled the best approach to the canal from the Caribbean Sea. Until 1931 the islands were administered by a naval governor; thereafter by a civilian appointed by the Department of the Interior. In addition to the islands of Saint Croix, Saint Johns, and Saint Thomas, the Virgin Islands of the United States comprise fifty smaller islets and cays.

Governors			
1917-1919	James Harrison Oliver	1935-1941	Lawrence William Cramer
1919-1921	Joseph Wallace Oman	1941-1946	Charles Harwood
1921-1922	Sumner Ely Wetmore Kittelle	1946-1949	William Henry Hastie
1922-1923	Henry Hughes Hough	1949-1954	Morris Filanque de Castro
1923-1925	Philip Williams	1954-1955	Archibald Alphonso Alexander
1925-1927	Martin Edward Trench	1955-1958	Walter Arthur Gordon
1927-1931	Waldo Evans	1958-1961	John David Merwin
1931-1935	Paul Martin Pearson	1961-1969	Ralph M. Paiewonsky
		1969—	Melvin Herbert Evans

Information from the Office of the Governor, Virgin Islands.

Bibliography: United States

Carano, Paul, and Sánchez, Pedro C. *A Complete History of Guam*. Rutland, Vt.: Charles R. Tuttle Co., 1964.

Darden, Thomas F., Jr. *Historical Sketch of the Naval Administration of the Government of American Samoa, April 17, 1900 - July 1, 1951*. Washington: U.S. Government Printing Office, 1952.

Hewett, Robert Foster. "United States Civil Administration of the Ryukyu Islands, 1950—1960: A Historical Analysis and Appraisal of a Decade of Civil Administration of an Asian Area." Unpublished Ph.D. dissertation, American University, 1966.

Mack, Gerstle. *The Land Divided. A History of the Panama Canal and Other Isthmian Canal Projects*. New York: Alfred A. Knopf, 1944.

Statesman's Year Book: Statistical and Historical Annual of the States of the World. London: Macmillan & Co., 1864 to date.

Todd, Roberto Henry. *Desfile de Gobernadores de Puerto Rico, 1898–1943*. 2d ed. Madrid: Ediciones Iberoamericanas, S.A., 1966.

U.S., Adjutant General's Office. *U.S. Army Register* [title varies], 1789—98, 1814, 1826—1916, 1918, 1920 to date. Washington, D.C.

U.S., Department of the Navy, Office of the Chief of Naval Operations. *Report on the Administration of the Trust Territory of the Pacific Islands, 1947/48 to 1950/51*. Washington, D.C.: U.S. Government Printing Office.

Who's Who in America: A Biographical Dictionary of Notable Living Men and Women of the United States. Chicago: A. N. Marquis Co., 1899 to date.

Appendix

The electorate of Brandenburg (after 1701 the kingdom of Prussia) and the duchy of Kurland, in what is now Latvia, engaged on a very limited scale in colonizing and commercial ventures in the 17th and 18th centuries. In 1651 Duke Jakob of Kurland purchased an island at the mouth of the Gambia River and other plots of lands nearby and established trading forts. In 1659 the Kurlander possessions in the area were, because of the captivity of the duke and the consequent inability of the Kurland government to administer them, leased to the Dutch West India Company. The Kurland commandant was expelled but returned the next year. In 1661 the Kurlanders were finally expelled by the English. Despite protests by Jakob, England refused their return and established its own posts permanently in the area (v. 132). Between 1642 and 1737 the Kurland rulers made several unsuccessful attempts to colonize the island of Tobago in the West Indies in competition with the English and Dutch.[1] The inability to settle Tobago rendered the Gambia posts almost nugatory since they were designed primarily as an entrepot for the export of slaves to the anticipated Tobagan plantations.

Brandenburg-Prussia established several posts along the Guinea coast of West Africa in what is today the Republic of Ghana, with headquarters at Gross Friedrichsburg, established in 1683. Plagued by the venality and incompetence of most of the directors-general and unable to compete commercially with the other European nations established in the area (v. Danish Gold Coast, 3, Gold Coast (British), 136, Gold Coast (Dutch), 268), the Brandenburger posts languished and were effectively abandoned after 1716. In 1720 they were sold to the Dutch. Gross Friedrichsburg was occupied at the time by John Konny, a local African merchant who had dominated the Brandenburg officials for several years before their departure. The Dutch succeeded in expelling him only in 1724.

---

1. For details of the Kurlander efforts to settle Tobago, see Anderson, pp. 129–55, 216–32, and Mattiesen, passim.

GAMBIA[1]

Governors		
1651-1654	Heinrich Vock (or Fock)	
1655-1659	Otto Stiel (1)	
1659-1660	(under the Netherlands)	
1660-1661	Otto Stiel (2)	

1. Duke Jakob appointed several other governors between 1652 and 1655 but none reached the Gambian posts.

Diederichs, passim; Mattiesen, pp. 118–272.

GROSS-FRIEDRICHSBURG

Governors		
1683-	Philipp Peterson Blonck	
-1684	Nathaniel Dilliger	
1684-1686	Karl Konstantin von Schnitter	
1686-1691	Johann Niemann	
1691-	Johann Tenhoof	
-1695	Jakob Tenhoof	
1695-1697	Gijsbrecht van Hoogveldt	
1697-1699	Jan van Laar	
-	Jan de Visser	
-	Adriaan Grobbe	
-1706	Johann Münz	
1706-1709	Heinrich Lamy	
1709-1710	Frans de Lange	
1711-1716	Nicolas Dubois	
1716-	Anton Günther van der Meden	

Schück, 337–45 and passim.

Bibliography

Anderson, Edgar. "Die kurländische Kolonie Tobago." *Baltische Hefte* 8 (1961/62):129—55, 216—32.

Diederichs, Heinrich. *Herzog Jakobs von Kurland Kolonien an der Westküste von Afrika.* Festschrift der kurlandischen Gesellschaft für Literatur und Kunst zur Feier ihres 75— Jährigen Bestehens. Mitau: n.p., 1890.

Mattiesen, Otto Heinz. *Die Kolonial- und Uberseepolitik der kurländischen Herzöge im 17. und 18. Jahrhundert.* Stuttgart: Verlag W. Kohlhammer, 1940.

Schück, Richard. *Brandenburg-Preussens Kolonial-Politik unter dem grossen Kurfürsten und seinen Nachfolgern, 1647—1721.* 2 vols. Leipzig: Verlag F. W. Grunow, 1889.

General Index

General Index

Index
of Governors' Names

The entries for compound surnames in this index are alphabetized in several different ways. French surnames, with very few exceptions, are entered under the first element of the surname. This conforms to the practice of the *Dictionnaire de biographie française* and the *Annuaires* of the various French ministries. Spanish surnames are likewise entered under the first, or paternal, element of the surname. The system adopted for Portuguese surnames is basically that used by the American Library Association. That is, the entry will be found under the last element of the surname, including compounds (e.g., Castelo Brance, Souto-Maior, etc.). It has not been possible, however, to determine adequately any rules of usage which could modify this system. Because of this it is unnecessarily procrustean and therefore less than satisfactory, but perhaps no more so than any other that could have been devised.

Titled British, Spanish, and Portuguese governors are listed under both the title and the family name. Normally the French did not assume titles different from the family name, but when this does occur both title and family name are listed. For purposes of alphabetization all connectives and participles except 'Le' and 'La', and sometimes 'du' have been ignored. Identical entries, particularly common with Portuguese names, are entered in chronological order.

Efforts have been made to ascertain whether individuals who had identical or similar names and who governed during roughly contemporaneous periods were in fact identical. If no evidence has been found showing such identity, then such individuals are entered separately.

It must be emphasized that the entries themselves are skeletal in form since their purpose is merely to distinguish any individual from all others rather than to provide complete forms of names. That is, they are designed only to serve as indicators for locating full names.

387

Calnein, 5
Calvel, 25
Calvert, B. L., 159
Calvert, Charles, 159
Calvert, Charles, 159
Calvert, G., 169
Calvert, L., 159
Calvert, P., 159
Calvo, 341
Calvo de Cáceres, 355
Calvo de la Puerte y O'Farrill Arango y Arriola, 352
Calzada, 355
Camacho, C., 406
Camacho, F., 294
Camacho, M., 303
Câmara, Francisco António da Veiga Cabral da, 313
Câmara, Francisco de Melo Manuel da, 299
Câmara, João Gonçalo da, 284
Câmara, João Pedro da, 300
Câmara, Jorge da, 297
Câmara, José Manuel da, 297
Câmara, José Pedro da, 309
Câmara, José Pinheiro da, 288, 308, 317
Câmara, L., 303
Câmara, Manuel da, 309
Câmara, Manuel António Pinheiro da, 288, 317
Câmara, S., 312
Camarena, 354
Camargo, A., 292
Camargo, M., 358
Camba García, 372, 377
Cambon, J.-M., 7
Cambon, P.-P., 67
Cambridge, 113, 237
Cameron, C., 88, 157
Cameron, D. C., 180, 227
Cameron, E. J., 110, 132, 209, 210, 235
Cameron, J., 102
Caminha, Duque de, 290
Camino y Alcobendas, 329
Campbell, Alexander A. M., 167, 235
Campbell, Archibald, 149, 155
Campbell, Archibald, 112, 168
Campbell, B., 180
Campbell, Clifford C., 149
Campbell, Colin, 134
Campbell, Colin, 118, 187
Campbell, David G., 157
Campbell, Donald, 198
Campbell, G., 97, 117
Campbell, H. D., 215
Campbell, James, 139
Campbell, James, 139
Campbell, John, 162
Campbell, John, 240
Campbell, John, 169
Campbell, John, 184
Campbell, John, 210

Campbell, John D., 113
Campbell, N., 136, 215
Campbell, P., 230
Campbell, W. T., 135, 231
Campbell, William, 187, 221
Campbell, William, 98
Campen, 265
Campero y Campos, 401
Camphuijs, 275
Campione, 250
Campo, Marqués de, 337, 362
Campo, Francisco Cristóbal del, 381
Campo Florido, Principe de, 329
Campofuerte, Marqués de, 329
Campos, A., 288
Campos, E., 289
Campos, J., 378
Campos, M., 302
Campo Santo, Marqués de, 368
Campos y Espinosa, 377
Cañada Ibáñez, Marqués de la, 327
Canal y Soldevila, 329
Canard, 61
Cañas y Merino, 399
Cañas y Portocarrero, 327
Cañas y Trujillo, 336
Cañaveral y Ponce, 328
Cáncer, 354
Canchy, 30
Cancio Sierra y Cienfuegos, 333
Candal, Barão de, 309
Candole, 253, 254
Cañedo Miranda, 337
Cañete, Marqués de. See Hurtado de Mendoza, Andrés; Hurtado de Mendoza y Manrique, García
Caneva, 254
Cangas, 340, 393
Canillas, Conde de, 369
Cañizares, 393
Cañizares Navarro, 391
Canning, C. J., 145
Cano, Antonio, 389
Cano, Pedro, 350
Cano de Aponte, 332
Cansano, Duque de, 368
Canseco de Quiñones, 361
Cantau, 19
Canterbury, Viscount, 168, 234, 239
Cantz'laar, 265, 281
Capagorry, 54
Capellen, 275
Capelo, 284
Capest, 36
Cappa y Rioseco, 329
Capsir y Sanz, 328
Caracciolo, 371
Carafa, 368
Carassa, 353
Caraway, 411

411

415

425

Metcalfe, C. T., 113, 145, 149, 238
Metcalfe, G., 125
Metcalfe, H. A., 90
Metcalfe, R. L., 408
Metelo, 317
Methuen, Baron, 157, 165
Methwold, 224
Meuron, 118
Mey, 276
Meyer, H., 3
Meyer, J., 3
Meyer-Waldeck, 76
Meyner, 369
Michaux, 22
Michener, 113
Micoud, Claude-Anne de, 57
Micoud, Claude-Anne-Gui de, 57
Middlemore, 139, 207
Middleton, A., 221
Middleton, G. H., 196
Middleton, Earl of, 228
Middleton, J., 127, 132
Midkiff, 407
Mier y Ceballos, 373
Mier y Noriega, 364
Mier y Torre, 364
Mijer, 275
Mikkelsen, 4
Milan, 4
Milbanke, 169
Mildmay, 96
Miles, H. S. G., 134
Miles, R., 136
Milius, 19, 54
Miller, J. O., 117
Miller, T., 183
Millet, J.-M., 27
Millet, R.-P., 67
Millot, 11
Mills, 136
Milne, 405
Milner, A., Viscount, 115
Milner, J. S., 184
Milnes, 41, 113
Milton, 222
Mina, Marqués de la, 369
Minami, H., 256
Minami, J., 255, 258
Minas, Marquês das, 286
Minto, Gilbert Elliot-Murray-Kynynmond,
    Earl of, 145
Minto, Gilbert John Elliot-Murray-Kynynmond,
    Earl of, 113, 145
Minuit, 277, 403
Mirabeau, 31
Miramende, 50
Miranda, Aires, 296
Miranda, Alonso, 350
Miranda, Aníbal, 296
Miranda, António, 314

Miranda, António José Bernardes, 296
Miranda, Fernão, 307
Miranda, Francisco Eugénio Pereira, 317
Miranda, Francisco Ribeiro, 292
Miranda, G., 339
Miranda, H., 339
Miranda, I., 307
Miranda, José, 329
Miranda, Juan, 346
Miranda, Manuel, 296
Miranda de Auta, Marqués de, 329, 362
Mirelis y González, 329
Mist, 261
Mitchell, C. B. H., 129, 154, 165, 223
Mitchell, J., 169
Mitchell, P. E., 129, 151, 236
Mitchell, R., 230
Mitchell, S., 139
Mittelhauser, 63
Miyares y González, 324, 355
Mizon, 43
Moçâmedes, Barão de, 284
Moctezuma, Conde de, 360
Modyford, 92, 149
Moens, 270
Mørch, 3
Moerman, 270, 271
Mogensen, 4
Moges, 41
Moir, 94, 110, 125, 208, 235
Moira, Earl of, 145, 157
Moisset, 60
Mola de Viñacorta, 373
Molenar, 319
Moles, 357
Molesworth, 149
Molina, 292, 294, 299
Molina y Minaño, 354
Moll, 11
Moloney, 103, 132, 180, 234, 247
Mombelli, 254
Momber van de Velde, 272
Moncada, 284
Monck, Charles Stanley Monck, Viscount, 113
Monck, Christopher, 149
Monckton, 178
Monckton-Arundell, 179
Monclova, Conde de la. See Portocarrero,
    Gaspar; Portocarrero Lasso de la Vega,
    Melchor
Mondon, 36
Mondragón, 329
Moneda, Pedro de la, 373, 395
Moneda, Rafael de la, 370
Monforte, Salvador de, 322
Monguillot, 35, 66
Monic, 53
Monjardim, 292
Monléon, 27, 28
Monro, C. C., 134

Index

450

Index

454

Index

Index